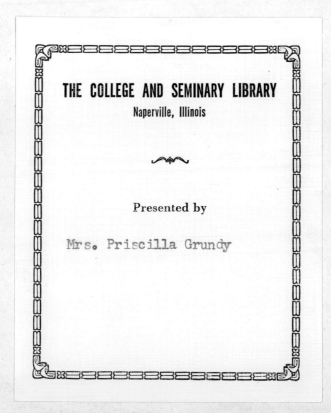

On the Literary Genetics of Shakspere's Plays, 1592-1594

ON THE LITERARY

GENETICS OF SHAKSPERE'S PLAYS

1592-1594

By T. W. Baldwin

THE UNIVERSITY OF ILLINOIS PRESS

Urbana, 1959

A grant from the Ford Foundation has helped to defray the cost of publishing this work.

In Memory of
Louisa Jane Anderson
b. January 3, 1822, *d.* February 7, 1895
"Aunt Lou"
who taught me to read
before I can remember

Preface

This volume takes up where *William Shakspere's Five-Act Structure* left off, both are supplemented by *On the Literary Genetics of Shakspere's Poems & Sonnets,* and all rest fundamentally upon *William Shakspere's Small Latine and Lesse Greeke,* and its "portico," *William Shakspere's Petty School.* The prefaces to these works have attempted to give the necessary explanations of procedures. The same mechanical makeup has been continued, as explained thus in *Small Latine.* "In the matter of references, I have done as I would be done by. At the first reference to a work, I have given fairly full, though not necessarily complete, information, my purpose being identification only. Thereafter I have abbreviated to significant words. If the reader does not understand the abbreviated form, he may turn to the proper place of author or title in the Bibliographical Index and be referred to the first occurrence, where I have given the fuller information. . . . I have thought that the best index would be a complete concordance of all names of persons, and of all significant places in the text, with some additions from the notes. I have ordinarily kept the Latin form of names of persons, since that is the form by which these men were universally known, unless the name has been anglicized. Very few will need any other form, and those who do ought already to know what it is. Usually, but not always, all titles of books have been normalized and placed under authors. Shakspere, of course, demands separate sections for his plays and characters."

In the present volume, it is my purpose to continue examining phases of Shakspere's composition upon the background of the universal methods of composition in his time, to see how he has arrived at some of his literary results. Since it was the fundamental business of grammar school to provide the basic training in composition, these methods were very widely spread and were the only methods of the time. If one had not the benefit of grammar school, nevertheless the grammar school materials were made available in English, for those who wished to avail themselves of them. But even if one did not have either the formal training of the Latin grammar school, or self-training, more or less, in English, still he would use these methods of composition if he used any at all. The question of Shakspere's languages, learning, education, however phrased, does not, therefore, enter fundamentally into such an enterprise, even though a minute knowledge of these things is evidently necessary for one who would understand and evaluate Shakspere's methods. So without apology I have tried to see how Shakspere has composed his raw materials into finished form. Since I do not believe in modern miracles, the accumulated and accumulating instances convince me that Shakspere did have such mastery of grammar school materials as the grammar school at Stratford would have made almost compulsorily available to the oldest son of a chief official of the town. But whether Shakspere ever spent a day in grammar school at Stratford or anywhere else, whether he was ever taught any language, Greek, Latin, English, what not; these and similar questions are for our present enterprise relatively unimportant, even though such equipment is obligatory on anyone who attempts to get at the bottom of Shakspere's methods, since they were the only methods of the day. The critic's scholarly equipment may be in question; Shakspere's is not.

Unfortunately, in the period covered, 1592-94, the various acting companies and their dramatists were so entangled with each other that it has been necessary to spend a considerable part of the volume in attempting to unscramble Shakspere from the mass. Here the study examines further, practices which were investigated partially in *The Organization and Personnel of the Shakespearean Company*. The examination, however, stands on its own, though the book is to be put back into print by the autumn of 1960, and so will be available for readers of the present volume. I have tried each time to base directly upon the relevant facts, not upon the previous conclusions of any volume. Inferences should be directly from facts, never from other inferences.

It has also been my intention always to let the arguments stand upon facts, not upon authority. For I sympathize with downright John Hester (*An excellent Treatise teaching howe to cure the French-Pockes*, 1590, ¶ 2ᵛ): "sure in my opinion, these fellowes that to fill large volumes, rather set downe what other men haue said . . . , thinking him the best Clark that voucheth most Authors, neyther waying theyr reasons, nor pondering their proofes, but hudling run on with *ipse dixit*, I say these fellowes, by blotting a great deale of good paper with much superfluous matter, lead a great many good wits a woolgathering, inforcing them to seeke for that they neuer finde, or els to find somewhat not woorth the seeking." I hope I have myself examined the pertinent authors, but present facts make many of the opinions of even the greatest of them now impertinent. It would be equally impertinent of me to pillory these false opinions. In so far as I could, I have tried to attribute facts to their proper discoverers, as also the just opinions to be derived from those facts. But what I consider to be unjustified opinion I have not usually troubled to mention.

Nor is it possible at this late day for work that has spread over so many years even to know the debts I owe to predecessors or to contemporaries. All that I have met has become some part of me. Students, colleagues, even many persons of whom I will never have heard must have left their impress. It is safest to assume that I have acquired even my errors from someone else. I am grateful that I have been permitted to use these materials of the common fund as if for the time they were my very own, in the hope that they may thus pass on to others and give them equal pleasure.

But to record some of my more immediate and obvious indebtednesses for this volume, the Research Board of the University of Illinois has over many years and in many persons supported my research in many ways. The executives of my university have been sympathetic and encouraging, and the librarians have continued to be my willing fellow researchers. The volume was put into final form and its materials checked during the school year 1953-54, while I was a Fulbright Senior Research Scholar to the United Kingdom, affiliated with Bedford College, London University, where my official mentor was the late Professor Una M. Ellis-Fermor. Blessed may her memory be. The staff of the British Museum gave more than duty; it gave also that good-will which makes a scholar know that he is welcome and at home.

Incidentally, because of that final checking in 1953-54, I have been wary of opening up the text, unless absolutely obliged, to materials which have appeared since then. To avoid confounding confusion, one must in work of this kind set a terminal date somewhere for both content and form, and that date is usually several years before the work can finally lumber into print. In that final painful ordeal of print, the staff of the University Press have used their professional skills to alleviate the process, made even more strenuous by the fact that I was at the time on leave from the University of Illinois as Visiting Professor at Southern Illinois University, commuting the two hundred miles week-ends. To all, my sincere appreciation of their patient aid and encouragement.

Finally, to use the words of Leonard Mascall (*The first Booke of Cattell* (1591),A3^v), though asking the reader to overlook their belligerent overtones, "If any thinke not well hereof, or despise this my trauell, I will friendly desire them with these wordes: *Quod melior nosti, candidus imparti, si non, his vtere mecum.* [Horace, *Epist.* VI, 67-68, adapted] Which is, If you know any better how to mend it, of your courtesie impart it, if not, take part of this with me." "Take part of this with me." Take part of me in this.

Contents

APPENDIXES

CHAPTER I

The Literary Genetics of Robert Greene's Shake-scene Passage[1]

In examining William Shakspere's work of 1592-94, we can hardly do better than to begin with Robert Greene's unfavorable appraisal, direct and implied, in 1592. Greene's diatribe against Shake-scene is known to everyone, and its possible meanings have been argued *ad nauseam*. But we have not yet been sufficiently conscious of the long train of events which led up to it, and in the light of which it must be interpreted. For Greene had acquired considerable experience in castigating opponents before Shake-scene fell under his lash, and even so, Shake-scene catches only a random blow from a particular thong which had been often used on his fellows.

So far as is at present known, Marlowe was the first to arouse Greene's literary ire. In his epistle "To the Gentlemen readers" prefixed to *Perimedes The Blacke-Smith* (S.R. March 29, 1588, published the same year), Greene says,

the small pamphlets that I haue thrust forth how you haue regarded them I know not, but that they haue been badly rewarded with any ill tearmes I neuer found, which makes me the more bold to trouble you, and the more bound to rest yours euerye waie, as euer I haue done: I keepe my old course, to palter vp some thing in Prose, vsing mine old poesie still, *Omne tulit punctum,* although latelye two Gentlemen Poets, made two mad men of Rome beate it out of their paper bucklers: & had it in derision, for that I could not make my verses iet vpon the stage in tragicall buskins, euerie worde filling the mouth like the faburden of Bo-Bell, daring God out of heauen with that Atheist *Tamburlan,* or blaspheming with the mad preest of the sonne: but let me rather openly pocket vp the Asse at *Diogenes* hand: then wantonlye set out such impious instances of intollerable poetrie, such mad and scoffing poets, that haue propheticall spirits as bred of *Merlins* race, if there be anye in England that set the end of scollarisme in an English blanck verse, I thinke either it is the humor of a nouice that tickles them with selfe-loue, or to much frequenting the hot house (to vse the Germaine prouerbe) hath swet out all the greatest part of their wits, which wasts *Gradatim,* as the Italians say *Poco à poco.* If I speake darkely Gentlemen, and offend with this digression, I

---

[1] I delivered a lecture excerpted from this chapter at Bedford College, London University, December 1, 1953, while I was affiliated with that institution as a Fulbright Senior Research Scholar.

craue pardon, in that I but answere in print, what they haue offered on the
Stage: but leauing these phantasticall schollers, as iudging him that is not
able to make choice of his chaffer, but a pedling chapman, at last to *Perymedes
the Black Smith*.[2]

It appears that two plays are here involved, one being Marlowe's *Tamburlaine* (both parts). In the other play, the two "mad men of Rome"
would have been fellow actors of "the mad preest of the sonne," who is
accused of "blaspheming." It is reasonably certain that these were actors
in *Heliogabalus*, which was entered S.R. June 19, 1594, but of which no
copy is known.[3] Elagabalus, priest of the Syro-Phoenician Sun-god, mad
enough in all conscience, would be "the mad preest of the sonne." He was
"Supposed to be the bastarde sonne of *Antonius Caracalla* emperour of
Rome, and (as *Lampridius* wryteth in his lyfe) of *Semiamitra:* or (as
Egnatus wryteth) of *Scenides,* his cosen: he was made emperour after
Macrinus, and *Diadumenus,* being but a boye of .xvi. yeres olde. He so
muche exceaded in detestable leachery and promoting of vyle persones, and
rybaldes, that fynally he was hated of all men, and at last slaine and
drawen through the city of Rome, and throwen into the ryuer of *Tyber.*
All be it he was warned afore of astronomers, that he should die a violent
death: and therefore hadde prouided ropes of sylke (if neede were) to
hange himselfe, swoordes of golde to kylle himselfe, strong poysons in
Jacinctes and Emerauldes, to poyson himselfe, if he were inforced. Moreouer he made a very high towre, hauing the floore of boordes keuered with
plates of golde, & bordered w^t precious stones, from the whiche he
would throwe himselfe downe, whan he were pursued. But al this nothinge auayled, for he was slayne by knaues."[4] The play should have been
sensational enough! The "propheticall spirits" would be the "astronomers," I suppose. The reference to these "propheticall spirits as bred of
Merlins race" may indicate that Marlowe had some responsibility for the
play, but I suppose the stunt of the "two mad men of Rome" from the
play would be a sufficient connection.

Upon what occasion had the "two Gentlemen Poets" caused "two mad
men of Rome" to deride Greene's motto of *Omne tulit punctum,* for the
reason that he wrote only love pamphlets, not blank-verse tragedies? It is
important here to clear the allusion in the beating of the motto out of
paper bucklers. The figure is of missile words aimed at a paper target, as
in Nashe, where Harvey is represented as having "cald forth the biggest

---

[2] *Perimedes* (1588), A3$^{r\&v}$; A. B. Grosart, *The Life and Complete Works in Prose
and Verse of Robert Greene, M. A.,* VII, 7-8.

[3] E. K. Chambers, *The Elizabethan Stage,* IV, 401. It will be well to remember,
however, that when Richard Jones printed "the two tragical Discourses of the
Scythian Shepheard, *Tamburlaine*" in 1590, he "(purposely) omitted and left out
some fond and friuolous Iestures . . . far vnmeet for the matter."

[4] Thomas Cooper, *Thesavrvs Lingvae Romanae et Britannicae* (1565).

gunshot of my thundring tearmes . . . to come and trie them selues on his paper Target."[5] Greene had shot his motto missile into the paper bucklers of the Romans, and they now beat it out on the stage. We must, therefore, look for a pamphlet of Greene's under this motto, in which he attacks Romans.

Before March 29, 1588, Greene had used this motto, so far as is at present known, only for *Arbasto* (S.R. August 13, 1584), and *Penelopes Web* (S.R. June 26, 1587). In the preface of the latter pamphlet, "To The Gentlemen Readers," Greene follows his usual formula in saying that he has found the gentlemen favorable, or at least they have not objected. He also admits, as usual, that, "It may be the forehead is not alwayes a true heralt of affections, neither the rules of Phisiognomie infallible principles: for they which smiled at the *Theatre* in Rome, might assoone scoffe at the rudenesse of the *Scaene,* as giue a Plaudite at the perfection of the action, and they which passe ouer my toyes with silence, may per-happes shrowde a mislike in such patience: if they doe, yet soothing my selfe in the hope of their courtesies, I sleepe content like *Phidias* in myne owne follies, thinking all is well, till proofe telles me the contrarie."[6] In *Euphues his censure to Philautus* (S.R. September 18, 1587), Greene was still complacently sleeping in his follies. But before his next pamphlet, *Perimedes,* Phidias Greene had a rude awakening. Because of the slur Greene had here cast upon the rudeness of the scene at Rome, that is, of the plays as distinguished from the acting, two gentlemen poets had caused two madmen of Rome to beat Greene's motto out of their bucklers in derision. But in spite of this Greene still keeps his formula to gentle-men in general, since while these madmen were set on by gentlemen, those were only gentlemen poets, upholding the plays (scene) of Rome (Lon-don) against the charge of rudeness; but Greene does not write tragedies, and merely continues to palter up love pamphlets in prose for the gentle-men who read the kind of things he writes under his motto; and they will know how to choose what they like. Why these two gentlemen poets (Marlowe and another), rather than others, should have taken Greene to task does not appear.

We need, however, to go beyond the fireworks of purely personal re-criminations and to get at the fundamentals of the quarrel. Greene had not attacked these gentlemen poets personally, and he intends to keep his "old course" of writing prose pamphlets for gentlemen readers. These gentlemen poets are said to allege that Greene "could not make . . . [his] verses iet vpon the stage in tragicall buskins" in such tragedies as they write. Greene's verses, be it remembered, were set in the ornate frame-

---

[5] R. B. McKerrow, *The Works of Thomas Nashe,* I, 321.

[6] *Penelopes Web* [1587], A3ᵛ; Grosart, *Greene,* V, 144.

work of his pamphlets. But Greene had rather be considered an ass in his old form than to "set the end of scollarisme in an English blanck verse" as they do, either because they are novices, or because they have sweated their brains out at the hothouse. Greene merely answers in print what these fantastical scholars have offered on the stage. The issue is thus clearly drawn as to the proper standards of art. Should gentlemen accept the bombast blank verse of the stage as the height of art, or should they continue to demand such ornate work as Lyly and Greene produced? It was the gentlemen poets who alleged that Greene could not write such verse tragedies as they, and Greene replies that he does not wish to do so, since the end of "scollarisme" is not an English blank verse, but such work as he is doing.

Though the contrary is regularly assumed, it will be seen upon this limiting background that Greene is quite clear that he has not yet written for the stage at this time, or at least has not written tragedies, about March, 1588.[7] Of the two gentlemen poets, one is certainly Marlowe, whose atheist Tamburlaine is alluded to. The other appears to be accused of "blaspheming with the mad preest of the sonne." Similarly, there are two explanations offered for their aberrations. The first is that to consider English blank verse the height of scholarship is the humor of a novice, which is certainly aimed at Marlowe, who had begun his literary career in London less than a year before. The second explanation is that the person must have sweated out his brains gradually at the hothouse (remember Nashe's Seneca let blood line by line and page by page, that is, *poco à poco,* as also the connected allusion to "French *Doudie*" next year!), which presumably explains the condition of Marlowe's companion poet, who is thus apparently an older man.[8]

Whether Marlowe and his companion poet made any reply, I do not know. But Greene neither forgot nor forgave. With the aid of Nashe, he continued the next year in *Menaphon* (S.R. August 23, 1589) his defense of true art, where Marlowe's *Tamburlaine* still draws his shafts, but being now joined with *The Taming of a Shrew.* "I reade that mightie *Tamberlaine* after his wife *Zenocrate* (the worlds faire eye) past out of the Theater of this mortall life, he chose stigmaticall trulls to please his humorous fancie."[9] The reference is, of course, to "Now, bright Zenocrate, the world's fair eye."[10] There is also the possible reference to Marlowe in the teller of "a *Canterbury* tale; some propheticall full mouth

---

[7] It seems now generally agreed that all surviving plays attributed to Greene are later than this. See pp. 56 ff.

[8] We shall later identify this companion poet. See pp. 31 ff.

[9] *Menaphon* (1589), F2ʳ; Grosart, *Greene,* VI, 84.

[10] U. M. Ellis-Fermor, *Tamburlaine the Great* (II), I, 4, 1; C. F. T. Brooke, *The Works of Christopher Marlowe, Tamburlaine,* line 2570.

that as he were a Coblers eldest sonne, would by the laste tell where anothers shooe wrings."[11] Since this occurs in the same connection as the reference to Zenocrate and only shortly after, it may very well be that Greene's proverbial expressions take the embodiment of Marlowe, eldest son of a cobbler of Canterbury. That would also explain the dark reference to this person in a "propheticall full mouth" as an allusive rephrasing of "propheticall spirits as bred of *Merlins* race." It would thus mean full-mouthed Marlowe. Why else "propheticall" if not referring to Merlin (Marlowe)?[12] Greene also parodies a speech in *The Taming of a Shrew*, which is itself a burlesque of a speech of Tamburlaine to Zenocrate in *Tamburlaine;* and Nashe is in on the joke, whatever it is.[13]

It is important to get at the fundamental satiric objectives of Nashe and Greene in *Menaphon*. In his preface Nashe carries on Greene's quarrel with Marlowe and his group along exactly the same lines that Greene had implied in *Penelopes Web* and had laid down in *Perimedes*. Here we must remember that Nashe himself was about to get published an "Embrion" of his own "infancie," *The Anatomie of Absvrditie*, which had been entered S.R. several months earlier, September 19, 1588, and to which he alludes as forthcoming toward the end of the epistle we are about to discuss. In this *Anatomie*, he feels "that little alliance which I haue vnto Arte, will authorize my follie in defacing her enemie," in spite of his "vnexperienst infirmities." He is thus a self-appointed puny champion of Art against Ignorance, the latter itself usually preferring to be called Nature. To that end he intends "to take a view of sundry mens vanitie, a suruey of their follie, a briefe of their barbarisme, to runne through Authors of the absurder sort, assembled in the Stacioners shop, sucking and selecting out of these vpstart antiquaries, somewhat of their vnsauery duncerie, meaning to note it with a *Nigrum theta,* that each one at the first sight may eschew it as infectious, to shewe it to the worlde that all men may shunne it."[14] The "vnlearned Idiots . . . are euery quarter bigge wyth one Pamphlet or other," whereas "those that are more exquisitly furnished with learning, shroude themselues in obscuritie." These unlearned idiots are "the very same . . . that obtrude themselues vnto vs, as the Authors of eloquence, and fountains of our finer phrases, when as they sette before vs, nought but a confused masse of wordes

---

[11] *Menaphon* (1589), F2^v; Grosart, *Greene*, VI, 86.

[12] Brooke makes the point that this is the Cambridge form of the name (Marlyn, Marlin, Marlen, or Malyn), in which he is followed by John Bakeless (*The Tragicall History of Christopher Marlowe*, I, 96), who believes that this fact "suggests that Greene had been personally acquainted with Marlowe while they were both at Cambridge, for the play that he makes on the name of the magician, Merlin, is intelligible only to those who know Marlowe as 'Marlin.' "

[13] See below, pp. 105 ff.

[14] *Anatomie* (1589), A1^r; McKerrow, *Nashe*, I, 9.

without matter, a Chaos of sentences without any profitable sence." Nashe is speaking in terms of the Erasmian statement of rhetorical doctrine as *Copia Rerum et Verborum*. These idiots think themselves "Authors of eloquence," *elocutio*, tropes and schemes, so that they are "fountains of our finer phrases." But they produce in fact "wordes without matter." They have *copia verborum*, but not *rerum*.

Nashe then anatomizes the unlearned matter of current literature, beginning with the matter of love, proceeding to ignorant divinity based upon translations only, yet presuming to correct even the magistrate, alleging the persuasions of the spirit (one should remember the Marprelate background), thence to the popular scientists, "astronomers," of the day with their prognostications of dire things to come, though they have only "a little Countrey Grammer knowledge god wote." Lest his purpose be mistaken, he then launches into a defense of poetry, and so on to "a rule for Students," wherein he points out that "he that estimats Artes by the insolence of Idiots,[15] who professe that wherein they are Infants, may deeme the Vniuersitie nought but the Nurse of follie, and the knowledge of Artes, nought but the imitation of the Stage. This I speake to shew what an obloquie, these impudent incipients in Arts, are vnto Art." Nashe goes on to admit that "Amongst all the ornaments of Artes, Rethorick is to be had in highest reputation, without the which all the rest are naked, and she onely garnished: yet some there be who woulde seperate Arts from Eloquence, whose [censures we] oppugne, because it abhorres from common experience." He then goes into detail to illustrate and warn against this fallacy. In all this Nashe is making his distinction in terms of the fundamental definition of rhetoric (*elocutio*, ornament) and logic (matter, art), where these primary definitions themselves regularly averred that the two could not be separated, rhetoric being the hand open, logic the hand closed, etc. So these "impudent incipients in Arts" are fundamentally wrong when they think that Art may be obtained by mere "imitation[16] of the Stage," without necessity of troubling about a thorough university training in matter. There must be sound matter (*copia rerum*, logic, etc.) as well as ornate words (*copia verborum*, rhetoric, *elocutio*) in true Art.

In the *Anatomie*, a very young man dons a tremendous grey beard of gnomic generalities. Certainly he is a credit to university Art. But in his

---

[15] This gets condensed into "their idiote art-masters" in *Menaphon*.

[16] Of course, everyone assumed imitation; the only questions were what to imitate and by what methods. Nashe had said earlier, "I am not ignorant, that farre more ardent is the desire of of [*sic*] knowing vnknowne thinges, then of repeating knowne things, this we see happen in Stageplayers, in Orators, in al things, men hast vnto nouelties, and runne to see new things, so that whatsoeuer is not vsuall, of the multitude is admired, yet must Students wisely prefer renowned antiquitie before newe found toyes" (*Anatomie* [1589], E1ᵛ; McKerrow, *Nashe*, I, 43).

preface to *Menaphon* this young man makes pungent application to personal cases. For as Nashe was finally about to be delivered of this burden of the *Anatomie,* the opportunity came to write a puff for *Menaphon* by Robert Greene, Master in Arts of either University. It is thus Nashe's cue to commend Greene's work "To the Gentlemen Students *of both Vniuersities."* He appeals to them as the only qualified judges, though he knows "how eloquent our gowned age is growen of late; so that euerie moechanicall mate abhorres the english he was borne too, and plucks with a solemne periphrasis, his *vt vales* from the inkhorne: which I impute not so much to the perfection of arts, as to the seruile imitation[17] of vainglorious tragoedians, who contend not so seriouslie to excell in action,[18] as to embowell the clowdes in a speach of comparison;[19] thinking themselues more than initiated in poets immortalitie, if they but once get *Boreas* by the beard, and the heauenlie bull by the deaw-lap." As we shall see,[20] Greene connects Marlowe with the Boreas figure.

The practitioners of the illiberal mechanic arts, relying upon the stage as the arbiter of art, now set themselves against the practitioners of the liberal arts in the Universities as the true arbiters of art. The dramatists, "their idiote art-masters," who write these speeches for the actors are even more foolish than the actors themselves. Nashe's phrase, "their idiote art-masters" is condensed from "he that estimats Artes by the insolence of Idiots" of the *Anatomie.* It has taken this form here because Marlowe, to whom he has just alluded through the Boreas figure, was a Master of Arts. These idiot art-masters "intrude thēselues to our eares as the alcumists of eloquence . . . [and] (moūted on the stage of arrogance) think to outbraue better pens with the swelling bumbast of a bragging blanke verse."[21] Now it may be that the "ouerflow of some kilcow conceipt" which overcloys "their imagination with a more than drunken resolution," "commits the disgestion of their cholerick incumbrances, to the spacious volubilitie of a drumming decasillabon," since they are "not extemporall in the inuention of anie other meanes to vent their manhood" (*cf.* "drunken resolution"). That is, the imagination being drunk with killcow conceits may vomit forth involuntarily or ex-

---

[17] This is the technical rhetorical term of the day.

[18] "Action," the proper art of the actor. The reference is technical and can only be to actors, not to writers.

[19] The technical rhetorical term, correctly applied to *this speech as a whole,* not to the figure alone.

[20] See below, pp. 105 ff.

[21] Ward was reminded here of *Faustus:* "It is quite possible that Nash may have intentionally chosen the expression 'alcumists,' and the phrase describing these alchemists as 'mounted' on a stage of arrogance, in remembrance of the alchemist Doctor Faustus in Marlowe's play, who for no mountebank purpose, 'mounts him up to scale Olympus' top'" (A. W. Ward, *Marlowe, Tragical History of Dr. Faustus; Greene, Honourable History of Friar Bacon and Friar Bungay* [1901], p. xviii).

temporally its incumbrances in drumming decasyllables, since it has no other form in which to vent itself.[22]

In "the spacious volubilitie of a drumming decasillabon" Nashe is echoing a figure he had used in *Anatomie*. There he had objected to those "that obtrude themselues vnto vs, as the Authors of eloquence, and fountains of our finer phrases, when as they sette before vs, nought but a confused masse of wordes without matter, a Chaos of sentences without any profitable sence, resembling drummes, which beeing emptie with in, sound big without. These authors have *copia verborum,* but not of *rerum; sententiae* without sense.[23] Their work is as empty as a drum and as noisy. So they require "the spacious volubilitie of a drumming decasillabon."

We need also to remember here Nashe's later statement of his objections to the theory of extemporal invention by black-pot inspiration. He believes the true scholar must have a black spot of the poet (be a "maker"), but he will not attain that black spot by black-pot inspiration.

But how euer their dissentious iudgements, should decree in their afternoone sessions of *an sit,* the priuat trueth, of my discouered Creede in this controuersie is this, that as that beast, was thought scarce worthie to bee sacrifised, to the Aegiptian *Epaphus,* who had not some or other blacke spotte on his skinne: so I deeme him farre vnworthie of the name of a scholler, & so consequentlie, to sacrifice his endeuors to art, that is not a Poet, either in whole or in a parte and here peraduenture, some desperate quipper, will canuaze my proposed comparison *plus vltra,* reconciling the allusion of the blacke spot, to the blacke pot; which makes our Poets vndermeale Muses so mutinous, as euerie stanzo they pen after dinner, is full poynted with a stabbe. Which their dagger drunkennesse, although it might be excused, with *Tam Marti quam Mercurio,* yet will I couer it as well as I may, with that prouerbiall *foecundi calices,* that might wel haue been doore keeper, to the kanne of *Silenus,* when nodding on his Asse trapt with iuie, hee made his moist nosecloth, the pausing intermedium, twixt euerie nappe. Let frugale scholares, and fine fingerd nouices, take their drinke by the ownce, and their wine by the halpeworthes, but it is for a Poet, to examine the pottle pottes, and gage the bottome of whole gallons; *qui bene vult* ποιειν, *debet ante* πινειν. A pot of blew burning ale, with a fierie flaming tost, is as good as *Pallas* with the nine Muses on *Pernassus* top: without the which, in vaine may they crie; ô thou my muse inspire mee with some pen, when they want certaine liquid sacrifice, to rouze her foorth her denne. Pardon me Gentlemen, though somewhat merely I glaunce, at their imoderate follie, who affirme that no man can write with conceit, except he take counsell of the cup.

Pot-fury may result extemporally in "the spacious volubilitie of a drumming decasillabon"; but it is not the true poetic fury divine.

---

[22] Cf. "Amongest all others, *M. Whyte,* then bishop of Lincolne (hys Poeticall vaine being drunken with ioy of the Mariage) spued out certain verses" (John Foxe, *Ecclesiasticall history contaynyng the Actes and Monumentes of thynges passed* (1570), p. 1642; slightly adapted in Holinshed (1587), III, 1120, col. 2, top). See p. 516.

[23] *Anatomie* (1589), A1ᵛ; McKerrow, *Nashe,* I, 10. See an illustration of the type in connection with English Seneca later.

It is advisable here to notice how a contemporary evidently interpreted this part of Nashe's epistle. When in his *Virgidemiarum* of 1597 Joseph Hall models upon and echoes Nashe's epistle, he makes some very significant applications. In Book I, Satire 2, Hall laments that some of the Muses had been deflowered of late

> And where they wont sip of the simple flood,
> Now tosse they bowles of *Bacchus* boyling blood.

So

> Ye bastard Poets see your Pedigree
> From common Trulls, and loathsom Brothelry.

Consequently, Hall opens Satire 3 with these bacchic bastards in pot-fury from wine, exhaling stenches.

> One higher pitch'd doth set his soaring thought
> On crowned kings that Fortune hath low brought:
> Or some vpreared, high-aspiring swaine
> As it might be the Turkish *Tamberlaine*.
> Then weeneth he his base drink-drowned spright,
> Rapt to the threefold loft of heauens hight,
> When he conceiues vpon his fained stage
> The stalking steps of his great personage,
> Graced with huf-cap termes, and thundring threats,
> That his poore hearers hayre quite vpright sets.
> Such soone, as some braue-minded hungry youth,
> Sees fitly fram[d] to his wide-strained mouth,
> He vaunts his voyce vpon an hyred stage,
> With high-set steps, and princely carriage:
> Now soouping in side robes of Royalty,
> That earst did skrub in lowsie brokery.
> There if he can with termes Italianate,
> Big-sounding sentences, and words of state,
> Faire patch me vp his pure *Iambick* verse,
> He rauishes the gazing Scaffolders:
> Then certes was the famous *Corduban*
> Neuer but halfe so high *Tragedian*.

From these "showes of Fortunes fall, / And bloudy Tyrants rage" Hall turns to the clown who "iustles straight into the princes place," with the poets sitting in judgment.

We are concerned with the quoted presentation of tragedy, not with the justling comedy. The tragedy is of two kinds: (1) of "crowned kings that Fortune hath low brought," or as rephrased, "showes of Fortunes fall"; (2) of "some vpreared, high-aspiring swaine" such as Tamburlaine, rephrased as "bloudy Tyrants rage." Nashe does not specify *Tamburlaine;* Hall does, and he might well have specified *Edward II* as a show "of Fortunes fall." The high-pitched author of such plays thinks "his base drink-drowned spright" rapt to the third heaven, and visualizes the stalking steps (see the allusions to Tamburlaine), huf-cap terms, and thundering threats of the character, which some wide-mouthed actor immediately presents, with "high-set steps," "soouping" in royal robes about the stage. The author uses "termes Italianate" to "patch me vp" his iambics and ravish the scaffolders, thinking himself twice as good a tragedian as Seneca. Here *Tamburlaine* is singled out specifically to go along with the Italianizers, Senecanizers, bombasters, etc. Nashe's allusions[24] had suggested Tamburlaine to Hall as they do to us, and Hall joins with it the plays of Fortune's fall. I am afraid we must add Hall to Nashe and Greene as one who did not approve of Marlowe's mighty line — and that exactly because it was so "mighty"! Nor may we overlook the alleged pot-fury inspiration.[25]

Nashe has alluded to Marlowe in the Boreas figure. His phrase "kilcow conceipt" is also an allusion, but not to Marlowe. In *Pappe with an hatchet,* "probably near the close of September," 1589,[26] Lyly had in effect taunted Gabriel Harvey to come in on one side or the other of the Martinist controversy. "And one will we coniure vp, that writing a familiar Epistle about the naturall causes of an Earthquake, fell into the bowells of libelling, which made his eares quake for feare of clipping, he shall tickle you with taunts; all his works bound close, are at least sixe sheetes in quarto, & he calls them the first tome of his familiar Epistle. . . . If he ioyne with vs, *periisti Martin,* thy wit will be massacred: if the toy take him to close with thee, then haue I my wish, for this tenne yeres haue I lookt to lambacke him."[27]

This attack touched up both Richard and Gabriel. Richard was first in print and evidently first in composition, with *Plaine Percevall,* which preceded his *Lamb of God* (S.R. October 23, 1589).[28] In *Plaine Percevall,* Richard Harvey as self-appointed "Peace Maker of England" poured hot water on both sides of the Martinist conflict. To Martin he says, "They haue plaguy Clubfists, the one with his Counter-Cuffe, the other with his Country-Cuffe, would quickly make a blew MARTIN. And you on the other side: what neede all this stir? this banding of kilcowes to fight with a shadow?" So Lyly with his *Countrie cuffe,* or *Pappe with an hatchet,* and the author of *Countercuffe* are now killcows "on the other side," fighting with a shadow.

Richard Harvey has here turned the killcow epithet in terms of its original background. For it was Captain Crackstone in *Fedele and Fortvnio* (S.R. November 12, 1584; printed 1585) who was at the bottom of these

---

[24] If Hall is independent of Nashe, then the case is all the stronger.

[25] Marlowe had died in a tavern brawl, and some contemporaries were beginning to make much more than the most of it.

[26] R. W. Bond, *The Complete Works of John Lyly,* I, 55.

[27] Bond, *Lyly,* I, 30, n. 2; III, 400.

[28] McKerrow, *Nashe,* V, 172.

allusions. While Fedele, Pedante, and their assistants lie in wait with a net, Captain Crackstone enters to exhibit his valerosity.

Crack-st. Now shall my valerositie appeare vnto all,
How I can kill men, and serue a woman at her call.
My gr[ea]test griefe is, that in dooing this feate,
I am sure my honour will not be so greate.
As when I giue a charger to my foes in the open feelde,
Or put Citties into sackes, and make thousandes to yeelde.

. . . .

I will make a great noyse before *Victoriaes* doore in the streete,
As though at this present with *Fedele* I did meete.
Then will I runne to her house amayne,
And make her beleeue that *Fedele* is slayne.
Then before that she heare any newes of his life,
I'le haue her to the Priest, and make her my wife.
Haue euen at it as well as I can,   *Fight with the Ayre.*
Ah Villaines, thus many of you set vpon a naked man.
Drawe on my good fellowes and spare not, strike home,
Ah cowardly Dastardes, so sone be you gone?

F]edele. Arme, Arme, Arme.
P]edante. Kill, kill, kill.
F]edele. Downe with *Crack-stone.*
P]edante. Giue me a Bill.   *Heere Crack-stone runnes into the net, Fedele*
F]edele. Followe, followe.   *after him, leauing Pedante on the stage.*
C]rack-st. Out alas where am I now?
P]edante. Faste ynough by this time I trow.
Is this my lusty kill Cow, that will eate vp so many men at a bit,
And when he deales with a shadowe will not stand to it?[29]

Notice Crackstone's "Fight with the Ayre," and the consequent taunt about fighting with shadows.

Is this my lusty kill Cow, that will eate vp so many men at a bit,
And when he deales with a shadowe will not stand to it?

So Pigmy Dick turns this into his conceit of the "banding of kilcowes to fight with a shadow." Evidently Captain Crackstone had impressed Dick, as he had impressed Nashe and many another.

We should also notice that the "kill Cow" conceit for Crackstone is really Mundy's own. Pasqualigo had ended the corresponding scene thus:

Fran. . . . ah codardi, ah vili, ah poltroni, ah infami tornate à dietro
ch'io non vi temo vna paglia, tutti in pezzi assassini da strada.
Nar. Ecco il vigliaco che combatte cõ l'aria adosso.
Comp. Amazza, amazza il traditore.
Fran. Ohime ch'io son morto da douero.[30]

---

[29] *M.S.R.,* 1338-43, 1354-72 (IV, 6).
[30] L. Pasqualigo, *Il Fedele* (1576), pp. 138-139.

Here in the original is the fighting with the air, as in Mundy's stage direction, but not the cow-killing. Frangipietra is called *codardi,* and cow was a term for coward. And Frangipietra was a coward pretending to be a killer. But there is no necessary suggestion of Mundy's "kill Cow" epithet.

Cows do get opprobrious mention in the play. As Narcissus sees the women approaching to do their conjuring for love, he says, "ò che cricca di Vacche."[31] Mundy gives this to Pedante, translating as "what cattell haue we heare?"[32] Again, when Narcissus is admitted by Attilia, servant of Beatrice, he says, "Non lo diss'io? mi racomando in furia, la uacca è nostra."[33] Narcissus had just overheard Frangipietra threatening to kill Fedele. But he then turns to the business in hand and his remark appears to apply to Attilia, as both Fraunce and Mundy also appear to think, though both adapt very generally here, and neither translates. The term *bestia* had been used more times than one, and had been applied to Frangipietra, while he himself had boasted "Io son un'huomo bestialissimo & terribile."[34] Florio will explain, *"Bestia,* any kinde of beast: it is taken for a mans priuy parts, a buls pizell." *"Vacca,* a cowe." *Vaccamente,* like a cowe, whorishlie, beastly." *"Vaccheggiare,* to play the cowe, the beast or filthie whore." I suppose these double-entendres could have suggested to Mundy that Frangipietra was a killcow, but still the actual invention would belong to Mundy.

Mundy had also insisted upon the "conceit" of the play. The title describes the play as "a very pleasaunt and fine conceited Comoedie," to which the headtitle adds "with the merie deuises of *Captaine Crack-stone,"* and Mundy in his dedication also praises "this prettie Conceit, as well for the inuention, as the delicate conueiance thereof." Here is "conceit" enough, combined with kill-cow Crackstone. So Mundy's *Fedele and Fortvnio* furnished Nashe his phrase "kilcow conceipt," just as it had furnished Richard Harvey his opprobrious label.

Both sides continue to bandy the term, and in the process it becomes clear that Nashe is quite conscious of the source of his phrase, just as Richard Harvey evidently shapes his opprobrious label with a full knowledge of its source. After Richard had labeled Lyly and another as cow-killers in his *Plaine Percevall,* he proceeded to his *Lamb of God* (S.R. October 23, 1589). In his preface, which appears to have been added after the book was published,[35] he pays his disrespects to Nashe as no

---

[31] Pasqualigo, *Il Fedele* (1576), p. 39.

[32] *M.S.R.,* 501.

[33] Pasqualigo, *Il Fedele* (1576), p. 88.

[34] Pasqualigo, *Il Fedele* (1576), p. 70.

[35] McKerrow, *Nashe,* V, 75, n. 6, 176.

better than Martin. "It becummeth me not to play that part in Diuinitie, that one *Thomas Nash* hath lately done in humanitie, who taketh vppon him in ciuill learning, as *Martin* doth in religion, peremptorily censuring his betters at pleasure, Poets, Orators, Polihistors, Lawyers, and whome not? and making as much and as little of euery man as himselfe listeth. . . . Iwis this *Thomas Nash,* one whome I neuer heard of before (for I cannot imagin him to be *Thomas Nash* our Butler of *Pembrooke Hall,* albeit peraduenture not much better learned) sheweth himselfe none of the meetest men, to censure Sir *Thomas Moore,* Sir *Iohn Cheeke,* Doctor *Watson,* Doctor *Haddon,* Maister *Ascham,* Doctor *Car,* my brother Doctor *Haruey,* and such like; yet the iolly man will needes be playing the douty *Martin* in his kinde, and limit euery mans commendation according to his fancy, profound no doubt and exceeding learned, as the world nowe goeth in such worthy workes."[36] Nashe himself later speaks of his alleged offense as having been given "in an epistle of mine,"[37] and the details refer to the epistle to *Menaphon,* not to the *Anatomie.* It is thus clear that Richard had read the epistle attentively, to find that Nashe was guilty of setting himself up as sole censor in civil learning exactly as Martin had in religion. He may there have been reminded by Nashe's killcow epithet of Captain Crackstone. For, as we have seen, Richard was in some way reminded of the play, and applied the epithet to Lyly and another pamphleteer. Is Richard accusing Mundy of being the author of *Countercuffe,* and is this why the epithet gets applied also to his yokemate Lyly, who has no killcows in his pamphlet? I do not know why else he was so careful to identify his allusion.[38]

The cause of Richard's displeasure against Nashe in the preface to his *Lamb of God* is all too clear. Anyone with the guilt of hexameters on his conscience as had Gabriel Harvey would certainly feel the sting of the lash when Nashe asked, "what can be hoped of those that . . . haue not learned so long as they haue liued in the spheares, the iust measure of the Horizon without an hexameter"? If, besides, that person prided himself upon having originated the English hexameter and Stanyhurst to boot, as Nashe later accused Harvey of doing, then unquestionably Nashe had been offensive in the highest degree to "my brother Doctor *Haruey.*" It would certainly appear to the brothers that while Nashe reprehends Martin in church and state, Nashe is himself guilty of the same sin of arrogance against the hierarchy of letters. Richard Harvey's accusation of Nashe arose quite naturally, whatever his wisdom in making it.

In the meantime, Gabriel Harvey had prepared to take John Lyly apart

---

[36] McKerrow, *Nashe,* V, 179-180.

[37] McKerrow, *Nashe,* I, 195.

[38] For Professor J. Dover Wilson's suspicions concerning Mundy, see p. 519.

for his challenge in *Pappe with an Hatchet*. Gabriel's reply is dated "At Trinitie hall: this fift of Nouember: 1589,"[39] but for some reason he did not publish it till *Pierce's Supererogation* in 1593. Here Harvey says of Lyly as Paphatchet, "Muster his arrant braueries togither: and where such a terrible killcowe, or such a vengeable bull-beggar to deal withall?"[40] Discussing in this section the fundamental weakness of "Consistories," Harvey threw in the aside "(some good fellowes are kill-cowes, and some poore neighbours all-hart)"[41] Gabriel has thus followed the lead of Richard in making Lyly a killcow, and with Lyly alone is he here concerned.

And here the matter rested for some years. Gabriel did not publish. Nashe did not reply to Richard. Lyly and the author of *Countercuffe* did not come out of their anonymity to reply. Evidently Tilney and his fellow inquisitors had laid down the law. Apparently it was Robert Greene who stirred up the hornet's nest again in his *Qvip for an Vpstart Courtier* (S.R. July 21, 1592).[42] Then Nashe himself in *Pierce Penilesse* (S.R. August 8, 1592) answered the attack which Richard had made upon him in the preface to his *Lamb of God*. Here Nashe also used the killcow epithet again, but apparently without personal application, though Nashe does insist upon Pride as one of Gabriel Harvey's deadly sins. *"Fraunce, Italy,* and *Spaine,* are all full of these false hearted *Machiuillions:* but properly Pride is the disease of the Spaniard. . . . Let a man sooth him in this vaine of kilcow vanitie, you may commaund his heart out of his belly, to make you a rasher on the coales, if you will next your heart."[43] Revival of the feud with the Harvey brothers has revived the epithet for Nashe.

Gabriel Harvey took up the cudgels for his brother Richard in *Fovre Letters,* saying of Nashe, "some odd wittes forsooth, will needes bee accompted terrible Bull Beggars, and the onely Killcowes of their age."[44] So in his preface to the Gentlemen Readers of *Strange Newes* (S.R. January 12, 1593), Nashe retorts, "I come to *The kilcow champion of the three brethren;* he forsooth wil be the first that shal giue *Pierce Penilesse* a *non placet,*"[45] and Nashe then explains that he had not attacked the Harveys before Richard attacked him in the *Lamb of God* two years

[39] A. B. Grosart, *The Works of Gabriel Harvey* (Huth Library), II, 221.

[40] Grosart, *Harvey,* II, 128-129.

[41] Grosart, *Harvey,* II, 195.

[42] McKerrow, *Nashe,* V, 77, n. 3. Someone, however, had echoed the controversy when in *A Prognostication* for 1591 he referred to an affirmation concerning "Martin the kill-hog" (McKerrow, *Nashe,* III, 387). Dr. McKerrow thinks that Nashe is probably not the author of this.

[43] McKerrow, *Nashe,* I, 176.

[44] Grosart, *Harvey,* I, 204.

[45] McKerrow, *Nashe,* I, 261.

before. If he thought Richard had attacked him in *Plaine Perceuall* as the author of *Countercuffe,* of which he has sometimes been accused, he gives no sign.

Gabriel Harvey then brought his heaviest artillery to bear in *Pierce's Supererogation* (1593). Gabriel here bombards all his foes, Greene, Lyly, Nashe, and Doctor Perne. We have already noticed the pamphlet against killcow Lyly, which occupies the middle of the book. In the *Precursor* to *Pierce's Supererogation* Harvey's championess is made to say of Nashe

> See, how He brayes, and fumes at me poore lasse,
> That must immortalise the killcowe ASSE.[46]

Then after Harvey has trounced Lyly as Pappadocio, he returns to Nashe as Braggadocio, Spenser's character and coined name. From him, "The newest Legendes of most hideous exploits, may learne a new Art to killcow men with peremptorie termes, and bugges-wordes of certaine death."[47] Both Nashe and Lyly are killcows to Gabriel Harvey. Lyly had been so in 1589, and is made to share the term with Nashe in 1592. Lyly was a killcow to Richard also in 1589-90, and the author of *Countercuffe* was at that time his yokefellow.

Later Nashe shows that he is aware of the source of this term of opprobrium which he and the Harveys had been tossing around all these years. When in 1596 Nashe produced *Haue with you to Saffron-walden,* he accused Harvey of having used the title of *Pierce Penilesse* to float his own venture. Nashe causes one of his characters to say of Gabriel Harvey, *"Yet for all he is such a vaine* Basilisco *and* Captaine Crack-stone *in all his actions & conuersation, & swarmeth in vile Canniball words, there is some good matter in his booke against thee."*[48] For Harvey's Braggadocio from Spenser, Nashe has returned as good measure the Italian and Spanish military braggarts Crackstone and Basilisco. Nashe has been conscious of killcow Captain Crackstone from his first allusion, as Richard Harvey also certainly was at the beginning.

On this background, it is thus clear that by "kilcow conceipt" in his epistle to *Menaphon* Nashe is alluding to Mundy along with Marlowe, though Mundy's conceit in *Fedele and Fortvnio* did not gush out into decasyllables. But this allusion is only by way of introduction, for Mundy next appears for his individual meed of dispraise. "Mongst this kinde of men that repose eternitie in the mouth of a player,[49] I can but

---

[46] Grosart, *Harvey,* II, 18.

[47] Grosart, *Harvey,* II, 224.

[48] McKerrow, *Nashe,* III, 102.

[49] Nashe's phrase, of course, alludes to the proud boast of Horace and Ovid that they would live forever by their works, specifically to Ovid's *ore . . . populi,* which Shakspere renders as "even in the mouths of men" (T. W. Baldwin, *On the Literary Genetics of Shakspere's Poems & Sonnets,* p. 292).

ingrosse some deepe read Grammarians, who hauing no more learning in their scull, than will serue to take vp a commoditie; nor Art in their brain, than was nourished in a seruing mans idlenesse, will take vpon them to be the ironicall censors of all, when God and Poetrie doth know, they are the simplest of all. To leaue these to the mercie of their mother tongue, that feed on nought but the crummes that fal from the translators trencher, I come (sweet friend) to thy *Arcadian Menaphon."* That is, there are some with a "learned grammarian's" grammar school smattering who have acquired only enough learning to be tradesmen,[50] or as servingmen have used such leisure as they had to improve their art, yet they set themselves up as "the ironicall censors of all, when . . . they are the simplest of all." These also set themselves up as arbiters of art among the mechanicals against the Universities, even though they are able to feed only on the crumbs of English translations, and they also repose eternity in the mouth of a player; that is they also write plays.[51] "Liberal Learning" had to defend itself against the "illiberal mechanicals" at every turn.

Mundy was at most a learned grammarian. How good a one I know of no competent evidence to show. Miss Turner can bring in evidence for his education the dedication to *The Mirrour of Mutabilitie* (1579), in which Mundy pays his respects to his parents for their "liberall enpences bestowed on vs in our youth, in trayning vs vp in verteous educations."[52] Also, in the *English Romayne Lyfe* he claims to have conversed in Latin at Rome. More important, if he was in any actual sense admitted to the English Seminary at Rome, as he procured an affidavit to prove, then he evidently passed muster as a sufficiently learned grammarian. It was not his Latin but his autobiography as the supposed son of an attributed father which troubled him. He has also a dedication of *Palmendos* in Latin verse to Sir Francis Drake,[53] as well as some Latin verses to Oxford at the end of the *Mirrour of Mutabilitie,* besides snatches of clownishly murdered Latin in his plays. But in each of these instances, we have primarily only Mundy's word. No doubt, Christopher Mundy, Draper, had seen to it that there was enough learning in Anthony's skull to take

---

[50] One was supposed to complete grammar school learning by fourteen at most, so that he could be apprenticed to trade for seven years to become master in a gild, or to university for seven years, so that he could become master in arts, etc.

[51] Nashe is speaking from the same point of view for literature as had Archbishop Parker for Religion. "That they should lay their Hands on none, but such as were instructed in good Learning, either in the University, or some lower Schools, or who well understood the *Latin* Tongue, and was conversant in the Scriptures . . . not brought up in Husbandry, or some other mean Trade or Calling" (John Strype, *The Life and Acts of Matthew Parker* (1711), p. 321).

[52] *Mutabilitie* Epistle, C3ʳ.

[53] Celeste Turner, *Anthony Mundy an Elizabethan Man of Letters,* p. 194.

up a commodity. Anthony had at first been apprenticed to the printing trade, but took up his freedom in 1585 by patrimony in the Drapers' Company.[54] He was at least in every respect qualified to take up a commodity. He had earlier, however, succeeded after considerable effort in becoming a "servant" of the Earl of Oxford.[55] He had, therefore, such Art in his brain as had been nourished in a serving man's idleness. His connection with translations will be more fully delineated when Nashe later returns to this subject.

Nashe's position with respect to these offenders will be even clearer if we notice his conclusion to the whole essay. "I cease to expose to your sport the picture of those Pamphleters, and Poets, that make a patrimonie of *In speech,* and more then a younger brothers inheritance of their *Abcie.* Reade fauourably, to incourage me in the firstlings of my folly, and perswade your selues, I will persecute those Idiots and their heires vnto the third generation, that haue made Art bankerout of her ornaments, and sent Poetry a begging vp and downe the Countrey. It may be, my *Anatomie* of *Absurdities* may acquaint you ere long with my skill in Surgerie, wherein the diseases of Arte more merrily discouered, may make our maimed Poets put together their blankes vnto the building of an Hospitall."

These pamphleteers and poets are insufficient scholars. They use their *Abcie;* that is, their petty school training in English, for the most part and have besides only *In speech;* that is, a smattering of grammar school knowledge. Consequently, these idiots have bankrupted art of her ornaments, specifically by their "blankes"; that is, blank verse.

So Nashe comes to Greene's *Menaphon,* a true exemplar in its "attire" of Tully's *temperatum dicendi genus.*[56] In a truly extemporal vein, Greene "will excell our greatest Art-masters deliberate thoughts," even though they take seven years (the usual length of time to reach the master's degree)[57] to their mouse, or wield an Italianate pen to afford the press "a

---

[54] Turner, *Mundy,* p. 75.

[55] Turner, *Mundy,* p. 11, etc.

[56] Greene was at the time trying his hand at being Cicero in *Ciceronis amor, Tullies Loue* (1589), and Nashe is no doubt aware of the fact.

[57] Since Nashe alludes to Horace's *ridiculus mus,* he may also have been thinking of Horace's parallel.

> ingenium, sibi quod vacuas desumpsit Athenas
> et studiis annos septem dedit insenuitque
> libris et curis, statua taciturnius exit
> plerumque et risu populum quatit.

A gifted man, that has chosen for home sequestered Athens, that has given seven years to his studies and grown grey over his books and meditations, when he walks abroad is often more mute than a statue and makes the people shake with laughter (H. R. Fairclough, *Horace* (Loeb), pp. 430-431 (Epistles, II, 2, 81-84)).

pamphlet or two in an age," of pilfries, vaunting besides Ovid's and Plutarch's plumes as their own.

It will be noticed that Nashe is here developing again one of his final and fundamental ideas in the *Anatomie.* There he pointed out that some "deeme the Vniuersitie nought but the Nurse of follie, and the knowledge of Artes, nought but the imitation of the Stage. This I speake to shew what an obloquie, these impudent incipients in Arts, are vnto Art." These are incipients in what is properly university work who have not gone far enough to cure their ignorance. Similarly, Nashe now appeals for Greene to university students, with their true standards of Art, not to the mechanicals who get their standards of Art from idiot art masters of the stage, nor to the mere learned grammarians who must depend on translation for such knowledge as they have. The condemnation is of the whole blankverse stage as the arbiter of Art as against the Universities. And in all forms of Art the Universities are the only arbiters.

These writers expect to win eternity by the bombastic rhetoric of mere stage plays, which goes no further than the mouths of the players. Stage rhetoric will not win eternity; the stage is not the arbiter of Art. Printed work, such as *Menaphon,* must perform that service, and the judges of Art must be the Universities, not mere learned grammarians, smattering ones at that. It would also appear from the Boreas allusion and the reference to "idiote art-masters" that when Nashe wrote of "the swelling bumbast of a bragging blanke verse" and of "a drumming decasillabon" he was thinking specifically of Marlowe, as we do, since Marlowe was at the time certainly writing such blank verse for that stage whose standards of Art Nashe condemns as against the standards of the Universities. In view of the past and future of Greene's quarrel with Marlowe, in which Nashe is here championing Greene along lines already laid down in *Perimedes* — in view of the past and future of this quarrel, it becomes certain that Nashe is here carrying on Greene's quarrel with Marlowe, though others than Marlowe are involved, notably Anthony Mundy.

Nashe next launches out on the theme of extemporal ability, which he has praised in Greene, it will be remembered, in contrast to that of the drunken "idiote art-masters," who could only show theirs in "a drumming decasillabon." He says that any real student with long labor can "bring forth (*tandem aliquando*) some or other thing singular," a sentence or a line a day. These students use all the stock methods of imitation (well and pungently described), even imitating the imitators so that "well may the Adage, *Nil dictum quod non dictum prius,* bee the most iudiciall estimate, of our latter writers." Still the hunger of the "vnsatiate humorists" of the public is such that it will swallow the apish devices of threadbare wits who have never been to university. "Gentlemen & riper iudgements" are advised how to "phisicke their faculties of seeing &

hearing" against this danger. "So woulde I haue them, beeing surfetted vnawares with the sweete sacietie of eloquence, which the lauish of our copious Language maie procure, to vse the remedie of contraries; and recreate their rebated witts . . . with the ouer-seeing of that *sublime dicendi genus,* which walkes abroad for wast paper in each seruing mans pocket, and the otherwhile perusing of our Gothamists barbarisme; so shoulde the opposite comparison of *Puritie,* expell the infection of absurditie; and their ouer-rackte Rhetorique, bee the Ironicall recreation of the Reader." The gentlemen are thus called back from this contemporary rhetorical absurdity to the true ideals of Tully, which are being treated so disrespectfully by ignorant serving men.

But Nashe must insist that "our vnexperienst punies" never do this and consequently admire the wrong things. Also, "Oft haue I obserued what I now set downe; a secular wit that hath liued all daies of his life by what doo you lacke [that is, was a tradesman], to bee more iudiciall in matters of conceit, than our quadrant crepundios,[58] that spit *ergo* in the mouth of euerie one they meete." Yet both the "vnexperienst punies" and the judicious tradesmen will greedily buy up pasquils of any Martin or Momus, however ignorant these may be, especially if they slander superiors. Nashe here echoes the attack upon these ignorant dabblers in divinity, at least one of whom has been at Cambridge, which he was making in full form in the *Anatomie,* and which preludes his own bouts with Martin. So Martin of the tradesmen and Momus of the "punies" are here joined.

Nashe next turns "backe to my first text, of studies of delight; and talke[s] a little in friendship with a few of our triuiall translators;" that is, translators with only the trivial training of the grammar school trivium behind them.

It is a cōmon practise now a daies amongst a sort of shifting companions, that runne through euery arte and thriue by none, to leaue the trade of *Nouerint* whereto they were borne, and busie themselues with the indeuors of Art, that could scarcelie latinize their necke-verse if they should haue neede; yet English *Seneca* read by candle light yeeldes manie good sentences, as *Bloud is a begger,* and so foorth: and if you intreate him faire in a frostie morning, he will affoord you whole *Hamlets,* I should say handfulls of tragical speaches. But ô griefe! *tempus edax rerum,* what's that will last alwaies? The sea exhaled by droppes will in continuance be drie, and *Seneca* let bloud line by line and page by page, at length must needes die to our stage: which makes his famisht followers to imitate the Kidde in *Aesop,* who enamored with the Foxes newfangles, forsooke all hopes of life to leape into a new occupation; and these men renowncing all possibilities of credit or estimation, to intermeddle with Italian translations: wherein how poorelie they haue

---

[58] This may mean men who put out a trifle every quarter. See the proverb *puerorum crepundia,* and Nashe's own statement in *Anatomie* (McKerrow, *Nashe,* I, 9) that these "vnlearned Idiots . . . are euery quarter bigge wyth one Pamphlet or other."

plodded, (as those that are neither prouenzall men, nor are able to distinguish
of Articles,) let all indifferent Gentlemen that haue trauailed in that tongue,
discerne by their twopenie pamphlets:[59] & no meruaile though their home-born
mediocritie be such in this matter, for what can be hoped of those, that thrust
Elisium into hell, and haue not learned so long as they haue liued in the
spheares, the iust measure of the Horizon without an hexameter. Sufficeth
them to bodge vp a blanke verse with ifs and ands, & other while for recreation after their candle stuffe, hauing starched their beardes most curiouslie,
to make a peripateticall path into the inner parts of the Citie, & spend two
or three howers in turning ouer French *Doudie,* where they attract more
infection in one minute, than they can do eloquence all dayes of their life, by
conuersing with anie Authors of like argument.

To begin with, we have not been sufficiently alert to Nashe's own warning that he will "turne backe to my first text, of studies of delight." It
will be remembered that he had ended that section with a fling at certain
would-be critics, "deepe read Grammarians, who hauing no more learning
in their scull, than will serue to take vp a commoditie; nor Art in their
brain, than was nourished in a seruing mans idlenesse," specifically Anthony Mundy, yet set themselves up as censors, and who also repose
eternity in the mouth of a player. These he left "to the mercie of their
mother tongue, that feed on nought but the crummes that fal from the
translators trencher." To these he statedly returns. It is thus clear on
this background that when he speaks of these as leaving "the trade of
Nouerint whereto they were borne," he merely means that they were born
to be tradesmen,[60] who were the chief dealers in such papers. Anthony
Mundy, son of Christopher, Draper, certainly was born to the trade of
Noverint, and had proved it by becoming a Draper by patrimony. He was
born to it. We have no record that he ever had occasion to read his neck-
verse. But it was the fashion of learned university men to take this
attitude, witness Ben Jonson (honorary degree) upon Shakspere — Jonson had need of his neck-verse and used it! Nashe does not necessarily
nor probably mean that a particular one of these dramatists was a scrivener or the son of a scrivener. Hence there is neither a necessary nor a
probable allusion here to Thomas Kyd, a son of one scrivener, as many
scriveners there were, and many sons.

These born tradesmen, who had enough Latin to deal with *Noverints*
but could scarcely Latinize their neck-verse at need, had drained English
Seneca dry for their sententious Senecan plays, which smell of the candle,
such as *Hamlet;* and they are now turning to Italian translations. One

---

[59] Compare Nashe's "first text," "the Italionate pen, that of a packet of pilfries,
affoordeth the presse a pamphlet or two in an age."

[60] In *Greenes, Groats-Worth of witte* (1592), the usurer was not "altogether
vnlettered, for he had good experience in a *Nouerint,* and by the vniuersall tearmes
therein contained, had driuen many a yoong Gentleman to seeke vnknowen countries"
(*Groats-Worth* (1592), B1ᵛ; Grosart, *Greene,* XII, 104, reading "many gentlewomen."

expression here, "intreate him faire in a frostie morning," has not been clear. Dr. McKerrow calls this "A meaningless tag," and gives reference to its use elsewhere. But Holland points out correctly that Nashe is alluding to "Fauste, precor gelida," etc., quoted by Shakspere's Holofernes and numerous others,[61] though Holland apparently does not know that the line is the first in Mantuan's *Bucolics,* a lower grammar school text, and the very gateway to all poetry.[62] In this opening line of Mantuan one swain evokes a story from another. Nashe means to say that when one of the writers of tragedy (in words known to every beginning grammarian) called on English Seneca for materials of composition, he got them; but that finally English Seneca is being bled dry.

So these writers of tragedy, who had got to Mantuan but could not read Seneca in Latin without the English translation, are now, like the Kid in Aesop, leaping into a new occupation of translations from the Italian, since they have bled English Seneca dry. It is apparently assumed regularly that Nashe is accusing these men only of turning to translating from the Italian. But since they had been using the English translation of Seneca till they had used it up, and are now turning to Italian translations, Nashe ought to mean also that they are now getting the subject matter of their plays and pamphlets from English translations as well as from their own personal mistranslation of Italian materials. This had been his accusation of them as censors and writers in his "first text," that they "feed on nought but the crummes that fal from the translators trencher." *Hamlet,* for instance, to which he alludes, is probably from an English translation, from the French of Belleforest, which was adapted from the Latin of Saxo Grammaticus. Of course, many of these plays were from the Italian, where the translated collections of Painter, etc., were a favorite source. And so far as popular Senecan drama of the period is concerned it is adapted Italianate Seneca rather than straight Seneca.

But to continue with our Kid in Aesop, Professor Koeppel pointed out long ago that Nashe is here alluding to a story told by Spenser in the *Shepheardes Calender,* May eclogue.[63] While the allusion seems certain, this is not the fundamental story in whose terms Nashe is speaking. Nashe is using the story of the fox and the goat as Phaedrus had adapted it from Aesop. The fact that Nashe had just been discussing goats' beards in connection with "our Gothamists barbarisme" might have helped induce Aesop's goat story for these barbarous Gothamists. Also, since Nashe is known to have been enamored of the *Vanitie and vncertaintie of Artes*

---

[61] H. H. Holland, *Shakespeare,* p. 25.

[62] See T. W. Baldwin, *William Shakspere's Small Latine and Lesse Greeke,* index.

[63] *Englische Studien,* XVIII, 130; see also K. Meier, in *Beiblatt zur Anglia,* XVI, 54, and XX, 119.

and Sciences by Henry Cornelius Agrippa, he may have had the suggestion of his fundamental figure from that source. For in his address to the reader Agrippa says that like Hercules he is setting out to "ouercome these monsters of Studies and Schooles. And I well perceiue what a blouddy battaile I haue to fighte with them hande to hande, and how daungerous this fight will bee, seeing that I am beset on euery side with an armie of so mightie enimies. O with howe many engins will they assail me, & with how many shames & villainies wil they lode mee? First of al the lowsie Grammarians wil make a stirre, and with their *Etymologies* vppon *Agrippa* will giue me a goutie name: The peeuishe Poetes wil put me in theyr verses for *Momus*, or for *Esopes Goate*."[64] Agrippa was also taking a leap, and expected to be taunted with gout and goat.

According to Aesop, a fox and a goat being thirsty jumped into a well. Using the goat as a springboard, the fox managed to leap back out, and then taunted the goat with having got into something before he had first planned to get out again. In the adaptation by Phaedrus (IV, 8), a fox had fallen into a well. A thirsty goat came by and asked if the water was plentiful and good. The fox, *fraudem moliens*, replied the water was so good that he could not get enough. Whereupon the goat jumped in, and the fox, using him as a springboard, jumped out, leaving the goat in the well. Nashe says that English Seneca, "must needes die to our stage: which makes his famisht followers to imitate the Kidde in *Aesop*, who enamored with the Foxes newfangles, forsooke all hopes of life to leape into a new occupation; and these men renowncing all possibilities of credit or estimation, to intermeddle with Italian translations," etc. These famished followers of Seneca now leap into the new occupation of Italian translations as the famished goat of Phaedrus (Aesop's Kid) jumped into the well. As the goat in fact forsook all hope of life, though he did not think of that when he jumped into the well, so these famished followers have renounced all possibility of credit or estimation by turning to Italian translations. The goat was enticed and deceived by the fine words of the fox, and these followers are "enamored with . . . newfangles." So the followers as the goat are "enamored with the Foxes newfangles." It is not necessary, therefore, to look for a specific fox who has lured these followers into Italian translations; their enamorment with newfangles, now that they have worn their old fangles out, has done that.

Touches, however, seem certainly to have come from a story in the Aesop collections of a fox and a kid as adapted by Spenser, to whom Nashe frequently refers. Says E. K. in a note, "This tale is much like to that in Aesops fables, but the Catastrophe and end is farre different." In

---

[64] *Henrie Cornelius Agrippa, of the Vanitie and vncertaintie of Artes and Sciences* (James Sanford's tr., 1575), A1ᵛ.

Aesop, the mother goat as she went to pasture shut her kid up at home and ordered him not to open to anyone till she returned. The wolf had overheard and immediately knocked at the door asking admission in a goatified voice. But the kid was too smart to open, for said he, though the voice goats, I see a wolf through the cracks.[65]

Spenser changed the villain from a wolf to a fox and reversed the catastrophe. Spenser's character, named Kidd, and affectionately called Kiddie, has been cautioned by his mother not to admit anyone. But the Fox, pretending to be a peddling sheep, shows Kiddie a glass from his pack. Kiddie is "so enamored with the newell" that he lets the Fox into the house. The Fox empties the pack for Kiddie's delight, all except a bell. When Kiddie reached for this, the Fox "popt him in, and his bas-ket did latch;" and that was that. Nashe's phrase, "enamored with the Foxes newfangles" seems certainly an echo of Spenser's phrase. So under Spenser's guidance the two stories of Aesop have coalesced for Nashe, and Aesop-Spenser's gullible Kid has taken precedence of what ought to have been a wise old Goat in the other Aesop story.

It was a Kid in Aesop who had the adventure which Spenser adapts and Nashe echoes. It was, however, a goat in Phaedrus which has the actual adventure that Nashe uses. But all these stories went under the name of Aesop, and Phaedrus had not yet been printed as such, though in various ways some of his stories had circulated before the *editio princeps* in 1596. Few of Nashe's contemporaries would have cavilled at the accuracy of his allusion.

Now it will be noticed that it is the changed occupation of these followers of Seneca, their newfangles, not the name of Kyd, which induces the comparison with Aesop's Kid. There is, therefore, nothing at all to indicate that one of these followers is named Kyd, rather than Fox, Wolf, or anything else. It was not the name of Kyd which suggested the story. Instead, the changed occupation of these famished followers of Seneca and its probable result suggested the story of the fox and the famished goat. The fox sweetly persuading the goat to destruction then brought in Spenser's vivid and recent picture of the Fox luring Kiddie to his destruction.

There is, therefore, nothing whatever in this passage to indicate that Nashe was accusing Thomas Kyd of having been a member of this group which has turned to Italian translations or of having been the particular member of the group who had written a play on Hamlet. Indirectly, Kyd is himself our warrant that he did not write this play. Nashe's allusion to this *Hamlet* was made about August, 1589. In the *Bestrafte Brudermord*,

---

[65] Incidentally, the touch about looking through the cracks shows that here Spenser used the regular collection of his day made by Erasmus and others, not the Planudes collection, nor the school collection by Camerarius.

which is in some way connected with the *Old Hamlet,* there is apparently an allusion to the ill-fated expedition of 1589 to Portugal. The story of a conscience aroused by a play, which plays so important a part in *Hamlet,* is localized in England to about the same date, but the evidence cannot be given here. Thus all our objective evidence, whether conclusive or not, points to 1589 as the date of composition for this *Old Hamlet.* Incidentally, if the *Old Hamlet* had just been produced, as this evidence indicates, one may well ask how Nashe could know that its author had already turned to Italian translations. Apparently, he is merely speaking of Senecanizers as a class and indicating that as a class they are now turning to translations from the Italian. Now Kyd himself, writing in 1593, indicates that he had forsaken the writing of plays six years previously; that is, about 1587.[66] Also, a competent contemporary places Kyd's work as having been done before that of Marlowe, who began in 1587.[67] If so, Kyd had ceased writing plays by 1587, a considerable time before the *Old Hamlet* was composed. So far as I know, these are the sole pieces of objective evidence on the problem. All the objective evidence, conclusive or not, denies that Kyd wrote the *Old Hamlet.* There is no objective evidence of any kind that Thomas Kyd was Nashe's Kid in Aesop.

We may as well notice here that *Hamlet* continued a favorite target for the satirists. For instance, Thomas Lodge takes a shot in *Wit's Miserie* (1596) by referring to "the Visard of ye ghost which cried so miserably at ye Theator, like an oister wife, Hamlet, revenge."[68] We are to remember that Lodge had written a puff for Greene in 1589, was connected with him in the same year on a play, and bade "penny knaves" farewell in a publication which was entered a few days after *Menaphon.* Thus Lodge in 1589 was closely associated with Greene and his feuds and feudaries, which would include Nashe. So his reference in 1596 may well be a memory of the original bout in 1589. For Lodge is describing the devil Hate-Vertue, and immediately shows how he operates among literary men, among whom Lodge mentions *"Th. Nash,* true English Aretine."[69] But the reference may be to time nearer 1596. For Henslowe records a performance of *Hamlet* June 9, really June 11, 1594, by the Admiral's and Chamberlain's at Newington.[70] The play is not marked as new, but

---

[66] T. W. Baldwin, "On the Chronology of Thomas Kyd's Plays," *Modern Language Notes,* XL, 343 ff.

[67] T. W. Baldwin, "Thomas Kyd's Early Company Connections," *Philological Quarterly,* VI, 311 ff.

[68] E. K. Chambers, *William Shakespeare,* I, 411. For the point to "oister wife," see below, p. 516.

[69] *The Complete Works of Thomas Lodge* (Hunterian Club), IV, 56, 57.

[70] W. W. Greg, *Henslowe's Diary,* I, 17; II, 164.

does not appear again in Henslowe's Diary either before or after. The fact that later the Shaksperean company had a *Hamlet* while the Admiral's had not indicates that at parting the play went with the former company. Lodge's allusion to the play in 1596 may thus be aimed at performance by the Shaksperean company. It is customary to explain posthaste that, of course, Lodge's reference must be to the *Old Hamlet,* and so the item is not even granted admission to possible allusions to Shakspere. For we are told that the ghost in *Hamlet* was Shakspere's greatest role. So if Lodge were alluding to Shakspere's play, he would be "ribbing" Shakspere both as author and as actor. What is more likely, especially if we remember Lodge's connections in the past feuds? If Shakspere was the ghost in his own version, then it is almost equally certain that he had merely continued the part from the time his company became possessed of the play. If the date of the actual allusion is 1596, here is pretty certainly one contemporary impression of Shakspere as the ghost in *Hamlet,* whether his own play or the *Old Hamlet.* But it is just as likely that Lodge is carrying over from the original flouting in 1589. Similarly, the satirists Dekker and Rowlands continue the satire well into the seventeenth century. Says Dekker in *Satiromastix,* IV, 1, 50, through Tucca, "my name's Hamlet revenge."[71] Again, so late as Samuel Rowlands' *The Night-Raven* (1620) we hear "I will not call Hamlet Revenge my greeves."[72] It appears, therefore, that "Hamlet, revenge" had become a cant expression among satirists, and that Lodge in 1596 gives us our first known instance of its use. And Lodge is carrying on the feud of 1589, whether his actual time of reference is 1589 or nearer 1596.[73]

Certainly, there is no allusion in the *Menaphon* passage to Thomas Kyd. To whom then does Nashe allude? The Stationers' Register and the *Short Title Catalogue* should show who was publishing at this period the kind of thing Nashe reprehends. Nashe is satirizing a group of mechanic critics who draw their ideas from the stage and, as a group, have only petty-school and a smattering of grammar school with which to support their art. They must rely, therefore, upon English translations for their basic knowledge. So far, his specific target continues to be Anthony Mundy. Already these smatterers have drained English Seneca dry and now have turned to Italian translations, which they are insufficiently equipped to make. Nashe had begun with an allusion to Mundy's *Fedele*

---

[71] Chambers, *Shakespeare,* I, 411.

[72] Chambers, *Shakespeare,* I, 411.

[73] The fact that Greene and his cohorts did not think highly of *Hamlet* and Shakspere would certainly not prejudice Gabriel Harvey; "The younger sort takes much delight in Shakespeares Venus, & Adonis: but his Lucrece, & his tragedie of Hamlet, Prince of Denmarke, haue it in them, to please the wiser sort." Nor was Gabriel among Mundy's detractors (Grosart, *Harvey,* II, 290).

and Fortvnio, translated, or rather adapted, from the Italian, as a sample
of Italian translations, and has stately returned in the present passage to
the attack on Italian translations. One of the specific thrusts, "nor are
able to distinguish of Articles," is likely aimed at the title of that play.
Mundy translated *Il Fedele,* the faithful one, simply as Fedele.

But another fault now alleged really concerns French translations:
"and these men, renowncing all possibilities of credit or estimation, to
intermeddle with Italian translations: wherein how poorelie they haue
plodded, (as those that are neither prouenzall men, nor are able to distinguish of Articles,) let all indifferent Gentlemen that haue trauailed in
that tongue, discerne by their twopenie pamphlets." While Nashe talks
of Italian translations, he is in fact thinking of French ones. For
"prouenzall" is Provençal, which *N.E.D.* defines as "Of or pertaining to
Provence and its inhabitants," giving this use in *Menaphon* as the first
instance. Similarly, these men, "after their candle stuffe, hauing starched
their beardes most curiouslie, to make a peripateticall path into the inner
parts of the Citie, & spend two or three howers in turning ouer French
Doudie, where they attract more infection in one minute, than they can do
eloquence all dayes of their life, by conuersing with anie Authors of like
argument."

Who were concerned in such enterprises in 1588-89? One man fits all
the characteristics perfectly, and so far as is at present known only one.
And that man is Anthony Mundy. Mundy certainly translated from
Italian and French. He had been prominently identified with Italian
affairs, and in 1585 published an adaptation of Pasqualigo's *Il Fedele* as
Fedele and Fortvnio. He may well be suspected of two-penny pamphlets
from the Italian along with his known activities as a ballad maker. But
neither pamphlets nor ballads were ordinarily entered S.R., and few
specimens of either class survive. There is the alleged translation of the
Titus Andronicus source story from an original printed at Rome. The
alleged translation survives only in one known copy of an eighteenth-
century chapbook; no Italian original has yet been found. For the French,
there is the *Hystorie of Hamblet* from Belleforest, surviving in a single
copy of 1608, but pretty certainly first published in the early 'eighties.
Neither of these pamphlets appears in the Stationers' Register, and no
representative of their class appears in the *Short Title Catalogue* for 1588
and 1589. So we have no surviving direct evidence of anyone's activity
in two-penny Italian translations in 1588-89 — and almost no direct record
of such activity at any time, for the reasons stated.

But when we turn to the French, at which Nashe makes his specific
thrust, then it is clear that Mundy was no "prouenzall" man, and among
other things was quite likely not "able to distinguish of Articles." The
first part of *Palmerin D'Oliva* is dated January 1, 1588, and dedicated to

the Earl of Oxford, whose servant Mundy had been; the second, March 9, 1588, to the same. Mundy advertized that the work was "Written in Spanish, Italian, and French, and from them turned into English."[74] Is this why Nashe speaks of Italian translations, but alludes specifically to weakness in the French? To continue, under date of April 23, 1588 (S.R. November 20, 1587) Mundy launched *The Famous . . . Historie of Palladine of England* from the French of Claude Colet, dedicated to the Earl of Essex.[75] On February 5, 1589 (S.R. January 9, 1589), came *The Honorable . . . Historie of Palmendos*, ultimately from the Portuguese of Francisco de Moraes, and dedicated to Sir Francis Drake. This also was "Translated out of French by A. M. one of the Messengers of her Majesties Chamber."[76] Mundy was certainly "flying high" in his pretensions as a translator of censorious prominence. But looking at the dedicatees, one will also do well to remember the interests of Sidney and Spenser.

As to the quality of Mundy's translation, there is and can be no dissenting voice. Long since, Southey set the tone in his depreciation of *Palmerin of England*. "If he had hanged himself before he translated Palmerin of England, he would have saved me a great deal of labour . . . He began it with some care, but he soon resigned the task to others less qualified than himself; for certain it is, that at least three-fourths of the book were translated by one who neither understood French, nor English, nor the story which he was translating. . . . Palmerin is decisive proof either that Anthony Munday sold his name to the booksellers, or had established a manufactory of translations himself, and set his mark upon what was produced in it, as being well known in the market. This will account for the rapidity with which his publications succeeded each other."[77] Certainly the mastery of French exhibited is no credit to the lessons Mundy earlier advertised that he was taking under Claudius Holyband (Desainliens), whatever may be true of his Italian. The French would well justify Nashe's description. And Nashe implies some such manufactory of translations as Southey posits. Mundy was thus very

---

[74] Turner, *Mundy,* p. 206.

[75] Miss Turner points out that Mundy dedicated his *Palladine of England* "to the Earl of Essex in April, 1588, comparing himself to a poor 'heardsman' who offered insense to Jove on pieces of broken 'potsheard,' much as Greene, in the same year, presented *Pandosto* to the Earl of Cumberland by comparing himself to Baucis, serving Jove in a wooden dish." It also opens "in a way remarkably similar to *Pandosto.*" She finds that "The similarity of dedication and opening passages is very striking" (Turner, *Mundy,* pp. 79-80, and n. 19). If either borrowed, it was Greene, since *Pandosto* was not entered S. R. till July 1, 1588, some months after Mundy's work should have been in print.

[76] Turner, *Mundy,* p. 207.

[77] *Palmerin of England,* corrected by Robert Southey (1807), Vol. I, pp. xlii-xliii. See also, Turner, *Mundy,* pp. 45-46.

prominent in such French translations in 1588-89, and if anyone else did any of such work no record exists of it. So far as we know, Mundy was the only man.

And because of these interests we may be certain that Mundy was one of the dramatists who would "bodge vp a blanke verse with ifs and ands, & other while for recreation after their candle stuffe, hauing starched their beardes most curiouslie, to make a peripateticall path into the inner parts of the Citie, & spend two or three howers in turning ouer French *Doudie,* where they attract more infection in one minute, than they do eloquence all dayes of their life, by conuersing with anie Authors of like argument."

Here we should remember that in his *Anatomie* Nashe, following the lead of Ascham,[78] had recommended that certain writers change their posies professing profit with pleasure, "when as in their bookes there is scarce to be found one precept pertaining to vertue." On the title page of *Palladine,* April 23, 1588, Mundy had tried to forestall such a criticism. "Heerin is no offence offered to the wise by wanton speeches, or encouragement to the loose by lascivious matter."[79] It should not offend those who seek profit, nor corrupt those who seek pleasure. Evidently Nashe does not agree, for he continues, "So shall the discreet Reader vnderstand the contents by the titel, and their purpose by their posie, what els I pray you doe these bable bookemungers endeuor, but to repaire the ruinous wals of *Venus* Court, to restore to the worlde, that forgotten Legendary licence of lying, to imitate a fresh the fantasticall dreames of those exiled Abbie-lubbers, from whose idel pens, proceeded those worne out impressions of the feyned no where acts, of Arthur of the rounde table, Arthur of litle Brittaine, sir Tristram, Hewon of Burdeaux, the Squire of low degree, the foure sons of Amon, with infinite others. It is not of my yeeres nor studie to censure these mens foolerie more theologicallie, but to shew how they to no Common-wealth commoditie, tosse ouer their troubled imaginations to haue the praise of the learning which they lack. Many of them to be more amiable with their friends of the Feminine sexe, blot many sheetes of paper in the blazing of Womens slender praises, as though in that generation there raigned and alwaies remained such singuler simplicitie, that all posterities should be enioyned by duetie, to fill and furnish theyr Temples, nay Townes and streetes, with the shrines of she Saints."[80]

---

[78] It was natural that Nashe and Greene of St. John's should follow the lead of Ascham (and Cheke), and that the succession should produce the Parnassus plays. The tradition of censorious scholarship is strong in St. John's from early in the century. Also, Hall, Harvey, and Marlowe were all Cambridge men, and many, if not most, of the cliques and animosities of these men stem from university days.

[79] Turner, *Mundy,* p. 207.

[80] *Anatomie* (1589), A1ᵛ-A2ʳ; McKerrow, *Nashe,* I, 11, reading *the* for *she.*

Nashe was in 1588 disturbed by this type of literature, which Mundy was bringing back to popularity. His specific references in 1589 can hardly be to any other than Mundy, who was besides a dramatist and translated from the Italian. But Nashe is not surprised at the deficiencies of the mere *Noverint* grammarian Mundy when he considers the aberrations in classical knowledge of some who are supposed to be learned. Though Mundy is one of those who was not a "prouenzall" man and could not distinguish of articles, "no meruaile though their home-born mediocritie be such in this matter; for what can be hoped of those, that thrust *Elisium* into hell, and haue not learned so long as they haue liued in the spheares, the iust measure of the Horizon without an hexameter." If gold rust, what will iron do? What can be expected of "home-born mediocritie," when even those who should be learned have thrust Elysium into hell and write only in hexameters? While Nashe has stated his opposition between home born mediocre and the learned quite clumsily, yet this is clearly his meaning. Nashe's attitude is well expressed some years later when he comments on Harvey's hexameters, "O Heathenish and Pagan Hexamiters, come thy waies down frō thy *Doctourship,* & learne thy Primer of Poetry ouer again."[81]

Here we need also to remember Nashe's scoffs at the hexameter elsewhere. Later in this address he objects to Stanyhurst because his "heroicall Poetrie infired, I should say inspired, with an hexameter furie, recalled to life, what euer hissed barbarisme hath bin buried this hundred yeare; and reuiued by his ragged quill such carterlie varietie, as no hodge plowman in a countrie, but would haue held as the extremitie of clownerie." Nashe then improves some of Stanyhurst's hexameters "being parte of one of his descriptions of a tempest," and comments, "Which strange language of the firmament neuer subiect before to our common phrase, makes vs that are not vsed to terminate heauens moueings, in the accents of any voice, esteeme of their triobulare interpeter, as of some Thrasonical huffe snuffe." For Nashe, therefore, Stanyhurst has connected hexameters with the heavens. So when Nashe returns to the hexameters of Stanyhurst and Harvey more than three years later, hexameters are still connected with the horizon. "In the Romaine common-wealths it was lawful for Poets to reproue that enormitie in the highest chairs of authoritie, which none else durst touch, alwaies the sacred Maiestie of their *Augustus* kept inuiolate: for that was a Plannet exalted aboue their Hexameter horizon, & it was capitall to them in the highest degree, to dispute of his setting and rising, or search inquisitiuely into his predominance and influence."[82] So "spheares" and "Horizon" of

---

[81] McKerrow, *Nashe,* I, 277.
[82] McKerrow, *Nashe,* I, 285-286.

the address to *Menaphon* belong to this complex of Nashe's on the hexameter. Nashe is simply gibing at those learned ones who use only hexameters, and so are no proper example for these unlearned writers of blank verse.

With the learned writers of hexameters he couples "those, that thrust *Elisium* into hell." Then he continues with "home born mediocritie" and its blank verse. Now, as Dr. McKerrow notes,[83] Marlowe wrote in *Faustus*

> This word "damnation" terrifies not me,
> For I confound hell in Elysium:
> My ghost be with the old philosophers![84]

For his third line, Marlowe quotes a commonplace statement of his day attributed to Averroes. As John Woolton puts it into English phrase in *The Christian Manuell* 1576, "*Auerrois* because the Christians eate that God whome they worshippe: my soule shall be with the Philosophers."[85] A side note refers us to "Auerrois in 12. Metaph." The Latin of Averroes is usually quoted as "Quandoquidem comedunt Christiani quod colunt, sit anima mea cum philosophis," the conclusion of which Woolton and Marlowe translate accurately. Marlowe's construction indicates that he is translating the Latin directly. Since this sentiment was called forth by transubstantiation, naturally it would be regularly quoted and echoed by the Protestant controversialists.[86] The sentiment as quoted by Faustus is a further reflection of Marlowe's anti-Romanism, and Marlowe's quotation would fall impressively and ominously on such trained ears as those of Nashe and Greene.

Faustus has dedicated himself to Beelzebub, Prince of Hell, and is not afraid to be damned, for that would send his soul to be with the old philosophers, such as Averroes on Aristotle, in pagan Elysium. So he confounds or defeats Hell by getting put into Elysium. He is thus to be in Elysium in Hell, which is thrusting Elysium into Hell with a venge-

---

[83] McKerrow, *Nashe*, IV, 450.

[84] W. W. Greg, *Doctor Faustus* (reconstruction), I, 3, 58-60 (294-296); compare Ellis-Fermor, *2 Tamburlaine*, IV, 2, 87-96 (3968-77), and the connection with the three preceding lines. Here also Marlowe in effect thrusts Elysium into hell. Cooper's definition of *Elysium* will help focus the idea, "A place of pleasure, where poetes did suppose the soules of good men to dwell."

[85] John Woolton, *Manuell* (1576), B8ʳ.

[86] For some early English allusions, see John Hooper, *Early Writings* (Parker Soc.), p. 70; and Thomas Becon, *Prayers and Other Pieces* (Parker Soc.), p. 278 and n. For later English statements, see J. C. Maxwell, "Two Notes on Marlowe's 'Faustus,'" *N.&Q.*, 194, 334-335, following G. T. Buckley, *Atheism in the English Renaissance*, p. 60. John M. Steadman, "Faustus and Averroes," *N.&Q.*, CCI, 416, cites John Collop, *Medici Catholicon* (1656), p. 87, as attributing the opinion to Averroes. For the French controversialists, note H of Bayle's article on Averroes gives several statements and references, whence Renan (E., *Averroes et L'Averroisme*, ed. 2, Paris 1861, p. 298) lifted his information.

ance.[87] Faustus holds lightly anyway "these vain trifles of men's souls," so much discussed by the theologians and philosophers. No one is likely to have thrust Elysium into Hell more spectacularly than did Marlowe in this speech of Faustus. Not only did Marlowe thrust Elysium into Hell; he advertised the fact in strongest terms, "I confound hell in Elysium."[88]

At any rate, Nashe has throughout his preface coupled Marlowe and Mundy. It now becomes clear that Marlowe's fellow poet, berated along with him by Greene in *Perimedes* (S.R. March 29, 1588), was Mundy. For in *A Looking Glasse* Adam, the Clown, is philosophising on ale. "The Ale is a restoratiue, bread is a binder, marke you, sir, two excellent points in phisicke; the Ginger, oh ware of that, the philosophers haue written of the nature of Ginger, tis expullsitiue in two degrees; you shal here the sentence of Galen, 'It will make a man belch, cough, and fart, And is a great comfort to the hart,' — a proper poesie, I promise you;[89] but now to the noble vertue of the Nutmeg; it is, saith one Ballad, I think an English Roman was the authour, an vnderlayer to the braines, for when the Ale gives a buffet to the head, oh, the Nutmeg, that keepes him for a while in temper."[90] For the ballad we turn to *Histrio-Mastix,* where "Enter Incle, Belch, Gutt, Post hast," singing "The Players Song."

> The nut-br[o]wne ale, the nut-browne ale,
> Puts downe all drinke when it is stale,
> The toast, the Nut-meg, and the ginger,
> Will make a sighing man a singer.
> Ale giues a buffet in the head,
>   But ginger under-proppes the brayne:
> When ale would strike a strong man dead,
>   Then nut-megge tempers it againe,
> The nut-browne ale, the nut-browne ale,
> Puts downe all drinke when it is stale.[91]

Here is certainly the ballad which Adam thinks was written by an English Roman. This ballad would belong supposedly to Posthaste, the poet of the company. Sir Edmund Chambers says, "Their poet Posthaste is clearly

---

[87] The idea is analogous to that in a contemporary thrust at "these puritans," who "woulde finde fault I thinke with Iohn of Cant. (if he beleeuing that Christe in soule went to Hell) should holde it vnlawfull for a man to pray vnto Christe being in hell" (*Hay any worke for Cooper* [1589], p. 46). One will remember also Shakspere's twiddles in Sonnet 133 and elsewhere.

[88] Incidentally, Marlowe's quotation makes it clear that the first person as in the edition of 1616 is correct, and that the edition of 1604 has leveled to the third person. So Sir Walter Greg may now with a clear conscience reach for his manuscript here — as he so badly wanted to do in his study of the texts (W. W. Greg, *Marlowe's Doctor Faustus, 1604-1616,* p. 314), and has done in his conjectural reconstruction.

[89] These sentiments concerning ginger and nutmeg are to be found in various popular books of the time on health, and the quote may be lifted from one of these.

[90] J. C. Collins, *The Plays & Poems of Robert Greene, Looking Glasse,* 249-258.

[91] *Histrio-Mastix,* A4[v]; I, 1.

Munday and not, as Simpson and others have vainly imagined, Shake-speare."[92] He adds of the date of the original play, "The style seems to me to be that of Peele or some imitator, the attitude to the players an academic reflection of the attacks of Greene, and the political atmosphere that of the years following the Armada, when the relief of peace was certainly not unbroken by fears of renewed Spanish attempts."[93] On the background we now have, it is quite clear that Sir Edmund is correct as to the approximate time, and as to Mundy as Posthaste. If the ballad was by, or generally supposed to be by, Mundy, he and his company are identified for the audience immediately by their singing of it in the play. It is also clear from all these interconnections, that Marlowe's English Roman companion in 1588 was Anthony Mundy.

It will be noticed also that the players turn from their trades exactly as Nashe says his censors have done.

Inc.   This *Peace* breeds such Plenty, trades serue no turnes
Bel.   The more fooles wee to follow them.
Post.   Lett's make vp a company of Players,
         For we can all sing and say,
         And so (with practise) soone may learne to play.
Incle. True, could our action answer your *extempore.*
Post.   I'le teach yee to play true *Politicians.*
Incle. Why those are th'falsest subtle fellowes liues."[94]

Here is Posthaste's extemporal facility, as in Nashe and Greene, and it is to be activated by the "action" of the players. Posthaste is always calling for drink, especially as he composes extempore. He is a black-pot poet. He uses "no new luxurie or blandishment,/ But plenty of old Englands mothers words;"[95] that is, he has "home born mediocritie," as Nashe phrases it. Posthaste is considered by his company to be "a Gentleman scholler," and Posthaste himself insists "A Gentleman's a Gentleman, that hath a cleane shirt on, with some learning, and so haue I."[96] Posthaste is given a theme

> Your Poetts and your Pottes,
> Are knit in true-Loue knots.[97]

and he sings; but the song evidently belongs to the later revision. Post-haste is a prodigious ballad writer, as was Antonio Balladino.

---

[92] Chambers, *E.S.,* IV, 18.
[93] Chambers, *E.S.,* IV, 18.
[94] *Histrio-Mastix,* B1r; I, 1.
[95] *Histrio-Mastix,* C1v; II, 1.
[96] *Histrio-Mastix,* C3r; II, 1. Mundy is a "gentleman" in the parish registers.
[97] *Histrio-Mastix,* C4v; II, 1.

> Faith Ile eene past all my ballads together,
> And make a coate to hold out pistoll-proofe.[98]

A Soldier says to one of the players

> Sirha is this you would rend and teare the Cat
> Vpon a Stage, and now march like a drown'd rat?
> Looke vp and play the *Tamburlaine:* you rogue you.[99]

When trouble brews, Posthaste will "boldly fall to ballading againe."[100]

It would appear, then, that it was Marlowe and Mundy who had caused two Romans to beat Greene's motto out of their bucklers before March 29, 1588. It is, therefore, presumably Mundy who is accused of writing *Heliogabalus.* In his preface to *Menaphon,* about August, 1589, Nashe is centering his attention upon the same pair, whether others are involved or not, as fellow upholders of blank-verse tragedy. Marlowe thus emerges in significant company. One thinks of the troubled degree in 1587, and remembers Mundy's spying activities for many years before. There is also the element of heroic romance in *Tamburlaine,* which has not been sufficiently emphasized, to be paralleled with Mundy's series of translations. The two men were much more "birds of a feather" to Nashe and Greene than they have been to us. Through Mundy we might be able to discover considerably more about Marlowe.

Nashe connects Marlowe certainly with *A Shrew,* and Marlowe was in some way certainly connected with the play. Nashe also has a fling at an exploit of which Marlowe certainly is guilty in *Faustus,* whether Nashe had this particular exploit in mind or not. Under the circumstances, most likely he did. The allusions to Mundy's plays are not so clear, probably because we do not have the plays. Someone in Mundy's

---

[98] *Histrio-Mastix,* F2ᵛ; V.

[99] *Histrio-Mastix,* G1ʳ; V.

[100] *Histrio-Mastix,* H1ᵛ; VI, 1. Miss Turner (*Mundy* pp. 96-97) would add another caricature of Mundy, this time a friendly one. Chettle depicts from the shades "an od old fellow, low of stature, his head was couered with a round cap, his body with a side skirted tawney coate, his legs and feete trust vppe in leather buskins, his gray haires and furrowed face witnessed his age, his treble violl in his hande, assured me of his profession. On which (by his continuall sawing hauing left but one string) after his best manner, hee gaue me a huntsvp: whome after a little musing, I assuredly remembred to be no other but old Anthony Now now" (Chettle, *Kind-Harts Dreame,* B2ᵛ). But Abraham Fraunce had paid his respects to Antony Now-Now some five years before.

> "*Antony Now-Now is good, and a singer,*   therefore
> *Antony Now-Now, is a good singer.*

For indeede these two thinges seuerally put downe are not essentiall partes of *Antony Now-Now,* but onely accidentall qualities" (A. Fraunce, *Lawiers Logike* (1588), f. 36ᵛ). In both cases, Anthony Now-Now is a musician, a singing fiddler, not an author of ballads, while Mundy was an author rather than a performer. Also, the obvious implication of Chettle's passage is that Anthony Now-Now was then dead. This is certainly not Mundy.

classification is accused of having written *Hamlet* on the basis of English Seneca. But there may have been others in that group besides Mundy. We remember, however, that in his first known attack upon Marlowe, Greene associated with him a dramatist who had written about the mad priest of the sun. This dramatist we have identified as Mundy. Mad Heliogabalus and mad Hamlet might well be bats from the same belfry. Since the one does not survive, and the other only in a very washed out form, we have no sufficient direct evidence on which to base an opinion. And whether fortunately or unfortunately, most of Mundy's surviving plays are later and in the tradition of the romances, so that we have no identified sample of what he could do in the 'eighties with a good gory subject in drama. But Southey thought Mundy could do well enough with a romance. "Sometimes, by way of making amends for what has been expunged, a little is added: in one place Palmerin is represented after he has killed a giant, as cutting his legs off, and hammering him about the head with the hilt of his sword till he has beaten out the teeth and the eyes!"[101] Mundy should have had no trouble in geremumbling satisfactorily the corpses in a tragedy. The Italianate machinery which was added to Saxo's Amleth would very readily have come from a man of Mundy's known background and interests. Perhaps a closer study of Mundy than we have yet given him, or than otherwise he deserves, may clear this background still further.[102]

Now to return to *Menaphon*. In August, 1589, Greene and Nashe both object to making the stage the arbiter of art, and both center attention upon Marlowe as the leader of the opposition, but Nashe also gives prominence to Mundy. Nashe is carrying on Greene's quarrel with Marlowe, Mundy, and their group along lines which Greene himself had already laid down more than a year before in *Perimedes*. Nashe is continuing exactly the same argument. So does Thomas Brabine Gent., one of his co-puffers to *Menaphon*.

> Come foorth you witts that vaunt the pompe of speach,
>   And striue to thunder from a Stage-mans throate:
> View *Menaphon* a note beyond your reach;
>   Whose sight will make your drumming descant doate:
> Players auant, you know not to delight;
>   Welcome sweete Shepheard, worth a Schollers sight.

The phraseology shows that Brabine's muse peeped over Nashe's shoulder. Brabine also takes his potshot at Marlowe's fair, crystal Zenocrate.

> One writes of loue, and wanders in the aire;
>   Another stands on tearmes of trees and stones:

---

[101] Southey, *Palmerin* (1807), I, xliii.

[102] I do not suggest that Mundy wrote the *Old Hamlet;* I merely suggest that on present evidence it is possible.

> When heauens compare yeeldes but the praise of faire,
> And christall can describe but flesh and bones.

Greene's pastorals are "mortall foes" to these. Brabine's target is evidently

> Now, bright Zenocrate, the world's fair eye,
> Whose beams illuminate the lamps of heaven,
> Whose cheerful looks do clear the cloudy air,
> And clothe it in a crystal livery.[103]

This quarrel, however, belongs properly to Robert Greene, and the opponent is the blank verse of the public stage, with Marlowe as an outstanding offender in a group of playwrights, and Mundy tumbling after.

In *Perimedes,* Marlowe has a comrade whom we have identified as Mundy, who seems to have written a play on the mad priest of the sun, and these appear to be the two gentlemen poets who caused Greene's motto to be so disrespectfully treated. In Nashe's preface to *Menaphon* Marlowe may have several comrades. One of the group has written the *Old Hamlet,* and Marlowe or another has written *The Taming of a Shrew.* The authors of these plays, or still another of the group, or others, have turned to translations from the Italian, whether as translators or for subject matter to their plays. One of these, at least, if there is more than one, was Mundy.

In the further course of his epistle to *Menaphon* Nashe has a glance at the actors also. In his survey of letters he eventually comes to the poets of London.

There are extant about *London,* many most able men, to reuiue Poetrie, though it were executed ten thousand times, as in *Platos,* so in Puritanes common wealth; as for example *Mathew Roydon, Thomas Atchelow* and *George Peele,* the first of whome, as hee hath shewed himselfe singular, in the immortall Epitaph of his beloued *Astrophel,* besides many other most absolute comicke inuentions (made more publique by euerie mans praise, than they can bee by my speache) so the second, hath more than once or twise manifested, his deepe witted schollership in places of credit; & for the last, thogh not the least of them all, I dare commend him to all that know him, as the chiefe supporter of pleasance nowe liuing, the *Atlas* of Poetrie, & *primus verborum Artifex:* whose first encrease, the Arraignement of *Paris,* might plead to your opinions, his pregnant dexteritie of wit, and manifold varietie of inuention; wherein (*me iudice*) hee goeth a step beyond all that write. Sundrie other sweete Gentlemen I know, that haue vaunted their pens in priuate deuices, and trickt vp a companie of taffata fooles with their feathers, whose beautie if our Poets had not peecte with the supply of their periwigs, they might haue antickt it vntill this time vp and downe the countrey with the King of *Fairies,* and dinde euerie daie at the pease porredge ordinarie with *Delphrigus.* But *Tolossa* hath forgot that it was sometime sackt, and beggers that euer they caried their fardles on footback: and in truth no meruaile, when as the deserued reputation of one *Roscius,* is of force to inrich a rabble of counter-

---

[103] Ellis-Fermor, *2 Tamburlaine,* I, 4, 1-4 (2570-73).

fets; yet let subiects for all their insolence, dedicate a *De profundis* euerie morning to the preseruation of their *Caesar,* least their encreasing indignities returne them ere long to their iuggling to mediocritie, and they bewaile in weeping blankes, the wane of their Monarchie.

Nashe is thinking of Roydon, Atchelow, and Peele as the outstanding poets of London — present company always excepted. He praises Roydon for his *Astrophel,* which had not then been published, and for "most absolute comicke inuentions," some of which could have been plays, does not specify for Atchelow, but is not overtly thinking of him as dramatist; and finally comes to Peele as the greatest of the dramatic poets, instancing his *Arraignment of Paris,* which was his only play in print, had very little blank verse, and that not of the "bragging" variety. From Peele, Nashe turns to "Sundrie other sweete Gentlemen . . . that haue vaunted their pens in priuate deuices, and trickt vp a companie of taffata fooles with their feathers."

Here we need to follow closely the line of Nashe's thought. If "our Poets" had not "trickt vp a companie of taffata fooles with their feathers," these crows would still be anticking up and down the country. But it is not surprising that they should forget that they are only crows, "when as the deserued reputation of one *Roscius,* is of force to enrich a rabble of counterfets; yet let subiects for all their insolence, dedicate a *De profundis* euerie morning to the preseruation of their *Caesar,* least their encreasing indignities returne them ere long to their iuggling to mediocritie." The poets, not some Roscius, have beautified the actors, even though just one genuine Roscius by using the borrowed feathers properly can enrich the rabble of counterfeits. The latent crow figure has also brought in Caesar's crow, with his *Ave Caesar* to procure Caesar's favor for the cobbler. Similarly, these crows had better say a *de profundis* every morning for their Caesar; that is, those who are subject to the Caesar of acting had better pray fervently that they may maintain their present favorable position, to which "our Poets" have helped them with their feathers, lest through "encreasing indignities" they be returned to their former state, which will happen if "our Poets"[104] under those "encreasing indignities" withdraw their support.

The passage has generally been interpreted as if "one *Roscius*" alone, and not the poets had given the company of actors its present condition, and could withdraw it. And naturally there have been attempts to identify Roscius as one individual, whereas the statement is general, "one *Roscius,*" any or a single Roscius, one actor who deserves to be called a Roscius.

---

[104] When Greene "rewrote" this passage in *Francescos Fortunes,* "our wittes," and "our knowledge" are equated with the cobbler who taught the crow to prate in the king's chamber (see below, p. 38).

The recognized Roscius of the period was Richard Tarleton. In print, at least, Dr. John Case started the tradition in his *Sphaera Civitatis* (1588). Case does not condemn all plays and players; "quippè *Aristoteles* hoc loco *Theodorvm* quendam peritum tragaediarum actorem laudat, *Cicero* suum laudauit *Roscivm,* nos *Angli Tarletonvm,* in cuius voce & vultu omnes iocosi affectus, in cuius cerebroso capite lepidae facetiae habitant."[105] This is adapted in *Tarltons newes* (1590, B1ʳ, p. 1) as: "after his death I mourned in conceit, and absented my selfe from all plaies, as wanting the merry *Roscius* of Plaiers, that famozed all Comedies so with his pleasant and extemporall inuention."

In 1598, Meres put Case's gem into one of his own choice settings, possibly with some suggestions from *Tarltons newes.* "As *Antipater Sidonius* was famous for extemporall verse in Greeke, and *Ouid* for his *Quicquid conabar dicere versus erat:* so was our *Tarleton,* of whome Doctour *Case* that learned physitian thus speaketh. . . . And so is now our wittie *Wilson,* who, for learning and extemporall witte in this facultie, is without compare or compeere, as to his great and eternall commendations he manifested in his chalenge at the Swanne on the Banke side."[106] Tarleton had been so before his death in 1588, and in 1598 "so is now our wittie *Wilson.*"

Then Howes in continuation of Stow's *Annales* wrote in 1615 of the formation of the Queen's Company in 1583; "amongst these xii. players, were two rare men, viz. *Thomas* [sic] *Wilson* for a quicke delicate refined extemporall witte, and *Richard Tarleton* for a wondrous plentifull pleasant extemporall wit, hee was the wonder of his time."[107] Howes finds both Tarleton and Wilson (whom he calls Thomas, and assumes to be the one of whom Meres wrote) in the patent of 1583, and varies the statement of Meres concerning the two. So Howes shows no independent knowledge, and Meres places the reputation of his Robert Wilson as in and near 1598, not 1589. It may also be well to remember that Jonson says Adams was Tarleton's fellow comedian. If Nashe was thinking specifically of any individual in 1589 as "one *Roscius,*" that individual was most likely Richard Tarleton, recently dead, certainly not Robert Wilson, for whom at that time there is no sign of such a reputation.

Some years after 1589 Nashe identified Edward Alleyn "improperly" as Roscius and properly as Aesop. In *Pierce Penilesse* (S.R. August 8, 1592), Nashe says, "Not *Roscius* nor *Aesope,* those admyred tragedians that haue liued euer since before Christ was borne, could euer performe

---

[105] John Case, *Sphaera Civitatis* (1588), p. 691.
[106] Francis Meres, *Palladis Tamia* (1598), 285ᵛ-286ʳ.
[107] John Stow, *Annales* (1615), p. 697.

more in action than famous *Ned Allen*."[108] As a matter of fact, Roscius was a comic, not a tragic, actor. This combination of the two actors in Nashe's mind was most likely at least part of the reason that the crow of the other Aesop got brought into juxtaposition with Roscius. Alleyn was also praised by Nashe in *Strange Newes* (S.R. January 12, 1593).[109] It is not likely, however, that Nashe was in 1589 thinking of Alleyn as Roscius, and there is nothing to indicate indeed that he was referring specifically to any particular actor. At any rate, the company itself, if it is a single company and not actors in general, gets anything but praise. And Greene was to use more times than one this warning of Nashe's to keep the actors in their place.

It would seem clear that Greene is in August, 1589, again attacking Marlowe, and that Nashe is attacking Marlowe, Mundy, and players, possibly, therefore, the Admiral's company specifically, for whom bepraised Peele was also writing, as were just possibly "Sundrie other sweete Gentlemen." This attitude of Nashe toward the public stage ought to mean that he was not yet connected with it. Greene, on the other hand, is here noncommital. It will appear that he had newly become a dramatist. But Nashe's admonition to the actors in 1589 remained with Greene the remainder of his life. A few months later than *Menaphon,* in *Francescos Fortunes* (1590), Greene causes Cicero to remind even Roscius that he is only Aesop's crow. Francesco had told the story of how he came in utter desperation to turn to the players with a first comedy which proved immediately successful. The Gentleman interrupted to ask Francesco's "iudgement of Playes, Playmakers and Players." Francesco then gave a pseudo-history of Roman drama, till the actors became mercenaries, and "grewe not onely excellent, but rich and insolent." And so Tully had to show even Roscius his proper place when "the prowd Comedian dared to make comparison with *Tully.*" Incidentally, to Greene Roscius was correctly a comedian. "Why *Roscius,* art thou proud with *Esops* Crow, being pranct with the glorie of others feathers? of thy selfe thou canst say nothing, and if the Cobler hath taught thee to say, *Aue Caesar,* disdain not thy tutor, because thou pratest in a Kings chamber: what sentence thou vtterest on the stage, flowes from the censure of our wittes; and what sentence or conceipte of the inuention the people applaud for excellent, that comes from the secrets of our knowledge. I graunt your action, though it be a kind of mechanical labour; yet wel

---

[108] McKerrow, *Nashe,* I, 215. Also, Jonson compares Alleyn with both Roscius and Aesop.

> Who both their graces in thy selfe hast more
> Out-stript, then they did all that went before.
>
> (Jonson, *The Workes of Benjamin Jonson,* 1616, p. 793)

[109] McKerrow, *Nashe,* I, 296.

done tis worthie of praise: but you worthlesse, if for so small a toy you waxe proud."[110] In spite of the rebuff from Tully, the actors waxed proud and "reueld it in *Rome* in such costly roabes, that they seemed rather men of great patrimonie," etc., causing Publius Servilius to give one of them a "frump." Greene now thinks "the play makers worthy of honour for their Arte: & players, men deseruing both prayse and profite, as long as they wax neither couetous nor insolent."[111] Greene had himself become a dramatist by the time he wrote this passage in 1590; at least one play-maker now had "Arte." But while a dramatist is now permitted to have Art, yet an actor is still only Aesop's crow.

We must not overlook the fact that Nashe merely alluded to the crow story without specifying whose crow. The playwrights have "trickt vp a companie of taffata fooles with their feathers." But to Greene the crow became inevitably Aesop's, for in this capacity he uses no other, which is an important fact to remember when we come to interpret the Shake-scene passage of 1592. In *Gwydonivs. The Carde of Fancie* (S.R. April 11, 1584, printed 1584), Castania reminds Gwydonius that the Duke, who had bestowed "feathers" on him "would vnplume thee of all his feathers, that like *Aesops* Crowe thou mightst receiue the reward of thy rash-nesse."[112] This fine feather was refurbished for *Orpharion* (S.R. February 9, 1590), where Lydia reminds Acestes that her father, the King of Lydia, "woulde vnplume thee of all thy feathers: and like *Esops* Crowe turne thee naked to the worlde: that they which grudged at thy hastie promotion, might laugh at thy sudaine fall."[113] Also, the fine feathers of the crow twice are said to be those of the phoenix,[114] the finest available and so the most incongruous. Once Greene defends himself from the possible charge of being Aesop's crow. When he retells the story of Susanna in the *Myrrovr of Modestie,* 1584, he says in his address to Lady Margaret, "But your honor may thinke I play like *Ezops* Crowe, which deckt hir selfe with others feathers, or like the proud Poet *Batyllus,* which subscribed his name to *Virgils* verses, and yet presented them to *Augustus:* In the behalfe therfore of this my offence, I excuse my selfe with the answere that *Varro* made, when he offred *Ennius* workes to the Emperour: I giue quoth he another mans picture, but freshlie flourished with mine owne coulours."[115] Greene is not Aesop's

---

[110] *Francescos Fortunes* (1590), B4ᵛ-C1ʳ; Grosart, *Greene,* VIII, 132. Notice that "action" is "a kind of mechanical labour"; the actors are properly mechanics. Compare Nashe's strictures above.

[111] *Francescos Fortunes* (1590), C1ʳ; Grosart, *Greene,* VIII, 133.

[112] *Gwydonivs* (1584), K3ᵛ; Grosart, *Greene,* IV, 103.

[113] *Orpharion* (1599), D1ᵛ; Grosart, *Greene,* XII, 37.

[114] Grosart, *Greene,* XII, 24, 252.

[115] *Myrrovr* (1584), Epistle; Grosart, *Greene,* III, 7-8.

crow — nor Horace's — the colors are his own. When, therefore, Nashe accused the company of players of being dressed in the playwrights' fine feathers, immediately and inevitably for Greene the players became Aesop's crow and none other.

The Roscius allusion has its equally inevitable apotheosis. Nashe had warned the company that only the deserved reputation of their Roscius enriched them, being, as they were, only "counterfeits." Now in *Mamillia* (S.R. October 3, 1580), Greene had said, *"Astorides* seeing *Roscius* gestures, durst neuer after come on the stage."[116] In *Penelopes Web* (S.R. June 26, 1587), "they which smiled at the *Theatre* in Rome, might assoone scoffe at the rudenesse of the *Scaene,* as giue a Plaudite at the perfection of the action."[117] To Greene, the perfection of Roscius and the Roman stage lay in the action. So when Greene inherits the Roscius figure from Nashe he is prepared to grant praise to the action, though it be only a mechanical labor. But Roscius himself, as well as actors in general, is nevertheless now specifically Aesop's crow.

And to add insult to injury he is besides Caesar's crow. For Greene had just used the "pye" story in *Orpharion* (where he had also warmed over Aesop's crow), so that in *Francescos Fortunes* the same year it naturally coalesced with the story of Aesop's crow. And no less than Cicero, the author of authors, must now administer the "frump" to Roscius the actor, since Greene had just presented *Tullies Loue* (1589). So it is clear that Greene has here in 1590 merely "varied" Nashe's passage into terms of his own mental processes.

But while the Roscius figure was suggested by Nashe, yet Roscius, a comedian, is not now in Greene necessarily any particular actor, but actors in general.[118] Since Greene has preserved the allegory of his story exactly, we have no evidence that he intended us to think of Alleyn as Roscius and Marlowe as the cobbler, though we inevitably do, and consequently suspect that contemporaries did.[119] But Greene here borrows the cobbler from Nashe and himself equates the cobbler with "our wittes," "our knowledge." Nashe had in the parent passage reminded the actors that they were only crows, even if they should have a deserving Roscius to support them. Then Greene reminds even Roscius that he too is the cobbler's crow, as well as Aesop's, both suggested by Nashe. Aesop the actor has also become the crow of the other Aesop and the resultant crow of both the Aesops has now in turn absorbed the cobbler's crow. But all these are actor crows, mere frippery crows by their very existence. The plagiarist crow (Horace's) does not appear here and has naught to do with these. And

[116] *Mamillia* (1583), F4r; Grosart, *Greene,* II, 79.
[117] *Penelopes Web* [1587], A3v; Grosart, *Greene,* V, 144.
[118] For further background on the cobbler's crow, see McKerrow, *Nashe,* IV, 105.
[119] Chambers, *E.S.,* I, 377n.

while Aesop's crow might become a plagiarist, that phase of his possible activities is not hinted at here, nor ever emphasized in Greene.

Just preceding this passage in *Francescos Fortunes,* Greene described how Francesco had been persuaded to write a comedy which was so successful that all the companies wanted plays from his pen.[120] Then followed the digression upon the actors, which we have just examined. Whether Francesco's experience is autobiographical, it is clear from external facts that Greene himself had already written one play, *Friar Bacon and Friar Bungay,* which was much imitated, first play or not.[121] One imitator of *Bacon* had by 1591 greatly disturbed Greene's admiring self-esteem. This was the author of *Fair Em,*[122] whom he identifies as Anthony Mundy again, the play being printed about 1593, "As it was sundrietimes publiquely acted in the / *honourable citie of London, by the right honourable* / the Lord Strange his seruaunts."[123] This is probably, therefore, a preliminary bout with Strange's organization in 1590-91 before the grand melee of 1592.[124] When the Shaksperean company came into contact with Anthony Mundy it inherited Greene's potential animosity.

But to continue with Greene's quarrels,[125] in allegedly his very last pamphlet, *Groats-Worth of Wit* (1592), Greene elaborates Nashe's warning in *Menaphon* (1589), to the other actors of what would happen to them if their Roscius were gone. Greene is generally supposed here to represent himself as Roberto and to give at least a partially autobiographical account of how he became a playmaker. Roberto asks one who proves to be a player how he may be employed.

Why, easily quoth hee, and greatly to your benefite: for men of my profession gette by schollers their whole liuing. What is your profession, said *Roberto?* Truly sir, saide hee, I am a player. A player, quoth *Roberto,* I tooke you rather for a Gentleman of great liuing . . . So am I where I dwell (quoth the player) reputed able at my proper cost to build a Windmill. What though

---

[120] *Francescos Fortunes* (1590), B3ᵛ; Grosart, *Greene,* VIII, 129.

[121] See below, pp. 262 ff.

[122] See below, pp. 514 ff.

[123] W. W. Greg, *A Bibliography of the English Printed Drama to the Restoration,* I, 192; R. B. McKerrow, *Printers' & Publishers' Devices . . . 1485-1640,* p. 55.

[124] A full discussion of this quarrel will be found in Appendix I.

[125] It has been suggested that Greene was still sneering at *Tamburlaine* in *Greenes farewell to Folly* (1591). Greene intimates that his *Mourning Garment* (S.R. November 2, 1590) had been quite successful, since a peddler "founde them too deare for his packe, that he was faine to bargain for the life of Tomliuolin to wrappe vp his sweete powders in those vnsauorie papers" (*Farewell* (1591), A4ʳ; Grosart, *Greene,* IX, 230). Some would see in "the life of Tomliuolin" an intended reference to Marlowe's *Tamburlaine,* both parts published together in 1590. But *Tamburlaine* was not published as a "life," and quite clearly proved to be a salable commodity. The suggestion of Tomolin for Tom of Lincoln is much more plausible. Greene would have written Tomlin, have struck out the *lin,* and have added *olin,* whereupon the printer took the whole, misreading the first *n* as *u.*

the world once went hard with me, when I was faine to carry my playing
Fardle a footebacke; *Tempora mutantur,* I know you know the meaning of it
better than I, but I thus conster it, its otherwise now; for my very share in
playing apparell will not be sold for two hundred pounds. Truly (said
Roberto) tis straunge, that you should so prosper in that vayne practise, for
that it seemes to mee your voice is nothing gratious. Nay then, saide the
Player, I mislike your iudgement: why, I am as famous for Delphrigus, & the
King of Fairies, as euer was any of my time. The twelue labors of Hercules
haue I terribly thundred on the Stage, and plaid three Scenes of the Deuill in
the High way to heauen. Haue ye so (saide *Roberto?*) then I pray you
pardon me. Nay more (quoth the Player) I can serue to make a pretie speech,
for I was a countrey Author, passing at a Morrall, for twas I that pende the
Morrall of mans witte, the Dialogue of Diues, and for seuen yeers space was
absolute Interpreter to the puppets. But now my Almanacke is out of date:

> *The people make no estimation,*
> *Of Morrals teaching education.*

Was not this prettie for a plaine rime extempore? if ye will ye shall haue
more. Nay its enough, said *Roberto,* but how meane you to vse mee? Why
sir, in making Playes, said the other, for which you shall be well paid, if you
will take the paines.[126]

It will be seen that Greene is here in 1592 "dilating" Nashe's passage
in 1589, concerning the players and their past experiences before "our
Poets" enabled "one *Roscius*" — or more — to support them. Greene's
player, too, had once carried his fardle "a footebacke," had been famous
for acting Delphrigus and the King of Fairies, etc., all as in Nashe. Thus
in fact the original picture belongs to Nashe in 1589, and Nashe's allusions are at narrowest to the adventures and repertoire of some group of
actors as a whole, not to those of an individual actor. In fact, if it were
not for "our Poets" supporting at least "one Roscius" they would be back
to their original status again. Greene in 1592 transfers all of Nashe's
satiric portrait to this one player, who is manager and author as well as a
famous actor, and Greene improves upon Nashe's efforts. Greene's portrait of this player is, therefore, certainly to some extent fictitious, though
some of the details might be actual, much depending upon how real
Nashe's original details were. Thus Greene's picture is an expansion and
adaptation of Nashe's, which had represented satirically circumstances at
some time before August, 1589. Further, it would seem that Nashe was
merely poking fun generally, though perhaps at the past of the Admiral's
men. Greene is now applying Nashe's jesting details specifically to one
person, who is a country author of moral plays, a principal actor, and
a manager.

In general, this is clearly Posthaste of *Histrio-Mastix;* that is, Anthony
Mundy again. Notice among Greene's additions to Nashe's list "the
Dialogue of Dives," which appears in *Histrio-Mastix* as *"The Diuell and*

---

[126] *Groats-Worth* (1592), D4^v-E1^r; Grosart, *Greene,* XII, 131-132.

Dives; (a Comedie)." Greene and *Histrio-Mastix* supply alleged details of Mundy's activities as a country author, manager, and player, while Nashe alludes to the same period generally by way of warning to the actors that but for "one *Roscius*" now and then and better poets they would be back to the country life again.

We should now notice that *Histrio-Mastix* and *Groats-Worth* are closely connected in time as well as in content. First, there is the allusion to "Callis Cormorants."

> The Callis Cormorants from Douer roade,
> Are not so chargeable as you to feed.[127]

Evidently straggling soldiers were returning from France. Volunteer forces had been sent to France as early as May, 1589, all being returned by the end of January, 1590.[128] There were no English troops in France in 1590 except a few volunteers.[129] The next expedition was in August, 1591, all troops being again withdrawn by November, 1593;[130] and here ended the "Callis Cormorants." It is true that there was an expedition to Picardy in October, 1596,[131] which remained throughout the next year, and its pressed soldiers showed remarkable facility in escaping to England;[132] but they were not Calais cormorants, since they had been sent chiefly to offset the taking of Calais March-April, 1598, by the Spanish.[133] Thus the allusion is not later than November, 1593. This last time, however, the French service proved so unpopular that it was soon hard to get men even by pressing, though many were idle.[134] The tone of the allusion, and of the pressing-scene both indicate this last expedition, August, 1591, to November, 1593.

The play also contains an allusion to Greene's *Qvip for an Vpstart Courtier,*[135] entered S.R. July 21, 1592, which further narrows the date to between August, 1592, and November, 1593. Within this period there was such a Spanish scare as is satirized in the Play,[136] occurring about August, 1592.[137] Also, the play refers to "This dreaming long vacation,"[138] "this

---

[127] *Histrio-Mastix,* D2ᵛ; III, 1.

[128] E. P. Cheyney, *A History of England,* I, 212-228.

[129] Cheyney, *History,* I, 238.

[130] Cheyney, *History,* I, 258, 293.

[131] *Acts of the Privy Council,* XXVI, Preface, xiv-xv.

[132] *Acts of P.C.,* XXVII, Preface, xvii-xix.

[133] *Acts of P.C.,* XXV, Preface, xxvi.

[134] Cheyney, *History,* I, 285-293.

[135] *Histrio-Mastix,* C2ᵛ; II, 1; Richard Simpson, *The School of Shakspere,* II, 35.

[136] *Histrio-Mastix,* G1ʳ; V, 1.

[137] *Acts of P.C.,* XXIII, 160; M. A. S. Hume, *The Great Lord Burghley,* p. 451.

[138] *Histrio-Mastix,* C2ʳ; II, 1.

summer season,"[139] and "when the terme comes."[140] Too, the satirized
players are traveling. Now because of disturbances the players were forced
to cease acting in London the summer of 1592, and because of the plague
the summer of 1593.[141] All these allusions occur in what authorities agree
was the first form of the play[142] except the allusion to the Spanish scare,
where Small would have a single line inserted in the old material, a very
improbable suggestion in view of the fact that there was such a scare at
the approximate date of the first version. It seems clear, therefore, that the
first form of *Histrio-Mastix* dates either late in the summer of 1592 or
that of 1593. The fact that at the same time soldiers are being pressed
while others return from France would indicate 1592 as the time rather
than 1593. Thus *Groats-Worth* and *Histrio-Mastix* are evidently closely
connected both in time and in intention.

We have seen that *Histrio-Mastix* satirizes Mundy. So does *Groats-
Worth,* where Greene has given a direct clue to the subject of his satire
in "So am I where I dwell (quoth the player) reputed able at my proper
cost to build a Windmill." Why build a windmill? The only windmills
listed by Kingsford in Stow (II, 370) are in Finsbury Fields, and all the
references known to Sugden are to these. In the case of *Fair Em,* Greene
accused the author of being familiar with the Sexton "of Saint Giles
without Creeple gate,"[143] the windmill parish. Mundy had been twitted
about happenings in Barbican, and in *A breefe Aunswer* (1582) gave
Barbican as his address. Stow places a watchtower "in the parish of
S. Giles without Cripplegate of London, commonly called the Barbican."[144]
When Mundy took up his freedom by patrimony in the Drapers' Company in 1585, he was described as living "By Creplegate a Poet."[145] His
family records are at St. Giles without Cripplegate. Greene has indicated
the same parish for his player or playwright in each case. Mundy's de-
precatively prideful statement in his will that his income had been "Fortie
or fiftie poundes yearlie"[146] is quite in keeping with the windmill boast.
Incidentally, there is nothing to indicate that Greene himself ever wrote
for such a company as that to which this player-dramatist belonged. Nor
that Greene ever wrote for Mundy. Probably the only autobiographical
fact here is that Greene did write a first play — and that he did thoroughly
detest Anthony Mundy. Nor may we use these satires as biographical

---

[139] *Histrio-Mastix,* C3^r; II, 1.

[140] *Histrio-Mastix,* C4^v; II, 1.

[141] Greg, *Henslowe's Diary,* II, 50; John T. Murray, *English Dramatic Companies,*
I, 65.

[142] Chambers, *E.S.,* IV, 17.

[143] *Greenes farewell to Folly* (1591), A4^v; Grosart, *Greene,* IX, 232-233.

[144] C. L. Kingsford, *A Survey of London by John Stow* (1908), I, 70.

[145] Turner, *Mundy,* p. 75.

[146] Turner, *Mundy,* p. 170.

fact for Mundy and his fellows. As we acquire the actual facts, we shall be able to interpret the satires.[147]

We are also to remember that in 1592 Mundy would have been connected with the Strange-Admiral company. It seems clear that the company satirized in *Histrio-Mastix* is one connected with the Alleyn stock, since all its attributed plays that can be identified were in some way connected with that stock. Thus the company had *The Prodigal Child*,[148] *The Devil and Dives*, [149] and *Mother Gurton's Needle*,[150] all performed by the German Admiral's, while one of the actors is advised now to "play the *Tamburlaine*,"[151] as if it were an accustomed part.[152]

Further, the organization of the satirized company is exactly that of the Shaksperean company 1588-94, certainly not that of the Admiral's men, nor so far as we can at present judge that of any other company of the time. Sir Oliver Owlet's men were "but four or five"; to be exact, there were five members in the company, as was exactly true of the Shaksperean company at this period. Perhaps we should not need to overstretch our imaginations to see in Incle the peddler, John Heminges the grocer; or in Gut the fiddlestrong maker, Augustine Phillips, the owner of miscellaneous stringed instruments.[153] Probably Sir Toby Belch, pretty certainly one of Pope's parts,[154] owes at least his name to Belch the beardmaker, pointing to Pope as Belch. Was he already acquiring belching rotundity in 1592? Clowt the clown would go by profession to Kempe, leaving Gulch for Bryane. But in all this we must remember that we are dealing with satire, not gospel history. It is likely, however, that *Histrio-Mastix* is aimed at some part of the Strange-Admiral combination about the summer of 1592, and does not concern any earlier company or set of circumstances.

So Nashe in 1589 furnished Greene with a figure which Greene was to vary till his last gasp. It was Nashe who provided Roscius and reminded other actors that they were only crows. Greene reminded even Roscius himself in 1590 that he too was only Aesop's crow, and the cobbler's crow besides. In 1592 Greene further develops Nashe's glimpse at Roscius and

---

[147] Evidently the satirists had a heap of more or less "commonplace" brickbats, to be heaved at any offending noggin that showed.

[148] *Histrio-Mastix*, C1ʳ; II, 1.

[149] *Histrio-Mastix*, C3ʳ; II, 1.

[150] *Histrio-Mastix*, C3ʳ; II, 1.

[151] *Histrio-Mastix*, G1ʳ; V, 1.

[152] The *Troilus and Cressida* (*Histrio-Mastix*, C3ᵛ ff.; II, 1) is not supposed to belong to the early version.

[153] J. P. Collier, *Memoirs of the Principal Actors in the Plays of Shakespeare*, Phillips.

[154] T. W. Baldwin, *Organization and Personnel of the Shakespearean Company*, Chapter IX.

his fellows into a full-length satirical portrait of one actor only. But the crow (Aesop's; that is, the actors') is now reserved especially for William Shakspere.

In the course of *Greenes, Groats-Worth of witte,* allegedly written upon what proved to be his deathbed, Greene addresses a letter "To those Gentlemen his Quondam acquaintance, that spend their wits in making plaies, R. G. wisheth a better exercise, and wisdome to preuent his extremities."[155] Greene hopes his experience will move them to "looke backe with sorrow on your time past, and indeuour with repentance to spend that which is to come." He calls first to the mourners' bench that "famous gracer of Tragedians," who has said "(like the foole in his heart) There is no God," and so has studied "pestilent Machiuilian pollicy."[156] Machiavelli's own fate and that of Greene should warn him to repent. This is clearly Marlowe.

"With thee I ioyne yong *Iuuenall,* that byting Satyrist, that lastly with mee together writ a Comedie," who is advised "get not many enemies by bitter wordes . . . then blame not Schollers vexed with sharpe lines, if they reproue thy too much liberty of reproofe." It is now apparently agreed that this is Nashe, not Lodge as was once suggested, since this is Nashe's reputation and age in 1592, but hardly that of Lodge. To my mind the strongest bit of evidence is that "Chettle feigning a letter from the dead poet to Nashe (*Robert Greene to Pierce Pennilesse*), makes Greene use almost the epithet of the *Groatsworth,* 'Awake, *secure boy,* revenge thy wrongs.' "[157] Since Chettle had caused *Groats-Worth* to be published, and in the publication quoted from had defended and apologized for Greene's passage, he would know who was the youth in the case.

Next comes George Peele, as is shown among other things by the turn on "sweet S. George," "no lesse deseruing than the other two, in some things rarer, in nothing inferiour; driuen (as my selfe) to extreme shifts . . . Base minded men all three of you, if by my miserie you be not warnd: for vnto none of you (like mee) sought those burres to cleaue: those Puppets (I meane) that spake from our mouths, those Anticks garnisht in our colours. Is it not strange, that I, to whom they all haue beene beholding: is it not like that you, to whome they all haue beene beholding, shall (were yee in that case as I am now) bee both at once of them forsaken? Yes trust them not: for there is an vpstart Crow,

---

[155] *Groats-Worth* (1592), E4^v ff.; Grosart, *Greene,* XII, 141 ff.

[156] Compare, "The Atheist saith in his heart, there is no God. The Machiuel with the Atheist wil not know that there is either God or deuil, hel or heauen, and in all their actions they quench the spirit of God, & that one day shal they know to their cost, except they turne againe" (W. Burton, *A Sermon Preached . . . in Norwich, the xxi. day of December, 1589,* F4$^{r&v}$).

[157] C. M. Gayley, *Representative English Comedies,* [I], 423.

beautified with our feathers, that with his *Tygers hart wrapt in a Players hyde,* supposes he is as well able to bombast out a blanke verse as the best of you: and beeing an absolute *Iohannes fac totum,* is in his owne conceit the onely Shake-scene in a countrey. O that I might intreat your rare wits to be imploied in more profitable courses: & let those Apes imitate your past excellence, and neuer more acquaint them with your admired inuentions. I knowe the best husband of you all will neuer proue an Usurer, and the kindest of them all will neuer proue a kind nurse: yet whilest you may, seeke you better Maisters; for it is pittie men of such rare wits, should be subiect to the pleasure of such rude groomes."[158]

Greene is accusing one particular organization of actors of having cast him off, and is advising Marlowe, Peele, and his own colleague in one play, supposedly Nashe, not to write for this organization any more, but to "seeke you better Maisters"; that is, to write for some other organization. The reference can only be to the cooperating Admiral-Strange organization, and within that to Strange's men. But Marlowe had written for the Admiral's since 1587, and Peele from before 1589. Why should Greene in August, 1592, warn these old timers of impending doom, "for vnto none of you (like mee) sought those burres to cleaue"? The answer clearly is that Greene is not warning against the Admiral's part of the organization (Alleyn), but against Strange's. It was Strange's[159] that had sought to cleave to Greene. But now they have cast him off and will cast them off too in favor of "an vpstart Crow, beautified with our feathers," who thinks he is as good a dramatist as "the best of you," though he is in fact but a *Iohannes fac totum,* and the only Shake-scene in the country. This Jack-of-all-trades, Shakspere, thinks he is as good a dramatist as the best, and Strange's company has agreed to the extent of discarding Greene, and will discard the other three.

We should notice immediately that several of these terms echo another passage on which Greene had just been engaged, in *A Qvip For An Vpstart Courtier.* In the course of it, a Poet is examined as a possible juror. Cloth Breeches thinks "him an honest man if he would but liue within his compasse, and generally no mannes foe but his owne"; but Velvet Breeches objects "this Poet is a proud fellowe," and prefers the Player and the Usher of a dancing school. To these Cloth Breeches objects, "they be so lowlie, that they be base minded, I meane not in their lookes nor apparell, for so they be peacockes and painted asses, but in their course of life, for they care not howe they get crownes, I meane how baselie so they haue them: and yet of the two I holde the Player to be the better Christian, although he is in his owne imagination, too full of selfe liking

---

[158] *Groats-Worth* (1592), E4ᵛ-F2ʳ; Grosart, *Greene,* XII, 143-144.

[159] Can there possibly be an intended echo in "Is it not strange"?

and selfe loue."[160] Upstart, proud, base-minded, peacocks and painted asses, too full of self-liking, self-love. Phraseologically, Shake-scene has fallen almost sole heir to this invention, so that it has important bearing in interpreting the Shake-scene passage.

Greene has in the *Groats-Worth* passage applied the evolving figure of Aesop's crow not only to the actors in general, "those Anticks garnisht in our colours," but also specifically to one individual, Shake-scene by name, whom we identify as Shakspere. What belongs generally to the figure, and what specifically to the person? Previously, Greene has always applied the figure to actors and has come to involve Roscius the actor with Aesop's crow as a borrower of fine feathers. The actors parade in the fine feathers of the dramatists. The same primary application is certainly made here to Shake-scene, the upstart actor, who is now singled out as one of "those Anticks garnisht in our colours." While the primary application of the figure to Shakspere is certainly as actor, yet as certainly Greene does glance at Shakspere's activities as a dramatist in "supposes he is as well able to bombast out a blanke verse as the best of you." The overt accusation is not of stealing but of bombasting blank verse, and the aggrieved person is "the best of you," which does not directly include Greene. The phraseology reminds us of Nashe's "swelling bumbast of a bragging blanke verse," and rightly or wrongly we think of Marlowe rather than of Peele or Nashe. But if so the overt accusation is of egotistic rivalry with Marlowe, and if not, then with someone else, certainly not of theft from Greene.

Between the two functions of upstart actor and bombasting dramatist the transition bridge has been "that with his *Tygers hart wrapt in a Players hyde.*" Greene is still taking it out on the "Players hyde," and immediately identifies the player here as Shake-scene. But Greene is also parodying a line from *3 Henry VI* (I, 4, 137) "O tiger's heart wrapp'd in a woman's hide!" Greene is turning the line from *3 Henry VI* to say that Shake-scene, the player, along with his fellow players, is acting the part of the tiger to Greene in thus casting him off. He had used the same device of parodying quotation in identifying Marlowe, also the author of *Fair Em,* etc. Presumably he is using his regular method here. There is nothing whatever in the total genesis of the crow figure, or in its specific application here, or in the turned line from *3 Henry VI* to indicate that Greene is accusing Shakspere of having "borrowed" that line. All that appears from the passage itself is that Greene has very cleverly turned a line from *3 Henry VI* upon Shake-scene. It happens, however, that the turned line is from a play which is included in the First Folio by those who knew the facts, as belonging to Shakspere,[161] though this attribution would not mean

---

[160] *Qvip* (1592, Scholar's Facsimiles, 1954), H2r; Grosart, *Greene,* XI, 291-292.

[161] In turn, this is our best warrant that Shake-scene is Shakspere.

that Shakspere wrote every word of every play so included. Still the burden of proof is on anyone who attributes any part of any one of the plays to anyone else. Until proved otherwise we must infer that Greene thought this was Shakspere's own line and sentiment, and that he exhibits it, wrong side out, as it were, as a specimen of that self-prized bombast blank verse of which he accuses Shake-scene in the same clause — and it is a grand line, we must admit! Greene may, of course, have been no better informed than we as to the actual authorship of the line, and as to its actual authorship I am not here called upon to commit myself. We simply have Greene's opinion to add to that of the First Folio. It is at least certain, however, that there is absolutely no evidence here to warrant an inference of a charge of plagiarism. These actors, including Shake-scene, are Aesop's frippery crow as usual, not a plagiarist crow of any feather.

It may be added that if Greene was aware of the context of the line, this application of it was peculiarly fitting. For the passage continues,

> How couldst thou drain the life-blood of the child,
> To bid the father wipe his eyes withal,
> And yet be seen to bear a woman's face?[162]

How could Shake-scene be seen to bear a dramatist's face and yet do this to father Greene?

And Shakspere certainly had not the excuse of ignorance or lack of acquaintance. For he knew well and used Greene's *Menaphon* shortly after its appearance in 1589 for his *Comedy of Errors*. He certainly knew the kind of criticism Nashe and Greene were leveling at such "learned grammarian" upstarts as he, and so he should not have been too much surprised when Greene in 1592 threw this twice-cooked bit — *bis cocta* — into his dish. And for Shakspere's borrowing Greene had repaid himself in kind. In 1590 he had borrowed and four times bettered a simile from *Two Gentlemen*.[163] This Shake-scene bur had been in Greene's fleece, and Greene had repaid himself in kind. Greene and Shakspere had long been aware of each other, whether favorably or unfavorably, before the incident of the "tiger's heart."

It should perhaps be emphasized, too, that the problem is not what from a detached reading we think Greene's passage might mean to us. Nor even what it could have meant to "the Elizabethan," since there must have been at least as many Elizabethans as there were Elizabethans — then as now. All that is pertinent here is what Greene himself meant. And the genesis and total evolution of the figure make that meaning essentially clear. Shakspere, as Shake-scene the actor, is Aesop's crow —

---

[162] *3 Henry VI,* I, 4, 138-140.
[163] See pp. 238 ff.

the frippery crow of both the Aesops, with perhaps the support of the cobbler's crow; the plagiarist crow does not enter here.[164] Shake-scene the actor is also incidentally accused of preferring himself as dramatist above all others, and by implication, of being preferred by his fellows.

It may also be well to add that the tiger line does not fit into Greene's menagerie. In Greene, the tiger is the symbol of fierceness and cruelty,[165] as it was to everyone else. For instance, the Roman Catholics accused Queen Elizabeth of having a tiger's heart toward them.[166] She had a tiger's heart wrapped in a woman's hide. But Greene usually substitutes the tiger for the wolf in the Biblical figure of the wolf in sheep's clothing, though twice in early work he has the original figure. In *Mamillia* (1583) Pharicles is accused of "framing a sheepes skin for his woolues backe," and in *The Myrrovr of Modestie* (1584), the judges who accuse Susanna have "vnder their sheepes skinnes, hidden the bloudie nature of a woolfe."[167] In all other instances the tiger gets substituted for the wolf, except that once the Pope gets the bad eminence, instead of either tiger or wolf, as a monster masking in a sheep's skin.[168] Mamillia says that Pharicles has "vnder the shape of a Lambe the substaunce of a Tigre."[169] Clarynda has designs on Pharicles, "Couering therefore the heart of a Tigre with the fleece of a Lambe."[170] Pharicles philosophizes that "It is more griefe (quoth he) to the silly Lambe to lie lingring in the gripe of the Tygre, thā presently to be deuoured."[171] In all these instances, the tiger is simply substituted for the wolf. By consequence, in one of these instances we get "the heart of a Tigre" in effect in a woman's hide; but it is statedly covered with the "fleece of a Lambe." In *Planetomachia,* Jupiter says Mercury causes man "to carry a Lamb in his shield, and a Tygre in his bosome."[172] In *Alcida* (1588), Telegonus cries out "cruell

---

[164] For some mediaeval applications of the crow story, see Helen Pennock South, "The Upstart Crow," *M.P.* (1927), XXV, 83-86. Sidney Thomas, "The Meaning of Greene's Attack on Shakespeare," *M.L.N.* (1951), LXVI, 483-484 cites two instances where literary purloining is figured as borrowed plumage. Because of Horace, such references are frequent, but for Greene they are impertinent; Horace's plagiarist crow nowhere enters into Greene's thinking.

[165] Grosart, *Greene,* II, 279; III, 205, 233; V, 57; X, 252.

[166] In Adam Blackwood's *Martyre De La Royne D'Escosse* (1587), Queen Elizabeth is regularly said to be worse than the Hyrcanian tiger. She is said also to have a soul more crooked than her body (p. 492) — infringing on the Essex copyright by some years!

[167] *Mamillia* (1583), B2ʳ; Grosart, *Greene,* II, 20; *Myrrovr* (1584), A2ᵛ; Grosart, *Greene,* III, 11.

[168] *Spanish Masqverado* (1589), B1ᵛ; Grosart, *Greene,* V, 249.

[169] *Mamillia* (1593), B2ᵛ; Grosart, *Greene,* II, 154.

[170] *Mamillia* (1593), E2ʳ; Grosart, *Greene,* II, 187-188.

[171] *Mamillia* (1593), I2ᵛ; Grosart, *Greene,* II, 235.

[172] *Planetomachia* (1585), B2ᵛ; Grosart, *Greene,* V, 43.

Fiordespine, borne of a Tyger, and nursed of the shee Wolues in Syria: whose heart is full of hate, whose thoughts are disdaine, whose beautie is ouerlaid with pride."[173] Thus Fiordespine also in effect has a tiger's heart wrapped in a woman's hide, though there is no suggestion of that phraseology. The wolf of the original figure also shows through. In the same pamphlet, "the Lambe and the Tiger" are not to be joined to- gether.[174] Greene has the elements of the figure as stated in *3 Henry VI,* but not the phraseology. Surely it is also apparent that the direct and violent statement for *3 Henry VI* does not fit Greene's flaccidly tumid style. It is exactly the kind of thing he has been objecting to from the beginning.

In this connection we should notice that "an Elizabethan" has at times been interpreted as thinking that Greene's accusation was more than that the actors had grown proud by wearing his fine feathers. In *Greenes Funeralls* (S.R. February 1, 1594; printed 1594), R. B., Gent. says in Sonnet IX

> *Greene,* is the pleasing Obiect of an eie:
>   *Greene,* pleasde the eies of all that lookt vppon him.
> *Greene,* is the ground of euerie Painters die:
> *Greene,* gaue the ground, to all that wrote vpon him.
> Nay more the men, that so Eclipst his fame:
> Purloynde his Plumes, can they deny the same?

The late Dr. McKerrow was of opinion that this is "Possibly, but not certainly, an allusion to the well-known passage."[175] If it is an allusion, then R. B. has misunderstood the charge, since he accuses "all that wrote vpon him," who are "the men, that so Eclipst his fame." Greene brings no such charges against the dramatists in his passage, and it was the actors, including Shake-scene, who were "garnisht in our colours," even the upstart crow being merely "beautified with our feathers." No one is accused of purloining anything. If. R. B. is referring to our passage, he has evidently misunderstood it even more completely than he has mis- represented it.

But, at least in general, R. B. makes the objects of his criticism clear. He continues with a sonnet containing "A Catalogue of certaine of his [Greene's] Bookes," and then Greene himself is represented as saying

> When my loathed life, had lost the light of *Olimpus,*
>   And descended downe, to the cursed caues of *Auernus,*
> Neuer more had I thought, of men to be inlie molested,
>   But now alas, I see my hope is vaine:
>   . . . .

---

[173] *Alcida* (1617), E3ʳ; Grosart, *Greene,* IX, 52.
[174] *Alcida* (1617), I2ʳ; Grosart, *Greene,* IX, 96.
[175] R. B. McKerrow, *Greenes Funeralls* (1911), p. 92.

For such foolish men, as I had neuer abused:

.   .   .   .

Not onely seeke to quench my kindled glorie,
But also for to marre my *vertues* storie.

.   .   .   .

Yet might my end, haue moued them to remorce:
And not to reake their teene, on sillie corse (Sonnet XI).

Here are the men who "so Eclipst his fame," "seeke to quench my kindled glorie." In the conclusion of each of the two sonnets preceding the "plume" passage, R. B. had said

For my selfe I wish, that none had written against him
But such men which had iust cause t'haue wr[i]tten against him,
   (Sonnet VII).

Yet will I euer write to defend and offend:
For to defend his friends, and to offend his foes (Sonnet VIII).

These men who unprovoked "wrote vpon him," that is, "against him," and "Eclipst his fame" by marring his "*vertues* storie" after his death — these men are the avowed objects of R. B.'s protests. Whoever these men were, among them Shakspere was not.[176]

As we look at Greene's statements in August, 1592, they show that Strange's men had made up their minds about Shakspere as a dramatist, and that Shakspere had also made up his mind about his own abilities. Other dramatists might at convenience be supplements to Shakspere but they could not be substitutes for him. And Greene found that he was not even wanted as a supplement. It will be noticed that such attachment as Greene had here was evidently through the Admiral's, not Strange's, as shown by the later history of Greene's plays. By August, 1592, Strange's was predominant, and Greene was out. So he warns the Admiral's former playwrights that the same thing will happen to them also. And Greene says these same actors had once sought like burs to cleave to him, as they had not to any of the others. This can only mean that the company had tried to get Greene as their chief regular writer, but now they prefer Shakspere.

But besides Greene himself, the three gentlemen-playwrights, and Shakspere, there are two other writers for the organization. "In this I might insert two more, that both haue writ against these buckram Gentlemen: but lette their owne workes serue to witnesse against their owne wickednesse, if they perseuere to maintaine any more such peasants. For

---

[176] Warren B. Austin, "A Supposed Contemporary Allusion to Shakespeare as a Plagiarist," *Shakespeare Quarterly,* VI, 373-380 argues that these lines are aimed at Gabriel Harvey.

other new-commers, I leaue them to the mercie of these painted monsters, who (I doubt not) will driue the best minded to despise them: for the rest, it skils not though they make a ieast at them."[177] Nashe had probably been the most outspoken against actors. If he was young Juvenal, then Mundy and Lodge are the only other two of whom I think in this role, though both defended against Gosson some acting. So one of the two referred to by Greene should probably be Mundy, who was also an old-timer with the Admiral's men, probably having helped Marlowe canvass Greene's motto about 1587. But Mundy had again offended Greene the preceding year; so, if the reference is to Mundy, Greene evidently rather hopes he will continue in the evil of his way and receive his just deserts. Unless the other dramatist was Lodge, I have no guess. He had sworn off in 1589, and may have been safely out of the country at the time, and so his case not urgent.[178] In the main the who and the why of Greene's disquisition are quite clear.

Since Chettle had put Greene's acrid disquisition into print after Greene's death, it fell to his lot to do some fervent explaining. Addressing "Gentlemen Readers" in *Kind-Harts Dreame* [1592], he says that this "letter written to diuers play-makers, is offensiuely by one or two of them taken, and because on the dead they cannot be auenged, they wilfully forge in their conceites a liuing Author: and after tossing it two and fro, no remedy, but it must light on me. . . . With neither of them that take offence was I acquainted, and with one of them I care not if I neuer be: The other" deserves an apology. "For the first, whose learning I reuerence, and at the perusing of *Greenes* Booke, stroke out what then in conscience I thought he in some displeasure writ: or had it beene true, yet to publish it, was intollerable: him I would wish to vse me no worse than I deserue." It is agreed that "the first" is Marlowe and "The other" Shakspere, to whom Chettle apologizes for not having ameliorated Greene's statements, as he says he did those directed to Marlowe, whose learning he reverences. So Greene had probably said much the same things about Marlowe here as he had been saying for several years past.

It seems not to have been sufficiently noticed that the terms of Chettle's apology give his interpretation of Greene's passage. Greene had called Shakspere "an vpstart Crow, beautified with our feathers," who "beeing an absolute *Iohannes fac totum,* is in his owne conceit the only Shake-scene in a countrey." On this charge, Chettle says, "my selfe haue seene his demeanor no lesse ciuill than he exelent in the qualitie he professes." Here is a handsome apology to the actor, covering the slurs both upon

---

[177] *Groats-Worth* (1592), F2ʳ; Grosart, *Greene,* XII, 144-145.

[178] But Professor C. J. Sisson, *Thomas Lodge and other Elizabethans,* p. 106, thinks Lodge may have returned about May, 1592.

his demeanor and upon his quality; he was not an "vpstart," and he was not a mere "Shake-scene." It is clear that Chettle understood "vpstart" to refer to demeanor and not to length of experience.

Of the dramatist, Greene had warned that he "supposes he is as well able to bombast out a blanke verse as the best of you." So Chettle continues, "Besides, diuers of worship haue reported, his vprightnes of dealing, which argues his honesty, and his facetious grace in writting, that aprooues his Art." At least, Gentlemen thought Shakspere wrote good comedy, whatever Greene might think of his bombast blank verse in tragedy. Since Greene had accused Shakspere of being the cause that he himself was shaken off by the actors, and had warned other dramatists of what would happen to them, Chettle brings from "diuers of worship" a character witness. Thus Chettle covers both charges against Shakspere as a dramatist. The apology to both actor and dramatist is categoric and complete. Greene was wrong on all counts. From both Greene and Chettle one learns that Shakspere was highly esteemed by Strange's in 1592, both as actor and as dramatist. As actor, he was to be taken into the membership in 1594. As dramatist, his plays were to be published by survivors of this group of actors as having been written for the one organization.

It must be remembered that the real object of Greene's attack is the company of players. Shakspere is berated because the company is alleged to prefer him to all others as a dramatist. Marlowe, Nashe, and Peele are warned so that they may not aid the company by writing for it. They are at least university men, and so for art's sake should side with Greene against the company, which thinks the artless Shakspere its greatest dramatist, an opinion Shakspere is accused of sharing. But whether he was already chief dramatist for the company as Greene implies or not, the importance for William Shakspere of his position in the company can not be too much emphasized. Both as actor and as dramatist he was "beautified with our feathers," from these four best dramatists of the day, two others later being added to the list. As an actor, he and his company were "garnisht in our colours." Whatever an actor could learn from acting in the plays of these the best dramatists of the day, that Shakspere had an opportunity to learn. There should be no mystery about any influences from these men found in Shakspere's own work. If he was at all sensitive to influence, the conditions warrant that there would be some.

This influence Shakspere would get, these things he would learn, from acting in the old plays of these authors, and of any others, such as Kyd, whose plays were still being acted. But if any of these authors wrote a new play for the company while Shakspere was an actor, there would have been other golden opportunities. As the play was being planned, constructed, and fitted, he would at least hear, and would doubtless partici-pate in, the discussions which arose between author and actors.[179] Was it some profferred and preferred suggestion of his which caused Greene to write that he "supposes he is as well able to bombast out a blanke verse as the best of you"? In our human frailty, no doubt we would like to know; but the present evidence does not tell us, and I have no revelation. It is also to be hoped that we have the charity to feel Greene's plight, even as we understand how essentially unjust he was to Shakspere. In the words of the Bishops' Bible, "Men we be all."

[179] For a brief sketch of the process, see my edition of *The Comedy of Errors*.

CHAPTER II

The Chronology of Robert Greene's Plays

Greene's castigations as arbiter of art have given us a very general sketch of literary coteries in the drama to 1592, furnishing a controlling framework for Shakspere's activities. The sketch can be made much more definite by an examination of the plays produced during this period by the various authors enmeshed with Greene, and we begin with Greene himself.

Robert Greene's habits of composition in procuring *copia* were such that it is easy to place *Orlando, Bacon,* his part of *Looking Glasse, James IV,* in that order, and to orient them with regard to his dated prose fictions. But *The Comicall Historie of Alphonsvs King of Aragon,* which was printed in 1599 as "Made by R. G.," does not connect with either the other plays or the prose fictions. We have only the attribution to R. G. to suggest that *Alphonsus* was written by Greene. Critics have usually made a wry face and then accepted the play as Greene's first. The prologue at least indicates that this is some kind of first play of its kind. There Venus is represented as saying that since Homer and Virgil are dead and modern poets have failed to give Alphonsus his due praise, she herself must turn Minerva.

> No, *Venus,* no, though Poets proue vnkind,
> And loth to stand in penning of his deeds,
> Yet rather then they shall be cleane forgot,
> I, which was wont to follow *Cupids* games
> Will put in vre Mineruaes sacred Art;
> And this my hand, which vsed for to pen
> The praise of loue and *Cupids* peerles power,
> Will now begin to treat of bloudie *Mars,*
> Of doughtie deeds and valiant victories.[1]

It is Venus who is to turn Minerva for the sake of Alphonsus. Venus has necessarily written habitually, if at all, of love and Cupid. The author who puts these lines into the mouth of Venus may or may not have written so. Venus and her apology are occasioned primarily by the mixed form, and not necessarily by the "mixed" author. The play is to end as a comedy, with Alphonsus winning the daughter of Amurack; but the deeds by which Alphonsus comes to this estate are those of Mars, not of Venus. So Venus apologizes for usurping.

---

[1] Collins, *Alphonsus,* 32-40.

Since the play refers to Tamburlaine and is generally agreed to imitate Marlowe's play, it could in that case hardly be earlier than 1588. To judge by alleged instances,[2] it would appear that the parallels of *Alphonsus* are entirely with *I Tamburlaine,* even those in phraseology, which are very weak indeed. If the borrowing is granted, and if it proves to have been only from *I Tamburlaine,* then the indication would be strong that *Alphonsus* was written immediately after *I Tamburlaine.* If the play be Greene's, he made a commonplace reference to Alphonsus the person in the *Epistle Dedicatorie* to *Gwydonivs. The Carde of Fancie* (S.R. April 11, 1584; printed in 1584). It is usual to have Greene in *Perimedes,* 1588, bewail an unsuccessful play in competition with *Tamburlaine,* and some would identify *Alphonsus* as that play.[3] Also, "In IV. i Mahomet speaks out of a brazen head. The play may therefore be alluded to in the 'Mahomet's poo [pow]' of Peele's . . . *Farewell* of April, 1589, although Peele may have intended his own lost play of *The Turkish Mahomet and Hiren the Fair Greek.*"[4] It will appear that the latter is the more likely interpretation.

But that *Alphonsus* is Greene's first play, or that it is Greene's at all, calls for more evidence. Its unlyrical verse is not that of the other plays, which Greene was to begin writing no long time if at all after *Alphonsus* is supposed to have been written, nor ever in any of his known verse did Greene write so. Critics have always known this but have attributed the recognized fact to youth and the awkwardness of a first play;[5] but Greene shows no such awkwardness, so-called, in his bits of early verse. The essential difference is in kind of verse, not in youth or awkwardness.[6]

Of Greene's fully acknowledged plays, three are closely interconnected with each other and with his prose works. The three plays are *Orlando, Bacon,* and his part of *Looking Glasse.* Since *Bacon* can be most definitely allocated, it will be well to consider it first. A favorite figure of the time[7]

---

[2] See Bakeless, *Tragicall History, I,* 249 ff., and the references there assembled.

[3] Chambers, *E.S.,* III, 327. See above, pp. 1-4.

[4] Chambers, *E.S.,* III, 327.

[5] The late Professor Una Ellis-Fermor ("Marlowe and Greene: A Note on their Relations as Dramatic Artists," *Studies in Honor of T. W. Baldwin,* p. 138) thought that, "The subjugation of Greene's genius to Marlowe's seems in this first play [*Alphonsus*] to be wholly disastrous, not so much because of his crude attempt to reproduce and outdo a popular figure as because his imagination is itself invaded; because, alongside an almost puerile attempt at superficial imitation, there is a poet's response to the vision of a poet, an imitation in the true sense."

[6] Miss Margaret P. McGlothlin, "The Channels and Sources of Spanish Influence on Elizabethan Drama, 1558-1603" (Master's thesis, U. of Illinois, 1930), pp. 11 ff., points out that *Alphonsus* "refuses to fit public opinion current in England in 1588." For further indications of its probable date, see below, pp. 277 ff.

[7] See Baldwin, *Small Latine,* II, 502; *On The Literary Genetics of Shakspere's Poems & Sonnets,* p. 308.

carries over from the prose to *Bacon*. In *Alcida* (S.R. December 9, 1588), Greene wrote that Time "stealeth on by minutes, and fareth like the Sunne, whose shadow hasteth on, yet cannot be perceiued."[8] This is the conventional similitude, the form of which given under the rule for the colon in Lily's grammar is: *Quemadmodum horologij vmbram progressam sentimus, progredientem non cernimus: & fruticem aut herbam creuisse apparet, crescere autem nulli videtur: ita & ingeniorum profectus, quoniam minutis constat auctibus, ex interuallo sentitur.*[9]

Then in *Menaphon* (S.R. August 23, 1589; printed 1589), Greene couples both the shadow and the grass of the simile with love, not with Time as conventionally. "Loue creepeth on by degrees . . . the grasse hath his increase, yet neuer anie sees it augment, the Sonne shadowes, but the motion is not seene; loue like those should enter into the eye, and by long gradations passe into the heart."[10] This version Margaret condenses in *Bacon*, when she tells Lacy "Loue ought to creepe as doth the dials shade."[11] *Menaphon* gives Greene's full form of the simile and *Bacon* the summary, so that the speech in *Bacon* is later, but probably very little later.

Still another passage in *Bacon* is closely connected with still another in *Menaphon*. In the latter, Menaphon "resting himselfe on a hill that ouerpeered the great *Mediterraneum*, noting how *Phoebus* fetched his *Laualtos* on the purple Plaines of *Neptunus*, as if he had meant to haue courted *Thetis* in the royaltie of his roabes: the Dolphines (the sweete conceipters of Musicke) fetcht their carreers on the calmed waues, as if *Arion* had touched the stringes of his siluer sounding instrument: the Mermaides thrusting their heades from the bosome of *Amphitrite*, sate on the mounting bankes of *Neptune*, drying their waterie tresses in the Sunne beames."[12] Here is the set picture fully developed.

In *Bacon*, Edward tells Margaret

> Like *Thetis* shalt thou wanton on the waues,
> And draw the Dolphins to thy louely eyes,
> To daunce lauoltas in the purple streames;
> Sirens, with harpes and siluer psalteries,
> Shall waight with musicke at thy frigots stem,
> And entertaine faire *Margret* with their laies.[13]

---

[8] *Alcida* (1617), B3ᵛ; Grosart, *Greene*, IX, 19-20.

[9] *Brevissima Institutio* (1567, facs.), A4ᵛ.

[10] *Menaphon* (1589), D2ᵛ-D3ʳ; Grosart, *Greene*, VI, 63.

[11] Collins, *Bacon*, 700; Allan H. MacLaine, "Greene's borrowings from his own Prose Fiction in *Bacon and Bungay* and *James the Fourth*," *P.Q.*, XXX, 22, has noted independently that the speech in *Bacon* is a "restatement" of the figure in *Menaphon;* Collins, II, 334, had noted the parallel with *Menaphon*.

[12] *Menaphon* (1589), B2ʳ; Grosart, *Greene*, VI, 36-37; A. W. Ward noted the parallel use of *lavolta* (*Faustus* and *Bacon* (1901), p. 263), and Collins, II, 338, quoted most of the parallel passage, omitting the mermaids.

[13] Collins, *Bacon*, 980-985.

This is evidently the focused rearrangement. The dolphins continue their own function and absorb that of Phoebus both in dancing and courting. The sirens now also take over the function of Arion in making music and entertaining.

Ward[14] points out yet another significant connection between *Menaphon* and *Bacon*. In Menaphon's Eclogue

> Her browes are pretie tables of conceate,
> Where Loue his records of delight dooth quoate.[15]

Edward says of Margaret

> Her front is beauties table where she paints
> The glories of her gorgious excellence.[16]

In *Menaphon*, the lady's brows are pretty, "conceited" notebooks, in which love records or displays his records of delight. In *Bacon*, beauty paints on the lady's front or forehead as a board or canvas the glories of beauty's gorgeous excellence. The passages belong close together, though I see no certain indication of precedence.

A reference in *Bacon* to Roscius fits into this same period.

> We must lay plots of stately tragedies,
> Strange comick showes, such as proud *Rossius*
> Vaunted before the *Romane* Emperours.[17]

At the beginning of his career, Greene had referred in *Mamillia* (S.R. October 3, 1580) to the acting of Roscius: "*Astorides* seeing *Roscius* gestures, durst neuer after come on the stage."[18] Addressing the Gentlemen Readers in *Menaphon*, Greene says, "If Gentlemen you finde my stile either *magis humile* in some place, or more *sublime* in another, if you finde darke Aenigmaes or strange conceipts as if *Sphinx* on the one side, and *Roscius* on the other were playing the wagges; thinke the metaphors are well ment, and that I did it for your pleasures, whereunto I euer aymed my thoughts: and desire you to take a little paines to prie into my imagination."[19] Roscius is equated with the "strange conceipts" of Greene's "more *sublime*" style. So far, Roscius is the very symbol of the ideal. Then in his prefatory puff to this same *Menaphon* one Thomas Nashe made way for the serpent of pride to enter this Garden of Eden. Nashe admits "the deserued reputation of one *Roscius*," but warns against

---

[14] Ward, *Faustus and Bacon* (1901), p. 221 .

[15] *Menaphon* (1589), I2ᵛ; Grosart, *Greene*, VI, 123.

[16] Collins, *Bacon*, 58-59.

[17] Collins, *Bacon*, 809-811.

[18] *Mamillia* (1583), F4ʳ; Grosart, *Greene*, II, 79.

[19] *Menaphon* (1589), *2ᵛ; Grosart, *Greene*, VI, 7-8.

the insolence of his counterfeit subjects. When in *Francescos Fortunes* (printed 1590) Greene adapted Nashe's thrust, the actors are still insolent and their insolence has made even Roscius a "prowd Comedian."[20] So Roscius became for Greene a proud comedian in 1589 under the influence of Nashe, and the reference in *Bacon*, which taints the accomplishments of Roscius with pride, belongs not earlier than this date. Thus in these four passages *Bacon* uses passages and concepts from *Menaphon* and must have been composed alongside, as it were, that work, which was entered S.R. August 23, 1589.

Another set of significant relationships has been pointed out by Mac-Laine.[21] In *Orpharion*, Acestes as a warrior reasons himself out of love, which of itself is a mere convention of the time. "Is it *Alcestes* loue that troubles thee? why thou art a Souldiour, sworne to armes, not to Armour: to incounter foes in the feelde, not to courte Ladies in the Chamber . . . thou seekest to be priuate friend to *Venus:* away fond foole."[22] The form of this reasoning is exactly reproduced by Edward in *Bacon*.

> *Edward,* art thou that famous prince of *Wales,*
> Who at *Damasco* beat the *Sarasens,*
> And broughtst home triumphe on thy launces point,
> And shall thy plumes be puld by *Venus* downe?
>
> . . . .
>
> Leaue, *Ned,* and make a vertue of this fault.[23]

But the content is in parallel with a later speech from *Orpharion*. When Greene puts Marcion through the same dilemma at length, that character reminds himself that he is "one that hath conquered both a Crowne and kingdom,"[24] just as Edward reminds himself that he "at *Damasco* beat the *Sarasens,*" etc., which apparently is pure fiction,[25] and may be from fictional sources. In form, Edward's speech parallels that of Acestes, but it embodies also the deed of Marcion. That should mean that Edward's speech is the later compact statement, rather than that the dilated speeches in *Orpharion* are expansions.[26] At any rate, it is clear that Edward's speech in *Bacon* must be close in time of composition to the two in *Orpharion*, these being the only three uses found by MacLaine in Greene. *Orpharion* was entered S.R. February 9, 1590, but Greene promised in the Epistle of *Perimedes* (S.R. March 29, 1588; printed 1588) to have

---

[20] *Francescos Fortunes* (1590), B4ᵛ; Grosart, *Greene,* VIII, 132.

[21] MacLaine, *P.Q.,* XXX, 22-23.

[22] *Orpharion* (1599), C2ᵛ; Grosart, *Greene,* XII, 28.

[23] Collins, *Bacon,* 1035-38, 1041.

[24] *Orpharion* (1599), H2ʳ; Grosart, *Greene,* XII, 87.

[25] Ward, *Faustus* and *Bacon* (1901), p. 213; Collins, II, 338.

[26] For further history of this idea in Greene, see pp. 96 ff.

Orpharion out the next term, and in the preface of *Orpharion* "To the Gentlemen Readers" Greene says the printer "had it long since," and with him "it hath line this twelue months in the suds."[27] So Greene's work was done upon *Orpharion* mostly in 1588, with possible overlap into 1589. Edward's speech in *Bacon* was thus probably written about 1589.

A bit of Greene's geographical finery connects *Bacon* with *Orpharion* and *Neuer Too Late*. In *Orpharion*, the Volga gets moved into Persia. "They (Madame) that seeke to stop the swift running *Volgo*, a Riuer that leadeth into *Persia*, by staying the streame, maketh the flood flow more fiercely."[28] Thus the Volga has been inserted as the specific river in the widely used formula of the stopped stream,[29] the dammed oven, etc. It was doubtless used as an example because conventionally it was swift-flowing. The statement concerning the Volga is ambiguous here, since the Volga could "lead into Persia," as in a way it did, without itself being physically in Persia. But there is no such ambiguity in *Bacon*, which reverses the flow, as it were, promising for the royal entertainment

> *Persia,* downe her *volga* by Canows [shall],
> Send down the secrets of her spicerie.[30]

While the Volga does not itself physically lead into nor flow out of Persia, yet, as Sugden puts it, "The V. is not a Persian river; but much of her merchandise came into Russia by way of the V." To Greene, therefore, the Volga has become the trade route to and from Persia.

Greene uses this river once more, in *Neuer Too Late* (1590), as "the *Volgo* a bright streame, but without fish."[31] This is pure mythological fiction. Of the two dated references, one was written about the end of 1588 or the beginning of 1589, the other about 1590. The reference in *Bacon* is close to that of 1588-89, but there is as yet no certain indication of precedence within the three certain references to the Volga. If we could find the source of Greene's miscue, it would probably show the direction of deterioration.

Sugden thinks there is also a misprint reference to the Volga in *Orlando*. There Mandricard of Mexico, speaking to the Emperor of Africa says that

> Seated beyond the Sea of Trypoly,
>
> .   .   .   .
>
> From thence, mounted vpon a Spanish Barke,
>
> .   .   .   .

---

[27] *Orpharion* (1599), A3^r; Grosart, *Greene*, XII, 7.

[28] *Orpharion* (1599), C4^v; Grosart, *Greene*, XII, 34.

[29] Baldwin, *Small Latine*, II, 433 ff.

[30] Collins, *Bacon*, 1351-52.

[31] *Neuer Too Late* (1590), D4^r; Grosart, *Greene*, VIII, 44.

> Come from the South, I furrowed Neptunes Seas,
> Northeast as far as is the frosen Rhene;
> Leauing faire Voya, crost vp Danuby,
> As hie as Saba, whose inhaunsing streames
> Cuts twixt the Tartares and the Russians:
> There did I act as many braue attempts,
> As did Pirothous for his Proserpine.[32]

The general intent of the journey is clear. Mandricard comes from Mexico, thus naturally on a "Spanish Barke," and proceeds to Tartary and Russia for his exploits. But Sir Walter Greg speaks with the authentic moderation of a Scot when he says, "The geography is bewildering."[33] From his native Mexico, Mandricard sails in his "Spanish Barke," "Northeast as far as is the frosen Rhene," which is at least possible. He then

> crost vp Danuby,
> As hie as Saba, whose inhaunsing streames
> Cuts twixt the Tartares and the Russians.

Since Mandricard sailed, he must have sailed to the mouth of the Rhine.[34] Next, he "crost vp Danuby." This should mean at least that he crossed over to the Danube, whether he went up the Rhine and crossed to the Danube, or whether he crossed over to the Danube and went up that stream. His objective on the Danube should help here. On the Danube, Mandricard went "As hie as Saba," which Sugden identifies as "Saba (the Savus, now the Save). A river rising in the Carinthian Alps and flowing E. along the borders of Bosnia and Serbia into the Danube." Also under Danube, Sugden says, "The Saba is the Save, which falls into the D. on its N. [sic] bank at Belgrade."[35] Mandricard should thus have gone up the Rhine, crossed to the Danube and have gone as far down it as to the Save at Belgrade. He is taking the Englishman's route instead of going through the Mediterranean, etc., as one would have expected from his Spanish ship.

In conformity to this routing is the peculiar description of the Danube itself

> whose inhaunsing streames
> Cuts twixt the Tartares and the Russians.

The actual river of separation was Tanais or the Don, which Cooper describes as "A great riuer in the north part of the world whiche diuideth Europa from Asia." Cooper tells us also that Tartaria "Is a countrey of

---

[32] Collins, *Orlando*, 55, 63, 65-71.

[33] W. W. Greg, *Two Elizabethan Stage Abridgements,* p. 205.

[34] The epithet "frozen" for the Rhine was conventional. Textor gives *gelidus* from Ausonius and *glacialis* from Priscianus.

[35] Ortelius, *Thesaurus Geographicus* (1611) gives it as *"Saus σάος,* Plinio & Straboni; Ptolemaeus, *Sauus σάουος,* & *Sauius σαύυιος,* habet. Trogus *Sabus.* Pannoniae fluuius est, in Danubium se exonerans."

incōparable greatnesse. It boundeth on the weast vpon *Russia* . . . it marcheth on the south vpon Persia, and India. . . . The people be fierce and cruell, and therewith vyle and beastly in their lyuynge. . . . the capitayne of the Tartarians was named Tamberlane. . . . Muche of Tartaria was that countrey whiche was sometyme called Scythia." Mandricard ought to have been able to find trouble enough in that region. One remembers also Caesar's difficulties along the Rhine, etc. Mandricard had chosen "rough" territory for his "many braue attempts."

The Tartars and Russians joined, but their common boundary was not in fact the "inhaunsing streames" of Danuby, which as Cooper tells us "receiueth into hym. lx. other ryuers, wel nygh the halfe of thē being nauigable." Textor describes it as "Danubius fluvius Scythiae perquam maximus." Greene is evidently confusing some such account of the Scythians and the Danube as is to be found in Mela. "At ille qui Scythiae populos a sequētibus dirimit, apertis in Germania fontibus, alio quā desinit nomine exoritur."[36] Olivarius notes on "At ille" that "Danubius est, qui Scythiam siue Vualachiam, siue Tartaros minores à sequentibus populis dirimit. à Bulgaris & Bosinis." Tartars are Tartars, whether major or minor, and the Danube separates the Tartars from the Bulgars and the Bosnians. But why from the Russians?

The ultimate source of this error was likely the confusion of *Rascia* with *Ruscia*. Along the Danube Ortelius places "Bosna, Servia, Rascia, & Bvlgaria."[37] Here are the Bulgars and Bosnians of Mela separated by the Danube from the minor Tartars, and along with them are the Servians and the Rascians; above are the Ruscians. And what is more, the Rascians are at the mouth of Greene's Saba along the Rhine. Mandricard had gone as far as Rascia. It would be interesting to know how Greene became possessed with this bit of misinformation.

We have still to account for one more item. When Mandricard had arrived at the mouth of the Rhine, "Leauing faire Voya," he "crost vp Danuby." That is, as we have just seen, he went up the Rhine, and crossed to the Danube, going down that river to the Save, where it separated the minor Tartars from the Rascians. Sugden thought Voya was a misprint for Volga. But surely misplacing his Persian Volga that far was too much even for Greene. Another possibility is that Greene simply wrote "voyage," since in fact Mandricard now left his fair voyage to take to the inland route of the frozen Rhine and the Danube. But when Peele borrowed the passage for his *Old Wives Tale*, he read "Leauing faire Po." That is, from the Rhine, instead of going down the Po into Italy, Mandricard had gone down the Danube. So far as sense and meter are concerned, Greene may well have written "Leauing faire Po, I crost vp

---

[36] *Dionysii Alex. et Pomp. Melae Situs orbis descriptio,* Paris, 1577, *Mela,* p. 20.

[37] J. A. Maginus, *Geographiae Vniversae* (1597), p. 270; see map opposite.

Danuby," though "Voya" does not appear to be an evident misreading for
"Po I." It might be well to remember, however, that "sometimes *Greenes*
hand was none ot the best."[38] But whether Greene's hand was good or
bad, the fact is that Peele read the name as Po, and the nonsense he makes
of the passage as a whole in adapting it does not indicate that he was
"correcting" an error. For in other respects Peele has made the geography
of this passage more completely absurd by making it more completely
definite.

> For thy sweet sake I haue crost the frosen *Rhine*,
> Leauing faire *Po,* I saild vp *Danuby,*
> As farre as *Saba* whose inhansing streames,
> Cuts twixt the *Tartars* and the *Russians*.[39]

It is evident that Greene's is the original passage and that Peele[40] admired
and lifted it.

Returning now to Greene, in 1589 he was also turning the love-friendship
theme in the direction it comes to take in *Bacon*. In *Ciceronis Amor.
Tullies Loue,*[41] printed 1589, Lentulus, the foremost Roman warrior, falls
in love with Terentia. His friend is the young orator-nobody, Cicero, who
also loves Terentia, who returns his love. Through floods of oratory, the
story finally trickles to the conclusion that Lentulus abdicates in favor of
Cicero. The rival friends are usually equals — by a cardinal rule of
friendship — but here it is the powerful noble and pauper friend, which in
Bacon becomes King and rival subject.

These several connections with *Menaphon, Orpharion,* and *Tullies Loue*
indicate certainly a date of composition for *Bacon* about 1589. Another
piece of evidence of a different nature also harmonizes with this dating.
In his address to the Gentlemen Students in *Greene's Farewell to Folly,*
at some time in the first half of 1591, Greene is critical of one who has
written *Fair Em* on the model of *Bacon*. Since Greene had not given any
hint in his criticisms prefixed to his next previous dated pamphlet, the
Mourning Garment (S.R. November 2, 1590), it is reasonably clear that
he had not at that time become aware of any infringement upon his
preserves. In fact, as Francesco in *Francescos Fortunes* (1590), Greene
was quite complacent over the success of a first comedy, which was
causing all companies to want plays from his pen. But when by 1591
other dramatists were attempting to supply the demand he had created,

---

[38] Chettle, *Dreame* [1592], Preface.

[39] *Old Wives Tale* (1595, *M.S.R.*), lines 1072-75.

[40] Also, "the expression 'Three blue beanes in a blue bladder, rattle bladder rattle'
(lines 819-820), which however was no doubt proverbial, recurs in the Dulwich manuscript of *Orlando* (lines 136-137, fol. 263)" (Greg, *Old Wives Tale* (*M.S.R.*), p. vi).

[41] The parallel had been noted earlier, but it is emphasized by MacLaine, *P.Q.,*
XXX, 25: "Lacy's part in II, 3, is almost certainly an adaptation of Cicero's situation
in *Ciceronis Amor*."

Greene rose to the defence of his patent rights. Greene intimates that the encroaching author had used a "whole year" in his imitation of *Bacon*. If so, *Fair Em* most likely dates at some time in 1590, and *Bacon* at some time in 1589.[42]

Also, I believe it is self evident and accepted that Mundy's *John a Kent and John a Cumber* owes its inception and much else to *Bacon*.[43] Since the surviving manuscript of *Kent* bears date 1590, it follows that *Bacon* can hardly be later than 1589.

In harmony with this dating is a detail pointed out by Fleay. It is, of course, well known that Greene changed his mottos at certain crucial times, so that Jordan, for instance, uses these variants as headings for his chapters. Now Fleay[44] pointed out correctly that *Bacon* has as its *finis* the full motto *Omne tulit punctum qui miscuit utile dulci,* which Greene used for the last time in some of his productions of 1589, only the abbreviated first half appearing in *Menaphon* (S.R. August 23, 1589).

There is a controllable and consistent evolution in Greene's mottos, which were selected to fit his evolving attitudes. Greene made his first dated gesture toward "repentance" in *The Spanish Masquerado* (S.R. February 1, 1589), upon which Lodge complimented him. In *Menaphon* six months later his friends thought that Greene was taking a step upward. Possibly as an outward reflection Green himself abbreviates for the first time his motto to *Omne tulit punctum,* though he advertizes in the title "A worke worthie the youngest eares *for pleasure, or the grauest censures for principles,"* and also assures the "Ladie Hales" that the book contains "as well humors to delight, as discourses to aduise." He is still pleasing and profiting, but emphasizing the profit. Henry Upchear, Gentleman, turns enthusiastically from Lyly to Greene, and is certain that *Menaphon*

> strained now a note aboue his vse,
> Foretels, he'le nere more chaunt of *Choas* sporte.[45]

Thomas Brabine, Gent., also thought that Greene's pastoral, especially in contrast with the matter of the dramatists, was quite superior morally. And even Thomas Nashe commends Greene to the Gentlemen of the Universities as "your scholler-like Shepheard." Greene was getting plenty of encouragement toward the upward path. In a work already written and then published soon after *Menaphon,* Nashe attacked severely the same writings and writers that he attacked in his preface to Greene's *Menaphon,* only there he accused them of using as their motto *Omne tulit punctum qui miscuit utile dulci,* as some had done for decidedly less

---

[42] Gayley, *Comedies,* [I], 411-412.

[43] See below, p. 270.

[44] F. G. Fleay, *A Biographical Chronicle of the English Drama,* I, 264.

[45] Choa is an evident misprint for Clora or Cloris; see below, pp. 83-84.

edifying work than Greene's. However, Nashe still declared himself to be "a professed *Peripatician,* mixing profit with pleasure, and precepts of doctrine with delightfull inuention."[46] Nashe had no objection to the motto and the ideal; he did object to the kind of material some were publishing under the motto — such as the translated romances of Mundy. Doubtless this associational background had its effect in determining Greene to change his motto at this time.

At any rate, the full motto is used after *Menaphon* only in *Orpharion* for dated work, which was entered S.R. Feb. 9, 1590, but had been written in 1588 or early 1589,[47] thus antedating *Menaphon.* The abbreviated motto appeared in *Menaphon* August, 1589, in *Neuer Too Late* about the middle of 1590, and in *James IV;* then not again. *Francescos Fortunes* and the *Mourning Garment* (S.R. November 2, 1590) bear the *Sero sed Serio* of the latter half of 1590, before *Nascimur Pro Patria* of 1591. Thus, if attached by Greene, the abbreviated motto is likely to mean that *James IV* was completed not later than 1590, hardly later than the summer. Similarly, the full form attached to *Bacon* would likely indicate a date before August, 1589. No one else besides Greene is known to have attached one of these mottos to Greene's work. Who else would have a motive for so doing anyway? And if attached by others, how do these mottos happen to fit in so pat with the other evidences of date? It scarcely needs pointing out, of course, that it makes no difference to our chain of evidence whether Greene was actually repentant. Here are the evolving and definitely controlled outer manifestations, whatever was the inner fact.

All our evidence points to a date for *Bacon* of 1589. Thus another fact becomes significant. As Fleay pointed out,[48] the play itself refers to St. James' Day, July 25, as falling on Friday,[49] which was the case in 1589. This reference would indicate a date of composition about the summer of 1589, which is in harmony with all our other evidence.

---

[46] McKerrow, *Nashe,* I, 27.

[47] See above, pp. 60-61.

[48] Fleay, *Biog. Chron.,* I, 264-265.

[49] Ward notes of Harleston that, "A fair is held there on July 5th; but St. James's day is the 25th of that month" (Ward, *Faustus* and *Bacon* (1901), p. 225). I do not know Ward's authority, but apparently the date has been transposed to new style. For in *A beautiful Bay-bush,* 1589, the fair is listed as occurring on June 24. Also, in 1570 there was a conspiracy for a rebellion "on Midsummer daie at Harlestone faire" (Holinshed (1587), III, 1221, col. 2, bottom). John Throckmorton of Norwich, Greene's home town, is said to have confessed that he had been the leader in this rebellion, which centered in Norfolk. Greene was old enough in 1570 to acquire vivid knowledge of these happenings. He would certainly know that Harleston was to have had a fair in 1570, whether or not he remembered it was to have been June 24. At any rate, the date now given is not the actual date of Harleston fair. Even if Greene did know the correct date, a London audience would not; but all should know their current calendar.

It would thus appear to be as certain as is possible with circumstantial evidence that *Bacon* was written about the summer of 1589. Because of the eulogy of Elizabeth at the end of the play, Gayley suggests that it must have been played at court, and "leans to" St. Stephen's day, December 26, when the Queen's appeared, as the probable date of performance there.[50]

When we turn to *Orlando,* it is apparent that the play is earlier than *Bacon* and *Looking Glasse. Bacon* shares a passage with *Orlando* in significant fashion. Collins has pointed out[51] three parallel passages in Greene which all derive from Genesis; but Collins does not notice the fact, though on Gihon in *Bacon* Ward had referred to Genesis.[52] Since Greene's details are nearer the Bishops' than Geneva, I quote the Bishops' (1568 folio).

10 And out of Eden there went foorth a flood to water the garden, and from thence it was deuided, and became into foure heades.

11 The name of yᵉ first is Pison, the same is it that compasseth the whole lande of Hauilah, where there is golde:

12 And the golde of the lande is very good. There is also Bdellium, and the Onix stone.

13 The name of the seconde riuer is Gyhon: the same is it that compasseth the whole lande of Ethiopia.

14 The name of yᵉ thirde ryuer is Hidekel, & it goeth toward the east side of Assiria: & the fourth ryuer is Euphrates.[53]

To understand the happenings in Greene, we need also to look at some such map as is presented in the Bishops' Bible (and others) for this chapter. Here Euphrates and Tigris are represented as having separate heads, then joining in such a way as to surround an unlabeled island, with the city of "Selevcia" on the Tigris arm and that of "Babilon" perforated by Euphrates, the island itself being between "The Land of Hevilah" on one side and "Babilone" on the other, after which the conjoined stream separates again into "The Fall of Evphrates" and "The Fall of Tigris," as these flow separately into "The Golphe of The Persian Sea." A note explains, "Moreouer, whereas Moyses sayde that a flood dyd proceede from that place: I do interpret it, from the course of the waters, as yf he shoulde haue sayde that Adam dyd inhabite in the flooddes syde, or in the lande which was watered of both sydes. Howbeit, there is no great matter in that, eyther that Adam hath inhabited vnder the place where both flooddes come together towarde Babylon and Seleucia, or aboue: It is sufficient yᵗ he hath ben in a place watered of waters. But the thing is not

---

[50] Gayley, *Comedies,* [I], 413.
[51] Collins, I, 305.
[52] Ward, *Faustus* and *Bacon* (1901), p. 301.
[53] Genesis 2, 10-14: slightly adapted in the translation of 1611.

darke nor hard to vnderstande howe this floodde hath ben deuided in foure heades. For they be two flooddes which be gathered in one, then they seperate them selues in diuers partes. So in theyr ioynyng and flowyng together, it is but a floodde, wherof there is two heades into two chanels from aboue, and two towarde the sea, when it begynneth to seperate it selfe abrode. But to declare vnto you the diuersities of the ryuers names, besydes their vsuall and principall appellations, and howe they be called as they passe through eche prouince, with the interpretations of the same, I thynke it rather tedious and combresome, then profitable."[54]

In *Orlando,* Greene bases a figure on these rivers. As Orlando is about to be charmed from madness, he says

> Else would I set my mouth to Tygres streames
> And drinke vp ouerflowing Euphrates.[55]

Here Greene has Tigris and Euphrates as in the Biblical map. There is, however, no Tigris in the text of either the Bishops' or the Geneva, but a side note in each identifies it as Hidekel, the third river. But Greene follows a different identification. Cooper has, *"Tigris,* One of the fowre ryuers whiche come out of Paradise called *Gion:* it passeth through Armenie and Media."[56] So Greene bases a sequence of three figures on Gihon and Euphrates.

Cuba in *Orlando* is

> like that wealthy Paradice
> From whence floweth Gyhon and swift Euphrates.[57]

"Paradice"[58] is the Garden of Eden, and inherits the gold, bdellium, and onix of Hauilah to become "wealthy." Thus the Biblical passage is smeared together for a "wealthy" simile. Then in *Bacon* the island resulting from Cuba gets into the figure itself, the "wealthy Paradice" becoming "wealthy Ile," and is now encircled by the two rivers, as is the unnamed island in the map, and as the islands of Cuba and England were not.

> faire *England* like that wealthy Ile,
> Circled with *Gihen,* and swift *Euphrates.*[59]

---

[54] For a digest of contemporary opinion as to these four rivers, see A. Willet, *Hexapla in Genesin* (1605), pp. 29-31.

[55] Collins, *Orlando,* 1143-44. "Whereas Moses here saith, *hu Perath,* this is Perath, both these ioyned together, make Huphrates, or Euphrates: so called, because by the inundation thereof, as Nilus, it maketh the land fruitfull, of the roote *pharah,* which signifieth to fructifie" (Willet, *Hexapla* (1605), p. 31).

[56] Cooper, *Thesaurus,* 1565.

[57] Collins, *Orlando,* 39-40. Cuba was connected with both Atlantis and the Fortunate Isles; see Ortelius, *Thesaurus Geographicus.*

[58] The Bishops' margin for "garden" reads "Or, *Paradise of pleasure."* Paradise is also used in the heading of the chapter, as it is in the heading of the Great Bible, but not, so far as I have found, in the Geneva, which, of course, is characteristic.

[59] Collins, *Bacon,* 2091-92. The epithet "swift" for Euphrates was conventional, appearing in Textor's *Epitheta* as *celer* from Claudianus.

The passage from *Bacon* is in the court compliment at the end, and if that performance occurred December 26, 1589, would have been written about December, 1589. The passage from *Orlando* would be earlier.

But Greene has not yet finished his worrying of this figure. In *Greenes Mourning Garment* (S.R. November 2, 1590), Greene wrote, "In the Citie of *Callipolis* seated in the lande of *Auilath,* compassed with *Gihon* and *Euphrates* two riuers that flowe frō Eden."[60] The setting is avowedly Biblical, and is based directly upon the passage in Genesis, but with Callipolis[61] inserted. Gihon and Euphrates still flow from Eden (or the garden of Eden) as in *Orlando,* and they encircle a place, as in *Bacon.* But Auilath now takes the place of "that wealthy Paradice" of *Orlando,* which became "that wealthy Ile" in *Bacon.* The wealth belonged, of course, to Auilath in the first place, but the surrounding rivers did not; its compassing river was Pison. Greene has simply substituted Auilath in the rivers figure he had developed in *Orlando* and *Bacon.* So, in fact, Auilath has taken the place of the island in the map, though obviously the figure and not the map is responsible for this rearrangement of contemporary Biblical geography.

Cuba's association with Atlantis and the Fortunate Isles induced the figure of "wealthy Paradice," which brought along its associated rivers. Inevitably, this figure had to be used as a compliment (in the court compliment) to that other fortunate isle, England. Then when a Biblical setting was needed for an *opus,* the figure as it had been developed was applied to the original source — all without any attempt to harmonize the factual details of the Biblical story, as then interpreted. The result is worthy of the genius that "invented" sea coasts for Bohemia and got Shakspere blamed for it. Such things are not the result of mere ignorance but of wilful improvement. An impression is to be conveyed, not facts.

Thus the passage in *Mourning Garment* is the latest of the three uses of the figure. Since the pamphlet was entered S.R. November 2, 1590, the passage in *Bacon* is earlier, and that in *Orlando* still earlier than that in *Bacon,* so probably not later than 1588 or early 1589.

Orlando is also tied with *Bacon* by a close and curious parallel in phraseology.

Hath Demogorgon, ruler of the fates?[62]

And *Demogorgon* maister of the fates.[63]

---

[60] *Mourning Garment* (1590), A4[r]; Grosart, *Greene,* IX, 127.

[61] Etymologically, Callipolis means the city beautiful, a famous instance of which is in Plato's *Republic* (Jonson (C. H. Herford and P. Simpson), X, 679.) The name was borne by various actual cities (See Ortelius).

[62] Collins, *Orlando,* 1272.

[63] Collins, *Bacon,* 1636. Ward, *Faustus* and *Bacon* (1901), 155 points out the parallel; Collins, II, 344, adds a few notes on the history of Demogorgon. Abraham Fraunce in *The Third part of the Countesse of Pembrokes Yuychurch* (1592), B2[r]

A few lines earlier in *Orlando* Greene had written

> Tuque Demogorgon, qui noctis fata gubernas,
> Qui regis infernum [64]

Demogorgon was *gubernator* and *rex*, "ruler of the fates" as elsewhere in *Orlando,* which has been varied to "maister of the fates" in *Bacon.* In the nature of the case, the line in *Bacon* was evidently written only a short time after that in *Orlando.*

Incidentally, Greene's allusion to Demogorgon goes back ultimately to Lucan, who had himself alluded to a power, identified by the commentators as Demogorgon, who

> Verberibusǫ; suis trepidā castigat Erinnym. [65]

The commentators on this passage embellished Lactantius Placidus on a similar passage in Statius, *Thebaid,* IV, 514 ff., who says that the philosophers, magi, etc. confirm that besides the known gods there was "alium principem, & maxime deum ceterorum numinum ordinatorem."[66] Demogorgon castigated the fates, because he was their *princeps* and supreme *ordinator* or ruler. But in an explanation of the passage in Lucan, Hortensius quotes Lactantius as having said "alium principem, & maximum dominum,"[67] so that we have in this version *dominus* or master. Hortensius, however, paraphrases the passage in Lucan as "Hunc Demogorgonem ut imperatorem. uindicē. & omnium rerum gubernatorem promittit se in eum immisurū. ni morē gerat." Here Demogorgon is quite decidedly a ruler.

Perhaps, while we have Lucan before us, we should insinuate as gently as possible that classicists had better let the end of Greene's line 1165 alone, "solemque, solumque, coelumque"; Demogorgon did rule hell, sun, earth, and sky as Greene means to say, whether he has said it in elegant and correct Latin verse or not. For the annotators point out that "Fingunt eum in Tartari abysso iacere . . . de cuius semine firmamentum, Solem, Lunam & Stellas[68] factas credebant."[69] Greene's ultimate model is Medea's

---

ff., gives a detailed account of Demogorgon or Demiurgon, basing upon Leo Hebraeus, who alleges an ancient poet Pronapides. See N. Comes, *Mythologiae* (1581), p. 452. We may add Cooper's description: *"Demogorgus,* An inchanter, whiche was supposed to be of suche exccllencie, that he had authoritie ouer all spirites that made men afearde." See Harris Fletcher, "Milton's Demogorgon," *J.E.G.P,* LVII, pp. 684-689.

[64] Collins, *Orlando,* 1164-65.

[65] Lucan, *Pharsalia,* Basle, 1578, p. 751 (VI, 747).

[66] Statius, *Opera,* Paris, 1600, pp. 143-144.

[67] Lucan, *Pharsalia,* Basle, 1578, p. 751.

[68] Greene's *filias* . . . *micantes,* line 1166, are the stars; exactly why the stars I do not know, unless as determiners of human fate.

[69] Lucan, *Pharsalia,* Basle, 1578, p. 751.

incantation in Ovid, where she also claims power over these last three. Incidentally, Greene's "noctis fata" is Ovid's "dique omnes noctis."[70]

While we are on the subject of Demogorgon, probably we should point out here also the parallel use in the invocation of Faustus, which as a whole looks to be the Christian job of a professional, not a bit of imitative pagan ornamentation as in Greene, so that one wonders where Marlowe found his model instructions. He too begins by invoking the gods of Acheron to be propitious, bids goodbye to the triple power of Jehovah, but hails the triple spirits of fire, air, and water (pointing out the balance by *valeo* and *salvo*).[71] Returning to the gods of Acheron, who were to be *propitii*, he now prays a certain one or ones (*propitiamus vos*) that Mephostophilis may appear and rise. The god specifically named is Beelzebub, as in the source, where no other is called upon; "then began Doctor *Faustus* to call for *Mephostophiles* the Spirite, and to charge him in the name of *Beelzebub* to appeare there personally without any long stay . . . [after delay, Faustus] began againe to coniure the spirite *Mephostophiles* in the name of the Prince of Diuels to appeare in his likenesse: where at sodainly ouer his head hanged houering in the ayre a mighty Dragon."[72] So in the play Faustus invokes this god as "Orientis Princeps, Belzebub, inferni ardentis monarcha." Here as in the immediate source passage the prince has become one instead of five kings of hell. For according to the

---

[70] Shakspere's fairies or elves are thus quite correctly

> You Moone-shine reuellers, and shades of night.
> You Orphan heires of fixed destiny.
>
> (*Merry Wives*, V, 5, 42-43.)

The first line is built on Ovid's *dique omnes noctis* (*Metamorphoses*, VII, 198), which Golding renders "Elves . . . of the Night" (W. H. D. Rouse, *Shakespeare's Ovid*, p. 142), and Shakspere "shades of night," also varying it as "Moone-shine reuellers." This same passage in Ovid Shakspere was later to use for one of his most famous speeches (*Tempest*, V, 1, 33-50). In the *Tempest*, these *di . . . noctis* are also elves, "Demy-Puppets, that / By Moone-shine" do various things. Shakspere has thus in the *Tempest* exactly rephrased the two lines from *Merry Wives*. The phrase "By Moone-shine" sums up the first line, the epithet demi-puppets sums up the second line. The idea that these elves or fairies were "Orphan heires of fixed destiny" or "Demy-Puppets" is not in Ovid's passage, and I have not found it in any note to the passage. But from some source Shakspere did know this bit of mythology.

[71] As Mephostophilis says

> the shortest cut for conjuring
> Is stoutly to abjure the Trinity
> And pray devoutly to the prince of hell.
>
> *Faustus* (Greg's reconstruction), I, 3, 52-54 (287-289)

It will be remembered that Archimago followed the same procedure.

> He bad awake blacke *Plutoes* griesly Dame,
> And cursed heuen, and spake reprochful shame
> Of highest God, the Lord of life and light
>
> (Spenser, *Faerie Queene*, I.i.37.4-6)

[72] H. Logeman, *The English Faust-Book of 1592*, pp. 4-5.

Faust Book the ten kingdoms of hell "are gouerned by fiue kings, that is, *Lucifer* in the *Orient, Beelzebub* in *Septentrio, Belial* in *Meridie, Astaroth* in *Occidente,* and *Phlegeton* in the middest of them all; whose rule and dominions haue none end vntill the day of Dome."[73] All these kings except Phlegeton (properly a burning river in the Lower World) are Biblical, and Beelzebub was "A heathen deity to whom the Jews ascribed supremacy among evil spirits."[74] In the New Testament he is regularly "the prince of the devils," and is so referred to in the parent passage from the Faust Book. Faustus addresses him, therefore, as Prince of the Orient and monarch of burning hell. But the classical Phlegethon is in the midst of the Biblical four; similarly the classical Demogorgon (demigorgon here by someone's error) is invoked as another name of Beelzebub.

In *Faustus* B, Dick, the clown, twice again uses demogorgon. In II, 3, he has stolen one of "Doctor *Faustus* coniuring bookes" and is trying to spell it out. *"A perse a, t. h. e the: o per se o deny orgon, gorgon."* His first attempt is upon *a* or a word containing *a.* Then he spells out *the,* before he comes to demogorgon. The first part of that name he thinks he recognizes, but the second part floors him. So he repeats conventionally *"o per se o,"* which enables him to get *orgon,* which in turn gives him *gorgon.* He should have read *demo,* if he had been actually reading, especially after he had so carefully sounded his *o.* But instead he is murdering his hearing of *demi* into *deny.* Later, however, in his actual attempt at hocus pocus he gets the name in correct form, though the *o* still troubles him; *"O per se o, demogorgon."*[75]

The three uses of the name are thus clearly in progression from *demigorgon,* to *denygorgon,* to *demogorgon.* In the first instance, someone has thrust the pagan Demogorgon into the Christian hell of Beelzebub. In the two instances of clownish parody it seems agreed that Marlowe did not write the scenes; Sir Walter Greg concurs in accusing Rowley. In the basic use the insert consists only of the name *demigorgon,* and that misspelled, followed by some corruption in the text. And this misspelling the clown finds also in his stolen book. Demogorgon does not belong to the Faust tradition and most likely was a complete later insert in Marlowe's play. There is no indication, however, from what source the inserter had the name. Demogorgon was evidently common knowledge at that period, in spite of our uncommon ignorance of him now.[76]

---

[73] Logeman, p. 20.

[74] Robert Young, *Analytical Concordance to the Bible.*

[75] *Faustus* B, 1156-57.

[76] Of course, *Selimus* and *Locrine* could not do without his horrific majesty.

> Black *Demogorgon,* grandfather of night,
> Send out thy furies from thy firie hall,
> The pitilesse *Erymnies* arm'd with whippes,

Continuing now with *Orlando,* a speech connects with one in *Farewell to Folly.* In his sweet thoughts of Angelica and a crown, Sacrepant says

> Sweet are the thoughts that smother from conceit:
> For when I come and set me downe to rest,
> My chaire presents a throne of Maiestie;
> And when I set my bonnet on my head,
> Me thinkes I fit my forhead for a Crowne;
> And when I take my trunchion in my fist,
> A Scepter then comes tumbling in my thoughts;
> My dreames are princely, all of Diademes.
> Honor, — me thinkes the title is too base:
> Mightie, glorious, and excellent, —
> I, these, my glorious Genius, sound within my mouth;
> These please the eare, and with a sweet applause,
> Makes me in tearmes coequall with the Gods.
> Then these, Sacrepant, and none but these;
> And these, or else make hazard of thy life.[77]

The figure is evolved in detail by application of the regal idea to Sacrepant's natural situation. There is nothing wrenched about it.

Greene uses the fundamental idea with equal naturalness in *Farewell to Folly,* where King Vadislaus had been "pulled out of his roabes and put into rags, in stead of a crowne . . . a scrip, for a scepter a palmers staffe," in which condition Vadislaus addresses himself thus, "bee still a Prince in thought . . . imagine thy palmers bonnet a princes diadem, thinke thy staffe a scepter, thy graie weeds costly attire, imaginations are as sweete as actions: and seeing thou canst not bee a king ouer nobilitie, bee yet a king ouer beggers: holde pouertie as a slaue, by thinking thy want store . . . [The] imagination [of Dionysius] soothed him in a princely content."[78]

In both passages, the villain is dreaming of the earthly fruition of a crown, Vadislaus of the one he has lost, Sacrepant of the one he hopes to gain. In both, a bonnet is fancied as a crown, a staff as a scepter. The

---

> And all the damned monsters of black hell,
> To powre their plagues on cursed *Acomat.*
> > (*Selimus, M.S.R.,* lines 1317-21)
>
> Alasse too soone by *Demagorgons* knife,
> The martiall *Brutus* is bereft of life.
> No sad complaints may moue iust *Lacus.*
> > (*Locrine, M.S.R.,* lines 276-278)

[77] Collins, *Orlando,* 246-260.

[78] *Farewell* (1591), E3ʳ-E4ʳ; Grosart, *Greene,* IX, 273-276. The three repeated oppositions of deposed king Vadislaus form the nucleus of a similar pathetical performance by about-to-be-deposed king Richard II, as I expect to demonstrate in treating of that play (*Richard II,* III, 3, 149-151; the theme of the solitary life being suggested by Halle, as Wilson notes), one of the items requiring only an "epithet" to be bodged into a blank verse, "My sceptre for a palmer's walking-staff."

fundamental conceit is the same, but to the two ideas in common Vadislaus adds costly attire and Sacrepant a throne. Vadislaus follows the order of bonnet, staff, weeds; Sacrepant chair, bonnet, truncheon. I see no certain indication of order between these passages, though Sacrepant's speech is more orderly in its development, probably indicating that Greene had already tried the idea at least once, on Vadislaus. *Farewell to Folly* was entered S.R. June 11, 1587, but our first print is 1591. If this speech of Vadislaus was in the original, as in the very nature of the case it must have been, then the speech of Vadislaus is pretty certainly the original and that of Sacrepant the further use.

But there is still another use of this bonnet and staff business. In *King Leir*, 1605,[79] the Gallian King, disguised as a Palmer, has fallen in love with Cordella at first sight — or maybe a wink or so after! As Palmer, he proposes for the Gallian King, and in the age-old convention Cordella advises him to speak for himself.

> Ile hold thy Palmers staffe within my hand,
> And thinke it is the Scepter of a Queene.
> Sometime ile set thy Bonnet on my head,
> And thinke I weare a rich imperiall Crowne.
> Sometime ile helpe thee in thy holy prayers,
> And thinke I am with thee in Paradise.
> Thus ile mock fortune, as she mocketh me,
> And neuer will my louely choyce repent:
> For hauing thee, I shall haue all content.

Here we have staff, bonnet, and assistance equated with scepter, crown, and Paradise, the third item being again a variant, as in the two instances in Greene. In *Farewell* and *Leir*, a Palmer's staff is the scepter and a Palmer's bonnet the crown, and like Vadislaus, Cordella will mock fortune and have "content." Cordella takes exactly the position of Maesia, another King's daughter in disguise, as she decides still to remain in the country instead of returning to court to be a daughter of the crown, and sings in the presence of the deposed Vadislaus, "Sweet are the thoughts that sauour of con[t]ent." The close connection of the two passages is unquestionable.

Equally unquestionable is the connection of Cordella's speech with that of Sacrepant in *Orlando*. The connections in phraseology, such as "set thy Bonnet" and "set my bonnet," "hold thy Palmers staffe within my hand" and "take my trunchion in my fist," are unmistakable. Cordella goes on through a choice to a conclusion, as does Sacrepant; that is, both speeches have the same technical form, as against content. As speeches, both are more fully and technically developed than the speech of Vadislaus.

---

[79] *M.S.R.*, lines 698-706; pointed out by Greg, *Abridgements*, p. 208, as a parallel to *Orlando*.

It should be noticed also that the speeches of Vadislaus and Sacrepant are "proper" to the character each time, while the speech of Cordella is "improper" to her and only applied in terms of the "proper" character. All these rhetorical relationships would appear to make it clear that Cordella's speech is the derivative, using for sources both the speech of Vadislaus and that of Sacrepant.

But how and when did the author of *Leir* come to combine these two passages? *Farewell* was entered S.R. June 11, 1587, but our first print is 1591. *Orlando* was on the stage about the latter date. If the author of the *Leir* passage was other than Greene, it is likely to have been written about 1591 or 1592. If the author were Greene himself, however, then the passage would follow soon after *Orlando*. It would be another interesting illustration of how Greene turned his materials into different forms. It is at any rate clear that *Farewell* and *Orlando* are connected by this common use of material.

Orlando shares significantly with *Perimedes* an allusion to the "Gordion" knot of love and marriage.[80] The figure is stated simply in *Perimedes,* S.R. March 29, 1588, printed 1588.

> To such as *Hymen* in his Saffron robe,
> Hath knit a *Gordion* knot of passions.[81]

This is twice-used — *bis cocta* — in *Orlando*. Angelica tells Sacrepant

> Braue Countie, know, where sacred Loue vnites,
> The Knot of Gordion at the Shrine of Ioue
> Was neuer halfe so hard or intricate
> As be the bands which louely Venus ties.[82]

Here the Gordion knot of marriage is not as strong as the knot of love tied by Venus.[83] Angelica goes on to say, with the Gordion knot now appropriated to love, that the knot of her love for Orlando can only be severed by cutting off her life. The figure is developed in terms of the original allusion, but now appropriated to love.[84] When later in the companion passage Orlando sees the name of Angelica "mixt with Medor," he says

> Angelica: — Ah, sweete and heauenly name,
> Life to my life, and essence of my ioy!
> But, soft! this Gordion knot together co-vnites
> A Medor partner in her peerlesse loue.[85]

---

[80] The parallel uses have been noted by Greg, *Abridgements,* p. 216.

[81] *Perimedes* (1588), G2ᵛ; Grosart, *Greene,* VII, 80.

[82] Collins, *Orlando,* 457-460.

[83] The knot of Venus had "properly" preceded in *Perimedes*.
> To such as sit at *Paphos* for releefe,
> And offer *Venus* manie solemne vowes.
>   (*Perimedes* (1588), G2ᵛ; Grosart, *Greene,* VII, 80)

[84] See Erasmus, *Adagia* on the proverb *Gordianus nodus*.

[85] Collins, *Orlando,* 578-581.

In this case, the "Gordion knot" is the true-love knot within which the names are entwined.

> these trees carued with true loue knots,
> The inscription Medor and Angelica.[86]

In *Perimedes* love is tied in a "Gordion knot" by Hymen. In the first passage in *Orlando*, the figure is applied in terms of the original story eventually to true love, but initially and specifically to marriage, Hymen. In the second passage in *Orlando*, the Gordion knot of true love is assumed and transferred to its symbol, the carved true-love knot. Thus the passages in *Orlando* are embroidered upon the simple material of *Perimedes*. Greene could have had the simple figure in mind only, have embroidered it in *Orlando*, and then have stated it simply in *Perimedes*, but for a man of Greene's known habits of composition that is not likely.[87]

It is also significant that Greene's pamphlets of 1588 reflect the Orlando story, and are apparently the only ones to do so. Greene's fullest use is in *Perimedes*, S.R. March 29, 1588, and *Orpharion* (Lydia story), written 1588; but two references to Angelica and Medor in *Alcida Greenes Metamorphosis*, S.R., December 9, 1588, are for our purpose quite significant. "*Angelica* forsooke diuers Kings and tooke *Medon* a mercenary Souldier."[88] Again, "yet *Omphita* the queene of the Indians loued a Barber: *Angelica Medes*, a mercinary souldier."[89] In *Alcida*, Greene had not yet transferred Angelica to Orlando.

In the light of Greene's known habits of using sources, this concentration upon 1588 is itself conclusive evidence of date. For instance, the previous year, 1587, the great source had been Primaudaye. As Hart has shown,[90] Greene used Primaudaye in the English translation of 1586 (S.R. July 6) heavily for *Farewell* (S.R. June 11, 1587, printed 1591), *Penelopes Web* (S.R. June 26, 1587, printed 1587), and *Tritameron*, as printed in 1587. *Perimedes* (S.R. March 29, 1588) has a few leftovers. After that, there is only a chance bit here and there for the next two or three years. Just as Greene used Primaudaye systematically in 1587, so he used Ariosto's *Orlando Furioso* systematically in 1588. The inception of Greene's *Orlando* was certainly at this period, at whatever time he may have concluded it.

---

[86] Collins, *Orlando*, 623-624.

[87] H. Dugdale Sykes, *The Authorship of "The Taming of A Shrew,"* etc., 1920, Shakespeare Association Papers No. 4, pp. 27-28, has pointed out connected uses of Gordion knot as marriage in *Taming of A Shrew* and *Wily Beguiled*, but does not connect them with the uses in Greene. If Greene was the first to develop this idea, then those two plays would be later than *Orlando*, and conversely *Orlando* earlier than they (see pp. 105 ff).

[88] *Alcida* (1617), C4[r]; Grosart, *Greene*, IX, 33.

[89] *Alcida* (1617), I2[r]; Grosart, *Greene*, IX, 96.

[90] H. C. Hart, *N.&Q.*, 10th S. V., 203-204, 343-344, 424-425, 442-445, 463-464. See also MacLaine, *P.Q.*, XXX, 22 ff. and his references — and their references.

These publications of 1588 also establish certain important details. In *Perimedes*, 1588, Sacrapant, so spelled, plays his part,[91] so that Greene did not borrow that form of the name from Harington in 1591.[92] Also, the form Ardenia appears in a passage in *Alcida*,[93] which is based on Ariosto.[94] This is the form which appears in the quarto of *Orlando*, but the Alleyn MS has Arden. It was long since suggested that this reference was occasioned by the forest of Arden in Lodge's *Rosalynde*. Certainly Lodge did not prompt the reference to Ardenia (fount) in *Alcida* (1588), since this came from Ariosto, and Ariosto is also a source of *Orlando*. And we must also remember that Greene had used the "fountaines of *Ardenia*" as early as *Mamillia*,[95] where Weld[96] suspects that Greene was borrowing from Wotton's translation, *Courtlie Controuersie*. Similarly, the form in the quarto of *Orlando* ties in with Greene's known interest and use of Ariosto's work in 1588. The Alleyn MS, which contains the Arden form, was presumably written about 1591, and so *could* have been influenced by Lodge, whether the change was made by Greene or by someone else.

Also, Greene parallels a speech in *2 Tamburlaine*. In his raging fury, Tamburlaine commands

> Theridamas, haste to the court of Jove;
> Will him to send Apollo hither straight,
> To cure me, or I'll fetch him down myself.[97]

Similarly, Orlando in his fury commands

> Clyme vp the clowdes to Galaxsia straight
> and tell Apollo, that orlando sitt*es*
> making of verses for Angelica
> yf he denye to send me downe the shirt
> that Deianyra sent to Hercules
> to make me brave, vpon my wedding day
> Ile vp the Alpes, and post to Meroe the
> watry lakishe hill, and pull the harpe
> from out the ministrills h⟨a d⟩es, and pawne
> ⟨it st ght⟩ to louely Proser⟨pin⟩e, y^t she
> may fetch me fayre Angelica.[98]

---

[91] *Perimedes* (1588), G3^v-G4^r; Grosart, *Greene*, VII, 83-84.

[92] Greg, *Abridgements*, pp. 126, 280; the form in the quarto of *Orlando* is Sacrapant, but in the Alleyn MS Sacrapant, as it is in Peele's *Old Wives Tale*. So Q has diverged.

[93] *Alcida* (1617), G4^r; Grosart, *Greene*, IX, 78. The earliest surviving print is 1617.

[94] Greg, *Abridgements*, pp. 216-217.

[95] *Mamillia* (1583), F2^r; Grosart, *Greene*, II, 72.

[96] John S. Weld, "Some Problems of Euphuistic Narrative: Robert Greene and Henry Wotton," *S.P.* (1948), XLV, 165, n. 2.

[97] Ellis-Fermor, *2 Tamburlaine*, V, 3, 61-63 (4453-55).

[98] Greg, *Abridgements*, pp. 170-172.

Greene's passage has the same framework as that of Marlowe. Since the milky way or galaxy led to the house of Jove along with the major gods, Greene's first line is in fact "varied" from that of Marlowe, whether there is any direct relationship or not. Tamburlaine demands that Jove send Apollo to heal him. Orlando demands of Apollo directly to send him the shirt of Hercules. Tamburlaine will himself fetch Apollo down if he refuses. Orlando will pull Apollo's harp out of his hand and pawn it to Proserpine to get what he wants, if Apollo refuses. Orlando furious has made Greene think of *Hercules Furens,* though apparently in terms of that atheist Tamburlaine daring God out of heaven. But Greene has completely denatured any suggested atheism of the passage by leaving out even Jove, who might be equated with God. Since we know that Greene had been strongly impressed by this scene of Marlowe's, it is highly probable that Greene is here borrowing his framework directly from Marlowe, perhaps even without realizing it, which would mean that this passage in *Orlando* is later than that in *2 Tamburlaine.*

Since Greene's *Orlando* is supposed to echo both parts of *Tamburlaine,*[99] it could hardly have been written earlier than *Perimedes,* where Greene makes very full use of Ariosto. If in fact *Orlando* refers to the Armada, as seems generally accepted, at least this reference would not be earlier than August, 1588.[100] All these bits of evidence, therefore, taken together would tend to place the play after the Armada, August, 1588, but before *Bacon,* the summer of 1589. The play was printed in 1594, "As it was plaid before the Queenes Maiestie." Such a detail as "Ardenia woods" would indicate that in this the quarto represents the original version, and consequently that the performance before the Queen was at that period. If the play was written 1588-89, and if the title page refers to court performance in this period, then it has been deduced that December 26, 1588, is the most likely date for that court performance.[101] It may be well to add that "The identification of *Orlando* with the play to which Peele alludes as 'King Charlemagne' in his *Farewell to Norris and Drake,* 1589 . . . sometimes proposed, is out of the question."[102]

Also, "There are over 100 classical allusions in *Orlando Furioso;* less than 100 in the other three plays taken together."[103] Such "literary" emphasis is likely to indicate the beginner.

Still another sequence establishes the order of Greene's plays as *Or-*

---

[99] C. W. Lemmi, "*Tamburlane* and Greene's *Orlando Furioso,*" *M.L.N.,* XXXII, 434-435.

[100] Storojenko, in Grosart, *Greene,* I, 176; Fleay, *Biog. Chron.,* I, 263; Gayley, *Comedies,* [I], 408-409; Chambers, *E.S.,* III, 329.

[101] Gayley, *Comedies,* [I], 409.

[102] Greg, *Abridgements,* p. 127n; cf. p. 8n.

[103] F. I. Carpenter, *Metaphor and Simile* (1895), p. 57 n. 6.

lando, Bacon, and *Looking Glasse.* Brandemart in *Orlando* speaks of the
"bordring Ilands"

> sprinkled with rich Orient Pearle,
> More bright of hew than were the Margarets
> That Caesar found in wealthy Albion.[104]

As Collins notes, "The allusion apparently is to Suetonius, *Life of Caesar,*
cap. 47: 'Multi prodiderunt. . . . Britanniam petisse spe margaritarum,
quarum amplitudinem conferentem, interdum sua manu exegisse pon-
dus.' "[105] Dyce[106] had paralleled with a passage from *Tullies Loue:*
"amongst manie curious Pearles I founde one Orient Margarite richer
then those which *Caesar* brought from the western shores of *Europe.*"[107]
One of these passages is certainly a rephrasing of the other and the two
were written close together. Notice how the descriptive "rich Orient
Pearle" of the verse in *Orlando* is gathered from the prose simile in
Tullies Loue; "Pearles . . . Orient . . . richer." *Tullies Loue* was printed
in 1589, and this passage in *Orlando* is later but closely connected in composition, hence is likely to date around 1589.

Next, these margarites become by echo, simile, and pun Margaret's
teeth in *Bacon.*

> Her teeth are shelues of pretious Margarites.[108]

Along with them in Edward's presentation of Margaret's "curious imagery" the margarites bring a rather startling setting.

> Richly enclosed with ruddie currol cleues.[109]

As Collins notes in a bepuzzled way, " 'cleve' means properly a steep
sloping ground, the steep side of a hill, cliff,"[110] referring us to *N.E.D.* by
way of washing his hands of the matter. In the parent passage in *Orlando,* these were cliffs. Brandemart went on to say

> The sands of Tagus all of burnisht Golde
> Made Thetis neuer prowder on the Clifts
> That ouerpiere the bright and golden Shore,
> Than doo the rubbish of my Country Seas.[111]

Collins is again a bit impatient, "The meaning of this rhodomontade is
plainly: The sands of Tagus never made Thetis prouder of the cliffs
that overhang that shore, than the rubbish of any [*sic,* should be "my"]

---

[104] Collins, *Orlando,* 75-77.
[105] Collins, I, 306.
[106] A. Dyce, *Greene,* I, 8.
[107] *Tullies Loue* (1589), E3ʳ; Grosart, *Greene,* VII, 145-146.
[108] Collins, *Bacon,* 60.
[109] Collins, *Bacon,* 61.
[110] Collins, II, 326.
[111] Collins, *Orlando,* 78-81.

country seas make her proud — the contrast being between 'sands of
Tagus' and 'rubbish.' "[112] So the "Clifts" of proud Thetis also get transferred to the mouth of Margaret along with the margarites to become
shelves or shores of margarite teeth enclosed within the ruddy "cleues"
or "Clifts" of her lips. What a sea-change is here! Wonderful are the
ways of true "art" — especially as practiced by a double-dosed master
from both universities! Incidentally, the margarites of Albion would
necessarily associate themselves with cliffs, since they were on

> *Englands* shore, whose promontorie cleeues
> Shewes *Albion* is another little world.[113]

At least, it is clear that the two lines of the margarite figure in *Bacon* are
derived from the seven of *Orlando*.

But we should notice that a passage in *Orpharion,* written probably in
1588, had also contributed to this result. There Lydia says, "the Mar-
guerites of the westerne Indies counted more bright and rich, then that
which *Cleopatra* quaft to *Anthonie,* the Corall highest in his pride vppon
the Affricke shoares, might well be graced to resemble my teeth and
lippes; but neuer honoured to ouerreach my purenes."[114] This general
figure gets localized through Caesar to Albion in *Orlando* to get transferred in *Bacon* to Margaret's lips. And thus the white cliffs of Dover
become "ruddie currol."[115]

But the end is not yet. In *Looking Glasse,* Rasni says,

> Ile fetch from Albia shelues of Margarites.[116]

The margarites of Albion had got into shelves to serve as Margaret's teeth,
so this passage is clearly later.[117] They are still accompanied by other

---

[112] Collins, I, 307.

[113] Collins, *Bacon,* 437-438. The ultimate reference is to Virgil, who in his first
eclogue (line 66) had said, "Et penitus toto divisos orbe Britannos."

[114] *Orpharion* (1599), C2[r]; Grosart, *Greene,* XII, 27.

[115] The coral may have had its effect upon the margarites in a passage in *Alcida*
(S.R. December 9, 1588), "the reddest Margarites had the most precious vertues"
(*Alcida* (1617), G2[r]; Grosart, *Greene,* IX, 73), where Grosart demurs, thinking the
description "more applicable to the opal" (*Ibid.,* p. 356). The passages from *Orpharion*
and *Tullies Loue* find a sequel in *Neuer Too Late.* There the margarites from "the
western shores of *Europe,*" from "the westerne Indies" become generalized for an
artful simile: "as the Margarites of the West are more orient then the Pearles of
the South: so womens affections are affected after the disposition of the clime
wherein they are borne" (Grosart, *Greene,* VIII, 24. This simile is culled by Francis
Meres in *Palladis Tamia,* f 43[v]), leading to a compliment to English ladies. The
contrast of the margarite and the pearl had been developed in *Euphues His Censure
to Philautus,* "lesse is the Margarite accounted of in the western world where it is
found, then the seede Pearle in a straunge countrey where it is vnknown" (*Euphues*
(1587), B4[r]; Grosart, *Greene,* VI, 165). The margarite serves for simple adornment
in various other places (Grosart, *Greene,* II, 41; V, 166; IX, 259).

[116] Collins, *Looking Glasse,* 100.

[117] Ward, *Faustus and Bacon* (1901), p. 221 has four of the margarite parallels.

jewels, but these do not appear to echo the earlier passages in any significant fashion.

It is thus clear that the line in *Looking Glasse* is later in composition
than the two in *Bacon,* and that the two in *Bacon* are in turn later than
the seven in *Orlando.* In view of this evolution, it is clear that the parent
passage of the Albion series is the one in *Tullies Loue,* printed in 1589,
and so composed at some time by or before that date.

Still another passage places *Orlando* before *Looking Glasse.* As Collins
notes, Ariosto had written in *Orlando Furioso*

> Mercurio al Fabro poi la rete inuola,
>   Che Cloride pigliar con essa uuole;
>   Cloride bella, che per l'aria uola
> Dietro à l'Aurora à l'apparir del Sole;
>   E dal raccolto lembo de la stola
> Gigli spargendo uà, rose, e uiole.[118]

This passage Greene uses three times, twice in *Orlando,* and once in
Looking Glasse. "The matchles beautie of Angelica" was

> Fairer than was the Nimph of Mercurie,
> Who, when bright Phoebus mounteth vp his coach,
> And tracts Aurora in her siluer steps,
> And sprinkles from the folding of her lap
> White lillies, roses, and sweete violets.[119]

Incidentally, this passage is certainly not based on Harington's version or
free paraphrase of *Orlando,* and it will be seen that between or within
Greene's second and third lines something has dropped out representing
"che per l'aria uola," thus leaving the sentence also up in the air. Again

> O Angelica, fairer than Chloris when in al her pride
> Bright Mayas Sonne intrapt her in the net
> Wherewith Vulcan intangled the God of warre.[120]

These passages are directly from Greene's source, the *Orlando* of Ariosto.
They have been lifted as pure embellishment, since they have no connection with the Orlando story proper.

Twice again in *Orlando* Chloris appears as the symbol of beauty, both
times in connection with the beauty of Angelica. Orlando craves pardon
of "faire saynt Angelica" in a passage of the Alleyn MS which does not
appear in the quarto.

> faire nimphe, about whose browes, sitts cloras pride
> & Clisias bewty trippes about thy looks.[121]

---

[118] Ariosto, *Orlando Fvrioso* (Venice, 1567), p. 155, Canto XV, 57; cf. 58.
[119] Collins, *Orlando,* 99-103.
[120] Collins, *Orlando,* 303-305.
[121] Greg, *Abridgements,* p. 196, lines 479-480; cf. p. 214, pp. 246-247.

Chloris is joined in alliterative beauty with Clitia. Phoebus of the original passage now has his Clitia to balance Mercury with his Chloris.[122] And both beauties are still doing honor to Angelica.

Orlando also prayed for Angelica

> Tread she these lawnds, kinde Flora, boast thy pride.
> Seeke she for shades, spread, Cedars, for her sake.
> Faire Flora, make her couch amidst thy flowers.[123]

The second Flora is Clora in the Alleyn MS, inserted as a correction by Alleyn himself. In *Tullies Loue,* there was "a groue that gaue a grace to *Cloris* excellencie;"[124] that is, a grove gracing the flowers of Chloris, as in *Orlando* there was a grove and the flowers of Chloris.[125] *Orlando* develops the picture by an allusion so far-fetched as to be well-nigh unintelligible unless one knows the past history of Chloris. Since *Tullies Loue* was printed in 1589, this passage in *Orlando* is not later. Notice that for the last two instances one is before *Tullies Loue,* the other after, which likely indicates that *Orlando* and *Tullies Loue* were "intercomposed," as it were.

We may now follow the further adventures of this bit of mythology, invented in *Orlando* from Ariosto. Chloris gets alluded to in *Looking Glasse* as

> The louely Trull that Mercury intrapt
> Within the curious pleasure of his tongue,
> And she that basht the Sun-god with her eyes,
> Faire Semele, the choyce of Venus maides.[126]

These "Were not so beautious as Remilia." It would appear to be obvious that the passage in *Looking Glasse* is later than the passage in *Orlando,* even if we did not know that *Orlando* rests directly on the source; and it must also be apparent that all these passages were written by Greene.

In *Looking Glasse,* Greene still connects Mercury and Phoebus, as in the original passage of *Orlando* from Ariosto. Only now the approach is from the point of view of their beautiful ladies, Chloris for Mercury and Semele for Phoebus. Semele was not in the original inserted passage from

---

[122] This pairing is, of course, conventional. Meres (*Palladis Tamia* (1598), f 142[r]) records it without source thus: "As *Cupids* dart caused *Diana* to loue the swaine *Endimion,* and *Calisto* to loue *Ioue:* so it caused *Clitia* to loue *Phoebus* and *Cloris Mercury.*"

[123] Collins, *Orlando,* 563-565.

[124] *Tullies Loue* (1589), H2[r]; Grosart, *Greene,* VII, 177.

[125] The Alleyn MS spoils the picture and the parallel, and Sir Walter Greg approves. Incidentally, when Sir Walter applies most excellent sense to Greene's fancies, he frequently demonstrates their nonsense but not thereby their lack of genuineness — merely that some other sensible person had also tried to make sense of Greene. Not logic but psychologic is frequently the test of artistic literature; here not logic but rhetorical pattern.

[126] Collins, *Looking Glasse,* 73-76.

Ariosto, and, of course belonged actually to Jove, not to Phoebus, causing Collins to note, "either Leucothea or Clytie. See the story of Ovid, *Met.* iii. 196 seqq. Clytie is probably meant . . . From the context it would seem that Semele was intended, but for Greene's credit it may be hoped that this was not the case."[127] But either Greene or Lodge knew also the correct pairing, for Rasni says

> Ope like th' imperiall gates where Phoebus sits,
> When as he meanes to wooe his Clitia.[128]

This figure then gets carried over into *Francescos Fortunes,* printed 1590. There first

> A vale of stormes had shadowed *Phoebus* face,
> And in a sable mantle of disgrace:
> Sate he that is ycleaptd heauens bright eye,
>   As though that he,
> Perplext for *Clitia,* meant to leaue his place.[129]

This is Phoebus and Clitia on a cloudy day. Only, Clitia is here really Semele (that mixup again), for whom Jove was perplexed so that he wanted "to leaue his place," and did assume only his second-rate thunder to try to save her. Next, in the same publication, this couple is reversed, and also Mercury-Chloris from Ariosto along with it.

> Clitia Phoebus, and Cloris eye
> Thought none so faire as Mercurie.[130]

It was Clytie who thought none so fair as Phoebus.[131] Her passion has now been attributed also to Chloris for Mercury. Phoebus and Mercury of the first passage of *Orlando* are joined with their ladies in *Looking Glasse,* only there the lady of Phoebus is Semele, as well as Clitia. Then in *Francescos Fortunes* Clitia finally gets her proper place with Phoebus. The approach in *Orlando* has been from the point of view of the males; in *Looking Glasse* and *Francescos Fortunes* the females. The evolution is clear. The development of this bit of mythology shows that the order of composition for these passages is *Orlando, Looking Glasse, Francescos Fortunes,* 1590. *Orlando* is also before and after *Tullies Loue,* 1589.

In this connection, we are to remember that Henry Upchear thought that *Menaphon* (S.R. August 23, 1589)

> Foretels, he'le nere more chaunt *Choas* sporte

---

[127] Collins, I, 291.

[128] Collins, *Looking Glasse,* 514-515.

[129] *Francescos Fortunes* (1590), H3ᵛ; Grosart, *Greene,* VIII, 200.

[130] *Francescos Fortunes* (1590), I4ᵛ; Grosart, *Greene,* VIII, 214. This parallel was pointed out by Greg, *Abridgements,* p. 206.

[131] Ovid, *Metamorphoses,* Book IV, fables 2 and 3. The reference in *James IV* (Collins, 1907), "And *Clitie* cannot blush but on the sunne," is purely conventional.

where Choa is clearly Clora. In the MS of *Orlando,* the form is consistently Clora, in one case corrected by Alleyn himself from Flora to Clora; but in the quarto of *Orlando* and elsewhere the form is consistently and correctly Chloris or Cloris (Cooper's form). Now Chloris was "florum dea, eadem cum ea, quae à Romanis Flora dicta est: quae cùm Zephyro nupsisset, à marito muneris loco impetrauit, vt florum omnium haberet potestatem. Ouid. 4. Fastorum, Chloris eram, quae Flora vocor."[132] The story followed by Greene, however, is not the classical one of Chloris, caught, forced, married, and dowered by Zephyrus, but Ariosto's story of Mercury catching her in Vulcan's net, which does not appear to be known to the classicists of the sixteenth century or of today. It is significant that Upchear uses the incorrect form Clora, attracted from Flora, as in the MS of *Orlando.* He thus ties in with *a* stage tradition, as at that time he ought to do. On this background, it will be seen that if Greene ever literally chanted of Clora's sport in any work that has survived, it was in *a* stage version of *Orlando,* where it was borrowed from the source in Ariosto. If Upchear had this suggestion from the use in Greene, then he had it from a stage version of *Orlando* before August 23, 1589.

Another passage in common between *Orlando* and *Looking Glasse* may also indicate that *Orlando* is the earlier. In *Orpharion,* composed in 1588 with possible overflow into 1589,[133] "I was ledde from *Erecinus* by *Mercury,* alongst the galupin or siluer paued way of heauen to the hie built house of *Ioue:* there woulde I haue gazde at the gorgious buildings, but my guide was in haste, and conducted me into the great Hall, wher *Iupiter* and the rest of the Gods were at a banquet," and Vulcan twitted Venus for the benefit of Mars.[134] This is based closely, of course, on Ovid's account of the *via lactea* and the council of the gods.

> Est via sublimis, caelo manifesta sereno;
> lactea nomen habet, candore notabilis ipso.
> hac iter est superis ad magni tecta Tonantis
> regalemque domum: dextra laevaque deorum
> atria nobilium valvis celebrantur apertis.[135]

Just as Jupiter had his "great hall," reached along the milky way, so did the rest of the superior gods have their *atria* or great halls thronging with clients. So mad Orlando jumbles this passage a bit and shifts it from Jove to Mars.

---

[132] Stephanus, *Dictionarivm Historicum ac poeticum* (Paris, 1570). The notes to the passage in *Fasti* (as in Basle, 1550, p. 303) will give the background in detail.

[133] Cf. above, pp. 60-61.

[134] *Orpharion* (1599), B3ʳ; Grosart, *Greene,* XII, 18 ff.

[135] Ovid, *Metamorphoses,* I, 168-172.

> Sirra, you that are the messenger of Ioue,
> You that can sweep it through the milke white path
> That leads vnto the Senate house of Mars.[136]

Mercury now "sweeps it" along the *via lactea* to the *atrium* of Mars. In the quarto, this *atrium* is a "Senate house," in the Alleyn MS a "synode" house. In this figurative and not overtly astrological use, most would have considered Senate the more "proper" term. Greene did use the terms "synod" and "synod house" astrologically,[137] but whether he used senate elsewhere, except for Caesar, I do not know.

But continuing along our milky way, the "sweep it" certainly belongs "properly" to one of the goddesses rather than to Mercury. In *Bacon*, Margaret "swept like *Venus* through the house."[138] In *Neuer Too Late*, printed 1590, the "sweeping" is along the milky way, only now it is the brass paved way.

> Her pace was like to *Iunoes* pompous straines,
> When as she sweeps through heuens brasse paued way.[139]

This passage in turn connects with one in *Looking Glasse*, which critics have regularly assigned to Greene.[140] Remelia asks,

> is not my state as glorious
> As Iunoes pomp, when, tyred with heauens despoile,
> Clad in her vestments, spotted all with starres,
> She crost the siluer path vnto her Ioue?[141]

Why in this one instance does Greene change from his normal silver paved way to have Juno "sweep" through "heuens brasse paued way"? The reader will probably be reminded immediately of Spenser's Pride who,

> stroue to match, in roiall rich array,
> Great *Iunoes* golden chayre, the which they say
> The Gods stand gazing on, when she does ride
> To *Ioues* high hous through heauens bras-paued way.[142]

---

[136] Collins, *Orlando*, 944-946. Greene agrees in his epithet "milke white" with Marlowe (Ellis-Fermor, *2 Tamburlaine*, IV, 3, 132 (4111)), "milk-white way." But Cooper, *Thesaurus*, 1565, defines, "*Lacteus* . . . Of, or like milke: white," "*Via* A way." The *via lactea* was thus inevitably a "milk-white way," as Marlowe has it, which Greene varies by a "path," not given as a synonym by Cooper.

[137] Grosart, *Greene*, VII, 201; VIII, 204; IX, 130.

[138] Collins, *Bacon*, 74.

[139] *Neuer Too Late* (1590), G1^r; Grosart, *Greene*, VIII, 70.

[140] Fleay, *Biog. Chron.*, II, 54; Gayley, *Comedies*, [I], 405, n. 3; Collins, I, 140-141; H. D. Gray, "Greene as a Collaborator," *M.L.N.*, XXX, 244-246.

[141] Collins, *Looking Glasse*, 407-410. The stars here are a naturally developed part of Juno's pomp as she crosses the milky way. Marlowe's parallel figure

> O, thou art fairer than the evening's air
> Clad in the beauty of a thousand stars

(Boas, *Faustus*, V, 1, 120-121 (1341-42)) is different and is wholly external ornament.

[142] *Faerie Queene*, I.iv.17.4-7.

The *Faerie Queene* was entered S.R. December 1, 1589, and printed in
1590 when Greene was working on *Neuer Too Late*. It is evident that
Greene read the work immediately and borrowed from Spenser's riding
Juno the "through heauens bras-paued way" for his pacing Juno to
"sweep" through.

It thus becomes clear that the passage in *Neuer Too Late* is a further
development of the idea in *Looking Glasse*, with "Iunoes pomp" becoming
"*Iunoes* pompous straines," as "she sweeps through heuens brasse paued
way," just as Mercury could "sweep it through the milke white path,"
and as Margaret "swept like *Venus* through the house." It is clear,
therefore, that the passage in *Orlando* is later than that in *Orpharion*,
1588, while that in *Looking Glasse* is earlier than that in *Neuer Too Late*,
1590. It is not directly clear, however, that the passage in *Looking Glasse*
is later than that in *Orlando*, but the chronological connections of the two
passages would imply as much.

In view of our past evidence, it would appear to be clear that the order
of composition for Greene's plays was *Orlando, Bacon, Looking Glasse*.
There are other connections to show that Greene's work upon *Looking
Glasse* was later than that upon *Bacon*, but not much later. For one of
these we uninitiate should remember that while the College of Brasenose
was founded only in 1509, yet Brasen Nose Hall, from which it derived
its name, goes back at least to the thirteenth century,[143] taking its name
from a nose of brass affixed to the gate.[144] Bacon's Brazen Head and the
Hall's brazen nose had a natural affinity for each other.[145] So in *Bacon*,
the brazen head within the setting of Brasenose College inexorably elicits
some puns. When Edward asks the clown Miles, "Sirha, where is
Brazennose Colledge?," the inevitable reply is, "Not far from *Copper-
Smithes hall.*"[146] There was no Coppersmiths' Hall, nor gild of copper-
smiths,[147] the hall being coined to balance the college, using university
parlance. As Collins makes clear, Coppersmiths' Hall would be a tavern,
where copper noses were to be acquired, and in the source Miles had called
the head copper-nose.[148] One suspects this jest of being a traditional

---

[143] F. Madan, *The Site of the College*, pp. 12 ff., in *Brasenose College Quarter-
centenary Monographs*, Vol. I, Monograph I.

[144] Madan, *The Name and Arms of the College*, pp. 12 ff., in *Ibid.*, Monograph II.

[145] See Ward, *Faustus* and *Bacon* (1901), pp. xxxviii, xlii, 228, etc.

[146] Collins, *Bacon*, 536-537. For another polishing of that shining nose, see
    Aeneus hic Nasus praelucet, vt insula ponto
    Prominet, aut reliquo nasus in ore nitet.
M. W[indsor], *Academiarvm Qvae Aliqvando Fvere et Hodie sunt in Europa* (1590),
p. 45.

[147] Collins, II, 332.

[148] Cf. "if your skill faile to make a brazen head, yet mother waters strong ale will
fit his turne to make him haue a copper nose" (Collins, *Bacon*, 204-206).

chestnut from hoary eld. Again, as this same clown Miles looks upon the brazen head, it is again inevitable that in Brasenose College the nose of the brazen head should have its due attention, "Now, Iesus blesse me, what a goodly head it is, and a nose! you talke of *nos autem glorificare*, but heres a nose that I warrant may be cald *nos autem popelare*[149] for the people of the parish."[150] The turn on the Latin phrase is likely also to have been a hoary chestnut.[151] When, therefore, the clown Adam in *Looking Glasse* has occasion to describe "an honest man . . . in great discredit in the parish," who "instructed me in the mysterie of a pot of Ale," he brings both jests together. "A proper youth he was . . . his nose was in the highest degree of noses, it was nose *Autem glorificam,* so set with Rubies that after his death it should haue bin nailed up in Copper-smiths hall for a monument."[152] The pun on *nos*-nose is developed in *Bacon* and adapted in *Looking Glasse,* where we need to know the Latin phrase from *Bacon* to understand how the pun in *Looking Glasse* has been derived. Adams had doubtless made a hit with the pun as Miles in *Bacon* and so was given another try with it as the clown in *Looking Glasse.* Incidentally, the speech obviously belongs to Greene, especially since in the next speech the Second Ruffian approves with "Well said, Smith, that crost him ouer the thumbs," which, as Collins notes,[153] occurs also in *Farewell to Folly* (S.R. June 11, 1587, printed 1591), "*Peratio* taking hold of Lady *Katherines* talke, thought to crosse *Benedetto* ouer the thumbs, and therefore made this reply,"[154] to which may be added, "*Tullie* had so roughly crost hir ouer the thumbs"[155] in *Tullies Loue,* 1589.

As Professor Law has pointed out,[156] the device of the clown (Adam) in *Looking Glasse* for fasting was no doubt suggested by a similar device in *The Famous Historie of Fryer Bacon,* which was the source of Greene's

---

[149] *Populo* . . . To gette the fauour of the people" (Cooper, *Thesaurus,* 1565). Cooper gives a diminutive *Popellus* for *Populus,* which may have influenced the form of the verb.

[150] Collins, *Bacon,* 1572-76.

[151] It looks as if John Heywood knew this *"nos autem"* jest. In epigram 86 of *An hundred Epigrammes,* 1556, he tells the story of a fool's blundering comment on a gentleman's nose, "Nose *autem,* a great nose as euer I sawe." The same story is told of Sir Thomas More's fool Pattison in *Il Moro* (1556, pp. 52-53) by Ellis Heywood, son of John. Since father and son published the same year, and since Ellis purveyed "fictitious conversations of Sir Thomas More" (*D.N.B., Epitome*), I take it that Ellis has dressed up and applied his father's story. There is no provocation in either story for "Nose *autem,*" which looks like an allusion to some well-known English jest, which is otherwise unknown to me.

[152] Collins, *Looking Glasse,* 193-203. Dyce had noted the parallel.

[153] Collins, I, 292.

[154] *Farewell* (1591), F3ᵛ; Grosart, *Greene,* IX, 285.

[155] *Tullies Loue* (1589), G4ʳ; Grosart, *Greene,* VII, 171.

[156] R. A. Law, "Two Parallels to Greene and Lodge's *Looking-Glass,*" *M.L.N.* (1911), XXVI, 146-148.

Bacon. If so, the probability, not certainty, would be that this section of *Looking Glasse* is later than *Bacon.* These various pieces of evidence make it clear enough that Greene's share in *Looking Glasse* is later than *Bacon.*

There is also a further network of allusions which helps to orient Greene's work in *Looking Glasse.* As has long been emphasized,[157] when Greene himself decided to don sackcloth and ashes, he did so with great elaboration in terms of Jonas and the Ninevites. Within *Greenes Vision* we have, "Onely this (father *Gower*) I must end my *Nunquam sera est,* and for that I craue pardon: but for all these follies, that I may with the Niniuites, shew in sackcloth my harty repentaunce: look as speedily as the presse wil serue for my mourning garment, a weede that I knowe is of so plaine a cut, that it will please the grauest eie, and the most precize eare."[158] The *Vision* was elicited by the attribution to Greene of *The Cobler of Canterbury,* which refers to *Tarltons newes* (S.R. June 26, 1590).[159] Greene intends to complete his *Neuer Too Late,* which was printed in 1590, and contained the admonition to "looke for *Francescoes* further fortunes, and after that my *Farewell to follies,* and then adieu to all amorous Pamphlets."[160] Accordingly, *Francescos Fortunes* appeared in 1590, and the *Farewell to Follie* in 1591. The *Farewell* had been entered S.R. June 11, 1587, and is echoed in "all these follies" of the *Vision.* Greene was evidently smiting mightily a hot iron to get out as many of his "papers" as possible while there was a demand. The *Vision* itself, however, did not appear till after Greene's death, having been found among his remnant papers.

The passage about the Ninevites which we have quoted from within the *Vision* was written later than June 26, 1590, but before the publication of *Greenes Mourning Garment* (S.R. November 2, 1590). In the dedication to this latter work, which would be written at the time of publication, Greene with great elaboration dons sackcloth in terms of the Ninevites. "While wantonnesse . . . ouerweaned the *Niniuites,* their sur-coates of bisse were all polished with gold; But when the threatning of *Ionas* made a iarre in their eares, their finest sendall was turned to sackcloath. . . . hauing my selfe ouerweaned with them of *Niniuie* in publishing sundry wanton Pamphlets, and setting forth Axiomes of amorous Philosophy, *Tandem aliquando* taught with a feeling of my palpable follies, and hearing with the eares of my heart *Ionas* crying, *Except thou repent,* as I haue changed the inward affectes of my minde, so I haue turned my wanton workes to effectuall labours, and pulling off their vaine-glorious

---

[157] Collins, I, 25-29, 43, 137-138; II, 395-397.

[158] *Greenes Vision* [1592], H1ᵛ; Grosart, *Greene,* XII, 274.

[159] See Waldo F. McNeir, "The Date of Greene's 'Vision,' " *N.&Q.,* 195, 137 (also 200, 282-283) for a suggested date before April 15, 1590.

[160] *Neuer Too Late* (1590), K3ᵛ; Grosart, *Greene,* VIII, 109.

titles, haue called this my *Mourning Garment.*"[161] In his Conclusion addressed to Gentlemen, Greene also says, "if you make the worst of it, weare it as the NINIUITES did their sackcloth, and repent with them; and I haue played the good Taylor."[162] The details of dress, the cry of Jonas, etc. are evidently reflections of the play.

Another passage in *Looking Glasse* embodies a figure which Greene used in numerous places in his love pamphlets. Remilia is

> She that hath stolne the wealth of Rasnis lookes,
> And tide his thoughts within her louely lockes.[163]

These intertwined looks and locks have a considerable history. Closest to the locks line is one in *Perimedes,* where the swain complains

> My thoughts are trapt within thy louely locks[164]

after

> Her locks, her lookes, did set the swaine on fire.

Closest to the looks line is one in *Tullies Loue*

> When Gods had framd the sweete of womens face,
> and lockt mens lookes within their golden haire.[165]

The looks, instead of the thoughts, get "trapt" or "wrapt" in *Mourning Garment*

> Oh that women are so faire,
> To trap mens eies in their haire[166]

> "wrapt their looks in the tramels of hir lockes."[167]

Under the influence of a "strange woman" the locks become "amber tramells" in *Neuer Too Late,* and *Francescos Fortunes,* being four times used in one form or another, but fortunately we do not need to quote the instances.[168] Then in *Groats-Worth* the "enticing *Curtizans*" take over the ornament entirely, "Who chaine blind youths in tramels of their haire," full Biblical style.[169] Thus the passage in *Looking Glasse* belongs to the pre-tramel stage, along with *Perimedes* (1588), *Tullies Loue* (1589), and *Mourning Garment* (1590), and before *Neuer Too Late* (1590), and

---

[161] Grosart, *Greene,* IX, 119-120.

[162] Grosart, *Greene,* IX, 220.

[163] Collins, *Looking Glasse,* 50-51.

[164] *Perimedes* (1588), H3ʳ; Grosart, *Greene,* VII, 92. Compare
> like to the Mirmydon
> Trapt in the tresses of Polixena
> (*Orlando Furioso,* 490-491)

[165] *Tullies Loue* (1589), C3ᵛ; Grosart, *Greene,* VII, 123.

[166] *Mourning Garment* (1590), G4ʳ; Grosart, *Greene,* IX, 203.

[167] *Mourning Garment* (1590), C4ʳ; Grosart, *Greene,* IX, 149.

[168] Grosart, *Greene,* VIII, 14, 93, 123, 178.

[169] *Groats-Worth* (1592), D4ʳ; Grosart, *Greene,* XII, 129-130.

Groatsworth (1592). Its closest affinities are with the passages of 1588 and 1589, though Remilia is at least on the border line of the "strange women" of 1590 and following. As a matter of fact, in another connection Remilia says

> I haue trickt my tramels vp with richest balme,
>
> .   .   .   .
>
> For womens locks are tramels of conceit,
> Which do intangle loue for all his wiles.[170]

We may thus be certain from these numerous indications that Greene had done his work upon *Looking Glasse* before the autumn of 1590. It is clear also that the incentive for the play came from Lodge, who as early as 1584 published *An Alarum against Vsurers* (S.R. November 4, 1583), since one of the three threads of the play is of the usurer and reflects this work. Greene's first dated gesture toward repentance is *The Spanish Masquerado,* (S.R. February 1, 1589), upon which Lodge complimented him; his first full-fledged announcement of purpose his preface to *Orpharion* (S.R. February 9, 1590).[171] Whether Greene was actually repentant has, of course, little or no bearing here. We are concerned with the overt and outward course. From this course we may be certain that Greene had done his work upon *Looking Glasse* not later than the middle of 1590.

Much of the other alleged evidence for dating of *Looking Glasse* is intangible or inconclusive, such as the relations with the work of Marlowe in *Tamburlaine* or *Faustus.* The undeniable parallels with *Faustus,* which are supposed to be the strongest evidence of influence one way or the other, are yet for the most part only the merest commonplaces, at least occasioned by the common background of the subjects discussed. For instance, as Faustus awaits the end he speaks properly in terms of the judgment day.

> see where God
> Stretcheth out his arm and bends his ireful brows.
> Mountains and hills, come, come and fall on me
> And hide me from the heavy wrath of God!
> No, no:
> Then will I headlong run into the earth.
> Earth gape! O no, it will not harbour me.[172]

Sir Walter Greg annotates, "Cf. *EFB,* ch. 60: 'Would God that I knew where to hide me, or into what place to creepe or flie. Ah, woe, woe is me, be where I will, yet am I taken.' But Marlowe has, of course, also in mind Hosea x. 8, 'and they shall say to the mountains, Cover us; and to the

---

[170] Collins, *Looking Glasse,* 426, 434-435.

[171] J. C. Jordan, *Robert Greene,* p. 53.

[172] *Faustus,* V, 2, 148-154 (Greg's reconstruction).

hills, Fall on us' (cf. Luke xxiii. 30), and Rev. vi. 16, 'And said to the mountains and rocks, Fall on us, and hide us from the face of him that sitteth on the throne, and from the wrath of the Lamb.' "[173] For the last two lines, we must add that they were suggested by the preceding verse, Revelation 6, 15, where all "hyd them selues in dennes and in rockes of the hylles."[174] Though suggested by the *History* of Faust, the passage is based squarely on scripture.

Similarly, as the Usurer in *Looking Glasse* expects the imminent destruction of Nineveh and all within it he says,

> Hell gapes for me, heauen will not hold my soule.
> You mountaines, shroude me from the God of truth:
> Mee-thinkes I see him sit to iudge the earth;
> See how he blots me out of the booke of life!
> Oh burthen more than Aetna that I beare!
> Couer me, hilles, and shroude me from the Lord;
> Swallow me, Lycus, shield me from the Lord.[175]

As has been pointed out by Collins,[176] this passage in the *Looking Glasse* grows out of Lodge's *Alarum Against Vsurers.* "In that day the horrour of your conscience shall condemne you, Sathan whom you haue serued shall accuse you, the poore afflicted members of Christ shall beare witnesse agaynst you, so that in this horror and confusion, you shall desire the mountaines to fall vpon you, and the hils to couer you from the fearfull indignation of the Lord of hostes, and the dredfull condemnation of the Lambe Iesus . . . the Lord shal place you among the goates, & pronounce his *Ve* against you, he shall thunder out this sentence, Goe you cursed into euerlasting fire."[177]

So the echo of Revelation 6, 16 and Hosea 10, 8 (with Luke 23, 30, all cross-referenced in the margins of the Bible) is in the *Alarum,* and shows in the phraseology of *Looking Glasse;* "the hils to couer you"; "Couer me, hilles." Cover, not hide, has also been varied into "shroude"; "shroude me from the God of truth," "shroud me from the Lord." The seventh line adds to the Biblical hills and mountains the local river Lycus,

---

[173] Greg, *Faustus 1604-1616,* p. 397.

[174] I quote the first Bishops' Bible, 1568, since Professor Robert Adger Law, *"A Looking Glasse and the Scriptures," Studies in English* (U. of Texas Pub.), 1939, pp. 31-47, has demonstrated that the Bishops' was used for the Biblical material in *Looking Glasse* as a whole, and also concludes that *Faustus* does not borrow from *Looking Glasse.* See the accompanying illustration in Bishops' at the opening of the sixth seal, "when the stars begin to fall," with the sun "blacke as sackcloth made of heere," and the moon presumably "all euen as blood"; and with the King and Queen down in the midst of the falling stars, and one head peering cautiously out from under the rocks on the left.

[175] Collins, *Looking Glasse,* 1948-54.

[176] Collins, I, 302-303.

[177] Lodge (Hunterian Club), I, *An Alarum Against Vsurers,* f. 20 a.

with which Greene — and the Bishops' Bible — surrounded Nineveh.[178] This is the only coincidence in source material with Marlowe. For the rest, the author has gone directly to Revelation 20, verses 11, 12, and 15.[179]

11 And I sawe a great whyte throne, and him that sate on it, frō whose face fledde away both the earth and heauen, and their place was no more founde.

12 And I sawe the dead both great and small stand before God, and the bookes were opened: and another booke was opened, which is [the booke] of lyfe, and the dead were iudged of those thynges whiche were written in the bookes, accordyng to their deedes.

. . . .

15 And whosoeuer was not founde written in the booke of lyfe, was cast into the lake of fire.

The first line of the passage from *Looking Glasse* is based on verses 12 and 15; the third is verse 11, the fourth is verse 15. The fifth line is mere classical adornment. There is thus no direct connection between the passages in *Faustus* and *Looking Glasse*. Each develops a source hint directly from the Bible.

The speech in *Looking Glasse* continues to the same climax as in its source.

> In life no peace: each murmuring that I heare,
> Mee-thinkes the sentence of damnation soundes,
> "Die reprobate, and hie thee hence to hell."[180]

This is a rephrasing of the source passage, "he shall thunder out this sentence, Goe you cursed into euerlasting fire."

This sentence of "Die reprobate" evokes the evil angel in behalf of accusing Satan of the source, offering a knife and rope for suicide.

> What fiend is this that temptes me to the death?
> What, is my death the harbour of my rest?
> Then let me die.[181]

"Curse God and die" had been the first solution of afflictions suggested by Satan at least from the time of Job.

The same solution is suggested visually to Faustus very early in his play.

Enter the two Angels.

Good Ang.	Faustus, repent; yet God will pity thee.
Bad Ang.	Thou art a spirit; God cannot pity thee.
Fau.	Who buzzeth in mine ears I am a spirit?
	Be I a devil, yet God may pity me;
	Yea, God will pity me if I repent.
Bad.	Ay, but Faustus never shall repent. *Exeunt Angels.*

---

[178] Collins, I, 290.
[179] I quote Bishops' 1568; Geneva is essentially the same.
[180] Collins, *Looking Glasse,* 1955-57.
[181] Collins, *Looking Glasse,* 1958-60.

Fau.   My heart is hardened, I cannot repent.
          Scarce can I name salvation, faith, or heaven,
          But fearful echoes thunder in mine ears
          "Faustus, thou are damned!" Then guns and knives,
          Swords, poison, halters, and envenomed steel
          Are laid before me to dispatch myself;
          And long ere this I should have done the deed
          Had not sweet pleasure conquered deep despair.[182]

While the evil angel is very liberal in his offering of lethal instruments, yet the despair of Faustus is conquered by the pleasure which Mephostophilis supplies. The parallel with *Looking Glasse* is in the stage business of a tempting angel, which was indigenous to such scenes.

And the good angel must, of course, oppose the evil. In *Looking Glasse*, Jonas had bade the Usurer repent, and had insistently repeated that same message to all Nineveh. Naturally, therefore, the Usurer continues

                    what second charge is this?
          Mee-thinks I heare a voice amidst mine eares,
          That bids me staie, and tels me that the Lord
          Is mercifull to those that do repent.
          May I repent? Oh thou, my doubtfull soule,
          Thou maist repent, the Iudge is mercifull.
          Hence, tooles of wrath, stales of temptation!
          For I will pray and sigh vnto the Lord.[183]

Here is only the ages-old convention of the good and evil angels.

          Two loves I have of comfort and despair,
          Which like two spirits do suggest me still.[184]

The angel of comfort wins repentance in the Usurer; the angel of despair (in his various embodiments) prevents repentance in Faustus. The connection between the two passages is in the time-honored machinery.[185]

The kill-devil passages[186] in *Faustus* and *Looking Glasse* certainly have

---

[182] *Faustus,* II, 2, 12-24 (Greg's reconstruction).

[183] Collins, *Looking Glasse,* 1960-67.

[184] Shakspere, Sonnet 144, 1-2.

[185] The parallels in *Faustus* to the speech in *Looking Glasse* were pointed out by Collins, I, 139; II, 2-3, who says "though the germ of the scene [part of a speech only] . . . is in Lodge's pamphlet, it is difficult not to suppose that it is a reminiscence of the famous scene in Marlowe's *Faust*." Muir (K., "The Chronology of Marlowe's Plays," *Proceedings of the Leeds Philosophical and Literary Society,* V, 354) is perceptive and persuasive, "The parallels between *A Looking Glass* and *Doctor Faustus* are very much closer than they are between the former play and the pamphlet. Apart from verbal echoes, we find in both plays the same attempt at repentance, the fearful echoes promising damnation, the Evil Angel — who does not otherwise appear in *A Looking Glass* — and the knife tempting the sinner to commit suicide. It can scarcely be doubted that Marlowe's lines were the original, and Lodge's the imitation." If direct connection were established, this conclusion would readily be accepted.

[186] Pointed out by Law, *M.L.N.* (1911), XXVI, 147.

some fairly close connection, but exactly what the connection is does not appear to me directly. Kocher points out that "The kill-devil business is an integral part of the scene in *A Looking Glasse* and, indeed, comprises most of the action. In *Faustus* it is merely lugged in, and there the Clown, far from killing the devils, is thoroughly frightened by them."[187] That is true, but the poorer tie-in could be merely the result of lack of skill on the part of the author. Other evidence, however, indicates that Kocher is correct in his conclusion.[188]

That *Faustus* and *Looking Glasse* share the alliterative "topless towers"[189] can hardly indicate direct relationship, since topless was a usual epithet for anything tall, and the alliteration made it an inevitable adjunct to tower. Greene had used it in *Menaphon:*[190] "The glister of the Sunne vpon the toplesse Promontorie of *Sicilia,*" so it was certainly rattling around in his head at the time he was working upon *Looking Glasse.* And Marlowe or Nashe used it in *Dido,*[191] where the waves are Neptune's "topless hills."

The allegations for connection of *Looking Glasse* with Kyd's *Spanish Tragedy* are even more intangible than those for *Faustus* and cannot be used helpfully.

Our evidence, therefore, is reasonably conclusive that the proper order of composition for these three plays is *Orlando, Bacon,* and Greene's part of *Looking Glasse.* There are also some hints as to the probable time of composition for the share of Thomas Lodge in *Looking Glasse.* Critics appear usually to assume that the play was a collaboration, though so far as I know there is no proof.[192] Now in *Scillaes Metamorphosis,* (S.R. September 22, 1589) Lodge vowed

> To write no more, of that whence shame dooth grow:
> Or tie my pen to *Pennie-knaues* delight,
> But liue with fame, and so for fame to wright.[193]

The reference to "penny knaves" has usually been supposed to refer specifically to spectators at plays. But Jordan objects[194] that "inasmuch as the lines occur at the end of a poem and not of a play, I cannot see that Lodge is referring to plays particularly and not to all kinds of writing for penny-knaves' delight." Even so, the reference would include plays, and

---

[187] P. H. Kocher, "Nashe's Authorship of the Prose Scenes in *Faustus*," *M.L.Q.* (1942), III, 35.

[188] See below, pp. 140 ff.

[189] N. B. Paradise, *Thomas Lodge,* p. 147.

[190] *Menaphon* (1589), D2ᵛ; Grosart, *Greene,* VI, 62.

[191] Brooke, *Dido,* IV, 3, 12 (1162).

[192] For a full discussion of opinions up to 1931, see Paradise, *Lodge,* pp. 142 ff.

[193] Lodge (Hunterian Club), I, *Scillaes Metamorphosis,* C4ᵛ.

[194] Jordan, *Greene,* p. 178.

so attain the same end. Besides, it could not apply to the pamphlets, since Lodge was now writing a pamphlet of Scilla's pride, and his previous pamphlets had been of like nature, not for penny knaves. Assuming that the reference is to plays, Professor Paradise had said, "there is nothing to show that he did not keep to his resolution. After that date, moreover, he was occupied with the writing of verse and prose of the non-dramatic sort."[195]

Here the date of the passage, so close to Menaphon, is also significant, for we must remember, too, that Lodge and Greene were closely enough associated at this period for Lodge to write some complimentary verses for Greene's *Spanish Masquerado* (S.R. February 1, 1589), a work in which Greene himself makes his first gesture toward repentance. Lodge is taking the same attitude toward plays by September that Nashe and Greene were taking by August.

There is another unusual coincidence, at least. There were, of course, numerous looking glasses.[196] But our play title shows a curious connection with the title of the one which appeared nearest to its date. On December 10, 1589, a book was entered S.R. to John Charlwood under the title *A lookinge glasse for England and the whole world*.[197] The book was printed by Charlwood in 1590, but with abbreviated title, *A Looking Glasse for Englande*.[198] A translation of a work attributed (spuriously) to St. Cyprian, *De duodecim abusiuis saeculi*, it shows no specific connections with the play by Greene and Lodge. Nor did Greene and Lodge get their title from the book, for in the book the parallelism of titles has been destroyed. The parallelism is only with the title of the book as entered S.R. Since Lodge and Greene are not at all likely to have had access to the S.R. entry, the only apparent possibility of the influence having been upon them is that they could have seen the manuscript of the translation before entry. But if there is any connection the titles themselves would be clear as to the order. Certainly the play title, which accurately describes the material of its play as presented, would be the original; and would have suggested the rather far-fetched title for the translation. Also, "London and England" would naturally suggest the "cap" of "England and the whole world," while the reverse is not true. If the book were one of Lodge's own early translations, then it would follow that he shaped the original title of the book in S.R. under the influence of the play title. The connection in titles may be mere coincidence. But if there should be

---

[195] Paradise, *Lodge*, p. 151.

[196] See G. J. Gray, *A General Index to Hazlitt's Handbook,* under Looking-Glass.

[197] E. Arber, *Transcript,* II, 536.

[198] *Catalogue of Books in the Library of the British Museum, Printed in England . . . To the Year 1640,* I, 533-534; S.T.C. 6155.

any direct connection at all, then the play title would precede that of the book, and hence would be earlier than December 10, 1589.

If the play was a collaboration by Greene and Lodge, and if Lodge's reference to "penny knaves" implies plays specifically, and if Lodge did keep his resolution, then the evidence would be reasonably conclusive that the work was done before September 22, 1589, though as Greene's reflections show, not long before. I do not know, however, of any absolutely conclusive proof that the play was a collaboration, though the facts given would indicate that it was. But even if Greene merely completed or revised the work, still the date of his share would be 1589, or just possibly early 1590.

We now turn to *James IV*, which has some slight connections with this group of plays and romances of 1588-89. After a close study of the parallels of *Bacon* and *James IV* with the later romances, MacLaine concludes, "Greene repeated considerably more material in *Bacon and Bungay* than he did in *James the Fourth*. Of the two plays *Bacon and Bungay* is the more derivative in the texture of its style, contains many more classical allusions (70 as compared with 20 in *James the Fourth*) and more particular plot ideas taken from the prose tales. The comparative purity of Greene's style in *James the Fourth* would seem to support the theory that it should be dated later than *Bacon and Bungay*."[199] The excessive "impurity" of style in *Bacon* is, of course, mostly occasioned by the university setting, where even Miles insisted on speaking naughty Latin. The important thing is that *Bacon* interlocks with the romances more fully than does *James IV*.

For parallels, MacLaine points out that Ateukin's speech in *James IV* to Ida

> Hee findes himselfe made captiue vnto loue;
> And though his power and Maiestie requires
> A straight commaund before an humble sute,
> Yet hee his mightinesse doth so abase
> As to intreat your fauour, honest maid[200]

is borrowed from "Pandosto's attempt to brow-beat Fawnia." While this is correct, the process is clearer upon the full background of the evolution of the figure. For Greene had in the story of Ninus and Semiramis developed at length this and the companion idea that a conquerer-king should conquer himself, where they form the text of the exemplum. In *Farewell to Folly*,[201] Ninus asks himself, "shalt thou gouerne a kingdome

---

[199] MacLaine, *P.Q.*, XXX, 29.

[200] Collins, *James IV*, 799-803.

[201] Farewell (1590), G4ᵛ; Grosart, *Greene,* IX, 298 ff. Both ideas are in *Soliman and Perseda*. Soliman says of Perseda, "She is my vassaile, and I will commaund" (F. S. Boas, *The Works of Thomas Kyd; Soliman and Perseda,* IV, 1, 102); but when this fails he checks himself with: "What should he doe with crowne and Emperie /

and canst not subdue thine owne passions?", instancing various who had done so. But he decides: "command *Semyramis*, nay, constraine *Semyramis* to loue thee, and vppon this resolue, for kings must haue power both ouer men and loue." He writes Semiramis that his eyes and ears have brought him into love. "Seeing then the Egyptian monarch, who hath triumphed ouer all the nations of the South and East climate with many bloudie conquestes, is by them brought as a captiue, seruile to thy beautie & his owne passions, boast that loue hath lotted thee such a victory . . . Then *Semyramis* pittie his plaintes, who is thy soueraigne and might command, and yet desirous to be thy paramour, seekes a conquest, not by constraint, but by intreaties." The story then evolves itself around these ideas, with various echoes of them. The balance between command (of sovereign power) and entreat has thus been evolved in *Farewell to Folly*.[202]

In *Orpharion*, King Marcion faces the same quandary as King Ninus and in much the same terms, "thou camst from *Sycilia* to be victor, & heere thou art arriued & [art] vanquished: thou hast beaten *Philomenes* in battaile, & art brought vnder by his wife in loue: thy resolution was to terrifie thy foes with thy sword, so thou hast don, but faine to please a woman with thy tongue: by this fond foolery I may note, y^t *Venus* frowne is of more force than the weapons of *Mars*, that affections are harder to be supprest then enemies to subdue: that loue is aboue King and Keiser: where *Cupid* commaunds, there dignity hath no priuiledge to withstand: then *Marcion* yeelde, sue and intreat, but whom, the wife of *Philomenes* thy captiue, rather commaund her, and what shee will not yeelde by intreaty, take by constraint: in so dooing should I reape infamy, and forced loue is neuer sweete: no *Marcion* allure her with wealth, promise she shal be thy paramore, to seat her next thy selfe in thy kingdome, women are won with fauors, and there is none so chast but time and gifts may intice."[203] So Marcion sends for Argentina and asks her consent to be his paramour. "I could *Argentina* y^u seest obtaine by force what I sue for by intreatie: but I couet rather to possesse my selfe of thy louely consent, then by constraint."[204]

Marcion is a soldier-conqueror as well as a king, which gives him a spring board of conqueror-conquered from which to jump into command-entreat. The conqueror-conquered had been developed earlier in *Orpharion* for Acestes[205] and now gets added to Marcion, the conqueror-king,

---

That cannot gouerne priuate fond affections?" (Boas, IV, 1, 145-146). The fundamental situation and ideas are the same, but the parallels are not close enough in statement to indicate certain connection.

[202] Sacrepant "nibbles" at the entreat-command figure (Collins, *Orlando,* 298 ff.).

[203] *Orpharion* (1599), H2$^{r\&v}$; Grosart, *Greene,* XII, 87.

[204] *Orpharion* (1599), H2^v; Grosart, *Greene,* XII, 88.

[205] See above, p. 60.

who thus inherits from both Ninus as king and Acestes as conqueror. Marcion decides upon entreat-constrain. Then in putting the antithesis to Argentina he splits it into force-(sue) entreat, and consent-constraint.

Now we turn to *Pandosto*, where Dorastus uses upon Fawnia the first form of the Ninus argument, centered upon command-constrain. "Why *Fawnia*, perhappes I loue thee, and then thou must needes yeelde, for thou knowest I can commaunde and constraine. Trueth sir (quoth she) but not to loue: for constrained loue is force, not loue."[206] Fawnia's reply is in turn summarized by Marcion in *Orpharion*, "forced loue is neuer sweete."

The final argument of King Ninus, however, is left for King Pandosto to use on Fawnia, as MacLaine notes (she should have been well prepared for it!). *"Fawnia*, I know thou art not so unwise in thy choice, as to refuse the offer of a King, nor so ingrateful as to dispise a good turne: thou art now in that place where I may commaunde, and yet thou seest I intreate, my power is such as I may compell by force, and yet I sue by prayers."[207] The argument has now been put into full double balance, command-entreat, power-sue. This double balance has also been used for Marcion's speech to Argentina in *Orpharion*, but because of the conqueror-conquered approach takes a slightly different form. The passage in *Orpharion* restates the conclusion of Pandosto's argument, and adds to it the balanced consent-constraint, instead of "sue by prayers."

The order of composition of these passages in the three publications is *Farewell to Folly* (S.R. June 11, 1587, first known print in 1591), *Pandosto* (S.R. July 1, 1588, printed the same year), *Orpharion* (composed for the most part in 1588). So the connection between these passages in the three works, temporally and rhetorically, is clear. When now we examine the passage in *James IV*, it becomes apparent that it is based on the double balance of King Pandosto's speech, command-entreat, power-sue. *James IV* interweaves the two. Now the king's power (power-sue) requires a command (command-entreat) instead of a humble suit (power-sue), but instead he entreats (command-entreat) her favor. The four terms of the double balance in Pandosto's speech have been interwoven in *James IV*, and thus the latter passage is clearly the later.[208] It follows that this passage in *James IV* is later than *Pandosto*, 1588; but there is no indication of how much later, since Greene might warm over such a choice bit after many years. And he had not previously had the occasion to use it in the verse of a play.

As King James faces the same problem as had King Ninus and King Marcion, the argument used by Ninus and sharpened up for Pandosto serves his situation also. Not only so, but the revival brings along with it

---

[206] *Pandosto* (1588), E2ʳ; Grosart, *Greene,* IV, 284.

[207] *Pandosto* (1588), G2ʳ; Grosart, *Greene,* IV, 310.

[208] The line preceding the double balance, "captiue vnto loue," goes back to Ninus.

the companion argument of King Ninus and King Marcion with themselves.

> *Ateu.* He will inforce, if you resist his sute.
> *Ida.* What tho, the world may shame to him account,
> To bee a King of men and worldly pelfe,
> Yet hath no power to rule and guide him selfe.[209]

This is nearer Marcion than Ninus. For Marcion had said that if he used constraint by command to get what Argentina would not yield by entreaty, "in so dooing should I reape infamy." Marcion had also thought of alluring with promises of wealth and rule, reflected in Ida's mention of king and worldly pelf. It was Ninus, however, who had asked himself if he could govern a kingdom and not his own passions. So here *James IV* has the full argument as in *Neuer Too Late* and *Orpharion*, showing traces of both. It is clear that each time the same situation evoked the same reactions. It is also clear that Greene had just been reminded of Semiramis and Ninus, since in the interact shows preceding these speeches he used the incident of Semiramis and Stabrobates, following the death of Ninus. The fact that the story of Semiramis and Ninus was to get into print in 1591 could have had some influence here. But it is the situation in *James IV* which sends Greene in memory at least to *Neuer Too Late, Pandosto,* and *Orpharion*, and no other incitement is needed. The composition of these passages in *James IV* is thus later than that of the passages in the three pamphlets, but there is no indication of how much later.

There is also a curious connection in a phrase used in *James IV* and *Orpharion*. In *Orpharion*, Lydia reminds Acestes that her father the King of Lydia, "woulde vnplume thee of all thy feathers: and like *Esops* Crowe turne thee naked to the worlde."[210] In the prologue to *James IV*, Bohan speaks of "leauing my two sonnes to the world,"[211] and advises these sons to "get you to the wide world."[212] There may be other instances of the phrase in Greene which I have failed to note, but at least here is another curious coincidence in expression between *James IV* and *Orpharion*.[213]

James IV has one quite significant connection with *Mourning Garment* (S. R. November 2, 1590), and Peele's lost play of *The Hunting of Cupid* (S.R. July 26, 1591). In the *Hunting*, a song is assigned to the "heardgroome vᵗ his strauberrie lasse," the first lines of which may be reconstructed as

---

[209] Collins, *James IV*, 823-826.

[210] *Orpharion* (1599), D1ᵛ; Grosart, *Greene*, XII, 37.

[211] Collins, *James IV*, 66-67.

[212] Collins, *James IV*, 91.

[213] The expression occurs also in *King Leir* (*M.S.R.*, line 602), where Cordella is "turnd into the world, to seeke my fortune."

> What thing is love? for wel I wot love is a thing.
> It is a pricke, it is a sting,
> It is a prettie, prettie thing.[214]

Now in *Mourning Garment* "The Shepheards wiues song" begins

> Ah what is loue   is it a pretie thing[215]

Also, in *James IV* Ida tells the King of Scots

> And weele I wot, I heard a shepheard sing,
> That, like a Bee, Loue hath a little sting.[216]

It is obvious that "The Shepheards Wife" as well as Ida had heard the shepherd sing before she sang her song in *Mourning Garment*. That is, Peele's play had been accessible upon some stage, no doubt, to all who had the means of access well before November 2, 1590, when Greene's pamphlet was entered for print. The echo-allusion in Greene's play of *James IV* is most likely to have been made while Peele's play *The Hunting of Cupid* was upon the stage. So Greene's *James IV* likely belongs to 1590, say not later than for the autumn, being composed alongside *Mourning Garment*.[217]

This being the approximate date of *James IV,* one further bit of evidence has its bearing. As Fleay[218] noted, the title page bore the abbreviated *Omne tulit punctum,* which, as we have seen above, probably indicates a date for *James IV* hardly later than the summer of 1590.

James IV has also a direct connection with *Looking Glasse* and an indirect one with *Bacon* in that John Adams of the Queen's men appears to have acted as one of the clowns in each play.[219]

There is besides an interesting structural connection between *James IV* and *Looking Glasse.* In *Orlando* and *Bacon,* the love theme of the play

---

[214] For the surviving texts of this song, see Malone Society *Collections,* I, 309-314. The first line seems certainly to have read "wel I wot," later changed to "sure I am," abbreviated to "sure."

[215] *Mourning Garment* (1590), C1ᵛ; Grosart, *Greene,* IX, 143a. With the later date of entry for Peele's *Hunting* firmly fixed in his mind, Gayley, *Comedies,* [I], 416, calls this "a premonition or echo" of Peele's verses.

[216] Collins, *James IV,* 231-232. Compare

> Altho a Bee be but a little thing,
> You know, faire Queen, it hath a bitter sting (890-891).

See also in *Mourning Garment* (S.R. November 2, 1590), "Loue, quoth she, is a queasie thing" (*Mourning Garment,* D2ʳ; Grosart, *Greene,* IX, 157; cf IX, 31); "Loue is a thing" (IX, 199); "the Bee hath a sting" (IX, 221). The only other possible parallel I have noticed is in *Orpharion* (S.R. February 5, 1590), "Women are false and loue a bitter thing" (XII, 21).

[217] I find nothing tangible in an article by Ruth Hudson, "Greene's *James IV* and Contemporary Allusions to Scotland," *P.M.L.A.* (1932), XLVII, 652 ff.

[218] Fleay, *Biog. Chron.,* I, 265. See above, pp. 65-66.

[219] Greg, *Henslowe's Diary,* II, 153.

had been permitted to meander to a happy and quite proper conclusion without overt moral guidance. But in *James IV* the story is embedded in elaborate machinery to display the corruption of the court of James IV and him in it, as in *Looking Glasse* the machinery displayed the various exempla of evil in Nineveh, morality style. Rasni's sycophant Radagon is reincarnated as Ateukin, the evil genius of James IV, etc. In view of the sequence in *Orlando, Bacon, Looking Glasse,* it is clear that *James IV* has been affected in its structure and tone by the last play of that sequence. *James IV* reflects the seriousness of 1590, which led Greene to abjure pamphlets of love. Here the ladies have become patient Griselda and chaste Susannah, all in two — good enough for the Reverend Victorians to sing their condign praise![220] One would like to know what turn Greene's plays took in 1591, as he devoted himself to the purposeful business of coneycatching. But we have no more known plays from his pen.

We have, then, three plays, *Orlando, Bacon,* and *Looking Glasse* intermeshed with each other and with Greene's prose romances of 1588-89. We have also *James IV* later but not so closely connected. Not only so, but the earlier three plays hold together in subsequent stage history. When Henslowe's *Diary* opens in 1592, we find Strange's men performing these three. We do not know, of course, how long before this opening Strange's company had been acting in these plays. Nor do we know that they had not acted in others of Greene's. All that we know is that these three plays are still grouped.

A contemporary, trying to embarrass Greene, gives a discreditable account of how *Orlando* came to Strange's company. Cuthbert Cunnycatcher in his reply to Greene's coneycatching exposures says in his *Defence of Conny catching,* "What if I should proue you a *Conny-catcher,* Maister *R. G.* would it not make you blush at the matter? . . . Aske the Queens Players, if you sold them not *Orlando Furioso* for twenty Nobles, and when they were in the country, sold the same Play to the Lord Admirals men for as much more . . . I heare when this was obiected, that you made this excuse: that there was no more faith to be held with Plaiers, than with them that valued faith at the price of a feather: for as they were *Comaedians* to act, so the actions of their liues were *Cameleon* like, that they were vncertaine, variable, time pleasers, men that measured honestie by profite, and that regarded their Authors not by desart, but by necessitie of time."[221]

As Simpson points out,[222] Greene was himself a few weeks later in a

---

[220] Even a secular modern is forced to his knees! See MacLaine, *P.Q.,* XXX, 28.
[221] *Defence* (1592), C3[r&v]; Grosart, *Greene,* XI, 75-76.
[222] Simpson, *School,* II, 387.

Groatsworth of Wit to put the philosophy here attributed to him into the mouth of Roberto, who is supposed in some degree to represent Greene. "But *Roberto* now famozed for an Arch-plaimaking-poet. . . . Marry this rule he kept, what euer he fingerd afore hand, was the certaine meanes to vnbinde a bargaine, and being askt why hee so slightly dealt with them that did him good? It becoms me, saith hee, to bee contrary to the worlde; for commonly when vulgar men receiue earnest, they doo performe, when I am paid any thing afore-hand, I breake my promise."[223] If it is suspected that this bit is autobiographical, Greene has only himself to blame.

Cuthbert Cunnycatcher's pamphlet was entered S.R. April 21, 1592. How long previously it had been written we do not know directly. But it must be significant that at this time the Admiral's company, whatever it was, was cooperating with Strange's, and Strange's performed *Orlando* on February 22, 1592 for a single performance. Since this is only two days after Henslowe's account book opens, it is likely that this is the end of the run for *Orlando* with Strange's. Further, Alleyn had at some time evidently himself played Orlando, and preserved his written part. If there had been only the one performance by the Admiral's (Strange's), Cuthbert Cunnycatcher is not likely to have known about the matter.

It must be significant that Cuthbert mentions only *Orlando*. For Strange's had also put on *Bacon*[224] the first day of Henslowe's account book, February 19, 1592, and continued to do so occasionally till January 29, 1593, a total of seven performances. It also put on *Looking Glasse* March 8, 1592, to June 7, 1592, four performances. There may, of course, have been earlier performances of all these plays before Henslowe's accounts in this particular book begin. But it appears that *Orlando* had already run its course and Cuthbert Cunnycatcher had heard of it alone. The first two parts of Greene's coneycatching pamphlets had been entered December 13, 1591 (printed as of 1591; that is, in the first quarter of what we would call 1592), and the third on February 7, 1592. Cuthbert says he is answering the "two iniurious Pamphlets published by *R. G.*" He is thus answering the two which were entered December 13, 1591, and first printed as of that year, and not the third part, which was entered February 7, 1592. It seems clear that Cuthbert had written this section by the middle of February, 1592, and knew only of *Orlando*.

In view of this situation, we must face squarely the fact that such a transaction as Cuthbert alleges must reflect at least as much upon the Admiral's (Strange's) company as upon Greene. For the Admiral's would

---

[223] *Groats-Worth* (1592), E1ᵛ; Grosart, *Greene,* XII, 134.

[224] As printed in 1594, *Bacon* had certainly been performed in Southwark; see Ralph's allusion to bringing things from the University to Southwark.

certainly know that some of these plays by Greene had been acted by the Queen's. If the incident were confined to *Orlando* as Cuthbert thought, his explanation might be accepted as a bit of Greene's coneycatching. But when *Bacon* and *Looking Glasse* are immediately added, the case is decidedly different. We should then need to conclude that if there was sharp practice, as Cuthbert charges, the company was equally implicated with Greene.

We shall need, therefore, to keep before us the fact that three of Greene's plays for the Queen's men by or before 1590 were accessible by 1592 to the Admiral's (Strange's) men, and that *James IV*, apparently also for the Queen's men, probably 1590, is not known to have followed the same channel. After *James IV*, we have no definite information as to what plays Greene wrote, for whom he wrote, or when he wrote. It is clear that Greene's play writing activities were still satisfactory to him well along in 1590, when Francesco, "getting him home to his chamber writ a Comedie, which so generally pleased all the audience, that happie were those Actors in short time that could get any of his workes, he grewe so exquisite in that facultie."[225] All the burs were supposedly at that time still willing to cleave to Francesco, and could even be rudely reminded that they were only Aesop's crow. Like Francesco, Robert Greene had by this time in 1590 written several successful comedies. But by the time *Farewell to Folly* came to print in 1591, the author of *Fair Em* had aroused Greene's ire by modelling the play closely on *Bacon,* no doubt with great success, since the play went through several editions in print, "As it was sundrietimes publiquely acted in the / *honourable Citie of London, by the right honourable* / the Lord Strange his seruaunts" (?1593). The structure of the play itself also indicates that it was written for Strange's company at this period. These particular burs were already causing Greene distress with a competitive dramatist (unfortunately Anthony Mundy), and they were forming a coalition with Edward Alleyn which gave them access to the old stock of plays of the Admiral's, and more important perhaps, to the outstanding corps of dramatists for the company, to which Greene did not belong.

Here it will not be amiss to notice the feverish spate of Greene's pamphlets beginning at the end of 1591. After Greene returned to pamphleteering in 1587, he produced steadily in print about three pamphlets a year through November 2, 1590, though one item in 1590 has two parts, and it is apparent that he also did some work on *Greene's Vision* that year. But in 1591 there is nothing of his own till December, except that the *Farewell to Folly*, entered in 1587, was printed. Then in December, 1591, began the flood of pamphlets which ended only after Greene's

---

[225] *Francescos Fortunes* (1590), B3^v; Grosart, *Greene,* VIII, 129.

death in September, 1592. It was this flood which impressed contemporaries. In *Strange Newes*, Nashe says Greene was "chiefe agent for the
companie (for hee writ more than foure other . . .)."[226] Nashe is certainly referring to the "companie" of writers, as the context makes clear,
and as is specifically indicated when Nashe continues later, "In a night &
a day he would haue yarkt vp a Pamphlet as well as in saeuen yeare."[227]
The author of *Greenes Newes* says that Green would "fit your fancies at
yᵉ least euery q[u]arter of the yere, with strange & quaint deuises."[228]
While "every quarter" was a stock phrase for facility, yet for Greene at
the finale it was probably literally true.

A reason for this activity beginning at the end of 1591 is suggested by
Cuthbert Cunnycatcher when he says that the Queen's had gone to the
country, and while their backs were turned Greene had made a double
sale of a play to the Admiral's. While the double sale was probably a
misinference, the Queen's had gone to the country in 1591, henceforth to
remain in fact a country company. It was thus probably in 1591 that
Greene lost the support of the Queen's and expected to get the support
of Strange's (Admiral's), only to find, then or later, that they were too
well satisfied with their Shake-scene. We have assumed apparently that
the actor-burs had tried to cling to Greene almost to his death bed,
casting him off only in his final illness in August, 1592, as nearly everyone else is said to have done. But if Strange's were the burs that sought
to cleave, we should notice that of Greene's known plays, only old ones
revived appear in their repertoire in 1592. It is only an inference that
Greene ever had anything to do with the *Henry VI* plays, for instance —
I do not say that he did or did not! Nor do we know that he had a hand
in any new play of the time for them, such as *Knack to Know a Knave* —
I do not say that he did or did not!

Thus inevitably when the Queen's company suffered eclipse in 1591,
that portended catastrophe for Robert Greene. He may have been retained for a time by Alleyn (the Admiral's men), as Cuthbert Cunnycatcher thought was true in February, 1592. But the burs may never
have availed themselves of Greene's services after the Queen's ceased as
a London company.

---

[226] McKerrow, *Nashe*, I, 271, 287.

[227] Fleay, *Biog. Chron.*, I, 262, makes a company of actors of this and says "the
Queen's company of course." Collins, *Greene*, I, 67-68 says Pembroke's.

[228] *Greenes Newes* (1593), A4ʳ.

CHAPTER III

Marlowe and *The Taming of a Shrew*

In 1588, Greene had reprehended *Tamburlaine*. Greene still displays his distaste for *Tamburlaine* in *Menaphon*[1] (S.R. August 23, 1589) and now joins with it, for some reason, *The Taming of a Shrew*. We have considered elsewhere the more direct references by Greene to *Tamburlaine* and Marlowe.[2] Here we must consider a whole parodying passage upon one in *The Taming of a Shrew*, since it clears up certain fundamental relationships. Hitherto our attention has been fixed upon it because it obviously parodies a simile to be found in *A Shrew*. As Professor Boas points out concerning this figure, "One simile, indeed, in Act II., i., 149-150, 'Whiter than . . . icy hair that grows on Boreas' chin,' was evidently in Greene's mind when he wrote in *Menaphon* (1589) of the ewe 'whose fleece was as white as the haires that grow on father *Boreas* chinne, or as the dangling deawlap of the silver Bull,' while Nash in his Preface to Greene's novel similarly refers to the vainglorious tragedians who 'get Boreas by the beard, and the heavenlie bull by the deaw-lap.' If Greene and Nash were here alluding to *The Taming of a Shrew*, the date of the play would necessarily be before 1589, but the author may well have borrowed the simile, which occurs in a speech pieced together mainly from fragments of Marlowe . . . from an older play, now lost. This is the more probable, as both Greene and Nash combine the reference to Boreas' chin with that to the dewlap of the Bull, to which there is nothing corresponding in *The Taming of a Shrew*."[3] Whether Marlowe himself wrote *The Taming of a Shrew*, or whether the author of *A Shrew* was here borrowing Marlovian passages, Greene is again centering attention upon Marlowe, and Nashe is following suit.

But in this proposed solution several vital facts of relationship have not been noticed. In *A Shrew* Ferando says

> Sweete Kate, lovelier than Diana's purple robe,
> Whiter than are the snowy Apennines,
> Or icy hair that grows on Boreas' chin!
> Father, I swear by Ibis' golden beak,

---

[1] The only known previous use of the name Menaphon is in *Tamburlaine*.

[2] See above, pp. 1 ff.

[3] F. S. Boas, *The Taming of a Shrew*, p. xxiii, n. 1.

> More fair and radiant is my bonny Kate,
> Than silver Xanthus, when he doth embrace
> The ruddy Simois at Ida's feet.[4]

In *Menaphon*, Greene causes his Arcadian shepherds to describe the loss of Samela under the figure of a marvellous ewe. "Marie sir quoth *Doron* bluntly, the flower of all our garland is gone. How meane you that sir, quoth he: We had answered *Doron,* an Eaw amongst our Ramms, whose fleece was as white as the haires that grow on father *Boreas* chinne, or as the dangling deawlap of the siluer Bull, her front curled like to the *Erimanthian* Boare, and spangled like the woosted stockings of *Saturne,*[5] her face like *Mars* treading vpon the milke white cloudes: beleeue me shepheard, her eyes were like the fierie torches tilting against the Moone: this paragon, this none such, this Eaw, this Mistres of our flockes, was by a wily Foxe stolne from our foldes; for which these shepheards as-semble themselues, to recouer so wealthie a prize."[6]

When Greene says that Samela, this "Eaw amongst our Ramms," had a "front curled like to the *Erimanthian* Boare, and spangled like the woosted stockings of *Saturne,*" he is thinking of contemporary illustra-tions of Aries, the Ram, who was represented with such a curly forehead and a star spangled in the midst of it, "in capite stellam vnam, in cornibus tres," etc.[7] The rest is the shepherd's own Arcadia or *Erimanthia,* where Hercules as one of his labors killed the boar, while Saturnus is the god of sowing. I suppose Saturn's "woosted stockings" are Greene's own ludicrous contribution to match Diana's purple robe. Diana, the moon, ought not to be purple. But Ovid had said "purpureus Lunae sanguine vultus erat,"[8] which Marlowe translated "The purple moone with sanguine visage stood."[9] In some such incongruous way Diana might get a purple robe, with which Greene matches Saturn's "woosted stockings." Saturn had a star, indeed, but I imagine the spangles (clocks) belonged to con-temporary "woosted stockings" rather than to Saturn. Saturn was also one of the planets, and was followed as such by Mars.[10] Representations of these planets usually scattered some clouds around for them to rest on. Saturn and Mars were, of course, the most malign of planets, this fact adding to the incongruity of the old shepherd's description.

---

[4] Boas, *A Shrew,* II, 1, 148-154.

[5] For the "coloring" of Saturn, see Guido Bonatus, *Astronomia* (Basle, 1550), pp. 99-100, especially "si iūgitur ei Mars, significat operationem coriorum de quibus fiunt solea." Is the cobbler's son in some way connected with this conjunction of Saturn and Mars? See also Agrippa, *Vanitie* (1575), f 138ʳ.

[6] *Menaphon* (1589), I1ʳ; Grosart, *Greene,* VI, 119.

[7] Hyginus (Paris, 1578), f 86ᵛ.

[8] Ovid, *Amores,* Bk. I, Elegy VIII, line 12.

[9] Brooke, *Marlowe,* p. 569.

[10] See Hyginus (Paris, 1578), ff 107ᵛ-108ʳ.

The Bull also got in through the same gate as the Ram, being the next constellation after him. I suppose it was Virgil in his *Georgics* who gave the Bull a silver dewlap.

> candidus auratis aperit cum cornibus annum / Taurus
> when the snow-white Bull with gilded horns ushers in the year.[11]

The star on the Bull's dewlap did the rest, "in pectore vnam."[12]

If the reader will now observe the genetics of the passage, he will notice that Greene begins with the hair on Boreas' chin from *A Shrew*, together with his own character Samela as the ewe among rams. This figurative mythology brings in Aries and his companion Taurus, good barnyard symbols both. Then "Diana's purple robe" of *A Shrew* occasioned "the woosted stockings of *Saturne*," and Saturn brought in his companion planet Mars, as Aries had brought in Taurus. The inciting force each time is from *A Shrew*. These items Greene works into the pattern of a formal description. The ewe's fleece makes Samela's hair snow white, but curled over her forehead, with spangles in it, also dangling as we learn from the Bull's dewlap. Next comes her face as a whole, followed inevitably by her eyes. It may not be amiss, incidentally, to remember here that Aries controlled the head and face, of which the shepherd is giving a formal description, while Taurus controlled the neck and throat.

Samela's eyes were "like the fierie torches tilting against the Moone." Her eyes were like stars trying to outshine Luna, another of the heavenly bodies. The Bull but not the Ram was represented as having stars for eyes, and this may have given part of the suggestion; but the parodied figure was a favorite of Marlowe's. To understand how this favorite figure gets in we must put the latter part of the speech in *A Shrew* into its proper background. For the inciting force here was

> Father, I swear by Ibis' golden beak,
> More fair and radiant is my bonny Kate,
> Than silver Xanthus, when he doth embrace
> The ruddy Simois at Ida's feet.[13]

It will probably be well first, omitting Ibis' golden beak for the moment, to put Ferando's total figure into its proper background, so that we may know how radiant Kate really was. The standard reference work on places by Stephanus says, "Simois, . . . fluuius Troadis, qui ex Ida monte labitur per campum Troianum, qui ab eo dicitur Simoësius, & mari appropinquans, commiscetur Xantho," etc.[14] Stephanus here systematizes the

---

[11] H. R. Fairclough, *Virgil* (Loeb ed.), I, 96-97 (*Georgics*, I, 217-218).

[12] Hyginus (Paris, 1578), f 87[r].

[13] Boas, *A Shrew*, II, 1, 151-154.

[14] Stephanus, *Dictionarivm* (Paris, 1570).

various bits of information given in the *Iliad*. It will be noticed that Stephanus says "Simois . . . commiscetur Xantho"; which *A Shrew* phrases

> Than silver Xanthus, when he doth embrace
> The ruddy Simois

The Simois is mixed with the Xanthus; the Xanthus embraces the Simois.[15] The Simois also flows from Ida; it is embraced "at Ida's feet." But *A Shrew* colors its rivers wrongly, for Stephanus (Henry this time) in his Greek dictionary defines Xanthus as "Flauus. Exponitur & Luteus. item Rufus . . . nomen fluuii Troiani, quòd flauos reddat qui eo se abluunt," Homer being given as authority. The same information is conveyed in the *Dictionarivm Historicum,* and in the *Thesaurus.* The Xanthus was ruddy, not the Simois, which was the "silver Simois," at least in *Locrine,* though Homer does not use the epithet, nor does Dinnerus record it for the Greeks, nor Textor for the Latins. Of course, the author of *A Shrew* is likely to have made this change consciously as part of the incongruity of Ferando's speech. The total pattern is in Stephanus under Simois, the standard source of information. While Stephanus gets his items from Homer, yet the total pattern is not in Homer. Various notes on Ovid say that *Simois commiscetur Xantho,* but say nothing of its happening at Ida's feet. It should be remembered also that a reviser of *A Shrew* quotes Ovid's passage on the Simois from the *Heroides.* Any mention of the river was likely to send one to Stephanus for information, either to the special dictionary which we have quoted or to the Latin dictionary, where the same information is given. Besides, as contemporary maps displayed for any who would look, the whole Trojan setting was only a short distance from Leander's Abydos, and Hero's Sestos opposite; and the father of Aurelius in *A Shrew* was Duke of the territory adjoining, as well as of Sestos. The Xanthus simile is, therefore, natural enough.

This fair and radiant jewel of a lady aroused in Greene memories of Tamburlaine's similarly radiant jewel Zenocrate.

> Zenocrate, the loveliest maid alive,
> Fairer than rocks of pearl and precious stone,
> The only paragon of Tamburlaine;
> Whose eyes are brighter than the lamps of heaven.[16]

Here is the point of reference for Greene's "her eyes were like the fierie torches tilting against the Moone: this paragon." Greene's Arcadian shepherd is thinking of the "paragon" Zenocrate of the Scythian shepherd Tamburlaine and her wondrous eyes, outshining the stars and moon.

---

[15] The embracing may have been suggested by the fact that there was a nymph of the same name, though not connected with the river.

[16] Ellis-Fermor, *1 Tamburlaine,* III, 3, 117-120 (1215-18); Boas, *A Shrew,* p. 93.

This figure had been so emphasized by reiteration that Greene seized upon it as characteristic. It appears first as above, together with three other lines.

> And speech more pleasant than sweet harmony;
> That with thy looks canst clear the darkened sky,
> And calm the rage of thundering Jupiter.[17]

This passage was redone in *2 Tamburlaine,* with verbal emphasis upon lines 1, 4, 6, and 7.

> Now, bright Zenocrate, the world's fair eye,
> Whose beams illuminate the lamps of heaven,
> Whose cheerful looks do clear the cloudy air,
> And clothe it in a crystal livery.[18]

I suppose the process of transposition into the second passage needs no further demonstration.

Now both these passages have parallels in *A Shrew.*

> But stay; what dames are these so bright of hue,
> Whose eyes are brighter than the lamps of heaven,
> Fairer than rocks of pearl and precious stone,
> More lovely far than is the morning sun
> When first she opes her oriental gates?[19]

Here two lines coincide with the first passage, but "bright Zenocrate, the world's fair eye" of the redone passage also gets reflected in the ladies "bright of hue," who are lovelier than "the morning sun" ("the world's fair eye").

Again, in *A Shrew* we have

> Come, fair Emelia, my lovely love,
> Brighter than the burnished palace of the sun,
> The eyesight of the glorious firmament,
> In whose bright looks sparkles the radiant fire,
> Wily Prometheus slily stole from Jove.[20]

This redoing is centered upon the "bright Zenocrate, the world's fair eye" of the redone passage in Marlowe. Emelia is brighter than the sun, the eye of the firmament. But she is lovely and does things with her looks as in the original passage. The four passages are subtly intertwined. It is not a matter of formal external patterning, but a reshaping each time from an internal fund of ideas. Marlowe was impressed with the figure, so was the author of *A Shrew;* and Robert Greene put a brickbat into this same bouquet to throw at Marlowe. The passages in *A Shrew* would,

---

[17] Ellis-Fermor, *1 Tamburlaine,* III, 3, 121-123 (1219-21).

[18] Ellis-Fermor, *2 Tamburlaine,* I, 4, 1-4 (2570-73). For the connection of these lines with *Dido,* see below, pp. 163 ff.

[19] Boas, *A Shrew,* I, 1, 22-26.

[20] Boas, *A Shrew,* II, 1, 56-60.

no doubt, have aided the reference to radiant Kate in connection with paragon Zenocrate. At any rate, Kate did cause the connection in Greene's mind. Kate's task was all the easier because in this same publication Greene is having his fun with Zenocrate as the world's fair eye, another application of the same figure.

We should notice, however, that only the fundamental figure of Emelia as the "eyesight of the glorious firmament" comes from Marlowe; the application does not.

> In whose bright looks sparkles the radiant fire,
> Wily Prometheus slily stole from Jove
> Infusing breath, life, motion, soul,
> To every object stricken by thine eyes![21]

This latter figure occurs in two forms in *Love's Labor's Lost,* one of them with direct verbal coincidence with *A Shrew.* These two, however, are the culmination of an evolving sequence. In the beginning situation, Biron opposes the projected academe with a long casuistic argument as to the true way to "seek the light of truth." If one does it by poring on a book, truth "Doth falsely blind the eyesight of his look." Instead

> Study me how to please the eye indeed,
>   By fixing it upon a fairer eye;
> Who dazzling so, that eye shall be his heed,
>   And give him light that it was blinded by.
> Study is like the heaven's glorious sun,
>   That will not be deep-search'd with saucy looks.[22]

Biron is for ladies' eyes instead of the dazzling sun of learning. The figure does not start with the sun, but with "the light of truth." That light should be sought in a lady's eyes, instead of in study, which latter is like looking directly at the sun. Ladies' eyes and the sun are both sources of light, but neither derives its light from the other, and the sun is not an eye.

When later Nathaniel reads "a staff, a stanze, a verse" which Biron has written to Rosaline but lost, he finds there

> Study his bias leaves and makes his book thine eyes,
>   Where all those pleasures live that art would comprehend
>
> . . . .
>
> Thy eye Jove's lightning bears.[23]

Biron is continuing his figure as to true learning. Now, however, the eye is not associated in its power with the light of the sun, but with the overwhelming power of Jove's lightning.

---

[21] Boas, *A Shrew,* II, 1, 59-62.
[22] *Love's Labor's Lost,* I, 1, 80-85.
[23] *Love's Labor's Lost,* IV, 2, 104-105, 110.

For the climactic decision a little later Biron continues his original argument to its full casuistic conclusion.

> From women's eyes this doctrine I derive:
> They sparkle still the right Promethean fire;
> They are the books, the arts, the academes.[24]

The ladies' eyes no longer bear Jove's lightning; now they "sparkle . . . the right Promethean fire."

To get the interconnections of this evolving figure, it will be well to refresh our minds with the contemporary account by Stephanus of the nuclear story. With the aid of Minerva, Prometheus got into heaven, "vbi cùm corpora omnia cęlesti igni videre animata, operi suo id vtilissimum fore ratus, ferulam, quam secum attulerat, rotae Solis admouit, eáque accensa, ignem detulit in terras, luteúmque suum hominem eo animauit." Since the heavenly bodies were animated with celestial fire, Prometheus stole some from the wheels of the sun to animate his mud man, because of which Jove (Zeus) was very angry and punished Prometheus severely.

So in the struggle between study and ladies' eyes as the source of the light of truth Biron reaffirms his original position for the eyes. They have the true generative fire of this world which Prometheus stole from the sun. But it was Jove's lightning which mediated the Promethean figure. Thus Shakspere has himself certainly in *Love's Labor's Lost* evolved the figure. Every stage is clear and needs no external influence. This is the direct line of evolution for the figure. Later, the concluding stage is restated indirectly.

> From women's eyes this doctrine I derive;
> They are the ground, the books, the academes
> From whence doth spring the true Promethean fire.[25]

This evolution of the figure[26] shows conclusively that Shakspere needed no suggestion from *A Shrew,* or from any other sources than those stated. The verbal coincidence of *A Shrew* is with the direct statement in *Love's Labor's Lost.* The evolution of the passage in Shakspere appears to preclude the possibility that both Shakspere and the author of *A Shrew* could have a common source which they echo independently. The probability is thus strong that the passage in *A Shrew* echoes that in *Love's Labor's Lost.* I would date this first form of *Love's Labor's Lost* the autumn and winter 1588-89. If this is the date, and if *A Shrew* borrows,

---

[24] *Love's Labor's Lost,* IV, 3, 346-348.

[25] *Love's Labor's Lost,* IV, 3, 298-300.

[26] I had not checked closely enough in *Five-Act Structure,* pp. 602 ff., on the details of this evolution and accepted the traditional opinion that the rewriting of these particular lines was the other way round. In other respects, the argument there remains essentially unchanged.

then this passage in that play would hardly be before 1589, but most likely about that date.[27]

Perhaps we should also notice the application of the figure in *A Shrew*.

> Infusing breath, life, motion, soul,
> To every object stricken by thine eyes!

Biron makes a different application, to the five senses from within, instead of to the objects without. *A Shrew* thus has the conventional application, as *Love's Labor's Lost* may once have had. But now *Love's Labor's Lost* has a specific application fitted to the particular situation. In this application, no suggestion was needed from either passage, and neither passage shows directly influence by the other.

On this background, I believe it is clear that Ferando's total speech in *A Shrew* begot the total passage in Greene. It is not a matter of a single parodying parallel, possibly lifted from an older play, but a case of total structure. And characteristic points in Kate connect in Greene's mind with similar characteristics in Zenocrate. Greene is certainly parodying Marlowe, and Ferando's speech in *A Shrew* is the only begetter of his parody. *A Shrew*, with at least that speech in it, must have existed before August, 1589.

It must be remembered also that Greene is not alone in his belaboring of *A Shrew*, but is seconded by Thomas Nashe, Greene's puny college mate at St. John's, Cambridge, and now his junior assistant in the salvation of literature. In a preface to *Menaphon*, Nashe, echoing Greene, reprehends the folly of "vainglorious tragoedians, who contend not so seriouslie to excell in action, as to embowell the clowdes in a speach of comparison; thinking themselues more than initiated in poets immortalitie, if they but once get *Boreas* by the beard, and the heauenlie bull by the dewlap."[28] It will be noticed that Nashe does not quote the "speach of comparison," or either simile, but alludes to them. Greene uses both of the similes to which Nashe refers, and only Boreas is from *A Shrew*, the heavenly Bull being Greene's parodying inspiration. Nashe is thus following Greene, as under the circumstances was to be expected. But Greene himself gives no direct hint that he is parodying a speech from a play. Nashe must have known from Greene, as possibly also from the play itself, what Greene was doing. The two likely had their heads together on this parody, but Greene furnishes the bell-wether of their resultant

---

[27] Various sonneteers get into trouble by stealing fire from beauty as Prometheus stole fire from heaven (S. Lee, *Elizebethan Sonnets* (1904), I, 205; II, 100, 362; cf. I, 118; II, 188; H. E., Rollins, *A Poetical Rhapsody 1602-1621*, I, 52, 145, 151), but the eyes of the ladies do not sparkle Promethean fire as in *Love's Labor's Lost* and *A Shrew*. The sonneteers use the simile, not the metaphor.

[28] *Menaphon* (1589), **1[r]; Grosart, *Greene*, VI, 9.

flock of parodies. We must remember also that their parodies were certainly aimed at Marlowe, whoever wrote the parodied speech in *A Shrew*. And most important, there is no dodging the fact that Greene and Nashe referred to a speech, essentially, at least, the surviving speech.

Since Greene and Nashe warrant that this speech was in *A Shrew* by August, 1589, we had best notice that it has various other connections with the Marlovian background. We must at once grasp the significance of the fact that it is modeled upon a speech in *1 Tamburlaine*. In *A Shrew* Ferando, "basely attired, and a red cap on his head," the incipient conqueror of the shrew Kate, says to her

> Sweet Kate, lovelier than Diana's purple robe,
> Whiter than are the snowy Apennines,
> Or icy hair that grows on Boreas' chin!
> Father, I swear by Ibis' golden beak,
> More fair and radiant is my bonny Kate,
> Than silver Xanthus, when he doth embrace,
> The ruddy Simois at Ida's feet.
> And care not thou, sweet Kate, how I be clad;
> Thou shalt have garments wrought of Median silk,
> Enchased with precious jewels fetched from far,
> By Italian merchants that with Russian stems
> Ploughs up huge furrows in the Terrene Maine,
> And better far my lovely Kate shall wear.[29]

Similarly, the incipient conqueror Tamburlaine, dressed still in shepherd's weeds, says to the lovely Zenocrate

> Zenocrate, lovelier than the love of Jove,
> Brighter than is the silver Rhodope,
> Fairer than whitest snow on Scythian hills,
> Thy person is more worth to Tamburlaine
> Than the possession of the Persian crown,
> Which gracious stars have promis'd at my birth.
> A hundred Tartars shall attend on thee,
> Mounted on steeds swifter than Pegasus.
> Thy garments shall be made of Median silk,
> Enchas'd with precious jewels of mine own,
> More rich and valurous than Zenocrate's.[30]

The first two lines of the speech in *A Shrew* correspond to the first three of that in *Tamburlaine,* and near the end are the "Median silk" lines as in *Tamburlaine*. Into this over-all pattern, the speech of *A Shrew* inserts materials from other parts of *Tamburlaine,* and from elsewhere, while the Pegasus item of the middle of the *Tamburlaine* speech is used elsewhere in *A Shrew*.

---

[29] Boas, *A Shrew,* II, 1, 148-160.
[30] Ellis-Fermor, *1 Tamburlaine,* I, 2, 87-97 (283-293).

First, we fill in the parallels for *A Shrew*. Kate was

> Sweet Kate, lovelier than Diana's purple robe.

parodying

> Zenocrate, lovelier than the love of Jove.

Similarly

> Whiter than are the snowy Apennines

parodies

> Brighter than is the silver Rhodope,
> Fairer than whitest snow on Scythian hills.

In the latter group, the line of *A Shrew* is patterned upon the first line of the *Tamburlaine* excerpt, and upon an analogue of the second line of it. For elsewhere Sigismund says his army looks as vast

> as the ocean to the traveller
> That rests upon the snowy Appenines.[31]

So "the snowy Apennines" get substituted for "the silver Rhodope." And the "Brighter" of silver Rhodope has given way to "Whiter" under the influence of the "whitest snow on Scythian hills." The whole subtle process of adaptation shows that the materials were in suspension in the poet's mind, as it were. This was not a matter of hunting out similar passages and pasting them together. They were there already in fusion and needed only to be poured into the requisite mold. Incidentally, the epithet "snowy" for the Apennines is the conventional *nivalis* of the Latin poets. Whiter than snow was and is even more conventional. So the similes themselves are not significant. But the total process is both conclusive and significant.

The alternative to the snowy Appenines, the "icy hair that grows on Boreas' chin," which gave Greene so much sadistic pleasure, has not yet been paralleled in Marlowe or elsewhere, though the current figurative mythology made it quite a natural simile.

Next comes the Ibis vow. Tamburlaine declares of Damascus

> The golden stature of their feathered bird,
> That spreads her wings upon the city walls,
> Shall not defend it from our battering shot.[32]

The reference is to the Ibis, the sacred bird of Egypt. So the Soldan of Egypt says

> A sacred vow to heaven and him I make,
> Confirming it with Ibis' holy name.[33]

---

[31] Ellis-Fermor, *2 Tamburlaine*, I, 2, 33-34 (2435-36).
[32] Ellis-Fermor, *1 Tamburlaine*, IV, 2, 105-107 (1549-51).
[33] Ellis-Fermor, *1 Tamburlaine*, IV, 3, 36-37 (1606-07).

These passages are in effect combined in *A Shrew* as

> Father, I swear by Ibis' golden beak.

Since the "stature" of the bird was gold, its beak was also gold, and in contemporary symbolism was the most important part of the bird.[34] In *A Shrew*, laid in Athens, there was no particular reason why anyone should swear by the Ibis rather than by some other sacred thing, though the Ibis was well known. If, therefore, there is any connection, *Tamburlaine* has the original and *A Shrew* the copy.

The silver Xanthus has not been found in Marlowe or elsewhere, but we have already examined its ultimate sources and its reflection in Greene's jest.

The next parallel is that of the Median silk, which involves wide interconnections.

> Thy garments shall be made of Median silk,
> Enchas'd with precious jewels of mine own.[35]

> And Christian merchants, that with Russian stems
> Plough up huge furrows in the Caspian Sea.[36]

> The Terrene main, wherein Danubius falls.[37]

The parallel in *A Shrew* runs

> Thou shalt have garments wrought of Median silk,
> Enchased with precious jewels fetched from far,
> By Italian merchants that with Russian stems
> Ploughs up huge furrows in the Terrene Maine.

In this connection we need to notice carefully Marlowe's "Terrene main." Orcanes expected to cut so many throats of Christians with "Our Turkey blades" that the field of battle would be a "bloody fen" and the Danube

> Shall carry, wrapt within his scarlet waves,
> As martial presents to our friends at home,
> The slaughtered bodies of these Christians;
> The Terrene main, wherein Danubius falls,
> Shall by this battle be the bloody sea;
> The wandering sailors of proud Italy
> Shall meet those Christians fleeting with the tide,
> Beating in heaps against their argosies.[38]

---

[34] See Ioannes Pierius, *Hieroglyphica* (Basle, 1556), ff 127-128.

[35] Ellis-Fermor, *1 Tamburlaine*, I, 2, 95-96 (291-292).

[36] Ellis-Fermor, *1 Tamburlaine*, I, 2, 193-194 (389-390).

[37] Ellis-Fermor, *2 Tamburlaine*, I, 1, 37 (2362).

[38] Ellis-Fermor, *2 Tamburlaine*, I, 1, 34-41 (2359-66); Ethel Seaton, "Marlowe's Map," *Essays and Studies by Members of the English Association*, X, 32-34.

Here is Othello's flood from the Euxine or Black Sea, into which the Danube flows, through

> the Pontic sea,
> Whose icy current and compulsive course
> Ne'er feels retiring ebb, but keeps due on
> To the Propontic and the Hellespont.[39]

In Marlowe, the "wandering sailors of proud Italy" in "their argosies" on their way against this flood to trade with Russia meet the Christian corpses in "The Terrene main, wherein Danubius falls." The Terrene main is the Mediterranean, into which this "icy current and compulsive course" from the Danube and the Euxine eventually flows, and Orcanes proposes that it shall become "the bloody sea" to match the Red Sea, its neighbor. I do not know why Marlowe should have specified Italian merchants here instead of Christian merchants, as earlier, unless the Terrene main recalled to him the Tyrrhene sea of Italy. For by his use of the phrase *Tyrrhenum . . . aequor* Virgil determined that we should hear interminably of the "*Tyrrhen* sea," as Phaer translates it.[40] Since the sailors of Italy go from their Tyrrhene sea and the "Terrene main" to the Danube, the Danube reciprocates by bearing the bodies and the blood to their "Terrene main" to make of it the bloody sea. It is in this sense that the Danube falls into the "Terrene main."

As we turn to the earlier passage in *1 Tamburlaine,* Christian Merchants, not necessarily Italian, are properly on Russian vessels in the Caspian sea. Here we have the same Russian trade, but from within the Russian orbit. Now the antics of Ferando's merchants can be understood only on the background of these two passages in Marlowe. The Italian merchants of *A Shrew* and their trade route to Russia are from *2 Tamburlaine,* but they have given up their argosies and have borrowed their Russian vessels and goods from the Christian merchants of the Caspian in *1 Tamburlaine.* About the feasibility of this swap, with no interconnecting stream I do not know.

We need now to notice that not merely this speech in *A Shrew* but the whole setting of the play is with relation to this trade route and its trade. Polidor assures Aurelius that he is

> Welcome to Athens .   .   .   .
>   from Sestos, famous for the love
> Of good Leander and his tragedy,
> For whom the Hellespont weeps brinish tears.[41]

---

[39] *Othello,* III, 3, 453-460. See T. W. Baldwin, "Shakespeare's Use of Pliny," *Parrott Presentation Volume,* pp. 167 ff. Musaeus alludes to this "compulsive course" in the Hellespont by his ἑλλήσποντον ἀγάρροον ("strong-flowing," Liddell and Scott). Incidentally, under the influence of the wintry description for Leander's last swim, this becomes to the author of *A Shrew* (see below, p. 118) the "boiling Hellespont."

[40] Virgil, *Aeneid* I, 67; Thomas Phaer, *The .xiii. Bookes of Aeneidos* (1584), B2ʳ.

[41] Boas, *A Shrew,* I, 1, 1-5.

We remember at once Marlowe's statement that on Hellespont

> In view and opposit two citties stood,
> Seaborderers, disioin'd by *Neptunes* might:
> The one *Abydos,* the other *Sestos* hight.
> At *Sestos, Hero* dwelt.[42]

And at Sestos good Leander's ("Amorous *Leander,* beautifull and yoong") tragedy ("Whose tragedie diuine *Musaeus* soong") occurred, though he "Dwelt at *Abidus,*" as the author of *A Shrew* later indicates incidentally. As for the "brinish tears" of Hellespont, Musaeus had said "even to this day they mourn the fate and love of Leander," which Marlowe rephrases

> since him dwelt there none,
> For whom succeeding times make greater mone.[43]

as the author of *A Shrew* also agrees they still do.

> For whom the Hellespont weeps brinish tears.

The author of *A Shrew* is struck by the same points of the original as is Marlowe,[44] even to coinciding in phraseology. But the trade background is not overt in Musaeus, nor strongly marked in Marlowe's *Hero and Leander.* Emphasis upon it belongs to the author of *A Shrew,* who could no doubt have cited excellent authority. For Strabo says, "Sestus optima est urbium, quę in Cherroneso sunt: & ob uicinitatem sub eodem quo Abydus duce ponitur. cùm ea aetate continentis partes & prouinciae nondum essent distinctae."[45] The Duke's son, Aurelius, was, therefore, of Sestos. Strabo adds quite a bit of information on crossing from one to the other so as to manage the current. Strabo notes also that Homer (*Iliad* B 835) in enumerating the ships had said

And they that dwelt about Perkote and Praktios and possessed Sestos and Abydos and bright Arisbe, these were led of Hyrtakos' son Asios, a prince of men.[46]

In *A Shrew,* Aurelius would have passed along the "icy current and compulsive course" from his native Sestos to Athens, and he would no doubt have met

> The wandering sailors of proud Italy

in their "argosies" on their way to Russia.

---

[42] Brooke, *Marlowe,* p. 492.

[43] Brooke, *Marlowe,* p. 493.

[44] See T. W. Baldwin, "Marlowe's Musaeus," *J.E.G.P.,* LIV, 478 ff.

[45] Strabo (Basle, 1571), p. 687. "Sestus is the best of the cities in the Chersonesus; and, on account of its proximity to Abydus, it was assigned to the same governor as Abydus in the times when governorships had not yet been delimited by continents" (H. L. Jones, *The Geography of Strabo* (Loeb ed.) VI, 41-43).

[46] Lang, Leaf, and Myers, *Iliad,* II, 835-839.

In reply to Polidor, Aurelius says it is love of him which

> Hath made me leave my father's princely court,
> The Duke of Sestos' thrice renownèd seat,
> To come to Athens.[47]

When Aurelius falls in love at first sight and decides to do his courting in disguise, the girl's father is to suppose

> I am a merchant's son of Sestos,
> That comes for traffic unto Athens here.[48]

Consequently, Polidor introduces him as "a wealthy merchant's son of Sestos,"[49] and Alfonsus, father of the girl, puts his merchandise at the disposal of Aurelius. The substitute father of Aurelius is "From Sestos, where our aged father dwells."[50] As Philema and Aurelius talk in terms of merchandise, he tells her

> when I crossed the bubbling Canibey,[51]
> And sailed along the crystal Hellespont,
> I filled my coffers of the wealthy mines,
> Where I did cause millions of labouring Moors
> To undermine the caverns of the earth,
> To seek for strange and new-found precious stones,
> And dive into the sea to gather pearl.[52]

Alfonsus, father of Philema, asks if Aurelius has notified his father who is

> a merchant of great wealth;
> And I have seen him oft at Athens here.[53]

Phylotus is introduced as a merchant of Sestos, father of Aurelius; and Valeria, servant of Aurelius, who is impersonating his master, is introduced as the son of the Duke of Sestos. Philema would not forsake Aurelius even for this son of the Duke of Sestos. She says:

> And should my love, as erst Leander did,
> Attempt to swim the boiling Hellespont
> For Hero's love, no towers of brass should hold
> But I would follow thee through those raging floods
> With locks dishevered and my breast all bare;
> With bended knees upon Abydos' shore
> I would with smoky sighs and brinish tears,
> Importune Neptune and the watery gods

---

[47] Boas, *A Shrew*, I, 1, 10-12.

[48] Boas, *A Shrew*, I, 1, 87-88.

[49] Boas, *A Shrew*, I, 1, 302.

[50] Boas, *A Shrew*, II, 1, 55.

[51] Anyone sailing from Sestos had to navigate a stretch of turbulent water before he could reach the Hellespont proper (see Strabo above). However Aurelius came by the name of Canibey for it, the reference appears to be to this rough stretch of water.

[52] Boas, *A Shrew*, II, 1, 74-80.

[53] Boas, *A Shrew*, II, 2, 114-115.

> To send a guard of silver-scalèd dolphins
> With sounding Tritons to be our convoy,
> And to transport us safe unto the shore.[54]

Aurelius thinks Philumena will be

> The fairest bride that ever merchant had.[55]

After the wedding, Phylotus, posing as the father of Aurelius says

> And now, Alfonso, more to show my love,
> If unto Sestos you do send your ships,
> Myself will fraught them with Arabian silks,
> Rich Afric spices, Arras counter-poins,
> Musk, cassia, sweet-smelling ambergris,
> Pearl, coral, crystal, jet, and ivory.[56]

And Valerius posing as the son of the Duke of Sestos says

> I'll yearly send you from my father's court,
> Chests of refinèd sugar severally,
> Ten tuns of Tunis wine, sucket, sweet drugs,
> To celebrate and solemnise this day;
> And custom-free your merchants shall converse
> And interchange the profits of your land,
> Sending you gold for brass, silver for lead,
> Cases of silk for packs of wool and cloth.[57]

Aurelius is the son "Of mighty Jerobel, the Sestian Duke."[58]

Thus *A Shrew* is set in the background of this Italian trade route to Russia, the same trade route Marlowe had envisioned from a different point in *1* and *2 Tamburlaine*. One of the lovers is son of the Duke of Sestos, the home of Hero whom Leander loved, whose exploits as a lover are alluded to here and were attempted in full form by Marlowe. The author of *A Shrew* borrows some material for this setting specifically from Marlowe's plays, and in doing so shows that he knew Marlowe's intentions completely, as we have not done till recently. Also, how would a mere rag-picking codger have happened to associate these passages in *Tamburlaine* in the first place, and how did he happen to do it through *2 Tamburlaine* to *1 Tamburlaine* in the second? The passage in *A Shrew* is the result of a mental evolution, not of mere agglomeration. The author

---

[54] Boas, *A Shrew*, III, 6, 35-45. This author knew the details of his Musaeus well. Here are the Hero and Leander of Musaeus and here are those marvelous dolphins, not in Musaeus, but to be found, for instance, in Ovid's epistle and in Chapter XXI of Solinus, which Golding in his translation heads, "Of *Hellespont, Propontis,* the Bosphor of *Thrace* and of the maruellous nature of the fishes called Dolphins."

[55] Boas, *A Shrew*, III, 6, 70.

[56] Boas, *A Shrew*, IV, 2, 12-17.

[57] Boas, *A Shrew*, IV, 2, 21-28.

[58] Boas, *A Shrew*, IV, 2, 123.

of these passages in *A Shrew* was certainly very intimately acquainted with Marlowe's mental processes.

It will now be seen that this speech of *A Shrew* upon which Greene centers his attention gathers together many Marlovian threads and is itself part of a complex in *A Shrew*. Not only that speech, but also the background complex must have been in *A Shrew* by August, 1589. The speech has involved five of the eleven parallels with *Tamburlaine* which Professor Boas considers of evidential significance. In these, it is clear that where there is borrowing at all, then *A Shrew* is the borrower.

The speech in *1 Tamburlaine* upon which the speech in *A Shrew* is modeled furnishes at least one other bit of figurative material to *A Shrew* elsewhere. Tamburlaine promises Zenocrate that when he attains the Persian crown

> A hundred Tartars shall attend on thee,
> Mounted on steeds swifter than Pegasus.[59]

We might overlook the connection here between Persia and Pegasus. "*Perses,* the sonne of Perseus and Andromeda, of whom came the Persians" (Cooper). In the mythology of the sixteenth century father Perseus had performed his exploit of rescuing and winning mother Andromeda by the use of Pegasus.[60] In fact, Perseus had supplanted Bellerophon in ownership of the beast. So Pegasus, the horse of Perseus, father of Perses, from whom the Persians were descended, was naturally connected with Persia.

A Shrew even more overtly makes this connection. Slie is promised

> if your honour please to ride abroad,
> I'll fetch you lusty steeds more swift of pace
> Than wingèd Pegasus in all his pride,
> That ran so swiftly o'er the Persian plains.[61]

Pegasus was the symbol of swiftness, and as the horse of Perseus had a perfect right to run so swiftly as he could over the Persian plains, without any incitement from *1 Tamburlaine*. There is thus no necessary direct connection between the two passages, nor consequently is there any indication of which preceded. But the close connection of the speech in *Tamburlaine* in which it occurs with one in *A Shrew* was probably occasioned by this speech.

There are also five other parallels in our list between *Tamburlaine* and *A Shrew* not directly connected with the two speeches we have been examining. There is certainly connection and clear indication of borrowing in the following set of parallels.

---

[59] Ellis-Fermor, *1 Tamburlaine,* I, 2, 93-94 (289-290).

[60] See T. W. Baldwin, "Perseus Purloins Pegasus," *Renaissance Studies in Honor of Hardin Craig,* pp. 169 ff.

[61] Boas, *A Shrew,* Induction, 2, 18-21.

Most happy king and emperor of the earth,
Image of honour and nobility,
For whom the powers divine have made the world,
And on whose throne the holy graces sit;
In whose sweet person is compris'd the sum
Of nature's skill and heavenly majesty.[62]

And yet I needs must love his second daughter,
The image of honour and nobility,
In whose sweet person is comprised the sum
Of nature's skill and heavenly majesty.[63]

The structural evolution of the *Tamburlaine* speech should be noticed. It evolves by balances. Tamburlaine is king and emperor, and as such the image of both honor and nobility. This leads to another pairing, that the divine powers made the world for him (as king and emperor), and also engraced his throne, so that it follows by another pairing that he combines both nature's skill and heavenly majesty. Here the idea is elaborately developed. In *A Shrew,* more or less relevant parts are applied to a beautiful woman, where nature's skill was presumably quite appropriate, but there is nothing to indicate "heavenly majesty," however much a lover could stretch the point.

In still another set of parallels the probabilities are with *Tamburlaine* as the original.

                    pale and ghastly death,
Whose darts do pierce the centre of my soul.
Her sacred beauty hath enchanted heaven,
And had she liv'd before the siege of Troy,
Helen, whose beauty summoned Greece to arms,
And drew a thousand ships to Tenedos,
Had not been nam'd in Homer's Iliads.[64]

O might I see the centre of my soul,
Whose sacred beauty hath enchanted me,
More fair than was the Grecian Helena
For whose sweet sake so many princes died,
That came with thousand ships to Tenedos![65]

Unquestionably, there is connection. The reference to the source of the Helen story in Homer's Iliads, the clearer explanation of "centre of my soul," a more likely origin for "sacred beauty," etc. make it probable that *Tamburlaine* has the original passage.

The next parallel is quite decisive as to its connections. In *1 Tamburlaine,* Zenocrate had said that Tamburlaine's

---

[62] Ellis-Fermor, *1 Tamburlaine,* V, 2, 11-16 (1855-60).

[63] Boas, *A Shrew,* I, 1, 61-64.

[64] Ellis-Fermor, *2 Tamburlaine,* II, 4, 83-89 (3051-57).

[65] Boas, *A Shrew,* I, 1, 81-85.

> exceeding favours have deserv'd,
> And might content the Queen of Heaven

but a further passion might

> Make me the ghastly counterfeit of death.

Agydas then replied

> Eternal heaven sooner be dissolv'd,
> And all that pierceth Phoebe's silver eye,
> Before such hap fall to Zenocrate![66]

On Phoebe, Professor Ellis-Fermor notes, "Dyce and some subsequent editors, following O₄, read Phoebus. But the Elizabethans, no more than the moderns, associated silver with the sun. The epithet has been the prerogative of the moon in many literatures." This ruling Textor supports, quoting Mantuan for the epithet

> *Argentea* . . . Atq; soporiferos niueis argentea bigis Luna uehit radios.

who also applies the same epithet to Phoebe.

> *Argentea* . . . Nox erat, & phoebe gelidis argentea bigis

The epithet is not quoted for Diana, nor for Apollo or Phoebus. It belonged to Luna or Phoebe, not to Phoebus. It was Phoebus or Sol, however, who traditionally saw all things. Here one needs to notice the echoed "heaven." Zenocrate's reference to the Queen of Heaven induced the reply of Agydas. The Queen of Heaven is thus not Juno, who bore the title traditionally, but Luna, who, as Textor notes from Horace (*Carmen Seculare*, 35), was "siderum regina," queen of stars. Zenocrate is saying that Tamburlaine's conduct toward her might please even the chaste Diana, who was also the chaste Phoebe, or Luna, queen of stars, hence a queen of heaven. The passage in *1 Tamburlaine* is thus quite clearly an original structure, growing out of the actual situation and in doing so taking some rather unexpected and even unconventional turns in its conventionality.

Now the passage in *A Shrew* is an exact parallel in structure and thought as well as in some of its verbiage. Here we begin with the man instead of the woman. Polidor had said that Emelia was

> Brighter than the burnished palace of the sun,
> The eyesight of the glorious firmament,[67]

and that he must enjoy her or die. Emelia replied

---

[66] Ellis-Fermor, *1 Tamburlaine*, III, 2, 10-20 (995-1005).

[67] Boas, *A Shrew*, II, 1, 57-58. For the first line, cf. "Brighter than is the silver Rhodope," which started this set of figures, and gave the structural formula. Also, Marlowe calls the sun "that bright eye of heaven" (*2 Tamburlaine*, IV, 2, 88 (3969)); "the golden eye of heaven" (*2 Tamburlaine*, IV, 3, 7 (3986)).

> Eternal heaven sooner be dissolved,
> And all that pierceth Phoebus' silver eye,
> Before such hap befall to Polidor.[68]

Under the circumstances, the eye must inevitably be that of Phoebus, as the repetition and sequence show, even though the "silver eye" was properly the perquisite of Phoebe, while the golden eye belonged to Phoebus. It is thus clear that *1 Tamburlaine* has the original passage and that *A Shrew* has the adaptation. And the whole sentiment and structure of two speeches has been adapted. This is not a case of borrowing a few frippery phrases of verbal finery. Further, the original passage is not without obscurity. The adapter knew the original passage completely. He did not merely hear or glance over; he had in some way completely mastered.

The next illustration is of interconnections.

> And shew your pleasure to the Persian,
> As fits the legate of the stately Turk.[69]

> And I sat down, cloth'd with the massy robe
> That late adorn'd the Afric potentate.[70]

> As was the massy robe that late adorned
> The stately legate of the Persian King.[71]

The structure shows that the passage in *A Shrew* is built on the passage from *2 Tamburlaine*. It begins by borrowing

> cloth'd with the massy robe
> That late adorn'd.

Then for "the Afric potentate," it substitutes a rephrasing of "the legate of the stately Turk" as "The stately legate of the Persian King." The man who performed this operation certainly knew the *Tamburlaine* plays authentically and accurately.

Finally, Tamburlaine warns his pampered jades of Asia

> The headstrong jades of Thrace Alcides tam'd,
> That King Aegeus fed with human flesh,
> And made so wanton that they knew their strengths,
> Were not subdu'd with valour more divine
> Than you by this unconquered arm of mine.
> To make you fierce, and fit my appetite,
> You shall be fed with flesh as raw as blood.[72]

Ferando soliloquizes on his system of starving Kate into submission.

> Were she as stubborn or as full of strength
> As were the Thracian horse Alcides tamed,

---

[68] Boas, *A Shrew*, II, 1, 67-69.
[69] Ellis-Fermor, *1 Tamburlaine*, III, 1, 43-44 (961-962).
[70] Ellis-Fermor, *2 Tamburlaine*, III, 2, 123-124 (3313-14).
[71] Boas, *A Shrew*, II, 1, 131-132.
[72] Ellis-Fermor, *2 Tamburlaine*, IV, 3, 12-18 (3991-97).

> That King Egeus fed with flesh of men,
> Yet would I pull her down and make her come
> As hungry hawks do fly unto their lure.[73]

The simile of the first two lines of the passage from *A Shrew* is quite obviously based upon the materials of the first and third lines of the passage from *2 Tamburlaine*. The *stubborn* is a variation for the epithet *headstrong*. The phrase "full of strength" sums up the third line. The second line from *A Shrew* then adapts the first from *2 Tamburlaine*, with the transferred and varied epithet *headstrong* omitted. Then the second line from *2 Tamburlaine* is shaped into the third of *A Shrew*. The conclusion in each passage is based upon the fact that the horses were subdued, though the phraseology does not coincide.

One other detail is also conclusive that the *Tamburlaine* passage is the original. In the section we have been examining, Marlowe's "jades of Thrace" are Ovid's "Thracis equos," to be found in Textor properly under Diomedes, which Golding renders as "pampred Jades of *Thrace*,"[74] a translation already adapted by Marlowe in the first line of the speech from which we have quoted as the now notorious "pampered jades of Asia." Certainly the *Tamburlaine* passage is colored directly by Golding's translation of Ovid. Quite clearly *A Shrew* then varies from this, as we have seen.

These verbal and structural relationships show the close connection of the passages, which are also bound together in a curious mythological aberration. For the Thracian steeds belonged to Diomedes, as any work of reference that I have seen for that day or for this would declare, even though no-one seems to have protested their transfer in these passages to Aegeus. For instance, Cooper would have done with the unpleasant master of the beasts quickly, "An other Diomedes was king of Thrace, whiche feeding his horses with mens flesh, was afterwarde by Hercules cast to them to be deuoured." Ovid, however, had not named Diomedes, though Regius and other annotators regularly stood ready to identify him. But there were no notes to Golding's translation, and for some reason Marlowe's memory slipped in substituting Aegeus for Diomedes in *Tamburlaine*. The author of *A Shrew* did not catch the slip, nor for that matter apparently has any one else to this day.

To these eleven instances collected by Professor Boas, Dr. Marion Bodwell Smith[75] adds a twelfth. Callepine in trying to persuade his keeper says

> Ah, were I now but half so eloquent

---

[73] Boas, *A Shrew*, III, 1, 49-53.
[74] Rouse, *Shakespeare's Ovid*, p. 186; IX, 238.
[75] M. B. Smith, *Marlowe's Imagery and the Marlowe Canon*, p. 148.

> To paint in words what I'll perform in deeds,
> I know thou wouldst depart from hence with me![76]

Similarly, the Boy (as wife) says to Slie

> Or were I now but half so eloquent,
> To paint in words what I'll perform in deeds,
> I know your honour then would pity me.[77]

One play evidently borrows and slightly adapts the speech from the other, but I see no indication of priority.

It must now be evident that *Tamburlaine*, both parts, and *A Shrew* are intimately and subtly interrelated, and that in the passages in common *A Shrew* is the later. Greene's parody in 1589 makes it clear that the six groups of parallel passages connected with the speech which Greene burlesques and its counterpart in *1 Tamburlaine* were already in *A Shrew* then essentially as they are now. It is a reasonable conclusion, therefore, that the other six groups of parallels also belonged to the same strata of construction.

The spread of these twelve parallels over most of the play must then be given its due evidential weight. "In the first place it is clear that though the borrowings are found chiefly in the underplot, they are by no means confined to it. Two of them occur in the Induction; several, including the most elaborate patchwork of quotations in the play, are put into the mouth of Ferando; another, the only prose bit 'conveyed,' is spoken by Ferando's man Sander. It is, therefore, in my opinion, a mistake to rest any argument against the unity of authorship of *A Shrew* upon the Marlowesque passages. They occur sporadically throughout the play in contexts of the most diverse kind, and they have every appearance of being the work, not of a collaborator, but of the original writer attempting at intervals to soar on borrowed plumes."[78] If it be granted that these parallels with *Tamburlaine*, both parts, do belong to one author, then *A Shrew* was already by August, 1589, in its essential structure and much of its verbiage, essentially as it was printed in 1594.

But *A Shrew* is also intimately connected in many passages with *Faustus*. Boas lists five instances of connection between the two plays. Naturally, Sir Walter Greg in his thoroughgoing bibliographical edition of *Faustus* has given characteristically close attention to the five parallel passages. In the first, *A Shrew* and *Faustus* have four lines in common. Sir Walter says that these four lines[79] "are reproduced verbatim in *A Shrew* (sig. A2, Introduction, i) and in one there is a variant, A reading

> Now that the gloomy shadow of the earth,

---

[76] Ellis-Fermor, *2 Tamburlaine,* I, 3, 9-11 (2500-02).

[77] Boas, *A Shrew,* Induction, 2, 41-43.

[78] Boas, *A Shrew,* p. xxxi.

[79] Greg, *Faustus 1604-1616,* I, 3, 227-230.

where B substitutes 'night' for 'earth'; and 'night' is the reading of *A Shrew.*"[80] *A Shrew* is thus closest to *Faustus* B. *A Shrew,* however, differs from both *Faustus* A and B "in having *lookes* in place of *looke.* Since B is here dependent on A, *lookes* may very well be the correct reading," as Boas had pointed out.[81] That is, *A Shrew* pretty certainly has the completely correct text, while *Faustus* A and B vary from this correct text and from each other. Their common ancestor may indeed have had the correct text; but they do not together prove it, and we have no way of knowing. Even if their common ancestor did have the completely correct text, we would still have no way of knowing from the texts themselves whether the common ancestor of *Faustus* A and B or *A Shrew* was the original. On the face of the present textual evidence, the presumption of originality is thus with *A Shrew,* as we shall now see also from the origins of the passage.

In the Induction to *A Shrew*

> *Enter a Noble man and his men from hunting.*
> Lord. Now that the gloomie shaddow of the night,
>   Longing to view Orions drisling lookes,
>   Leapes fron th'antarticke World vnto the skie
>   And dims the Welkin with her pitchie breath,
>   And darkesome night oreshades the christall heauens,
>   Here breake we off our hunting for to night,
>   Cupple vppe the hounds and let vs hie vs home,
>   And bid the huntsman see them meated well,
>   For they haue all deseru'd it well to daie.[82]

The first four of these lines appear also in *Faustus,* both A and B; and their textual relationships in the different versions have just been considered to the conclusion that *A Shrew* presents the correct version. Their setting shows that they were originated for *A Shrew.*

Correctly, Sir Walter Greg, following previous authority, refers Orion as described here to Virgil. "The constellation appears in northern latitudes at the beginning of winter; hence Virgil, *Aeneid,* i, 535, 'nimbrosus (*sic*) Orion,' and iv. 52, 'aquosus Orion.'"[83] Textor stood ready to tell aspiring poets of the sixteenth century all this and more: "estq́; signum tempestuosum, pluuijsq́; et procellis idoneum, cuius tempore hyems ortum habet, turbatq́; terras et maria tempestatibus." Textor's first epithet for Orion is *nymbosus,* and his second *aquosus,* in the lines from Virgil referred to by Sir Walter. In his epithet *drisling* for Orion's looks our author is thinking of actuality in terms of Virgil's *aquosus,* which Cooper

---

[80] Greg, *Faustus 1604-1616,* pp. 31-32.
[81] Greg, *Faustus 1604-1616,* p. 310, 32n.
[82] *A Shrew,* A2^r&v.
[83] Greg, *Faustus 1604-1616,* p. 311.

defines as "Ful of water: watrish." The hunting had been good under "Orions drisling lookes," for the scent would lie well on such a drizzly day.

Sir Walter raises a query here. "The four lines mean no more than 'now that it is night': but how came Marlowe to put forward the astonishing view that night comes not from the east but from the southern hemisphere?"[84] The answer is that Marlowe didn't, and lies in the first passage from Virgil cited by Sir Walter, which we had best, therefore, quote as a whole.

> cum subito adsurgens fluctu nimbosus Orion
> in vada caeca tulit penitusque procacibus Austris
> perque undas superante salo, perque invia saxa
> dispulit.

"when, rising with sudden swell, stormy Orion bore us on hidden shoals and with fierce blasts scattered us afar amid pathless rocks and waves of overwhelming surge."[85]

Phaer translates

> Whan sodenly there rose at south a winde and tempest wood
> That toward shore enforst to fall, and so tooke on the flood,
> That in the rockes we be disperst.[86]

Marlowe had himself in *Dido* put into the mouth of a follower of Aeneas a fairly close translation of this passage.

> When, suddenly, gloomy Orion rose,
> And led our ships into the shallow sands,
> Whereas the southern wind with brackish breath,
> Dispers'd them all amongst the wrackful rocks.[87]

So to Marlowe *nimbosus Orion* was "gloomy Orion," and *Auster* was, properly, a southern wind. We need to remember also for all these passages that Orion is "a large and brilliant constellation south of the zodiac" (*N. E. D.*).

We can now watch our passages materialize. The *Dido* passage is based directly on the original of Virgil, but also reflects the earlier description of the actual storm, as in the case of the epithet "gloomy" for *nimbosus Orion*. For in Cooper's words *nimbosus* is "Stormie, tempestuous: clowdie." But one will remember that in the description of the actual storm, "In a moment clouds snatch sky and day from the Trojans' eyes; black night broods over the deep" (I, 1, 88-89). So to Marlowe *nimbosus*

---

[84] Greg, *Faustus 1604-1616*, p. 310. "Nox aliud nihil, nisi terrae umbra est, quae surgente Sole occidit, oritur occidente" (I. F. Ringelbergius, *Opera* (Lyons, 1531), p. 68). Night is itself only the shadow of the earth; but in our passage Night is itself given a shadow.

[85] Fairclough, *Virgil*, I, 278-279 (*Aeneid* I, 535-538).

[86] *Aeneidos* (1584), B8ʳ.

[87] Brooke, *Dido*, I, 2, 26-29 (274-277).

Orion becomes "gloomy Orion" because of this storm-shadow of night. Consequently, when Marlowe employs Orion in our four-line passage, this sudden night-darkness of "gloomy Orion" becomes the "gloomy shadow of the night," not night itself, leaping to the sky to view "Orions drisling looke." Thus the leaping reflects the *subito adsurgens* and the *eripiunt subito nubes* of "gloomy Orion." Orion is obscured by sudden darkness of the clouds; but this obscuration is the shadow of night, not night itself. Since Orion was a southern constellation, the shadow of the night, not night, would be obliged to do its leaping to view Orion in "th'Antarticke world." The figurative approach has been from the Orion of Virgil, not from Night. This is not a matter of actual astronomy, but of conventional figures. And what a mess they do get into! And we too when we cannot find their conventional background. There is nothing wrong with Marlowe's astronomy in the four-line passage. He is not talking about night, but the shadow or semblance of night which Orion occasions with his storms, *a la* Virgil.

On the four-line figure of the shadow of the night both *A Shrew* and *Faustus* agree. But *A Shrew* is not content with the shadow of night and proceeds to night itself.

> And darkesome night oreshades the christall heauens,
> Here breake we off our hunting for to night.

Not merely Orion's shadow or appearance of night but actual night forces the end of the hunting. The line on night itself is not a mere lame repetition; it belongs. It is also Marlovian, fitting into a sequence on crystal, which begins in *Dido,* gets shaped in *2 Tamburlaine,* and is here reversed, as it were.[88] So also does the hunting line belong, as will shortly appear.

The setting, therefore, is at nightfall on a drizzly day toward winter. In all known versions of the source story, the setting is at the beginning of night. The author has here localized this setting to an English Lord returning from the hunt. So the Lord orders

> in my fairest chamber make a fire.

And in the morning, when the Tapster finds Slie sleeping where he left him the previous night, he says

> I thinke he's starued by this,
> But that his belly was so stuft with ale.

Here "starved," of course, means frozen, as in Aesop's starved snake.

Now we are likely to overlook the fact that Orion was "a very handsome giant and hunter" (Smith), but everyone in the sixteenth century would be aware of Orion and his dogs. For instance, in Nashe's *Summers Last Will* Vertumnus is ordered to call in Orion. "*Orion,* gentleman

---

[88] See below, pp. 163 ff.

dogge-keeper, huntsman, come into the court: looke you bring all hounds, and no bandogges. Peace there, that we may heare their hornes blow. *Enter Orion like a hunter, with a horne about his necke, all his men after the same sort hallowing and blowing their hornes.*"[89] Incidentally, this suggests the kind of action one would have had for the entry in *A Shrew*. After the entry, in *Summers Last Will* Orion's dogs are accused of various alleged evils of the dog-days,[90] but get defended as dogs in full form (courtesy of Sextus Empiricus). Since Nashe is writing a play of the weather, his jest is upon the dog-days, of which everyone then would be conscious. He is interested in Orion primarily as gentleman dog-keeper, and not as huntsman. But Nashe and everyone else knew that Orion was conventionally a patron of the chase, as Nashe himself indicates.

Thus the four lines in *A Shrew* are "fitting" to, and in detail fitted to, the assumed setting. Upon the night-setting of the source, the "gentleman dogge-keeper, huntsman" Orion begot this passage; and every stage of its propagation is accounted for from the original of Virgil, through *Dido*, through *A Shrew*. And certainly this passage is not a parody, but a serious poetic flight — however we may be impressed by its coruscations! Surely it is clear that the passage was written for this particular setting in *A Shrew*. And surely it is clear that it evolves through the mental processes of Christopher Marlowe, and none other.

It is now easy to see what has happened in *Faustus*. For the four-line passage as set in *Faustus* may in some respects be "fitting," but the lines certainly are not in any detail fitted to their setting. Following a scene heading which Sir Walter Greg stigmatizes as not belonging to the original, Faustus speaks these four lines, and continues, *"Faustus,* begin thine Incantations." The speech of Faustus might as readily have begun here without the four-line fanfare. But the *History* of Faust says that Faustus came into the wood to do his conjuring "towards euening" and began to conjure about "nine or ten of the clocke in the night." The evening setting has caused Marlowe to lift these four lines from *A Shrew* as fitting background. The weight of the evidence from the setting is thus for *A Shrew* as the original and *Faustus* the borrower, as it is from the textual relationships. And who save Marlowe could have written the

---

[89] McKerrow, *Nashe*, III, 253.

[90] Each one of those foule-mouthed mangy dogs
Gouernes a day, (no dog but hath his day,)
And all the daies by them so gouerned,
The Dog-daies hight (648-651).

See the names of some of these dogs in Comes, *Mythologiae* (1581), p. 882, and his unintentionally amusing argument that Orion must have been a hunter to have so many dogs — unless he was insane. See also his *De Venatione* in the same volume, p. 1088. Servius explains on the lines in Virgil how Orion became a *venator*, and Textor, of course, has a line of verse to exhibit this epithet of *venator* for Orion.

passage in *A Shrew,* with its subtle relationship to Virgil's original through *Dido,* and then have transplanted the relevant four lines to *Faustus?*

For the second parallel noted by Boas, Sir Walter rules justly that "the resemblance is not very close and may be accidental."[91]

For the third parallel, again *A Shrew* has the more nearly correct text, and *Faustus* B is again nearest to it. In *A Shrew* (sig. C4^v), the passage runs

Boy.   Come hither sirha boy.
San.   Boy; oh disgrace to my person, souns boy
          Of your face, you haue many boies with such
          Pickadeuantes I am sure.

In *Faustus* B this runs

Wag.   Come hither sirra boy.
Clo.   Boy? O disgrace to my person: Zounds boy in your face,
          you haue seene many boyes with beards I am sure.[92]

Assuming that *A Shrew* borrows, Greg says, "This agrees with B except for the error *Of* for *in,* the omission of *seene,* and the reading *such Pickadeuantes,* in which last it agrees with A. The term 'pickedevant' for a pointed beard came in about 1587, and it was still common in 1616, though it had doubtless lost the spice of novelty. It was presumably on this account that the editor substituted *beards.*"[93] It is thus agreed that the original reading in *Faustus* was "pickadevaunts," as it still is in A. For the other two instances of variation, there is no direct evidence that *Of* is an error for *in,*[94] nor that *seene* has been omitted from *A Shrew.* That conclusion follows only in case we assume in the first place that *A Shrew* borrows here. Instead, the version behind *Faustus* A and B took over the passage, merely "popularizing" it by substituting the more usual *in* for *of* and expanding *haue* to *haue seene.* It should be noticed also that here as in our first instance the man who transplanted the passage to *Faustus* originally either had in his head an intimate knowledge of the passage in *A Shrew,* or had access to some form of accurate manuscript, or to the printed form. So again the presumption in this third parallel as in the first is with *A Shrew,* and the genetics of the scene in which the parallel occurs will also imply that the presumption is correct. *A Shrew* presents the original and *Faustus* borrows.

For the whole scene in which this passage occurs is a late compilation. Kocher[95] has noted that this scene in *Faustus* shares a bawdy jest with

---

[91] Greg, *Faustus 1604-1616,* p. 303.

[92] Greg, *Faustus 1604-1616,* B, 341-344.

[93] Greg, *Faustus 1604-1616,* p. 316.

[94] As an imprecation the construction may very well follow the analogy of "a plague of."

[95] Kocher, *M.L.Q.* (1942), III, 36.

Bacon. Pride says, "I am like to *Ouids* Flea, I can creepe into euery corner of a Wench: Sometimes, like a Perriwig, I sit vpon her Brow: next, like a Neckelace I hang about her Necke: Then, like a Fan of Feathers, I kisse her [lippes]; And then turning my selfe to a wrought Smocke do what I list."[96] Now in "Ovid's flea," the author would like by Circe's charms or Medea's incantations to be transformed into a flea.

> His ego mutatus, si sic mutabilis essem:
> Haererem tunicae margine virgineae:
> Inde means per crura meae sub veste puellae,
> Ad loca, quae vellem, me citò surriperem.
> Cúmque illa dudum laedens nil ipse cubarem:
> Donec de pulice rursus homo fierem.[97]

"Ovid's flea" would get as quickly as possible to the point, and at the earliest opportunity become a man again. He had no wish to go gallivanting on a sightseeing trip, as, for instance, did the not in-famous prose flea of Caelius Calcagninus, which because of its ability to go places "etiam apud homines magnam illi inuidiam concitauit. Subiens enim reginarum cubilia, & in puellarū sinus se recipiens, lectissimę cuiusq; formę primitias libat. Est em̄ sanè ingeniosus formarū spectator: & sicubi purpureas genas aduertit, sicubi candidas papillulas, aut aureum femur inspexit, ibi mira cum uoluptate solet lasciuire: ibi molles ac teretes lacertulos amplexatur, ibi castigatissimum ac multis expetitum pectus exosculatur. Quid igitur mirum, si omnes illi populariter inuident?"[98]

Pride's flea has a similar idea. Not as a flea, however, but as Pride in the guise of different personal perquisites, he would enjoy his progressive metamorphoses downward till he became a smock. Evidently, Pride's device for attainment belongs to the smock, not to the flea, whether he be Ovid's or anyone else's. The flea is only a notorious analogue, and is brought in by way of comparison for his ability at creeping into every corner.

We have been considering the passage in the B version. In A, the smock does not appear as such. Instead, Pride says, "indeede I doe, what doe I not?"[99] But in A, as Greg has noticed, the flea device had appeared in another connection. When Wagner promises to teach the Clown how to turn himself into anything, naming various animals, the Clown says, "if you turne me into any thing, let it be in the likenesse of a little pretie frisking flea, that I may be here and there and euery where, O Ile tickle

---

[96] Greg, *Faustus 1604-1616*, II, 2, 681-687.

[97] *P. Ovidii Nasonis Heroidvm Epistolae* (Antwerp, 1578), pp. 334-335.

[98] Caelius Calcagninus, *Opera* (Basle, 1544), pp. 406-407, *Pvllicis Encomion*. Such encomia were a regular literary exercise, with Homer's battle of the frogs and mice to lead the way and the praise of folly by Erasmus to follow after. See Baldwin, *Small Latine*, II, 339.

[99] Greg, *Faustus 1604-1616*, A, 745.

the pretie wenches plackets Ile be amongst them ifaith."[100] This is exactly
the wish and purpose of the lover in "Ovid's flea." Thus the placket
passage has no necessary intermediary connection with the smock passage. Indeed, the placket passage materalizes naturally out of the situation
as a clownish version of "Ovid's flea," and must have been in the parent
version of both A and B. For both the device of the smock and that of
the placket are from *Bacon,* where they played their parts in Ralph Simnell's plot to procure Margaret for Edward. Bacon should turn Edward
into "a silken purse, full of gold, or else a fine wrought smocke."[101] For
"if thou beest a silken purse full of gold, then on sundaies sheele hang thee
by her side, and you must not say a word. Now, sir, when she comes into
a great prease of people, for feare of the cut-purse on a sodaine sheele
swap thee into her plackerd; then, sirha, being there you may plead for
your selfe."[102] We need not repeat the device of the smock. The placket
and the smock are two separate devices to attain the same purpose, without progression or necessary connection between them. It hardly needs to
be repeated that Ovid's flea has no need for such devices; in his own right
he *is* the device. It will be seen that both of Ralph's devices do in fact
appear in *Faustus,* both times connected with "Ovid's flea," and that their
transplantation there lies behind both A and B. But "Ovid's flea" shows
that the placket passage is the primary one and the smock passage the
derivative. And "Ovid's flea" attracted both the placket and the smock
device from *Bacon.*[103]

Here we must consider another of these clown borrowings from Greene.
As Professor Law has pointed out,[104] in *Faustus* and *Looking Glasse* a
clown enjoys the prospect of being known as the man who killed the devil.
The kill-devil passage of *Faustus* appears in A but not in B. Sir Walter
Greg believes it was an insert upon A. The preceding case makes it likely
that this transplantation took place during the same operation and that it
likely lies behind both A and B, being part of the process of fitting the
clowns into this version of the play. At any rate, it is clear that the
transplantation has been from *Bacon* and *Looking Glasse* to *Faustus,* but
this applies only to the present version or versions of *Faustus,* and might
not apply at all to the original form of the play.[105]

---

[100] Greg, *Faustus 1604-1616,* A, 424-427.

[101] Collins, *Bacon,* 102-117.

[102] Collins, *Bacon,* 106-111.

[103] Of course, plackets are indigenous to such an idea, but here they are already
connected with another item which is taken over. A variant of the smock device
appears in *King Leir* (*M.S.R.,* 617-618).

[104] Law, *M.L.N.* (1911), XXVI, 147.

[105] It may be added that another item could have come in at this stage of revision
in *Faustus.* Wolfgang Bernhardi (*Robert Greene's Leben und Schriften,* p. 39)

The primary genetics of the parent version of this fourth scene of
Faustus are now clear and of unusual significance. The scene begins with
a transplantation from *A Shrew*, proceeds to devil-beating from *Looking
Glasse*, and continues with the placket device from *Bacon*. The interlarded
jests may be similar adaptations for the most part, though at least one of
them appears to be topical at the time of construction. The clowns, or
their closely cooperating agent under direction, have simply gathered
together choice bits from earlier clown roles to compile for themselves
parts for this scene, as a parody on the main action. One should remember
Kempe's applauded merriments and other analogous instances of clownish
devices. If it is a matter of heads, Greene is the only one besides the
clowns who would naturally have had all this material in one head.
Certainly Marlowe had not, and certainly we know nothing to indicate
that he would have gone to this trouble to pillage from these particular
plays. If it were not for the connection with the smock passage later, one
might think that only the clowns had been concerned in concocting this
scene. But we must not forget that the Clown's placket begot Pride's
smock. Nor may we assume that the clowns had no previous scene upon
which to build. The beard jest may be a relic of an earlier version, to
which the Greene items and topical jests were added. What a fate for
Robert Greene; to be used as patching for Christopher Marlowe! But at
whatever time it happened, it would appear probable that the beard passage was transplanted from *A Shrew* to *Faustus*.

For the fourth parallel,[106] both plays coincide in the greater part of a
line, "rauishing sound of his melodious harpe." In *Faustus*, the line was
occasioned by the source of the play. When "Mephostophiles came for his
writing," and had blared in a singing manner, etc., "Lastly, was heard by
Faustus all maner Instruments of musick, as Organs, Clarigolds, Lutes,
Viols, Citerns, Waights, Hornepipes, Fluites, Anomes, Harpes, and all
maner of other Instruments, the which so rauished his minde, that hee
thought hee had been in another world, forgat both body and soule, in so
much that he was minded neuer to change his opinion concerning that
which he had done."[107] Faustus is thinking of this when in the play he

---

pointed out that Faustus intended to surround Germany with a wall of brass, as Bacon
also intended to do with England, and opines that Marlowe was the borrower, since
Bernhardi can find in *Bacon* no borrowings from *Faustus* — which could just as well
be stated the other way around! As has been pointed out, Bacon, according to his
History, had intended to wall England with brass. So Greene clearly gets the item
from his source, not from Marlowe. But, on the other hand, Marlowe may as readily
have transferred this item from the Bacon tradition as from Greene's play. It is at
least possible, however, that it was inserted in *Faustus* at the same time and by the
same person or persons as were Ralph's devices.

[106] Greg, *Faustus 1604-1616*, p. 335.

[107] Logeman, pp. 12-13; Nan Cooke Carpenter "Music in 'Doctor Faustus' . . . ,"
NQ, 195, 181.

refers to the delights which conquered despair and prevented him from
repenting.

> hath not he that built the walles of *Thebes,*
> With rauishing sound of his melodious Harpe,
> Made musicke with my *Mephostophilis?*[108]

The harp, the last of the instruments mentioned in the source, has become
the representative of the group and has a "rauishing sound," as in the
source the instruments "rauished his minde." Quite clearly, then, the
occasion of the line in *Faustus* is from the source.

But Amphion, a master of the harp, is introduced to assist Mephostophilis. The *locus classicus* for his exploit was the *Ars Poetica* (391-396) of
Horace, where the doublet musicians Orpheus and Amphion are coupled.

> Silvestris homines sacer interpresque deorum
> caedibus et victu foedo deterruit Orpheus,
> dictus ob hoc lenire tigris rabidosque leones.
> dictus et Amphion, Thebanae conditor urbis,
> saxa movere sono testudinis et prece blanda
> ducere quo vellet.

"While men still roamed the woods, Orpheus, the holy prophet of the
gods, made them shrink from bloodshed and brutal living; hence the fable
that he tamed tigers and ravening lions; hence too the fable that Amphion,
builder of Thebes's citadel, moved stones by the sound of his lyre, and
led them whither he would by his supplicating spell."[109] Amphion did
build the walls of Thebes by persuading the stones into place by the sound
of his lyre, but the stones were not ravished. To base our translation on
Cooper, they were merely persuaded by flattering entreaty whither
Amphion willed.

The source has thus occasioned the allusion to Amphion as master of
the harp and has furnished the word ravished to describe the effect of its
sound. But why is the echo "turned"? For now the emphasis is upon the
"rauishing sound" of the harp, not upon the ravished mind of Faustus.
The answer is that "ravishing sound" was a conventional phrase for the
harp and for music generally. The earliest use of the epithet ravishing in
connection with music recorded in *N.E.D.* is from Lydgate, where it is
used for the music of the sirens. "c1430 Lydg. *Reas. & Sens.* (E. E. T. S.)
3656 Whan they harpe, pley, and synge, The noyse is so ravysshynge."
Still earlier Chaucer had said

> Of instruments of strenges in acord
> Herde I so pleye a ravysshyng swetnesse.[110]

By our period the epithet was commonplace for the effect of music. One

---

[108] Greg, *Faustus 1604-1616,* B, 597-599.

[109] Fairclough, *Horace,* pp. 482-483.

[110] *Parlement of Foules,* 197-198.

remembers Shakspere's fair queen singing "With ravishing division, to her lute."[111] Or

> Dowland to thee is dear, whose heavenly touch
> Upon the lute doth ravish human sense.[112]

Under the influence of the conventional epithet, the ravished mind of Faustus became the ravishing sound of the harp, and brought along Amphion as master to make the sound. Thus the genetics of the passage in *Faustus* are completely clear, except that we do not know what form of the epithet was in the author's head, whether the elementary form, or whether already shaped to the form of the line we are considering. The elementary form would have been sufficient; the shaped form would have made present results inevitable. But the genesis of the passage, with its occasion in the source, makes it clear that the passage belongs to the original version of *Faustus*.[113]

We turn now to a passage in *A Shrew* which uses the same part of a line without verbal and almost without literal variants. In *A Shrew* Emilia says

> And should my loue as erste did *Hercules*
> Attempt to passe the burning valtes of hell,
> I would with piteous lookes and pleasing wordes,
> As once did *Orpheus* with his harmony,
> And rauishing sound of his melodious harpe,
> Intreate grim *Pluto* and of him obtaine,
> That thou mightest go and safe retourne againe. (Sig. E3ʳ)

The passage in *A Shrew* rests consciously and allusively upon Ovid's account of the expedition of Orpheus to bring back Eurydice from the underworld. "As he spoke thus, accompanying his words with the music of his lyre, the bloodless spirits wept; Tantalus did not catch at the fleeing wave; Ixion's wheel stopped in wonder; the vultures did not pluck at the liver; the Belides rested from their urns, and thou, O Sisyphus, didst sit upon thy stone. Then first, tradition says, conquered by the song, the cheeks of the Eumenides were wet with tears; nor could the queen nor he who rules the lower world refuse the suppliant."[114] Grim Pluto and all within the burning vaults of hell were ravished by the sound of Orpheus' harp. Certainly, the figure is "proper" to *A Shrew*.

Further, the lines

> I would with piteous lookes and pleasing wordes,
> As once did *Orpheus* with his harmony,
> And rauishing sound of his melodious harpe

---

[111] *1 Henry IV*, III, 1, 210.

[112] *Passionate Pilgrim*, 107-108.

[113] Greg attributes this section to Marlowe, correctly as to these items, it would appear.

[114] F. J. Miller, *Ovid* (Loeb), II, 67 (*Met.* X, 40-47).

expand Ovid's statement

> Talia dicentem nervosque ad verba moventem
> "As he spoke thus, accompanying his words with the
> music of his lyre."

The epithet "ravishing" has been introduced to suggest the consequent effect. These minds also were ravished, though the epithet is not used. But if one knew the conventional epithet, it was certain to be suggested. And certainly it was suggested in some form, whether as simple epithet or as some variant, including the form in the line we are discussing.

So in both *A Shrew* and in *Faustus,* the source of each passage has suggested the conventional epithet. There is no sign that either passage has suggested the other as a whole, though Amphion and Orpheus were yokemates. Nor is there any certain indication that either author shaped the conventional epithet into our line. They may both have borrowed from some current version, say a song, which has not survived or we have not yet discovered. In that case, there would be no direct connection between the passages and so no indication of priority. Against this possible solution is the fact that there was certainly some direct connection between the two plays. But so far as the authorship of our line is concerned we are left just about where we began — except that we know how in each case the mind of the author worked. And if there is connection it was mediated in a very subtle way by the yoking of Orpheus with Amphion.

The fifth parallel[115] appears only in *Faustus* B, not in A, and Sir Walter considers that it belongs to Samuel Rowley. But he feels that "unfortunately this passage is one of the least convincing of the parallels, and cannot be taken by itself to prove anything at all."[116] So far as textural relationships are concerned, so be it. But the two passages share the simile of hewing a body with the sword into pieces as small as sand. In *A Shrew* it runs

> This angrie sword should rip thy hatefull chest,
> And hewd thee smaller then the *Libian* sandes . . .
>   (sig. F2ʳ)

In *Faustus* B

> And had you cut my body with your swords,
> Or hew'd this flesh and bones as small as sand.[117]

Because of its repeated use as the symbol of number, sand occurs interminably in similes of number or smallness. *A Shrew* adds a conventional epithet in *Libian*. For instance, Textor gives under Libya,

Arenosa   Quint. Intrat arenosam Libyen, ubi torrida semper Ardet humus.

---

[115] Greg, *Faustus 1604-1616,* p. 368.

[116] Greg, *Faustus 1604-1616,* p. 28.

[117] Greg, *Faustus 1604-1616,* B, 1449-50.

Libya was a conventional butt for such similes.[118]   There is thus no indication whether the epithet, being merely conventional, has been added or has been omitted. But the complete simile of body-hewing was not widely used,[119] and if connection be granted between the two plays — as it must — then it is likely that the simile in one of these plays has suggested its use in the other. But which borrowed from which is not directly apparent.

In his examination of these five parallels, Sir Walter simply assumed that "it is unquestionably *A Shrew* that is the debtor";[120] but the evidence of the first and third parallels appears to show conclusively that the debt was the other way round, though this opposite conclusion strengthens rather than weakens Sir Walter's case as to the relation of *Faustus* A and B. The next question is as to the time when these materials were taken into *Faustus*. The night setting in the source could readily have been the occasion for borrowing the first of our parallels for appropriate ornamentation to *Faustus,* as eventually it was certainly so borrowed. If the occasion was from the source, then this parallel was borrowed by Marlowe himself for his original version. Of the other parallels, only the third and fourth are accepted by Sir Walter as strong enough for certainty. Sir Walter attributes these along with the first to Marlowe. This also would likely mean that they belonged to the original structure of the play.

We must now face certain facts. *Faustus* borrows as intimately, though not as widely[121] from *A Shrew* as *A Shrew* borrows from *Tamburlaine*. *A Shrew* has not been connected by comparable borrowing with any other play. The connection is with Marlowe only, and with two of his plays only. And the play is sandwiched between, with borrowing both ways. What is the explanation of this intimate relationship, which is certainly beyond the ordinary process of imitative borrowing? No other plays of the period are bound together more intimately by borrowings than these three (four), not even those of Greene. And why did Greene parody a speech in *A Shrew* to poke fun at Marlowe's style? The obvious answer is that Greene thought Marlowe was guilty of the speech. And some of his choicest bits, such as Boreas' chin, to which he adds the bull's dewlap, are not in any of the accepted works of Marlowe. How could he expect

---

[118] H. N. Hillebrand, *Troilus and Cressida* (Furness Variorum), pp. 74-75.

[119] One is likely to remember the thorough "dismay" of Guyle at the hands of Talus.

> he with his yron flayle
> Gan driue at him, with so huge might and maine,
> That all his bones, as small as sandy grayle
> He broke (*Faerie Queene,* V. ix, 19, 2-5).

[120] Greg, *Faustus 1604-1616,* p. 28.

[121] The fact that the comic business of *Faustus* has been so completely revamped might partially account for this.

anyone to recognize Marlowe as the butt of his fantasy, if that person did not also think that Marlowe was the author of this outstanding "flight of fancy" in *A Shrew?* An unknown imitative author whom Greene took to be Marlowe will not do if, as the evidence indicates, Marlowe in *Faustus* in turn borrowed from *A Shrew,* as *A Shrew* borrowed from *Tamburlaine.*[122]

After a careful study of the materials of Marlowe's figures (not actually his "images" at all) and the parallel uses in *A Shrew,* Dr. Marion Bodwell Smith[123] concludes, "But the problem of the Marlovian imagery in *The Taming of A Shrew* is more than one of plagiarism; its author seems at times to have almost thought like Marlowe. It appears probable that, whether as collaborator in an original play, or as assistant in the piracy of an existing one, the author of certain parts of *The Taming of A Shrew* was a member of the company that acted Marlowe's plays and so heard his 'high astounding terms' rolled off the tongues of his fellows day after day until they became second nature to him." But why should his "second nature" extend only to *Tamburlaine?* and why did Marlowe then lift some of the resultant passages in *A Shrew* for *Faustus?* And why did this saturated imitator produce no more such adaptations? Whether I like it or not, I cannot account for the demonstrated facts in any other way than by common authorship for these Marlovian passages, especially since Greene so obviously assumed that Marlowe was the author of the passage he burlesques.[124]

If Marlowe had at least a hand in *A Shrew,* the same explanation of repetitions would then serve as has been given for a similar phenomenon in Chapman. "Chapman very frequently used material in the same or a slightly different form twice or more often in his poems and plays. Apparently, he kept a commonplace-book for verses of his own composition, and drew upon it as occasion served, and was not careful to avoid the repetitions which abound in his plays and poems with such extraordinary frequency, such repeated passages sometimes containing as many as nine lines."[125] Chapman ought to be able to keep Marlowe in countenance upon this quite usual procedure, whether Marlowe kept a commonplace-

---

[122] If we should break the evidence that *Faustus* borrowed from *A Shrew,* then we would place both *Tamburlaine* and *Faustus* before August, 1589. We would then have explained why these two plays are coupled in *A Shrew.* But we would still not have explained the mental processes of the author of the Marlovian passages in *A Shrew,* nor why nothing else of his is known.

[123] Smith, *Marlowe's Imagery,* pp. 142-149.

[124] J. M. Robertson, *The Shakespeare Canon,* Pt. II, pp. 139 ff., argues Marlowe's revision in *A Shrew.* The objections of Boas to Pegasus and to Ibis are, as we have seen, groundless (Boas, *A Shrew,* pp. xxxi-xxxii). Nor is the argument of absurdity and grotesqueness valid, especially when the author's whole aim in the presentation of Ferando's "fantastic . . . humour" was to be absurd.

[125] Charles Crawford, *Englands Parnassus,* p. 517.

book or not. Imitative transplantation and variation was a fundamental literary device in the age, and can be demonstrated in any literary figure of the age. They had not our prejudices for "originality." But it is not my purpose here to argue for or against the authorship of Marlowe in *A Shrew;* I am, however, decidedly puzzled to know how anyone else could have selected and used Marlowe's work in quite this way. And I must believe that Greene knew what he was about in pointing the finger at Marlowe.

At any rate, the *Tamburlaine* element was in *A Shrew* before August 23, 1589, approximately, at least, in the same form as now. Nor is there anything to show that the whole play had not already taken approximately or entirely the shape in which it was printed in 1594. Presumably Greene and Nashe thought it was Marlowe's latest play when they were writing in the summer of 1589.

CHAPTER IV

The Chronology of Christopher Marlowe's Plays

The girdings of Greene fortunately give us a considerable amount of information as to the chronology of Marlowe's plays. In probably our first literary reference to Marlowe,[1] Greene is attacking Marlowe and another. With the last scratches of a pen made vitriolic by an alleged surfeit from too much Rhenish wine and pickled herring Greene was still attacking, among others, Christopher Marlowe.

In the epistle prefixed to *Perimedes the Blacke-Smith*, S.R. March 29, 1588, Greene speaks with considerably less than respect of "that Atheist *Tamburlan*," "daring God out of heauen," an exploit of *2 Tamburlaine*.[2] Sir Edmund Chambers has identified a reference which shows that *2 Tamburlaine* was being performed by the Admiral's men just before November 16, 1587.[3] It follows that both parts of *Tamburlaine* are earlier than November 16, 1587.[4] They were entered S.R. August 14, 1590, and printed the same year as having belonged to the Admiral's men. On the other hand, Marlowe took his M.A. from Cambridge in 1587.[5] It is thus reasonably established that *1 Tamburlaine* was written hardly earlier than the summer of 1587, and that *2 Tamburlaine* followed before November 16, 1587, both for the Admiral's men.

We have seen that Nashe in his preface to *Menaphon* about August, 1589, probably alludes to a speech in *Faustus*.[6] Kocher has located a bit of evidence which shows Nashe's interest in *Faustus*, recorded in a book to which Nashe refers in this preface. Sir Walter Greg sums soundly and adds to the evidence thus: "A copy of John Leland's *Principum*

---

[1] Tucker Brooke, "The Reputation of Christopher Marlowe," *Transactions of the Connecticut Academy of Arts and Sciences* (1921), XXV, 351.

[2] See Malone in Brooke, "The Marlowe Canon," *P.M.L.A.* (1922), XXXVII, 390.

[3] *T.L.S.,* August 28, 1930, p. 684.

[4] For the puzzling connection with Paul Ive's *Practise of Fortification* (1589), see Ellis-Fermor, *Tamburlaine,* pp. 8-10, 45. Marlowe has the Latin form *quinqueangle,* Ives the French *cynqueangle*. Surely Marlowe is quite thoroughly misunderstanding some Latin original common to both him and Ives, as he could hardly have done so well from the English and illustrations of Ives. Incidentally, the *quinqueangle* is not a five-pointed star; that would give the five acute angles of a triangle, the most objectionable of all figures; it is a pentagon.

[5] Brooke, *Life of Marlowe,* p. 32.

[6] See above, pp. 112 ff.

ac illustrium aliquot et eruditorum in Anglia virorum encomia (London, 1589) from the Harmsworth collection, now in the Folger Library, contains what Kocher believes to be the signature and autograph marginalia of Thomas Nashe. I have examined photostats of these. That the signature is his there appears to me little doubt, and that the notes in question are also in his hand is at least highly probable. One of these is 'Faust*us*: Che sara · sara deuinynitie adieu' (*sic?* but the 'y' looks more like a 'g' . . .); in another the last two words appear to be repeated (but the writing is obscure and the spelling at least is different) together with what Kocher deciphers as 'Faust*us*: studie in indian silke'. . . . That the writer was recalling Marlowe's play is obvious. Further, it would appear that Nashe was acquainted with Leland's work soon after its publication (preface to Greene's *Menaphon* (entered 23 Aug., 1589), ed. McKerrow, iii. 320, line 28) and it is likely enough that he wrote his name in the volume the same year. But that the references to *Faustus,* supposing them to be his, were entered at the same time is admittedly a matter of doubtful inference. They have no relevance to anything in the text, and there is therefore no reason to suppose that they were written in the course of reading the book. Like some other scribbles in the volume they are evidently pen trials."[7] While there is no certainty, yet it is at least granted that Nashe had in his physical possession a copy of this book to which he refers in work entered August 23, 1589. The natural inference, therefore, is that he had come into possession of this copy in 1589 before he refers to it in August, and had examined it for use in his work. McKerrow does not note any further use of the book by Nashe. The expected time for pen trials within a book would be while the writer was going through the book — fly-leaves are likely to catch anything at any time, and these jottings are perilously near the end! While, therefore, the evidence is not conclusive, it nevertheless does give a probability that Nashe had *Faustus* on his mind while he was writing the preface to *Menaphon,* and this in turn bolsters the probability that Marlowe is the person who is accused in that preface of thrusting Elysium into Hell.

Another way of approaching the date of *Faustus* is through its source, which is customarily said to have been "The Historie of the damnable life, and deserued death of Doctor Iohn Faustus, Newly imprinted, and in conuenient places imperfect matter amended: according to the true Copie printed at Franckfort, and translated into English by P. F. Gent.," this being the title page of the first known edition, printed at London in 1592 by Thomas Orwin for Edward White. Since the title page states that this is not the first edition, the question becomes: When would an earlier edition have been available for the use of Marlowe?

---

[7] Greg, *Faustus 1604-1616,* p. 8, n. 2.

Our most definite point of departure is a record made December 18, 1592, by the Court of the Stationers' Company.

Abell Ieffes   Yt is ordered: that if the book of D[oct]ʊɾ ſauſtuſ ſhall not
Tho. Orwin   be found in the hall book entred to Richard Oliff before Abell
                Ieffes claymed the same w[hich] was about May last · That
then the seid copie shall Remayne to the said Abell as his prop[er] copie from
the tyme of his first clayme w[hich] was about May Last as aforesaid/[8]

The implication of "Remayne" would seem to be that the first claim of Jeffes about May had been recognized, and that before December 18, Thomas Orwin in the name of Richard Oliff had disputed the claim. The test is to be whether Oliff had made a prior claim by an official entry. Otherwise, the first claim of Jeffes in May was to stand. This ruling would not imply that Oliff did have a claim before May; he simply must have made an official claim before Jeffes did in May, if his claim was to be recognized. The entry does not, therefore, as a matter of fact imply that anyone thought he had a claim before May except possibly Jeffes. No such entry survives for either Oliff or Jeffes, then or later, though the eventual right of Jeffes is recognized indirectly when Edward White entered the book April 5, 1596, "he havinge th[e]interest of ABELL IEFFES thereto."[9] The book had thus evidently "remained" with Jeffes "as his prop[er] copie" from the time of his "first clayme" about May, 1592.

But while White entered the book only so late as April 5, 1596, yet Orwin had printed an edition for him in 1592, and the order of the Court in some way connects with this fact, the question before the Court being whether Jeffes or Orwin had the right to the book. Orwin claimed by December 18 through Oliff; Jeffes had made a claim about May. Orwin and Jeffes were printers and would expect to make their money by printing for a publisher. Thus in December, 1592, Orwin the printer wanted the right to print for some publisher, and Jeffes the printer had blocked him with his claim of about May, 1592. Apparently Orwin was not planning to print for Oliff, since in that case Oliff should himself have pressed his own claim. Since Orwin did print for White, it would appear that Orwin had presumed that he had in some way acquired from Oliff, a publisher, a right to print, but that he wished to do so for White, as eventually he did.

On what the rival claims of Oliff the publisher and Jeffes the printer were based we do not know. It is certain that by or before May, 1592, Jeffes had printed or had hoped eventually to print an edition for some publisher. About May he found it advisable to defend his claim. He did not then enter the book; he simply claimed it, as already his. In the light of later events, we infer that the occasion was probably the desire of

---

[8] W. W. Greg and E. Boswell, *Records* (1930), p. 44.

[9] Arber, *Transcript*, III, 63.

others to print an edition. As to the claim of the publisher Oliff, we have no hint further than that it must depend upon his having made an official entry previous to the claim of Jeffes, as he had not done. Consequently, the claim by Jeffes of previous ownership stood. Since there were no penalties attached in December, there was no question of offensive action having already been taken on either side. Presumably, therefore, White the publisher procured the right of Jeffes the printer as recognized by this ruling, under such terms that Orwin could proceed with the edition of 1592, after December 18. How far Orwin had already gone or could have gone without being liable to penalty we do not know.

It should be noticed also that this order does not stand alone. For Jeffes had been in trouble with these authorities for several months, and this session of the Court was devoted almost entirely to clearing up his misordered affairs. It is not likely, therefore, that the order had been elicited by a second claim of Jeffes, as a strict interpretation of the wording of the order would imply. Apparently "the tyme of his first clayme" means merely the time when he first made his claim. In all this, the primary antagonist of Jeffes was Edward White. White and Jeffes had swapped trouble over *The Spanish Tragedy,* entered to Jeffes October 6, 1592, and *Arden of Feversham,* entered to White April 3, 1592. Each had offended by printing the other's play. So all the books of each impression were to be confiscate, forfeited, and "disposed to thuse of the poore of the companye." Each was also to pay a ten shilling fine, and the Court would defer the question of imprisonment, to which the offenders were liable besides, "till some other convenient tyme." The penalties imposed here are a sufficient indication that no overt offense had been committed in the case of the *History.*

This edition of the *History* in 1592 indicates specifically on its title page that it is not the first, just as the counter claims of Jeffes and Oliff have done by implication. By its statement that it has been "Seene and allowed," it also claims to have followed authorized procedure, though this gives no indication of when or by whom. All these statements may have appeared on one or more preceding editions, since such title pages were ordinarily set up with little change except accumulative errors. The title page claims that the *History* is "Newly imprinted, and in conuenient places imperfect matter amended: according to the true Copie printed at Franckfort, and translated into English by P. F. Gent." It is possible to wrest the meaning of this piecemeal. But it is clearly intended to convey the information to the public that this is an emended edition. When this statement is taken in conjunction with the records of 1592, I believe there can be no question that there had been at least one previous edition. That edition would have been before May, 1592. For if Oliff was concerned with it, the Court ruled that he should have made an entry before May,

1592. Jeffes did not enter the work in May; he simply claimed it then, and later his claim was recognized and passed to White, who eventually made record in 1596 of the transfer. Jeffes had in some way already acquired the eventually recognized right before May, 1592, which he claimed at that time. Thus the indications are that there had been at least one edition before May, 1592. There is no indication, of course, of how long before May, 1592, the next preceding edition had been, nor that there had been only one.

The first English edition of the *History* could have been at any reasonable time after the appearance of the German *Historia* at Frankfort in 1587. The preface to the German book is dated September 4, 1587,[10] and the volume would have been ready for the October Fair. It is said to have had two reprints and an enlarged edition the same year. Such a sensation was certain to come back to England, at least as likely to London as to either university, from the Frankfort Fair in October, 1587, and it was this first form of 1587, not the enlarged form of 1587, or later enlargements, etc., that P. F. used for his translation. The story had reached the ballad stage in England by February 28, 1589, *"A ballad of the life and deathe of Doctor FFAUSTUS, the great Cunngerer."*[11] The ballad does not survive, and so we do not know whether it was based upon German or English materials. I should judge from custom that such a ballad was far more likely to be based upon an English book or play. It is simply too much to believe that such a sensation had to wait five years to get translated and into print — to prove popular for a century! The natural inference from the known habits of the booktrade is that copies of the first form of the *Historia* came back to England from the October Fair at Frankfort in 1587, that P. F. Gent immediately translated one of these (not the enlarged form later that year), and that his work became available in print not later than 1588. Marlowe could then have used the translation, and the ballad could have been based upon either the translation or Marlowe's play. At any rate, the first edition by P. F. could have been as early as 1588, and hence Marlowe's *Faustus,* if based upon it, may also be that early. In the nature of the case, it is likely to have followed hard upon the first edition of the *History.*

Boas believes that "there is no doubt that the English *History* was Marlowe's only authority."[12] It is easily possible to doubt, and it has been doubted, that the English *History* was Marlowe's only source. Jantz

[10] Greg, *Faustus 1604-1616,* p. 1, n. 1.

[11] Arber, *Transcript,* II, 516. For various other instances of English interest in the story of Faust and Wagner 1589-92, see Kocher, *M.L.N.* (1940), LV, 95-101; (1943), LVIII, 539-542; Greg, *Faustus 1604-1616,* p. 5, n. 1; H. Jantz, "An Elizabethan Statement on the Origin of the German Faust Book," *J.E.G.P.,* LI, 137-153; and the references cited in these.

[12] Boas, *Faustus,* p. 11.

contends that Marlowe may have known the hypothetical Latin original of the Faust story from which all traditions, including that in German, are alleged to derive, that this would explain how Marlowe knew some things in the German Faust tradition which are not to be found in the English tradition, and that the question of date for a first printing of the English translation thus has no bearing upon the date of Marlowe's *Faustus;* "its date can confidently be determined only on the basis of other evidence, external and internal."[13] But granting a Latin original, no copy survives for inspection; and consequently we have no way of knowing that it contained all the details which P. F. did not find in the Frankfort book, some of which were used by Marlowe. They may, indeed, have been there; but then again they may not; we simply do not know. The first surviving edition of the English *History* claims to be "according to the true Copie printed at Franckfort," not according to a manuscript in any language. And not a single copy of such a manuscript in Latin is known to survive; copies could not have been widely available. While there could be no evidence that Marlowe did not use the hypothetical original, there can equally be no evidence that he did, until we have the *corpus delicti,* or at least some relevant fragments thereof. The English version does account for Marlowe's knowledge of fact as at present verifiable, as Boas contends.[14] But it is highly precarious to assume that it was Marlowe's only authority, especially since it is unnecessary to assume it. The upshot is that we are perfectly free to date Marlowe's *Faustus* wherever other evidence may place it.

We have examined above what I would consider strong evidence that *Faustus* was written probably before August, 1589. Of further evidence there is not much. In Middleton's *Black Booke,* 1604, we read, "He had a head of hair like one of my devils in *Doctor Faustus,* when the old theatre cracked and frighted the audience."[15] As Chambers says, "This was presumably before 1592, as *Dr. Faustus* seems to have been continuously in Henslowe's [Alleyn's] hands from the beginning of that year."[16] There may be another reference to this occurrence. In his *Orlando Furioso,* Ariosto writes that when Astolpho blew his magic horn

> Si nel cor de la gente il timor preme,
> Che per disio di fuga si trabocca
> Giù del theatro sbigottita, e smorta;
> Non che lasci la guardia de la porta.

> Come talhor si gitta, e si periglia
> E da finestra, e da sublime loco

[13] Jantz, *J.E.G.P.,* LI, 153.
[14] Boas, *Faustus,* 13-14.
[15] Bullen, *Middleton,* VIII, 13.
[16] Chambers, *E.S.,* II, 395, n. 2.

> L'esterrefatta subito famiglia:
> Che uede appresso, e d'ogn'intorno il foco,
> Che mentre le tenea graui le ciglia
> Il pigro sonno, crebbe à poĉò à poĉo.
> Cosi messa la uita in abandono
> Ogn'un fuggia lo spauentoso suono.[17]

Catching at the word *theatro,* Sir John Harington in his translation of 1592 changes the simile entirely.

> So great a terrour in their minds was bred,
> That straight as if with sprits they had been scard,
> This way and that, confusedly they fled,
> And left the gates without defence or guard,
> As tumultes often are at stage playes bred,
> When false reportes of sudden fires are heard,
> Or when the ouerloden seates do cracke,
> One tumbling downe vpon an others backe.[18]

Here the audience is frightened into panic by spirits as in the *Black Book,* or when the overloaded seats crack (break), as the Theatre is said to have cracked. It looks as if Middleton is referring to some actual occurrence at the Theater before 1592, which Harington may be echoing in his translation, which was entered February 26, 1591. But if *Faustus* was the play, as Middleton alleges, then the incident hardly took place after 1590, when Alleyn, who owned the play, and the Admiral's men had left the Theater, following upon the events of November 24.

For internal evidence of dating, there is a "very dubious reference" to Cavendish's circumnavigation of the globe, July 21, 1586, to September 10, 1588.[19] Again, Faustus says

> I'll levy soldiers with the coin they bring,
> And chase the Prince of Parma from our land,
> And reign sole king of all the Provinces;
> Yea, stranger engines for the brunt of war,
> Than was the fiery keel at Antwerpe bridge,
> I'll make my servile spirits to invent.[20]

The"fiery keel" refers to an anti-Parma exploit of April 4, 1585. Parma was "the Spanish Governor-General of the Netherlands, then technically part of the Empire, from 1579 to 1592."[21] But "After 1590 Parma was fighting in France, and the boast would have no point."[22]

The evidence, therefore, would indicate that *Faustus* was written in

---

[17] Ariosto, *Orlando Furioso* (Venice, 1567), p. 233, Canto XX, 88, 89.

[18] John Harington, *Orlando Furioso* (1591), Bk. XX, 61. For the cracking of the seats, the notorious instance at Paris Garden would do quite well.

[19] Brooke, *P.M.L.A.* (1922), XXXVII, 380, n. 43.

[20] Boas, *Faustus,* I, 1, 93-98 (120-125).

[21] Boas, *Faustus,* p. 62.

[22] Bakeless, *Tragicall History,* I, 276.

fairly close sequence with *Tamburlaine,* and *A Shrew,* after the latter play, which was in existence by August, 1589, when *Faustus* itself may also be referred to. Its relation to its source as well as such echoes of contemporary matters as have been noticed harmonize with such a date about the first half of 1589. It survives only in forms which were certainly the outcome of severe rehashing, but nothing is to be gained for our present purpose by shedding tears over its later awful fate.

The Jew of Malta appears in Henslowe's Diary as an old play February 26, 1592. On the other hand, its prologue refers to the death of the Duke of Guise, December 23, 1588. Machiavel says as prologue (1-8, Bennett's edition)

> Albeit the world think Machiavel is dead,
> Yet was his soul but flown beyond the Alps;
> And, now the Guise is dead, is come from France,
> To view this land, and frolic with his friends.
> To some perhaps my name is odious,
> But such as love me, guard me from their tongues,
> And let them know that I am Machiavel,
> And weigh not men, and therefore not men's words.

Being now again disembodied, Machiavelli's soul could have come to England immediately after December 23, 1588 — as soon, in fact, as the news could reach England. Machiavelli's first application is to religion, leading to the summary statement "I count religion but a childish toy," which serves as transition to the state, where his topic view is that might makes right. Here it will be well to remember Meyer's surprise; "Having heard from the prologue of the 'Jew of Malta' that Machiavelli's spirit had once taken up habitation in the Guise, we would naturally expect to find a disciple of his in the 'Massacre at Paris'; but, although he is a murderer, dissembler, and poisoner, there is no Machiavellian feature in this mutilated play except the Guise's hypocrisy in religion."[23] That fact calls for careful consideration, both as to what Marlowe meant when he referred to Machiavelli and as to what others meant when they called Marlowe a Machiavellian. It will not do to assume with Meyer that we can interpret in terms of Gentillet's Machiavelli — or "true" Machiavelli either.

We can get the French background for Marlowe's statement in its proper contemporary perspective from Antony Colynet, *The True History of the Ciuill Warres of France . . . vntill this present October. 1591.* Colynet represents Henry III as being under the domination of his mother and the Guise, Machiavellians all. "Up then old MEDEA, you must shewe yet once againe some of your olde Italian trickes. Old CATIE must bee the market woman, she shall make the bargayne. But for as much as two eyes doo see more than one, she shall haue some counsellers appoynted

---

[23] Edward Meyer, *Machiavelli and the Elizabethan Drama,* p. 56.

her in that negotiation, such as would not suffer her to doo any good vnto the King and the Realme, if she had been willing so to doo; for they were al the Kings enemies, addicted to the Leaguers, and such as would haue taught Italian trickes the busiest head of all *Florence,* yea such as would haue sent the great Prophet of *Italy* MACHIUELL, with all his diuellish Prophecies, to his Christcrosse."[24]

"Thus hee weakened his royall authority, by following the counsell of Italians, thrusted into his seruice by the cunning of the *Guyzes* for that intent. These Italian scholemasters did endeuour alwaies to rule him by the preceptes of MACHIAUELL the Italian prophet: so that after he came to the Crowne, the *Guyzes* with their adherents interrupted diuers times the peace made with them of the religion."[25]

"There is no doubt but he had a will and purpose to be reuenged of them: but being a scholler of the villanous and prophane Atheist the Italian MACHIAUELL, whose philosophie he had hardly studied by the counsell of his godles mother, and of some villanous scullions Italians which were about her, hee supposed that he could be reuenged better by craftinesse and surprising of them, then by force."[26] Whatever his exact source, Marlowe is presenting this Huguenot view of the role of the Guise in France.

As we turn to England, who were the religious and political Machiavellians there following December 23, 1588, to replace Guise in France as a repository for Machiavelli's soul? The answer is Martin Marprelate and his followers. *Antimartinvs* (1589) shows considerable kinship to Marlowe's statement. "I had thought Nicolaus Machiavelli was dead long since; but perhaps he descended living to hell and when he was about to descend left his redoubled spirit to these politicians. For he taught princes to contemn religion; these not that only but also show a most cunning and artificial means of contemning."[27]

The earliest instances I have noticed of coupling Martin and Machiavelli directly are in *Martins Months minde,* published about October, 1589.[28] Under the figure of a school divided into four forms, the author says, "I meddle not here with the *Anabaptists, Famely louists, Machiauellists,* nor *Atheists;* neither doo I mention them in *Martins formes;* not for that they are strangers vnto his schoole; but because in trueth they are so generallie scattered, thoroughout cuerie forme: as all his formes are ful of them, and therefore can make no one forme of them selues" (D2[r&v]). In reporting to his sons the causes of his death, one of Martin's

[24] Antony Colynet, *True History* (1591), p. 37.

[25] Colynet, *True History* (1591), pp. 41-42.

[26] Colynet, *True History* (1591), p. 263.

[27] *Antimartinvs* (1589), p. 25.

[28] McKerrow, *Nashe,* V, 53, n. 2.

items is labeled "A Macheuillein tricke of the Martinists yet in practise."
Martin confesses it was a mistake to attack the Queen's Council. "Againe
(which worse was) manie of them I slandered against mine owne knowledge; & thought it enough, if I might but deuise against them the vilest
things of the world, to bring them in hatred with the credulous multitude:
(a diuellish tricke, my sonnes, which I learned in Machiuell, but take
heede of it for it asketh vengeance). As some to be Papists, whom I
knew to be sound Protestants: some to fauour the Spaniards, who I
knew detested them: Some to bee traitors, who my conscience tolde me
were good subiects" (F2ᵛ-F3ʳ). In Martin's will, "Item, I bequeath to
my lay brethren, my works of Machiuell, with my marginall notes, and
scholies therevpon; wishing them to peruse, and mark them well, being
the verie Thalmud, and Alcoran of all our *Martinisme*" (G2ʳ). This item
is labeled in the margin, "His workes of Machiuell." One of the epitaphs
by N. N. runs

> Lament you fooles, ye vices make your moane,
> Yee *Ribaulds,* railers, and yee lying lads:
> Yee Scismatiques, and Sectaries, each one:
> Yee *Malcontents,* and eke ye *mutinous swads:*
> Yee *Machiuelists, Athiests,* and each mischieuous head:
> Bewaile, for *Martin* your great Captaine's dead (H1ᵛ).

The author himself contributes a Latin epitaph, a stanza of which runs

> O vos Martinistae
> Et vos Brounistae,
> Et Famililouistae,
> Et Anabaptistae,
> Et omnes sectistae,
> Et Machiuelistae,
> Et Atheistae,
> Quorum dux fuit iste,
>   Lugete singuli (H2ᵛ).

As the title put it, Martin was "the great makebate of *England,* and father
of the Factious." He was the Machiavellian of the Machiavellians in
exactly the same sense and role that Guise had harbored the soul of
Machiavelli in France.

Another pamphlet shortly after, which is dated October 20 and refers
to the preceding, links Martin, Machiavelli, and Savonarola. This is *The
Returne of the renowned Caualiero Pasquill of England.* "Howe odious
and how dangerous innouations of Religion are, Secretarie *Machiauell,* a
pollitick not much affected to any Religion, discloseth by the example of
Fryer *Sauanaroll.* He was a man like *Martin,* sprong vp in such a time as
Martin, when Spayne, Fraunce, Rome, Arragon, and the Emperour,
entred a league to make warre altogether vppon the Venetians. . . . I
muse howe any state man can abide to heare of innouasions in Religion

where the trueth is preached?"[29] When this treatment of Savonarola was
objected to, the author replied in *The First parte of Pasquils Apologie*
(dated July 2, 1590), "I thinke well with M. *Foxe* and M. *Beza* of that
which was good in Fryer *Sauanaroll*, though I compared him with *Martin*
for hys factious head, pleading in Florence as Martin did in England, for
a newe gouernment, at such a time as Armes and inuasion clattered about
their eares. It may be I am of some better sente then you take me for,
and finding a Machiauellian tricke in this plot of innouation, I was the
more willing to lay *Sauanarols* example before your eyes, that hauing
recourse vnto *Machiauell* in whom it is recorded, you might see *Machiauels*
iudgment vpon the same. His opinion is, that when such a peaze may be
drawne through the noses of the people as to beare a change, the Maisters
of the Faction are most happie; they may doe what they lust without
controlment."[30]

Thus Martin is accused of "innovation" against both church and state at
exactly the time when England was being attacked from without. For as
A Whip for an Ape had put the case, probably early in October, 1589,

> Yes, he that now saith, Why should Bishops bee?
> Will next crie out, Why Kings? The Saincts are free.
>
> The *Germaine* Boores with Clergie men began,
>   But neuer left till Prince and Peeres were dead:
> *Iacke Leydon* was a holie zealous man,
>   But ceast not till the Crowne was on his head.
> And *Martins* mate *Iacke Strawe* would alwaies ring
> The Clergies faults, but sought to kill the King.
>
> . . . .
>
> The thing that neither Pope with Booke nor Bull,
>   Nor *Spanish* King with ships could do without,
> Our *Martins* here at home will worke at full;
>   If Prince curbe not betimes that rabble rout.
> That is, destroy both Church, and State, and all;
> For if t'one faile, the other needes must fall.[31]

Pappe with an hatchet, about the same date as the preceding pamphlets,
agrees with them; "when we finde that to the rule of the Church, the
whole state of the Realme is linckt, & that they filching away Bishop by
Bishop, seeke to fish for the Crown, and glew to their newe Church their
owne conclusions, we must then say, let Bishops stand, & they hang; that
is, goe home" (C3[v]). More specifically, "Because they say, *Aue Caesar,*
therefore they meane nothing against *Caesar.* There may bee hidden
vnder their long gownes, short daggers, and so in blearing *Caesars* eyes,

---

[29] McKerrow, *Nashe,* I, 79.

[30] McKerrow, *Nashe,* I, 113; cf. III, 348-349.

[31] *Whip for an Ape,* pp. 5-6. Some of these items are to be found in the anti-
Martinist pamphlets of Leonard Wright.

conspire *Caesars* death. God saue the Queene; why it is the Que which
they take from the mouthes of all traytors, who though they bee throughly
coninced, both by proofe and their owne confessions, yet at the last
gaspe they crie, God saue the Queene. GOD saue the Queene (say I) out
of their hands, in whose hearts (long may the Queene thus gouerne) is
not engrauen" (D3^r).

Marre Mar-Martin [1590] pronounces "a plague o' both your houses,"
coupling both Martin and Mar-Martin with the Jesuits and Machiavel,
since "All helpe to pull Religion downe."

> my name (said he) is *Lucian.*
> This is a *Iesuite,* quoth he,
> These *Martin* and *Mar-martin* be:
> I seeke but now for *Machyuell,*
> And then we would be gone to hell.

These literary opponents of Martin agree that through this religious
factionalism both church and state will be pulled down, and they cite
various instances. Marlowe implies that the Machiavellian Guise had
attempted this same kind of "innovation" in France and that Guise being
dead Machiavelli's soul has now come to frolic with friends in England.
After the death of Guise in France December 23, 1588, it was said in
England by October, 1589, that the Martinists were Machiavellians, and
this was certainly the first large issue with which Machiavelli's name was
strongly associated in England after the death of Guise.[32] The concatenation of events makes it certain that Marlowe is here showing an anti-
Martinist bias, which is immediately coupled with an anti-Roman
pronouncement, as is characteristic of Marlowe, also of the anti-
Martinists. But probably as early as May, 1589, Martin was accused
of being the friend of the Pope.

> Here hangs knaue *Martine* a traitorous Libeler he was
> Enemie pretended but in hart a friend to the Papa.[33]

Martin was a traitor to England, and really a friend to the Pope. Marlowe's Machiavelli was indifferent; he made popes only to pull them down.

---

[32] For early uses of "Machiavellian" in England, see *N.E.D.* In 1572, Parker admitted that he sometimes used the term "Machiavel-governance," but did not think it
advisable for Bartholomew Clerke to use it in a reply to Nicholas Sanders. "In one
or two Places the Author had given a stroke of his Pen, against the secret Favour
and Connivence, that some enjoyed, who opposed the Ecclesiastical Rites and Customs
established in the Church; which the Archbishop used to stile *Machiavel-governance,*
or by such like Terms" (Strype, *Parker,* p. 382). This "secret Favour and Connivence" stemmed from Leicester, the champion of the Protestant non-conformists,
whom the Roman Catholics also regularly labeled as a Machiavellian (see, for instance, *The Copie of a Leter,* 1584). The argument that the dissenters would not stop
with the church but would also subvert civil rule goes back at least to Pope Adrian,
writing November 25, 1522 (Foxe, John, *Actes* (1583), p. 855).

[33] *Mar-Martine* (1589), end of pamphlet.

He was equally indifferent to the church and state in England. It was merely the best theater for his endeavors now that Guise was dead.

Marlowe's anti-papal pronouncement is also identifiable.

> Though some speak openly against my books,
> Yet will they read me, and thereby attain
> To Peter's chair; and, when they cast me off,
> Are poison'd by my climbing followers.
> I count religion but a childish toy,
> And hold there is no sin but ignorance (10-15).

This allusion belongs to the same background of international intrigue as does that to Guise. Of this, Antony Colynet contributes his picturesque account in 1591. "After the death of Frier SIXTUS, which was hastened by the Spanish faction with a little slubber sauce, was elected a newe Vicar of *Rome,* of the house of *Sfondraty,* if I remember well, and is as much to say as burst bellie, naming himselfe GREGORY the 14."[34] Nashe knows the same story. "In Rome the Papal Chayre is washt, euery fiue yeare at the furthest, with this oyle of Aconitum. I pray God, the King of Spayne feasted not our holy father *Sextus,* that was last, with such conserue of Henbane, for it was credibly reported hee loued him not."[35] Following Sixtus V, the mortality of popes was very high. As G. B. puts it in *A Fig for the Spaniard* (1591, S.R. January 31, 1592), "The last pope finely, and wittily denied the king of Spaine manie requestes: These and such like dealinges haue caused the deathes of 5. Popes within these 17. monethes" (C4^v). Dr. McKerrow gives the statistics thus, "The succession of Popes was very rapid at this time, namely Urban VII (Sept. 15-27, 1590), Gregory XIV (Dec. 5, 1590-Oct. 15, 1591), Innocent IX (Oct. 29-Dec. 30, 1591), Clement VIII (Jan. 30, 1592-1605). As Sixtus V had been hostile to the Spanish party great efforts were made at his death to secure the election of an adherent, and Urban VII and Innocent IX were strongly Spanish in sympathies, while Gregory XIV and Clement VIII were, though less devoted partisans, considered as satisfactory and supported by the Spanish cardinals."[36]

The allegations of poisoning center upon Sixtus V, who had played the Machiavellian finely to get the papal chair. Under his predecessor, "On le voyait rarement en public, et s'il lui arrivait de se montrer, sa demarche penible, son corps voute, sa voix faible, une toux continuelle, enfin tous les symptomes d'une vieillesse anticipée faisaient croire que sa fin etait prochaine. S'il faut ajouter foi a ses chroniqueurs, qui a la verite sont pour la plupart ses ennemis, il parait que ces considerations determinerent le conclave a l'elire pape, le 24 avril 1585. On dit encore qu' a peine

---

[34] Colynet, *True History* (1591), p. 545.

[35] McKerrow, *Nashe,* I, 186-187.

[36] McKerrow, *Nashe,* IV, 114.

l'election faite, il jeta son baton, et montra aux cardinaux stupefaits sa taille encore droite et son regard encore plein du feu . . . Les Espagnols, par compensation, finirent par vouer au pape une telle haine qu'on les soupconna de l'avoir fait empoissonner."[37]

Marlowe is describing quite accurately these impressions of Sixtus V. This section of the prologue, therefore, must have been written after August 17, 1590, but while the Marprelate issue was still alive. The most likely time would be the autumn of 1590.

The prologue continues its allusive echoes.

> Birds of the air will tell of murders past:
> I am asham'd to hear such fooleries.
> Many will talk of title to a crown:
> What right had Caesar to the empery?
> (16-19)

Leonard Wright will furnish a proper background for Marlowe's allusion. He is essaying upon "The dutie of subiects to their Prince," warning that "Whosoeuer therefore resisteth the authoritie of the ciuil Magistrate: resisteth not man, but the ordinance of God himselfe, to his owne damnation [Rom. 13. 2. Exod. 16. 7]. He that prouoketh his soueraigne vnto anger (sayth Salomon) offendeth against his owne soule [Prou. 20. 2.]. Yea he that shall but euen thinke euill against the Lords annoynted (sayth he) the very bird of the ayre, with the fluttering of her wings, will bewray his secret thoughts [Preach. 10. 18]."[38] Wright makes application to "certaine seditious preachers, possessed with proud erronious spirits, euery one hauing a Church plot, or common wealth in his head."[39] These he finds "more dangerous enemies to y[e] state, then open professed Papists."[40] Wright is controverting the Martinists, of course.[41]

Marlowe is similarly alluding in terms of Ecclesiastes, 10, 19 (Bishops', not Geneva), "Wishe the king no euil in thy thought, and speake no hurt of the riche in thy priuie chamber: for a byrde of the ayre shall betray thy voyce, and with her fethers shal she bewray thy wordes." A side-note explains, "Treason can not be wrought so secretly, but it wilbe knowen." Machiavelli does not[42] fear what the birds of the air can do in bewraying

---

[37] J. C. F. Hoefer, *Nouvelle Biographie Generale* (Paris, 1865), XLIV, 48-50.

[38] L. Wright, *Display of dutie* (1589), p. 13.

[39] *Ibid.*, p. 13.

[40] *Ibid.*, p. 14.

[41] See his *Summons* (1589), Epistle, etc., especially p. 18; also *Hunting of Antichrist* (1589).

[42] As the Earl of Northampton assured Garnet in 1606, "God . . . by his word assureth vs that the birds of heauen shall bring those proiects and Inuentions to light that are contriued in the secret thought, or priuy cabinet of any wicked and false hearted Subiect against the King" (*Proceedings against the late Traitors* (1606), Ccc2[r]).

his treasonable dealings, including murders. In "murders past" Marlowe's contemporaries would doubtless have seen specific allusion to the assassination of the French king in 1589, which the Machiavellian Sixtus V had defended, to the great scandal of England. One resultant English pamphlet was entitled *Martin Mar-Sixtus,* entered November 8, 1591, by its title also echoing the anti-Martinist pamphlets.

This network of allusions in the prologue to the *Jew of Malta* makes it quite clear that it echoes the anti-Martinist controversy as it stood about the autumn of 1590. These allusions show that Marlowe found Martin no more to his liking than he did the Pope. Incidentally, it is time a bit of sober hard work was being done in placing Marlowe in his actual contemporary political-religious background.

As we turn to *Edward II,* our best evidence for the date comes from parallels with other plays. After a summary of these, Brooke concluded: "This evidence indicates the latter part of 1591 and the year 1592 as the time of the play's production."[43] The majority of these parallels are only the common phraseology of the stage at the time, without any necessary implication of immediate and direct relationship — they could be simply common-form stage patter. But a few do indicate direct relationship.[44]

Assuming that everybody borrowed from *Edward II,* H. M. Dowling[45] would place that play before October 29, 1591, since it has a close parallel with Peele's *Descensus Astraeae* for that date.[46] But Sampley saw no indication of which borrowed, and I see none.

It has been suggested that there is direct connection between "this cry" of Edward II in *Edward II* (V, 5, 113), and the "tragicke cry" of the same person in Peele's *Honour of the Garter* (223). It must be remembered that in these works both authors are using Holinshed as source, where Mortimer makes a "wailefull noise" (III, 341). Peele merely varies Holinshed's phraseology by synonyms, while Marlowe refers to the same outcry as it had evidently been rendered by the actor on the stage. There is thus no direct connection between Peele and Marlowe.

There are so many close parallels between *Edward II* and Peele's

---

[43] Brooke, *P.M.L.A.* (1922), XXXVII, 376; for parallels, see Brooke, "The Authorship of the Second and Third Parts of 'King Henry VI,'" *Transactions of the Connecticut Academy of Arts and Sciences* (1912), XVII (1913), [141]-211; Charles Crawford, "The Authorship of Arden of Feversham," *Shakespeare Jahrbuch* (1903), XXXIX, 74-86; H. B. Charlton and R. D. Waller, *Edward II,* pp. 8-15; Bakeless, *Tragicall History,* II, 28 ff., 231 ff.

[44] We shall see later that *Edward II* adapts a passage from *1* and *2 Henry VI,* and hence is later (see pp. 279 ff). For a parallel with *Arden,* see below, pp. 162-163.

[45] H. M. Dowling, "The Date and Order of Peele's Plays," *N.&Q.* (1933), 164, 184; rediscovered by Arthur M. Sampley, "Peele's *Descensus Astraeae* and Marlowe's *Edward II,*" *M.L.N.* (1935), L, 506.

[46] Charlton and Waller, *Edward II,* III, 2, 32-33 (1338-39); Horne, D. H., *Peele,* I, 215 (38-39).

Edward I that there has clearly been borrowing.[47]   One of these parallels, noted by Verity,[48] is probably significant.

> Hence feignèd weeds! unfeignèd is my grief.[49]
>
> Hence feigned weeds! unfeigned are my woes.[50]

"The line is the only indication in *Edward II* that the king is disguised as a monk. The action does not require him to be, nor does Holinshed say he was. In Peele, however, the king has dressed in 'friar's weeds' to discover his wife's secret."[51] Consequently, Charlton and Waller "incline to think . . . that *Edward I* is the earlier play and that it lent a few lines to *Edward II*."

Another set[52] of these parallels indicates that Marlowe borrowed in *Edward II* and adapted in *Massacre*. In *Edward I* we find

> Not Caesar, leading through the streets of Rome
> The captive kings of conquered nations,
> Was in his princely triumphs honoured more
> Than English Edward in this martial sight.[53]

> It shall suffice me to enjoy your love,
> Which whiles I have, I think myself as great
> As Caesar riding in the Roman street,
> With captive kings at his triumphant car.[54]

> As ancient Romans o'er their captive lords,
> So will I triumph o'er this wanton king;
> And he shall follow my proud chariot's wheels.[55]

The figure in *Massacre* is generalized from that in *Edward II*. Thus the figure is developed in *Edward I,* applied in *Edward II,* and generalized in *Massacre*.

But other facts on dating indicate that the *Massacre* passage echoes also *2 Henry VI*.

> Sweet Nell, ill can thy noble mind abrook
> The abject people gazing on thy face,
>
> .   .   .   .
>
> That erst did follow thy proud chariot-wheels,
> When thou didst ride in triumph through the streets.[56]

---

[47] Charlton and Waller, *Edward II,* pp. 8-10.

[48] A. W. Verity, *Edward II,* p. 131.

[49] A. H. Bullen, *Edward I,* Sc. 25, 123.

[50] Charlton and Waller, *Edward II,* IV, 6, 96 (1964).

[51] Charlton and Waller, *Edward II,* p. 10.

[52] Parallel between *Edward I* and *Edward II* noticed by C. Tzschaschel, *Marlowe's Edward II und Seine Quellen* (Halle, 1902), p. 46.

[53] Bullen, *Edward I,* Sc. I, 91-94.

[54] Charlton and Waller, *Edward II,* I, 1, 171-4 (171-174).

[55] H. S. Bennett, *Massacre,* XVIII, 51-53 (989-991).

[56] *2 Henry VI,* II, 4, 10-11, 12-14; *Contention* essentially the same.

It would seem that this passage occasioned the generalization in *Massacre* from Caesar to the Romans generally. The "triumph" passage in *2 Henry VI* is one of a long tradition, not showing any specific relationship to either Edward play.[57] The two instances of relationship that we have examined are together reasonably conclusive that *Edward II* succeeded *Edward I*. If so, we can go a stage further, since *Edward I* is itself later in its fundamental structure than *Bacon*,[58] which belongs to 1589.

The present group of parallels is a significant illustration of Marlowe's methods. Marlowe does not think in figures. His figures do not as figures grow, develop, evolve; they are simply appropriated full grown, and then adapted as ornamentation. And that is the fact, however much we might prefer them to the results of others.[59] By consequence, there is no series of some evolving figure in successive works as in Greene or Shakspere. At most, a new incentive, as in the illustration above, may coalesce with some former similarity. Thus this powerful instrument for looking into the progression of literary ornament in Greene and into the mind of Shakspere is almost useless for Marlowe.

But there are compensations, as the following parallel with *Faustus* will indicate. Briggs points out parallel passages in *Faustus* and *Edward II*, and says "Both passages might be contrasted with the earlier lines in *Edward II*, 1709 ff.: 'Gallop apace, bright Phoebus,' etc., and all three may be regarded as outgrowths of the influence of Ovid, *Amores,* I, xiii. 40: lente currite, Noctis equi, which Marlowe uses in the *Faustus* passage and had translated in his *Ovid's Elegies*."[60] The "Gallop apace" is in the Ovid tradition, but connecting with a parallel in *Romeo and Juliet* from Brooke. Elsewhere I have presented the evidence that Marlowe's passage echoes that in *Romeo and Juliet,* which I would date in 1591.[61] Consequently, the passage in *Edward II* would be not earlier than 1591. The corresponding passage in *Edward II* has also the day-night pattern of the other passages in *Edward II;* but desires day and night to shorten time instead of lengthen it, and shows no specific connection with the other two passages cited by Briggs.

For these other two, as the clock strikes eleven and Doctor Faustus realizes that he has but one hour before he is perpetually damned, he says

> Stand still, you ever-moving spheres of heaven,
> That time may cease and midnight never come;
> Fair nature's eye, rise, rise again and make

---

[57] Brooke, *Connecticut Academy* (1912), XVII, 174, overlooks this fact in his analysis.

[58] See below, pp. 264 ff.

[59] See the "Recapitulation" in Carpenter, *Metaphor,* p. 47.

[60] W. D. Briggs, *Edward II,* pp. 183-184.

[61] Baldwin, *Five-Act Structure,* 765 ff.

> Perpetual day; or let this hour but be
> A year, a month, a week, a natural day,
> That Faustus may repent and save his soul.
> *O lente lente currite noctis equi!*
> The stars move still, time runs, the clock will strike,
> The devil will come, and Faustus must be damned.[62]

With this passage Briggs parallels *Edward II* (Sc. XIX, 2017-23), where Edward II wishes to be king till night, and then exhorts

> Continue ever thou celestial sun;
> Let never silent night possess this clime:
> Stand still you watches of the element;
> All times and seasons, rest you at a stay,
> That Edward may be still fair England's king.
> But day's bright beams doth vanish fast away,
> And needs I must resign my wished crown.[63]

The passage in *Faustus* is built consciously on Ovid, whose germinal line is quoted. Here it should be remembered that Marlowe himself translated that line as "stay night and runne not thus."[64] So in *Faustus* "stay" becomes "Stand still," and "night . . . runne not thus" becomes

> you ever-moving spheres of heaven,
> That time may cease and midnight never come.

Then follow alternative statements. As correlative to night, the sun is to make perpetual day, or if this perpetual time be not granted for this single remaining hour, then let it be stretched to a year, month, week, day; that is, to any unit more than its natural length. To close the idea, the line of Ovid is quoted from which all this has been consciously developed. But Faustus continues that in spite of this exhortation all the markers of time continue to move, and at the end of the allotted hour the devil will come. Thus it is clear that this passage has been built from the line of Ovid exactly into the situation. There is no possible overt effect of the passage in *Edward II* upon it. In contrast, the speech in *Edward II* deals wholly in generalities. The sun is to continue and thus prevent night from ever coming, and the "watches of the element; All times and seasons" are to stop so that Edward may still be king; but day is vanishing fast, and Edward must resign the crown. The over-all rhetorical form is the same, using the statement of the wish, and the "but" of its non-fulfillment. This is, however, too general to indicate specific connection. Only one line in each is in actual verbal parallel.

> Stand still, you ever-moving spheres of heaven.
> Stand still you watches of the element.

---

[62] *Faustus, V.* 2, 134-142 (Greg's reconstruction).

[63] Charlton and Waller, *Edward II,* V, 1, 64-70 (2050-56).

[64] Marlowe (Brooke), *Ouids Elegies,* I, xiii, 40.

In *Faustus* these "ever-moving spheres of heaven," paraphrased from Ovid's "night," are later equated with the stars and are desired to be replaced by the sun. In *Edward II,* the sun and night (moon) have preceded and are apparently the "watches of the element." The verbal parallel thus reduces itself to "Stand, still you," which hardly shows conscious — or unconscious — parallel; it is merely a conventional repetition. But, as we have seen, the *Faustus* line is paraphrased from Ovid. There the line was elicited directly by its source, even in its general form and "varied" phraseology. In *Edward II,* it is the secondary mention of night in contrast to day which elicits the accompanying line. This should mean that the association was formed in the passage of *Faustus,* based directly upon Ovid's line, and has been revived in *Edward II* by the secondary mention of night. It is not a matter of consciously formal rhetoric, but of the unconscious associative processes of Marlowe's mind.

There are also parallels of *Edward II* with *Soliman and Perseda,* and one of these appears certainly to indicate that, if there was direct borrowing at all, then *Edward II* was the borrower.[65] A "pretty sentiment" is developed in *Soliman,* but merely applied in Marlowe, who, besides, is not given to fabricating "pretty sentiments." Perseda presents Erastus with a carcanet, which her grandmother had given her and she had vowed to keep

> vntill my wandring eye
> Should finde a harbour for my hart to dwell.
> Euen in thy brest doo I clect my rest;
> Let in my hart to keep thine company.[66]

This elicits from Erastus an equally grand flourish.

> And, sweet *Perseda,* accept this ring
> To equall it: receiue my hart to boote.[67]

This is a pretty posy for a ring, all developed in the approved tradition.

In *Edward II,* Gaveston says, "My lord, these titles far exceed my worth," and Edward replies

> Thy worth, sweet friend, is far above my gifts,
> Therefore, to equal it, receive my heart.[68]

The conceit is not evolved and does not grow out of the situation, but is simply applied to it. If there is direct connection, then this should certainly mean that *Soliman* evolved the original figure which *Edward II* applied. But the parallel is chiefly in the conceit, not notably in the phraseology, so that it is not certain that there is any direct connection.

---

[65] Charles Crawford, *Shakespeare Jahrbuch* (1903), XXXIX, 82; *Collectanea,* I, 116.

[66] Boas, *Soliman,* I, 2, 35-38.

[67] Boas, *Soliman,* I, 2, 39-40.

[68] Charlton and Waller, *Edward II,* I, 1, 157, 161-162 (157, 161-162).

Other parallels with *Soliman* are close but offer nothing conclusive.[69] *Soliman* was entered S.R. November 20, 1592; but the borrowing, if any, may have been from manuscript or more likely from the stage, since the parallels are not extended verbal copies. But again the relationship, if proved, would not help us much on dating, since we do not know enough about the history of *Soliman*.

There is also in *Edward II* an undoubted coincidence with Lodge.

> Immortall powers that know the painefull cares,
> That waight vpon my poore distressed hart,
> O bend your browes and leuill all your lookes
> Of dreadfull awe vpon these daring men.[70]

> Immortal powers! that knows the painful cares
> That waits upon my poor distressed soul,
> O level all your looks upon these daring men.[71]

Charlton and Waller think "The padding of the passage in Lodge makes it look dependent on Marlowe."[72] My own impression, nothing more, would be exactly the opposite, that the passage in *Edward II* is an abridgement of the passage in *Wounds*. But in any case, *Wounds* itself is in need of a date.

Professor Rupert Taylor claims that there is connection between *Edward II* and *The Troublesome Reign of King John,* printed 1591, and assumes that the latter is the borrower.[73] Few of the parallels are at all specific. It is possible, perhaps probable, that Marlowe borrowed Pandulph's threatened curse and excommunication in *Troublesome Reign*.[74] If *Edward II* did so borrow, and from the printed form, then this borrowing in *Edward II* would be not earlier than the latter part of 1591.

Thus *Edward II* borrows from *Romeo and Juliet*, 1591, *2 Henry VI* in some form, probably 1592, Peele's *Edward I*, which is later than *Bacon*, 1589, *Faustus*, by 1589, perhaps *Soliman and Perseda*, printed 1592, possibly *Wounds of Civil War*, usually dated early, and possibly from *Troublesome Reign*, printed 1591. Incidentally, *Edward II* makes it abundantly clear that, like his contemporaries, Marlowe did not hesitate to borrow suitable ornament. The upshot is that *Edward II* would appear to have been written in 1591 or 1592, as the wealth of these parallels with other plays would of itself indicate. We shall see that its relationship to *Massacre, 2* and *3 Henry VI*, and *Arden* probably indicates a date after

---

[69] Charlton and Waller, *Edward II,* pp. 17-19.

[70] Thomas Lodge, *Wovnds of Ciuill War,* G4[r].

[71] Charlton and Waller, *Edward II,* V, 3, 37-9 (2302-4).

[72] Charlton and Waller, *Edward II,* p. 21.

[73] Taylor, R., "A Tentative Chronology of Marlowe's and Some other Elizabethan Plays," *P.M.L.A.,* LI, 643 ff.

[74] Baldwin, *Five-Act Structure,* pp. 770-772.

April 3, 1592. The relationship to *Romeo and Juliet,* together with the acting conditions of the period, would indicate probably but not certainly a date before the closing of the theaters of June 11, 1592.[75] So *Edward II* was most likely written for the summer of 1592.

The *Massacre at Paris* appears in Henslowe's Diary as "ne" on January 26, 1593, as acted by Strange's men.[76] But after Strange's and the Admiral's became separate aggregations, it remained with the Admiral's. As is well known, the play alludes to the Armada (XVIII, 105), presents the death of Henry III, August 2, 1589, and refers to "Sixtus' bones" (XXI, 100), this being Sixtus V, who died August 17, 1590,[77] and is also alluded to in the prologue to *Jew of Malta.*

Just as *Edward II* borrowed from *2 Henry VI,* so *Massacre* has unmistakable parallels with *3 Henry VI,* though the order of composition between them is not directly clear.

> we are grac'd with wreaths of victory[78]

> Thus far our fortune keeps an upward course,
> And we are graced with wreaths of victory.[79]

> Thus still our fortune giues vs victorie,
> And girts our temples with triumphant ioies.[80]

> Sweet Duke of Guise, our prop to lean upon,
> Now thou art dead, here is no stay for us.[81]

> Sweet Duke of York, our prop to lean upon,
> Now thou art gone, we have no staff, no stay.[82]

> Sweet Duke of *Yorke* our prop to leane vpon,
> Now thou art gone there is no hope for vs.[83]

In both instances, the parallel is with *3 Henry VI* rather than with *True Tragedie.* In neither instance is it clear to me whether *Massacre* or *3 Henry VI* precedes in composition.[84] But the fact that *Edward II* borrows from *2 Henry VI,* and that *Massacre* is close to *3 Henry VI* ought to mean that *Massacre* is later than *Edward II.* In fact, as Dyce noted, the

[75] Baldwin, *Five-Act Structure,* pp. 769-770.

[76] Greg, *Henslowe's Diary,* II, 157.

[77] Bennett, *Massacre,* p. 170.

[78] Bennett, *Massacre,* XV, 2 (794).

[79] *3 Henry VI,* V, 3, 1-2.

[80] *True Tragedie,* Scene XXIII, 1-2.

[81] Bennett, *Massacre,* XX, 4-5 (1122-23).

[82] *3 Henry VI,* II, 1, 68-69.

[83] *True Tragedie,* Scene V, 45-46.

[84] Brooke, *Connecticut Academy* (1912), XVII, 174, thinks the Guise passage more closely fitted to its situation than the York passage and hence the earlier. On the other hand, Sir Walter Greg thinks, "It is pretty clear that the borrowing was on the part of *The Massacre*" (Greg, *Massacre* (*M.S.R.*), p. ix).

two plays certainly have a rousing patriotic passage in common, though again it is not directly certain which precedes.

> Why should a king be subject to a priest?
> Proud Rome, that hatchest such imperial grooms,
> For these thy superstitious taper-lights,
> Wherewith thy antichristian churches blaze,
> I'll fire thy crazed buildings, and enforce
> The papal towers to kiss the lowly ground.
> With slaughter'd priests may Tiber's channel swell,
> And banks rais'd higher with their sepulchres.[85]

>   the papal monarch goes
> To wrack, and [th'] antichristian kingdom falls.
> These bloody hands shall tear his triple crown,
> And fire accursed Rome about his ears;
> I'll fire his crazed buildings, and enforce
> The papal towers to kiss the lowly earth.
> Navarre, give me thy hand: I here do swear
> To ruinate that wicked Church of Rome,
> That hatcheth up such bloody practices.[86]

The "antichristian" and "hatcheth" are parallel phraseology, and the awkwardly repeated "fire" probably means that the two lines in common have been let into *Massacre* from *Edward II*, though the sadly mangled form of *Massacre* calls for caution.

And now we have an awkward piece of evidence.

> Sweete *Mosbie* is the man that hath my hart:
> And he vsurpes it, hauing nought but this,
> That I am tyed to him by marriage.[87]

> Sweet Mugeroun, 'tis he that hath my heart,
> And Guise usurps it 'cause I am his wife.[88]

Arden was entered S.R. April 3, 1592; *Massacre* was new January 26, 1593. This should mean that Marlowe borrowed from *Arden,* and the passages themselves confirm the relationship, since the idea is developed in *Arden* but applied in *Massacre.*

But *Edward II* also has an unmistakable connection with *Arden.*

> Is this the end of all thy solemne oathes?
> Is this the frute thy reconcilement buds?[89]

> Is this the love you bear your sovereign?
> Is this the fruit your reconcilement bears?[90]

---

[85] Charlton and Waller, *Edward II,* I, 4, 96-103 (392-399).

[86] Bennett, *Massacre,* XXI, 60-68 (1210-18).

[87] *Arden of Feversham,* A3[r].

[88] Bennett, *Massacre,* XII, 3-4, (665-666).

[89] *Arden,* A4[v].

[90] Charlton and Waller, *Edward II,* II, 2, 30-31 (832-833).

Charlton and Waller say, "If there was ever a clear case of borrowing this is one. However it came into *Arden,* it surely shows that *Edward II* existed before 3 April 1592,"[91] when *Arden* was entered S.R. The coincidence is in the second line of each passage, that line being identical except for the last word. I suppose that in this one variant Charlton and Waller have been impressed by the fact that "bears" is a more "proper" term than "buds," and so they give primacy to Marlowe. But even Marlowe has the "proper" figure only at the expense of the awkward repetition of "bear." It is quite possible, therefore, that Marlowe is the borrower here, and since he was the borrower in *Massacre,* we would expect the same relationship here. Since the borrowing in *Massacre* must have been well after *Arden* was in print, it may be that both the passage in *Edward II* and that in *Massacre* rest on the printed form, entered April 3, 1592; though Marlowe's access could have been acquired, of course, in other ways.

Another suggested parallel between *Edward II* and *Arden* is too general to be of evidential value. Says Edward

> Or, like the snaky wreath of Tisiphon,
> Engirt the temples of his hateful head.[92]

This is the simple classical allusion to Tisiphone's "permanent" of snakes. But in *Arden* Alice says

> I shall no more be closed in Ardens armes,
> That lyke the snakes of blacke Tisiphone
> Sting me with their embraceings[93]

Comes, under the title of *Tisiphones amores,* refers us to his version of the story. "Fabulati sunt antiqui neque has quidem seuerissimas Deas Cupidinis vim potuisse deuitare, quādo scriptum reliquit Maenander in rebus fabulosis Tisiphonem in amorem cuiusdam pueri formosi Cytheronis nomine incidisse, cuius desiderium cùm ferre non posset, verba de congressu ad illum perferenda curauit. at is formidandum aspectum veritus, neque responso quidem dignam fecit, quo illa vnum è suis draconibus è capillis conuulsum in eum coniecit, quem serpens intra nodos constringens interemit, vbi Deorum misericordia mons ab illo dictus fuit, qui priùs Asterius dicebatur."[94] Mrs. Arden's allusion is quite apt if one knows this story. The irony of the allusion also appears when one remembers that, as Cooper puts it, Tisiphone was "One of the furies of hell, which was supposed to tourment homicides, or slears of men." Either way, Mrs. Arden was doomed to Tisiphone's attentions. Thus in these passages the

---

[91] Charlton and Waller, *Edward II,* p. 17.
[92] Charlton and Waller, *Edward II,* V, 1, 45-46 (2031-32).
[93] *Arden,* H3ᵛ — H4ʳ.
[94] Comes, *Mythologiae* (1581), p. 220.

parallel between *Edward II* and *Arden* consists only of a reference to the snakes of avenging Tisiphone. I suppose one passage could have suggested the other, but there is no necessary indication that such was the case.

These are Marlowe's plays for the public stage. Of authenticated plays we have *Dido* left, attributed to Marlowe and Nashe. We have seen that a passage in *Dido* is earlier than a passage in *A Shrew* — which is earlier than a passage in *Faustus*. It would appear probable also that passages in *Dido* are earlier than certain corresponding passages in *Tamburlaine*. In *Dido*, Aeneas sums up a section of Virgil thus

> Yet flung I forth, and, desperate of my life,
> Ran in the thickest throngs, and, with this sword
> Sent many of their savage ghosts to hell.[95]

To this, Crawford[96] noted a parallel in *2 Tamburlaine*.

> But then run desperate through the thickest throngs,
> Dreadless of blows, of bloody wounds and death.[97]

Two separate passages in *Dido* finally coalesce in *2 Tamburlaine*. Crawford[98] had noted that a line in *Dido*,[99] "And clad her in a crystal livery," is paralleled by *2 Tamburlaine*, which is embedded in the following speech of Tamburlaine.

> Now, bright Zenocrate, the world's fair eye,
> Whose beams illuminate the lamps of heaven,
> Whose cheerful looks do clear the cloudy air,
> And clothe it in a crystal livery.[100]

On the parallel of the last line with that in *Dido* Brooke[101] notes, "The setting of the line is much more appropriate and natural here [in *Dido*]: Carthage is to be clad in a garment (encompassing wall) of crystal rocks."

The three lines preceding the "crystal livery" are a redoing of a speech in *1 Tamburlaine*, by Tamburlaine also, of course.

> Zenocrate, the loveliest maid alive,
> Fairer than rocks of pearl and precious stone,
> The only paragon of Tamburlaine;
> Whose eyes are brighter than the lamps of heaven,
> And speech more pleasant than sweet harmony;
> That with thy looks canst clear the darkened sky,
> And calm the rage of thundering Jupiter.[102]

---

[95] Brooke, *Dido*, II, 1, 210-212 (505-507).

[96] Crawford, *Collectanea*, I, 92.

[97] Ellis-Fermor, *2 Tamburlaine*, III, 2, 139-140 (3329-30).

[98] Crawford, *Collectanea*, I, 92.

[99] Brooke, *Dido*, V, 1, 6 (1414).

[100] Ellis-Fermor, *2 Tamburlaine*, I, 4, 1-4 (2570-73).

[101] Brooke, *Dido*, p. 214.

[102] Ellis-Fermor, *1 Tamburlaine*, III, 3, 117-23 (1215-21); the "looks" parallel was pointed out by Knutowski (Brooke, *Dido*, p. 138).

Now as Knutowski noted, there is a parallel in *Dido*. There Achates, addressing Aeneas as "our god" (Jupiter), says

> Do thou but smile, and cloudy heaven will clear,
> Whose night and day descendeth from thy brows.[103]

The figure begins in *Dido,* with Aeneas as Jupiter properly making heaven smile with his looks. Then in *1 Tamburlaine* Zenocrate illuminates heaven and Jupiter himself. Finally the figure is shrunk in *2 Tamburlaine* and supplemented by the "crystal livery" from *Dido*. The progression is thus clear from *Dido* through *Tamburlaine*.

A similar progression from *Dido* to *Faustus* is pointed out by Muir, who argues that *Dido* belongs to Cambridge days because it contains the germs of many passages to be found in Marlowe's later plays. "The most famous example is the passage in which Dido addresses Aeneas —

> So thou wouldst proue as true as *Paris* did,
> Would, as faire *Troy* was, *Carthage* might be sackt,
> And I be calde a second *Helena*.
> (1554-6)

Shortly afterwards Dido cries to Anna —

> Tell him, I neuer vow'd at *Aulis* gulfe
> The desolation of his natiue *Troy,*
> Nor sent a thousand ships vnto the walles. . . .
> (1610-2)

In an earlier passage Dido declares —

> If he forsake me not, I neuer dye,
> For in his lookes I see eternitie,
> And heele make me immortall with a kisse.
> (1327-9)

All three passages are echoed in the famous speech of Faustus, addressed to the shade of Helen of Troy —

> Was this the face that lancht a thousand shippes?
> And burnt the toplesse Towres of *Ilium?*
> Sweete *Helen,* make me immortall with a kisse. . . .
> I wil be *Paris,* and for the loue of thee,
> Insteede of *Troy* shal *Wertenberge* be sackt. . . .
> (1328-6)

It is almost certain that Marlowe created the perfection of Faustus' lines from the tentative attempts in *Dido*. It is quite improbable that, having written the Faustus lines, he should produce a weakened version of them in *Dido*. Moreover it is more in keeping with Marlowe's poetic method that one passage should be combined from three earlier ones, than that three separate passages should be echoed from one."[104]

---

[103] Brooke, *Dido,* I, i, 155-156 (155-156).
[104] Muir, *Chronology of Marlowe's Plays,* V, 346-347.

The second of the passages from *Dido,* lines 1610-12, is based directly on the *Aeneid,* the source of the play.

> Non ego cum Danais Troianam exscindere gentem
> Aulide iuravi classemve ad Pergama misi.[105]

Similarly, in the first passage from *Dido,* the preceding lines, 1549-53, were based closely on the *Aeneid,*[106] and the quoted passage is an application in parallel to that situation. It is thus the Trojan parallel, suggested by Virgil himself, as we have just seen. It is evident that these two passages in *Dido,* being based directly on Virgil, the source of the play, are certainly the originals, and the passage in *Faustus* the later adaptation. Further, in the third parallel from *Dido,* "heele make me immortall with a kisse" is evolved as the climax of three lines, whereas in *Faustus* it is simply applied. Certainly, then, the three passages in *Dido* are the originals, the passage in *Faustus* the adaptation.

Brooke[107] lists various other parallels of *Dido* with *Tamburlaine* and the other plays, but those noticed are the only ones for which I see the direction of change.

It is probable that Marlowe wrote other plays in whole or in part, and some of these may survive, but we are not here concerned primarily with authorship, and the attributed plays will appear in other connections. As in the case of Greene, so for Marlowe we have now a fair idea of the order and progression of the plays as a background for interpreting the evidence on Shakspere.

----

[105] *Aeneid,* IV, 425-426. See Dr. Earl Oliver's *Studies in the Background and Source of* Dido Queene of Carthage (U. of Ill. Master's thesis, 1943), p. 55.

[106] Oliver, p. 53.

[107] Brooke, *P.M.L.A.* (1922), XXXVII, 372-373.

CHAPTER V

The Chronology of George Peele's Plays

To continue with Greene's group of authors, the generally accepted canon of George Peele's surviving plays consists at present of *The Arraignment of Paris, The Battle of Alcazar, The Old Wives Tale, The Hunting of Cupid* (fragments), *David and Bethsabe,* and *Edward I,* being five and a piece. Some others of which Peele has been accused in whole or in part will appear in other connections.

The first known play by Peele is *The Arraignment of Paris,* printed in 1584 as it was "Presented before the Queenes Maiestie, by the Children of her Chappell." As a play for children, it does not here concern us further.

Peele's first surviving play for a company of men was apparently the *Battle of Alcazar,* which belongs to the autumn and winter 1588-9, and was printed in 1594, "As it was sundrie times plaid by the Lord high Admirall his seruants." It used for a chief source John Polemon's English translation of John Freigius' *Historia de bello Africano* under the title *The Second Part of the Booke of Battailes,* 1587.[1] As Dyce noted,[2] *Alcazar* refers definitely to *2 Tamburlaine.*

> Convey Tamburlaine into our Afric here,
> To chástise and to menace lawful kings:
> Tamburlaine, triumph not, for thou must die,
> As Philip did, Caesar, and Caesar's peers.[3]

This echoes *2 Tamburlaine* directly

> For Tamburlaine, the scourge of God, must die.[4]

Alcazar is supposed also to refer to the Armada of August, 1588.

> The wallowing ocean hems her round about;
> Whose raging floods do swallow up her foes,
> And on the rocks their ships in pieces split.[5]

---

[1] W. G. Rice, "A Principal Source of *The Battle of Alcazar,*" *M.L.N.* (1943), LVIII, 428-431.

[2] Dyce, *Peele* (1828), II, 221.

[3] Bullen, *Alcazar,* I, 2, 33-36.

[4] Ellis-Fermor, *2 Tamburlaine,* V, 3, 248 (4641).

[5] Bullen, *Alcazar,* II, 4, 117-119.

When Dyce sought parallels to substantiate the authorship of Peele for *Alcazar*,[6] he found one in *David and Bethsabe,* one in the *Honour of the Garter,* one in *Descensus Astraeae,* four in *Farewell,* three in *Tale of Troy.* Since *Farewell* and *Troy* were published together in 1589 and are short items besides, this is a very strong argument that *Alcazar* was written about the same time. The *Farewell* was entered S.R. February 23, 1589, and being an occasional poem, was evidently written but a short time before. Since it is only about an eighth of the length of *Troy,* and contains but seventy-six lines, its four parallels with *Alcazar* against three for *Troy* place *Alcazar* nearer *Farewell.*

Peele says that *Troy* was an old poem, though it was no doubt refurbished for publication. Interestingly enough, the three parallels with *Troy* are all from the same connection, and evidently were transferred to *Alcazar.* In *Alcazar,* it is reported that Sebastian is coming

> Top and top-gallant, all in brave array.

He has been deceived by the Spaniard

> For which he storms as great Achilles erst
> Lying for want of wind in Aulis' gulf.[7]

In *Troy,* Peele recounts the story of how the Greeks

> In Aulis' gulf they mightily assemble.[8]

He continues the story of Iphigenia, and the sending

> To fetch to Aulis' gulf the Argive queen.[9]

After the sacrifice, there is wind, and the Greeks sail

> Top and top-gallant in the bravest sort.[10]

It is clear that *Alcazar* simply echoes the story as Peele had told it in *Troy.* Consequently, it appears that *Alcazar* was written around February, 1589, when *Troy* was refurbished and *Farewell* written, all three belonging to the same patriotic fervor aroused by Drake's expedition.

Another group of parallels is also important here. Stukely states as a fact, whether so or not

---

[6] Dyce, *Peele* (1828), I, xxv-xxvi. Richard Laemmerhirt, *George Peele* (Rostock, 1882), pp. 20-22 makes additions of sorts.

[7] Bullen, *Alcazar,* III, 3, 26, 39-40.

[8] Dyce, *Peele* (1828), II, 98.

[9] Dyce, *Peele* (1828), II, 99; reading of Q 1589.

[10] Dyce, *Peele* (1828), II, 100; reading of Q 1589. Apparently Peele changed these readings later because he had used the passages in *Alcazar.* The *Anti-Spaniard* (1590), C2[v] (translated from Antoine Arnauld; Mundy suspected by Turner), has the figure as "our ship, that erst with full spred sayles did with top and top gallant sayle so stately" (I have not checked the French original).

> In England's London, lordings, was I born,
> On that brave bridge, the bar that thwarts the Thames.[11]

In *Farewell,* the heroes are invited to say farewell to the Thames, which runs

> To that brave bridge, the bar that thwarts her course.[12]

In *Descensus Astraeae,* a pageant for October 29, 1591, the allusion needs explanation

> And by the bar that thwarts this silver stream.[13]

In the sequence, the alleged fact, as stated in *Alcazar,* evidently comes first. So we have *Alcazar* written before *Farewell,* doubtless in a way as a piece of propaganda, fitting into the political interest toward the end of 1588, which culminated in the expedition of April, 1589, sometimes alluded to as the counter-Armada, equally disastrous eventually, and alluded to so sourly a few months later in the *Old Hamlet.*

Indeed, it has been usually assumed that *Farewell* itself refers to *Alcazar.* Dyce says, "I believe it is to the battle of Alcazar, not to the Famous History of Stukeley, that Peele himself alludes in his Farewell to Norris and Drake:

> 'Bid Mahomet's Poo, and mighty Tamburlaine,
> King Charlemagne, Tom Stukeley & the rest
> Adieu.' "[14]

The latest editor thinks the reference "more probably [to] *Captain Thomas Stukeley* than Peele's *The Battle of Alcazar.*"[15] But why should Peele advertise a rival play? Since the evidence shows that *Alcazar* precedes *Farewell,* surely Peele is referring to his own play. Besides, there is no evidence that *Captain Thomas Stukeley* had been written by 1589.

Because of the fact that there is some flattery for Elizabeth within the play, Dowling[16] thinks it was presented at court by the Admiral's men in one of their performances the Christmas season 1588-89, when they appeared December 29, 1588, and February 11 or March 3, 1589. The play may very well have been so presented, though it did not have a characteristic court ending.

The *Old Wives Tale* was entered S.R. April 16, 1595, and printed the same year as "played by the Queenes Maiesties players. Written by G. P." Since the Queen's made its last known appearance in London May 8, 1594, it is customary to place the play before that date. As Malone noted, the "frozen Rhine" passage of *Old Wives Tale* is lifted from

---

[11] Bullen, *Alcazar,* V, 1, 136-137.

[12] Dyce, *Peele* (1828), II, 87.

[13] Dyce, *Peele* (1828), II, 80.

[14] Dyce, *Peele* (1828), II, 4.

[15] Horne, *Peele,* p. 277; cf. p. 77, n. 47.

[16] Dowling, *N.&Q.* (1933), 164, 167.

Orlando Furioso,[17] as are other details. Since *Orlando* appears to have been written about 1589, this fact gives an over-all date of 1589-94.

Further indication for dating has been found in the satire upon Gabriel Harvey in the character Huanebango, which apparently all recent critics admit. For as Dyce points out,[18] Huanebango quotes at least one of Harvey's hexameters, though he is even more liberal with those of Stanyhurst, as Dyce also notes.[19] Larsen points out that "Nashe had been making fun of Stanyhurst's hexameters ever since 1589, when he wrote the Epistle prefixed to *Menaphon*. But he does not connect Harvey with this metrical folly until Harvey in 1592 came forward proudly boasting that he was the inventor of the English hexameter and acknowledging Stanyhurst as his disciple."[20] Now as a matter of fact, Nashe does not make fun of Stanyhurst's hexameters in 1593. There and thereafter he centers attention on Harvey's hexameters, justly accusing Harvey of claiming that Harvey had invented the hexameter in English, and that Stanyhurst was his disciple. Nashe specifically refers to Greene as the man who had "awakte" Harvey on this subject; "tyll *Greene* awakte him out of his selfe admiring contemplation, hee had nothing to doe but walke vnder the Ewe tree at Trinitie hall"[21] and compose such hexameters as are given in two samples. But Greene had not mentioned Stanyhurst. It was in the address to *Menaphon* some three years earlier that Nashe had given an improved selection from the hexameters of Stanyhurst. Eventually, then, in following Harvey's own lead Nashe brings Stanyhurst into momentary connection with Harvey in his *Strange Newes,* entered S.R. January 12, 1593. This accounts for Nashe's sequence.

Larsen next assumes that Peele followed Nashe's lead of January, 1593. But the evidence alleged does not certainly connect Nashe with Peele. For if one were going to satirize Harvey's hexameters, he would inevitably use *Encomium Lauri,* as both Peele and Nashe do, though they do not use the same passage. But Stanyhurst furnished much the more ridiculous hexameters, whether one credited him to Harvey or not. Here again in their selections from Stanyhurst, Nashe and Peele do not notably coincide; each makes a natural selection for his purpose. While Peele and Nashe both satirize both Harvey and Stanyhurst for their hexameters, yet their selections are at least for the most part independent, and show no necessary connection. And Harvey and Stanyhurst were at that time in fact the notorious writers of hexameters. It was thus natural for Peele, and Nashe, or anyone else to connect the two; but Peele gives no hint that

---

[17] Dyce, *Peele* (1828), I, 244n. See above, p. 64.

[18] Dyce, *Peele* (1828), I, xxix-xxx, 235n.

[19] Dyce, *Peele* (1828), I, 234n.-235n.

[20] T. Larsen, "The date of Peele's *Old Wives' Tale*," *M.P.,* XXX, 27.

[21] McKerrow, *Nashe,* I, 277.

Harvey claims to have invented Stanyhurst, as Nashe justly accuses him of having done.

Here Nashe offers us a significant hint. In *Strange Newes,* S.R. January 12, 1593, Nashe tells Harvey, "though Greene be dead, yet I may liue to doe thee good. But *by the meanes of his death thou art depriued of the remedie in lawe, which thou intendedst to haue had against him for calling thy Father Ropemaker.* Mas, thats true: what Action will it beare? *Nihil pro nihilo,* none in law: what it will doe vpon the stage I cannot tell; for there a man maye make action besides his part, when he hath nothing at all to say: and if there, it is but a clownish action that it will beare: for what can be made of a Ropemaker more than a Clowne? *Will Kempe,* I mistrust it will fall to thy lot for a merriment, one of these dayes."[22] Nashe is alluding to "KEMPS *applauded Merrimentes* of the men of Goteham, in receiuing the King into Goteham" in *A Knack to Know a Knave,* performed by Strange's men as new June 10, 1592, and thence till January 24, 1593, and is threatening Harvey through his father with a like fate. Had Peele's supposed endeavors in *Old Wives Tale* been fresh in Nashe's mind he would certainly have taunted Harvey with them. On the other hand, Nashe's hint could have given Peele the suggestion to satirize Harvey, but Peele does not produce the kind of "merriment" at which Nashe hints.

Horne thinks it possible that "Peele may have satirized Harvey in 1589 during the skirmish between Harvey and Lyly, adding the Stanyhurst tags later."[23] The conjecture of later addition for this satire has probability against it. For in 1589 Nashe was praising Peele as "the chiefe supporter of pleasance nowe liuing, the *Atlas* of Poetrie, & *primus verborum Artifex,*" and in the same connection was ridiculing Stanyhurst's hexameters. Surely Peele would have known of this particular passage and have had the satiric possibilities of Stanyhurst thrust on him by Nashe in 1589 — for that matter, surely he would already have known of these hexameters. One might as readily argue that Nashe had *Tale* in mind when in 1589 he praised Peele and ridiculed Stanyhurst's hexameters. The upshot is that the satire upon Harvey would on present evidence fit 1589 as well as it would 1593.

Sir Edmund Chambers points out that *"The Old Wive's Tale* was evidently staged in a way exactly analogous to that adopted by Lyly, or by Peele himself in *The Arraignment of Paris.*"[24] In form, therefore, it connects with the plays for the children's companies. Dowling makes a suggestion which would help to explain this fact. "In the stage-direction

---

[22] McKerrow, *Nashe,* I, 286-287.

[23] Horne, *Peele,* p. 89.

[24] Chambers, *E.S.,* III, 48.

at line 552 of the 1595 quarto, the churchwarden is called 'Simon' though we know from l. 597 that his name is Steeven Loache. The 'Simon' may be a relic of the prompt copy and as such may refer to the actor John Symons who in 1588-9 and perhaps later is found with the Queen's."[25] Simonds had a company of tumbling boys under Stanley's patronage as early as 1583, which cooperated in some way with the Admiral's from the season of 1588-89 through the season of 1590-91, though George Ottewell is the payee in that last season.[26] But Simonds had also connected with the Queen's in the country by 1588, and this connection appears to have lasted at least into 1590. Apparently, Ottewell continued with the Queen's some years further. If the reference in *Old Wives Tale* is to Simonds with the Queen's, then the date of reference would probably be 1588-90. This suggested dating would harmonize with the borrowings from *Orlando Furioso,* a play of 1589, and with a date of 1589 for the satire on Harvey. These facts make it highly probable that *Old Wives Tale* was written about 1589-90, whether the Harvey satire belongs to this version or is an insertion or revision about 1593.

Fragments survive from a work of Peele's which appears to have been a play, *The Hunting of Cupid,* entered S.R. July 26, 1591,[27] and evidently printed as later quotations show, though only fragments survive. One of its songs was particularly liked, and Robert Greene echoes it in the latter half of 1590.[28] This fact and the entry of 1591 indicate that it was current about 1590, though it may, of course, have been written much earlier. It was evidently of the pastoral variety, most closely akin to *Arraignment.* If it was a play, we have no means, as yet, of knowing for what company it was written.

The Love of King David and Fair Bethsabe was entered S.R. May 14, 1594, but the first surviving edition is of 1599, without attribution to acting company. Dyce[29] noticed that in *David and Bethsabe* Peele borrowed a passage from Spenser's *Faerie Queene,* which was entered December 1, 1589, and printed in 1590. Another passage appears to belong to 1590, since Marlowe borrowed from it in *The Jew of Malta.*

> Like as the fatal raven, that in his voice
> Carries the dreadful summons of our deaths.[30]

---

[25] Dowling, *N.&Q.* (1933), 164, 184. The Lord in the Induction to *The Taming of a Shrew* also gives his name as Simon, which Slie abbreviates to Sim. If the reference should be to Simonds, it would connect the play with either the Queen's or the Admiral's, other circumstances perhaps indicating the latter.

[26] See below, pp. 246 ff.

[27] Arber, *Transcript,* II, 591.

[28] See above, pp. 99 ff.

[29] Dyce, *Peele* (1828), I, 286n.

[30] Bullen, *David and Bethsabe* [Second] Chorus, 4-5.

Dyce noted correctly that the source of Peele's lines is Du Bartas, *L'Arche.*
Marlowe then adapted these lines in *The Jew of Malta.*

> Thus, like the sad presaging raven, that tolls
> The sick man's passport in her hollow beak.[31]

Even if we did not know that Peele based his lines on Du Bartas, it is
clear that Peele's is the simple, fundamental statement, giving the summons only. Marlowe then varies summons to passport, and colors the
passage with "tolls," to make the raven's voice the actual passing bell.
Still later, in a passage noted by Collier,[32] Edward Guilpin in *Skialetheia*
(1589, A4^r) puts Marlowe's figure, in italics, fully after death by having
the raven toll the dirge at the funeral (summons, passport, dirge).

> Like to the fatall ominous Rauen, which tolls,
> The sicke mans dirge within his hollow beake.

Guilpin has certainly adapted Marlowe, though in doing so he shows some
coincidence with Peele, "Like to the fatall . . . his." It would appear
that Peele's passage in *David and Bethsabe* is earlier than that in the *Jew
of Malta,* which was not far from the autumn of 1590. This date thus
harmonizes with the use of Spenser's *Faerie Queene,* printed 1590. The
two instances indicate a date of 1590 for *David and Bethsabe.*

This dating, in turn, puts another set of figures in order.

> climbs
> The crookèd zodiac with his fiery sphere.[33]
>
> Gallop the Zodiacke, and end the yere.[34]
>
> gallops the Zodiack in his fierie [wayne].[35]

It would have been hazardous to deduce this order directly, but now that
the order is established by other facts, it is seen to be a natural one.[36]

Cheffaud believes that Peele used Du Bartas heavily in this play.[37]
I believe that his parallels do prove that Peele used "Les Artifices" of
Du Bartas in Scene XV, as well as other bits elsewhere. But I see no
reason to believe that "Les Trophees" of the second week of Du Bartas
gave Peele the seminal conception of his drama. The moral framework
of the play is not more evident to me in "Les Trophees" than in the
Biblical story. Surely both Peele and Du Bartas are merely using current

---

[31] H. S. Bennett, *Jew of Malta*, II, 1, 1-2 (640-641).

[32] Collier, *History*, III, 136.

[33] Bullen, *David and Bethsabe*, Scene I, 108-109.

[34] *Descensus Astraeae* (1591), 4.

[35] *Anglorum Feriae* (1595), 24.

[36] For further significance of these parallels, see Baldwin, *Literary Genetics,* pp. 5-8.

[37] P. H. Cheffaud, *George Peele,* pp. 136 ff., 176 ff. Independently, H. Dugdale
Sykes later discovered the borrowings in Scene XV, as well as a chance bit or two
elsewhere ("Peele's Borrowings from Du Bartas," *N.&Q.,* 147, 349-351, 368-369).

Biblical commentary in their interpretations. If it could be shown that Peele did borrow from "Les Trophees," published in 1591, that would push *David and Bethsabe* past that date, and with it *The Jew of Malta*.

Sir Edmund Chambers brackets *David and Bethsabe* with *Tale* as two plays he cannot accept for the public theaters. "The extant text apparently represents an attempt to bring within the compass of a single performance a piece or fragments of a piece originally written in three 'discourses.' I mention it here, because somewhat undue use has been made of its opening direction in speculations as to the configuration of the back wall of the public stage. It uses the favorite assault motive, and has many changes of locality. The title page suggests that in its present form it was meant for public performance. But almost anything may lie behind that present form, possibly a Chapel play, possibly a University play, or even a neo-miracle in the tradition of Bale; and the staging of any particular scene may contain original elements, imperfectly adapted to later conditions."[38] For *David and Bethsabe* the datable elements are of 1590; and there is nothing, so far as I can see, to indicate that the play was not constructed originally in three discourses, presumably at that time.[39] At any rate, it is not characteristic for the companies of men in the public theaters, but is rather to be paired with *Tale* and to be dated 1590. This pairing and dating may in turn be thought to offer some slight support to the dating of about 1589 for *Tale*.

Edward I was entered S.R. about October 8, 1593, and printed without attribution to company. Fleay suggested a date for the play of 1590-91, but after November 17, 1590, on the ground that it borrows from Peele's own *Polyhymnia*.[40] These parallels[41] point to the priority of *Polyhymnia*. The latest editor[42] doubts that the *Sonet* attached to *Polyhymnia* was by Peele. It ends

> Goddesse, allow this aged man his right,
> To be your Beads-man now, that was your Knight.

With these words Sir Henry Lee ended his career as Queen Elizabeth's champion. The flourish grows out of the situation. In *Edward I,* we have the counter speech. As a hospital and pensions are being provided for Edward's soldiers, the Queen Mother says

> And whilst this ancient standard-bearer lives,
> He shall have forty pound of yearly fee,
> And be my beadsman, father, if you please.[43]

---

[38] Chambers, *E.S.,* III, 48-49.

[39] See Appendix II.

[40] Fleay, *Biog. Chron.,* II, 157.

[41] See Cheffaud, *Peele,* p. 87 and n.

[42] Horne, *Peele,* pp. 169 ff.

[43] Bullen, *Edward I,* Sc. I, 127-129. Two of the other six parallels belong to the same speech and connection.

Here is the answer to Sir Henry Lee, as it were. Thus the speech in
Edward I is more likely to be the later, especially if the *Sonet* was not
written by Peele. Again, in *Polyhymnia*, there is the classical allusion

> Entring the listes like Tytan, arm'd with fire,
> When in the queachy plot Python he slew.[44]

Mortimer says of Elinor

> were she his, I wot,
> The bitter northern wind upon the plains,
> The damps that rise from out the queachy plots,
> Nor influence of contagious air should touch.[45]

It would seem likely that the "queachy plot" belongs to the classical figure
in *Polyhymnia* and gets transferred as ornamentation in *Edward I*. For
the first recorded use of "queachy" in *N.E.D.* is from Golding's translation of the *Metamorphoses*. In line 16 of his "Too the Reader" (ed. 1565)
he writes

> Eche queachie groue, eche cragged cliffe the name of Godhead tooke.

In the B. M. copy, someone has cross-referenced from this line to "B. 4.
leaf 6." where Salmacis "hides her in a bushie queach" to spy upon
Hermaphroditus. After instances c. 1450, and 1486, the next illustration
of "queach" in *N.E.D.* is also from Golding, *Metamorphoses*, I, 137-138,
who says of the people of the silver age, "their houses were the thyckes,
And busshie queaches." So Golding's "queachie groue" probably becomes
Peele's "queachy plot" for Titan's exploits with the Python. Peele would
then have transferred the phrase as ornamentation to *Edward I,* where
he is still speaking in terms of the Ovid background.

Further, *Polyhymnia* pays its respects to

> Elizabeth great Empresse of the world,
> Britanias Atlas, Star of Englands globe,
> That swaies the massie scepter of her land,
> And holdes the royall raynes of Albion.[46]

In two separate sections of *Edward I* we hear that Edward

> lives to wear his father's diadem,
> And sway the sword of British Albion[47]

while next Sir David addresses him as

> Renowmèd Edward, star of England's globe.[48]

It seems evident that the *Polyhymnia* passage is the original, and the split

---

[44] Horne, *Peele,* I, 239 (212-213).
[45] Bullen, *Edward I,* Sc. VII, 75-78.
[46] Horne, *Peele,* I, 232 (3-6).
[47] Bullen, *Edward I,* Scene II, 320-321.
[48] Bullen, *Edward I,* Scene V, 47.

passages in *Edward I* the later echoes. Particularly, the first quotation from *Edward I* restates the last three lines of the quotation from *Polyhymnia,* Britannia appearing as British, and the last two lines being reversed and entwined.

In each of our three instances of certain connection, the weight of evidence is that *Polyhymnia* precedes *Edward I.* Since *Polyhymnia* was written for November 17, 1590, this relationship would mean that *Edward I* was written shortly after, perhaps still for the autumn and winter season of 1590-91, as further evidence tends to indicate.

Cheffaud,[49] following Fleay, convinced himself of this proximate date for the play from the anachronistic statement that England's

> neighbour realms, as Scotland, Denmark, France,
> . . . .
> Have begged defensive and offensive leagues.[50]

He pointed out that in 1590 King James of Scotland married Anne of Denmark (he married her in 1589, but got her home in 1590), and that he and Henry of Navarre received the order of the garter from Elizabeth at the same time, while she was engaged in helping Henry win the crown of France. In the reference to the quakings of barbarous people at England's name,[51] Cheffaud saw an allusion to the truce Queen Elizabeth obtained in 1590 from the Emperor of the Turks for the Polonians and the Vaivod of Moldavia. It seems probable that Cheffaud was correct, though the evidence is hardly conclusive. Probably, then, Fleay's date of 1590-91 for *Edward I* is to be sustained.

Also, Peele's treatment of history indicates that the play was probably written to be performed about December of some year. The coronation date in the play is set for "14 December next," which is considered by Queen Elinor to be only a short time away. Actually, Edward was crowned, according to Holinshed, at Westminster on August 19, in the second year of his reign. Peele's history is fictitious, as one may illustrate by a further date. Luellen's birth-year is given in the play as 1272. Actually, this is the year in which Edward's reign began. Evidently Peele's dates are quite as romantic as his story.

Why should Peele have invented December 14 as the coronation day? Another allusion in the play would seem to suggest an answer. When Queen Elinor is acting the expectant mother, she repeatedly refers to the heat. Since Edward II was born on April 15, 1284, presumably Peele has here, for once, taken in a very general way his cue from history. But when shortly afterward the Welsh would present the child with a

---

[49] Cheffaud, *Peele,* 87-88.
[50] Bullen, *Edward I,* Scene I, 22, 24.
[51] Bullen, *Edward I,* Scene I, 16 ff.

mantle of frieze, proud Elinor objects, and says "For God's sake lay it up charily and perfume it against winter; it will make him a goodly warm Christmas coat."[52] These lines concerning winter and Christmas are in prose at the end of a speech in blank verse, and so may represent an insertion of some kind. The change of the date of coronation from August 19 to December 14, and the orienting of this other allusion by winter and Christmas would suggest that the play was being written about or for that season. These seasonal allusions couple with the parallels in *Polyhymnia,* written about November 17, 1590, with its relation to *Friar Bacon,*[53] which dates it after the summer of 1589, and with its echoes of the general political situation of 1589-90, to indicate that the play was written hardly earlier than the end of 1590, probably along with *Polyhymnia.*

For Peele as for Greene, the record of canonized surviving plays ends about 1590, unless *Tale* is later, though their days did not end there; and in the case of Peele, at least, his dramatic activity did not. It is thus evident from our examination that we have here only a small part of Peele's dramatic output, and that much of that is but wretchedly preserved.

---

[52] Bullen, *Edward I,* Scene X, 193-194.

[53] See p. 269.

CHAPTER VI

The Chronology of Thomas Kyd's Plays

We have considered Greene, Marlowe, and Peele as the three principal playwrights in Greene's early background. The probable dates and connections of the plays of other authors can be investigated more profitably in other connections. But because of the fundamental influence of his work we must also examine here the play or plays of Thomas Kyd.

It is now clear that Thomas Kyd preceded Marlowe, Greene, and Shakspere as a dramatist. To begin with, we have Kyd's own statement in a letter to Sir John Puckering in May, 1593, that he had served "my Lord" "almost theis vj yeres nowe."[1] Kyd's statements in this letter imply that he had not written plays in this period, but had been in some capacity which involved his attending prayers regularly in the household, as Marlowe, who merely wrote for the players, had not. In fact, in another letter to Puckering[2] Kyd refers to the kind of work he had in mind at the time he was associated with Marlowe "by some occasion of *our* wrytinge in one chamber twoe yeares synce" from about May, 1593. Marlowe is alleged to have said to Kyd "That for me to wryte a poem of St paules conversion as J was determined he said wold be as if J shold go wryte a book of fast & loose, esteming paul a Jugler." So "aswell by my lord*es* commaundm*ent* as in hatred of his Life & thoughts J left & did refraine his companie." Thus Kyd says he entered the service of "my Lord" about 1587, and implies that he had not since been a dramatist, but meditated poems on such subjects as St. Paul's conversion.

In *A Knight's Conjuring*, 1607, Dekker envisions in Phoebus' grove two companies of dramatists.[3] In the first, "sat learned Watson, industrious Kyd, ingenious Atchlow, and (tho hee had bene a player, molded out of there pennes) yet because he had bene their louer, and a register to the Muses, inimitable Bentley."[4] In the second company, were Marlowe, Greene, and Nashe, with Chettle just arriving out of breath.

---

[1] Boas, *Kyd,* facsimile; see T. W. Baldwin, "On the Chronology of Thomas Kyd's Plays," *M.L.N.,* XL, 343 ff.

[2] B.M. Harleian 6848, fol. 154; Brooke, *Marlowe,* pp. 107-108.

[3] See T. W. Baldwin, "Thomas Kyd's Early Company Connections," *P.Q.,* VI, 311 ff.

[4] *A Knight's Conjuring,* Percy Society, V, 74-77.

Thus Dekker places Kyd earlier than Marlowe, Greene, etc., which would date his efforts as a dramatist before 1587, as Kyd himself implies they were. This much Dekker should certainly have known. Dekker also gives some indication of time and the company for which Kyd wrote by his statement that Bentley the actor sat with Kyd's group because he had been "molded out of there pennes." Now Bentley was buried August 19, 1585,[5] and had belonged to the Queen's company 1583-85. The implication is that Kyd had written plays before 1585, probably for the Queen's, though possibly for some company with which Bentley acted before 1583.

Dekker's grouping of Kyd with Watson and Atchelow is also significant in other ways. Here we must look at the circle in which Watson moved. Watson was in the patronage of Sir Francis Walsingham from 1581 to the latter's death in 1591. It was at Walsingham's request that the Queen's company was formed about March 10, 1583.[6] About a year before this, we get a roster of the Watson circle in the puffers for his *Hekatompathia*, entered S.R. March 31, 1582, printed in 1582. These were John Lyly, Sir George Buc, Thomas Acheley or Atchelow, C. (probably Gregory) Downhall, Matthew Roydon, and George Peele.[7] Kyd, of course, does not belong to this select circle, though he pays his respects by borrowing from the *Hekatompathia* in his *Spanish Tragedy.*

On this particular occasion the Earl of Oxford is the central figure. It is his praise of *Hekatompathia* which is alleged to have created the demand for printing it. Oxford's "servant," John Lyly, leads the commendations under the title of Watson's "friend." But here the known Oxford connection ceases. Oxford's patronage of Watson is not known to have continued further. It would appear rather that Secretary Walsingham was Watson's regular patron from 1581. Through him, Watson would have been brought into contact with Sidney, Walsingham's son-in-law. This may have occurred before publication of *Hekatompathia,* since in it Watson praises Sidney and Dyer.

This group, then, is of the courtly reformers, a leading spirit in which was Sidney. Whether a leader or not, Oxford also had, at least, some literary interests. It is thus significant to watch the later combinations in which we find the members of this group. By 1584, both Peele and Lyly have been writing for the children's companies. Dekker implies that by 1585, Watson, and Atchelow had been writing for some company of which Bentley was a member, and Kyd had written for the same company. By 1589, Robert Greene is writing for the Queen's, and he and Thomas Nashe have much to say of praise and blame. For praise, Nashe

---

[5] Chambers, *E.S.,* II, 106; *M.L.N.,* XLI, 34.

[6] Chambers, *E.S.,* II, 104.

[7] For a competent summary of what is known about the literary interests of these men at the time, see Horne, *Peele,* pp. 66-70.

singles out Matthew Roydon, Thomas Atchelow, and George Peele, to which group Meres in 1598 adds Watson. In 1589, Thomas Watson gives Greene a puff. In this same year also, Lyly and Nashe waged war on Martin Marprelate, in behalf of orthodoxy. Later, Gabriel Harvey accuses Lyly of having set Greene and Nashe upon him, and groups the three as intimates. Here again is our circle of 1582, to which Greene and Nashe have been added. It includes still at least Watson, Atchelow, Roydon, Peele, and Lyly. Nor is there anything to show that the other members no longer belonged. Thus this background group had remained intact and still reflected courtly interests. It had regularly aligned itself with the children's companies and the Queen's company.[8]

Consciously opposed to this group in certain strictly dramatic matters, though not necessarily in others, was Christopher Marlowe and his crew of rebel angels for the Admiral's. Marlowe and his myrmidons on the one side bombarded Greene and his on the other. But this dramatic bombardment is merely one phase of a larger literary contention between the courtly, cultured group, and the more or less self-made men and rebels, a contention into which we need not now enter.

Here was Kyd's dilemma. By birth, background, and ability he should have been on the side of the self-made men, just as Marlowe should by virtue of his academic degrees have been on the side of the courtly group — and in certain respects was on their side. But Kyd desired to affiliate with the courtly group. In *The Spanish Tragedy,* he draws his models from their type of literature. By implication, he is said to have written before 1585 for the same company as Watson and Atchelow, probably the Queen's. By 1587, he withdraws from active service as a playwright, but does a certain amount of translating, still carrying on the courtly tradition. In 1593, he is unsympathetic to popular plays and to Marlowe as a dramatist. Now that he has lost his place, he turns to the Pembroke circle, which was leading the battle against the popular stage. The Pembroke circle was the innermost group of the orthodox courtly party, worshiping at the shrine of Sidney and striving to kill those elements in drama which Sidney had condemned, but which were now in full possession of the popular stage. Thomas Kyd had not been in sympathy with popular drama, though his work had by the irony of fate become one of the most potent and prolific forces in the popular movement. Nor was Kyd alone in his disappointment. There is Robert Greene's deathbed invective against these unlearned players who are now the masters, and have no place for art and Robert Greene.

The courtly circle had lost its control on drama. The children's companies were forced out of the fight by 1591, and the Queen's company

---

[8] There is no suggestion that this circle was in any sense an "organized band."

made its last appearance at court December 26, 1591. Watson had turned to other means of subsistence. Of Atchelow and Roydon we hear nothing further as dramatists, if indeed they were actually dramatists for the public stage, though we do hear quite a bit of Roydon in connection with Marlowe,[9] Chapman, etc. Lyly is not known to have written any more plays. Greene died in bitterness of heart, September, 1592, warning his old opponent Marlowe of the fate which the success of his own movement must bring him, and advising Peele and Nashe to withdraw from the drama while there was yet time. Unfortunately for their personal happiness neither heeded the warning, and Robert Greene proved to be a prophet without a single error. The actors catering to the popular taste had won that campaign, though they had by no means won the whole war. But that is another story.

When we turn to actual product, we find that the only play for the popular stage assigned to Kyd on contemporary evidence is *The Spanish Tragedy,* which was entered S.R. October 6, 1592, and printed the same year. The numerous datable reflections of life and literature in the play all belong to the years 1578-82. For the Soliman and Perseda story in the play, Kyd is supposed to have turned to Henry Wotton's *Courtlie Controuersie of Cupids Cautels,* entered S.R. July 1, 1578. Boas shows that the play clearly reflects the stylistic tricks of *Euphues,* first part entered S.R. December 2, 1578, second part July 24, 1579. The play adapts a passage from Watson's *Hekatompathia,* entered S.R. March 31, 1582. It is not possible to date the numerous borrowings from Seneca, but the ten tragedies were collected in English translation and published in 1581, entered S.R. July 4-9.

Boas would also have Kyd borrow from Garnier's *Cornélie,* which was printed in 1574, reissued in *Huit Tragédies,* 1580,[10] and again in the collected edition of 1585; but the parallels alleged appear to me either too commonplace to indicate connection, or else are Kyd's own habitual tricks of phraseology, uninfluenced by Garnier's original French. Witherspoon's detailed analysis of the influence of Garnier also makes it clear that *The Spanish Tragedy* was written before Garnier had begun to exert appreciable influence upon Kyd. "A good illustration of the difference which the invasion of the influence of Garnier into Elizabethan drama made in the chorus, may be had from a comparison of a portion of a chorus from Kyd's *Spanish Tragedie,* which is absolutely without any influence of Garnier, with a passage from one of the choruses of

---

[9] In 1593, Kyd says that Marlowe "conversd . . . w[th] *Harriot, Warner, Royden* and some stationers in Paules churchyard," and that inquiry will show he himself was not "of their consort" (Boas, *Kyd,* facsimile, and p. cix).

[10] Chambers, *E.S.,* III, 397.

Cornelia, his paraphrase of Garnier's tragedy."[11] As in the important matter of the chorus, so in that of "ink-horn" terms. "It is highly significant that, while Kyd's *Spanish Tragedie* is entirely lacking in such 'ink-horn' terms, and while his *Soliman and Perseda* contains just enough of them to number on the fingers of one hand — *guidresse, edicate, muliebritie, misintend, tralucent* — his translation of Garnier's *Cornélie* abounds in them. . . . Several of these are taken directly from Garnier."[12] Again, "To use the works of Kyd once more as an illustration of the difference made by the influence of Garnier, we may note that, whereas his *Spanish Tragedie* is entirely without such compounds, and *Soliman and Perseda* has only a few unimaginative expressions like *drie-shod, lambe-like,* and *milke-white,* his translation of Garnier's *Cornélie,* on the other hand, is brimful of them. . . . Several compounds are found in Marlowe, but their use is not nearly so extensive, and they do not show the variety of formations exhibited in the compounds found in our group."[13] "There were, at least, no more *Spanish Tragedies* after the period of the influence of Garnier."[14] "Garnier's *Cornélie* was translated by Thomas Kyd, who had several years before produced one of the most popular of all Elizabethan tragedies, and the one which is perhaps most unlike the type of drama that Lady Pembroke was encouraging."[15]

Such an analysis makes it clear, at least, that Kyd had written *The Spanish Tragedy* before he had made any careful study of Garnier. It also makes it clear that if Kyd wrote *Soliman and Perseda,* it is later than *The Spanish Tragedy,* and shows the beginnings of Garnier's detailed influence upon Kyd. It is said that Kyd used the collected edition of Garnier's plays, 1585, for his translation of *Cornélie* in 1594. If this is correct, it would not mean either that Kyd had procured this edition in 1585, or that he had not known Garnier previously. But it is at least a curious coincidence that *Soliman and Perseda,* which we date for the Christmas season 1585-86, is the first of the plays attributed to Kyd to show demonstrably the influence of Garnier's style. If the play is his, then Garnier's influence seems to have been made specific by the publication of Garnier's collected plays in 1585. Even if the play is not Kyd's, the coincidence in dates is itself equally significant.[16]

---

[11] A. M. Witherspoon, *The Influence of Robert Garnier on Elizabethan Drama,* p. 160.

[12] Witherspoon, *Influence,* pp. 167-168.

[13] Witherspoon, *Influence,* pp. 170-171.

[14] Witherspoon, *Influence,* p. 188.

[15] Witherspoon, *Influence,* pp. 91-92.

[16] For style in general, we must also allow for the influence of other popular French authors, such as Du Bartas, to mention only one, not to mention authors in other languages, etc. I suspect that much of the alleged influence of Garnier as stated by Witherspoon is mere parallel development in a common background. See, for instance,

If, then, there was any influence from Garnier upon Kyd's *Spanish Tragedy*, it was general and not specific. Boas gives evidence which he thinks shows influence. Witherspoon accepts the conclusion of Boas,[17] but without giving an examination of the point, even though his own detailed study makes it certain that Kyd shows little, if any, specific influence in *The Spanish Tragedy*. If there is any influence from Garnier at all, it is of the general nature which preceded the more accurate imitations following publication of the complete edition of Garnier in 1585. Such influence as is alleged, then, would indicate a date before 1585 rather than after. Thus Kyd's three datable reflections of literature cluster around 1578-82, and the other more general reflections are more in harmony with such a dating than with a later one. If Kyd did indeed write *The Spanish Tragedy* late in the 'eighties, he was suffering from a most curious case of arrested literary development.

The reflected contemporary events are of the same period as the reflections from literature. The "late conflict"[18] of Spain and Portugal is that of 1580. Again, as Schick points out, "such a detail from Portuguese history as that there was a special *Capitāo Donatorio* of Terceira (see *Spanish Tragedy*, I. iii. 82 and note) could hardly have been generally known in England before Terceira had come into prominent notice in the course of the Hispano-Portuguese war. It is well-known that, in 1582, the island distinguished itself by its stubborn resistance to the Spaniards. The Spanish leader, Alvaro de Baçan, Marquis de Santa Cruz, one of the greatest naval officers of the time, wrote accounts of his expeditions to the Azores, which were translated into English about 1582 and 1584. . . . About the same time, Drake had formed a great plan to crush the King of Spain's power, with the Azores as a centre of operations."[19] Of the two translations mentioned, one was printed in 1583, the other was entered S.R. October 16, 1583, and printed probably late in 1583 or in 1584. Schick also examines the historical background to the conclusion

---

T. W. Baldwin, "Parallels Between *Soliman and Perseda* and Garnier's *Bradamante*," *M.L.N.*, LI, 237-241. But even in that case the mere fact of type of parallel is still significant for chronology.

Because of the intensive nature of Hart's search for parallels, a finding of his has some significance. "There is little evidence or none of community between *Tamburlaine* and *The Spanish Tragedy*. But that does not at all apply to Kyd's later plays *Cornelia* and *Soliman and Perseda*, which show many signs of *Tamburlaine*. The absence of *Tamburlaine* from Kyd's tragedy is unexpected; Kyd was not addicted to self-restraint of that sort. Possibly they were simultaneous, or else Kyd had no acquaintance with it" (H. C. Hart, *3 Henry Sixth* (English Arden), p. xxxi). The true explanation appears to be that *The Spanish Tragedy* preceded *Tamburlaine* by several years.

[17] Witherspoon, *Influence*, p. 93.

[18] Boas, *Spanish Tragedy*, I, 1, 15.

[19] J. Schick, *The Spanish Tragedy* (1898), p. xxii.

that the list of exploits by Englishmen in Spain fits best before 1585, and that the echoes of Spanish affairs fit best around 1583-85.[20]

Further, Professor Boas points out that Kyd's reference to the extempore acting of the Italians[21] is probably a reflection from "the 'comedians of Ravenna,' whose visit to England is mentioned by Whetstone in 1582."[22] The first surviving notice of Italian actors in England is in September, 1573, and there are several records of such actors in 1574. There were Italian players of some kind at court in 1576, and Drusiano Martinelli and his company were performing in 1577-78,[23] after which we have no further records of Italian players as companies for many a year. Drusiano Martinelli, the last of these to appear, later became famous in the *commedia dell' arte,* and presumably he and his companions were acting this type of play. If Kyd gained his knowledge of Italian *commedia dell' arte* from the acting of Italian players in England, it was most likely from this company in 1577-78. So far as we now know, he could not have had a later opportunity.

Here, then, is an unusual number of references and echoes. But why are they all confined to this short period 1578-82? The only logical answer is that the play belongs directly at the end of this period, else so allusive an author, or an author in so allusive a mood, would also have reflected later events. Thus the allusions indicate not only that *The Spanish Tragedy* is later than the last absolutely definite reference of this series March 31, 1582, but also, by their clustering around the period 1578-82, that the play can not be any considerable length of time later than March, 1582.

Now Robert Greene adds his accustomed mite. In Part I of *Mamillia,* entered S.R. October 3, 1580, printed 1583, there is a reference to the story of Erasto and Persida which has some connection with *The Spanish Tragedy.* As Pharicles catches his second wind in a very long-winded address to Mamillia, he says, "Though the free stone is apt for euery impression: yet the Emerauld will sooner breake, then receiue any new forme: Though the Polipe chaungeth colour euery houre: yet the Saphyre will cracke before it consent to disloyaltie."[24] This would seem certainly to be derived from the passage of Wotton's *Courtlie Controuersie* in which Erastus "in establishement of this bargaine" of "their desired mariage" gives Persida "a iewell, wherein was a Diamante and an

[20] Schick, *Spanish Tragedy* (1898), xxiii-xxiv. In a Master's thesis (University of Illinois, 1930), on "The Channels and Sources of Spanish Influence on Elizabethan Drama, 1558-1603," Miss Margaret P. McGlothlin examines the historical background, with similar results.

[21] Boas, *Spanish Tragedy,* IV, I, 163-165; pp. 411-412.

[22] Boas, *Kyd,* p. xxiii.

[23] Chambers, *E.S.,* II, 261 ff.; K. M. Lea, *Italian Popular Comedy,* II, 352 ff.

[24] *Mamillia* (1583), E2ᵛ; Grosart, *Greene,* II, 61.

Emeralde," "Requiring his beloued maistresse, in beholding this gage of hys good wil, always to resemble in loue the Emeralde, which doth rather cracke than consente to any disloyaltie: promising for hys parte, euer to be like the Diamante, whiche throughe constante and decreed stedfastnesse, sooner breaketh vnder the toole, than endureth any newe shape, so muche the nature thereof abhorreth exchaunge,"[25] in requital of which Persida bestowed upon him the chain which was to cause so much trouble. This was, in fact, their betrothal, though it is not so called. Greene has interchanged the qualities of the two stones, but keeps the echoes. In Wotton "the Emeralde . . . doth rather cracke than consente to any disloyaltie"; in Greene, "the Saphyre will cracke before it consent to disloyaltie." In Wotton, "the Diamante . . . sooner breaketh vnder the toole, than endureth any newe shape"; in Greene, "the Emerauld will sooner breake, then receiue any new forme." The close phraseology makes it clear that Greene is here nearer to the translation of Wotton than to the original of Yver.

Since Greene next proceeds in regular rhetorical sequence to his instances, including Erasto and Persida, I take it that he has certainly used Wotton. For Pharicles continues: "And sure *Mamillia*, I call the Gods to witnesses, I speake without fayning, that sith thy bewtie, either by fate or fortune, is shrined in my heart, my loyaltie shall be such, as the betroathed fayth of *Erasto* to his *Persida,* shal not compare with the loue of *Pharicles* to *Mamillia.*"[26] The form of the name, Erasto, does not trace through Jacques Yver, *Printemps d' Iver* (1572), who has Eraste and Perside, nor through the translation by Henry Wotton as *Courtlie Controuersie* (1578), who has Erastus and Persida. *Soliman and Perseda* follows Wotton with Erastus and Perseda. But *The Spanish Tragedy* agrees with Greene in using Erasto in the actual play, though the form is Erastus in the preliminary casting. Also, in Hieronymo's recital of the argument we are told

> The Chronicles of Spaine
> Record this written of a Knight of Rodes:
> He was betrothed, and wedded at the length,
> To one *Perseda,* an Italian Dame.[27]

---

[25] Henry Wotton, *A Courtlie Controuersie of Cupids Cautels* (1578), pp. 43-44. On Greene's use of Wotton, see John S. Weld, *S.P.* (1948), XLV, 165-171.

[26] When Greene redid this section for *Gwydonius; the Carde of Fancie,* entered S.R. April 11, 1584, printed 1584, he omitted the figure of the emerald and the diamond, and adapted the Persida passage thus, "And sure Madame, I call the Gods to witnesse, I speake without faining, that sith your beautie and vertue eyther by fate or fortune is so deepely shrined in my heart . . . I will repaie such duetifull seruice, as the betrothed fayth of *Erasta* to his *Persida,* shall not compare with the loue of *Valericus* and *Castania*" (*Gwydonius* (1584), F1ʳ; Grosart, *Greene,* IV, 54-55). The passages have other connections, not pertinent here.

[27] Boas, *Spanish Tragedy,* IV, I, 107-110.

There is no emphasis upon betrothal as such in Yver, in Wotton, or in *Soliman and Perseda,* and Greene emphasizes betrothal in statement more than does *The Spanish Tragedy.* Boas thinks the *Soliman* insert "far more likely to have been written expressly for its function in *The Spanish Tragedie,* as the plot of the tale is modified to suit the peculiar exigencies of the situation in the main play. Wotton's *Courtlie Controuersie . . .* was probably the source of the Marshal's piece; though in narrating its 'argument' he cites the 'Chronicles of Spaine,' and calls Perseda 'an Italian Dame,' though Wotton speaks of her as 'borne in the Isle of Rhodes.' "[28] The form Erasto may be due to the fact that Italian was used as one language in the original *Soliman* play in *The Spanish Tragedy.* This seems the more likely since the character is referred to as Erastus in the casting of the play. It is possible, however, that there was an Italian — or Spanish — source. But if there was no Italian or Spanish original behind the *Soliman* play in *The Spanish Tragedy,* then it would seem necessarily to follow that Greene has the form Erasto from *The Spanish Tragedy,* and in his emphasis upon "betrothed truth" is echoing the "argument" in the play. And it must be remembered that there is no emphasis on "betrothal" as such in other known versions, as well as that at that point the hero is Erastus, not Erasto as in the actual play and in Greene.

If Greene is here echoing *The Spanish Tragedy,* then that play is not later than 1583, when Greene's allusion went into print. Greene's pamphlet was actually entered S.R. October 3, 1580, but is not known to have been printed before 1583, so that the reference may be an insert upon his original manuscript. The fact that it is a complete rhetorical duplication of the preceding paragraph may also indicate that it is an insert. At the very least, here is another instance of parallel between *The Spanish Tragedy* and a printed item of 1583.

Certain analogues to the story of Pedringano as told in *The Spanish Tragedy* help further to narrow the date of the play. These analogues occur in the printed work, *Copie of a Leter* (1584), now usually referred to by its later title of *Leycester's Common-wealth,* and in the manuscript first version of that book, referred to as a *Letter of Estate.*[29] Before considering these analogues, it is necessary for us to clear up certain facts

---

[28] Boas, *Kyd,* p. lvi.

[29] "Our manuscript is, Record Office, MS., *Domestic Elizabeth, Addenda,* Vol. xxviii, no. 113, ff. 369 to 388. The title page has got widely separated, and may be found in *Domestic,* clxxv, no. 101" (*Pub. Cath. Rec. Soc.,* XXI, 59). My direct knowledge of the manuscript is derived from a photographic copy permitted to the library of the University of Illinois in October, 1930. I came upon the abstract of it in working the background for *William Shakespeare Adapts a Hanging* (1931), sketched its significance, applied for a photographic copy, and put the present section into form at that time.

concerning these two versions in which the analogues are found. The printed version bears date of 1584 upon its title page. Copies of it were brought from France to England in September, 1584, by Ralph Emerson, who himself said on April 17, 1593, that he had been imprisoned "for bringing over of books called *My Lord of Leicester's books,* as he saith."[30] In another record of June 14, 1586, Emerson is said to be detained "for bringinge over sartayne books touching some of the honorable Counsell, who was comytted the xxvj. of September, anno 1584."[31] Robert Parsons had written from Paris on August 20, 1584, to the Father General of the Jesuits that "Ralph is just returned from the sea, where he has done wonders. He has planned two new ways of passage, by which he has sent in four priests and eight hundred and ten books, but it has cost us dearly. Father Weston in another twenty days will be at the sea with Ralph." Ralph Emerson set out with his cargo of priests and books about September 18 (n.s.). He succeeded in getting his books to London, but his errand "got wind and was reported to the Privy Council," who were thus on the watch for him, capturing both him and the books, though his companions escaped.[32] Thus the first attempt of Robert Parsons to launch this libel, which was popularly known as "Father Persons' Green-coat" (because of the color of the binding) had failed, though Parsons soon found means to send in other copies. Still the watchfulness of the English government made this very dangerous business. For "Government suppressed the book by a letter of Privy Council: a special law against it was introduced into Parliament but dropped. The government were so used to punishing the sale or possession of prohibited books, sometimes even by death, that further powers proved unnecessary."[33] A proclamation was issued October 12, 1584, for the suppression of seditious and slanderous books which were being imported, though the books are not mentioned by name.[34] So it was reported as late as April 11, 1585, that "1000 of the lord of lecester his book" were still at Roan in the custody of one Flynton, who printed at Rheims most of the books of propaganda which were to be sent to England.[35]

In the meantime, the book had been translated and enlarged in French. Throgmorton had started to translate it when the English version came out; but Stafford had stopped him at that time.[36] Sir Edward Stafford

---

[30] John Morris, *The Troubles of Our Catholic Forefathers* (2 ser.), p. 43.

[31] H. Foley, *Records of the English Province,* III, 35; Morris, *Troubles* (2 ser.), p. 41; *C.S.P., Domestic,* CXC, no. 32; *P.C.R.S.,* II, 249.

[32] Foley, *Records,* III, 30 ff; Morris, *Troubles* (2nd ser.), pp. 37 ff., 68.

[33] *P.C.R.S.,* XXI, 63.

[34] Robert Steele, *A Bibliography of Royal Proclamations . . . 1485-1714,* No. 775 (I, 83).

[35] *P.C.R.S.,* XXI, 72-73.

[36] *C.S.P., Foreign,* 1584-85, p. 387.

wrote March 30, 1585, of its appearance, and advised against making efforts to suppress it.[37] It also appeared the same year in Latin at Naples. Sir Philip Sidney wrote an answer to it. Queen Elizabeth thought it necessary to state officially on June 20, 1585, "Her Highness . . . knoweth to assured certainty the books and libels against the said Earl to be most malicious, false and scandalous, and such as none but an incarnate devil himself could dream to be true."[38] Numerous records show that many people were in serious difficulties over it.[39] It was a grand scandal, perhaps the greatest of Elizabeth's reign.

It is clear from all this that the *Copie of a Leter* had been printed by September 18 (n.s.), 1584, and probable that it was nearing completion about August 20, when Emerson was making arrangements for its transportation. The variant form surviving in manuscript certainly represents an earlier version of the work.[40] It is dated 1584,[41] and contains a reference to the death of Leicester's son (folio 382[v]), Lord Denbigh, July 19 (o.s.), 1584.[42] It is possible, of course, that the passing reference to the death of Denbigh was inserted later; but it is not probable. In view of the fact that the book was being printed late in August, 1584, it seems clear that this earlier draft, dated 1584, and referring to an event of July 19 (29 n.s.), had been written late in July or early in August, and had then been immediately revised and put into print. The two forms are thus very closely connected in time and authorship.

The authorship and purpose of the work are also sufficiently clear for our present purposes. "With our present fairly full information we can say with some certainty that the editor was Charles Arundell; with assistance from other exiled followers of Mary Stuart. Robert Heighington is mentioned as assisting him in a later political tract, and Thomas Fitzherbert is named as aiding with the French Translation.[43] Father

---

[37] *C.S.P., Foreign,* 1584-85, pp. 386-387; cf. 1585-86, p. 306.

[38] F. J. Burgoyne, *History of Queen Elizabeth,* p. viii.

[39] Leicester and Walsingham caused Sir Edward Stafford's man William Lilly a great deal of trouble on the ground that he had some connection with or knowledge of the libel (*C.S.P. Foreign,* 1584-85, 267; 1585-86, 306; 1586-88, 131). Thomas Morgan wrote a letter Jan. 15, 1586, to Mary Queen of Scots, telling her that Leicester believed the libel was in behalf of the Queen and against him, so Leicester was likely to injure Mary. It was reported that Leicester had sent an Englishman to kill Charles Arundell (Historical MSS. Comm., *Calendar . . . Manuscripts . . . Salisbury,* Pt. III, 129).

[40] *P.C.R.S.,* XXI, 58-59.

[41] Date at end of title on folio 1. The 8 is perfect, the 1 and 5 are damaged, but visible to the naked eye. A powerful magnifying glass makes clear in the photographic copy the very faint traces of the 4.

[42] R. Savage and E. I. Fripp, *Minutes and Accounts of the Corporation of Stratford-Upon-Avon,* IV, xiv.

[43] It is said on August 11, 1585, to be stored in Thomas Fitzherbert's room (*C.S.P., Foreign,* 1584-85, 716).

Robert Persons also had something to say to the book. At least he promoted its circulation, and though he denied authorship, it may well be that he encouraged the writing, or perhaps helped to correct or print it. The style . . . is not that of Persons; but the ulterior object of the volume, to promote the succession of the Queen of Scots, against the Protestant candidates proposed by Leicester, was quite to that Father's mind."[44] Charles Arundell and his group of agitators fled England for France because of the Throgmorton plot about November, 1583.[45] It is thus to be presumed that their work on the *Copie of a Leter* is later than this date, though they may have had previous collections of such stories on which to work.[46]

The printed form, *Copie of a Leter,* is a free and fictitious revision of the manuscript form, *Letter of Estate.* The revision was made with a purpose. "In the Catholic council of war held in the Spring of 1582 (at which both Allen and Persons were present), it had been agreed that books . . . should be encouraged . . . 'to explain the brutality, dishonesty, cruelty and crimes of the present queen . . . and to make manifest to all the right of the Queen of Scotland.' "[47] "Charles Arundell and his friends . . . resolved to re-edit [the first version] in conformity with the recommendations of the Council of War, quoted above. The principal thing was to work up to the succession of Queen Mary or King James; and they were among the first English writers to do this, undeterred by the unconstitutional opposition of the English Ministers.

"Such an addition involved great changes. The *Letter of Estate* had avoided raising the worst charges (such as the murder of Amy Robsart);[48] now they should be given plainly. Though the tone should still be quite restrained and Queen Elizabeth should not be touched, the accusations against Leicester should be open and unfaltering. This involved entire rewriting. The whole was thrown into dialogue form (this is openly stated in the French Title *q.v.*) though thereby the diffuse, antique style of the *Letter of Estate,* with its perhaps affected dialect, had to be abandoned. Great numbers of further allegations were worked into the story. So complete is the freedom in rewriting, that I can find no literal quotation from the manuscript in the printed page. If, however, the second and shorter passage [quoted by the editors] is compared with its original, we see that the paraphrasing is absolutely studied. It must really have been more deliberate than mere copying would have been.

---

[44] *P.C.R.S.,* XXI, 58.

[45] Conyers Read, *Mr. Secretary Walsingham,* II, 387.

[46] *P.C.R.S.,* XXI, 57-58.

[47] *P.C.R.S.,* XXI, 58.

[48] But it is there!

"Such alterations, however, do not make for increased authenticity. Partizanship is plainly more rife now than before."[49]

To minor details in this account one must raise objections; but from this description of the book as a whole and of what has been done in other instances, one can readily see what value to attach to the printed version of our story. The changes from the first version are merely fictitious, made for the purpose of literary effect. The story in the manuscript which is analogous to the story of Pedringano in *The Spanish Tragedy* has been thoroughly rewritten for the printed version. The manuscript version runs thus:

lett me a littell shewe you how hee rewards them that haue spente all they haue in his seruis mary deales wth them for the moste pte as men do wth there horses who while they ar stronge lusty and servishable feede them and cherish them as men should doe but when they wax lene ould and profitable [sic] and that there is no more servise to be had of them torne them to grase on an ould dich banke or els take forty pence of the dogmaster for there scinne and for an instance of the like dealinge of his lordship I will sett you downe the whole ma[nn]or thereof allthough it will seme some what tedius vnto you yet is it well worth the notinge and markinge and therby [y]oue may iudge of his pestelente nature wch in mannor and forme followinge insues [There] was not longe since dwellinge [in Yor]ckeshere a gentillman of [good birth] and caulinge wch ought of yearly reauenewes to the value of thr[ee] hundred pounds att the leaste wch genti[l] mann had a longinge desiere to gett the whit beare and raged stafe on [his] backe thinkinge if once hee might [but] get that one his sleve hee might [lorde] it wth the beste gentillman or syr [in] the country and therefore made [all] the frends that possible hee might [to] effecte and bringe the same to pass so after some frends made and no small bribes bestowed this gentill man had what so much hee desired wch whe[n] hee had obteyned his state was sone [seene] both in his countenance and in his ap[pearell] for havinge occation to atte[n]d in the [chamber] and all waies to be in his lords pr[esence he] was faine to sute him selfe according[ly] where as a fore a semly sute [wold haue] serude to haue worne among[st his] honest neybors now no thin[ge but] velvet and sattine wolde [serve his turne] his chaine of gould f[olded twice] doble about his necke [silver] braclets aboute his w[rists rings on] every finger of [his handes] wth all the reste of his appearell corespondent so as if his three hundred pound had bine three thousand a yeare it wold not haue sufficed to haue borne out his prodigall expences in so much as wth in for or five yeares expirance hee was ronne so far in the marchants books that hee hardly knew wch waie to g[e]t forth for that hee ought more by five hundred pound then all that was lefte wold make satisfaction so as cheapside Poules nor the exchange were no walkinge places in so much that hee was driven to play leaste in sight and walkt for the moste pte as oules doe by night and that in such feare and timeritie that every naile that cought hould of his [s]leve hee tooke for a sargante to carie him to the counter and livinge in this loth some life not knowinge how to remedie the same thought good to acquaint his lord wth [his] cause in what miserable state hee

---

[livde] hopinge for that in his honnors [service] and ⟨to⟩ do him credit he
had consumed [his patri]mony he wold nowe att this instant [stande his]
good lord and rid him out of These feares and preasently put his determina-
tion in practyse so as hauinge gott excess vnto his Lordchip and to h[im]
made knowne his miserable state w[th] desire of his Lordshipes favora[ble
mind he] preasently receaved this ansere of [his] Lordship how that hee had
well [and favorably] considered of his state and that he was not altogether
unmin[d]full of him but that hee shoulde finde that h[e] wold stande his
good Lord / mary well you may thinke that it should not bee for nought for
moste suttely seinge to what desperat state hee was bro[ught] and that for
hope of rewarde hee [wolde] attempte any thinge ca[l]ls him [into] his
secret chamber and there [breaks] w[th] him about his matters tell[ing him]
that if his hart wold serue [him] to attem[pt] a matter hee wold [mention to]
him and therein bee both f[aithfull and secret] hee should finde that hee
[wolde bee a good] Lord vnto him and that [when he had this] pformed and
done hee [when he should] any thinge commaunde [to have it accomplished]
Hee should make full accompte and there wth all manifestinge the same vnto
him w[ch] was no less then wilfull murther wth some what in hand as good lucke
to beegine wth all and promisse of mountains when the dede was finished
presently goes about to performe the same w[ch] ere it was longe moste wickedly
hee effected and being for the same worthely apprehended was caste amongste
other malefactors in the goale from whence wth all possible sped that may be
hee in formes his Lordship of all that had happened and wth all desires his
honnor to be mindfull of him who preasently againe sends woord by the same
messenger that he shold not not nede to put him in mind for that of him
selfe hee was mindfull enough and that it stod so much vppon his honnor as
that hee could not forgett him if hee wold but hee wilde him to be mery and
feare nothinge and for that hee could not [change] the corse of the law but
that the [law] muste nedes haue his corse yet [he must] not therefore doubt
of any thinge and as for death not so much as a thought thereof should once
troble him for that it was as far for him as from his Lordship and that his
pardon was alre[adie] sealed and thereto hee bad him [tru]ste his honnor
and all though this ch[ea]red him somwhat yett was it no smale greef vnto
him beinge a gentillmann of g[oode] birth to bee ar[ra]ind att an open sise
there was no other reamedy and session beinge att hand hee amōgste other
was called to the barr and vppon his owne confession found guiltie had
se[n]tence of death pronounste againste hi[m] w[ch] he semed littell or nothinge
to [feare] hopinge vppon that w[ch] was neve[r meant] to be sente him in so
much as whe[n the] reste of the condemned prisoner[s were] prayinge vnto
god for forgiuenes [of their] sinnes hee on the otherside was [bousinge] of
wine and drinkinge car[ouses to the] health of his lorde but nowe the da[ye
of] execution beinge come hee [among the] reste was conueied to the s[caf-
fold time] passinge a waie and he[e still lookinge] for that w[ch] was never
meant to be sent him and the executioner hasteninge to performe his office
and seinge how fowly hee was deluded wth the smale tyme of repent tance
for his sinnes wth many grevous exclamations on his lordship as on the
aughther of all his mishap wth great penitense ended his life and to this great
prefermente hee preferd him after he had consumed all his patrimony in his
servis and lastly his life who although he sofered worthely yet the blood
both of him and the other be onday asked att his wicked hands   but twenty

of these devises hath hee to rid those out of the waie that may any waie discry any of his wicked practices and devises[50]

The corresponding story in the printed version is much altered.

Ther was also this last sommer past, one, Gates hanged at Tiborne, amonge others, for robbing of Carriars, which Gates had bene latelie clark of my Lords kitchinge, and had layed out much mony of his owne, (as he said) for my L. prouision, being also otherwise, in so greate fauour and grace with his L. as no man lyuing was thought to be more priuy of his secrets thē this mā wher vpō also it is to be thought, that he presumed the rather to commit this robberie, (for to such thinges doth my Lordes good fauour most extende:) and being apprehēded & in daunger for the same, he made his recourse to his honour for, protectiō, (as the fashon is) and that he might be borne out, as diuers of lesse merite had bene by his Lordship, in more heynous causes before him.

The good Erle answered his seruant and deare Priuado curteouslie, and assured him, for his lyffe, how so euer for vtter shew or complement the forme of law might passe against him. But Gates seing him self cōdemned, & nothing now between his heade and the halter, but the worde of the Magistrate which might come in an instante, when it would be to late to send to his Lorde: remembring also the smal assurance of his said Lords word by his former dealinges towardes other men, wherof this man was to much pryuie: he thought good to sollicit his case also by some other of his frindes, thoughe not so puisant as his L. and master, who dealinge in deed, both diligentlie and effectuallie in his affaire, founde the mater more difficult a great deal then ether he or they had imagined: for that my Lord of Leycester, was not onely not his fauorer, but a great hastener of his death vnder hād and that with such care, diligence, vehemencie, and irresistable meanes, (hauing the law also on his syde,) that ther was no hope at all of escaping: which thing when Gates heard of, he easelie belieued for the experience he had of his Masters good nature, and said, that he alwayes mistrusted the same, considering how much his Lordship was in debt to him, and he made pryuie to his Lordship fowle secretes, which secrets he would, ther presentlie haue vttered in the face of all the world, but that he feared tormētes or speedie death, with some extraordinarie crueltie, if he should so haue donne, and therefore he disclosed the same onely to a Gentleman of worshippe, whom he trusted speciallie, whose name I may not vtter for some causes (but it beginneth with H.) & I am in hope ere it be long, by means of a friēd of myne, to haue a sight of that discourse & reporte of Gates, which hytherto I haue not sene nor euer spake I with the Gētleman that keepeth it, though I be wel assured that the whole mater passed insubstance as I haue here recounted it.

SCHOL. Wherunto I answered, that in good faith it were pittye that this relation should be lost, for that it is very lyke, that many rare thinges be declared therin, seing it is donne by a man so priuie to the affayres them selfes, wherin also he had bene vsed an instrument. I will haue it (quoth the Gentleman) or els my friendes shal fayle me, howbeit not so soone as I would, for that he is in the west countrie that should procure it for me, &

---

[50] Folios 17ʳ-20ʳ, pp. 385ʳ-388ʳ. For a condensed report of this story, see *C.S.P., Domestic, Addenda,* 1580-1625, 138.

will not returne for certaine monethes, but after I s[h]all see him agayne, I will not leaue him vntil he procure it for me, as he hath promissed.[51]

The accompanying tabulation will serve to bring out the relationships between the Pedringano story and these analogues.

It is at once evident that the printed version is essentially fiction. Even if there was such a person as Gates, and even if he had been clerk of Leicester's kitchen, and even if he was hanged for robbing carriers as alleged, still the general point of the story is merely carried over from the earlier version. It is the setting which has been made specific and concrete to procure a greater effect of verisimilitude — excellent literary art. The printed version may thus have been a lie which was half a truth, proverbially the most difficult kind to fight. More likely it was wholly a lie, both in setting and in fact.

The fact that the earlier version was so altered to become the printed version is sufficient proof that the former also is fictitious. The truth could not and would not thus have been manipulated.

Whence, then, had Charles Arundell and his group of conspirators their fictional suggestions? Where did they get this story which they have served up in two very different forms? It is clear that the story was not original with them. Its relations with the story of Pedringano in *The Spanish Tragedy* are sufficient proof of that. Further, their first telling of the story is much closer to the play than their second, printed, version. This first version closely parallels, and even echoes verbally the play. The second version agrees with the play rather in general motivation than in details. One may be startled, indeed, on reading in this version that the confession of Gates came into the hands of a gentleman whose name "beginneth with H." Pedringano's letter of confession came into the hands of a gentleman whose name begins with H., Hieronimo. The side-note, however, explains the motive for this addition. "This relation of Gates, may serue hereafter for an addition in the secōd editiō of this boke." The addition is merely a fictitious device to permit any number of future insertions alleged to be from the confession of Gates. The device may readily have been suggested by the play, but it is the merest possibility that the H. was suggested by Hieronimo.

Likewise, Gates' feat of robbing carriers reminds one of the old play of *Henry V*, which must have been available about this time; but the actuality occurred so frequently in life that we can establish no inherent probability that the authors turned for the suggestion to a play. Still the Oldcastle story appealed to Parsons, at least, as good anti-Protestant ammunition. In a publication of 1604 on "Protestant Saintes," he says

---

[51] *Copie of a Leter* (1584), pp. 56-58. Opposite the last paragraph is the sidenote "This relation of Gates, may serue hereafter for an addition in the secōd editiō of this boke."

Spanish Tragedy	*Leter*	*Copie*
Lorenzo, nephew of the King of Spain, and Balthazar, son of the Viceroy of Portugal, aided by the servants Pedringano and Serberine, entrap and slay Horatio, son of Hieronimo, Marshal of Spain.	A gentleman of Yorkshire became one of Leicester's retainers, and in five years was so badly in debt that he dared not appear in public.	One Gates was hanged last summer for robbing carriers. He had been clerk of Leicester's kitchen, had spent much of his own money for Leicester, and knew Leicester's secret.
Suspecting that Serberine has betrayed the murder to Hieronimo, Lorenzo hires Pedringano to kill Serberine. Says Pedringano (III, 3, 5-6) Heere is the golde, this is the golde proposde; It is no dreame that I aduenture for. Lorenzo had won him originally (II, 1, **52-53**) Not with faire words, but store of golden coyne, And lands and liuing ioynd with dignities. and is thus contemptuous of Pedringano and Serberine (III, 2, 113-114). For, They that for coine their soules endangered, To saue my life, for coyne shall venture theirs.	The gentleman appealed to Leicester, who seeing his desperate case told him if he would commit a murder he should command Leicester in anything. Also, Leicester gave him "some what in hand as good lucke to beegine wᵗʰ all and *promisse* of mountains when the dede was finished."	Relying on Leicester's favor and protection, Gates committed robbery.
Pedringano has received the money, and reasons (III, 3, 12-14) As for the feare of apprehension, I know, if needs should be, my noble Lord Will stand betweene me and ensuing harmes. Pedringano kills Serberine, but is captured by the Watch, which has been posted by Lorenzo.	The gentleman committed the murder, but was captured and put in prison.	Gates was captured and put in prison.
Pedringano is defiant, and sends a letter to Lorenzo, asking him "To stand good L⟨ord⟩" (III, 4, **56**). Lorenzo sends him a purse and a message (III, 4, 64-67) Bid him be merry still, but secret; And though the Marshall Sessions be to day, Bid him not doubt of his deliuerie. Tell him his pardon is already signde.	The gentleman sends information to Leicester, who had promised to "stande his good Lord," and claims aid. Leicester "wilde him to be mery and feare nothinge," that he must stand trial, but "his *pardon* was alreadie sealed."	Gates asked Leicester for protection, and was assured his life would be saved, though for appearances, he must stand trial.

Spanish Tragedy	Leter	Copie
Meantime Lorenzo had prayed Balthazar, who knows nothing of the plot (III, 4, 30-33):		Knowing how little Leicester's promises were to be trusted, Gates decided to solicit his case through other friends, who found that actually Leicester was "not onely not his fauorer, but a great hastener of his death vnder had and that with such care, diligence, vehemencie, and irresistable meanes, (hauing the law also on his syde,) that ther was no hope at all of escaping."

My lord, let me entreat you to take the paines
To exasperate and hasten his reuenge
With your complaintes vnto my L⟨ord⟩ the King.

Balthazar leaves, saying (III, 4, 36-37)

    ile haste the Marshall Sessions:

For die he shall for this his damned deed.

Whereupon Lorenzo moralizes (III, 4, 38-46):

Why so, this fits our former pollicie,
And thus experience bids the wise to deale.
I lay the plot: he prosecutes the point;
I set the trap: he breakes the worthles twigs,
And sees not that wherewith the bird was limde.
Thus hopefull men, that meane to holde their owne,
Must look like fowlers to their dearest freends.
He runnes to kill whome I haue hope to catch,
And no man knowes it was my reaching fatch.

Lorenzo gives a box to a Boy, in which he is to tell Pedringano there is a pardon; the Boy takes a peep into the empty box, but decides to carry out his part of the jest. Relying on the supposed pardon, Pedringano says (III, 6, 29-30),

First I confesse, nor feare I death therfore,
I am the man, twas I slew *Serberine*.

Hieronimo pronounces sentence of death.

The gentleman "was called to the barr and vppon his owne confession found guiltie had sentence of death pronounste againste him wᶜʰ he semed littell or nothinge to feare hoping vppon that wᶜʰ was never meant to be sente him."

Gates was deeply repentant.

Pedringano is immediately turned over to the hangman, with whom he jests, while the boy stands by and points at the empty box. The executioner is shocked and advises him to "hearken to your soules health" (III, 6, 75). Pedringano calls for the King's pardon, but is suddenly turned off.	Gates was executed
	Instead of praying god for forgivenness of his sins, as did the other condemned prisoners, the gentleman spent his time at the wine, drinking carouses to his lord. He continued thus merry and confident to the scaffold itself, still looking "for that wch was never meant to be sent." It was only when the executioner was "hasteninge to performe his office," that the gentleman repented his sins.
In the meantime, Pedringano had written to Lorenzo another letter just before the Boy appeared with the empty box (III, 6, 19-21): For I had written to my Lord anew A neerer matter that concerneth him, For feare his Lordship had forgotten me. The hangman discovered this letter and took it to Hieronimo (Lorenzo had thought of "fixing" the hangman, but had decided it was not necessary). Hieronimo thus finds out that Lorenzo has done these deeds.	The gentleman uttered "many grevous exclamations on his lordship as on the aughther of all his mishap."
	When Gates found that Leicester was against him, he repented of his sins. He did not dare tell the foul secrets of Leicester to the world for fear of torments or speedy death with extraordinary cruelty, so he "disclosed the same onely to a Gentleman of worshippe, whom he trusted speciallie, whose name I may not vtter for some causes (but it beginneth with H.)." This discourse the author hopes to see and use as an addition to the second edition of his book.
Lorenzo had promised Pedringano that he should "mount" (III, 2, 93) for committing the murder, meaning mount the gallows; but Pedringano thinks he means mount in worldly position.	Leicester had promised the gentleman "mountaines"; but "to this great prefermente [the gallows] hee preferd him after he had consumed all his patrimony in his servis and lastly his life."

"The second moneth of *February* is more fertile of rubricate Martyrs, then *Ianuary,* for that yt hath 8. in number, two Wickliffians, *Syr Iohn Oldcastle,* a Ruffian-knight as all England knoweth, & commonly brought in by comediants on their stages: he was put to death for robberyes and rebellion vnder the foresaid *K. Henry* the fifth."[52] Had Parsons been seeking slanderous material against that Puritan saint, Leicester, in 1584; and had he at the time known the presentation of Oldcastle in the *Famous Victories,* he would certainly have considered it a fitting story to confer on Leicester. But we know only that his colleagues were in 1584 seeking such stories.

The first and second versions together of the Leicester libels supply practically the whole of the Pedringano story from the time Lorenzo hires him to kill Serberine; and the printed version even hints at precedent villainies, under which the former part of the story might be included. At least, it is clear that the libel and the play are not independent in this particular story.

What then is their relationship? Did Kyd use the libel for his purposes? He could not have done so, since the first version remained in manuscript abroad, and was not widely propagated, while the printed second version would not have given him the story he used. He would have needed both versions to construct his story. Even if he could, he would not have used these stories from the libel, for no one dared admit connection with the forbidden thing, least of all such a cringing coward as was Kyd. Whatever the relationship of these stories, Kyd had used his version in *The Spanish Tragedy* long enough before Arundell's versions appeared in the libel to free Kyd from suspicion of complicity. Kyd could not have launched such a story after September, 1584. *The Spanish Tragedy* must have been written long enough before that date to free it from suspicion. This fact strongly confirms our previous evidence for a dating of about 1583.

Did Arundell and Kyd use a common source for their story? On that point there seems to be no satisfactory evidence. So far as I can find, no other really close possible source or analogue has been suggested for this story in Kyd. If Kyd's source could be located, it would probably enable us to answer this particular question. But the numerous verbal parallels and identities in the play and the first version of the libel count against a double adaptation by Kyd and Arundell from a common source. In case of such an adaptation, we should expect the kind of general relationship that we find between the play and the second version. It is highly unlikely, though not certain, of course, that the relationship of *The Spanish Tragedy* to the libel is to be accounted for by a common source.

Did Arundell and his group simply use their memories of *The Spanish*

---

[52] Chambers, *Shakespeare,* II, 213, cf. 217-218.

Tragedy? That solution seems highly likely. *The Spanish Tragedy* was written not earlier than March, 1582, and our accumulated evidence would indicate that it appeared at some time in 1582-83. These young men from the play-going courtly class were forced out of England in November, 1583. It is thus highly probable that some one or more of them had seen the play before ejection in November, 1583, and so naturally turned to its most ghastly story when, in July or August of 1584, the group was seeking the worst available fictions to tell upon Leicester. If this proves to be the case, then *The Spanish Tragedy* dates between March, 1582, and November, 1583. But even if libel and play merely use a common source, still the play must date several months, at least, before September, 1584. In any case, then, the play is not later than 1583; hence dates 1582-83, most likely in 1583, where considerable other evidence has placed it.

After I had written this section, Professor Fredson T. Bowers published an article calling attention to the analogue in the printed *Copie of a Leter,* but not to the much closer preceding manuscript.[53] I had myself, however, overlooked a telling point which he makes in connection with "Leycesters Ghost," affixed to *Leycesters Commonwealth* in 1641, the author of which, as Bowers argues, "manifestly based Leicester's character on Lorenzo, although he used the incidents of *The Copie of a Leter* (1584) as a foundation on which to elaborate. Thus he recalls Lorenzo's comment on Pedringano (*The Spanish Tragedy* III, ii, 113-119) when speaking (in Leicester's person) of the disposal of Salvatour:

> But what reward should such a man expect,
> Whom Gold to any Lewdnes could entice,
> Ons turne, on'st serv'd, why should wee not reject
> So vile an instrument of damned vice,
> What if hee were dispatched in a trice,
> Was it not better this mans bloud to spill,
>   Then let him live the World with sinne to fill.[54]

The final proof leaps from the page, however, when in 'Leycesters Ghost,' the poet adds the incident of Pedringano's empty box to his narration of the Gates execution.

> Of pardons, I did put him still in hope,
> When hee of felony was guilty found
>
> . . . .
>
> For his reprivall, (like a crafty Fox,)
> I sent no pardon, but an empty Box."[55]

---

[53] F. T. Bowers, "Kyd's Pedringano: Sources and Parallels," *Harvard Studies and Notes in Philology and Literature* (1931), XIII, 241-249.

[54] *Leycesters Common-wealth* (1641), "Leycesters Ghost," p. 22.

[55] *Ibid.,* p. 23. It would seem that the box device was part of regular practice. Of Hooper, Foxe tells us, "Now after he was somewhat entred into his prayer, a boxe was brought & layd before him vpon a stoole with his pardon (or at the least wise it was fayned to be his pardon) from the Queene, if he would turne" (Foxe, *Actes* (1570), p. 1683).

Though the author of "Leycesters Ghost" was writing after the reign of Queen Elizabeth, apparently but shortly after, he still sees at least the connection of the Gates story with that of Pedringano. He is likely indeed to have been aware of the original relationship, but that does not yet appear as a certainty.[56] I believe the evidence is conclusive that the *Spanish Tragedy* was the source for these variant versions in the libel.

Boas[57] sums up the evidence to the conclusion that there was a forepiece to *The Spanish Tragedy*, but that it is not the surviving *First Part of Jeronimo*, printed in 1605, and probably composed a few years before for a company of children. There is a reference in the play to the year of Jubilee, 1600. Forsythe[58] later pointed out parallels with Shakspere's *Cymbeline,* and *Julius Caesar,* 1599, and with Marston's *Second Part of Antonio and Mellida.* The parallels with *Julius Caesar* were still later emphasized independently by Bernhard Neuendorff.[59] K. Wiehl also decided against the play as Kyd's on metrical grounds.[60] It would thus appear to be generally agreed that the surviving *First Part* is not Kyd's, is not early, and so does not concern us here.

There has been considerable belief that *Soliman and Perseda* was written by Kyd, though I find no convincing evidence for such an attribution, and the style of the blank verse is oratorically quite different from that in *The Spanish Tragedy* and from that in Kyd's translation of Garnier's *Cornélie.*[61] The play was entered S.R. November 20, 1592, and printed the same year. It certainly borrows from *The Spanish Tragedy,* whether Kyd wrote it or not,[62] and so is probably not earlier than 1583. Since it is a court version, the praise of Spain and Spanish bravery must date a considerable time before the Armada.[63] The compliment of Death

---

[56] R. S. Forsythe, "Notes on the Spanish Tragedy," *P.Q.* (1926), V, 78-79 finds a parallel between "Venus Tragedie" in *Planetomachia* (printed 1585) and the Pedringano story of *The Spanish Tragedy,* concluding "One cannot be certain, however, as to whether dramatist or novelist was the borrower. That an indebtedness exists, seems in any case probable." I see nothing to indicate direct connection.

[57] Boas, *Kyd,* pp. xxxix-xliv.

[58] R. S. Forsythe, "Some Parallels to Passages in *The First Part of Jeronimo,*" *M.L.N.* (1912), XXVII, 110-111.

[59] B. Neuendorff, "Zur Datierung des First Part of Jeronimo," *Shakespeare Jahrbuch* (1914), L, 88-90.

[60] K. Wiehl, "Thomas Kyd und die Autorschaft von . . . *The First Part of Jeronimo,*" *Englische Studien* (1912), XLIV, 343 ff. J. E. Routh, Jr., "Thomas Kyd's Rime Schemes and the Authorship of *Soliman and Perseda* and of *The First Part of Jeronimo,*" *M.L.N.* (1905), XX, 49-51 had also decided against Kyd's authorship for *The First Part of Jeronimo.*

[61] After a thoroughgoing technical examination of its verse structure in comparison with that of *The Spanish Tragedy* and *Cornelia,* Wiehl decided against *Soliman and Perseda* as Kyd's (Wiehl, "Thomas Kyd und die Autorschaft von *Soliman and Perseda,*" etc., *Englische Studien* (1912), XLIV, 343 ff).

[62] *M.L.N.* (1925), XL, 348.

[63] *M.L.N.* (1925), XL, 346.

to the Queen refers to events of 1584-5, leading to an act of March, 1585.[64] Such a reference would presumably be attached to the first play the company performed at court after March, 1585. If the company was the Admiral's, as I once supposed, the first performance of that season was December 27, 1585. If it was the Queen's, as now seems more likely, their first appearance of the season was December 26, 1585. It would appear likely, therefore, that the play was written about 1585.

We have examined elsewhere the evidence for Kyd's supposed authorship of the *Old Hamlet,* to the conclusion that there is no evidence that he was in any way connected with it.[65]

The net result of our examination in this chapter is that Kyd wrote *The Spanish Tragedy* about 1583, probably for the Queen's, that someone wrote *Soliman and Perseda* about 1585, probably for the Queen's, and that someone wrote the *Old Hamlet* about 1589, probably for the Admiral's. And "someone" is not here necessarily in the singular, but is intended to include "person or persons unknown" — at least to me.

---

[64] *M.L.N.* (1925), XL, 346-347.

[65] See above, pp. 21-24.

CHAPTER VII

The Casting Pattern of the Queen's Company
before 1590

With this background of fact concerning the dramatists, their plays, and company connections, we can now differentiate at least roughly the casting patterns in the plays for the different companies at different periods and thereby still further clear the background for Shakspere's work of 1592-94.

In *Five-Act Structure* I have traced Shakspere's career with Strange's company into 1591. At that time, or shortly before, Shakspere came into contact with the plays and playwrights which had been accumulated by Edward Alleyn as a member of the Admiral's company. This connection was not finally severed until 1594. It thus becomes necessary to sift Shakspere out from the agglomerated chaos surrounding Henslowe's Diary, 1592-94. Because of the peculiar nature of Alleyn's stock, this sifting process will involve eventually a consideration of practically all the surviving plays for men's companies from about 1583 through 1594. It will be necessary first to attempt to assign the plays to their proper companies and to put them into their correct chronological order. The structure of the plays themselves is of primary importance here, since the plays were written each time for the company, and in consequence each company had its own particular characteristics of play structure.

We know that Shakspere did some writing for Strange's company at the Rose in 1592. We look, therefore, to Henslowe's Diary for light and leading. Strange's began at the Rose — or at least Henslowe's account for them began — February 19, 1592, and played till June 23, six days a week for eighteen weeks, a total of 105 performances, presenting twenty-three plays, of which eighteen were old, and of these probably seven survive.[1] The probable survivors are Greene's *Orlando, Bacon, Looking Glasse* (with Lodge), and Tarlton's *Seven Deadly Sins,* second part as *Four Plays in One,* the plot of which survives with Alleyn's papers; these four being old plays from the Queen's stock. The other three old plays were probably Kyd's *Spanish Tragedy* as *Jeronimo,* ultimately from the Queen's, apparently; probably Peele's *Battle of Alcazar* as *Muly Molocco,* apparently from the Admiral's stock; and Marlowe's *Jew of Malta,*

---

[1] Chambers, *E.S.,* II, 121-122.

apparently from the Admiral's. Thus the old plays were heavily from
the Queen's (because of Greene), and involved Greene, Peele, and Marlowe. We need, therefore, to differentiate the structure of the plays of
Strange's, Admiral's, and Queen's before 1592.

I have pointed out elsewhere[2] that Shakspere's earliest plays are constructed on a regular pattern of two young men, two comedians, and an
old man. Was this pattern peculiar to Shakspere? Was it peculiar to his
company? Did each dramatist have his own casting pattern? Did each
company have its casting pattern? We shall now examine the pertinent
facts for Strange's, the Admiral's, and the Queen's before 1592, beginning with the Queen's.

The Queen's casting pattern came nearest to that of Strange's, since
both had two principal comedians. Excluding the plays of Shakspere and
of others attributed or attributable to Strange's company, we find two
comedians in (1) *The Famovs Victories of Henry the fifth* (Dericke and
John Cobbler), entered S.R. May 14, 1594, first surviving print 1598,
"As it was plaide by the Queenes Maiesties Players," (2) *Frier Bacon,
and Frier Bongay* (Miles and Ralph Simnell), entered S.R. May 14, 1594,
printed 1594, "As it was plaid by her Maiesties seruants," (3) *A Looking
Glasse for London and England* (Adam the Clown and Alcon), entered
S.R. March 5, 1594, printed in 1594, without attribution to company,
(4) *Solyman and Perseda* (Basilisco and Piston), entered S.R. November 20, 1592, printed without date or attribution to company, and (5) *The
Old Wiues Tale* (Huanebango and Chorebus), entered S.R. April 16,
1595, printed in 1595, as "played by the Queenes Maiesties players."

We could hardly consider Ferando of *The Taming of a Shrew*, entered
S.R. May 2, 1594, printed 1594, as "acted by the Right honorable the
Earle of Pembrook his seruants," a comedian in quite the same sense
these others are, and so include that play, with Ferando and Sander as
the comedians. But if we should, then Strange's company would have
the better claim, since the total structure of the play would then be
characteristic for them.

(6) *James the fourth*, entered S.R. May 14, 1594, printed 1598 without
attribution, could belong to this classification, since, while it has three
principal comedians (Andrew, Slipper, and Nano), yet only two are men,
Nano, the dwarf, being evidently a boy.

What company or companies owned these five plays that certainly, and
the one that probably had two principal comedians? Of these, *Famous
Victories, Bacon,* and *Old Wives Tale* are attributed by their title pages
to the Queen's company. *Looking Glasse* and *James IV* have a clown
Adam, who is supposed to be Adams, the famous clown of the Queen's.

---

[2] In *Five-Act Structure* particularly.

For *Soliman* there is no direct clue to ownership. It is thus clear that we are here dealing predominantly, if not wholly, with Queen's plays.[3] It appears then that all surviving two-comedian plays for men before 1595 certainly or probably belonged to the Queen's company, or to the Strange-Derby-Chamberlain organization.

It is important, too, to note that no known surviving comedy for the Queen's company fails to show this two-comedian structure, unless it be *Orlando,* entered S.R. December 7, 1593, transferred May 28, 1594, printed 1594, "As it was plaid before the Queenes Maiestie," or *Three Lordes and three Ladies of London,* entered July 31, 1590, and printed 1590 without attribution to company.[4] We shall examine the case of *Orlando* later. In the other possible exception, *The Three Lords and Three Ladies of London,* a printed ballad is sung by the one chief comedian, Simplicity, upon Tarleton's death, and a long eulogy is given upon Tarleton. If the play belonged to the Queen's, as is usually inferred, Tarleton's death may explain why there is but one major comedian. Unfortunately, the evidence is not conclusive that the play did belong to the Queen's. The claim of Wit that he had always been with Tarleton, and of Will that he had sometimes been, though Wealth never was, has generally been taken literally; but basically it is certainly allegorical. It may also be literal; though there seems to be no clear indication of the fact. Further, the author, R. W., has been usually identified as Robert Wilson, who is supposed to be the actor Robert Wilson of the Queen's company. But no other of Wilson's known or attributed plays belonged to the Queen's. Nor is it certain that Robert Wilson, the Queen's actor, was still a member of the company after Tarleton's death.[5] Possibly our strongest reason for believing this to be a Queen's play is that no other company is so likely to have given the long eulogy of Tarleton which is to be found in this one. If it does so belong, its departure from the two-comedian pattern is doubtless to be explained by Tarleton's recent death. The evidence, however, is too tenuous and too contradictory to warrant inclusion of *Three Lords* as a Queen's play.[6]

---

[3] Chambers, *E.S.,* II, 114, agrees on five of these plays, leaving *Soliman* neutral.

[4] The negative fact, however, that a play does not have two comedians does not of itself argue against attribution to either Strange's or the Queen's, since the comedians might be employed in other ways, as in *Knack to Know a Knave,* or the comic parts may have been cut or altered, as in the Alleyn MS of *Orlando.*

[5] See Appendix, pp. 515 ff.

[6] Also, *The Three Ladies,* written about 1581, printed in 1584 as by R. W., and mentioning Paul Bucke, presumably as an actor, is closely linked with *Three Lords,* the same actor having played Simplicity in both plays. *Clyomon and Clamydes,* written about 1570, printed 1599, "As it hath bene sundry times Acted by her Maiesties Players" can hardly throw light on our problem, even if its attribution should be correct.

It is at least clear that a casting[7] with two principal comedians is characteristic of the Queen's company in this early period. We should, of course, expect such a casting for the company which numbered among its principal actors Richard Tarleton and John Adams. Says the stage-keeper in *Bartholomew Fair* (1614), "I am an Asse! I! and yet I kept the *Stage* in Master *Tarletons* time, I thanke my starres. Ho! and that man had liu'd to haue play'd in *Bartholomew Fayre,* you should ha' seene him ha' come in, and ha' beene coozened i' the Cloath-quarter, so finely! And *Adams,* the Rogue, ha' leap'd and caper'd vpon him, and ha' dealt his vermine about, as though they had cost him nothing. And then a substantiall watch to ha' stolne in vpon 'hem, and taken 'hem away, with mistaking words, as the fashion is, in the *Stage*-practice."[8] One of the chief comic characters in *Looking Glasse* is named Adam, and Oberon in *James IV* is similarly connected with the name Adam. It seems generally agreed that these two parts were acted by Adams. Tarleton was buried September 3, 1588. It does not follow, however, that all these two-comedian plays were written before Tarleton's death, since there would necessarily have been a successor of some variety. Nor do we have any record of Adams after the subsidy list of June 30, 1588, in which both he and Tarleton appeared as Queen's men.[9] We cannot, therefore, use either Tarleton or Adams to date these plays, nor can we assume that either was necessarily an actor in each of these plays, since successors would have carried on the traditional parts, at least for a time. The important fact is that the Queen's company had parts included in its comedies for two chief comedians, since from establishment in 1583 it had Tarleton and Adams as chief comedians. Its tragedies, of course, would be a different matter.

But while the Queen's plays regularly have two comedians in their comedies, yet it will appear that these plays are built on a casting pattern which is clearly distinguishable from that of Strange's company. It thus becomes necessary to distinguish this pattern, a problem which, in turn, demands the establishment of the canon and chronology of the plays for the Queen's company from 1583 to around 1595. We have already checked the plays with two comedians. For the non-comic plays, (1) *The True Tragedie of Richard the third* was entered S.R. June 19, 1594, and printed in 1594, "As it was playd by the Queenes Maiesties Players," (2) *The Troublesome Raigne of Iohn King of England* (both parts) was printed in 1591, without entry, as "(sundry times) publikely acted by the

---

[7] It must be remembered always that plays for the men's companies were at that period normally cast as to the principal lines before they were written.

[8] Jonson (Herford & Simpson), *Bartholomew Fayre,* Induction, 36-45.

[9] Chambers, *E.S.,* II, 107.

Queenes Maiesties Players, in the honourable Citie of London," (3) *The First part of the Tragicall raigne of Selimus* was printed in 1594, "As it was playd by the Queenes Maiesties Players." We shall find evidence to attach (4) *The Lamentable Tragedie of Locrine,* entered S.R. July 20, 1594, and printed in 1595 without attribution to company, as also (5) *King Leir,* entered S.R. May 14, 1594, re-entered May 8, 1605, and printed in 1605 without attribution to company, but which was performed by the Queen's and Sussex's companies at the Rose in April 1594.[10]

We may notice first that by their structure these plays fall into groups. *The Famous Victories of Henry the Fifth, Soliman and Perseda,* and *The True Tragedie of Richard the third* form one group. *Soliman and Perseda,* and *True Tragedie* are built on exactly the same plan, except that the two principal comedians are omitted from *True Tragedie.* Without these two comedians, we find two men, and two principal boys, one of the latter appearing as a boy, the other as a woman. Similarly, *Famous Victories* has the two non-comic men, and the two comedians, as in *Soliman,* but lacks the two principal boys.

1 and *2 Troublesome Raigne, Orlando,* and *Bacon* form a second group, differing for the men only in that the boy-page of the earlier group has become a man, while another boy is starting on the same progress from boy-page to young manhood. The first and second groups are tied together, and *True Tragedie* is shown to precede *Troublesome Raigne* by the fact that the former play has both of these actors as pages, while in the latter the elder page has become capable of a heavier part.

Since the *Old Wives Tale* as it survives is only half the length of a standard play, many of its distinguishing characteristics will have been lost, but it matches up best with the plays of this period, since it evidently had six principal parts for men (Jack, Eumenides, Sacrapant, Erestus, and the two comedians, Huanebango and Corebus), and one for a boy, Madge. But it has also numerous boys, as in the third group.

A third group of Queen's plays, chronologically and structurally, consists of *A Looking Glasse, Three Lords and Three Ladies,* and *James IV.* This third group, so far as men are concerned, remains the same structurally as the second, except that it adds an old man as a seventh principal character in all the plays, and another young man as a principal character in one of the four, as a distinguishable minor character in a second. The most noticeable difference, however, in this group is the unusual number of boys in these three plays. This consideration of the plays for the Queen's company before 1591, then, shows that the company had a fundamental pattern, to which additions were made at different periods of its history.

We have seen that structurally *The Famous Victories, Soliman and*

---

[10] Of these plays, Sir Edmund Chambers puts only *Leir* under unknown ownership.

Perseda, and *True Tragedie of Richard the third* form one group, with the latter two closely connected. *Soliman* would appear to date about 1585,[11] and the *True Tragedie* reflects the same general background. A few suggestions have been made, indeed, which might indicate for *True Tragedie* a later date. Hopkinson[12] noticed a parallel between *True Tragedie,* and Peele's *Alcazar.* As Richard enters wounded, with his Page, he demands

> *King.* A horse, a horse, a fresh horse.
> *Page.* A flie my Lord, and saue your life.
> *King.* Flie villaine, looke I as tho I would flie.[13]

In a corresponding situation in *Alcazar,* the Moor and his Boy enter.

> *The Moor.* Villain, a horse!
> *Boy.* O, my lord, if you return, you die!
> *The Moor.* Villain, I say, give me a horse to fly,
>   To swim the river, villain, and to fly.[14]

Again

> *The Moor.* A horse, a horse, villain, a horse!
>   That I may take the river straight and fly.
> *Boy.*   Here is a horse, my lord.[15]

Now, "the drowning of the Moor in the river when on a horse he had taken, on which to escape, and the recovery of the body" are in the source of *Alcazar.*[16] At least, then, the fact is here historical, whatever be true of its presentation; the Moor had to have a horse.

But why was the Moor's demand twice presented? It should be noticed that the second presentation in *Alcazar* is the historical one; the Moor wants a horse on which to get drowned, and the Boy presents him one, with no questions asked. Then the author has inserted a preliminary statement with question asked. Why did the Boy suppose the Moor wanted the horse in order to return to the battle instead of to fly? Most likely because in *True Tragedie* Richard wanted a horse to return to battle and not to fly. Incidentally, this horse business evidently had quite a history before Shakspere impressed it indelibly in the memories of us all. It is probable, therefore, that *True Tragedie* is earlier than *Alcazar,* which we have seen cause to date the winter 1588-89.

For another suggestion as to date, Sir Edmund Chambers points out "Collier, *Shakespeare,* V, 342, put the play earlier than 1588 on the ground that the epilogue in praise of Elizabeth makes no mention of the Armada. But 'She hath put proud Antichrist to flight' may pass for such

---

[11] See pp. 198-199.

[12] A. F. Hopkinson, *True Tragedy.*

[13] *M.S.R.,* 1985-87.

[14] *Peele,* (Bullen, I, 287); *Alcazar,* V, 1, 71-74.

[15] Peele (Bullen, I, 289); *Alcazar,* V, 1, 96-98.

[16] Peele (Bullen, I, 223).

a mention."[17] Professor Churchill had long before expressed his belief
that the passage "probably refers to the defeat of the Armada, but may
refer to the restoration of the Protestant religion."[18]

If we examine the passage in its context, it appears to be clear that
Professor Churchill's alternative interpretation, that Elizabeth has overthrown "the Catholic religion prevailing under Mary,"[19] is the correct one
after all. For at the end of the play history is brought from the conquering Richmond down to date. In due order, after Mary, succeeded
"Worthie Elizabeth, a mirrour in her age, by whose wise life and ciuill
gouernment, her country was defended from the crueltie of famine, fire
and swoord, warres, fearefull messengers."[20] Elizabeth the peacemaker
and peacekeeper, which at this period was historically the role she chose
to play,[21] is the theme of this long epilogue-speech upon her.

The particular lines suggested by Churchill occur in the sequent address
to "happy England."

> And through her faith her country liues in peace:
> And she hath put proud Antichrist to flight,
> And bene the meanes that ciuill wars did cease.
> Then England[22] kneele vpon thy hairy knee,
> And thanke that God that still prouides for thee.[23]

That is, by putting the Roman Catholic faith to flight and establishing her
own, Queen Elizabeth has caused the civil wars to cease. Since this is
in an address to England, this establishment of religion and stopping of
civil wars must refer to England. This settlement was determined at the
beginning of her reign and had been her continuing policy. There is thus
no specific reference to the Armada.

The epilogue-speech then turns to England's position abroad, as opposed
to the position at home. We are told that abroad the Turk admires to
hear her government and has sworn never to injure her. In 1584, Elizabeth's representative, one Harborne, reported that the Sultan's councillors
had sworn to him to help her against Spain. The English government was
seriously fostering the proposal late in 1585.[24]

---

[17] Chambers, *E.S.,* IV, 43-44.

[18] G. B. Churchill, *Richard the Third up to Shakespeare,* p. 469; cf. p. 527.

[19] Churchill, *Richard the Third,* p. 527.

[20] *M.S.R.,* 2192-95. I suppose few will agree with A. F. Hopkinson, *True Tragedy,* p. vii, that the last line of the quotation is "an undoubted allusion to the destruction of the Spanish Armada in 1588."

[21] See Read, *Walsingham,* III, Chapter XV.

[22] Since this is the official "kneeling" by the actor, this speech must have been spoken by a character representing England, with a "hairy knee."

[23] *M.S.R.,* 2203-7.

[24] Read, *Walsingham,* III, 225 ff.; *C.S.P., Venetian,* 1581-91, sec. 383, Introduction, pp. xxix-xlvi.

In this epilogue also, Queen Elizabeth is said to have helped the war-oppressed, and has done good to Geneva, France, and Flanders. The Geneva reference is to a semi-enforced contribution for the relief of Geneva begun early in 1583. Maillet had come from Geneva to England in December, 1582, to negotiate a contribution, and was ready to leave in May, 1583,[25] with promise of help. "Although the demand is ostensibly for voluntary gifts, they really are almost obligatory . . . if the sum given was small, they frightened the givers by saying that the Queen and Council would be very angry at their conduct in refusing to help generously so charitable a work."[26] The authorities at Geneva were hoping for the final instalment of this contribution May 12, 1585. It was reported in January and February, 1586, that the Pope and the King of Spain were preparing expeditions against England and Geneva,[27] so that Geneva was prominently in the minds of English people 1583-86, but especially so early in 1586. Again, after long preparation, Queen Elizabeth sent Leicester to Flanders in December, 1585,[28] whence he returned in November, 1586. She was also busying herself with the civil wars in France, begun in 1585.[29] Reference to all these things together would probably be most natural late in 1585 or in 1586. It is not likely to have been much later.

In all this and more, it is clear that the author is basing upon and echoing the official *An order of prayer and thankesgiuing, for the preseruation of her Maiestie and the Realme, from the traiterous and bloodie practises of the Pope, and his adherents,* printed 1586. The *Preface* to this says, "Considering the great peace and quietnesse, wherewith God hath continually blessed this Noble Realme of England, since the time that it pleased him by the hand of her Maiestie to haue the sincere trueth of the Gospel of our Sauiour planted among vs, and his great blessings of all sortes, wherewith he hath enriched vs, and giuen vs our heartes desires to our comfort, and the admiration of our neighbours rounde about vs: It were too great impietie, not to shewe our selues dayly thankefull for these great mercies, and not to craue the continuance of Gods holy hand ouer vs. But weighing further, with what perill of violent death, by meanes of wicked popish practises, our gracious soueraigne hath mainteined the trueth, which we professe, vpon whose life (next

---

[25] Thomas Birch, *Memoirs of Queen Elizabeth,* I, 26, 27, 34.

[26] *C.S.P., Spanish,* 1580-86, pp. 454, 456; cf. *C.S.P., Foreign,* 1583-84, p. 60; 1584-85, p. 473; *C.S.P., Domestic,* 1581-90, pp. 104, 106, 297; also p. 646; and John Strype, *Brief Annals* (1731), 17, 19.

[27] *C.S.P., Venetian,* 1581-91, sec. 322; cf. sec. 459; *C.S.P., Foreign,* 1585-86, p. 297; cf. pp. 327, 360, 362, 415, etc.; cf. *Cambridge Modern History,* III, 414.

[28] Read, *Walsingham,* III, 124 ff., 164-166.

[29] Read, *Walsingham,* III, 195 ff.

vnder God) the profession of the same in this land, and the continuance of the liues and welfare of vs her faithfull Subiects, doe depend . . . : with what zeale ought euery one of vs to be inflamed to prayse the Lord, for the detecting and confusion of our secret foes, whō his right hand hath bruised? And howe ought we to detest that doctrine which bringeth foorth so traiterous and bloodie fruites?" Likewise, the prayer itself begins with thanks for the preservation of Elizabeth, "First, according to her right to come to this kingdome and Royall seate of her Noble Father, and next, by her (being therein established) to deliuer vs thy people, that were as captiues to Babylon, out of thraldome of yᵉ enemies of thy true Church, and to restore vs agayne to the free fruition of yᵉ Gospel of thy Sonne our Sauiour Christ."

It will be seen that for his epilogue the author of *True Tragedie* follows the same outline as the quoted section of the *Preface* and echoes its phraseology. He begins with the peace and quietness of her reign since she brought in the true gospel incurring the enmity of Antichrist, the pope, all this to the admiration of the neighbours round about, ending also, as in the *Preface*

> For if her Graces dayes be brought to end,
> Your hope is gone, on whom did peace depend (2222-23)

Since the pamphlet was entered August 25, 1586, the epilogue would be for court performance the winter season of 1586-87.[30]

Professor Churchill believed, also, that the *True Tragedie* has connections with Marlowe's works which put it later than *Tamburlaine, Faustus,* and *Edward II.* No one of these connections is supposed to be a specific imitation. Rather, Professor Churchill assumes that Marlowe was the first to invent certain types of dramatic character and situation. Then, since he sees these types in *True Tragedie,* he assumes that the play must be later. His strongest argument is that Richard has been made to conform to the Tamburlaine type. Yet Professor Churchill admits, "Like Tamburlaine, the chronicle Richard was the ruthless and determined follower of an ambition to be king; and like Faustus, he was pictured as suffering fearful conflict with his conscience."[31] Since these are outstanding characteristics of the source, we must have either specific imitation, which is not alleged, or such an intensification of the characteristics as cannot be accounted for without assuming the influence of Marlowe. This latter alternative becomes chiefly a matter of opinion. To me, Shakspere's *Richard III* does show the intensification one would expect after *Tamburlaine* has set the type. It out-Tamburlaines Tamburlaine. But just as clearly, I think, the *True Tragedie* does not. Surely the author of that

---

[30] For the use made of this epilogue by *A Knacke to Knowe a Knaue,* see below, pp. 239 ff.

[31] Churchill, *Richard the Third,* p. 470.

play would have made a more effective Richard had he known Tambur-laine, and surely there would have been more specific influence from Mar-lowe. This alleged relationship, then, does not seem clear enough to cast doubt on the more definite evidence for an earlier date.

Professor Churchill has much stronger evidence, though he admits it is not fully conclusive, that some form of the Henry VI story similar to that in *3 Henry VI* had preceded the *True Tragedie*. This seems probable, but the story of the Contention was so well known and so thoroughly alive in the political thinking of the day that the assumptions in the *True Tragedie* of precedent knowledge may be due to this fact. For instance, in speaking of Huntingdon's claim to the throne *The Copie of a Leter* in 1584 says: "Which challenge being deriued from the title of Clarence onlie, in the house of Yorke, before the vnion of the two great houses: rayseth vp againe the olde cōtention, between the families of Yorke and Lancaster, wherin so much English blood was spilt in tymes past, and much more like to be poured out now, if the same contention shoud be set on foot againe. Seing that to the controuersie of titles, would bee added also the controuersie of religion, which of al other differences is most daunger-ous."[32] Later the author gives as his authority on this contention "Pol. lib. 23. hist. Angl." Polydore Vergil's account of this contention so inter-preted, as was the universal habit of the time, is sufficient to account for the connections between *The Contention* and *True Tragedie*.

But even if the *True Tragedie* does refer to a precedent play, it was certainly not to the present *3 Henry VI*, which is too late on Professor Churchill's own admission. Rather it was to an earlier version of this or a similar play. If there was an earlier version of *3 Henry VI*, it may have preceded the *True Tragedie* for all we know. Indeed, since the Queen's had the old *Henry V*, and the *True Tragedie*, probably written in proper chronological order at that, it is possible, even probable, that they also had an intermediate play or plays, presumably written 1583-85. But I cannot see that the evidence is as yet at all certain that they did have such a play.

It would appear, then, that the allusions in the body of *True Tragedie* date its composition about 1585-86, and that the epilogue was for court performance 1586-87. If so, it would be a reasonable conjecture that a ballad upon this subject, entered S.R. August 15, 1586, was based upon the play, as Fleay once suggested.[33] This dating would also harmonize well with the fact that the structure, as we have seen, is so close to that of *Soliman and Perseda*, which may have been presented by the company as its first court play the preceding season, December 26, 1585.

On the dating of *The Famous Victories*, we know only that the play was produced before Tarleton died in September, 1588. We have seen

---

[32] *The Copie of a Leter* (1584), pp. 120-121.

[33] Fleay, *Biog. Chron.*, II, 28.

that its structure indicates that it belongs near the group of 1585-86, probably at some time before, since the boy-page is not provided for among the principal characters. Indeed, it may be one of the earliest of the Queen's plays, produced shortly after the company was formed in 1583.

Our second group structurally of Queen's plays is *1* and *2 King John, Orlando,* and *Bacon.* We have seen that *Orlando* and *Bacon* date about 1589.[34] Since the boy-page was still a page in *Orlando,* but a young man in *Bacon,* while seemingly he is a mere boy as Prince Arthur in the two parts of *King John,* it would appear that the latter plays are earlier, and hence date 1586-88, probably nearer 1586 than 1588. The concluding couplet of King John:

> If *Englands* Peeres and people joyne in one,
> Not Pope, nor *Fraunce,* nor *Spaine* can doo them wrong.

by its hypothetical statement would seem to belong to the pre-Armada years 1585-88, when this was precisely the doubt that England faced. When hostility opened with Spain in 1585, it was rightly assumed that the Pope would help Spain. It was the fear of English diplomacy that France and Scotland might also side actively with Spain. There was especially the great fear that England's peers and people might not join in one. This fear the Armada dispelled.[35]

A reference in the play to the Friars as "bald and barefoot *Bungie* birds"[36] does not refer specifically to *Friar Bacon and Friar Bungay.* Friar Bungay was well known long before Greene put him in a play. For instance, Fabyan reported about 1504 the belief that Bungay raised mists to help King Edward in his struggle against the lords.[37] A reference to Tamburlaine in the prologue is clearly to the printed version which appeared just before *King John* itself went into print.

Our third group of Queen's plays consists of *Looking Glasse,* which we have dated 1589, and *James IV,* 1590. By virtue of its two comedians, Peele's *Old Wives Tale* should fit here. It was entered S.R. April 16, 1595, and printed the same year as "played by the Queenes Maiesties players. Written by G. P." We have seen that the satire in Huanebango fits either about 1589 or in 1593. Also, the satire, occurring only in one spot, may readily have been an insert. If it was indeed a Queen's play, the *Tale* ought probably to belong not later than 1590.

But, as is usual with Peele, the structure of the play is not clear-cut. Besides, the play is only about half of the ordinary length, indicating apparently that we have only an abridged version. As a consequence, there is nothing beyond the title page to show with any degree of definite-

---

[34] See above, pp. 57 ff.

[35] See Read, *Walsingham.*

[36] Shakspere, *King John* (Furness Variorum), p. 498.

[37] Churchill, *Richard III,* pp. 68-69.

ness that the play belonged to the Queen's. That company could have found itself parts in the play. The Ghost of Jack is the principal part, and as is usual in Queen's plays, directs the action. The villain appears as Sacrapant, third character, who fits well enough with the other villains constructed for this company. The old man Erestus, fifth character, also could be cared for. Corebus, the clown, sixth character, is not different from other clowns of the company. The wandering knight Eumenides, second character, is of a type which was never in any other play for the company of anything like the same importance. If we had confidence in Peele's judgment in fitting a play, we should consider this part a strong argument against attributing the play to the Queen's. Neither is the braggart Huanebango, fourth character, a characteristic type, though he might readily be provided for. The rather numerous women could also be satisfactorily presented by the company. But the most that can be said is that the play could have been performed by the company. Also, it would have fitted the Queen's very much better than it would the Admiral's or Strange's.[38] At least, its closest connections are found with the Queen's plays.

Fleay[39] would attribute *Arden of Feversham,* which was entered S.R. April 3, 1592, and printed in 1592, without attribution to company, to the Queen's and date it before the *True Tragedie of Richard the third* because Black Will belongs to the source of *Arden* and he thinks the actor of this part then got inserted for the sake of his name as an unhistorical supplementary murderer in *True Tragedie* as "Will Sluter, yet the most part calles him blacke Will."[40] But if the name of the actor in *True Tragedie* is William Slaughter, that would itself account for the nickname Black Will, without any need to suppose an allusion to Black Will of *Arden.* No such actor is known, of course, but Fleay would permit William to be the father of the actor Martin Slaughter. There is thus no evidence to connect *Arden* with the Queen's, and its structure is impossible for a period before *True Tragedie,* and not really characteristic for the company at any period, though it could just possibly be better fitted to the Queen's after 1590 than it can to any other company. The reason that it is not fully characteristic for any company may be that an actual story had to be presented realistically, not an invented story fictitiously. Thus fact took precedence over casting formula; a modern company faces the same problem when it would cast an old play; it must conform to a play already made, not shape to itself a story yet to be made. I believe it to be the part of discretion, therefore, to leave the play unassigned.

---

[38] This structure suggests that the play was in fact designed for Simonds and Stanley's boys, as there is other evidence to indicate. See above, pp. 170-171.

[39] Fleay, *Biog. Chron.,* II, 28.

[40] *M.S.R.,* line 1215.

c.1583-5 4+0		1585 4+2		1586 2+2		1586-8 3+1		1586-8 3+0	
Famous Victories		*Soliman and Perseda*		*True Tragedy*		*1 King John*		*2 King John*	
1 Henry V	654	1 Soliman	479	1 Richard	451	1 John	413	1 John	280
3 Henry IV	131	6 Brusor	119	3 Richmond	136	4 French King	111	3 Lewes	149
		2 Erastus	332	2 Page	137	2 Bastard	321	2 Bastard	198
				Prince Edward	51	3 Arthur	121	Arthur	26
2 Dericke	258	3 Basilisco	314						
4 John Cobbler	125	5 Piston	213						
Katherine	30	4 Perseda	242	Shore's Wife	127				
John's Wife	10	Lucina	52	Queen	78	Elinor	95		
				Elizabeth	22	Constance	93		
				York	16	Mother	52		
						Blanche	16		
						Nun	13		
						Boy	5		

NOTE: This tabulation is merely to suggest the casting pattern of the plays. It is not intended to indicate that only one actor took each of the lines of principal parts, since we do not know enough about the succession of actors and of the types they performed to be able to hazard even a guess. In some instances some of the lines themselves are not clearly distinguishable.

As we look at these plays for the Queen's before 1590, it appears that this company also had its structural pattern for a play. It is equally clear that this pattern was different from that of Strange's. To consider only those Queen's plays which have two comedians, it is clear that they are not constructed on the five-man pattern of Strange's. The *Famous Victories* has an old man, Henry IV, but only one young man, Henry V. *Friar Bacon* has the two young men, Lacy, and Prince Edward, but it has, besides the two comedians, two other principal characters, Bacon and Edward, instead of only one. King Edward might correspond to the old man, but Bacon is the lead in the play, whereas one of the young men, or one of the clowns, is always the lead in Shakspere's plays. Thus *Friar Bacon* is constructed for six principal men actors instead of five, and for

1589 4+0		1589 6+1		1589 6+1		1589 7+1		1590 6+3	
Orlando		*Old Wives Tale*		*Bacon*		*Looking Glasse*		*James IV*	
Orlando	517	2 Eumenides	102	1 Bacon	337	1 Rasni	376	2 K. of Scots	286
3 Marsilius	121	5 Erestus	72	7 Henry III	102	6 Oseas	149	8 Sir Bartram	121
2 Sacripant	192	3 Sacripant	99	3 Edward	245	3 Jonas	259	1 Ateukin	350
4 Orgalio	103			5 Lacy	150	8 Thrasybulus	101	Eustace	70
		4 Huanebango	78	4 Miles	231	2 Adam	345	Oberon	75
		6 Corebus	56	6 Ralph Simnell	111	4 Alcon	176	7 Andrew	126
		1 Jack	104			7 Usurer	115	5 Bohan	147
								4 Slipper	207
		7 Madge	56					3 Queen Dorothea	251
						5 Alvida	159	9 Ida	105
Angelica	87			2 Margaret	289	Remilia	87	Lady Anderson	46
Melissa	38			Elinor	34			6 Nano	126
				Hostess	16				

a company which had a different type of lead from Strange's. *James IV* is also constructed for six principal men characters. *The Old Wives Tale* does not have the two young men and in other respects fails to conform. *Soliman and Perseda* is the nearest of all these plays to the Strange model. But Soliman is not a typical young man of the variety regularly used, nor especially is Brusor an old man. Also, the play is not a comedy. Too, the play seems to have been of too early a date for the Strange company. It is apparent, then, that these two-comedian plays of the Queen's company were constructed on a different pattern from that of Strange's.

Presumably this pattern for the Queen's company was based directly upon the personnel of the company, as apparently it was originally in the case of the two principal comedians, and in consequence the progressive alterations of that pattern were dictated by changes in the personnel of the company; but our knowledge of the changing personnel is not yet sufficiently definite to warrant a connection of lines of characters with individuals.

CHAPTER VIII

The Casting Pattern of the Queen's Company
after 1590

It will be most convenient to consider in this connection another group of plays, not earlier than 1590, and attributed directly or by inference to the Queen's. *Selimus* was printed without entry in 1594, "As it was playd by the Queenes Maiesties Players." It is closely connected with *Locrine,* entered S.R. July 20, 1594, and printed in 1595 without attribution to company. *Alphonsus King of Aragon* was printed in 1599, without entry and without attribution to company, but as "Made by *R. G.,*" supposedly Robert Greene. This reputed authorship and its affinities with *Selimus* and *Locrine* call for its discussion here. *Locrine* was entered by Thomas Creede, and all three of these precedent plays were printed by him, but any significance this fact may have does not yet appear. *King Leir* was entered S.R. May 14, 1594, re-entered May 8, 1605, and printed that year without attribution to company. But it was performed by the Queen's and Sussex's men as an old play in April, 1594.[1]

Selimus and *Locrine* are closely connected by a patchwork of borrowings, much of it concerned with material taken from Spenser. It is thus necessary to determine priority between the two, as well as their relationship to Spenser. Since *Locrine* borrows from Spenser's *Complaints* (entered S.R. December 29, 1590; printed 1591), it is in its present form not earlier than 1591.[2] *Locrine* appears also to have borrowed a line from the printed version of Wilmot's *Tancred and Gismond,* an epistle to which is dated "From Pyrgo in Essex, August the eight, 1591." Since some copies of the quarto are dated 1592, it would seem that *Tancred* was not available in print till an appreciable time after August, 1591, probably late in the year, and hence that the passage in *Locrine* could not have been written till late in 1591. The fact that *Locrine* borrows from two publications of 1591 would indicate pretty certainly that a version of it dates in 1591 or early in 1592. The play may thus well have been the occasion of a reference to the Locrine story in *A Knack to Know a Knave,* which

---

[1] Greg, *Henslowe's Diary,* II, 162.

[2] For the best summary of the facts, see J. W. Cunliffe's résumé of the conclusions of F. G. Hubbard, in the *Cambridge History of English Literature* (1910), V, 94-98.

appeared in Henslowe's Diary as new June 10, 1592, was entered S.R. January 7, 1594, and printed the same year.

Locrine has also several parallels with Greene's *Orlando Furioso,* collected by Sir Walter Greg.[3] These, too, are borrowings on the part of *Locrine*. Mad Orlando in poetic fury instructs his page Orgalio to tell Apollo

> Ile passe the Alpes, and vp to Meroe,
> (I know he knowes that watrie lakish hill,)[4]

The Alleyn MS reads

> Ile vp the Alpes, and post to Meroe the
> watry lakishe hill[5]

Greene knew the "Ile *Meroe*" as early as *The Anatomie of Fortune.*[6] Cooper calls it "An yle in the great ryuer of *Nilus* in Aegypte,"[7] which is essentially Stephanus. But Cooper also places the isle under *"Aethiopia, A great countrey in Affrike, conteyning two regions: the hyther and the further Aethiope. The hither that is aboue Aegypt, hath on the north Aegypt. . . . In this coūtry is the Ile Meroe, where S. Mathewe is reported to haue preached the gospell.*[8] The further Aethiope. . . . In this countrey be the mountaynes out of the whiche Nilus issueth." As Greg explains, "In reality, the 'Island' of Meroe is the district between the Nile, the Atbara, and the Bahr el-Azrak or Blue Nile, east of Khartum. . . . Meroe is in fact a hilly district almost surrounded by rivers."[9] But to Cooper and his contemporaries[10] Meroe was "An yle in the great ryuer of *Nilus,"* though here Cooper places it specifically in Egypt, not generally in Ethiopia as he does elsewhere.

Solinus also gives information upon the Nile, which "inuironeth many and great Iles, whereof some are of so large and huge bignesse, that a man can scarce lakey through them in fiue dayes, runne he as fast as he can. The noblest of them is *Meroe,* about which, the Ryuer beeing de-

---

[3] Greg, *Abridgements, passim.*

[4] Collins, *Orlando,* 1086-87.

[5] Greg, *Abridgements,* p. 172.

[6] *Arbasto* (1584), C3[r]; Grosart, *Greene,* III, 195.

[7] Cooper, *Thesaurus* (1565).

[8] *"Meroë* is an Iland of *Nilus,* sometime called *Saba,* and nowe *Elsaba,* where S. *Matthew* did preache ye Gospel. From thence came the Queene of *Saba* to heare the wisedome of *Salomon.* From hence also came *Candaces,* the Queenes Eunuch, which was baptized of *Phillip* the Apostle. But at this present it is the seate of the mightie Prince, that we call *Preter Iohn"* (*The Rare and Singuler worke* of Pomponius Mela (tr. by Arthur Golding, 1590), p. 112).

[9] Greg, *Abridgements,* p. 234.

[10] Most contemporary maps show Meroe as an island in the Nile; but Greene must have been innocent of any map here.

uided, is named on the right Channell *Astusapes,* and on the left *Asta-bores.*"[11] A note on Meroe says, "Nowe called Guaguera."

To Greene also Meroe is an island and as such a "watrie lakish hill," for as Greg remarks, "a hill in a lake *is* an island."[12] The descriptions emphasize the wide spread of the Nile, frequently mentioning its lakes, causing Greene to think of it as a lake surrounding the Isle Meroe. Orlando may have selected this hill for his threatened exploit to "pull the harpe out of the minstrelis hands" (1088), because of its notoriously difficult situation. The Egyptian army having driven the Ethiopians "euen vnto Saba, the chiefe citie of Ethiopia (which *Cambyses* called Meroë, for the loue which he bore vnto his sister, who was so called) they besieged them. The Citie was strong, and verie hard to be assailed, by reason of the riuer Nilus, which enuironed it round about: on the other side, the riuers of Astapus and Astaborra did flow in so freshly, as they could neither breake the course of the water, nor wade ouer the streame: for the citie is builded in an Island, inuironed with a strong wall round about, hauing great rampiers betwixt the riuers and the walles built, to resist the inundations of the waters; which are the cause that the Citie may be very hardly taken, although the opposite armie had found meanes to passe the water."[13] Quite a "watrie lakish hill" was Meroe, and worthy of Orlando's prowess.

On this background, it is now clear that our passage in *Locrine* (1595) is the imitation in the following line, as Bernhardi[14] pointed out, and that the line borrows from the form printed in the quarto, not that surviving in the Alleyn MS.

Ile passe the Alpes to watry *Meroe.*[15]

The author has simply dropped "and vp" from the first line, fitting in "watry" from the second line instead. It is evident also, as Bernhardi also pointed out, that the whole speech in *Locrine* is based upon that in *Orlando,* and that another line is closely imitated, appearing in *Locrine* as "Ile pull the fickle wheele from out her hands" (869). The imitated line in *Orlando* reads in the quarto, "And pull the harpe out of the minstrelis hands," but in the Alleyn MS, "and pull the harpe / from out the ministrills h⟨a d⟩es."[16] Here the "from out" of *Locrine* agrees with the Alleyn MS, not the quarto. Thus the *Locrine* speech reflects both quarto and Alleyn MS, showing that the form available to the author of *Locrine* con-

---

[11] Solinus (Golding's tr., 1587), U2ᵛ.

[12] In the index of Solinus, *meroe insula* is followed by *meros mons,* which by faulty association could have made a hill of Meroe.

[13] T. Lodge, *The Famous and Memorable Workes of Iosephvs* (1602), p. 44.

[14] Bernhardi, *Greene's Leben* (1874), p. 34.

[15] *Locrine* (M.S.R.), line 856.

[16] Collins, *Orlando,* 1088; Greg, *Abridgements,* lines 250-251.

tained features of both — a "pretty kettle of fish" which we pass very hastily with out compliments to the bibliographers.[17]

Again, *Locrine* has

> Et vos queis domus ect nigrantis regia ditis,
> Qui regitis rigido stigios moderamine lucos.[18]

These lines are in the same scene as the preceding borrowing. Greg[19] finds "a certain distant resemblance, and apparently some obscure relation, between these lines" and some in *Orlando*.

> O vos qui colttes lacusque laeosque profundos,
> Infernasque domus, & nigra palatia Ditis:
> Tuque Demogorgon qui noctis fata gubernas,
> Qui regis infernum[20]

Since we know the ultimate source of Greene's lines,[21] it is clear that they are the original and those in Locrine the borrowing. The first line of *Locrine* is cut from the first two of *Orlando;* the second is a restatement of the second two of Orlando, but with "lucos" of the first line carried over.[22] Further, the quarto of *Orlando* reads "angry Nemesis sits on my sword to be reuengd."[23] The Alleyn MS has "Ride Nemesis, vpon this angry steel."[24] Greg compares *Locrine*

> For *Nemesis* the mistresse of reuenge,
> Sits arm'd at all points on our dismall blades.[25]

Here again *Locrine* is connected with the quarto version, not the Alleyn MS. It would not be possible, I believe, to infer directly which was the borrower here. Nor for that matter, could we infer directly that the two passages are necessarily connected, since this is a widespread figure.

Thus the author of *Locrine* has had access predominantly to the quarto version, not to that of the Alleyn MS of *Orlando Furioso*. The latter play appears to have been written in 1589,[26] but was being acted by the Strange-Admiral combination early in 1592, and presumably had been acted late in 1591. A contemporary, however, thought that Strange's had

---

[17] It is to be remembered that Greene himself is here apparently modelling on a passage in Marlowe's *Tamburlaine* (see above, pp. 77-78). These "beauties" were turned and re-turned!

[18] *Locrine* (*M.S.R.*), lines 895-896.

[19] Greg, *Abridgements,* p. 240.

[20] Greg, *Abridgements,* 1277-80.

[21] See above, pp. 69 ff.

[22] This proves Greg's emendation of *laeosque* to *lucusque* is correct (*Abridgements,* p. 240).

[23] Collins, *Orlando,* 1380.

[24] Greg, *Abridgements,* 372.

[25] *Locrine* (*M.S.R.*), lines 1956-57.

[26] See above, p. 78.

only a second sale of the play. If *Locrine* was for the Queen's, and if *Orlando* belonged to them, then naturally the author would agree with the Queen's version, not with that in the Alleyn MS, which was apparently for the Strange-Admiral organization. Thus the quarto of *Orlando* should represent the version of the Queen's company. But since *Locrine* does agree in at least one point with the Alleyn MS, it is clear that the Queen's version used by *Locrine* had some features which do not appear in the quarto. In general, these borrowings of *Locrine* from *Orlando* thus indicate the same approximate date of construction for *Locrine* as do the others.

It has been suggested that there was an earlier version of *Locrine* than that of 1591. Collier discovered a manuscript notation on a copy of the play, which Sir Walter Greg transcribes and reconstructs as follows: "Char. Tilney wrote ⟨a⟩ / Tragedy of this mattr ⟨wᶜʰ⟩ / hee named *Estrild*: ⟨& wᶜʰ⟩ / J think is this. it was l⟨ost?⟩ / by his death. & now [?] s⟨ome?⟩ fellow hath published ⟨it.⟩ / J made dūbe shewes for it. /wᶜʰ J yet haue. G. B⟨.⟩"[27] Sir Walter and Professor R. C. Bald have amassed what appears to be conclusive evidence that the note is genuine and in the hand of Buc.[28] If so, Charles Tilney wrote a play of *Estrild* before his execution in 1586; but even Buc, who had written dumb shows for that play and still had them, was not certain that *Locrine* was that play, though he thought so.

The evidence is clear, however, that if *Locrine* has any direct connection with *Estrild* at all, yet it must at least be a pretty thorough reconstruction and rewriting. Besides the evidence already given, Harper points out that Debon of *Locrine* first appears in Spenser's *Faerie Queene*.[29] Debon appears in Act I, 1, 139-140; gets killed in a scene direction of II, 5, is mentioned II, 5, 64-65; and III, 1, 34-36. Harper concludes "The part that Debon plays is on the one hand too slight and on the other hand too closely interwoven with the texture of the whole, to be the result of revision."[30] At any rate, the scenes in which Debon occurs, I, 1; II, 5; and III, 1, must have been at least thoroughly recast after 1590. The fact that II, 5, 1-18 and III, 1, 5-12 contain borrowings from Spenser's *Complaints* also indicates that these scenes were at least rewritten after 1590. But since *Selimus*, which was printed in 1594, borrows II, 5, 1-18 from *Locrine*, then these borrowings from *Complaints* were evidently already in the manuscript of *Locrine* which was entered S.R. July 20, 1594. The

---

[27] Greg, "Three Manuscript Notes by Sir George Buc," *The Library,* 4th Ser., XII (1932), 314.

[28] R. C. Bald, "The *Locrine* and *George-a-Greene* Title-Page Inscriptions," *The Library,* 4th Ser., XV (1935), 295-305.

[29] C. A. Harper, " 'Locrine' and the 'Faerie Queene,' " *M.L.R.,* VIII, 369.

[30] *M.L.R.,* VIII, 370.

companion borrowings from *Complaints* in the prologues to Acts I and III, would indicate that these two prologues were also written not earlier than 1591 nor later than July 20, 1594, and would imply that the other three prologues and the final speech of Ate, which belong to the same thread, were written at the same time. But the final speech of *Locrine* refers to

> that renowned mayd,
> That eight and thirtie yeares the scepter swayd.

Queen Elizabeth's thirty-eighth regnal year began on November 17, 1595, and ended November 16, 1596. The play was entered S.R. July 20, 1594, and printed in 1595 as "Newly set foorth, ouerseene and corrected, By W. S." Part of the overseeing and correcting presumably included the regnal line, and if so was done later than November 17, 1595, in order to conform more nearly to the date of publication. It seems clear, then, that the Spenser borrowings were all inserted into the story at one time later than 1590, but earlier than July 20, 1594 (*Selimus*). The last speech of V, 4, just preceding Ate's final speech, because of its borrowing of a line from *Tancred and Gismond,* is also not earlier than late in 1591, and presumably was inserted with the Spenser borrowings. If so, this revision or writing of *Locrine* occurred not earlier than late in 1591, nor later than July 20, 1594. If there was an earlier version, these borrowings show that Ate and Debon were inserted, and at least the end of V, 4 was written for this version of not earlier than late 1591.

There is some connection between *Locrine* and Lodge's *The Complaint of Elstred,* published 1593.[31] Professor Baldwin Maxwell[32] believes that the dramatist was the more likely borrower.

Another section may not have entered the play before 1593. Steevens (Amner) thought that an item in Strumbo's letter to Dorothy reflects the invitation of Venus in *Venus and Adonis*. At least, both passages do reflect the same Platonic tradition. As early in English as the *Petite Pallace* Germanicus makes suit to Agrippina. "Therefore, may it please you to understand, that since not long since I took large view of your virtue and beauty, my heart hath been so inflamed with the bright beams thereof, that nothing is able to quench it, but the water which floweth from the fountain that first infected me."[33]

Strumbo's letter is based upon the same conceit. "So it is, mistresse *Dorothie,* and the sole essence of my soule, that the little sparkles of affection kindled in me towards your sweet selfe, hath now increased to a great flame, and will ere it be long consume my poore heart, except you

---

[31] See the summary of *Elstred* in G. B. Harrison, *An Elizabethan Journal . . . 1591-1594,* p. 271.

[32] Baldwin Maxwell, *Studies in the Shakespeare Apocrypha,* pp. 33 ff.

[33] I. Gollancz, *A Petite Pallace of Pettie his Pleasure,* I, 90.

with the pleasant water of your secret fountaine, quench the furious heate of the same."[34] Strumbo has translated the Platonic ideal into the vulgar literal by localizing the fountain.

The fountain had been given some impulse toward the vulgar literal in *Soliman*. In itemizing the physical attractions of Perseda, Soliman pursues his downward way:

> Brests, like two ouerflowing Fountaines,
> Twixt which a vale leads to the Elisian shades,
> Where vnder couert lyes the fount of pleasure
> Which thoughts may gesse, but tongue must not prophane.[35]

Here is at bottom the unmentionable or secret fountain and here is the basic form of the figure underlying Shakspere's embroidery.

> I'll be a park, and thou shalt be my deer;
> Feed where thou wilt, on mountain or in dale:
>   Graze on my lips; and if those hills be dry,
>   Stray lower, where the pleasant fountains lie.
>
> Within this limit is relief enough,
> Sweet bottom-grass and high delightful plain,
> Round rising hillocks, brakes obscure and rough,
> To shelter thee from tempest and from rain (231-238).

The same fountains as in *Soliman,* not merely the unmentionable fount of pleasure, have been adapted to the deer-park figure. It is possible that Venus had some suggestion from Soliman. While Strumbo is in the direct tradition of the conceit, as in *Petite Pallace,* yet his phraseological degradation of "fountain" into "the pleasant water of your secret fountain" may have been suggested by Shakspere's "pleasant fountains," as Steevens suggested, rather than by Soliman's unmentionable "fount of pleasure." But the relationship is not certain.

Since *Venus and Adonis* was entered S.R. April 18, 1593, and printed the same year, if the echo were proved it would place Strumbo's borrowed fancy later than April of 1593. It is not "gag," since it is in an authentic version. It could, of course have been inserted by W. S. for the printed version, though one does not see why. I suppose some might argue that W. S. is William Shakspere and that he bestowed this choice bit on Strumbo at revision; but I shall not uphold that thesis. It would seem certain then that *Locrine* was either written or thoroughly rewritten not earlier than the autumn of 1591, nor later than July, 1594, that at least one insert may have been made not earlier than the autumn of 1593; and probable that the play was slightly "corrected" as it was "overseen" through the press the autumn of 1595.

---

[34] *Locrine* (*M.S.R.*), 345-351.

[35] Boas, *Soliman and Perseda,* IV, 1, 84-87.

Now *Locrine* has some connections with *Selimus* which cannot be accidental. The one really definite piece of evidence as to the relation between the two plays has been interpreted as showing that *Selimus* is the borrower. Professor Hubbard examines the fact that both plays have an adaptation of the same passage from Spenser's *Complaints*.[36] Since the adaptation agrees almost word for word in the two plays, one of them has evidently borrowed from the other. Suspicion falls at once on *Selimus,* because it borrows only the one passage from *Complaints,* while *Locrine* has several. The natural suspicion is that *Selimus* did not go directly to

---

[36] I insert the passages here as they are arranged in the *Cambridge History of English Literature,* V, 96-97, n. 2.

The Ruines of Rome, 149-160:

> Then gan that Nation, th'earths new giant brood,
> *To dart abroad the thunder bolts of warre,
> *And, beating downe these walls with furious mood
> Into her mothers bosome, all did marre;
>> To th' end that none, all were it Jove his sire,
>> Should boast himselfe of the Romane Empire.

> XII

> Like as whilome the children of the earth
> *Heapt hils on hils to scale the starrie skie,
> And fight against the gods of heavenly berth,
> Whiles Jove at them his thunderbolts let flie;
> All suddenly with lightning overthrowne,
> *The furious squadrons downe to ground did fall.

(The lines copied are marked with an asterisk.)

Locrine, 800-811:

> How bravely this yoong Brittain *Albanact*
> †Darteth abroad the thunderbolts of warre,
> Beating downe millions with his furious moode;
> And in his glorie triumphs over all,
> †Mo[w]ing the massie squadrants of the ground;
> †Heape hills on hills, to scale the starrie skie,
> †When *Briareus* armed with an hundreth hands
> †Floong forth an hundreth mountains at great *Jove,*
> †And when the monstrous giant *Monichus*
> †Hurld mount *Olimpus* at great *Mars* his targe,
> †And shot huge caedars at *Minervas* shield.

(The lines copied in *Selimus* are marked with a dagger.)

Selimus, 415, 416:

> Ide dart abroad the thunderbolts of warre,
> And mow their hartlesse squadrons to the ground.

Selimus, 2423-29:

> As those old earth-bred brethren, which once
> Heape hill on hill to scale the starrie skie,
> When *Briareus* arm'd with a hundreth hands,
> Flung forth a hundreth mountaines at great *Jove,*
> And when the monstrous giant *Monichus*
> Hurld mount *Olimpus* at great *Mars* his targe,
> And darted cedars at *Minervas* shield.

Complaints at all, but borrowed the passage through *Locrine*. The suspicion is strengthened by the fact that the passage borrowed from *Complaints* is used in *Locrine* in a single connection, while in *Selimus* it is broken into two sections quite distantly separated. This fact would seem to indicate that *Locrine* adapted the passage from *Complaints,* and that *Selimus* then broke it up into two sections. It would be a remarkable occurrence if *Selimus* had used the passage from *Complaints* in two widely separated places, and if *Locrine* had then caught the two widely separated passages and brought them back together again.

Clearly, too, *Locrine* is in certain details nearer Spenser. It has a line and an echo from the adapted Spenser passage which do not appear in *Selimus.* Spenser writes

> And, beating downe these walls with furious mood
> . . . . all did marre.

Locrine

> Beating downe millions with his furious moode;
> And in his glorie triumphs over all.

Thus *Locrine* could not have borrowed the passage from *Selimus* alone, but must certainly have consulted Spenser. Too, *Locrine* reads with Spenser "hills on hills," instead of "hill on hill," which is the reading of *Selimus.*

On the other hand, *Locrine* has mangled line 804, and has clearly omitted what must have been line 805.[37] Why should only these two lines be inferior? It will be noticed that line 804 is the end-line of the second passage common with *Selimus.* The suggestion is that someone had so marked these passages on the manuscript of *Locrine* that he obscured these two lines for the printer, causing him to mangle the first and omit the second entirely. This is most likely to mean that the passages were marked for omission from the acting version of *Locrine* and that the author of *Selimus* transplanted them to try again to get them on the stage. Another very intimate connection between the two plays is the fact that while both *Selimus* and *Locrine* should read "heapt" as does Spenser, or possibly "heapd," yet both wrongly read "heape." Surely in each case the author wrote "heapt" or "heapd." If so, the handwritings of these two authors or transcribers must have been decidedly alike in the formation of the final "t," or more likely it was "d," since the printers mistook it in each case for an "e."

Not only did the authors or transcribers have remarkably similar handwritings, but they also had remarkably similar tastes; and, further, they

[37] Kenneth Muir, "'Locrine' and 'Selimus,'" *The Times Literary Supplement,* August 12, 1944, p. 391, argues that this line has dropped out of *Locrine,* and hence that *Selimus* does not itself use Spenser's *Complaints* directly.

must have been in some way very intimately associated. It is a peculiar fact if we have at the same time two men so ardent plagiarists of Spenser, and one of whom was so over-ardent a plagiarist of the other. Since it is safe to assume that neither play had been printed at the time the borrowing occurred,[38] the plagiarist must have had very free access to the manuscript of the plagiarized. It is hard to see how he could have used the whole framework of the other man's play, and have quoted numerous passages of some length from that play, with word for word, perhaps even letter for letter, accuracy at that, unless he had continuous access to the manuscript until those passages were for some reason burned into his memory. Spenser, even though he was in print and was the ultimate model, had not been impressed on the plagiarizing author with anything like the same fullness and accuracy as had the passages adapted from Spenser in the plagiarized play. The most logical explanation is a common authorship for these passages. I do not, however, commit myself for or against that thesis.

In any case, it seems clear that *Selimus* borrows from *Locrine,* and hence could hardly in these borrowings be earlier than 1592, though it might just possibly belong very late in 1591.[39] It was printed in 1594. The nature of its relations to *Locrine,* on this supposition, would indicate proximity, especially since both plays appear to have been for the same company. *Selimus* would thus date very late in 1591 or early in 1592. That it is not likely later than this date is also indicated by the fact that it borrows from *The Faerie Queene,* and *Arcadia,* both printed in 1590, and from *Complaints,* 1591. It would seem to have been calculated to help *Locrine,* and probably *Titus and Vespasian,* in 1591-92 to satisfy, if not to satiate, the appetite of London audiences for blood.

As has been pointed out above, *Selimus* borrows numerous and widely separated passages from *Locrine.* Each of these passages would represent at least an insertion; but perhaps it is not desirable to make a complete collection of these passages here, though such a collection would make it clear that *Selimus* must at least have been thoroughly rewritten after *Locrine.*[40] Too, Aga, a principal character, will have been completely refurbished. Since the basis of the incident in which Aga figures is historical, there must have been some such character in the first version of

[38] If the question were one of borrowing from the printed form, then *Locrine,* printed 1595, would certainly have borrowed from *Selimus,* printed 1594.

[39] Baldwin Maxwell, *Studies in the Shakespeare Apocrypha,* pp. 56 ff., admits the weight of evidence that parts of *Locrine* precede *Selimus,* but is not convinced that Strumbo precedes Bullithrumble. It would appear possible that Strumbo was at least "fattened" not earlier than the autumn of 1593, to that extent bolstering Professor Maxwell's suspicions.

[40] See *Cambridge History of English Literature,* V, 95 ff. and the bibliography there given.

the play. For source, Bang[41] gives it as his opinion that "The author of Selimus, whoever he may have been, seems to have drawn his material from the Turkish Chronicles of Paulus Jovius, but whether from the original or from a translation is at present uncertain." Jovius would be readily accessible in Latin, and an English translation by P. Ashton was published in 1546. Jovius says that Acomat "caught his fathers oratour and cut of his nose and stow[n]ed of bothe his eares."[42] This is not bad, of course; but in the play it has been improved and adorned with the Senecan beauties of eye-gouging and hand-cutting.

Whence came these beauties? The only other eye-gouging English play of the period seems to be Shakspere's *Lear*. This incident is in the sub-plot of that play, not found in the old *Leir*, but added by Shakspere from Sidney's *Arcadia* (Book II, chapter 10). In the *Arcadia*, the son removes his father's eyes, and deposes him from his throne. In *Selimus*, too, the son is attempting to gain his father's throne, though it is only his father's ambassador that he mutilates. It would appear that the author or reviser of *Selimus* saw the parallels in the stories, and borrowed the eye-gouging from Sidney. The *Arcadia* was entered S.R. October 23, 1588, and printed in 1590, the same year with the *Faerie Queene*, from which also, the author or reviser of *Selimus* pillages heavily. The source for the hand-cutting is not directly demonstrable, belonging as it does to so ancient and honorable a stage tradition. But since the eye-gouging was inserted apparently not earlier than 1590, there is some presumption that the hand-cutting was added at the same writing or revision. Since, as we have seen, this version of *Selimus* can hardly be earlier than 1592, it is to be suspected, though not to be proved, that the hand-cutting was borrowed and bettered from *Titus Andronicus*. These parallels would indicate, then, that this version of *Selimus* was made in or about 1592.

There is also a parallel which indicates the same approximate date.

> Will fortune fauour me yet once againe?
> And will she thrust the cards into my hands?
> Well if I chance but once to get the decke,
> To deale about and shufle as I would:
> Let *Selim* neuer see the day-light spring,
> Vnlesse I shuffle out my selfe a king.[43]

Marlowe has a parallel to this in *Massacre*.

> Since thou hast all the cards within thy hands,

---

[41] *Selimus* (M.S.R.), p. vi. To use Grosart's own words, "we may safely assume" that Grossart had not looked at the work he suggests as source (A. B. Grosart, *The Tragical Reign of Selimus* (1898), p. ix), since the story of Selimus is not there.

[42] Paolo Giovio, *A shorte treatise vpon the Turkes Chronicles*. Translated by P. Ashton, 1546, G8ᵛ.

[43] *Selimus* (M.S.R.), 1539-44.

> To shuffle or cut, take this as surest thing,
> That, right or wrong, thou deal thyself a king.[44]

Selimus develops the figure in perfect consonance with the situation. Fortune is favoring him in the letter he has just received, and cards are the game of fortune. But Guise in *Massacre* simply assumes the figure, as is usual with Marlowe. This should mean that Marlowe borrowed. Since *Massacre* was "ne" January 26, 1593, this parallel would indicate a date about 1592-93 for *Selimus,* and if Marlowe borrowed, then *Selimus* is earlier than January 26, 1593, while *Locrine* is still earlier than *Selimus.* And the wide distribution of the Spenser and *Locrine* borrowings in *Selimus,* and the complete refurbishing of one of the principal characters shows that if the play was not written in 1592, it must have been, at least, thoroughly altered at that time.

It may be added that a parallel between *Selimus* and Kyd's translation of Garnier's *Cornelia* probably does not aid with chronology, since it is due to the fact that *Selimus* is merely translating the same passage.[45] The passage in Garnier reads

> Ie l'aime cherement, ie l'aime, mais le droit
> Qu'on doit à son pays, qu' à sa naissance on doit,
> Toute autre amour surmōte: & plus qu' enfant, que pere,
> Que femme, que mary, nostre patrie est chere.[46]

In print, these lines are set off by quotes to indicate that they are a sentential plum, and for such the author of *Selimus* has taken them. Kyd translates:

> I loue, I loue him deerely. "But the loue
> "That men theyr Country and theyr birth-right beare,
> "Exceeds all loues, and deerer is by farre
> "Our Countries loue, then friends or chyldren are.[47]

In *Selimus* we have:

> I loue, I loue them dearly, but the loue
> Which I do beare vnto my countries good,
> Makes me a friend to noble *Selimus.*[48]

It will be seen that the only coincidence between the translation of Kyd and that of the author of *Selimus* is that both render "Ie l'aime . . . ie

---

[44] Bennett, *Massacre,* II, 89-91. There is a related figure in *3 Henry VI,* V, 1, 43-44.
> Whiles he thought to steal the single ten,
> The king was slily finger'd from the deck!

where Hart (*3 Henry VI,* p. 144) quotes Peele's reversed figure in *Edward I* (Bullen, VII, 30-32) "since the king hath put us amongst the discarding cards, and, as it were, turned us with deuces and treys out of the deck."

[45] Crawford, *Englands Parnassus,* pp. 399-400.

[46] R. Garnier, *Les Tragedies* (1592), p. 113.

[47] Garnier, *Cornelia* (1594), G1ʳ; (1595), G1ʳ; IV, 1, 63 (Clarendon Press ed.).

[48] *Selimus* (M.S.R.), 945-947.

l'aime" as "I loue, I loue," bringing the repetition together, since the remaining coincidence is the result of literal translation. For the rest, it will
be seen that the author of *Selimus* is closer to the original than is Kyd.
Thus it is clear that the author of *Selimus* has merely lifted this gnomic
passage from Garnier. Consequently, we know only that this passage in
Selimus is later than the publication of Garnier's *Cornélie* in 1574.[49] Like
Locrine, Selimus also has been under strong suspicion, however, of being a refurbished older play. To begin with, the title page has a puzzling
reference to "Selimus, sometime Emperour of the Turkes, and grandfather to him that now raigneth." Now Selimus, the first, the subject of
this tragedy, succeeded his father Bajazet II in 1512. Then Soliman, the
second, succeeded in 1520; Selimus, the second, in 1566; Amurath, the
third, in 1574; and Mahomet in 1595 (1596).[50] Since the play *Selimus*
was printed in 1594, "him that now raigneth" at the time of printing was
Amurath, 1574-95, not the grandson, but the great-grandson of Selimus
the first.[51] In view, however, of the looseness with which such terms of
kinship were then generally used, we can not rely too heavily on this
seeming inconsistency.

But the face of the title page does seem to refer to a time other than
that of printing in 1594. To quote again, it reads, "Selimus, sometime
Emperour of the Turkes, and grandfather to him that now raigneth."
Selimus the first, the subject of the play, was grandfather of Selimus the
second, who should thus be "him that now raigneth." Seemingly this is
the point to the title statement; i. e., Selimus, though not the one who is
now reigning, but Selimus his grandfather. Now this second Selimus,
grandson of the first came to the throne in 1566, and died April 28, 1574.
Is the present play, then, a revision of an older play, which was written
1566-74? Collins[52] says that *"Selimus* is plainly the recast of an earlier
play," "it seems perfectly clear that the play was originally one of the
old-fashioned rhymed plays, and that it had been re-cast and interpolated
with blank verse in consequence of the popularity of Marlowe's innovations." If the title page is correct, the old play would have been written
between 1566 and April, 1574. The old *Selimus* would have been a companion play to *Cambyses,* printed 1570. If so, *Selimus* would represent
the earliest known English play on Turkish history.[53] But how would a

---

[49] Gayley, *Comedies,* I, 421, notices that a similar jest about godfathers occurs in
both *Looking Glasse* (Collins, *Looking Glasse,* III, 2, 1123-27) and *Selimus* (*M.S.R.,*
1954-57); but I see no necessary direct connection.

[50] Jean François de La Croix, *Abbrégé Chronologique De L'Histoire Ottomane,* I,
344, 362, 540, 604.

[51] Compare *"Solyman* king of the Turkes, grandfather to him that now raigneth"
(Pierre de La Primaudaye, *French Academie* (1586)), p. 239 [230].

[52] Collins, *Greene,* I, 66, 63.

[53] F. E. Schelling, *Elizabethan Drama,* I, 446.

play printed in 1594 come to have a title page fitted to 1566-74? That it
does seems highly improbable. But whether there was or was not an
earlier form of the play, the present form of *Selimus* was written or
revised not earlier than 1591. We may thus be reasonably certain that it
fairly represents the structure of Queen's plays about 1592.

We have noted the close connections in expression between *Locrine* and
Selimus. This connection also extends to structure. *Selimus* has exactly
the same number and types of principal characters for men as *Locrine*,
except that the clown Bullithrumble in *Selimus* is not given a principal
part, even though he is only a miniature replica of Strumbo in *Locrine*.
Since *Selimus*, which has the typical structure of plays of this period for
the Queen's company, uses the same casting pattern as *Locrine*, then
Locrine must also have been a Queen's play. Otherwise, *Selimus* in modeling upon it would have been warped from the Queen's formula.[54] The
three women among the principal actors in *Locrine* place the play close
alongside *James IV*, certainly preceding *Selimus*, as other facts have
already demonstrated.

Another play attributed to the Queen's inferentially is *Alphonsus, King
of Aragon*, printed without entry in 1599, "As it hath bene sundrie
times Acted. Made by *R. G.*" It has been supposed that R. G. is Robert
Greene, whose plays, so far as is known, were all written for the Queen's.
As we have seen, the play is supposed to be post-*Tamburlaine*,[55] and if by
Greene does not reflect his romances, as all his other known plays through
James IV do. If it belonged to Greene, it would date hardly earlier than
1591. Collins, indeed, decided upon that date. "From internal evidence
I am inclined to think that this play was produced early in 1591, in any
case that its composition was subsequent to the publication of Spenser's
Complaints in that year."[56] But his parallels with Spenser are intangible.

Alphonsus in its male cast pairs most closely with *Selimus* and *Locrine*,
being closer, however, to *Locrine* in the female lines. It also shares with
Locrine the device of an ambushed army. Alphonsus orders Laelius

> Go haste and fetch the youths of *Aragon*,
>
> . . . .
>
> and bring them back again
> Into this wood; where in ambushment lie.[57]

This Laelius does with decisive results. But little is made of the device.
In *Locrine*, Humber orders his son Hubba to take soldiers

---

[54] See, for instance, below, pp. 261-264, how *A Knacke to Knowe a Knaue,* and
Fair Em were modelled to Strange's company from *Friar Bacon*.

[55] See above, p. 57.

[56] Collins, *Greene,* I, 70.

[57] Collins, *Alphonsus,* 414, 416-417.

> And place them in the groue of *Caledon,*
> With these, when as the skirmish doth encrease
> Retire thou from the shelties of the wood,
> And set vpon the weakened Troians backs,
> For pollicie ioyned with chiualrie
> Can neuer be put back from victorie.[58]

Here is the same staging of a wood to conceal an army, as well as the same military device. The military ruse is executed successfully and is later referred to repeatedly as treachery, since an English hero — a Trojan with his back turned to "the grove of Caledon"! — was here the victim of a Scythian. In *Alphonsus,* all were "foreigners," so a plague of all your houses! There is apparently nothing of this ambush in any preceding version of the Locrine story. Until we know more of the sources of *Alphonsus* we cannot say whether the device belongs there. But the device and the staging of it link closely *Locrine* and *Alphonsus.*

As we examine the casting pattern in *Locrine, Alphonsus,* and *Selimus,* we find that the lead is regularly a young hero-warrior, somewhat tinged with love; Locrine (a "venerian squire,"(1850)), Alphonsus, Selimus. This lead has usually about half the number of lines of an Admiral's lead, as was also true of the corresponding parts before 1590. There is then the King-father of the young warrior lead, Brutus, Carinus, Bajazet. The young hero-warrior must have an opponent of more villainous cast, not necessarily young, Humber, Amurack, Acomat. In *Locrine* and *Selimus,* there are two other young men. Albanact and Mustapha are noble young warriors, not too well distinguishable perhaps from Thrasimachus and Corcut. *Alphonsus* has only one of these, the faithful warrior Albinius, who probably fits with Albanact and Mustapha. The other line was doubtless supplied by some minor character or characters, such as Laelius. Besides these five, there is a sturdy prop of virtue, the aged Corineus in *Locrine* and mutilated Aga in *Selimus.* Though not so virtuous, King Belinus of *Alphonsus* in other respects fits this line well enough. The clown has a principal part only as Strumbo in *Locrine,* and we have seen that Strumbo may have been "fattened" not earlier than 1593. His replica in *Selimus,* Bullithrumble, is a minor part. There is no corresponding characteristic part in *Alphonsus.*

For the female characters, *Locrine* and *Alphonsus* pair, with three principal characters each, against *Selimus,* with none. There are two viragos, Guendoline-Fausta and Ate-Medea, and a more pleasant woman, Estrild-Venus. The women in *Selimus* are all quite minor. Evidently the company had lost its large group of very capable boys. This group of three principal females appears first in *James IV,* 1590, which is the last

---

[58] *Locrine* (*M.S.R.*), 772-777.

play of the group through 1590, thus joining properly the two groups of plays. In fact, this later group of plays matches quite exactly with *James IV*, which matches most closely in structure with *Looking Glasse*. All these were evidently constructed for approximately the same aggregation of actors.

As we have seen, *Leir* was performed by the Queen's and Sussex's men as an old play April 6, 9, 1594, so that there is nothing in the record to show that it had belonged originally to either company. When we examine *Leir*, it is apparent that it does not fit the casting pattern for the Queen's at all well. Its lead is aged King Leir, who does not fit with the young hero-warrior lead of the other plays. Equally aged Perillus could be fitted to the King-father line, but is not characteristic. By villainous function the Messenger-murderer could be joined to the "villain" opponent, but is not characteristic. The Gallian King should have been the lead in the Queen's casting pattern, but could be taken by the actor of Albanact and Acomat. But jesting Mumford has no counterpart in any of the plays for the Queen's organization. Nor is there any clowning in *Leir*. The large number of principal parts for women, three, is characteristic of the Queen's casting pattern around 1590. But as a whole *Leir* is not built on the same casting formula as the Queen's.

The reason for the non-conformity of *Leir* is at once evident. It will be remembered that it was performed by the Queen's and Sussex's together. Now the Queen's men of this combination did not belong to the main group of Queen's men which we have been tracing. The structure of *Leir* indicates the same thing. It was not constructed for the Queen's company. Whether it was constructed for Sussex's alone, for this other Queen's organization alone, for the Sussex's-Queen's combination, or for some other company entirely, I know of no evidence to show.

These facts of structure for Queen's plays correlate significantly with the facts known about the company at this period. It had been made up from various companies in 1583, and had continued to appear as separate groups, especially in the provinces. There had been a particularly significant break about 1590. For the two plays at court 1589-90, "John Dutton and John Lanham" received the pay. Then the next season 1590-91, "Lawrence Dutton and John Dutton" received pay for four plays, and "John Laneham" received pay for one. There were thus two Queen's organizations at court this season. That there were two groups is also shown by the fact that while the Dutton group was performing one of its four court plays on February 14, 1591, another Queen's company was playing with Sussex's men at Southampton. This Queen's and Sussex's combination appears occasionally as late as 1594, and it was by it that

Leir was acted.[59] There were at least two Queen's companies in 1591. The following court season of 1591-92, there was only one play by a Queen's company at court, with no payee named. For the first time since 1583, the company is almost unrepresented. For 1592-93, the Queen's do not appear at all. For 1593-94 once, doubtless the Queen's-Sussex's group, payee unspecified, and never again. It is evident that the main organization of Queen's men deteriorated or ceased about 1591. It is evident also that our Queen's plays are for the main organization at this period, the coincidence of dates being exact.

Apparently, *Selimus* belongs at the very end, when in some way the group of able boys had already been lost. This group of boys shows first about the summer of 1590 in *James IV*, and this fact also correlates with something. As we have seen, the plays of Robert Greene previous to *James IV*, and also Tarleton's *2 Seven Deadly Sins* had passed to the Strange-Admiral combination by 1592, the latter, and presumably all, through Edward Alleyn of the Admiral's. The corresponding facts indicate that some change occurred in the Queen's about 1589-90, leading to their final exit as a London company in 1591-92.

---

[59] For the date of *Leir,* "Though 'The most famous Chronicle historye of Leire kinge of England and his Three Daughters' was registered for publication on May 14, 1594, and a King Leir play is recorded by Henslowe to have been acted several times in May, 1594, Greg doubts its actual publication in that year and sees possibility of revision before 1605. Aside from stylistic evidence, the argument for its early composition is strengthened by the dates of its sources, viz., Warner's *Albion's England* (1586), *The Mirour for Magistrates* (1587), Spenser's *Faerie Queene* (1590), and Lodge's *Rosalynde* (1590). Add to these dates Shakespeare's *Richard III* (*ca.* 1593) and Yarington's *Two Lamentable Tragedies* (probably composed 1594), both of which, I believe, echoed lines from *King Leir*" (R. A. Law, *"King Leir* and *King Lear,"* *Studies in Honor of T. W. Baldwin,* pp. 121-122, n. 10).

Locrine 7+3		*Alphonsus* 5+3		*Selimus* 6+0	
1 Locrine	306	1 Alphonsus	372	1 Selimus	635
6 Brutus	143	3 Carinus	179	2 Bajazet	545
2 Humber	274	2 Amurack	243	3 Acomat	278
5 Albanact	145	5 Albinius	153	4 Mustaffa	163
4 Corineus	166	7 Velinus	143	6 Aga	103
7 Thrasimachus	136	Laelius	72	5 Corcut	115
3 Strumbo	262			Bullithrumble	82
Trumpart	19				
8 Guendoline	120	8 Fausta	113		
9 Estrild	100	4 Venus	162		
10 Ate	100	6 Medea	145		
Sabren	62	Iphigina	72	Queen of Amasia	35
Madan	4	Melpomene	11	Solyma	27
Page	4	Clio	5	Zonara	14
		Calliope	22	Page	15
		Six other Muses			

NOTE: This tabulation is merely to suggest the casting pattern of the plays. It is not intended to indicate that only one actor took each of the lines of principal parts, since we do not know enough about the succession of actors and of the types they performed to be able to hazard even a guess. In some instances some of the lines themselves are not clearly distinguishable.

CHAPTER IX

The Casting Pattern of the Admiral's Company
before 1590

We have now checked upon the Queen's plays, some of which were available to Strange's in 1592. At that period, Strange's was cooperating in some fashion and form with the Admiral's of some fashion and form, whose plays before 1590 we now examine.

We have seen that Marlowe wrote *1* and *2 Tamburlaine* for the Admiral's in 1587, *Faustus* probably in 1588, *Jew of Malta* probably 1590. Of these, *1* and *2 Tamburlaine* were entered S.R. August 14, 1590, and printed the same year "as they were sundrie times shewed vpon Stages in the Citie of London. By the right honorable the Lord Admyrall, his seruantes." *Doctor Faustus* was entered S.R. January 7, 1601, and printed 1604. "As it hath bene Acted by the Right Honorable the Earle of Nottingham his seruants." *The Jew of Malta* was entered S.R. May 17, 1594, but the first known print is 1633. It is known to have been performed by the Admiral's company among others, and remained with them. Peele's *Battle of Alcazar* belongs to the autumn and winter of 1588-89.[1] It was printed without entry in 1594, "As it was sundrie times plaid by the Lord high Admirall his seruants."

Besides these plays by Marlowe and Peele, Lodge's *Wounds of Civil War* also belongs to this period. This was entered S.R. May 24, 1594, and printed the same year, "As it hath beene publiquely plaide in London, by the Right Honourable the Lord high Admirall his Seruants," but does not appear in Henslowe's Diary, so is presumably earlier than 1592. Its chariot drawn by four Moors is clearly later than *Tamburlaine,* thus hardly earlier than 1588, where writers on Lodge seem disposed to leave it.

Greene and Nashe in *Menaphon,* August, 1589, assign *Hamlet* by inference to the Admiral's and the torso of its structure survives as *Bestrafte Brudermord.* That structure is nearest to that of the *Jew of Malta,* about 1590, and the indications are that this *Hamlet* was a current play the summer of 1589. So was *A Shrew,* referred to in the same connection. Besides these, *Titus Andronicus* has the typical structure for an Admiral's play at this period. This fact is in accord with Jonson's statement in 1614 that *Titus* and the *Spanish Tragedy* had been on the stage "these fiue and

---

[1] See above, p. 167.

twentie, or thirtie yeeres."[2] That would place the dates of the two plays between 1584 and 1589. The structure of *Titus* is closest to that of *Alcazar,* which is earlier than April 1589. The *Spanish Tragedy* also conforms to the Admiral's plays of this period. *By structure only,* the play of *Edward III,* entered S.R. December 1, 1595, and printed in 1596, without attribution to company, also claims a place among Admiral's plays. There is some evidence, however, that the English comedians had performed a play of Edward III in Danzig by 1591,[3] which would indicate the same general date, the play being possibly connected with the wandering contingent of the Admiral's in 1590.

As we look at the structure of the plays for the Admiral's before 1590, one outstanding characteristic is at once apparent. The lead has usually about three times as many lines as anyone else in the play. This fact is doubtless due to the prominence of Edward Alleyn as an actor; he came nearest to being "starred" of any actor of the period. A second line of characters works with or against this lead: Jeronimo-Lorenzo, Tamburlaine-Bajazeth, Tamburlaine-Callipine, Scilla-Marius, Faustus-Mephistophilis, Sebastian-Moor, Titus-Aaron, Hamlet-King, Barabas-Ithamore, Edward III-King John. This second line usually ranks second in number of lines for men. The lead is ordinarily of the dominating, Tamburlaine type; the second line is ordinarily his only less dominating opponent, or else his chief assistant in his mighty ambitions. The third major part is a rather oratorical dignitary, frequently, though not necessarily, of some age: King, Cosroe, Orcanes, Anthony, Emperor of Germany, Abdelmelec, Marcus, Corambis, Farneze, Warwick. The fourth major part is a rather young warrior: Balthazar, Theridimas, Theridimas, Young Marius, ?Wagner, Stukeley, Lucius, Horatio, Calymath, Prince Edward. There is a fifth major part, at times in penumbra, which may be best described as a Lord, sometimes of a slightly humorous turn. A remarkable fact here is that there is no major comedian. The clowns are incidental. The greatly preponderating serious lead and the lack of major comedian give the Admiral's plays a distinctive structure. For the boys, there is usually one major woman, a second less prominent one, and occasional small parts both as women and as boys. But the feminine interest is not strongly marked in the plays for the Admiral's company. The play of Lodge and that of Peele do not give the male lead quite so preponderating a role as do the others, but in other respects are typical.

It may be well to point out here how typical are the plays that partly or wholly because of structure we have assigned to the Admiral's at this period. To begin with *Titus,* this is closest akin structurally to *Alcazar.*

---

[2] Chambers, *Shakespeare,* II, 206.

[3] E. Herz, *Englische Schauspieler . . . in Deutschland* (1903), pp. 5-6.

Titus, the lead, has more than twice the number of lines of the second man, who is Aaron, the villainous Moor, corresponding to the Moor of *Alcazar*. This pairing of the lead and villain as the two chief characters is characteristic also of the plays for the Admiral's company. The third character is the elderly dignitary, in this play Marcus. The young warrior who is usually fourth for men is in this case fifth by thirteen lines, appearing as Lucius. The five major parts for men, all serious, are completed by Saturninus, who here is the fourth character for men. There is also but one major part for a woman, Tamora, who ranks fourth in total lines, as happens regularly in the plays for the Admiral's at this period. Clearly, *Titus Andronicus* was first written for the Admiral's men around 1588 or 1589, where Jonson places it, and — what is more important — clearly its fundamental structure has not been altered in revision. I need not point out the bearing of this fact on the question of authorship.

The German *Hamlet (Bestrafte Brudermord)* also shows the characteristic structure of this period, representing as it does the *Old Hamlet* referred to by Nashe and Greene. While the play is badly mauled, yet the torso is still recognizable. Hamlet, the lead, has more than twice as many lines as his villain opponent the King. Here is the characteristic Admiral's pairing, both in relative importance and in lines represented. True to form, the elderly Corambis occupies the third place, as is consistently true of the Admiral's plays. The other two men are characteristically Horatio and Leonardo. So in *Bestrafte Brudermord* Horatio is consistently emphasized as a military leader, as is characteristic of the line for the Admiral's. Though he still in Shakspere is a member of the watch, yet his military connection is not emphasized. There is also a significant point in connection with the casting of the women. The Queen is now first and Ophelia second, as was true of these types for the Admiral's at the period of writing. But Shakspere in revision has heightened the part of Ophelia and lowered that of the Queen. It is thus at least clear that the *Old Hamlet* referred to by Nashe and Greene in August, 1589, was typical of the Admiral's structure at the time. It is curious that it also, like *Titus Andronicus,* tends to pair best with Peele's *Alcazar,* but also with the *Jew of Malta.*

The *Spanish Tragedy* also belonged eventually to the Admiral's men. The first company to be connected directly with the play, however, is Strange's, during its period of cooperation with the Admiral's, which performed it March 14, 1592, and following.[4] After the Admiral's reformed, they began another series of performances of the play January 7, 1597, later had "additions" written for it, etc. Dekker implies that Kyd wrote for the Queen's, which might be supposed to give some indication

---

[4] Greg, *Henslowe's Diary,* II, 153.

that the *Spanish Tragedy* was originally written for that company and passed with other Queen's plays to the Admiral's. But the structure of the play is typical of the Admiral's company, whether it was written originally for that company or had already had "additions" to fit it to that company when it first came to print.

The *Spanish Tragedy* does not conform to the formula for the Queen's, since it has no comedians, its lead has far more lines than were customary in the Queen's, and it has about twice as many serious characters as were usual in that company. On the other hand, Hieronimo, with 781 lines, is a typical Admiral's lead. His opponent Lorenzo, is second, with 343 lines, not half as many as the lead, which is also characteristic. As usual, the King dignitary is third with 232 lines. The fourth man (fifth character) is the typical young warrior Balthazar, with 181. The Viceroy, with 147 lines, is the occasional fifth character. The Ghost, with 156 lines, belongs to the framework, and is extraneous to the play and to the system. He is not an actor but an orator. For the women, Bel-imperia, with 214 lines, and Isabella with 73 would fit the Admiral's as well as any, though the shifting nature of the "women" actors makes it difficult, if not impossible, to distinguish the differing practices of the different companies. At least, Bel-imperia is fourth, as in *1 Tamburlaine,* and *Jew of Malta.*

For *Edward III* the lead is King Edward, who has nearly three times as many lines as the next nearest character to him. Opposed to him in true Admiral's style is King John of France, who fails of being second character, as this opponent nearly always is, by nine lines only. The second part is taken by the young warrior Prince Edward, who is usually the fourth character; but the heroic tradition would demand the enhanced position of the Black Prince. The fourth man is Warwick, the role of the dignitary who was usually third, but who has in this play, together with the second man, been forced down one place by the Black Prince. The occasional fifth man appears as Lord Audley, barely passing by five the minimum of one hundred lines. In *Edward III,* the leading lady ranks fourth in total number of lines, as she did in *1 Tamburlaine* and *Jew of Malta.* It is thus evident that *Edward III* was built on the same formula as the plays for the Admiral's men about 1589, whatever this fact may mean.

It is clear that the Admiral's company of 1587-89 was predominantly a company of tragedians. Unfortunately, we do not know directly how this tragic group adapted itself to comedy. We have, therefore, no means of testing the inferential assignment of *A Shrew* to the company by the satire of Nashe and Greene upon it in August, 1589. The tamer Ferando takes the lead. He is really a villain, and unmercifully bludgeons Kate into submission. He does the dirty-work for the two nice young lovers,

s 1587 4+1		w 1587 5+0		c 1588 4+0		w 1588 2+0		spring 1589 5+0	
1 Tamburlaine		*2 Tamburlaine*		*Wounds of Civil War*		*Faustus*		*Alcazar*	
1 Tamburlaine	758	1 Tamburlaine	876	1 Scilla	652	1 Faustus	683	1 Sebastian	223
2 Bajazeth	213	4 Callepine	164	2 Marius	443	2 Mephistophilis	179	2 Moor	211
3 Cosroe	189	2 Orcanes	212	3 Anthony	193	Emperor of Germany	50	4 Abdelmelec	165
Theridimas	80	3 Theridimas	190	4 Young Marius	163	7 Wagner	77	5 Stukeley	132
Techelles	54	5 Techelles	106	?Lucretius	82			3 Presenter	175
5 Mycetes	113			?Cynna	73			?Muly Mahomet Seth	92
4 Zenocrate	173	Zenocrate	40	Cornelia	78	Duchess		Moor's Son	64
Zabina	77	Olympia	81	Fulvia	35	Hostess		Rubin Archis	19
Anippe	14					Helen		Calipolis	18
Ebea	3					Devil		Queen	5
1 Virgin	34	Turkish Concubines				Leachery	3	Ladies	
2 Virgin	16	Captain's Son	5			Alexander's Paramour			
3 Virgin	2								
4 Virgin	2								

NOTE: This tabulation is merely to suggest the casting pattern of the plays. It is not intended to indicate that only one actor took each of the lines of principal parts, since we do not know enough about the succession of actors and of the types they performed to be able to hazard even a guess. In some instances some of the lines themselves are not clearly distinguishable.

Polidor, second, and Aurelius, third. One of these, Aurelius, is the son of the Duke of Sestos (compare Marlowe's *Hero and Leander*); that is, the gilded nobleman; the other is just a nice young man. The fourth character is a clown, Sander. No other major clown appears in any Admiral's play of the period, though some of the plays are known to have had their comic matter cut out. The fifth character is a dignified old man to serve as father to the three girls; a sixth man, just below the mechanical deadline of 100 lines, and outside of the play proper, is a humorous Lord who conceives and humors the practical joke on Sly. There are

5+1		>Aug. 1589 2+0		>Aug. 1589 6+1		1590 3+1		5+1	
Titus Andronicus		*Bestrafte Brudermord*		*Taming of a Shrew*		*Jew of Malta*		*Edward III*	
1 Titus	715	1 Hamlet	452	1 Ferando	267	1 Barabas	1138	1 Edward III	738
2 Aaron	355	2 King	211	3 Aurelius	155	2 Ithamore	227	3 King John	272
3 Marcus	311	(5) Corambis	55	5 Alfonso	122	3 Farneze	216	5 Warwick	121
6 Lucius	187	(3) Horatio	80	2 Polidor	165	Calymath	85	2 Prince Edward	281
5 Saturninus	200	(7) Leonardo	49	7 Lord	94	Pilia Borza	87	6 Lord Audley	105
?Demetrius	94					?Jacomo	61		
?Bassianus	63								
4 Tamora	257	(4) Queen	55	6 Kate	120	4 Abigail	147	4 Countess of Salisbury	214
Lavinia	59	(8) Ophelia	45	Emelia	37	Bellamira	58	Philippa	17
Young Lucius	44			Philema	41	Katharine	16		
Nurse	19								
						Nuns, Abbess			

then several fifty-line (half-part) dignitaries and servants to fill in. For the boys, there is the shrew Kate, who ranks sixth in lines. The other two girls are merely beautiful figurines for the young men to fall in love with. A few more small parts are taken by boys.

I have done the best I could to match these comic lines with corresponding tragic lines of the Admiral's plays. But it would be much easier to fit the play to Strange's company. The two young men, Polidor and Aurelius, are second and third, the old man Alfonso is fifth, the country clown Sander is fourth. The trouble in casting for Strange's is with Ferando, first man, as the higher comedian. Perhaps he is not too far from the braggarts Armado and Parolles of Shakspere's plays, while the quality of Bremo the wild man is much nearer to him. The women give no particular indication of any company. We simply do not yet have sufficiently definite evidence to solve this particular problem concerning *A Shrew*.

Our survey makes it abundantly clear that the Admiral's company before 1590 had its own characteristic and clearly distinguishable casting pattern, at least for tragedy. It should be relatively easy to distinguish between its casting formula and that of Strange's company.

CHAPTER X

The Casting Pattern of Strange's Company
before 1591

It is evident that the Queen's and Admiral's had casting patterns which are distinguishable from each other and from that of Strange's as reflected by Shakspere. For Strange's before 1591, Shakspere had written at least the first form of *Love's Labor's Lost, The Comedy of Errors,* and *Two Gentlemen of Verona,* and in that order.[1] Robert Greene furnishes us a further crucial fact for the dating of *Two Gentlemen.* I have pointed out[2] that Shakspere closely adapts a figure of Plutarch's, if not from the Greek or a Latin translation, yet from a very close adaptation. Robert Greene uses this figure of Plutarch's four times in *Neuer Too Late,* printed in 1590. The Palmer says, "if I come amõgst youth, I will shew them that the finest buds are soonest nipt with frosts, the sweetest flowers sorest eaten with cankars, & the ripest & yongest wits soonest ouergrowen with follies."[3] Isabell reasons with herself, "the fairest Roses haue prickes . . . the most beautifull men of the most imperfect conditions, for nature hauing care to pollish the body so farre . . . leaues their mindes imperfect," a position which she argues at length, pro and con.[4] Her deliberations result in a letter to Francesco, in which she says, "the brightest blossoms are pestred with most caterpillers, the sweetest Roses wyth the sharpest prickes, the fairest Cambrickes with the fowlest staines, and men with the best proportion, haue commonly least perfection."[5] Yet again Francesco in fancying Infida found that "the fairest blossoms, are soonest nipt with frost, the best fruite soonest touched with Caterpillers, and the ripest wittes most apt to be ouerthrowen by loue."[6]

It is at once apparent that both Greene and Shakspere have substituted love for envy in Plutarch's figure, and that both have omitted the grain

---

[1] Baldwin, *Five-Act Structure,* pp. 579 ff.

[2] Baldwin, *Small Latine,* II, 350-352.

[3] *Neuer Too Late* (1590), B2^r; Grosart, *Greene,* VIII, 16. Adapted into a simile by Meres, *Palladis Tamia* (1598), f 65^v.

[4] *Neuer Too Late* (1590), D4^r&v; Grosart, *Greene,* VIII, 45. Adapted into a simile by Meres, *Palladis Tamia* (1598), f 151^r.

[5] *Neuer Too Late* (1590), E1^r; Grosart, *Greene,* VIII, 47.

[6] *Neuer Too Late* (1590), G1^v; Grosart, *Greene,* VIII, 71. Adapted into a simile by Meres, *Palladis Tamia* (1598), f 135^r.

(wheat as the *French Academie*[7] and Holland translate), keeping only the rose for the canker to prey upon. But Shakspere keeps also the original form of the figure as a simile, and phrases accurately, while Greene states the figure generally, varying and adding analogous instances to the details. Shakspere could not have derived his simile from Greene. Then did Greene borrow this phoenix feather from crow Shakspere, or do both use a common source adapted from Plutarch?

We should notice first that various parts of Plutarch's figure had been applied to love traditionally long before Shakspere and Greene, so that their coincidence in this respect is not necessarily of particular significance. Tilley[8] gathers various instances of one tradition under the heading "The *Best* wits are soonest subject to love," from which collection it will appear that Shakspere's epithet "finest" for these wits is the repeated epithet of Pettie in his *Petite Pallace,* though this gives no indication, of course, that Shakspere had it directly from that source. Greene preferred "ripest" as in the *Mirour for Magistrates* (1578, f 179ʳ), "The rypest wits are soonest thralles to loue."[9] The simile of the canker and the rose, used by both Shakspere and Greene, was also traditional.[10] Also, the canker might have the caterpillar as a kind of deputy to prey on the fruit, as in Greene. But while Shakspere's materials are traditional and by his day traditionally applied to love, yet Shakspere keeps the materials he uses closely phrased to the pattern of Plutarch.

Plutarch has, according to the Latin translation of Stephanus, "quemadmodum cantharides . . . floridissimis quibusque rosis innascuntur," which becomes quite accurately in Shakspere, Proteus speaking,

> as in the sweetest bud
> The eating canker dwells[11]

restated immediately by Valentine in patterned parallel

> as the most forward bud
> Is eaten by the canker ere it blow.

In Greene (1) "the finest buds . . . the sweetest flowers sorest eaten with cankars,"(2) "the brightest blossoms are pestred with most caterpillers,

---

[7] Plutarch "compareth it [envy] to the flies called Cantharides. For as they alight especially vpon the fairest wheate, and most blowne roses: so enuie commonly setteth it selfe against the honestest men, and such as haue most glorie & vertue" (La Primaudaye, *French Academie* (1586), p. 459).

[8] M. P. Tilley, *Elizabethan Proverb Lore* (1926), pp. 76-77, and cross-references. Tilley's *Dictionary* (1950), C 56, W 576, and cross-references, does not alter the facts.

[9] L. B. Campbell, *The Mirror for Magistrates,* p. 378.

[10] Tilley, *Proverb Lore,* pp. 89-90.

[11] *Two Gentlemen,* I, i, 42-50. For Shakspere's own reshaping of this figure in *Romeo and Juliet,* I, i, 157-159, see Baldwin, *Five-Act,* pp. 753-754.

the sweetest Roses"[12] (which evidently varies 1), (3) "the fairest blossomes . . . soonest touched with Caterpillers," which further varies 1 and 2. Thus 1 is the fundamental form in Greene, from which he has varied progressively the other two. Further, Greene agrees with Shakspere's Englishing of "sweetest bud" and "eating canker." For as a matter of fact there is neither an "eating" canker in Plutarch nor a "sweetest" bud. It is Shakspere who has bestowed these epithets in the Plutarch pattern. Either Shakspere has preserved quite accurately some English adaptation of Plutarch's simile (not the original Greek nor the Latin translation), which Greene also varies, or Greene has borrowed from Shakspere.

The conclusion of the Plutarch simile shows the same kind of relationship. In Plutarch, "sic inuidia eos potissimùm mores eásque personas incessit quibus probitas inest."[13] In Shakspere this becomes

> so eating love
> Inhabits in the finest wits of all.

Shakspere's "inhabits in" reflects the *incessit* of the Plutarch translation, and his "finest wits of all" gives Plutarch's sense, the "finest wits" being one traditional phraseology of one simile from the present passage in Plutarch. In Valentine's restatement, the conclusion is rephrased as

> Even so by love the young and tender wit
> Is turn'd to folly.

Greene in his first and fundamental version reflects both the statement of Proteus and the restatement of Valentine significantly, "the ripest & youngest wits soonest ouergrowen with follies," which his third version rephrases, and his second adapts to the situation. Greene has substituted "ripest" for "finest" in "finest wits," and then has been betrayed into coupling "ripest" with "youngest" by his restatement of Shakspere's "young . . . folly." Greene substitutes "ripest" from one tradition for Shakspere's "finest" from another, and combines it improperly with Shakspere's "young" to couple exact opposites. It will now be seen that the same kind of thing has happened to the restatement of the premise by Shakspere as "eaten by the canker," which Greene phrases as "eaten with cankars." Also, the "finest wits" of Shakspere's first conclusion becomes Greene's "finest buds" in the parallel premise. Such relationships can only mean that Greene has adapted Shakspere's own phrasing of the

---

[12] This is the only detail in which Greene agrees overtly with Plutarch against Shakspere. But while Shakspere does not specifically say rose, most of us will be surprised to realize that he does not, since it is clear that he is speaking of the rose in bud.

[13] Holland's translation, "even so envie taketh commonly unto the best conditioned persons."

Plutarch simile, from whatever source Shakspere may have had his version, Greek, Latin, English, what not.

The reader should not overlook the marvelous but characteristic proliferation of this simile from Plutarch. Shakspere has first trimmed and stated it, and then immediately turned it in restatement. Next, Greene varies Shakspere's statement and restatement through four different figures. Then Meres turns at least three of Greene's four uses back into similes for his collection of similes, the *Palladis Tamia.* He may have the fourth, since I merely guessed the commonplace each time under which the other three were placed, and have not read through the collection to be sure. And this is only one tradition from Plutarch's simile. These beloved beauties were turned and re-turned *ad infinitum;* they belonged to the common fund, and no one had the slightest idea that he was plagiarizing.

But to continue, this relationship between Shakspere and Greene is of fundamental importance in dating Shakspere's play of *Two Gentlemen of Verona,* in which this simile occurs. For Greene's *Neuer Too Late* was printed in 1590. It and its second part, *Francesco's Fortunes,* were written before Greene's *Mourning Garment*[14] was printed (entered S.R. November 2, 1590), but after *Orpharion,* entered S.R. February 9, 1590.[15] Thus these speeches of Shakspere's play impressed Greene at some time in 1590. There is, therefore, now direct evidence for the date 1590 for some form of this speech of this play, a date which I have elsewhere inferred for the whole play on other grounds.[16]

It would appear that *Two Gentlemen* was available to Greene hardly later than the summer of 1590. But it is built upon a framework from *The Comedy of Errors,* which was derived from the sources of *The Comedy,* and in other respects shows itself to be later than that play. In turn, *The Comedy* is not earlier than the latter part of 1589. Thus *The Comedy* and *Two Gentlemen* are *dos a dos,* the latter part of 1589 and the first part of 1590, a dating which gives us a long sought "place to stand." Incidentally, the close connection in use of sources, etc., between *Two Gentlemen,* and *Romeo and Juliet* further confirms a date of 1591 for the original construction of the latter play. Preceding *The Comedy* and *Two Gentlemen* is the first form of *Love's Labor's Lost,* so not later than 1589.

These three comedies before 1591 are all built on a standard pattern of two young men, two comedians, and an old man, with women and minor

---

[14] In *Mourning Garment,* the address to the "Gentlemen Schollers of both Vniuersities" still has a faded form of the figure; "of all floures the Rose soonest withereth . . . the most pregnant wit soonest tainted with affection," Grosart, *Greene,* IX, 123.

[15] Jordan, *Greene,* p. 172.

[16] Baldwin, *Five-Act Structure,* p. 782.

characters added according to the need and the company's ability. This was the pattern of the original form of *Love's Labor's Lost*, though upon revision in 1598 a third comic part was inserted or enlarged.[17] The original five-man pattern is very clear-cut in *The Comedy of Errors*, and *Two Gentlemen of Verona*.

It should perhaps be emphasized, however, that the extraordinarily clear-cut five-man casting pattern of *Comedy* and *Two Gentlemen* is due in part to the Latin sources of *The Comedy*. Thence Shakspere has taken the *Senex* Aegeon; the reduplicated *Juvenis*, Antipholus of Syracuse and Antipholus of Ephesus; and the reduplicated *Servus* of comic turn, Dromio of Ephesus and Dromio of Ephesus.[18] That these should be clear-cut types was determined by the Latin drama, that they should be five principal ones for men was determined by the casting pattern of the company. This pattern was then carried over to *Two Gentlemen*. It is not, therefore, to be expected that all comedies for the company at the period would be quite so clear-cut. And about the tragedy of the company at this period we know nothing directly.

It is now certain that there was a play called *Love's Labor's Won*,[19] which Meres attributes to Shakspere. If so, then it is reasonably certain that, while the quarto under that name has so far been lost, yet the play under some other name has most likely survived in the First Folio. Its pairing in name with *Love's Labor's Lost*, the mention of the two together by Meres in 1598, and the occurrence of the two together for sale in 1603, cause us to look for a companion play to *Love's Labor's Lost*. Such a companion play is *All's Well that Ends Well* in its original form. As I have shown elsewhere, the structure and cast of characters for this form fit best between *Love's Labor's Lost* and *The Comedy of Errors*.[20] If it should so belong, we would then have Shakspere's first four plays, beginning with *Love's Labor's Lost* for the autumn and winter of 1588-89, though both of the *Love* plays have been revised. It appears also from *The Comedy* and *Two Gentlemen* that Shakspere was already producing the normal two plays a year expected of the ordinary dramatist for a company, and from the *Love* plays that he had begun to do so by the autumn and winter 1588-89.

It may be added here that in the period 1591-95, the *Midsummer-Night's Dream* conforms to this early casting pattern, as was probably true also of

[17] Baldwin, *Five-Act Structure*, p. 653.

[18] See E. W. Robbins, *Dramatic Characterization in Printed Commentaries of Terence 1473-1600*, on these types in the Renaissance.

[19] It was listed by a stationer along with *Love's Labor's Lost* in August, 1603, as shown by a manuscript in the Ernest Ingold collection of the University of Illinois Library. See T. W. Baldwin, *Shakspere's Love's Labor's Won*.

[20] Baldwin, *Five-Act Structure*, pp. 728-736.

the first form of *Merry Wives*. In the later periods, *As You Like It* comes nearest to this pattern, and *Measure for Measure* might well have been first constructed on this pattern and then enlarged, somewhat after the fashion of *The Taming of the Shrew*. The clearest instances, however, of this pattern in Shakspere belong before 1591, and all probable ones are not later than 1594, while all Shakspere's known comedies through 1594 are on this pattern.

The question arises whether this pattern was merely peculiar to Shakspere or whether other dramatists also used it, and, if so, for what company or companies. So far as I know, the play outside of Shakspere which shows the pattern most completely[21] is *Mucedorus*, which has for its principal characters two young men, rivals in love, Mucedorus and Segasto; two comedians, the clown Mouse, and the wild man Bremo; and a fatherly old man, the King of Arragon. So far as is known, *Mucedorus* was first printed in 1598, without attribution of ownership, but was printed for at least the third time under date of 1610, with amplifications, as performed by the King's company, which historically had once been Strange's. While, therefore, the proof is not complete that the play belonged originally to this organization, yet the company at least did eventually own it, and there is no evidence that any other company ever did. Thus such evidence as is known indicates that the play which most nearly approaches the early Shaksperean pattern was written for Strange's as were Shakspere's plays.

As to date, *Mucedorus* was printed in 1598, "Newly set foorth, as it hath bin sundrie times plaide in the honorable Cittie of London." This phraseology may indicate that there had been an earlier edition or editions. Since the play is supposed to be based upon Sidney's *Arcadia*, it is not likely to be earlier than the printed form of 1590. Incidentally, since the bear belongs to the Mucedorus story, this fact upsets Sir Edmund Chambers' theory that this bear and the one in *Winter's Tale* were inspired by that in Jonson's *Masque of Oberon*.[22] Kocher points out that *Faustus*[23] presents the stealing of a goblet, which was suggested by the source. *Mucedorus* has a similar incident of stealing a pot. Thus, if there is any connection at all, then *Mucedorus* has borrowed from *Faustus*, which would harmonize with the borrowing from *Arcadia*, which was probably not before 1590. Also Gayley[24] noticed another borrowing. In *Selimus*,[25] Bullithrumble, the clown, has been asked his name, the first question in

---

[21] It is possible that *The Taming of a Shrew* also belonged to Strange's. See pp. 201, 235-237.

[22] Chambers, *E.S.*, IV, 35.

[23] *M.L.Q.*, III, 37-38.

[24] Gayley, *Comedies*, I, 421, n 4.

[25] *Selimus* (M.S.R.), 1953-79.

the *Little Catechism.* This sets him off on godfathers and godmothers, who according to the next question and answer had given him that name, leading to his obliging offer, "and it please you ile goe forward in my catechisme." He asks his interlocutors, "if I should entertaine you, would you not steale?", and decides they shall be his "seruitures," if they will keep his sheep truly and honestly, "keeping your hands from lying and slandering, and your tongues from picking and stealing," All this is according to the *Little Catechism* of 1549, where after the echoed preliminaries the catechumen recognizes under his duty to his neighbor, "To bee true and iust in al my dealing. . . . To kepe my handes from picking and stealing, and my tongue from eiuill speaking, liyng and slaundring. . . . Not to couet nor desire other mennes goodes. But learne and laboure truely to geate my owne liuing, and to doe my duetie in that state of life: vnto which it shall please God to cal me." The intermixed tongues and hands of *Selimus* are then reversed in *Mucedorus,*[26] where the clown, Mouse, who has just been "entertained" as a servant, tells what he can do; "I can keepe my tongue from picking and stealing, and my handes from lying and slaundering." It would appear that the clown parts generally are highly synthetic, with the comedians themselves likely dictating the materials. As we have seen, *Selimus* itself dates probably late in 1591, or in 1592. This borrowing in *Mucedorus* is thus not likely earlier than 1592. Thus the play dates 1590-1598, and its characteristics indicate the earlier rather than the later date.

It may be well at this stage to point out that in our present investigation we seek merely to establish a fact, not to explain it. It is apparent as a purely mechanical fact that each of the two other companies we have been examining in detail had a different and distinguishable casting pattern, though for various reasons some plays do not conform fully. But, whatever the explanation of conformity or nonconformity, the fact of differing pattern is all that we seek here to establish.

I have, indeed, elsewhere examined the facts for one company to find that its surviving plays with known casts[27] were constructed for the principal actors, and in consequence would vary with the actors. I then used this known and demonstrated procedure as a framework by which to interpret all other surviving facts of that category. Presumably the same explanation will apply to the different casting patterns of the three companies we are now examining, since no other contemporary procedure has as yet been found. Some moderns, indeed, have thought that this was a very uneconomical procedure, etc. But the fact is that there is no known

---

[26] C. F. T. Brooke, *Apocrypha,* I, 4, 128-130.

[27] *Organization and Personnel.* I should have added *The Swisser,* which merely helps to establish the principles more fully.

evidence to show that Elizabethan actors thought so, and we should not be putting anachronistic ideas into their heads. So, to repeat, it is no part of our present investigation to explain the fact of the differing casting patterns for these companies; it is merely our concern to establish the fact, if it is a fact.

CHAPTER XI

Cooperation between the Admiral's Company
and Strange's

We have differentiated the casting patterns for Strange's, the Admiral's, and the Queen's before 1590. How do these correlate with known facts concerning the companies? We center attention upon the connections of the Admiral's and Strange's. The first record of cooperation between the Admiral's company and an organization definitely labeled as Strange's is in the Christmas season 1590-91, when for December 27, 1590, and February 16, 1591, payment was made to "George Ottewell and his companye the Lorde Straunge his players for [plays] . . . and for other feates of Activitye then also done by them."[1] But "P. C. Acts do not name Ottewell, and call the company the Admiral's." So some organization under the patronage of Strange was cooperating with the Admiral's the winter season of 1590-91, and presented feats of activity as well as plays.

What was the past history of the Strange organization which connects with the Admiral's in 1590? It will be noticed that the combined organizations also put on feats of activity as well as plays. The preceding Christmas, 1589-90, Strange's is not mentioned, but there is record on December 28, 1589 for "the Servauntes of the Lorde Admirall . . . for shewinge certen feates of activitie," and on March 3, 1590, "the servauntes of the Lorde Admirall . . . for playinge." So also the preceding Christmas, December 29, 1588, and February 11, 1589, "the Lorde Admyrall his players . . . for twoe Enterludes or playes . . . and for showinge other feates of activity and tumblinge." An item of "a paire of fflannell hose for Symmons the Tumbler" gives a clue as to who had been furnishing these feats of activity and tumbling, for Simons and his group can be traced.

The first record of appearance for Simons at court is January 1, 1583, "John Simons . . . for showing c̄ten ffeates of actiuitye and Tomblinge," also labeled "the Lord Straunge his seruantes."[2] Strange's servants had been presenting feats of activity previously, but this is the first mention of Simons. Next, on January 1, 1585 "John Symons and other his fellowes Servantes to Therle of Oxforde . . . for . . . feates of actiuitye and

---

[1] Chambers, *E.S.,* IV, 163.

[2] Chambers, *E.S.,* IV, 159.

vawtinge." Also, "Dyuers feates of Actiuytie were shewed and presented . . . on newe yeares daye . . . by Symons and his fellowes."[3] The next Christmas on January 9, 1586, "John Symondes and M[r]. Standleyes Boyes . . . for Tumblinge and shewinge other feates of activitie." There is no record the next Christmas, but on December 28, 1587, "John Simons . . . for certein feates of actiuitie by him and his Companie." So Simons had a company of tumbling boys under the patronage of Stanley (Strange) at least from 1583, though in 1584-85 Oxford is said to be the patron.[4] Simons was still carrying on his feats independently December 28, 1587, but by the season of 1588-89 had in some way joined forces with the Admiral's to continue presenting feats with that company through the season 1590-91, though George Ottewell is in that season mentioned as the payee for "Lorde Straunge his players." Thus the Admiral's had cooperated for a considerable period with Strange's boys and that cooperation tapers into its cooperation with Strange's men, after which we hear no more of Strange's boys in connection with the Admiral's or elsewhere. But though Simons appears with the Admiral's at court the season 1588-89, yet he had been connected with the Queen's in the country by 1588,[5] and the connection with the Queen's in the country appears to have lasted at least into 1590. It is clear, therefore, that Simons led a company of tumblers, which retained its identity as such under its own patron through the court season 1590-91, though it is known to have cooperated in the country with the Queen's and at court with the Admiral's. Simons himself is replaced as manager in the record at court 1590-91 by George Ottewell, and his tumbling organization appears no more thereafter at court as such, nor so far as I know elsewhere, though Ottewell seems to continue with a country group of Queen's.[6]

It is also pertinent to notice here that the connection of Simons with both companies at this period correlates with a known physical fact. Both the Queen's and the Admiral's had played regularly at the Theater and the Curtain during the merger of these theaters, through 1589.[7] Further, it seems clear that the Queen's company was at the Theater in 1589, and the Admiral's in 1590.[8] But we cannot assume that at this period any one of these companies had an exclusive right to any one of the possible acting places. In fact, it seems clear that in general the same situation prevailed as at the Rose later. But the close connection at the Curtain

---

[3] Chambers, *E.S.*, IV, 161.

[4] This was most likely due to some connection with the Oxford-Lyly scheme, not to any change of patronage.

[5] Chambers, *E.S.*, II, 111, 119; *Shakspere,* I, 33, etc.

[6] Chambers, *E.S.*, II, 115, etc.

[7] Baldwin, *Organization and Personnel,* pp. 322 ff.

[8] Chambers, *E.S.*, II, 395.

and Theater and the possible succession at the Theater in 1589-90 correlate with something else. In 1592, we find that Edward Alleyn, the Admiral's "men," had become possessed of Tarleton's *ε Seven Deadly Sins,*
and of Greene's three plays before 1590, but not of those after. While we
do not directly know the details of why, when, or how, yet the correlations
between connection in playhouses and plays must have some real basis,
even if the actual transfer of plays should not have occurred till 1592.

We must also consider in this connection a tantalizing undated letter of
one W. P. to Edward Alleyn, which interlocks various names of persons
connected with these two companies.[9] "The remarkable thing about the
letter . . . is that it is not a forgery."[10] Even more remarkable, however,
are the implications of the contents of the letter. W. P. had made a wager
with some gentlemen, and Alleyn's answer "the other nighte" had haz-
arded it. Apparently Alleyn had made some refusal on the ground that
acquiescence would "preiudice Peeles credit," though W. P. says it
would not have done so. The matter is "now growen farther into question" and "the partie affected to Bentley, (scornynge to wynne the wager
by yor deniall), hath now giuen yo^u libertie to make choice of any one
playe, that either Bentley or Knell plaide, and least this advantage, agree
not wth yor minde, he is contented, both the plaie and the tyme, shalbe
referred to the gentlemen here p^{r}sent. J see not, how yo^u canne any waie
hurte yor credit by this acc^{i}on; for if yo^u excell them, yo^u will then be
famous, if equall them; yo^u wynne both the wager and credit, yf short of
them; we must and will saic Ned Allen still."

Whatever the details, certain assumptions are clear. Fundamentally, it
is assumed that Edward Alleyn would have access to the plays in which
Bentley and Knell had played, who were Queen's men; that is, that Edward Alleyn, who, so far as we know had been an Admiral's (formerly
Worcester's) man only had access to Queen's plays after the death of
Bentley (buried August 19, 1585) and Knell (dead probably before 1588).
The time of writing is evidently only a short time after the death of
Bentley and Knell, since their memories are still green and the plays in
which they acted their most famous parts are still alive. It is likely also
to be at the very beginning of the career of Edward Alleyn as actor,
before he became "famous" Ned Alleyn. We, at least, would think this
must have been before Tamburlaine in 1587 (when Alleyn was just turning twenty-one), a dating which correlates well enough with Bentley's
death in 1585. Apparently, the original wager concerned a specified play
by Peele, in which Bentley had acted, but it is now broadened to some

---

[9] Greg, *Henslowe Papers,* p. 32.

[10] Greg, "Edward Alleyn," *A Series of Papers on Shakespeare and the Theatre*
(Memb. of Shak. Assn., 1927), p. 6.

play in which either Bentley or Knell had acted, the particular play to be chosen by Alleyn, or, if he thought that too great an advantage, then the play and the time for acting it to be set by the gentlemen. At least, the sometime personnel of both Queen's and Admiral's is here closely inter-locked, and it is assumed that Alleyn had access to Queen's plays.

It will be seen also that Peele had written a play in which Knell of the Queen's had acted some famous part, and in which Alleyn of the Ad-miral's so far as we yet know directly, could now act if he would. Peele had also written for the Admiral's.

The facts of the letter are in consonance with the known facts of physical proximity of the two companies and of Alleyn's later ownership of Queen's plays. It is possible, indeed, whether probable or not, that Edward Alleyn, or a syndicate to which he eventually belonged, furnished plays at the Theater in much the same fashion as later at the Rose, and that thus he became possessed finally of Queen's plays. At any rate, the Queen's and Admiral's had physical proximity and something more, and Simons cooperated with each.

This group with Simons under the patronage of Strange is thus one of tumblers and seems to have lost its identity in 1591. Simons himself ap-pears to have died or withdrawn by 1590, being succeeded by George Ottewell. Since Ottewell has some connection with the Queen's several years later, it would appear that the most important part of its personnel likely continued with the Queen's in the country. There is no record nor any known person to connect Strange's tumblers with Strange's men. This does not mean, of course, that there was no connection.

But it is a curious, and has been a confusing coincidence (we have sinned all; *peccavimus!*) that Strange's tumblers were succeeded immedi-ately by Strange's men in cooperation with the Admiral's. For, the next season, 1591-92, it was "yᵉ seruantes of yᵉ lo: Straunge" who received pay for six plays from December 7, 1591, to February 8, 1592, while there was only one performance each by the Queen's, Sussex's, and Hertford's. Strange's was now *the* company, as the Queen's had been the preceding season. Though it had not appeared at court before, now it becomes almost the only organization, and it was thenceforth good enough to hold a leading place. A few days later than the end of the court season Henslowe's surviving account book opens with Strange's company, though we learn that it is also the Admiral's as well. In the following summer, Strange's had appealed an adverse ruling on the ground that they would not be prepared for the coming court season.[11] They had acquired a defi-nite and recognized expectation as a court company. Consequently, the coming Christmas season 1592-93, Strange's performed three plays at

---

[11] Cf. below, pp. 257 ff.

court, while Pembroke's performed two, no other company appearing. And these two companies had some close connection at the time as shown by certain plays which they shared. The plague intervened for the season of 1593-94, and by the season of 1594-95, Strange's had been reorganized and was upon its own again.

These facts of connection correlate with a piece of inferential evidence. Since Shakspere continued to use the Abbey wall through *Romeo and Juliet*,[12] the inference is that he and the company expected to be at the Curtain the summer of 1591. The further inference would be that they went to the Rose not earlier than the summer of 1591, where they appear definitely in February, 1592. These various pieces of evidence thus indicate that the alliance with the Admiral's occurred probably about the autumn or winter of 1591.

What are the origins of Strange's company? In such a case, personnel is the important thing, not patronage. When we get the personnel of the membership May 6, 1593, it consisted of "Edward Allen, servaunt to the right honorable the Lorde Highe Admiral, William Kemp, Thomas Pope, John Heminges, Augustine Phillipes and George Brian, being al one companie, servauntes to our verie good the Lord the Lord Strainge."[13] First, to look at the personnel of the Admiral's, which on May 6, 1593, consisted of Edward Alleyn alone.[14] Both before and after this date the Admiral's had consisted of eight members. About 1589, these were Robert Browne, James Donstall, Edward Alleyn, Richard Jones, and John Alleyn certainly; E. Browne, Thomas Sacheville, and John Bradstreet probably. Then on February 10, 1592, the Lord Admiral granted license to Robert Browne, John Bradstreet, Thomas Sacheville, and Richard Jones to travel in Germany, passing through Zealand, Holland, and Friesland, as they proceeded to do,[15] thus leaving in England only Edward and John Alleyn, James Donstall, and E. Browne, of whom only Edward Alleyn can be connected with Strange's at the Rose.

Moreover, there is no certain indication of an Admiral's group in the country from this split by February 10, 1592, till after the inhibition of June 22 (23), 1592.[16] It is equally doubtful that there had been an

---

[12] Baldwin, *Five-Act Structure,* pp. 782-783.

[13] Chambers, *E.S.,* II, 123.

[14] Baldwin, *Organization and Personnel,* pp. 321 ff.

[15] A. Cohn, *Shakespeare in Germany,* p. XXIX; Murray, II, 120-121. For a compact account of this German branch of the Admiral's, see L. M. Price, *English > German Literary Influences,* pp. 134 ff.

[16] A reference to the Admiral's and Derby's supposed to date March 7, 1592, at Ipswich has proved to be an error for August 7, 1592 (Malone Society *Collections,* II, iii, 259, 277). The reference to Derby's at Shrewsbury in 1591-92 (Murray, II, 392) could belong to this period, though the account may be misdated. An entry to the Admiral's at Aldeburgh for 1591-92 probably refers to the same tour.

Admiral's group in the country since the autumn of 1590. The only record definitely purporting to be of the period is one said to occur in the accounts of 1591-92 at Shrewsbury, "The iii of feb: 1592. Bestowed vppo the players of my Lorde Admyrall . . . x^s".[17] On the face of it, this should be February, 1593, and Derby's men, mentioned later in the same accounts, should have come at the very end of the accounting period, though this record may have the same occasion as the Ipswich record to Derby's of 1592.

At any rate, the licence of 1593 shows that Edward Alleyn was the Admiral's company which cooperated with Strange's from February, 1592, when half of the Admiral's went abroad and Henslowe's account book opens with Strange's playing at the Rose. It should be noticed that the license to travel is February 10, just two days after Strange's, possibly in connection with the Admiral's, who are not mentioned, had presented the last of six plays at court the preceding court season. These dovetailing facts might mean that the complete Admiral's had cooperated with Strange's this season, and that then the disintegration of the Admiral's occurred in February, 1592, half going to Germany and the others ceasing to act, thus leaving Alleyn alone as the Admiral's men cooperating with Strange's till a couple of years later the Admiral's reunited and reorganized.

But the Admiral's are not mentioned at court this season, and the process of disintegration had been going on for some years before February 1592. From a legal document of January 3, 1589,[18] we learn that the ownership "of playinge apparell*es*, playe Bookes, Instrument*es*, and other comodities whatsoeu*er* belonginge to the same" was at that date vested in an inner circle of the company, consisting of Edward Alleyn, John Alleyn, Robert Brown, and Richard Jones, the last of whom was then selling his share to Edward Alleyn, thus leaving the ownership with the Alleyn brothers and Robert Brown. Then the next year we learn that Robert Brown and "his fellows" were in Holland and that Sacheville was in Vienna. These are two of the four who were licensed by the Lord Admiral on February 10, 1592, to go abroad. Whether the other two, Bradstreet and Jones, were also abroad in 1590 does not directly appear, nor is it indicated when Robert Brown and his fellows returned to England. Events of the season of 1590-91 make it clear, however, that Robert Brown, like Jones, had withdrawn from the group which owned the plays, etc., leaving that function entirely in the control of John and Edward Alleyn. So Fynes Moryson tells us that in the autumn of 1592 he saw Brown and his companions, whom he labels "some of our cast

---

[17] Murray, II, 392.

[18] Greg, *Henslowe Papers*, p. 31.

dispised Stage players," act at "Franckford in the tyme of the Mart, hauing nether a Complete number of Actours, nor any good Apparell, nor any ornament of the Stage . . . , speaking English . . . , and pronowncing peeces and Patches of English playes, which my selfe and some English men there present could not heare without great wearysomenes."[19] Since the Alleyn brothers owned the play manuscripts, Brown and his companions had only the "peeces and Patches of English playes" which they had retained in their heads — unless some of them had saved their parts.[20] We should be warned of this known situation when we consider the German *Hamlet,* etc.

Much the same situation was evidently true of the other acting properties besides plays. John and Edward Alleyn now in 1590 owned the accumulated furnishings of the Admiral's company, including their accumulated plays. We have seen that Richard Jones sold his share to Edward Alleyn on January 3, 1589, and Browne had sold out or withdrawn by 1590. A haberdasher's release to John and Edward Alleyn alone February 5, 1589,[21] doubtless means that the complete change had occurred between January 3 and February 5, 1589. Incidentally, the English actors would be obliged to retain these manuscripts of their plays as authorization; the actors in Germany would not.

A group of Admiral's men was in the country the summer and autumn of 1590 but there is no direct indication as to its personnel. At least the Alleyn group, however, was at the Theater by November 1590, and were drawn into the quarrels of James Burbadge with Mrs. Brayne. According to his affidavit of February 6, 1592, John Alleyn had exhorted James Burbadge to have a conscience toward Mrs. Brayne, pointing out that she had Chancery, the highest court of conscience, on her side, and that James might find himself in contempt; but James said he was not afraid of twenty contempts and as many injunctions. Since James was in fact cited for contempt on November 26, 1590, this conversation evidently purports to have occurred on Monday November 16, 1590, at the time of the grand altercation. Then "when this Depo^t about viij Daies after came to him for certen money wch he deteyned from this depo^t and his fellowes / of some of the Dyvydent money betwene him & them / growing also by the vse of the said Theater / he denyed to pay the same / he this depo^t told him that belike he ment to deale w^t them / as he did w^t the

[19] C. Hughes, *Shakespeare's Europe,* p. 304.

[20] Their plays must have been assembled from parts, written or in their heads, much after the fashion of Professor J. Dover Wilson's theory of assembled texts. Also, the plays of the German branch from Marlowe and Greene are those we have dated before 1590.

[21] G. F. Warner, *Catalogue of the Manuscripts and Muniments of Alleyn's College of God's Gift at Dulwich,* pp. 123, 126.

po^r wydowe / meani*n*g the now comp^l / wishing him he wold not do so / for yf he did / they wold compleyne to ther lorde & M^r the lord Admyrall / and then he in A Rage litle Reu*e*rencing his hono^r / & estate / sayd / by a great othe / that he cared not for iij of the best lord*es* of them all."[22] In a supplementary affidavit of May 6, 1592, Alleyn says the contempt statement was made in the Theater yard when Mrs. Brayne and Miles came to claim the receipts, "wch he thinketh to be about A yere past," and the disrespect to the Admiral "about viij daies next after / in the hearing of one James Tunstall this depo^t and others."[23]

The altercation had occurred on Monday November 16, 1590. Now the sharing of the receipts was usually weekly and the next time of division was most likely on the following Saturday, at the end of the week. The statement of Alleyn implies that at this time James Burbadge detained some of the divident money which the actors should have had. So about the following Tuesday John Alleyn "came to" James Burbadge to demand that money also, with resultant fireworks. The later supplementary affidavit is merely to make more definite the times, places, and persons of his first. He points out that the contempt explosion was in the Theater yard in connection with the main altercation. The disrespect to the Admiral is still about eight days later and is now localized to the tiring-house of the Theater, with James Tonstall and others as witnesses. The time of the altercation "he thinketh to be about A yere past." The period of time so stated in round terms is likely to mean anything from more than half a year to some appreciable time less than two. Since this supplementary statement was made in May, 1592, a year preceding was May, 1591, and "about A yere past" might well stretch that year back to November 24, 1590. At any rate, the second statement merely adds to the first, and the first certainly refers to events between November 16 and 26, 1590. Eventually, the Admiral's left the Theater, but we do not know when. But whether the Admiral's left the Theater at once in November 1590, or whether they continued through the season, this season cannot have been a particularly prosperous one for them. This may be part of the reason that, whereas the feats of activity were merely mentioned for the preceding seasons, yet for the performances at court on December 27, 1590, and February 16, 1591, it was "George Ottewell and his companye the Lorde Straunge his players" who received the pay in March, 1591, the Admiral's being mentioned only by cross-reference as it were. Then this company of Strange's tumblers disappears from collaboration with the Admiral's and from court.

---

[22] C. W. Wallace, "The First London Theatre," *The University Studies of the University of Nebraska* (1913), XIII, 101.

[23] Wallace, *First London Theatre*, pp. 126-127.

There is no indication that Strange's tumblers had been involved with
the Admiral's at the Theater. It will be noticed that John Alleyn is the
business representative of the actors and that it was in this capacity that
he demanded a fair division of the receipts from James Burbadge, and
threatened him with the company's master, the Lord Admiral. It is also
significant that John Alleyn says that this demand was made in the presence of James Tonstall. Here we need to remember that on November 23,
1590, the day before the probable date of disagreement with Burbadge,
James Tonstall had witnessed the sale of a cloak to John Alleyn, evidently
for theatrical purposes.[24] He also witnessed the sale of another cloak to
John and Edward Alleyn on May 6, 1591.[25] The cloak sales show what we
already know, that John and Edward Alleyn now owned all the accumulated furnishings of the Admiral's, and were evidently continuing to add
to them for furnishing the company. Tonstall serves as a witness[26] here,
and was a witness when John Alleyn, in still another capacity as business
agent for the actors themselves, demanded a proper division from James
Burbadge. So these records show that in the season 1590-91 three of the
four Admiral's men who did not leave England are involved. Of the
fourth, E. Brown, we have no certain further record at this period. There
is no indication that the members who had gone abroad in 1590 had
returned to rejoin these who are known to have remained in England.
It is curious that Edward Alleyn is not mentioned as having been involved directly and personally in these conflicts. It is also curious that
the bill of sale on November 23, 1590, exactly in the midst of the conflict,
was to John Alleyn alone, while that of May 6, 1591, was to John and
Edward, just as a similar transaction of July 25, 1591 involves both.[27]
It seems pretty clear that John Alleyn and James Tonstall were the only
active members, and that Edward was not present and active in the company in November, 1590. That may be another reason for the topsy-turvy
record at court this season. Further, the furnishings of the Admiral's
were still in the joint ownership of Edward and John Alleyn as late as
July 25, 1591. The only possible later connection of John Alleyn with
acting of which I know is the fact that he signed a bond with Thomas
Goodal, mercer, and Robert Lee to John Allen of London, gentleman,

[24] J. P. Collier, *Alleyn Papers*, p. 12; Warner, *Catalogue*, p. 3.

[25] Collier, *Alleyn Papers*, p. 13; Warner, *Catalogue*, p. 4. John Alleyn bought a
cloak August 8, 1589 (Warner, *Catalogue*, p. 3; cf. 4, 127). A general release from
"Nich. Harrison, of London, haberdasher" on February 5, 1589, to John and Edward
Alleyn was also doubtless connected with furnishings (Warner, *Catalogue*, 123, 126).

[26] James Tonstall was otherwise closely associated with the Alleyns, serving as
witness to documents of personal business October 28, 1585 (Warner, *Catalogue*, p.
251), and July 6 and 8, 1590 (Warner, *Catalogue*, p. 253).

[27] Collier, *Alleyn Papers*, pp. 14-15; Warner, *Catalogue*, p. 127.

May 18, 1593;[28] but he was not included in the reorganized Admiral's in 1594, and died about May, 1596. Returning now to Edward Alleyn, when he is next localized, in 1592, he has control of the Admiral's plays and furnishings and is cooperating with Strange's at the Rose. This change would most likely have taken place about September, 1591, in preparation for the autumn and winter season of 1591-92.

We have no trace, therefore, at this period of E. Brown or of the four Admiral's men who got the license to go abroad in February, 1592. So far as I see, we have no conclusive evidence whether these returned to the company in 1590 or not. Nor do we know that even Strange's tumblers were with the Admiral's at the Theater this season of 1590-91, though the two companies in some way continued their cooperation at Court. And there is nothing whatever to indicate that Strange's men were in any way directly involved. Richard Burbadge, who later grew up to be their greatest actor, was very decidedly "at home" at the Theater on November 16, 1590, and apparently enjoyed the occasion hugely. But I know nothing to indicate that he had at that time connected with Strange's. Indeed, the plot of the *Dead Man's Fortune* connects him early with the personnel of some other company, presumably one with which Edward Alleyn was connected, while the plot of *2 Deadly Sins,* pretty certainly for the season 1591-92, is the first record to connect Richard with Strange's. There is nothing to indicate that either he or his father ever had any quarrel with Strange's men, and Richard did certainly become the chief actor in Strange's company while the controlling personnel was still as it was in November, 1590. If there were any grudges toward Strange's men engendered in 1590, they were certainly more than healed by 1594. There is nothing whatever to indicate that there were ever any grudges to be in need of healing.

It is at any rate now clear that the personnel of Strange's men as given in the license of 1593 was not derived from the personnel of the Admiral's. Two of the members, George Bryane and Thomas Pope, had belonged to Leicester's "instrumentister och springere" in Denmark June 17, 1586,[29] and on July 17, 1587, that organization is described as "Funf Instrumentisten und Springern aus England." This group under the patronage of Leicester was thus of musicians and tumblers.

But Leicester also had players, of whom William Kempe was one. This company had five members but we do not know the names of the other four at this period, though James Burbadge had been a member of an earlier group. It is thus not at all surprising that his son Richard should turn up with the remnant of Leicester's men later, to become the chief

---

[28] Warner, *Catalogue,* p. 127.

[29] Baldwin, *Organization and Personnel,* pp. 74 ff.

actor of their company. We know, then, that Leicester had a company of five players and another of musicians and tumblers, which abroad consisted of five members. Strange's men in 1593 have five members, two of whom are eventually from Leicester's muscians and tumblers abroad, one from his players. The other two have no previous record of membership. Since, therefore, Strange's has the same number of members as Leicester's companies had, and since three out of five members are from the membership of these companies, the inference is obvious. At Leicester's death in 1588, his men were evidently reorganized into one company under another patron, Lord Strange, so that Strange now had a company of men as well as a company of tumblers, just as had been the case of Leicester.[30]

Before 1593, the fullest list of the company is in the plot of *2 Deadly Sins,* which appears to date the latter part of 1591. Here Bryan, Phillips, and Pope appear, Heminges and Kempe do not. Since this is only the second part, presumably they too would have appeared in the first. Kempe is referred to apparently at the Curtain in 1590, but the name of his company is not indicated.

Strange's men got into difficulties at the Cross Keys on November 5, 1589, some of them landing in prison; but we do not yet have their names. As we have said, Kempe appears to have been at the Curtain about February-March, 1590, though his company is not mentioned. But Shakspere's plays themselves offer curious confirmation of a shift from the Cross Keys to the Curtain. It will be remembered that *Love's Labor's Lost,* 1588, mentions Banks' horse, which was at the Cross Keys in 1588. Then *The Comedy of Errors,* late in 1589, uses Holywell Priory as a fundamental element in its setting, while an abbey wall plays its part in both *Two Gentlemen,* 1590, and *Romeo and Juliet,* summer 1591.[31] Thus these reflections are at least consistent to indicate that Strange's went from the Cross Keys in 1589 to the Curtain, where they remained to the summer of 1591, after which they went to the Rose, probably for the autumn 1591, certainly by February, 1592. During this period, so far as I can find, there is no record for Strange's men in the country. Nor is there any record of connection between Strange's tumblers and Strange's men. But if one looks at the sources of the personnel for the company of men, he can readily see one reason why Shakspere's early plays show so much kinship with those for the children's companies. Also, whether Shakspere himself had been abroad or not, his masters had, and would make demands and supply materials accordingly.

---

[30] We must not forget that patronage had been limited to rank, was now in process of becoming allocated to offices, and at the accession of James became attached to the royal family, the Lord Chamberlain's becoming naturally the King's, and so in effect remaining the Lord Chamberlain's, etc.

[31] Baldwin, *Five-Act Structure,* p. 782.

Since the Theater and the Curtain as buildings were close together and under joint control, the Admiral's at the Theater and Strange's men at the Curtain would inevitably have some association together. But there is no record of direct cooperation between the companies. There is nothing, therefore, to connect Strange's with the quarrels of James Burbadge and John Alleyn at the Theater in November, 1590. The association of Strange's men with the Admiral's was close enough to account for the cooperation in 1591 and following, but not close enough to have forced them out with the Admiral's in 1590, if the Admiral's were forced out.

Thus Strange's men connected with Edward Alleyn pretty certainly not later than at some time in 1591. Whether they went to the Rose at the time of connection or only when Henslowe's jottings begin on February 19, 1592, we do not directly know. But if Sir Walter Greg is correct concerning the refurbishing of the Rose at this time, then most likely the association had begun elsewhere. At any rate, Strange's acted at the Rose from February 19, 1592, to February 1, 1593, with intermission because of the plague from June 22 (23) to December 29, 1592.

It is necessary to note with some care the facts connected with this intermission. Strange's company travelled at least part of this time, since it was at Canterbury on July 13, 1592.[32] But it seems clear that Henslowe and his cohorts were attempting to get the Rose reopened for Strange's. In some long vacation, apparently 1592, Strange's pointed out to the Privy Council that, "Forasmuche (righte honorable) our Companie is greate, and thearbie our chardge intollerable, in travellinge the Countrie, and the Contynuaunce thereof wilbe a meane to bringe vs to division and seperacion, whearebie wee shall not onelie be vndone, but alsoe vnreadie to serve her maiestie, when it shall please her highenes to commaund vs," and since their "dismission" from the Bankside "nowe in this longe vacation" hurts the business of the Thames watermen, they beg that the Privy Council will "recall this our restrainte, and permitt vs the vse of the said Plaiehowse againe."[33] Henslowe and the watermen petition Lord Admiral Howard that since he has given warrant "for the restraynte" of the Rose, he will now "give leave vnto the said Phillipp Henslo to have playinge in his saide howse duringe suche tyme as others have, according as it hathe byne accustomed."[34] In lifting their order the Privy Council recites part of its terms. "Wheareas not longe since vpon some Consideracions we did restraine the Lorde Straunge his servauntes from playinge at the Rose on the banckside, and enioyned them to plaie three daies at Newington Butts, Now forasmuch as wee are satisfied that by reason of the tediousnes of

---

[32] Murray, I, 108.
[33] Chambers, *E.S.*, IV, 311-312.
[34] Chambers, *E.S.*, IV, 312.

the waie and that of longe tyme plaies haue not there bene vsed on working daies, And for that a nomber of poore watermen are therby releeved" the Rose may be reopened, conforming only to plague regulations.

As Sir Walter Greg points out, "On 11 June there had been riots in Southwark and on 23 June the Privy Council issued letters forbidding all plays till Michaelmas."[35] This fits exactly the conditions of these undated documents. The Rose had been closed and Strange's men were traveling in July, as their petition points out that they were when it was written. Nevertheless, they could have been acting "three daies at Newington Butts," presumably each week; but evidently had preferred to travel. The petitions also intimate that the restraint was only on the Bankside, as was the case in 1592.

While we can hope for further facts to make the details of cooperation between Strange's and Alleyn, and of the Admiral's and the Queen's, more definite, still we already have enough to stand us in good stead as we examine the plays produced in the period of recorded cooperation between Strange's and Alleyn.

---

[35] Greg, *Henslowe's Diary*, II, 156.

CHAPTER XII

The Casting Pattern of Strange's Company, 1591-92

Now that we have examined the provenance and casting pattern for the old plays which were to be performed by Strange's men February 10–June 23, 1592, we turn next to the plays marked as new, which were five,[1] though two do not survive. The three possibly surviving "new" plays were probably *Titus Andronicus, Henry the Sixth* (number of parts not indicated), and *A Knacke to knowe a Knaue.*[2] If *Titus* does appear, it is built squarely on the Admiral's casting pattern, and yields us no information as to Strange's practice at this period. Of the other two (or more), *A Knacke to knowe a Knaue* is the only comedy, and so the fittest place to begin, since we know the casting pattern of Strange's directly only for comedy. *Knacke* was entered S.R. January 7, 1594, "newlye sett fourth as it hath sundrye tymes ben plaid by Ned Allen and his companie, with Kemps applauded merymentes of the menn of Goteham," and was printed 1594 with the same statement on its title page. Confirmatory of the statement is the fact that "Strange's men produced 'the Knacke to Knowe a Knave' on 10 June 1592, and played it seven times to 24 Jan. 1593."[3] Since *A Knacke* is based in part on the *Defence of Conycatching,* entered S.R. April 21, 1592, and refers to the story of Titus in the form that it occurs in the play, some form of which appears to have been put on by Strange's men April 11, 1592,[4] it is apparent that at least in some respects it was "new" when it was put on in June, 1592.

It appears to be certain, however, that the entry and title page are more nearly accurate in saying that the play was "Newlie set foorth," since there was evidently an earlier form of *Knacke,* about 1586-87, as shown chiefly by its connections with the epilogue of *True Tragedie* (Richard III). Two lines of *True Tragedie*

> Then England kneele vpon thy hairy knee,
> And thanke that God that still prouides for thee.[5]

---

[1] Chambers, *E.S.,* II, 122.

[2] We shall see that neither *Titus* nor *Knacke* was wholly "new" but at most "newly set forth," and that was most likely true of *Henry VI,* play or plays.

[3] Chambers, *E.S.,* IV, 24.

[4] Chambers, *E.S.,* IV, 24-25.

[5] *True Tragedie (M.S.R.),* 2206-7.

are lifted into the first speech of Dunston in *Knacke* (A2^v), in reply to the King's first speech, lauding his own regime.

> Then *England* kneele vpon thy hartie knee,
> And praise that God, that so prouides for thee.

The King's first speech had opened the play with a somewhat freer rephrasing of the sentiment

> Dunston, how highlie are we bound to praise
> The Eternall God that still prouides for vs.

The author of *Knacke* in both instances substitutes *praise* for *thanke,* and once uses *still* as in *True Tragedie,* and once substitutes *so,* better to fit the context. In *True Tragedie,* England has the *hairy* knee of actuality; in *Knaue,* the *hartie* knee of far-fetched figure, if indeed the epithet is not a misreading.[6] Further, when this author of *Knacke* comes to his own "kneeling" he borrows both the reason and the rhyme of two further lines from the epilogue to *True Tragedie.*

> For if her Graces dayes be brought to end,
> Your hope is gone, on whom did peace depend.

In *Knacke* (G4^r), Honestie kneels to the same sentiment.

> And Honestie wil pray vpon his knee,
> God cut the[m] off that wrong the Prince of Communaltie.
> And may her dayes of blesse neuer haue end,
> Upon whose lyfe so many lyues depend.

It needs no arguing that in all these instances *Knacke* borrowed.

But it seems clear that in his two ending lines this author was also mindful of the prayer of 1586, upon which this part of the epilogue to *True Tragedie* was based. "But weighing further, with what perill of violent death, by meanes of wicked popish practices, our gracious soueraigne hath mainteined the trueth, which we professe, vpon whose life (next vnder God) the profession of the same in this land, and the continuance of the liues and welfare of vs her faithfull Subiects, doe depend." While the author of *Knacke* bases the form and sentiment of his final two lines on two from the epilogue of *True Tragedie,* yet he certainly echoes the "liues . . . depend" of the prayer.

This use of an occasional prayer of 1586 by both plays, with one play also modeling upon the other, can mean only close connection both in time and authorship. The author of *Knacke* here had a completely accurate knowledge of the corresponding passage in *True Tragedie,* either through eye or ear, if two authors are involved, for his variants are

---

[6] I suppose the conventional epithet *hearty* for praise has been transferred to knee.

intentional and purposeful, and would appear even to go beyond the accuracy likely to be obtained by the ear alone. If two authors are involved, then the author of *Knacke* must have been imitating currently in order to recognize the occasional prayer of 1586 as the basis of the epilogue of *True Tragedie* and to have used further the material from that prayer independently. Even if but one author is involved in the two sets of passages — and at least one author has been suspected in connection with both plays — this evidence would point strongly to close chronological connection for the passages. It is thus reasonably clear that *Knacke* received its first two speeches and its final "kneeling" in approximately the present form in 1586 or 1587.[7]

Other borrowings would most likely have come in by this date. Among other things, *Knacke* has two passages based upon Greene's *Carde of Fancie*, S.R. April 11, 1584, printed 1584 and again 1593. Also, two passages based upon *Euphues*.[8] All these things taken together appear to make it certain that the "new" *Knacke* of June 10, 1592, was merely "Newlie set foorth" by such additions as we have mentioned above. The printed version of *Knacke* is said on the title page of 1594 to have belonged to the Strange-Admiral combination, and the play is traceable with them from June 10, 1592. There is no direct evidence as to whence they had it, but the inferential evidence points toward the Queen's. At any rate, the connections of *Knacke* with *True Tragedie* would appear certainly to belong originally to the version of 1586-87, not to the "new" version of June 10, 1592.

Though we could have wished *Knacke* to have been constructed completely "new" in 1592, its reconstruction or adaptation still remains our best landmark for the casting practice of the company in comedy at this date. *Knacke* has been fitted to the typical five-man pattern of the early Shaksperean company, but with additions and adaptations. Kempe's applauded merriments form a separable unit and were evidently added for the performance of June, 1592. The coneycatchers, Perin in court life, and Cuthbert Cutpurse in city life, have either been added or refurbished in deference to Greene's work,[9] which is used.

The casting pattern of the play shows why this solution was suggested for adapting the old *Knacke*. The low comedian, Kempe, does not appear among the principal characters of the play proper, since he was busy with the device of "Kemps applauded Merrimentes of the men of Goteham."

---

[7] H. D. Sykes, "The Authorship of 'A Knack to Know a Knave,'" *N.&Q.*, 146, 412, would have Peele work on the earlier version about 1588.

[8] Sykes, *N.&Q.*, 146, 411, from W. Creizenach, *The English Drama in the Age of Shakespeare* (1916), pp. 77, 342, n. 2, who refers to the text of Hazlitt-Dodsley, *Old Plays*, VI, 522, 557, 569, 581, etc.

[9] Chambers, *E.S.*, IV, 25.

This method of caring for the clown must have been common, and needs always to be remembered in dealing with play structure. The high comedian appears as gruff, dialect speaking Honesty. The old man is the councilor Dunston. The young men lovers, King Edgar and Ethenwald, correspond to Valentine and Proteus, and their ilk. The additions to the scheme are the two coneycatchers, Perin in court life, and Cuthbert Cutpurse in city life. Thus the basic pattern of the earlier play (which may not be completely represented in the "new" play) was not the five-man pattern of the Shaksperean company but has been adapted to it, with two extras added of villainous tendencies. This does not mean, of course, that the extraneous actors are to be looked for as the performers of these particular parts, since other actors may have been substituted in parts which belong to the primitive pattern. Neither does extraneous mean that the actors were necessarily from another company, since they may well have been the company's own cadets, as they were in Tarleton's *Sins*.

Because it shows similar characteristics, it will be best to examine next another comedy printed about this time with attribution to Strange's company, though it was not recorded at the Rose. This is *Fair Em,* whose author Greene takes to task early in 1591 for imitating *Bacon*.[10] *Fair Em* was put on probably late in 1590 or early in 1591, and was printed, without entry S.R., about 1593,[11] "As it was sundrietimes publiquely acted in the honourable citie of London, by the right honourable the Lord Strange his seruants."

In *Fair Em,* the author has entwined mechanically two plays, the two sets of characters having no necessary and little assigned connection. In the title play, Manvile is the favored suitor of Fair Em, the title character, who is the daughter of the Miller of Manchester, in reality Sir Thomas Goddard, who is in hiding from William the Conqueror. As rivals to Manvile, we have the clown Trotter, Mountney, and Valingford, who finally gets assigned to Em by King William. Here we have the complete casting pattern for Strange's company. The Miller is the old-man father, and the two young men and two comedians are all rivals for Em. Trotter the clown is thus prominent and in the play, but has not a major part. The true and successful Valingford (Valentine) is, of course the faithful young man, who will not let a little thing like blindness stand in his way, while the jealous (Antipholus of Ephesus, Proteus) deserter Manvile is the fickle young man. This leaves Mountney for the high comedian. The "deaf routine" would doubtless give him sufficient scope. This, therefore, is the comedy of *Fair Em,* and conforms to the typical casting pattern for Strange's company.

---

[10] See Appendix I, pp. 514 ff.

[11] McKerrow, *Devices,* p. 55; Greg, *Bibliography,* I, 192.

For a kind of background setting to this title play, we have the court of William the Conqueror, from whom Sir Thomas Goddard as a miller and his daughter Fair Em are in hiding. Valingford and Mountney are gentlemen from King William's court, and King William himself must, of course, eventually bestow Em upon Valingford and reconcile all difficulties — arbitrarily, equally of course.

But King William also has his own play, built on the theme of the king and rival subject, with King William and Lubeck as the rival young men for Mariana, though King William has finally to be content with Blanche, daughter of King Zweno, the usual father in the case. So in the second play we have the rival young men and the father, who could be fitted into the casting pattern of Strange's company; but in this play no comedians. Its three chief male characters are involved in a very serious comedy in high estate, threatening tragedy till the very last lines of the play.

We have, therefore, the comedy of *Fair Em* written on Strange's casting pattern, with three other main characters for men cared for by a truncated enveloping background play of serious cast. The structure of the play itself makes it clear that by the end of 1590, there was some kind of occasion for adding to the normal casting pattern in Strange's company. Again, as in the case of the two additional parts in *Knacke,* we cannot be certain that the extraneous three actors were confined to the King William plot, etc.

Greene early in 1591 ridiculed the composition of *Fair Em.* If it was the first, it certainly was not the last of the imitations of *Bacon.* In fact, *Bacon* is as much a landmark in comedy as *Tamburlaine* is in tragedy. Since the Henry VI plays and *Knacke* for Strange's, as well as other plays, also show its influence, it will be well to examine some phases of its influence upon structure here. In *Bacon,* we have the prince, Edward, rivalled in love by the nice but unfaithful noble, Lacy. The lead is Friar Bacon, who by his magic gives the play such guidance as it receives. There is a dignified father, Henry III, and two clowns. One of these is a "scholar" clown, Miles, the other is a "fool" clown, Ralph Simnell. There is, of course, a very sweet leading lady to occasion the rivalry of Edward and Lacy. This is Margaret, with second largest number of lines in the play.

As we have seen, rivalry of king and subject furnishes a background for the title play of *Fair Em.* William the Conqueror and the Marquis of Lubeck are the rival king and noble subject, but they are not rivals for the lovely country maid. Instead, they struggle for another, and in the end each is matched with a princess fair. Also, their rivalry is built specifically and explicitly upon the love-friendship theme as in *Bacon.* The author has adapted here a story in which the country maid could not well be included. So he splits the *Bacon* triangle, as it were, and provides the country maid her own special circle of rivals to the number of four. The two nobles from King William's court involved in this second rivalry are friends, but there is no specific reference to the love-friendship theme. To these two were added the fickle, favored lover and the clown, so that there is a double set of rivals, each set from a different class in society. The latter two are more nearly of Fair Em's supposed social standing, but the former two are nearer what is later found to be her actual position in society. Of course, the clown hadn't a chance, and his fellow rival in low society proved inconstant, as does one of the pair from higher society. So Em is worthily matched with a companion of the rival prince, and of his antagonist noble. The author of *Fair Em* has produced his play by writing variations upon Greene's central theme, though some of his ingenuity would better have been expended upon tying his two triangle plays together. No wonder that a man of Greene's haughty and egoistic nature was offended at the clever manipulation. So, as we have seen, when next he took pen in hand he proclaimed his spite to the world. It appears, then, that *Fair Em* was written hardly earlier than the autumn of 1590, upon the model of *Bacon*. But its casting pattern is not that of *Bacon*. For now the rivals themselves become the leading characters in a play of their own, and there are various other divergencies.

In two other plays which are not far in time of composition from *Fair Em,* this rivalry in love of king and subject is also fundamental. First of these is Peele's *Edward I,* which was entered S.R. October 8, 1593, and printed in 1593, without attribution to company, though it is usually supposed to be the "longe shanke" which was played by the Admiral's in 1595-96.[12] Elsewhere we have seen reason to date the play about the Christmas of 1590, but it is not among the plays performed by the Admiral-Strange combination at the Rose, though it could have had its run there or elsewhere before Henslowe's Diary begins.

As in *Bacon,* so in *Edward I,* the leading man is not used in the rival king and subject plot. In *Bacon,* the lead is Friar Bacon, whose magic is supposed to guide, or at least condition, the events of the play. In *Edward I,* the lead is Longshanks himself, who is the titular king, around whom the events of the play revolve. It turns out indeed that Longshanks has had various rivals, including his brother, but nothing is made of that rivalry in the play itself. The person with the second greatest number of lines in each play is the leading lady, Margaret in *Bacon,* Queen Elinor in *Edward I.* In *Bacon,* however, the leading lady was the object of contention between the prince and subject; in the story of *Edward I,* she was needed for the leading man's partner, and so the young prince and the

---

[12] Horne, *Peele,* p. 91; Chambers, *E.S.,* III, 461.

noble were forced to be content with a less well trained paragon as the object of their rivalry. In *Bacon,* these rival young men, Edward and Lacy, are fourth and fifth in number of lines, Miles the clown ranking third by virtue of thirteen lines more than the prince. In *Edward I,* they are third and fifth, Lluellen and Mortimer, the clown this time having seventy-one lines less than the prince, and so in this respect being placed between the rivals. In *Bacon,* the sixth character was another comedian, the fool, Ralph Simnell. There is no corresponding major character in *Edward I,* though the comedians did not always have parts written into the play. Consequently, omission of a comedian is not so significant as his inclusion. There was quite a bit of incidental clownery in *Edward I,* in which another comedian could have found his place. Nevertheless, the fact is that *Edward I* varies its structure from *Bacon* in having only one clown. Again, *Bacon* had a seventh character with barely more than one hundred lines, King Henry III, with 103 lines. The story demanded him as a major character, but Greene and the Queen's company did as little for him as they could. The corresponding character in *Edward I* could be considered to be "John Baliol, elected King of Scotland," who has eighty-four lines, though something might be said for Edmund, Duke of Lancaster, brother and confidant of Longshanks. Lancaster has sixty-one lines. Thus each major character in *Bacon* has some corresponding character in *Edward I,* except that there is only one major comedian in *Edward I,* and that some of the corresponding characters are not major ones. But the parallels are close enough to show that one play is modeled on the other.

Which borrows from the other, *Bacon* or *Edward I?* Both chronology and the relationships of the plays would seem to indicate that *Edward I* is the borrower. For chronology, it would appear that *Bacon* dates 1589 and *Edward I* 1590-91.[13] For structural relationships, *Bacon* is accounted for from its sources without any reference to *Edward I.* So far as the organization of its story is concerned, it is thus independent of *Edward I.* *Bacon* is constructed from three chief elements. The guiding one is the story of *Bacon.* This story, in turn, was laid in the reign of Henry III, thus demanding the historical background as a second element. But this historical background involved only the use of prominent historical names, mostly suggested by the source story, and the sketching in the most casual and general way of a few historical events. Into the Bacon story and the historical background, Greene wove as his third element a wholly independent and self-contained romance. He attached the romance to prominent historical characters, and sent some of the characters to Bacon for help in tangling and untangling the romance, thus tying it into the

---

[13] See above, pp. 57 ff., 173 ff.

Bacon story in a purely mechanical way. Bacon's connection with the romance is entirely professional and perfunctory. It is merely another occasion for exercise of his all-powerful art. So whether Greene found or invented the romance, it came to him whole and as a unit; it did not grow out of either of the other two elements. Nor is there anything to indicate that Greene is adapting this romance of rival prince and subject from Peele's rival prince and noble in *Edward I*. Greene's romance is founded on the love-friendship theme, further complicated by the idea of wooing by the unfaithful friend as proxy. It is only an accident that the lover is a prince, and that the rival, unfaithful, wooer-friend is his subject. Peele's romance is merely that of a rival prince and noble, without any theme at all. The love-friendship theme was a stock one at the time, and Greene most likely invented his own story upon it. At any rate, the whole story of *Bacon* is accounted for without reference to *Edward I*.

But *Edward I* is not independent of *Bacon*, as is evident when it is checked against its sources. To these sources Peele himself has been kind enough to give us the clue. Luellen and his men will "get the next day from Brecknock the Book of Robin Hood,"[14] Luellen will act as Robin Hood, Meredith as Little John, Friar David as Friar Tuck, and Lady Eleanor as Maid Marian. Later Mortimer appears as the Potter, and continues the rivalry for Lady Eleanor, though Mortimer's actual physical battle for Lady Eleanor is with Friar David. The "Book of *Robin Hood*" would presumably be "A mery geste of Robyn Hoode," the first surviving edition of which dates around 1560. This version brings Robin Hood into personal encounter with "Edward our comely kynge," who by the descriptions is evidently Longshanks. It thus brings in the historical background of the reign of Edward I.

From these two sources, (1) the traditional and invented Robin Hood stories (not merely the "mery geste"), and (2) history, Peele has borrowed, adapted, and invented his material. But from neither does he get the shaping idea. From history, he learned that Lady Eleanor had been captured and turned over to Edward I as she was on her way from exile in France to marry Luellen, Prince of Wales. Thereupon, Luellen went to war with Edward, was beaten into submission, but in the terms of settlement procured his bride. Luellen kept rebelling periodically, and finally in one of these rebellions Lord John Gifford and Lord Edmund Mortimer were sent to subdue him. Luellen was killed, his head brought to Mortimer, and by him transmitted to King Edward. This historical struggle between Edward and Luellen, originating over Lady Eleanor, Peele has retained. The general idea of rivalry between Luellen and Mortimer would be furnished by the events of Luellen's last rebellion; yet

---

[14] Bullen, *Edward I*, Scene VII, 27-28.

there was nothing in history to suggest that these two were rivals in love. But Luellen's struggle for his lady love, and his later struggle with Mortimer, might suggest connecting the two struggles as a rivalry in love between prince and noble, provided Peele already had the idea of such a rivalry, and was seeking an opportunity to apply it. The idea, however, is not suggested by history itself.

Whence did this idea come? One turns next to the Robin Hood element. But the idea is not from this source. In the ballads, at least, Robin Hood and the Potter were not rivals for the love of Maid Marian. Nor does the Potter have any known connection with Marian. While Maid Marian was being paired with Robin Hood in May games early in the sixteenth century, yet it is not till toward the end of the century that we find the two cast as lovers. In the ballads proper, Maid Marian had been coupled wih Friar Tuck. But even there the two were late additions, coming from the May games and morris dance. It is in accord with this pairing that Friar David, as Friar Tuck, makes advances to Lady Eleanor, as Maid Marian, although Peele had already supplied him with his trull. Incidentally, Friar Tuck's Maid Marian is the one whom Falstaff knew. Neither is there any reason from the ballads why the Potter should struggle with Friar Tuck for Maid Marian. The motive for this struggle does not come from the ballads, but from the love attributed to Lord Mortimer, as the Potter, for Lady Eleanor, as Maid Marian. The struggle itself between Friar Tuck and the Potter is merely the customary bout through which a newcomer won admission to Robin's band, though that bout was regularly with Robin himself. And so one might go on.[15] Clearly, Peele has merely selected characters and materials from the Robin Hood tradition to carry on his main idea of rivalry between Luellen and Mortimer for Lady Eleanor. The setting is a Robin Hood setting but the story is not a Robin Hood story.

This idea of rivalry between prince and noble for a lady fair does not derive either from history or from the story of Robin Hood. These two sources account for the materials of the story, indeed; but the structural idea, which is the heart of the play, is missing. This idea had to be strong enough in the first place to pull these particular two stories of the reign of Edward I together, and in the second place to give them a common denominator which warps both of them from their true forms. This idea has shaped the materials of both of the stories into its own likeness. *Edward I* is neither the story of Luellen, nor the story of Robin Hood, nor a combination of the two. It is a story based upon the idea of the rivalry of prince and noble for the hand of lady fair, which merely finds

---

[15] On these matters, see F. J. Child, *English and Scottish Popular Ballads* (1956), III, 43 ff., 218, etc.

its materials in the story of Luellen, and of Robin Hood. Whence did the basic idea come?

It is to be remembered here that the structural formula of *Bacon* and *Edward I* is the same, and that the plays are not independent, that the structure of one play has clearly been modeled upon that of the other. But the story and basic idea of *Bacon* can be accounted for without reference to *Edward I*. So could the number of characters also be accounted for, and their arrangement to form the structure of the play. Each major character has his or her function, and that function follows naturally from the source materials. Not so, as we have seen, in *Edward I*. Some major characters are thrust in to fill up, and their arrangement has been determined by an idea external to the source stories. *Edward I* must thus have from some source such a model as *Bacon* to furnish the basic idea, and to determine its fundamental structure. Since *Edward I* and *Bacon* are not independent, since *Bacon* can be accounted for from its source materials without the influence of *Edward I,* but since *Edward I* cannot be accounted for without some such model as *Bacon,* it seems reasonably clear that *Edward I* is the borrower, and hence the later play.

With *Bacon* as a model, it is easy to see how Peele shaped the story of *Edward I*. In *Bacon,* the rivalry of Prince Edward and Lord Lacy was to the fore. Peele takes the reign of this same Prince Edward, now become king. In it he finds the story of Luellen fighting King Edward for the love of Lady Eleanor, and finally losing his life before the army of Mortimer. So Luellen, Mortimer, and Eleanor are fitted into the triangle of *Bacon*. For his pastoral setting to correspond to that in *Bacon,* Peele turns to the Robin Hood stories, popularly supposed to belong to the reign of Edward. Thus was his triangle all fitted up. The lead could be cast in the central guiding and directing role of Edward I, corresponding in importance and structural purpose with Bacon. Edward's wife Eleanor was tinkered in as the bloodthirsty Spaniard of popular tradition, thereby casting a sop to current popular hatred of Spain. One comedian was cared for as Friar David, borrowed from Friar Tuck of the Robin Hood cycles. Other characters were inserted according to need.

A play connected with *Edward I* also shows the king and subject rivalry. This is Marlowe's *Edward II,* which is later than Peele's *Edward I*. In *Edward II,* Edward and Mortimer are the rivals. This rivalry was known to history, but was not emphasized there. Too, as in history, the triangle does not develop at once; but in the beginning of the play is rather reversed, with the Queen and Gaveston struggling for Edward's affections. It is only in the latter half of the play, as in history, that the prince-subject triangle develops. Around the leading characters, Marlowe has grouped the other important personages from history who were necessary to carry on the main story. Since *Bacon* had made the prince-subject triangle prominent, and others had followed suit, Marlowe would be the more alive to its possibilities, though I see no indication that he has modeled directly in any way upon *Bacon*. But, at any rate, Marlowe has emphasized this theme in *Edward II*.[16]

Marlowe was also aware of this triangle as it appeared in *2 Henry VI*, since in *Edward II*[17] he echoes the climactic scene of the triangle in the former play. There are touches of this king and subject triangle in both *1* and *2 Henry VI*. There the suggested but not fully developed rivalry is between Henry VI and Suffolk, with Queen Margaret as the object of it. In *1 Henry VI* Talbot dominates the play as do Bacon and Edward I in their plays; but he does not direct events as do they. Talbot's story is separate from the triangle, and has no connection with it. As in *Edward I,* so in *1 Henry VI,* the lady of the triangle is not the leading lady of the play. Instead, the haughty Spaniard Eleanor and the French witch Joan are the corresponding leading ladies in the two plays. Thus three of the six chief male characters, and the leading ladies correspond in the two plays, and occupy relatively the same structural places. The other three main characters of *1 Henry VI* do not correspond so specifically to the other characters in *Edward I*. But quite clearly *1 Henry VI* was originally constructed on much the same formula.

While *1 Henry VI* is partially constructed on the same general formula as *Edward I,* yet *2 Henry VI* is not so clear. It is a continuation of *1 Henry VI,* with four of its six major characters necessarily continuing, and certain others because of historical facts necessarily being added. Talbot and Joan have necessarily dropped out, and history furnished no corresponding characters for the other two parts. Therefore the play had to be constructed according to the new conditions, though, since all the members of the triangle are still alive, it is continued.

The triangle does not continue into *3 Henry VI,* the sequel play, since Suffolk is dead. It is possible, therefore, that *1 Henry VI* was originally constructed for the same company as *Edward I,* and probable that *2* and *3 Henry VI* were first written for the same organization. It will appear that at least the three Henry the Sixth plays in their present form were written for the Strange-Admiral combination. As we have seen, *Edward I* may also have belonged here. Similarly, *Edward II* belonged eventually to the Admiral's, though Pembroke's had something to do with it, as they

---

[16] It should be noticed in this connection that, in effect, *Bacon, Edward I,* and *Edward II* form a trilogy, with *Bacon* as the basis. The other two Edward plays followed *Bacon,* and in historical order. Peele and Marlowe may have fallen into this sequence initially by personal inspiration, but the actors, whether the same group or rival groups, may have had something to do with planning a sequence. In any case, both the dramatists and the actors were probably aware of these relationships.

[17] See below, pp. 292 ff.

had with the *True Tragedie* (York) and other plays connected with either or both the Admiral's and Strange's.

The *Knacke to knowe a Knaue* also has its connections with the *Bacon* type, though it is not modeled directly upon it or upon any of the other plays we have been considering. The play is really a morality, constructed on the idea of coneycatching, *a la* Robert Greene; and the rival king and subject illustrate coneycatching in love. Characters are so selected as to represent coneycatching in the different orders of the commonwealth, and some person is needed to act as judge upon them. This is, of course, the duty of the sovereign. Since coneycatching was being practiced throughout the commonwealth at the sovereign's expense, it was but natural that the coneycatching in love should also be at his expense, especially since that idea offered opportunity for another presentation of the popular theme of rival prince and subject. Doubtless, then, it was the popularity of this theme which suggested its inclusion as the illustration of coneycatching in love.

Another play of the time is generally admitted to have modeled upon the rival magicians of *Friar Bacon and Friar Bungay.* This is Mundy's *John a Kent and John a Cumber,* the surviving manuscript of which is dated 1590.[18] Here Mundy centers attention upon the rivalry of the two magicians, John a Kent and John a Cumber, the lovers being the pawns in the game between the two. Mundy has borrowed the idea of rival magicians from *Bacon* and made much fuller use of it. Some Robin Hood touches might be caused by *Edward I,* but I see no conclusive evidence of it. We shall see that *Kent* fits well enough structurally with the plays of this period.[19]

---

[18] I. A. Shapiro, "The Significance of a Date," *Shakespeare Survey* (1955), VIII, 100 ff.

[19] *John a Kent* calls for at least a note on *Sir Thomas More,* where the original MS is also in Mundy's hand and was preserved along with that of the former play. The structure of *More* is typical of the Admiral's before 1590, since the part of Sir Thomas More is six times that of the second person. But since it is a "one-man" play, some such preponderance would likely have occurred at any time and place. The latest full-scale review of the evidence, by Professor Bald (*"The Booke of Sir Thomas More* and its Problems," *Shakespeare Survey* (1949), II, 51 ff.), tends to place the revision as probably some years after 1594, without establishing, however, the date of the original form. For critics do not appear to have cleared their minds as to the order of events. The original manuscript in Mundy's hand was submitted to Tilney, who ripped it to pieces. Then or later it was decided to rework the play. The fact that the original author, Mundy, had nothing to do with the revision would likely indicate that this reworking was later. It would no doubt have been a good idea to let Tilney cool off. If the revision was made when and as Professor Bald thinks, there is little probability that Shakspere had anything to do with it. Still, Mundy's original version may well have belonged to the early 'nineties where handwriting experts have suggested, but in any case what we have of Mundy's original version would not particularly aid our present enterprise. At revision, after all hands and the cook (except the original author) had done their endeavors, the surviving

Such facts as those we have been examining — and there are more — show why Robert Greene might well in 1590 represent himself as Roberto, who had written so successful a first play that all companies were bidding for his services. Whether first or not, *Bacon* had been such a play, and even *Orlando,* his probable first, was evidently much admired and pillaged. But quite understandably Greene was not pleased when other dramatists, such as the author of *Fair Em,* had by 1591 begun to invade his market. Still less was he pleased when he himself by 1592 was cast aside in favor of others. If one wishes to know what Robert Greene meant in August, 1592, let him look around him.

We have been looking at these plays from the point of view of Strange's men. But in this period Strange's were in some way cooperating with the Admiral's. We have examined the structure of the plays for the Admiral's through 1589. The same basic pattern but slightly modified continues in plays which belong to the Admiral's tradition up to and into the known connection with Strange's in 1592. These are Mundy's *John a Kent,* his *Fair Em*[20] (attributed to Strange's), and Peele's *Edward I,* all probably in 1590, and Marlowe's *Edward II,* probably 1591 or 1592. To these we may add *Knacke* of May, 1592, because of its kinship in structure. Strange's is connected directly with *Fair Em* and *Knacke,* and we have seen how these plays are adapted to their casting pattern. Strange's had no known direct connection with the other three, and these do not show the same kind of adaptation to Strange's formula as the other two.

In these five plays, we still have the lead and a second line of characters working with or against the lead: Longshanks-Luellen, John a Kent-John a Cumber, William the Conqueror-Lubeck, Edward-Mortimer, Edgar-Honesty. In this period, however, the lead does not have quite the old preponderance over the second man. The lead is now receiving much more support from the remainder of the company, not so much by cutting down the lines of the lead as by raising those of the other parts. The third line, that of the oratorical dignitary, is also evident as Lancaster, Chester, Miller, Lancaster, Dunston. The fourth major line, the young lover and warrior, appears as Mortimer, Sir Griffin, Valingford, Gaveston, Ethenwald. The fifth part, a Lord in penumbra, seems to fade out or at least not to develop, King Baliol, King Zweno, Kent. But there is now a second young lover, Gloucester, Powis, Mounteney, Spenser, Perin.

---

mess was the result. It would then have been the luckless task of someone to put this mess into fair form so as to try again to get it by the censor. Whether it passed or failed this time we do not know. It might be well to remember here that such a hashing could happen to any play — even to one from the sacred pen of Shakspere himself.

[20] See Appendix I.

Since these plays are now for the most part love stories, such an addition was necessary to the starkly tragic cast of the early Admiral's plays. Before 1589, the *Spanish Tragedy* was in the ascendant. Thereafter *Bacon* took the lead. Only one clown still appears occasionally in a major capacity. Friar Hugh, Turnop, Trotter. Even the turning from tragedy to romantic love has not much benefited the clown. While the first four lines for men remain approximately in place, this does not necessarily mean that exactly the same actor was acting each line throughout. We shall need to know much more about the actual personnel before we can form any reasoned and reasonable guess as to that. But the same tradition continued for these, and adaptations were made by adding additional types. The women occupy about the same position as earlier, even though these are love stories. After all, the heroes of those days required slight incentive!

In our discussion so far, we have laid aside the three parts of *Henry VI* as history. But it will now be seen that the historical characters have also been shaped toward these traditional rôles. There is, however, a further significant deviation. The Strange-Admiral company is known to have performed in the *Henry VI* plays and the *Knacke*. It will be seen that these plays provide for still another principal line, Dauphin, Young Clifford, Cuthbert Cutpurse. This further adaptation of the casting formula is doubtless due to the composition of the cooperative company. It will be remembered that before it entered this combination Strange's company provided typically for two young men, an old man, and two comedians among its principal parts. The old man would be at home in the Admiral's line. The two young men could be reasonably satisfied after *Bacon* produced its transformation of the old type. The high comedian would find life more difficult, though he could usually adjust himself. But the clown would find himself technically excluded.

The structure of these plays thus shows progressive deviation from the old Admiral's formula, and it is clear that the ultimate deviation was occasioned by the cooperation with Strange's. Apparently that cooperation for the Admiral's consisted of only Edward Alleyn as actor and the accumulated and accumulating stock of plays for the Admiral's organization in the hands of Edward Alleyn. Both actors and dramatists would need to adapt themselves to this new situation. Habitually the long-time dramatists for the Admiral's would continue the old rôles as far as possible. Just as naturally Strange's men would want to be cast as they had been accustomed. And inevitably there would have to be adjustment of these conflicting desires. We can see that some adjustment did occur, but we do not yet know the conditioning circumstances well enough to go into details.

But as we look at our accumulated facts, it appears that there are some significant known adaptations of the casting pattern of Strange's company at the period. One of these concerns the clown. He may not be written into the play proper at all but given his own business, which he may even himself provide. There is the case in a *Knacke* of "Kemps applauded Merrimentes of the men of Goteham, in receiuing the King into Goteham." Kempe has been given his own comic business of a "play within a play," which he himself may have provided, though the statement is ambiguous. And Kempe's play gets equal billing with the main play, a *Knacke*, both in the entry S.R. and on the printed title page. It was not a matter of suppressing the clown — the audiences would not tolerate that. It was a question of how to care for the clown, whether to write him into the play and let him speak no more than is set down, or whether to provide space for his own devices in the cracks of the action. It was this latter solution which drew the satire of the youthful Cambridge authors of the Parnassus plays, who hauled the clown in with a cart-rope to symbolize the devices of the professional companies. The method of caring for the clown is frequently that obvious. Some author of *Hamlet* preferred the former method. "Let those that play your clowns speak no more than is set down for them," etc.[21] In the poor quarto, the quoted illustrations of the clown's witticisms are traceable to Tarleton, hence probably belonged to the *Old Hamlet*. This is the solution of *Fair Em*, where the clown is written into the play as Trotter but is given quite a restricted part. One may also instance Kempe as Peter in *Romeo and Juliet*, though this is a tragedy, where one would expect the clown to be more restrained.

Such a solution represents the view of the Admiral's men, who went in heavily for tragedy, though apparently they also were obliged to furnish some comic matter. The reader will remember at once the statement of "R. I. Printer" to the Gentlemen Readers, "I haue (purposely) omitted and left out some fond and friuolous Iestures, digressing (and in my poore opinion) far vnmeet for the matter, which I thought, might seeme more tedious vnto the wise, than any way els to be regarded, though (happly) they haue bene of some vaine cōceited fondlings greatly gaped at, what times they were shewed vpon the stage in their graced deformities: neuertheles now, to be mixtured in print with such matter of worth, it would prooue a great disgrace to so honorable & stately a historie." One is reminded of the Romans beating Greene's motto out of a buckler, of which Greene accuses the Admiral's along with the blasphemies of Tamburlaine and Heliogabalus, though evidently the Roman clownery belonged to the latter play.

The Admiral influence, then, upon Strange's would be pro-tragedy and

---

[21] *Hamlet,* III, 2, 37-39.

anti-clown. We have seen both these influences at work, whether they came in wholly from the Admiral's or not, in the addition of serious parts to the casting formula of Strange's in *Fm* and *Knacke,* and in the treatment of the clown in both plays. Another significant illustration of the Admiral influence is the adaptation of Greene's *Orlando,* which was written for the Queen's two-clown organization, as that adaptation is indicated by the Alleyn MS. Sir Walter Greg finds of the clownage scenes that "not one of them can be traced to the original."[22] Only, since we now know that Q represents more nearly the original form for the Queen's, we must reverse his statement in application; that is, the clownery of Q has been cut completely from the form represented by the Alleyn MS. This latter form is presumably the adaptation made for the Strange-Admiral performances early in 1592. Whether other comic material was substituted and what it was we do not know. Sir Walter also finds indications that the part of Orlando was heightened for the version represented by the Alleyn MS. All these pieces of evidence point in the same direction. The Admiral's influence would induce serious parts to Strange's casting formula and heighten the serious lines already in it. It would also minimize the clown within the play. Kempe is not likely to have been very happy with this turn of events. Too much ranting; too little fun!

But the combination of two groups of actors would create an uneasy problem in construction for the dramatist. He might solve it as did the author of *Fair Em* by lashing together two plays. A mature Shakspere can join two plays together in a *Lear* and get praised "beyond beyond" for artistic balance, etc. The artistic balance is there, and is praiseworthy in the highest; but the prosaic fact is that the need for this solution of artistic balance arose from the circumstance that the old *Leir* did not provide enough vehicles for the available and necessary number of major actors. So Shakspere balanced with another play taken from the *Arcadia.* We believe that even the immature Shakspere, having as he did a so highly developed respect for structural form, would have done a much better job with *Fair Em* than did its author. But we must never forget that this author had this problem thrust upon him by the circumstances of play production; his solution had nothing to do with his free artistic choice of an ideal form. Only we critics can indulge in such luxury!

Unaccustomed size, at this early period, in play construction results, not in added size of the fundamental unit, but in an agglomeration of several units. Even Tamburlaine swashes through a "life" and a "death," not the unit of a story. This difficulty was inherent in "history" plays generally, since the authors had not learned how to subject loose story-

---

[22] Greg, *Abridgements,* pp. 306 ff.

narrative to close-wrought exposition — hardly indeed had they learned this even with their small units modeled on the Roman plays. It is, therefore, interesting to have some clues as to how Strange's adapted themselves to an inherited play of pageants, such as Tarleton's *Seven Deadly Sins*. Unfortunately, we have only the plot for one of the halves. This gives some light as to the kind of parts some of the actors took; but it does not show the whole company in action, nor very clearly the relative importance given to the various actors. The play consisted really of seven plays or pageants, divided four and three for two performances, with a purely mechanical over-all linking to hold them together.

For the surviving plot, "The piece consists of three plays or episodes illustrating the sins of Envy, Sloth, and Lechery, in the stories respectively of Ferrex and Porrex, Sardanapalus, and Tereus, set in an historical framework dealing with an episode of the reign of Henry VI. This framework comprises the two introductory scenes (divisions I and II as marked in the transcript), the conclusion and epilogue (XXIII and XXIV), and the two interludes that separate the Sin plays (IX and XVII). The first Sin play begins and the last ends with a dumb-show to which Lydgate (a framework character) acts as expositor (ll. 25, 80). But it will be observed that Henry and Lydgate also break into the middle of the first Sin play (ll. 33-5) and Lydgate into the middle of the second (l. 52). This serves to divide the first and second Sin plays into two acts each, while the third is undivided; so that the three Sin plays together constitute five acts.[23] . . . Evidently Henry and Lydgate remain present as spectators throughout, commenting at appropriate points on the action of the Sin plays."[24]

It will be seen that this was a sit-and-see play, with the shows being presented to Henry VI by Lydgate. Thus Lydgate is the typical oratorical presenter outside the action. In lines, he would have had a major part, but the passive Henry VI would not. Since these two were fixtures, there was no need to mention the actors for them. It has been plausibly suggested that Heminges took the part of Lydgate; but we have only our wishful will to believe that Shakspere was Henry VI, as has been suggested, though such an assignment is in keeping with what we know of his acting.

The first Sin to be shown is Envy as exemplified in the well-known story of Gorboduc and his two sons, Ferrex and Porrex. Here three

---

[23] Since this act-division evidently goes back to original construction by 1585, I could have used it in *Five-Act* as further illustration of stage practice. Notice that the acts are indicated, as partially in *Romeo and Juliet*, for instance, but not denominated as acts. The plot of *The Dead Man's Fortune* also indicates the acts but does not so denominate them. So for that matter do the tragedies of Seneca.

[24] W. W. Greg, *Dramatic Documents from the Elizabethan Playhouses*, p. 113.

cadets of Strange's company take the principal parts. Young Richard Burbadge is aged and unwise Gorboduc, while the envious and murderous sons are personated by Henry Cundall as Ferrex, and Will Slye as Porrex. Apparently all three of these, along with Shakspere, were taken into the membership at one time at the reorganization of 1594.[25] So coming events are casting their shadows before.

The second Sin show is of Sloth as exemplified by Sardanapalus, represented by Augustine Phillips, who was opposed by General Arbactus, represented by Thomas Pope. Both these are members of the company and principal actors in it. The third Sin is Lechery, exemplified by the story of Tereus, represented by Richard Burbadge.

Thus Richard Burbadge has the lead in two of the three shows, being Gorboduc and Tereus, an unwise old man and an equally unwise young one. Burbadge was thus already playing leading roles, though he did not become a member till 1594. Phillips as Sardanapalus and Pope as Arbactus pair against each other in leading roles, as do Cundall and Slye. All four take vigorous and possibly villainous parts. Heminges does not appear, but was most likely Lydgate, the presenter. For some reason Kempe does not appear either, though we would have expected him to be Will Fool in Sloth, played by John Duke.

It is clear from this plot of *2 Deadly Sins* that Strange's at this period put on a play with one lead, Burbadge; one pair consisting of an effeminate dignitary Sardanapalus-Phillips, and a gruff general Arbactus-Pope; another pair, consisting of two sparring young men Ferrex-Cundall, and Porrex-Sly. A sixth principal part of dignified and oratorical cast, Lydgate, does not have the actor named, but is probably Heminges. Brian has only minor roles here, appearing as Warwick and probably as Damasus, a councilor to Gorboduc, and Kempe does not appear at all. By using their three cadets, Strange's men could, therefore, and did put on a play with seven principal roles for men, exclusive of the clown.

The next question is that of date of this performance. It is clear that the plot passed through Alleyn, hence that Strange's had access during its connection with Alleyn, who was at the time the Admiral's company. In the plot itself there is no sign of Alleyn, nor for that matter of any actor, principal or minor, who can be connected with the old Admiral's men. Since the play had belonged to the Queen's men along with at least *Orlando, Bacon,* and *Looking Glass,* it is evident that Alleyn had acquired control of these from the Queen's. We have seen that this was probably about the end of 1589 or the beginning of 1590. Strange's were performing the other three plays in 1592, and it has been supposed that the plot was for *Four Plays In One,* performed by Strange's March 6,

---

[25] Baldwin, *Organization and Personnel,* p. 83.

1592. This was Sir Walter Greg's first conclusion,[26] but later he and Sir Edmund Chambers succeeded in persuading each other that this identification and date were wrong.[27] As has been explained,[28] their fears have been unfounded. If this plot is for *Four Plays In One*, as Sir Walter first thought, then the plot is doubtless for the revival by Strange's men, in which one performance is recorded March 6, 1592. If this is *Three Plays In One*, then its companion play was *Four Plays In One* and was doubtless referred to in the entry of March 6, 1592. In either case, the plot is likely to belong about 1591-92. It cannot date far on either side, since Strange's had access through Alleyn during this period of co-operation with him, which can hardly be earlier than 1590, nor can be later than 1594. Had the performances been after March, 1592, we ought to have some record. So the plot is not likely earlier than 1590, nor later than March, 1592. Most likely it belongs late in 1591 or early in 1592. This fits the fact that Gabriel Harvey refers to Tarlton's play in his *Four Letters* of 1592,[29] where Harvey calls it a "most liuely playe, I might haue seene in London: and was verie gently inuited thereunto at Oxford, by *Tarleton* himselfe." This may mean that the London performances referred to were also before the death of Tarlton. But at least Harvey had in some way been reminded of the play in 1592.

The upshot of the matter is that we know that by 1591-92, Strange's company alone, whatever its connection with Alleyn and the Admiral's, could and did put on a play with the number of serious principal parts which we find in *Romeo and Juliet* and the three Henry VI plays. Elsewhere I have endeavored to match up the parts in these four plays with those in Tarlton's play of the Deadly Sins.[30] It is evident also that Strange's would at this period have no difficulty in putting on the tragedies of the Admiral's.[31] They could also have put on the two-clown plays of the Queen's, as they were written, had they wished. But *Orlando* and the general submergence of even the country clown in the plays of the period indicate that they did not wish. One reason for this *may* very well be that inheriting his line traditionally from the mediaeval devil, Pope preferred to be a villain rather than a high comedian, and even a high comedian, to

---

[26] Greg, *Henslowe Papers*, p. 129.

[27] Greg, *Dramatic Documents*, p. 113.

[28] See p. 255.

[29] Grosart, *Harvey*, I, 194.

[30] Baldwin, *Organization and Personnel*, Chapter IX and tabulation.

[31] It seems certain that Edward Alleyn himself acted with Strange's, at least occasionally, as the entry S.R. of *A Knacke to know a Knave* "as it hath sundrye tymes ben plaid by Ned Allen and his companie" (title page also), the license of 1593, and the part of *Orlando* would indicate. But there is as yet no evidence that any other major actor from the Admiral's was involved, and not even Alleyn appears in Tarlton's *Sins*.

being a clown. At any rate, in these serious plays, the clown is submerged and the villains get stronger parts. Even the comedies of the period as represented by *Fair Em* and *Knacke* show a similar strengthening of the serious side. In tone, at least, they are tragicomic. We are not dealing here with a mere whim of Shakspere's or of any other dramatist. The dramatist, no doubt, had his influence. But the audience by its response at the box office determined what the actors could put on to earn a living, and they hired a dramatist to write plays that would take. Marlowe and the Admiral's had found a certain kind of tragic history quite successful. Greene and the Queen's had won interest in a certain kind of romantic comedy. Strange's and Shakspere in 1592 are capitalizing on both traditions, and Shakspere will eventually please his audiences and us through having learned further from both these traditions — and from many another.

CHAPTER XIII

The Relation of *Contention* to *2 Henry VI*

In a work which went to press in June, 1925, and was published in September 1927, I wrote, "as I hope to show in later publication, the First and Second *Contentions* are only *2* and *3 Henry VI* printed from damaged manuscript."[1] Later, Mr. Peter Alexander has argued a similar thesis, and the conclusion has generally been accepted in recent years that *Contention* and *True Tragedie* (York) are derivatives. We are not here concerned with the nature of *Contention* and *True Tragedie* further than to establish their general relationship to *2* and *3 Henry VI*. Perhaps our best point of departure is the relationship of certain passages in Marlowe's *Edward II* to other passages in *1* and *2 Henry VI*. Here I have taken as a soundly appraised basis, the passages accepted by Charlton and Waller as being related,[2] though I have examined carefully all suggested parallels that I could find.

In our first instance of parallel between *2 Henry VI* and *Edward II* it is necessary to take into consideration the full parallel between *2 Henry VI* and *Contention*. Gloucester has been summoned by a *Messenger*.

> *Glou.* I go. Come, Nell, thou wilt ride with us?
> *Duch.* Yes, my good lord, I'll follow presently.
> > *Exeunt Gloucester and Messenger.*
> > Follow I must; I cannot go before,
> > While Gloucester bears this base and humble mind.
> > Were I a man, a duke, and next of blood,
> > I would remove these tedious stumbling-blocks
> > And smooth my way upon their headless necks.[3]

In *Contention*, the corresponding passage runs

> *Humphrey.* . . .
> > Come *Nell,* thou wilt go with vs vs I am sure.
> > > *Exet Humphrey.*
> *Elnor.* Ile come after you, for I cannot go before,

---

[1] Baldwin, *Organization and Personnel*, p. 140, n. 81. Evidence not yet presented.

[2] Charlton and Waller, *Edward II*, pp. 10-15. Dyce published a collection in 1850 (A. Dyce, *Works of Christopher Marlowe* (1850), I, lxii-lxiii), including from *2 Henry VI* (1) the tilt passage, (2) the wild O'Neill, (3) revenues on back; and from *3 Henry VI* (1) the narrow seas, (2) the cedar, (3) aspiring blood, (4) the arms as a sepulchre.

[3] *2 Henry VI*, I, 2, 59-65.

> But ere it be long, Ile go before them all,
> Despight of all that seeke to crosse me thus.[4]

It is obvious that the first three lines of the passage from *Henry VI* belong to the necessary machinery for leaving Eleanor upon the stage. In *2 Henry VI,* Eleanor answers properly, Gloucester exits, and then Eleanor continues her speech in soliloquy. The "follow" of her answer to Gloucester has evoked a proverbial statement, "They that cannot go before must come behind,"[5] taking for her the form "Follow I must; I cannot go before." It is obvious that the first two lines of her speech have been shrunk to one in the *Contention* by cutting and rephrasing the repetition of "follow," which originally evolved the point she is to make. *Contention* simply states in one line the point which *2 Henry VI* has evolved in two lines. So the first three lines of our quotation from *2 Henry VI* must have stood approximately as now in the version which *Contention* represents.

It is also obvious that in its "Ile go before them all," *Contention* is continuing its rephrasing, which had begun with "I cannot go before," taken over from *2 Henry VI.* It is obvious also that in idea this rephrasing takes the place occupied in *2 Henry VI* by the line, "And smooth my way upon their headless necks." If so, then these two lines are a restatement of the three in *2 Henry VI.* In *2 Henry VI,* Eleanor says if she were in Gloucester's place, she would remove these stumbling blocks by taking off their heads. There the idea is developed conditionally. But in *Contention* Eleanor states the idea absolutely; before long she herself will get rid of all opposition. It must be remembered also that these passages in *2 Henry VI* and *Contention* are known certainly to be one from the other, whichever way the relationship runs. Whatever the relationship, it is a primary one.

We are now prepared to look at a secondary, two-line parallel in *Edward II* to Eleanor's last two lines in *Contention.*

> Nay, all of them conspire to cross me thus;
> But if I live, I'll tread upon their heads.[6]

The parallel with *Contention* is unmistakably exact; there must be some fairly direct relationship. The two passages have the same rhetorical structure, but with the two lines reversed as to order. The "crosse me thus" lines are indifferent, since each is merely adapted to its own situation. But in the other line, where *Contention* has substituted "Ile go before them all" for an original equivalent of "And smooth my way upon their headless necks," *Edward II* has "I'll tread upon their heads." This

---

[4] *Contention,* Scene II, 42-46.

[5] Tilley, *Dictionary,* G 156, quoted in *2 Henry VI,* ed. Wilson, p. 127.

[6] Charlton and Waller, *Edward II,* II, 2, 95-96 (897-898).

must, therefore, have been the approximate reading in the version known to Marlowe.

Thus the passage in *2 Henry VI* represents the original form of these lines. *Contention* then rephrases them, and Marlowe adapts two of them in *Edward II*, though one of these lines in *Contention* has later been further debased in form. The order of events here is of primary importance. In this passage, *2 Henry VI* preserves the earliest form known to us, while *Contention* is a rewriting of this earlier form. Marlowe used this revision, and this revision was then later debased to its present printed form.

The ultimate source of another of the parallels between *Edward II* and the plays on Henry VI is in the chronicles. Halle had said under the 25th year, "This woman perceiuyng that her husbande did not frankely rule as he would, but did all thyng by thaduise and counsaill of Hūfrey duke of Gloucester, and that he passed not muche on the aucthority and gouernaunce of the realme, determined with her self, to take vpon her the rule and regiment, bothe of the kyng and his kyngdome, & to depriue & euict out of al rule and auchthoritie, the-said duke, then called the lord protector of the realme: least men shoud saie & report, yᵗ she had neither wit nor stomacke, whiche would permit & suffre her husband, beyng of perfect age & mās estate, like a yong scholer or innocent pupille, to be gouerned by the disposicion of another man."[7] Grafton takes over this statement exactly.[8] Holinshed also quotes Halle's pupil statement only slightly altered, "This ladie disdaining that hir husband should be ruled rather than rule, could not abide that the duke of Glocester should doo all things concerning the order of weightie affaires, least it might be said, that she had neither wit nor stomach, which would permit and suffer hir husband being of most perfect age, like a yoong pupill to be gouerned by the direction of an other man."[9]

In the *Mirour for Magistrates* (1578), 45ᵛ, which confessedly is based upon Halle, Gloucester is made to say that his enemies plotted his downfall and death.

> Which by slye driftes, and wyndlaces aloofe,
> They brought about, perswading first the Queene,
> That in effect it was the kinges reproofe,
> And hers also, to be exempted cleane,
> From princely rule, or that it should be seene
> A king of yeares, stil gouerned to bee
> Lyke a Pupil, that nothing could forsee.

[7] Halle, Edward, *The Vnion of the two noble and illustrate famelies of Lancastre & Yorke* (1548), CLᵛ-CLIʳ.

[8] *Grafton's Chronicle* (1809), I, 628-629.

[9] Holinshed (1587), III, 626.

This pupil passage from the sources passes over into the plays on Henry VI in three places. In *1 Henry VI*, Gloucester himself turns it upon his opponents.

> None do you like but an effeminate prince,
> Whom, like a school-boy, you may over-awe.[10]

In *2 Henry VI*, the Queen levels the charge at Gloucester as he is about to be deposed, where it occurs in the sources.

> I see no reason why a king of years
> Should be to be protected like a child.[11]

The Queen's phrase, "a king of years," is from Gloucester's speech in the *Mirour for Magistrates*, presenting the Queen's view, and does not occur in Halle, Grafton, and Holinshed. Earlier in *2 Henry VI*, the Queen had exclaimed to Suffolk

> What, shall King Henry be a pupil still
> Under the surly Gloucester's governance?
> Am I a queen in title and in style,
> And must be made a subject to a duke?[12]

Queen Margaret had been represented in the *Mirour* as resenting that Henry should

> stil gouerncd to bee
> Lyke a Pupil

which is again a trifle closer to our passage than is the source of the *Mirour* passage in Halle, or in its repetition in Grafton and Holinshed. It is thus clear that the view attributed to the Queen in the *Mirour,* or some close repetition of it, is the source for the Queen's two repetitions of the speech in *2 Henry VI.*

Then *Contention* conflates and restates these two speeches from *2 Henry VI.* At the first occurrence of the Queen's speech, at I, 3, 44-47, we now have in *Contention*, Scene III, 48-50, the Queen's angry statement that King Henry

> nere regards the honour of his name,
> But still must be protected like a childe,
> And gouerned by that ambitious Duke.

It will be seen that this is based on the corresponding passage at I, 3, 44-47, but with conflation of "be protected like a child" from the passage at II, 3, 28-29, which passage has in turn been omitted from *Contention.* This evolution from the view attributed to the Queen in the *Mirour,* through the Queen's two speeches in *2 Henry VI,* to the Queen's one conflated speech on the subject in *Contention* is completely clear. The corresponding pas-

---

[10] *1 Henry VI,* I, 1, 35-36.
[11] *2 Henry VI,* II, 3, 28-29.
[12] *2 Henry VI,* I, 3, 44-47.

sage in *1 Henry VI* is a free restatement by Gloucester of this charge leveled at him by the Queen, which he himself had been caused to report in the *Mirour*. Its only possible coincidence phraseologically with the source is Halle's "yong scholer or innocent pupille," which could have influenced "school boy," but is hardly necessary for such a result. The charge against Gloucester has thus in *1 Henry VI* been used once by Gloucester, who reports it in the *Mirour* and so is quite entitled to it, and then twice in *2 Henry VI* by Queen Margaret, whose view it had been reported to be. There can be no question; these passages do not come from Marlowe but from the sources of the Henry VI plays — quite certainly, I think, from the *Mirour*.

Now in parallel with the passage in *1 Henry VI* Hart[13] quoted Marlowe's *Edward II,* where schoolmaster Baldock resents the treatment of Edward II

> As though your highness were a schoolboy still,
> And must be aw'd and govern'd like a child.[14]

It will be seen that Baldock (quite properly as a schoolmaster) uses the same simile as Gloucester, sharing "schoolboy" and "awe." But Baldock's speech also shares with the Queen's in *Contention* "like a childe" and "And gouerned." In turn, the "gouerned" is from the corresponding speech in *2 Henry VI* and "like a childe" from the Queen's later speech in the same play, from which two speeches the Queen's speech in *Contention* has been conflated. Since the whole idea and some of the phraseology belong to the sources of the Henry VI plays, it is clear that Marlowe borrows and transfers the idea and some of the phraseology to *Edward II.*[15]

It will be seen that Marlowe's two-line simile is a mosaic from the two-line simile of the passage in *1 Henry VI,* with additions from the analogous three-line passage in *Contention*. The author or authors of *1* and *2 Henry VI* were impressed with the parent statement in the sources to the extent of using it three times, and Marlowe was impressed to the extent of combining one of their statements and a conflation of the other two into one. It should be noticed that Marlowe uses the conflated form appearing in *Contention,* not the original forms in *2 Henry VI.*

Here again, as in our first example, it is evident that the passages in *2 Henry VI* represent the earliest form known to us, that there was then revision for the form underlying *Contention,* and that Marlowe used the revised form found in *Contention*. Also, what is much more important

---

[13] Hart, *1 Henry VI,* I, 1, 36, note (Arden ed.).

[14] Charlton and Waller, *Edward II,* III, 2, 30-31 (1336-37).

[15] Presumably Marlowe also borrows "Did you regard the honour of your name" (III, 2, 17; 1323), which occurs a few lines before, from "nere regards the honour of his name" (*Contention,* Scene III, 48).

for us, there was a form of *1 Henry VI* containing this speech before
Marlowe borrowed from it for *Edward II*.

Besides this pupil passage, I, 3, of *2 Henry VI* has two other parallels
with *Edward II* immediately following. After the Queen has objected to
being the subject of a duke, she continues,

> I tell thee, Pole, when in the city Tours
> Thou ran'st a tilt in honour of my love,
> And stolest away the ladies' hearts of France,
> I thought King Henry had resembled thee.[16]

which appears in *Contention* thus

> I tell thee *Poull,* when thou didst runne at Tilt,
> And stolst away our Ladaies hearts in *France,*
> I thought King *Henry* had bene like to thee.[17]

Similarly, Edward II says

> Tell Isabel, the queen, I look'd not thus,
> When for her sake I ran at tilt in France,
> And there unhors'd the duke of Cleremont.[18]

As Charlton and Waller (p. 15) point out, "*2 Henry VI* is much closer."
Brooke[19] notes that Queen Margaret's "words are admirably adapted to
the speaker's character and to the facts of history. The chroniclers all
give special attention to the magnificent jousts in which Suffolk was the
chief figure, both during his negotiations with the French king for Henry's
marriage and later when he returned to France as Henry's representative
to escort the new queen to England."[20] On the other hand, Edward II
was far from such exploits. It is thus clear that the passage in *2 Henry
VI,* resting as it does on a historical basis, is earlier than that in *Edward
II.* Also, the passage in *2 Henry VI* is nearer the historical sources than
is that in *Contention.*

A few lines later in this same scene of *2 Henry VI* the Queen complains

> Not all these lords do vex me half so much
> As that proud dame, the lord protector's wife.
> She sweeps it through the court with troops of ladies,
>
> . . . .
>
> She bears a duke's revenues on her back,
> And in her heart she scorns our poverty:
> Shall I not live to be avenged on her?
> Contemptuous base-born callet as she is.[21]

---

[16] *2 Henry VI,* I, 3, 48-51.
[17] *Contention,* Scene iii, 59-61.
[18] Charlton and Waller, *Edward II,* V, 5, 67-69 (2516-18).
[19] Brooke, *Connecticut Academy* (1912), XVII, 175.
[20] See W. G. Boswell-Stone, *Shakspere's Holinshed,* p. 248.

Similarly, Mortimer, Jr., complains of Gaveston

> Uncle, his wanton humour grieves not me;
> But this I scorn, that one so basely born
> Should by his sovereign's favour grow so pert
>
> . . . .
>
> He wears a lord's revenue on his back,
> And, Midas-like, he jets it in the court,
> With base outlandish cullions at his heels.[22]

In *Contention,* the whole section containing the Queen's speech is summed up by Suffolk in a connective line, "And as for proud Duke *Humphrey* and his wife."[23] Thus the parallel is between *2 Henry VI* and *Edward II*. In view of the two preceding parallels from the same scene and connection, it is probable that these two passages are also connected.

It is not directly clear, perhaps, from the passages themselves, as to which borrowed. In the *Mirour,* Eleanor admits she was "base," though as a matter of fact she was of good birth, even if not of the rank of her husband. As for the "callet," Halle says of Gloucester, "Wherfore he, by wanton affeccion blinded, toke to his wife Elianor Cobham doughter to the lord Cobham, of Sterberow, whiche before (as the fame wēt) was his soueraigne lady and paramour, to his great slaunder and reproche."[24] But in fact Margaret and Eleanor had never been rivals, since Eleanor had been condemned some years before Margaret came to England. "The historic Queen Margaret was not troubled by any ambitious hopes which the Duchess may have cherished; for Eleanor Cobham did penance in November, 1441, and Margaret was . . . crowned on May 30, 1445."[25]

Nevertheless, the author of *2 Henry VI* was not the first to bring these two into opposition. In the *Mirour,* which we have previously established as a source, George Ferrers had caused Dame Eleanor to confess

> Thus of a Damsel a Duchesse I became,
> My state and place aduanced next the Queene
> Whereby me thought I felt no ground, but swam
> For in the Court myne equall was not seene
> And so possest with pleasure of the splene
> The sparkes of pride so kyndled in my brest
> As I in court, would shyne aboue the rest.
>
> . . . .
>
> Grudge who so would, to him I was most deere
> Aboue all Ladyes aduaunced in degree

---

[21] *2 Henry VI,* I, 3, 73-75, 78-81. Margaret later gets the "baseborn callet" returned upon herself (*3 Henry VI,* II, 2, 143, 145).

[22] Charlton and Waller, *Edward II,* I, 4, 401-403, 406-408 (699-701, 704-706).

[23] *Contention,* Scene III, 66.

[24] Halle, *Vnion* (1548), f xciii[r].

[25] Boswell-Stone, *Holinshed,* p. 248.

> (The Quene except) no Princesse was my peere
> But gaue me place, and lords with cap and knee
> Dyd all honour and reuerence vnto me
> Thus hoysted high vpon the rolling wheele
> I sate so sure, me thought I could not reele.[26]

At the end she hopes

> My graue I trust, shal purchasse me good peace
> In such a world, where no wight doth contend
> For highest place, whereto all flesh shal wend.[27]

It hardly seems possible that "the Queene" of these passages could be the Queen Mother, and I doubt if anyone would have thought of her here. Also, while various ladies were "sweeping" through the drama at this time,[28] the description for Eleanor, "She sweeps it through the court with troops of ladies," was likely suggested by her swimming around in the court, as above. Also, Gloucester's enemies had used Eleanor in their efforts to pull him down. Margaret joined them in their later efforts and thus inherited an antagonism to Eleanor. So the adapted presentation of Eleanor here is in consonance with her past history, and apparently was suggested by the *Mirour.*

Gaveston would also be "so basely born," and the other details are in consonance with the source of *Edward II.* But while it is not directly clear that Marlowe borrowed, yet it is clear that the parallel is with *2 Henry VI,* not with *Contention.*

The three parallels from less than forty lines, all three of the parallels belonging to Queen Margaret, indicate that Marlowe was in some way impressed with the lady. Also, the pupil passage had already been conflated as in *Contention* before Marlowe used it, but the sequent lines were still as in *2 Henry VI.* That is, the form of *Contention* which Marlowe knew here was derivative from that preserved in *2 Henry VI.*

Perhaps this is as good a place as any to point out that the *Mirour* is an important source for the plays on *Henry VI.* We have just seen its influence upon the interpretation of the character of the Duchess, and shortly before, its use in the presentation of Gloucester, where there was verbal echo in "a king of years." Similarly, Gloucester asks the Duchess, "Art thou not second woman in the realm?",[29] rephrasing statements we have quoted from *Mirour.* There is also a verbal echo in *1 Henry VI.* Winchester says to Gloucester

---

[26] *Mirour* (1578), f C2ᵛ.
[27] *Mirour* (1578), f C3ᵛ.
[28] See above, pp. 85 ff.
[29] *2 Henry VI,* I, 2, 43.

I do, thou most usurping proditor,
And not protector, of the king or realm.[30]

In *Mirour,* it was Somerset who complained of York

And thus was Yorke declared Protectour,
Protectour sayd I, nay Proditor playne.[31]

Also, *Mirour* at least clarifies a scene direction in *True Tragedie* (Scene X), "Enter *Clifford* wounded, with an arrow in his necke." The fact that Clifford was killed by a headless arrow in the neck is given by the chronicles. But *Mirour* invites us to "suppose you see this Lord Clifford al armed saue his head, with his Breast plate all gore bloud running from his throate, wherein an headlesse Arrowe sticketh, through which wound, he ratleth out this Rhime."[32] Evidently the person who wrote the scene direction for *True Tragedie* hoped for a similar illusion of Clifford rattling out blank verse.

Further, a figure from Halle appears to trace through *Mirour*. Halle had said in condemnation of Clifford's brutality to Rutland, "The propertie of the Lyon, which is a furious and an vnreasonable beaste, is to be cruell to them that withstande hym, and gentle to such as prostrate or humiliate them selfes before him."[33] In *Mirour,* this becomes, "Pore sely Lambes the Lyon neuer teares."[34] Then in *3 Henry VI* Rutland's lines to Clifford are a kind of reverse lend-lease.

So looks the pent-up lion o'er the wretch
That trembles under his devouring paws;
And so he walks, insulting o'er his prey,
And so he comes, to rend his limbs asunder.[35]

In *True Tragedie,* the victim is a "lambe" instead of a "wretch." Thus "lambe" is likely to be the original reading, and "rend his limbs asunder" a variation of "teares." That is, the figure is apparently developed from *Mirour* rather than directly from Halle. If so, then *True Tragedie* has the original reading and *3 Henry VI* the secondary one.[36]

---

[30] *1 Henry VI,* I, 3, 31-32.

[31] *Mirour* (1578), f 68ʳ.

[32] *Mirour* (1578), f 80ʳ.

[33] Halle, *Vnion* (1548), f C.lxxxiiiᵛ; Boswell-Stone, *Holinshed,* p. 298.

[34] *Mirour* (1578), f 80ᵛ.

[35] *3 Henry VI,* I, 3, 12-15.

[36] I suppose that in his suggestion of Ovid as the source of the passage, Hart in his edition is thinking of Lucrece

Sed tremit, ut quondam stabulis deprensa relictis
Parva sub infesto cum iacet agna lupo.

(Ovid, *Fasti,* II, 799-800), where the villain is a wolf (cf. *Metamorphoses,* VI, 527-528), not a lion.

For a further instance, as Gloucester waits to see his punished Duchess pass by, he says

> Uneath may she endure the flinty streets,
> To tread them with her tender-feeling feet.[37]

Then "Enter the Duchesse in a white Sheet, and a Taper burning in her hand, with the Sherife and Officers." Boswell-Stone notes that these particulars are not mentioned by Halle or Fabyan, but 2 Holinshed says "Polychronicon saith she was inioined to go through Cheapside with a taper in hir hand,"[38] and Stow has a similar note. I suppose the sentence of "open penance" was likely to imply to an Elizabethan the usual trappings. But Gloucester in *Mirour* gives part of the sentence thus

> And fyrst she must by dayes together three,
> Through London streetes passe a[l] along in sight
> Bare legde and barefoote, that al the world might see,
> Bearing in hand a burning taper bright.[39]

Here is the taper, and the bare feet; but not the sheet.

These instances are from the *Henry VI* plays. For *Richard III*, Churchill[40] pointed out that the tragedy of Clarence in the *Mirour* first made Richard III directly guilty in the death of his brother Clarence, so that it is at least an ultimate source for this item in *Richard III*. Professor J. Dover Wilson has now pointed out the direct dependence of two passages in *Richard III* upon passages from the *Mirour* quoted, among other passages, by Churchill but without any hint from him of direct connection. "The eighteenth tragedy of *The Mirror* is that of George, Duke of Clarence, who tells us, in Baldwin's doggerel,

> A prophecy was found, which sayd a G,
> Of Edwardes children should destruccion be.
> Me to be G, because my name was George
> My brother thought, and therfore did me hate.
> But woe be to the wicked heades that forge
> Such doubtful dreames to brede vnkinde debate.

And in Shakespeare's version, Richard tells us,

> Plots have I laid, inductions dangerous,
> By drunken prophecies, libels and dreams,
> To set my brother Clarence and the king
> In deadly hate the one against the other . . .
> About a prophecy, which says that G
> Of Edward's heirs the murderer shall be.

---

[37] *2 Henry VI*, II, 4, 8-9.
[38] Boswell-Stone, *Holinshed*, p. 261.
[39] *Mirour* (1578), f 45^v.
[40] Churchill, *Richard the Third*, pp. 239-245.

. . . Holinshed speaks of 'grudge' and 'malice' between the brothers; the word with Shakespeare and *The Mirror* is 'hate.' Holinshed says nothing, as they do, about the murder of Edward's heirs. Finally, the two couplets which state the prophecy have the same rhyme, the same rhythm, and are in other respects so similar that one is a palpable echo of the other. . . . Baldwin's Clarence concludes the account of his death in the Tower with these lines:

> Howbeit they bound me whether I would or no,
> And in a butte of Malmesey standing by,
> Newe christned me, because I should not crie.

The quibble in the last line is the more arresting that light touches are rare in *The Mirror*. It certainly arrested Shakespeare, who gave it, how-ever, a wittier and more pregnant point by associating it with the 'G' prophecy. Informed by Clarence that the crime for which he is sent to prison is the name George, Richard exclaims:

> Alack, my lord, that fault is none of yours;
> He should, for that, commit your godfathers:
> Belike his majesty hath some intent
> That you should be new-christ'ned in the Tower.

And by turning the old jest and setting this fresh nap upon it, Shake-speare loses nothing of its former relevance; on the contrary he adds irony and depth to it, since every spectator who knew anything of history would know of the baptism that awaited Clarence. Baldwin's wise-crack becomes in Richard's mouth charged with hideous omen."[41]

It now becomes evident that the *Mirour* is of much more importance for our tetralogy than can be indicated by mere parallels, since, while the chroniclers give the raw materials, *Mirour* shapes them to a tragic view in an interpretation which has directly and indirectly influenced that of the author or authors of the tetralogy. Baldwin is quite conscious of the defect in the chronicles.

> Unfruiteful Fabian followed the face
> Of time and dedes, but let the causes slip,
> Which Hall hath added some with better grace,
> For feare I thinke lest trouble might him trip:
> For this or that (sayth he) he felt the whip.
> This story wryters leaue the causes out,
> Or shew them so as they were in some dout.
>
> But seyng causes are the chefest thinges
> That should be noted of the story wryters,
> That men may learne what endes al causes bringes,
> They be vnworthy the name of Chroniclers
> That leaue them cleane out of their registers,

---

[41] Wilson, *Richard III,* pp. xxv-xxvi.

> Or doubtfully report them for the fruite
> Of reading storyes standeth in the suite.
>
> Wherfore Baldwin either speake thou vpryght
> Of our affaiers, or touch them not at all.[42]

The *Mirour* attempts to give an interpretation of the causes behind the face of events, its interpretations being, of course, in terms of sin against the moral law. Each character must show what dereliction caused his downfall. The interpretation of the Duchess, for instance, was particularly important because she was used to pull Humphrey down, and *Mirour* had explained her motivation. So while the direct borrowings from *Mirour* may appear to be slight, yet its influence is basic.

With present knowledge, it is now unnecessary to reconstruct an arid and abstract universe, hypothetic and synthetic, as a macrocosm into which to fit the microcosm man in order to interpret these plays. The specific takes precedence over the general. The person who conceived the tetralogy did so in terms of the *Mirour* as applied to the chronicles. Here we are on firm ground, with no fictional quicksands. As we look for fundamentals, we find that the shaping idea of moralizing history was of primary importance in these plays. This idea was of great antiquity, and came to the author or authors of the Henry VI plays specifically as one source through the *Mirour,* which had itself further pointed the materials and views it found in Halle, as also no doubt in the air to which the author or authors of the Henry VI plays was or were also exposed. We need, therefore, to examine more fully the evolution of the materials in these plays in order to determine exactly what the air contained from those materials in the early 'nineties of the sixteenth century. Such a study was undertaken by Mr. E. H. Peterson for *1 Henry VI,* and he had completed the section upon the chronicles up to the printed forms for his doctoral dissertation in 1940; but death intervened before he could bring his materials through the printed chronicles and make application to the play. With such studies made for the three parts of *Henry VI,* we should be in position to judge accurately what happened so far as materials are concerned. In the meantime, Churchill has offered a great deal of material, though we have mostly neglected him, on the background of *Richard III,* even though he began at the wrong place, and especially though some have permitted Saint Thomas More's halo rather to dazzle their critical eyes. For the *Mirour* itself, we are fortunate. Editing it as it should be done, Professor Lily Bess Campbell has seen the differentiating characteristics of the *Mirour* and the plays. Approaching from the mediaeval view, Professor Farnham has emphasized the tragic content of this kind of material and its shaping influence upon the tragic concept

---

[42] *Mirour* (1578), f 83ᵛ.

of the plays. We need now to see how the plays were evolved from these known materials in accordance with these known shaping ideas. The problem is of paramount importance, for whether Shakspere wrote all of all these plays, or whether only a part, yet it was here that he began to acquire his ultimate tragic view. Following these ideas on through other illustrations from English and Roman history, he finally arrived at his own tragic view. And what he came to think of man's place in the universe gave substance also to his comedy. Here is the highway of Shakspere's questing mind. May we follow him patiently therein!

Returning now to our parallels, in another instance the parallel of *Edward II* is again with *Contention* rather than with *2 Henry VI*.

> The wild Oneyl, with swarms of Irish kerns,
> Lives uncontroll'd within the English pale.
> Unto the walls of York the Scots made road,
> And unresisted drave away rich spoils.[43]

In *Contention,* we have

> *Messen.* Madame I bring you newes from Ireland,
> The wilde Onele my Lords, is vp in Armes,
> With troupes of Irish Kernes that vncontrold,
> Doth plant themselues within the English pale.
>
> . . . .
>
> And burnes and spoiles the Country as they goe.[44]

The corresponding passage in *2 Henry VI* is a different statement, without parallel in *Edward II.*

> *Post.* Great lords, from Ireland am I come amain,
> To signify that rebels there are up,
> And put the Englishmen unto the sword.[45]

"Parallel with *Contention* only. There was no historical O'Neill in either case. Alexander takes this as a clear case of incorporation of a passage of *Edward II* by the *Contention* pirate."[46] But while strictly speaking there may have been no historical O'Neill in either case, yet, as Brooke points out,[47] the Irish were historically up and active in *2 Henry VI* and *Contention,* while at the date of the play there was a very wild O'Neill who is here accurately described.[48] So in *2 Henry VI* (*Contention*) the

---

[43] Charlton and Waller, *Edward II,* II, 2, 162-165 (966-969).

[44] *Contention,* IX, 133-136, 140.

[45] *2 Henry VI,* III, 1, 282-284.

[46] Charlton and Waller, *Edward II,* pp. 12-13.

[47] Brooke, *Connecticut Academy* (1912), XVII, 175-176.

[48] Gabriel Harvey in 1592 has the exact moralization of O'Neill.

> Iesu, that we should band, like Iohn Oneale,
> That tenderly should melt in mutuall zeale.
>
> (Grosart, *Harvey,* I, 248)

wild O'Neill represents the historical fact; in *Edward II,* the Irish and the Scotch are illustrative fiction.[49] Consequently, Marlowe evidently borrowed from some form which had the passage approximately as in *Contention.* Yet while the fact of Irish rebellion is historical for *2 Henry VI,* the details are not, but are contemporary. We have no means, therefore, of deciding between *2 Henry VI* and *Contention* here as to which is the earlier. In previous instances, *2 Henry VI* represents the original and *Contention* the revision. Presumably that is also the case here.

In another instance, I have no conviction that there is necessary connection; but if so, then the relation is between *Edward II* and *Contention.*

> But haue you no greater proofes then these[50]

> But hath your grace no other proof than this?[51]

Charlton and Waller comment, "The contriver of a murder in both cases faced by an accuser. Absent from *2 Henry VI*" (p. 15). The phraseology seems to me to be so inevitable under the circumstances that I am not impressed by so general a coincidence.

In our next instance, Marlowe connects with a sequence of figured passages in Shakspere on banishment. Following Brooke, Shakspere had in *Two Gentlemen*[52] developed the thesis that banishment is death, and in *Romeo and Juliet*[53] had enlarged upon that theme.[54] In *Two Gentlemen* the idea is given syllogistic form, which may be represented thus:

> Death is banishment from self.
> Silvia is myself.
> Therefore banishment from Silvia is banishment from self,
>   or death.

The conclusion is, therefore,

> To stay is to await death.
> To go is to leave life.

Similarly, in *Romeo and Juliet,* the syllogism is

> Hence banished is banished from the world.
> Banishment from the world is death.
> Therefore banishment is death.

---

[49] See Briggs, *Edward II,* p. 142; Bakeless, *Tragicall History,* II, 232.

[50] *Contention,* X, 70.

[51] Charlton and Waller, *Edward II,* V, 6, 43 (2611).

[52] *Two Gentlemen,* III, 1, 170-187. There was nothing novel about the conceit itself, of course. For instance, John Heywood has in his *Dialogue Concerning Proverbs,*

> Thus though loue decree, departure death to bee,
> Yet pouertie parteth felowship we see
>   (Burton A. Milligan, *John Heywood's Works,* p. 56)

[53] *Romeo and Juliet,* III, 3, 12 ff.

[54] Baldwin, *Five-Act Structure,* pp. 752-753.

The conclusion is

> Heaven is here where Juliet lives (stay).
> But Romeo is banished to hell (go).

The treatment in *Romeo and Juliet* is much less formal, but it has the same fundamental framework as in *Two Gentlemen*.

Elements from both these treatments are found in *2 Henry VI*.[55] Now it is a woman, the Queen, who inverts the situation by threatening to go into banishment herself and says to the man, Suffolk,

> banished I am, if but from thee.
>
> . . . .
>
> Yet now farewell; and farewell life with thee!

This is the syllogism of *Two Gentlemen,* but assumed and not stated syllogistically. Suffolk replies

> where thou art, there is the world itself
>
> . . . .
>
> And where thou art not, desolation.

Here is the syllogism of *Romeo and Juliet,* but again assumed, not stated in syllogistic form. Now that each has had a syllogism, the man, who is the actual banishee, is given the conclusion.

> If I depart from thee, I cannot live (go)
>
> . . . .
>
> To die by thee were but to die in jest; (stay)
> From thee to die were torture more than death: (go)
> O, let me stay, befall what may befall! (stay).

This is the same conclusion as in *Two Gentlemen.* It is thus clear that the order of construction for these passages is *Two Gentlemen, Romeo and Juliet, 2 Henry VI.* Since the topic-line introducing the Queen's sentiment on banishment and the introductory two lines of Suffolk's speech survive in *Contention* as printed in 1594, these speeches evidently all date not later than 1594. That is, these passages in *Two Gentlemen, Romeo and Juliet,* and *2 Henry VI* are not later than 1594. It must be evident also that all three passages are from the same brain, that of William Shakspere.

It is well to note too that Queen Margaret in *Richard III* is to take Romeo's position.

> Glou.   Wert thou not banished on pain of death?
> Q. Mar.   I was; but I do find more pain in banishment,
>   Than death can yield me here by my abode.[56]

---

[55] *2 Henry VI*, III, 2, 349 ff.

[56] *Richard III*, I, 3, 167-169. This is not the historical fact, and these lines do not occur in the quartos. They are thus an "insert" in this sequence of ornamentation.

This is Romeo's conclusion, elaborated by the Queen and Suffolk in *2 Henry VI.* If we had only the passages out of sequence, we could hardly tell which precedes, except that the idea is developed in *Romeo and Juliet,* elaborated in *2 Henry VI,* but simply stated in *Richard III.*[57]

Returning now to the passage in *2 Henry VI,* the Queen turns the situation by saying she will herself go into banishment, whereupon Suffolk says that then he will not be banished, for leaving the country is not important, but leaving her is banishment. In *Richard II,* the love connection is dropped; but this turned situation is used, when Gaunt tells Bolingbroke

> Think not the king did banish thee,
> But thou the king.[58]

The paradox is now fully recognized. Further, as Suffolk would have "every several pleasure in the world" if the situation were reversed by the Queen's going into banishment, so Bolingbroke is to suppose that he is going to everything he holds dear, including fair ladies. The paradox is thus continued. Here is a sequence of passages on banishment, from a known source, Brooke, and most of them known to be in this order. For whatever reason, here is another instance of how Shakspere's mind *did* work.

Into this evolving sequence a passage of *Edward II* fits. There we have

K. Edw.   .   .   .   .

> And long thou shalt not stay, or if thou dost,
> I'll come to thee; my love shall ne'er decline.

.   .   .   .

> Thou from this land, I from myself am banish'd.

Gav.

> To go from hence grieves not poor Gaveston;
> But to forsake you, in whose gracious looks
> The blessedness of Gaveston remains.[59]

This parallels *2 Henry VI.*

Queen   .   .   .   .

> I will repeal thee, or, be well assured,
> Adventure to be banished myself:
> And banished I am, if but from thee.

Suf.   .   .   .   .

> 'Tis not the land I care for, wert thou thence;
> A wilderness is populous enough,
> So Suffolk had thy heavenly company;

---

[57] There is also a colorless presentation of the general idea in the statement of the Duchess, "Welcome is banishment; welcome were my death" (*2 Henry VI,* II, 3, 14).

[58] *Richard II,* I, 3, 279-280.

[59] Charlton and Waller, *Edward II,* I, 4, 114-115, 118-121 (410-411, 415-418).

> For where thou art, there is the world itself,
> With every several pleasure in the world,
> And where thou are not, desolation.[60]

Since the total passage in *2 Henry VI* is developed from a passage in *Romeo and Juliet* (based on Brooke) with the aid of another passage in *Two Gentlemen*,[61] it is clear that the passage in *2 Henry VI* is the original and that Marlowe has borrowed slightly here; that is, this passage in *Edward II* is later than that in *2 Henry VI*. The relationship, however, is complicated by the two-line representation in *Contention* of the first two lines of *2 Henry VI*, the other quoted lines not being represented there.

> And long thou shalt not staie, but ile haue thee repelde,
> Or venture to be banished my selfe.[62]

The second line of the *Henry VI* passage is retained essentially, but the first is summed up and preceded by "And long thou shalt not staie," which Marlowe also has, the only coincidence in him with these two lines. Since Marlowe is the borrower from the total passage in *2 Henry VI*, this coincidence ought to mean that the two lines of the *Contention* stood essentially so in the version from which Marlowe borrowed. Otherwise, we have a case of borrowing and reborrowing — though that is not, of course, impossible. This instance ought to mean that the passage as we now have it in *2 Henry VI* has been slightly revised in a line or two for the form underlying the *Contention,* which Marlowe used, the whole passage being later cut to the minimum.

We may notice in passing that another speech in this dithyramb on banishment indicates that *2 Henry VI* more nearly represents the original form of the speech.

> *Queen* . . . .
>   So, get thee gone, that I may know my grief;
>   'Tis but surmised whiles thou art standing by,
>   As one that surfeits thinking on a want.
>   I will repeal thee, or, be well assured,
>   Adventure to be banished myself;
>   And banished I am, if but from thee.
>   Go; speak not to me; even now be gone.
>   O! go not yet. Even thus two friends condemn'd
>   Embrace and kiss and take ten thousand leaves,
>   Loather a hundred times to part than die.
>   Yet now farewell; and farewell life with thee!
> *Suf.*   Thus is poor Suffolk ten times banished;
>   Once by the king, and three times thrice by thee.[63]

---

[60] *2 Henry VI*, III, 2, 349-351, 359-364.
[61] Baldwin, *Five-Act*, pp. 752-753.
[62] *Contention*, X, 174-175.
[63] *2 Henry VI*, III, 2, 346-358.

The King has banished Suffolk once, and in the preceding speech the Queen has thrice told him to "get thee gone," "Go," "now farewell." Suffolk then goes on to explain that each banishment from her is triple.

> 'Tis not the land I care for, wert thou thence;
> A wilderness is populous enough,
> So Suffolk had thy heavenly company:
> For where thou art, there is the world itself
> With every several pleasure in the world,
> And where thou art not, desolation.[64]

To be banished from her is to be banished also from the country, from the world itself, and every pleasure in it. Each banishment being triple, she has thus in three times pronouncing it banished Suffolk "three times thrice." So Suffolk's "ten times banished" ties this whole passage mathematically together.

Now in *Contention* Suffolk still makes his mathematical assertion as in *2 Henry VI*, but it no longer represents the fact. Quite economically, the Queen now banishes him only once and a piece — "hie thee hence to France," "Away, I say" and there is no explanation of how she has each time of three banished him thrice. Quite clearly the passage in *Contention* is essentially a cut-down of that in *2 Henry VI*.

Charlton and Waller include also among the parallels

Edward II, I, 2, 83

> Ay, if words will serve; if not, I must
> [i.e., levy arms against the king.]

2 Henry VI, V, 1, 139-140

> Edw. Ay, noble father, if our words will serve.
> Rich. And if words will not, then our weapons shall.[65]

Contention, Scene XXI, 102-103

> Edward. Yes noble father, if our words will serue.
> Richard. And if our words will not, our swords shall.

Edward II is nearer to *2 Henry VI* by an "Ay," which is not much. If there has been borrowing, the passage in *Edward II* is perhaps most readily, though not necessarily, accounted for as the adaptation.

Our facts are thus capable of consistent interpretation. In each instance, the form in *2 Henry VI* represents certainly, probably, or possibly the earliest form known to us. That conclusion is also indicated by another class of evidence not yet considered here. Boswell-Stone does not once quote *Contention* as possibly having material from the historical sources not found in *2 Henry VI*, nor so far as I know has anyone else

---

[64] *2 Henry VI,* III, 2, 359-364.

[65] Charlton and Waller, *Edward II,* p. 11.

found a clear and considerable instance of this.[66] Alexander has analyzed passages in *2* and *3 Henry VI* where these plays are not only closer to the historical sources than *Contention* and *True Tragedie*, but where the latter plays even miss the point completely.[67] However wretchedly *Contention* may represent its original, if that original had contained considerable historical material not found in *2 Henry VI*, at least some of it would have shone through.

The Biblical allusions also point in the same direction. The majority of these in *2 Henry VI* do not appear in *Contention;* but where they do appear, if there is significant variation, *2 Henry VI* is always nearer the Biblical original.

(1) I, 2, 73
> Your grace's title shall be multiplied.

"In play on 1 Pet. i. 2: 'Grace and peace be multiplied vnto you.' "[68]

Contention has "Your graces state shall be aduanst ere long."[69]

(2) II, 3, 24-5
> God shall be my hope,
> My stay, my guide and lantern to my feet.

"Ps. xxxix. 8: 'truly my hope is even in thee.' Ps. lxxi. 4: 'thou art my hope, even from my youth.' Ps. xviii. 18 B: 'but God was vnto me a sure stay' (G, 'but the Lord was my stay'; L 'upholder'). Note this Psalm is also in 2 Sam. xxii. Ps. xlviii. 13: 'he shall be our guide unto death.' Ps. cxix. 105: 'Thy word is a lantern unto my feet' (B, 'candel'). In 'lantern to my feet,' Mr. Robertson also detected the hand of Greene."[70] Only "guide" comes through in *Contention*.

(3) III, 1, 69-71
> Our kinsman Gloucester is as innocent
> From meaning treason to our royal person,
> As is the sucking lamb or harmless dove.

"For the innocence of lambs see Isa. xi. 6 and Luke x. 3, and for the 'harmless dove' see Matt. x. 16: "harmlesse as the Doues' (G, 'innocent,' R, 'simple').[71] *Contention* shifts the epithets away from the Bible.

> For as the sucking childe or harmlesse lambe,
> So is he innocent of treason to our state.[72]

---

[66] If Q does use Grafton as a source, as Dr. A. D. Richardson is said to be about to demonstrate (Charles T. Prouty, *The Contention and Shakespeare's 2 Henry VI*, p. 75), then such a fact might have some bearing here.

[67] P. Alexander, *Shakespeare's Henry VI and Richard III*, pp. 61 ff.

[68] R. Noble, *Shakespeare's Biblical Knowledge*, p. 120.

[69] Scene II, 52.

[70] Noble, *Biblical Knowledge*, p. 124.

[71] Noble, *Biblical Knowledge*, p. 124.

[72] *Contention*, Scene X, 14-15.

The use of classical material has been so superficial that it gives practically no aid. But one instance is at least a clear substitution. In *2 Henry
VI*, there is an allusion to "Bargulus the strong Illyrian pirate."[73] As
Warburton pointed out, this is a clear and correct allusion (according to
sixteenth century knowledge) to a character in Cicero's *De Officiis*. But
in *Contention*, a wholly different character appears, "mightie Abradas,
The great Masadonian Pyrate."[74] As Steevens pointed out, Abradas is
known only in Greene, "*Abradas* the great *Macedonian* Pirat thought
euery one had a letter of mart that bare sayles in ye Ocean."[75] One character has been substituted for another, but it does not appear to me which
was which.

All these classes of material give a definite basis for judging direction,
and all point to *2 Henry VI* as the earliest form of the play known to us.
It is also clear that in the form underlying *Contention* several passages
have been rewritten from the form in *2 Henry VI*. It is this underlying
rewritten or revised form which was known to Marlowe. The number
and nature of the instances of Marlowe's agreement with *Contention*
against *2 Henry VI* would suggest that the stylistic or rhetorical revision
was considerable. Unfortunately, the extent, and to some degree the
nature, of this revision have been obscured by the drastic debasement
suffered by this revision as it survives in *Contention*.[76]

There may also be some significance in the fact that *Edward II* was
printed in 1594 "As it was sundrie times publiquely acted in the honourable citie of London, by the right honourable the Earle of Pembrooke his
seruants." If Marlowe wrote *Edward II* for Pembroke's, and if Pembroke's was acting the form of *2 Henry VI* represented by the *Contention*, then Marlowe's borrowing from that form rather than directly from
2 Henry VI might be readily accounted for. But there are at least these
two "ifs" between us and certainty.

It is also certain that *Edward II* is later than the surviving versions of
2 Henry VI, as well as at least part of *1 Henry VI*. Charlton and Waller[77]
were inclined "to believe that *Edward II* was written after *2 and 3 Henry
VI*," and Wilson is justifiably emphatic, "Once, however, the parallels are
studied in relation to the sources of *Henry VI*, Marlowe is revealed as

---

[73] *2 Henry VI*, IV, i, 108.

[74] *Contention*, Scene XII, 51-52.

[75] *Penelope's Web* [1587], E3^v; Grosart, *Greene*, V, 197; repeated verbatim in
Menaphon (1589), E3^v; Grosart, *Greene*, VI, 77-78.

[76] With the best will in the world, I am still at a loss to know how the numerous
comparative parallels recently instanced by Professor Prouty in "The *Contention*
and Shakespeare's *2 Henry VI*" can be placed on any objective bases to show
priority of Q over F or the reverse.

[77] Charlton and Waller, *Edward II*, pp. 16-17.

unquestionably the borrower, since, in three cases, the passages in *Edward II* are neither guaranteed by history nor required by the dramatic context, while those in *Henry VI* are obviously taken from the chronicles."[78] As to Shakspere's authorship of the whole or parts of *2* and *3 Henry VI*, it now appears that the *Contention* and the *True Tragedie* can throw no light. If the three parts of *Henry VI* were revisions of older plays, we must find our evidence in a different set of facts. If Shakspere here revised old plays or collaborated on new or old, we shall need to determine this by other evidence.

[78] Wilson, *2 Henry VI*, pp. xxv, 165.

CHAPTER XIV

The Relation of *True Tragedie* to *3 Henry VI*

It is also clear that *True Tragedie* (York) is a derivative from *3 Henry VI*, though our evidence is not so full, and the form underlying *True Tragedie* has been much better preserved than that underlying *Contention*. Here Marlowe is by no means so helpful. Charlton and Waller[1] list five parallels between *Edward II* and *3 Henry VI*, but rightly reject the fifth, since it is only partial, and even that partial procured by emendation.

Of the remaining four, the first is a figure of the cedar and the eagle, without parallel in phraseology. The cedar originates in *2 Henry VI*, where Warwick boasts to Clifford

> Now, by my father's badge, old Nevil's crest,
> The rampant bear chain'd to the ragged staff,
> This day I'll wear aloft my burgonet,
> As on a mountain top the cedar shows
> That keeps his leaves in spite of any storm,
> Even to affright thee with the view thereof.[2]

The cedar "That keeps his leaves in spite of any storm" had been suggested by Warwick's advice to Clifford to "keep thee from the tempest of the field," and by Clifford's reply

> I am resolved to bear a greater storm
> Than any thou canst conjure up to-day[3]

together with the challenge to Warwick to wear "thy household badge" on his burgonet for identification. Thus the figure of the mountain cedar has been elicited by the situation.

Then as this same Warwick is about to die in *3 Henry VI*, he further develops his figure of the lofty cedar by putting an eagle in it.

---

[1] Charlton and Waller, *Edward II*, pp. 12-14.

[2] *2 Henry VI*, V, 1, 202-7. With "age" for "badge," essentially the same in *Contention*. I am reminded of Marlowe's

> And in my helm a triple plume shall spring
> ....
> Like to an almond tree ymounted high
> Upon the lofty and celestial mount
> Of ever green Selinus
> (Ellis-Fermor, *2 Tamburlaine*, IV, 3, 116, 119-121)

[3] *2 Henry VI*, V, 1, 198-199.

> Thus yields the cedar to the axe's edge,
> Whose arms gave shelter to the princely eagle,
> Under whose shade the ramping lion slept,
> Whose top-branch overpeer'd Jove's spreading tree,
> And kept low shrubs from winter's powerful wind.[4]

The lofty cedar, with appurtenances, is now made to symbolize more or less exactly the role of Warwick the kingmaker.

The figure is further adapted in *Richard III*. Queen Margaret warns

> They that stand high have many blasts to shake them;
> And if they fall, they dash themselves to pieces.

Richard replies

> Our aery buildeth in the cedar's top,
> And dallies with the wind and scorns the sun.[5]

The figure thus has a definite origin and a traceable sequence in the tetralogy.

Marlowe uses the figure at the stage it had reached in *3 Henry VI*. Mortimer, Jr., gives as his device

> A lofty cedar-tree, fair flourishing,
> On whose top-branches kingly eagles perch.[6]

Here are the cedar and eagle as in *3 Henry VI*, figuring directly in a device, as the cedar alone did indirectly in *2 Henry VI*. If there is direct connection, and it seems likely, then *Edward II* is later than *3 Henry VI*. Also, whether Marlowe had the figure from *3 Henry VI* or from some other source, he is here displaying his usual habit of borrowing a figure full-grown, not himself developing it. That is, the passage in *Edward II* is dependent indirectly if not directly upon the passage in *3 Henry VI*, so either way it is later.

While we are considering the cedar, it may be noticed that its contrast with the shrub has further use. In *3 Henry VI*, the cedar "kept low shrubs from winter's powerful wind." The protection is reversed into fatality in *Lucrece*.

> The cedar stoops not to the base shrub's foot,
> But low shrubs wither at the cedar's root.[7]

The relationship of cedar and shrub is alluded to in *Titus*

> Marcus, we are but shrubs, no cedars we.[8]

---

[4] *3 Henry VI*, V, 2, 11-15. Essentially the same in *True Tragedie*, except that the last line does not appear there.

[5] *Richard III*, I, 3, 259-260, 264-265.

[6] Charlton and Waller, *Edward II*, II, 2, 16-17 (818-819).

[7] *Lucrece*, 664-665.

[8] *Titus*, IV, 3, 45.

It is hardly possible, however, from the uses themselves to be certain of their order, except that the reversed passages in *Lucrece* and *Titus* are later than that in *3 Henry VI*. That is, the passage in *3 Henry VI* is, therefore, earlier than May 8, 1594.

In the second suggested parallel between *3 Henry VI* and *Edward II*, Queen Margaret says

> Stern Falconbridge commands the narrow seas.[9]

Mortimer, Jr., says

> The haughty Dane commands the narrow seas.[10]

We have thus the stock phrase "the narrow seas," coupled with the word "command," which is also common to the type of expression. With over half of the verse line determined by common locution, the remainder of the line almost necessarily conforms to the same rhetorical pattern. There is thus no certainty of direct connection. But Boswell-Stone,[11] and Wilson[12] consider the line in *3 Henry VI* to be probably historical, while the one in *Edward II* is not so. Thus if there is direct connection, then again the indication is that *Edward II* borrowed.

The third instance of parallel is another common pattern built on "Forslow." In the fourth case, "The parallel [is] not very exact, but the sentiment and the repetition are similar." Further, *Massacre* borrows a line from the same speech in which this passage occurs. The upshot is that *Edward II* probably borrowed slightly from *3 Henry VI*. The parallels are always with *3 Henry VI* as against *True Tragedie*. We have seen[13] that the same is true in the case of Marlowe's *Massacre at Paris*.

As we have seen, Marlowe was clearly the borrower in *Edward II* from a derivative of *2 Henry VI*.[14] Consequently, the borrowings in *Massacre* from *3 Henry VI* are also doubtless due to Marlowe, not to inserts by someone else. As we have seen, Marlowe borrowed also from other plays; it was evidently a characteristic of his. Whether these borrowings have any bearing on the question of authorship is not pertinent to our present investigation.

---

[9] *3 Henry VI*, I, 1, 239; same in *True Tragedie*.

[10] Charlton and Waller, *Edward II*, II, 2, 166 (970).

[11] Boswell-Stone, *Holinshed*, pp. 293-294.

[12] Wilson, *3 Henry VI*, p. 128.

[13] See above, p. 160.

[14] It is at least clear that presence of these parallels with *Edward II* in *Contention* is not due to transplantation by a pirate (a most appreciative and ingenious person — to be such a muttonhead!). "Bibliographers" have shown quite a fascination for a sugar-plum pirate, with a thumb in almost every pie. If ever a pirate of any sort existed — he is only a hypothesis; so far no one has discovered an authentic specimen — or if he be only some plodding official or officials merely doing a necessary duty in the hum-drum routine of fitting plays for the stage — in any case, it is probable that

In contrast to the case in *Contention*, Boswell-Stone noticed several instances where *True Tragedie* in its stage directions sums up actions from the source,[15] but *3 Henry VI* simply gives general directions. It is not that *3 Henry VI* has changed the details of acting; it simply does not record them, while *True Tragedie* does. In one instance, one word, "disguisde," is also in the text of *True Tragedie*.[16] Hart thinks that in *True Tragedie* the statistics given at II, 1, 177-181 are nearer the sources than they are in *3 Henry VI*. The fact is, of course, that neither *True Tragedie* nor *3 Henry VI* agrees in these statistics with the sources — and in such matters a miss is as good as a mile. There is also a possible but not probable "squinting reflection" of the source at *3 Henry VI,* II, 3, 52. In Halle, Edward promised "great rewardes" to those who should remain to fight and "great remuneraciō and doble wages"[17] to anyone who should kill a flying coward. In Holinshed, "remuneracion" is changed to "reward." In *3 Henry VI*, those who stay are promised "rewards" as in Halle and Holinshed. But in *True Tragedie* the promise is to "remunerate" those who stay, not those who kill cowards as in Halle. Someone in *True Tragedie* has probably used a synonym. We have seen that at *3 Henry VI*, I, 3, 12, *True Tragedie* has probably the original reading "lambe" instead of "wretch." It would appear from these instances that some of the scene directions of *True Tragedie* are nearer the originals than are those in *3 Henry VI,* and there is some indication that this relationship may extend to the text.

In *3 Henry VI*, in contrast to *2 Henry VI*, the Biblical allusions are considerably fewer; but nearly all of them are represented in *True Tragedie,* and I find no significant variations in the forms of them.

One bit of classical lore contributes its mite to indicate direction.

> But you are more inhumaine, more inexorable,
> O ten times more then Tygers of *Arcadia*.[18]

3 Henry VI has correctly Hircania, so represents the original.

Again, a four-line passage in *3 Henry VI* (II, 1, 21-24) is derived from four in Spenser's *Faerie Queene* (Bk. I, C. V, st. 2). "Since the four-line figure in *3 Henry VI* is derived from four lines in Spenser, it is clear that this version represents the original form while the two-line

---

such an individual would share with his age their interest in rhetorical ornamentation; but we must remember that the primary responsibility for supplying these "sallets" belonged to the literary artists, not to some tag-happy actor.

[15] II, 6; III, 1, 12; V, 5. The instance at V, 5, 50 (Boswell-Stone, *Holinshed,* p. 341, n. 1) does not appear to me to be a clear case. Hart (*3 Henry VI,* V, 1, 81n) adds another illustration.

[16] Scene XI, 5.

[17] Halle, *Vnion* (1548), f clxxxvi[v].

[18] *True Tragedie,* Scene IV, 139-140.

version in *The true Tragedie* is only a further derivative. In other words, *The true Tragedie* is in this passage only a debased form of *3 Henry VI*, as is now generally agreed for that form of the play as a whole."[19]

In another case, a long passage in *3 Henry VI* evidently represents the original. Queen Margaret develops very elaborately the figure of a wrecked ship.

> Great lords, wise men ne'er sit and wail their loss,
> But cheerly seek how to redress their harms.
> What though the mast be now blown overboard,
> The cable broke, the holding-anchor lost,
> And half our sailors swallow'd in the flood?
> Yet lives our pilot still. Is't meet that he
> Should leave the helm, and like a fearful lad
> With tearful eyes add water to the sea,
> And give more strength to that which hath too much,
> Whiles, in his moan, the ship splits on the rock,
> Which industry and courage might have saved?
> Ah, what a shame! ah, what a fault were this!
> Say Warwick was our anchor; what of that?
> And Montague our topmast; what of him?
> Our slaughter'd friends the tackles; what of these?
> Why, is not Oxford here another anchor?
> And Somerset another goodly mast?
> The friends of France our shrouds and tacklings?
> And, though unskilful, why not Ned and I
> For once allow'd the skilful pilot's charge?
> We will not from the helm to sit and weep,
> But keep our course, though the rough wind say no,
> From shelves and rocks that threaten us with wreck.[20]

The ship of state has been wrecked indeed, but it can be repaired and next time must succeed.

The body of this speech is built on three lost things, (1) mast, (2) anchor, (3) sailors, balanced against one (4) a saved pilot. The first two lines state the commonplace moral. Then a line is devoted to each of the three lost elements, balanced against the "Yet" of the saved pilot, who gets six lines. Finally, comes the one-line commonplace moral conclusion. Next, we go through the scheme again, designating the lost elements, Warwick the anchor, etc.; and finally "Ned and I" as pilot get five lines. This structure clears up at least one debated line, "The cable broke, the holding-anchor lost," which means simply that the anchor which should hold the ship has been lost because the cable broke. The third element needs to be grasped clearly. In the first statement, it is "sailors," to represent the lost forces. In the second, these sailors become, therefore, "Our slaughter'd friends the tackles," so as to have substituted

---

[19] Baldwin, *Literary Genetics,* p. 5 and n. 11.
[20] *3 Henry VI,* V, 4, 1-24.

for them finally "The friends of France our shrouds and tacklings." This analysis should make clear the elements out of which the speech was constructed. It may be added that the unquoted remainder of the speech identifies Edward as the sea, Clarence as the quicksand, Richard as "a ragged fatal rock," warns that there is no escape from them, and exhorts to courage. Someone must have been very proud of this speech.

In the Renaissance, an ode of Horace was the great model for such ships of state, and Queen Margaret's elaborate flourish belongs to this tradition, as Collins pointed out.[21] Horace wrote

> O Navis, referent in mare te novi
> fluctus. o quid agis! fortiter occupa
>   portum. nonne vides, ut
>   nudum remigio latus
>
> et malus celeri saucius Africo
> antemnaeque gemant, ac sine funibus
>   vix durare carinae
>   possint imperiosius
>
> aequor? non tibi sunt integra lintea,
> non di, quos iterum pressa voces malo.
>   quamvis Pontica pinus,
>   silvae filia nobilis,
>
> iactes et genus et nomen inutile:
> nil pictis timidus navita puppibus
>   fidit. tu, nisi ventis
>   debes ludibrium, cave.
>
> nuper sollicitum quae mihi taedium,
> nunc desiderium curaque non levis,
>   interfusa nitentis
>   vites aequora Cycladas.

To the Ship of State

O SHIP, new billows threaten to bear thee out to sea again. Beware! Haste valiantly to reach the haven! Seest thou not how thy bulwarks are bereft of oars, how thy shattered mast and yards are creaking in the driving gale, and how thy hull without a girding-rope can scarce withstand the overmastering sea? Thy canvas is no longer whole, nor hast thou gods to call upon when again beset by trouble. Though thou be built of Pontic pine, a child of far-famed forests, and though thou boast thy stock and useless name, yet the timid sailor puts no faith in gaudy sterns. Beware lest thou become the wild gale's sport! Do thou, who wert not long ago to me a source of worry and of weariness, but art now my love and anxious care, avoid the seas that course between the glistening Cyclades![22]

Horace does not want his ship of state to risk another storm; Margaret is arguing that hers should do so. Horace has a shattered mast, but no

---

[21] J. C. Collins, *Studies in Shakespeare*, p. 27; Baldwin, *Small Latine,* II, 503.
[22] C. E. Bennett, *Horace* (Loeb ed.), *Carmina* I, 14, pp. 42-43.

anchor, though the Renaissance may have thought he had, and no sailors, etc., though the allegory of Quintilian upon the passage in effect furnished them.

Garnier modeled a speech upon this ode of Horace in his *Cornélie*.[23] Addressing Rome, Garnier says,

> Tu es comme un navire errant en haute mer,
> Lors que la bise fait les vagues escumer;
> Tu roules périlleuse, et le vent, qui te berse,
> Deçà delà flotante, à demi te renverse.
> Ton mas est tout brisé, tes voiles abatus,
> Tes costez entrouverts de rames dévestus;
> Tu n'as plus de cordage, et toutefois sans cables
> Les vaisseaux ne sont point contre l'eau défensables.
> Regarde que de rocs lèvent sur toy le front:
> Si tu les vas heurtant, ils te mettront en fond,
> Despouille de Neptune, et jouet misérable
> Des Glauques et Tritons au coeur impitoyable.
> Tu te vantes en vain de tes faicts victorieux;
> Cela ne sert de rien: ainçois fait que nous sommes
> En l'envieuse haine et des dieux et des hommes.[24]

Thomas Kyd in his paraphrase of 1594 renders this:

> For Rome thou now resemblest a Ship,
>   At random wandring in a boistrous Sea,
>   When foming billowes feele the Northern blasts:
>   Thou toyl'st in perrill, and the windie storme,
>   Doth topside-turuey tosse thee as thou flotest.
>   Thy Mast is shyuer'd, and thy maine-saile torne,
>   Thy sides sore beaten, and thy hatches broke.
>   Thou want'st thy tackling, and a Ship vnrig'd
>   Can make no shift to combat with the Sea.
>   See how the Rocks do heaue their heads at thee,
>   Which if thou sholdst but touch, thou straight becomst
>   A spoyle to *Neptune,* and a sportfull praie
>   Toth' Glauc's and Trytons, pleased with thy decay.
> Thou vaunts't not of thine Auncestors in vaine,
>   But vainely count'st thine owne victorious deeds.
>   What helpeth vs the things that they did then,
>   Now we are hated both of Gods and men?[25]

---

[23] W. P. Mustard, "Notes on Thomas Kyd's Works," *P.Q.* (1926), V, 85.

[24] R. Garnier, *Oeuvres Complètes* (L. Pinvert, 1923), I, 99.

[25] Garnier, *Cornelia* (1594), A2ᵛ; Boas, *Kyd, Cornelia,* I, 79-95. I cannot resist appending another of these adaptations, because of its characteristic view of democracy.

> DEMOCRACIE is as a tossed Ship
> Void both of *Pole* and Pilot in the Deep:
> A *Senate* fram'd of thousand Kinglings slight;
> Where, voices pass by number, not by waight;
> Where, wise men do propound, and Fools dispose:
> A Fair, where all things they to sale expose:

Garnier's ship has a broken mast, is "sans cables," which could readily have suggested Queen Margaret's broken cable and consequently lost anchor, and has no "cordage," which Kyd translates as "tackling," a term which is used by Queen Margaret in two of her three references to the third element. Thus Garnier seems to have suggested these three elements of mast, anchor, and tackling for Queen Margaret's speech. But neither Horace nor Garnier furnished Queen Margaret with a pilot. Behind Ned, she was to be that herself. Garnier also supplies the rocks against which Margaret warns. These may be implied in Horace, but definitely threaten in Garnier, as in Margaret's speech. Also, "the mast . . . blown overboard" is more likely to have been suggested by Garnier's intensives, "ton mas est tout brisé, tes voiles abatus," than from Horace's more sober statements. Generally, Garnier is much more violent than Horace, and Queen Margaret loses none of the force. There may be adaptations of this ode of Horace unknown to me. But as between Horace and Garnier, Queen Margaret's speech appears to derive through Garnier.

But if the author of Queen Margaret's speech knew Garnier's passage, he would also certainly know the parent passage in Horace. Every learned grammarian had Horace thrust upon him, even William Shakspere.[26] In the annotated editions, such as those of Lambinus, upon the passage the interpretation of Quintilian usually leads the way, with various embroiderings upon it by later commentators. Even in the unannotated editions, such as those of Plantin, there is likely to be a shoulder note condensing Quintilian. Everyone was supposed to know the significance of this ode. On the other hand, Garnier would be known to only a small coterie. It is likely then that Horace is in the background, but Garnier would appear to be the immediate model, unless there is still some rendering of this figure which I have not seen.

But whatever the model, it is certainly evident that Queen Margaret's speech belongs to this tradition from Horace. In view of this known relationship, it is obvious that the corresponding eleven lines of *True Tragedie* are a murderous abbreviation of the passage in *3 Henry VI*.

> Welcome to *England* my louing friends of *Frāce,*
> And welcome *Summerset,* and *Oxford* too.
> Once more haue we spread our sailes abroad,
> And though our tackling be almost consumde,

> A Sink of Filth, where ay th'infamousest,
> Most bold and busie, are esteemed best:
> A Park of savage Beasts, that each-man dreads:
> A Head-les Monster with a thousand heads.
> (*Bartas* (tr. by Sylvester, 1608), p. 531)

[26] Baldwin, *Small Latine,* II, 497 ff.

> And *Warwike* as our maine mast ouerthrowne,
> Yet warlike Lords raise you that sturdie post,
> That beares the sailes to bring vs vnto rest,
> And *Ned* and *I* as willing Pilots should
> For once with carefull minds guide on the sterne,
> To beare vs thro[u]gh that dangerous gulfe
> That heretofore hath swallowed vp our friends.[27]

Much of this condensed allegory is not clear without the original speech. Now, of the three elements only the mast has been retained, though the tackling is referred to but not identified. And for the mast only the substitution is retained, but even so there is no identification of the substitute, "that sturdie post," as Oxford — unless Margaret points at him! It is thus clear that this speech is a clumsy condensation. It is also clear that the condensation is freely done, "with malice aforethought." The author has no excuse; he knew or had known the original text. He did no better because this was the best his clobberly muse could do — even if he should have been following someone else's memory of the original.

Besides this full figure, there was also, however, the simile of the mastless ship, which may belong to this same tradition. This appears in *Soliman and Perseda*, I, 2, 2-3 as

> But shall I, like a mastlesse ship at sea,
> Goe euery way, and not the way I would?

Boas cross-references to Garnier's speech as translated by Kyd, calling the latter "an elaborated form of this simile." But there is nothing to show direct connection.[28] *Wily Beguiled* has "My mind, sweet friend, is like a mastless ship."[29]

In *True Tragedie*, King Henry says

> How like a mastlesse ship vpon the seas,
> This woful battaile doth continue still,
> Now leaning this way, now to that side driue,
> And none doth know to whom the daie will fall.[30]

3 Henry VI has a different, though analogous figure.

> This battle fares like to the morning's war,
> When dying clouds contend with growing light,
> What time the shepherd, blowing of his nails,
> Can neither call it perfect day nor night.
> Now sways it this way, like a mighty sea
> Forced by the tide to combat with the wind;
> Now sways it that way, like the selfsame sea

---

[27] *True Tragedie*, Scene XXIV, 1-11.

[28] Bel-imperia's "My hart (sweet freend) is like a ship at sea" (*Spanish Tragedy*, II, 2, 7) is still another simile — as many more there be!

[29] Hazlitt-Dodsley, *Wily Beguiled*, IX, 281, 19.

[30] *True Tragedie*, Scene IX, 3-6.

Forced to retire by fury of the wind:
Sometime the flood prevails, and then the wind;
Now one the better, then another best;
Both tugging to be victors, breast to breast,
Yet neither conqueror nor conquered:
So is the equal poise of this fell war.[31]

Boswell-Stone noted, "The long struggle at Towton is spoken of by Halle (256) in terms not unlike these: 'This deadly battayle and bloudy conflicte continued .x. houres in doubtful victorie, the one parte some tyme flowyng, and sometime ebbyng. . . .' "[32] Thus the figure in *3 Henry VI* is from the historical source and so represents the original form of the speech. Consequently, it is evident that the author of the speech in *True Tragedie* has reduced the elaborate figure of *3 Henry VI* to terms of the mastless ship simile. He keeps the swaying battle. The statement, "Now sways it this way . . . Now sways it that way" like the sea becomes, "Now leaning this way, now to that side driue," with the terms no longer specifically applicable to the sea only but generalized to any see-saw. This is prefaced, however, with the simile of the mastless ship. The battle swaying like the sea in *3 Henry VI* has suggested the mastless ship simile; but neither the original nor the simile it suggested was sufficient to keep the author to this specific figure, which is characteristic of him. He juggles words to fit his purposes without any respect to the images they convey. Clearly, this is the same deflationary genius who reduced Queen Margaret's speech to plodding tatters. Also, this particular transplantation is typical of a process in *Contention* and *True Tragedie* which has been accounted for as "Marlowe's repetitions." It is now clear that this characteristic feature does not belong to Marlowe but is the result of the revisionary process, whatever it was and by whomever performed.

The main figure of Margaret's ship speech had also carried over into *Richard III*. For the ship speech had continued with an application

And what is Edward but a ruthless sea?
What Clarence but a quicksand of deceit?
And Richard but a ragged fatal rock?
All these the enemies to our poor bark.[33]

This application to Richard as "a ragged fatal rock" for the Lancastrian bark later stands Queen Elizabeth in good stead. As Richard woos her for his niece, her daughter, she says

But that still use of grief makes wild grief tame,
My tongue should to thy ears not name my boys,

---

[31] *3 Henry VI*, II, 5, 1-13.
[32] Boswell-Stone, *Holinshed*, p. 306.
[33] *3 Henry VI*, V, 4, 25-28.

> Till that my nails were anchor'd in thine eyes;
> And I, in such a desperate bay of death,
> Like a poor bark, of sails and tackling reft,
> Rush all to pieces on thy rocky bosom."[34]

It is clear that Queen Elizabeth is indebted to Queen Margaret for this bit of tinsel.

The elaborate ship speech was very "artificially" done, and evidently impressed even the botcher of it for *True Tragedie*. It may be well to note here that at least one wave from this ship spreads through the remainder of Shakspere's work even into his final *Tempest*. In the speech we have the simile

> like a fearful lad
> With tearful eyes add water to the sea,
> And give more strength to that which hath too much.

This came directly from the *Adagia* of Erasmus and was elicited by the figure of a ship's pilot, in which it occurs. Under *In syluam ligna ferre*, Erasmus says, "In syluam ligna ferre, est aliquem ijs rebus augere uelle, quibus ipse maximè abundet." Then as a sub-instance, with side note *In mare aquā*, he says, "In mare deferre aquam: quorum utrunq; nos in epigrammate quodam coniunximus:

> Largiri numeros tibi Petre, hoc est,
> Syluae ligna, uago mari addere undas.

Vtrunq; congruit cum eo, quod alio retulimus loco, Vlulas Athenas."[35] This proverb is indexed as *mari aquam addere*.

This proverb and its interpretation is not again used till *As You Like It*, II, 1, 46-49. Jacques moralizes on the stag, "weeping into the needless stream" and so

> giving thy sum of more
> To that which had too much.

The stream has been substituted for the sea. The structure and word echoes show that in the passage in *As You Like It* Shakspere has adapted directly the passage in *3 Henry VI* (not in *True Tragedie*). This doubtless occurred about the time of *Henry V*, when the *Henry VI* plays appear to have been again in production. The fundamental figure is also adapted in *Hamlet*, IV, 7, 186-187.

> Too much of water hast thou, poor Ophelia,
> And therefore I forbid my tears.

I see nothing to indicate which of the two passages above has been adapted. But the *Hamlet* passage is adapted in *Twelfth Night*, II, 1, 26-28, "She is drowned already, sir, with salt water, though I seem to

---

[34] *Richard III*, IV, 4, 229-234.
[35] Erasmus, *Adagia* (Basle, 1574), I, 196.

drown her remembrance again with more." Sebastian thinks Viola has been drowned in the sea, and he drowns her memory with more salt water, his tears. The "too much" echo has been lost, and we have only the "more." This statement of the idea has been influenced by another.

> The pretty-vaulting sea refused to drown me,
> Knowing that thou wouldst have me drown'd on shore,
> With tears as salt as sea, through thy unkindness.[36]

There is also a final restatement of *3 Henry VI*, V, 4, 8, without the "more."

> When I have deck'd the sea with drops full salt.[37]

The evolving ideas would show the order, though it happens that we know the relative order of the plays involved from other facts. Here is how Shakspere's mind *did* work with figures, however it came to do it. Whatever the elapsed time, it picks up where it left off. And apparently it never completely forgot. And always the figures are visualized and vital.

It now appears that among other things *True Tragedie* is a purposefully cut version from the form represented by *3 Henry VI*. In some of its scene directions, it preserves an original version for acting, and its text may also have some readings earlier than those of *3 Henry VI*. *True Tragedie* is attributed to Pembroke's men, so presumably this is the version which they acted. It does not follow, however, that this version was made for them. For all we know yet, it could represent the acting version for the Shaksperean company, simply taken over by Pembroke's.

Contention has also been purposely cut as was *True Tragedie*. But, in addition, that cut form has suffered disastrous maiming. It is usual to assume that *Contention* was for Pembroke's; but if so, then, as in the case of *True Tragedie*, it does not follow that it was cut for Pembroke's rather than for the Shaksperean company. Still less is there any ground to accuse Pembroke's of the disastrous maiming. If we knew how *John of*

---

[36] *2 Henry VI*, III, 2, 94-96.

[37] *Tempest*, I, 2, 155. Most of these instances have been gathered by P. Reyher, *Les Idées*, p. 215, n. 59. Another use of the proverb in the Shakspere corpus does not fit into this evolving tradition. When already lamenting Titus is presented with mangled Lavinia he asks

> What fool hath added water to the sea,
> Or brought a faggot to bright-burning Troy?
> My grief was at the height before thou camest,
> And now, like Nilus, it disdaineth bounds.
>
> (*Titus*, III, 1, 68-71)

This is the straight proverb, and yokes another with it to illustrate folly. It is a more distant rephrasing of the proverb than that in *3 Henry VI*, and of its conventional application. If by the same author, this would give some slight indication that it was later.

Bordeaux[38] "got that way," we would probably have a pretty good idea of how *Contention* came to its final degradation.

Here we should pause to notice that much the same thing has happened in the case of *2* and *3 Henry VI* as happened in Marlowe's *Faustus* and Greene's *Orlando*. In the case of *Orlando*, Q represents the full version and the Alleyn MS an altered and shortened stage version, but the Alleyn MS preserves some details from the parent version which are not in Q.[39] Similarly in the case of *Faustus*, B represents the full version and A an altered and shortened stage version, but neither gives quite the full original version. Anyone who is conversant with surviving stage versions of the time will know that the full manuscript of a play was whittled down by some official to the two hours' traffic of the stage. It is clear in the instances cited that this is one thing which has happened to *Orlando*, *Faustus*, *Contention*, and *True Tragedie*. And one could cite astounding instances of the liberties taken by such company officials in "improving" the author's expression, etc. But the individual parts still had to be fitted to the actors, where the actor himself had further opportunities to "improve." We need to disabuse ourselves completely of the old and inherited prepossession that a play was put on word for word as the dramatist handed it in. Actually, the play as play still had to be cut out of the author's literary manuscript — and the cutting is likely to have been frequently painful to the dramatist — editors always know so much better than the author how it should be done! Nor was the ultimate result of all this cutting and fitting carried back to the original manuscript — or for that matter set down completely in any manuscript. It is impossible to recover completely the actual acting form of any play of the period.

Instead of inferring stage practice from "bibliographical" facts — of fundamental importance for their legitimate purposes — and then in turn using the inferred stage practice to explain the bibliographical facts, thus indulging in the scholar's favorite occupation of lifting himself by his own bootstraps, it would be well to establish stage practice independently and historically, only then using the established procedures to interpret bibliographical facts. Bibliographical fact, whatever the term may mean to whomever, is one thing; interpretation of bibliographical fact in terms of stage practice is quite another. For "bibliographical" evidence, as such, faces both ways, as do all parallels, as such. If we would only interpret in terms of known contemporary procedures, or not attempt to interpret at all till we did know those procedures, we might get on a bit faster.

---

[38] For a description of its characteristics, see Harry R. Hoppe, "*John of Bordeaux: A Bad Quarto That Never Reached Print*," *Studies in Honor of A. H. R. Fairchild* (U. of Missouri Studies, Vol. 21, 1946), pp. 119-132.

[39] See above, pp. 77 ff.

Among other things, we need to center our attention intensively on the actual process of cutting the play out of the manuscript and fitting it to the stage. We shall then doubtless find that our pirates are for the most part well meaning officials doing their best to make "good" plays for their particular organization and immediate clientele out of the stuff that such poets as Marlowe and Shakspere handed in!

CHAPTER XV

The Figured Complex of 1592-94

As we turn now to the relationships of the plays of the period 1592-94, *Venus and Adonis* and especially *Lucrece* form very useful landmarks. Several of Shakspere's figures evolve through these compositions, and so enable us to put dates on certain stages of development, thereby giving a relative dating for other parts of a sequence.

We may begin with a sequence of figures which has its origin definitely in the source of *Richard III*. When Dr. Shaw was inferring the bastardy of Edward's children and of Edward himself he is represented by Sir Thomas More as "takyng for his Theme. *Spuria vitulamina nō dabunt radices altos. Sapien. iiii.* that is to saie, bastarde slippes shal neuer take depe rootes: whereupon when he had shewed the greate grace that God geueth & secretely infoundeth in right generacion after yᵉ lawes of matrimony, then declared he that those children cōmenly lacked yᵗ grace (& for the punishement of their parentes) were for yᵉ most part vnhappy which wer gotten in baste, and specially in aduoutry, of whiche (though some by the ignorauncie of the worlde and the truthe hid from knowlege) haue enherited for a season other mennes landes, yet God alwaie so prouideth that it continueth not in their bloude longe, but the truethe commynge to lighte the rightefull enheritoures bee restored, and the bastard slippes plucked vp or it can bee rooted depe."[1]

Naturally, therefore, this theme of bastardy reflects in the tetralogy, even before it is handled at its necessary place in *Richard III*. In *2 Henry VI*, Queen Margaret taunts

> The bastard boys of York
> Shall be the surety for their traitor father.[2]

For Shaw was to include Clarence along with Edward in bastardy. And here Richard gets a monitory tarring with his own stick along with Edward.

The theme had also appeared earlier in the play as a grafting which had produced the expected fruit of bastardy. Here we need the Biblical passage before us in the Geneva version (1560), since it is echoed verbally in our following passages.

---

[1] Halle, *Vnion* (1548), Edward V, f XIXᵛ.
[2] *2 Henry VI*, V, 1, 115-116.

314

3 But the multitude of the vngodlie which abunde in children, is vnprofitable:
& the bastard plātes shal take no depe roote, nor laye any fast fundacion.
4 For thogh they budde forthe in the branches for a time, yet they shal be
shaken with the winde: for they stand not fast, and thorowe the vehemēcie
of the winde they shalbe rooted out.
5 For the vnperfect branches shalbe brokē, & their frute shalbe vnprofitable
& sower to eat, and mete for nothing.[3]

Now as Suffolk and Warwick quarrel, Margaret speaks up for Suffolk,
whereupon Warwick reminds her pointedly

> Madam, be still; with reverence may I say;
> For every word you speak in his behalf
> Is slander to your royal dignity.[4]

Suffolk resents the insinuation

> Blunt-witted lord, ignoble in demeanour!
> If ever lady wrong'd her lord so much,
> Thy mother took into her blameful bed
> Some stern untutor'd churl, and noble stock
> Was graft with crab-tree slip; whose fruit thou art
> And never of the Nevils' noble race.[5]

The Biblical statement that the fruit "shalbe vnprofitable & sower to eat"
has suggested the grafting of a crab-tree "slip" (More's translation of
vitulamina), the crab being the sourest of fruits, upon a noble stock to
produce the naturally resulting fruit. So through "slip," the figure of
grafting as bastardy has entered in, which is probably not suggested by
the translation of the Biblical passage itself, though the "budde forthe
in the branches" in the same connection might suggest it.

This figure, thus developed, occurs again at its expected place, when
Buckingham, echoing Shaw's role as reported by More, refers to England's "royal stock graft with ignoble plants."[6] The Biblical figure of
bastard plants, as in the Geneva version, or bastard slips, as translated by
More in the source, has become a bastard graft producing fruit, as in the
earlier use. The graft of bastardy has coalesced with the bastard plants
of the Geneva version to produce grafted plants. The resultant figure is
itself, therefore, something of a bastard or mixed one, grafting the Biblical figure of bastard plants, from the source, upon the earlier figure of
graft upon stock.

---

[3] The Bishops' version (1568) does not have "bastard plātes," though in it also the
fruit is "vnprofitable, & sowre to eate," following earlier translations.

[4] *2 Henry VI,* III, 2, 207-209.

[5] *2 Henry VI,* III, 2, 210-215.

[6] *Richard III,* III, 7, 127. Omitted from the quartos, but certainly in the original
version.

Then under the influence of this mixed figure Lucrece resolves

> This bastard graff shall never come to growth:
> He shall not boast who did thy stock pollute
> That thou art doting father of his fruit.[7]

Lucrece does not propose to allow this bastard graff (plant in Geneva, slip in More) to come to growth as in the Bible and More. Lucrece substitutes graff for plant in the Biblical phrase. Buckingham in *Richard III*, echoing the source, had used plants in his figure of bastardy, instead of slips as in More's translation and in *2 Henry VI*. The author of the passage, therefore, also had in mind the Biblical phrase of the Geneva version "bastard plātes." But instead of bastard plants, Lucrece uses the figure of grafting as bastardy, as in the first use in *2 Henry VI*. Lucrece's application, however, is that of More upon the Biblical passage, in reverse. Lucrece resolves that there will never be a bastard child to be mistaken as her husband's, as in More. Lucrece and More make the same application of the Biblical passage, both agreeing fundamentally with the Geneva version ("posthumously" in the case of both!). The order of progession for these three uses is thus clear.

There is, however, a fourth use in this same period. In *Titus Andronicus*, Lucius has captured the "incarnate devil" Aaron with "the base fruit of his burning lust," "This growing image of thy fiend-like face," and orders

> A halter, soldiers! hang him on this tree,
> And by his side his fruit of bastardy.[8]

There is no allusion to grafting in this passage, the figure being simply of bastard fruit. But Lucrece is determined that her "bastard graff shall never come to growth"; Aaron may produce a "growing image" of his face, but Tarquin shall not. Aaron's child was actual and from the source; that of Tarquin hypothetical and never to be, thus reversing also the actual expectation of nature. Consequently, the passage in *Titus*, as well as the two in *2 Henry VI*, and the one in *Richard III* should in order of composition have preceded that in *Lucrece*. And the passage in More is evidently the only begetter of the sequence, though Lucrece echoes also the Biblical phrase directly, as do the passages in *2 Henry VI* and *Richard III*.

The full, double-rooted figure is developed in this known early group of plays and is exploited but once again. In *Winter's Tale*, Perdita objects to "streak'd gillyvors"

---

[7] *Lucrece*, 1062-64. Steevens pointed out the ultimate Biblical echo (Baldwin, *Literary Genetics*, p. 138), though Carter does not notice it and Noble does not mention it, since he considers only the plays.

[8] *Titus Andronicus*, V, 1, 47-48.

> Which some call nature's bastards: of that kind
> Our rustic garden's barren; and I care not
> To get slips of them.[9]

But Polixenes objects

> You see, sweet maid, we marry
> A gentler scion to the wildest stock,
> And make conceive a bark of baser kind
> By bud of nobler race.[10]

This presents the grafting figure in its better aspect, though Perdita still stigmatizes it as bastardy, as it had been without demur in our earlier group of figures.

It would appear, then, that the order of our group of early passages is *2 Henry VI* and *Richard III*, suggested directly by their historical source, but shaped in terms of the Geneva Bible and in the form of the induced figure of grafting as bastardy. Then *Titus Andronicus* and *Lucrece* fit into the sequence. The use in *Titus Andronicus* is before that in *Lucrece* and presumably later than the development of the figure in *2 Henry VI* and *Richard III*. Since *Lucrece,* the last in this sequence, was entered S.R. May 9, 1594, these other uses would be before that date. The figure then recurs, still in the fully developed form, only once more, in *Winter's Tale*.

The nature of the process shows that all these passages belong to the one mind, that of Shakspere. Before he wrote the passage in *2 Henry VI* he knew the Geneva version of the Bible for this passage well enough to reflect its phraseology, else More's reference in the historical source caused him to look the passage up in a Geneva version, which was by that time the only current version in less than folio form. It is more likely that he looked the passage up, as he is known to have done for a passage in *Lucrece,*[11] also in the Geneva version. He also had already or at that time acquired the idea that grafting is bastardy. So More's reference was the occasion of synthesizing these various ideas from various sources, and they remain in this resultant complex at least as late as *Winter's Tale*. Thus did the mind of Shakspere work.

The historical sources of *Richard III* occasion another chain of figures linking several plays into relative order. The fundamental figure in this

---

[9] *Winter's Tale,* IV, 4, 83-85.

[10] *Winter's Tale,* IV, 4, 92-95.

[11] *Literary Genetics,* pp. 135-136, 138. The Geneva was by the 'nineties the only current version in less than folio. Anyone in England purchasing a new Bible for ordinary use after the supply of the 'seventies had been exhausted could have only a Geneva. If Shakspere consulted a Bible directly in his working days, the odds are almost unanimous for the Geneva. He might remember the Bishops' of his youth, and his memories would be kept alive by the church services; but he would almost nec-

complex is a variant of Nature's Molds, which I have treated elsewhere.[12]
In our present particular complex of figures, Natures mold takes the
form of a mold for coins, with a consequent chain of figures from that
process. Angelo says of Claudio's trespass

> It were as good
> To pardon him that hath from nature stolen
> A man already made, as to remit
> Their saucy sweetness that do coin heaven's image
> In stamps that are forbid: 'tis all as easy
> Falsely to take away a life true made,
> As to put metal in restrained means
> To make a false one.[13]

Here the stamp is thought of as the mold into which metal is poured to
mold the coin with a stamp upon it, as one would mold bullets. The
fundamental figure on Nature's molds has somewhat muddled the coining
process. The figure of molded metal without specific allusion to coining
appears in a speech of the Duchess of Gloucester.

> Ah, Gaunt, his blood was thine! that bed, that womb,
> That metal, that self-mould, that fashion'd thee
> Made him a man.[14]

The figure of coining with consequent stamp appears also in *Cymbeline*.
Posthumus, in the belief that Imogen has been false says

> We are all bastards;
> And that most venerable man which I
> Did call my father, was I know not where
> When I was stamp'd; some coiner with his tools
> Made me a counterfeit.[15]

The father coins his likeness, legitimate or counterfeit. So for Aaron's son

> The empress sends it thee, thy stamp, thy seal[16]

and Aaron tells the half-brothers

> Nay, he is your brother by the surer side,
> Although my seal be stamped in his face.[17]

The father coins his offspring, setting his stamp upon it. The cognate

---

essarily consult the Geneva. Noble's statistics show that throughout his career Shakspere relied more upon his youthful memories of the Bishops', though the Geneva gradually improved its position. He evidently consulted the handiest Bible on emergent occasion, which was the Geneva, and the general use of this version outside the church services would also tend to impress his memory.

[12] Baldwin, "Nature's Moulds," *Shakespeare Quarterly* (1952), III, 237-241.

[13] *Measure for Measure*, II, 4, 42-49.

[14] *Richard II*, I, 2, 22-24.

[15] *Cymbeline*, II, 5, 2-6.

[16] *Titus*, IV, 2, 69.

[17] *Titus*, IV, 2, 126-127.

figure of the seal in wax is twice in *Titus* put in parallel with the stamp on the coin, and is echoed elsewhere.

But returning to Posthumus in *Cymbeline,* when he realizes his mistake, he prays the gods to take his life and spare Imogen's.

> 'tis a life; you coin'd it:
> 'Tween man and man they weigh not every stamp;
> Though light, take pieces for the figure's sake.[18]

The gods, or Nature, have coined a life, and one coin is taken ordinarily to be as good as another of the same stamp. Thus when she molds, Nature puts her stamp upon the individual, though "use almost can change the stamp of nature."[19] This stamp, if of defect, may be only for identification, as in *Cymbeline*

> *Cym.*   Guiderius had
> Upon his neck a mole, a sanguine star;
> It was a mark of wonder.
> *Bel.*   This is he;
> Who hath upon him still this natural stamp:
> It was wise nature's end in the donation,
> To be his evidence now.[20]

Lucrece would like to think that such marks may be only a fault of Nature and not necessarily a mark of infamy.

> Worse than a slavish wipe or birth-hour's blot:
> For marks descried in men's nativity
> Are nature's faults, not their own infamy.[21]

Hamlet apparently goes distinctly further than Lucrece in his thinking that even if the mark of Nature destines the individual to evil it is not his fault

> some vicious mole of nature in them,
> As, in their birth — wherein they are not guilty,
> Since nature cannot choose his origin, —[22]

Since man is not responsible for the origin of his nature, these faults of birth belong to Nature, not to the individual, even if the fault is a vicious mole of character.

This fundamental idea of Nature putting a stamp upon a person in the mold of birth receives elaborate treatment in accounting for the character of Richard III. Richard's own mother says

> Thou camest on earth to make the earth my hell.
> A grievous burthen was thy birth to me.[23]

[18] *Cymbeline,* V, 4, 23-25.
[19] *Hamlet,* III, 4, 168.
[20] *Cymbeline,* V, 5, 363-368.
[21] *Lucrece,* 537-539.
[22] *Hamlet,* I, 4, 24-26.
[23] *Richard III,* IV, 4, 166-167.

Queen Margaret explains why.

> Thou elvish-mark'd, abortive, rooting hog!
> Thou that wast seal'd in thy nativity
> The slave of nature and the son of hell!
> Thou slander of thy mother's heavy womb![24]

Richard himself itemizes some of the details.

> Why, love forswore me in my mother's womb:
> And, for I should not deal in her soft laws,
> She did corrupt frail nature with some bribe,
> To shrink mine arm up like a wither'd shrub;
> To make an envious mountain on my back,
> Where sits deformity to mock my body;
> To shape my legs of an unequal size;
> To disproportion me in every part,
> Like to a chaos, or an unlick'd bear-whelp
> That carries no impression like the dam.[25]

These details Richard recapitulates as he sets his own play in motion.

> I, that am rudely stamp'd, and want love's majesty
> To strut before a wanton ambling nymph;
> I, that am curtail'd of this fair proportion,
> Cheated of feature by dissembling nature,
> Deform'd, unfinish'd, sent before my time
> Into this breathing world, scarce half made up,
> And that so lamely and unfashionable
> That dogs bark at me as I halt by them.[26]

Nature had "sealed" or "stamped" Richard as her slave to be a slander to his mother's womb by making him "elvish-mark'd, abortive," in numerous physical respects, with "no impression like the dam."

Fundamentally, Richard's physical characteristics were historical, and the interpretation of them in *Richard III* is at least suggested historically. According to More, Richard himself claimed that his physical deficiencies were caused by "yonder sorceresse my brothers wife, and other with hir," who "by their sorcerie and witchcraft, wasted my bodie," though "no man was there present, but well knew that his arme was euer such since his birth." Richard claimed sorcery, but everyone knew he was born so; that is, if there were any such dealings at all, Richard was "elvish-mark'd, abortive"

> seal'd in thy nativity
> The slave of nature and the son of hell!

The details of deformity are also at least sketched in the historical sources. Halle says "As he was small and litle of stature so was he of body grrately

---

[24] *Richard III,* I, 3, 228-231. Cf. IV, 4, 47-48.

[25] *3 Henry VI,* III, 2, 153-162.

[26] *Richard III,* I, 1, 16-23.

deformed, the one shoulder higher then the other, his face small but his cōtenaunce was cruel, and such, that a man at the first aspect would iudge it to sauor and smel of malice, fraude, and deceite," etc.[27] Thus Shakspere has simply developed the historical hints as to Richard's deformities and the significance of them.

In *King John* we have these developed characteristics brought together in a single speech. Constance says to Arthur

> If thou, that bid'st me be content, wert grim,
> Ugly and slanderous to thy mother's womb,
> Full of unpleasing blots and sightless stains,
> Lame, foolish, crooked, swart, prodigious,
> Patch'd with foul moles and eye-offending marks,
> I would not care, I then would be content,
> For then I should not love thee, no, nor thou
> Become thy great birth nor deserve a crown.
> But thou art fair, and at thy birth, dear boy,
> Nature and Fortune join'd to make thee great:
> Of Nature's gifts thou mayst with lilies boast
> And with the half-blown rose.[28]

If Arthur had been so sealed, Constance would not care, since in that case he would not become his birth or deserve a crown. Richard was so marked, did not become his birth or deserve a crown, and his mother at least eventually did not care.

Richard was "elvish-mark'd, abortive"; he was grim, ugly, a "slander of thy mother's heavy womb" in more senses than one, made "lamely" and halted, was a "crook-back prodigy," but probably not swart, and certainly not foolish in the sense here intended. The phrases from the description of Richard ring in Constance's description. I believe it is clear that this picture of Richard was developed directly from the historical sources, and that it is equally clear that Constance has her eye on this picture as she draws the one that Arthur is not. That is, I take it to be clear that the speech of Constance in *King John* was written later than was *Richard III*.

But a third passage must also fit closely into this sequence. For the fairies in *A Midsummer-Night's Dream* ban Constance's fundamental list of elf-marks from the bridal bed.

> And the blots of Nature's hand
> Shall not in their issue stand;
> Never mole, hare lip, nor scar,
> Nor mark prodigious, such as are
> Despised in nativity,
> Shall upon their children be.[29]

---

[27] Halle, *Vnion* (1548), Richard III, f 59ʳ.

[28] *King John*, III, 1, 43-54.

[29] *Midsummer-Night's Dream*, V, 1, 398-403.

Nature is not to blot, as she had not blotted Arthur. Positively, both Nature and Fortune have joined to make Arthur great.

Richard's mother, Margaret, and Richard himself had alluded to the seals of nativity which showed that Richard was "the slave of nature and the son of hell." Constance specifies them as in *Midsummer-Night's Dream.*

unpleasing blots	blots of Nature's hand
sightless [that is unsightly] stains[30]	mark prodigous such as are
	Despised in nativity
Patch'd with foul moles and eye-offending marks	
	Never mole, hare lip, nor scar,
	Nor mark prodigious, such as are
	Despised in nativity

The remaining characteristics are for the most part, as we have seen, directly those of Richard III. I see nothing to show directly which is the earlier of these two passages. But the passage in *Midsummer-Night's Dream* is positive and is developed out of and adapted directly to the actual dramatic situation, while the speech of Constance is negative and is entirely and freely fictional, however well or ill adapted it may be to the emotional situation. The probability is, therefore, that the fairy-ban precedes the speech of Constance, though I see no necessary connection between it and anything in *Richard III.* I regard it as certain, therefore, that Constance's speech was written later than *Richard III,* and at least probable that it was written after the fairy-ban in *Midsummer-Night's Dream.*

It is noticeable also that the passage in *Lucrece* has close verbal connections with both *Richard III* and *Midsummer-Night's Dream.* On the background of our fundamental figure, Lucrece's "slavish wipe" is only a variant way of saying

> seal'd in thy nativity
> The slave of nature.

It is not necessarily, however, a specific, allusive restatement of the passage in *Richard III,* though that is the probability. If it could be shown that the passage in *Lucrece* is in fact specifically a reminiscent variant allusion to that in *Richard III,* then the latter passage would date before May 9, 1594.

Further, Lucrece says

> For marks descried in men's nativity
> Are nature's faults

where the phraseology is close to that in *A Midsummer-Night's Dream.*

---

[30] The fundamental phrase "blots and stains" is used in *Richard III,* III, 7, 234, and in *King John* itself II, 1, 114. In our passage, each noun has received an epithet. These are the only three instances of the phrase.

> Nor mark prodigious, such as are
> Despised in nativity.

I have a "feeling," nothing more, that the lame line "Despised in nativity" was occasioned by rephrasing from "descried in men's nativity." But whatever the precedence, one passage simply varies the other. We are also reminded that *Titus* uses the fundamental figure of stamping or coining. At least, therefore, we have yet another instance in which these plays show themselves as a group in their closely interrelated uses of a fundamental figure, which was occasioned by the historical sources of *Richard III*.[31]

Various other instances of this figured complex of 1592-94 can probably be best presented under particular plays,[32] especially those which link *Titus* and *Lucrece*. Those we have examined here place *Richard III* definitely before *Lucrece*, that is, before May 9, 1594, and give useful information on the relationships of various other plays.[33]

---

[31] The dictum *Cave tibi ab iis quos natura signavit* was, of course, commonplace. See, for instance, the seventeenth-century summary by Edward Reynolds in his *A Treatise of the Passions* (1640), pp. 78-79, which alleges Aristotle's *Ethics*, lib. 8, as its basic authority and Homer's Thersites (cf. *Troilus and Cressida*) as its illustration.

[32] See also Baldwin, *Literary Genetics*, pp. 219, 252-253.

[33] A thoroughgoing examination of the sources and evolution of the figures in these early plays would certainly illuminate Shakspere's processes of composition, and give insight to his mind at work.

CHAPTER XVI

Dating of the Lancaster-York Tetralogy

We have now some cardinal facts of relationship in the Lancaster-York tetralogy by means of which to control our indications of date. I take it as certain that *Contention* and *True Tragedie* (York) are derivatives from *2* and *3 Henry VI* and hence later in date. *True Tragedie* was printed in 1595 as having been performed by Pembroke's men. What of the parent version, *3 Henry VI? 1, 2,* and *3 Henry VI* were printed in the First Folio of 1623 as Shakspere's. Chief guarantors are Heminges and Cundall. There is no reasonable doubt, therefore, that in some sense the plays included are Shakspere's and equally no doubt that most if not all of these plays had belonged to the one organization, which at this early period was under the patronage of Strange.

Now both *2* and *3 Henry VI* as printed in the First Folio bear witness that they are taken from manuscript which had belonged to the early Strange-Admiral combination. Both *2* and *3 Henry VI* preserve the names of a few actors for minor parts, these two originals pairing as to type of text, as do their derivatives *Contention* and *True Tragedie*. In *2 Henry VI*, John Holland and perhaps some actor named Bevis took small parts. John Holland played minor parts for Strange's men in *2 Seven Deadly Sins*, probably about 1591. He was also a general handy-actor in a badly hashed play surviving in manuscript of the early 'nineties, which has been dubbed *John of Bordeaux*. If Bevis was an actor, he does not appear in the plot of *2 Seven Deadly Sins*, nor is anything known of such an actor. Thus *2 Henry VI* is through Holland directly connected with Strange's men and that at an early period.

In *3 Henry VI*, John Sinkler, Humfrey Jeffes, and Gabriel Spencer have their names connected with minor parts. Sinkler has record only with the Shaksperean company, as a minor actor over many years, beginning with the plot of *2 Seven Deadly Sins*. Jeffes and Spencer appear as important actors with the Admiral's men after the junction of Pembroke's with that company in 1597. Spencer had certainly been with Pembroke's in 1597, and Jeffes almost certainly also had been.[1] Neither Spencer nor Jeffes had appeared with Strange's in *2 Seven Deadly Sins*, as Holland and Sinkler had done. Thus Spencer and Jeffes evidently

---

[1] Chambers, *E.S.,* II, 133, 200; Baldwin, "Posting Henslowe's Accounts," *J.E.G.P.,* XXVI, 42 ff.

appeared in *3 Henry VI* in connection with the Admiral's part of the combination as minor actors, whence Spencer and probably Jeffes passed at least eventually through Pembroke's, back to the Admiral's again, now as important men. Also, this text of *3 Henry VI* is later than *2 Seven Deadly Sins,* which was about 1591.

Further, we know directly from Henslowe that Strange's company had at this period a play or plays on Henry the Sixth. It is usually assumed that these entries by Henslowe for Strange's company refer to *1 Henry VI.* Perhaps Hart states the presuppositions as well as any. "It is perhaps a slight evidence in favour of the Henslowe Diary play being the same as the Folio play, that it was known always in the Diary as *Henry VI.* The subsequent parts in their earliest forms had distinct titles, and were not known as *Henry VI.* until they reached the final stage. We have no record of the acting of those earlier forms."[2] But the fact is that Strange's company is connected only with a play or plays entitled *Henry VI,* and that when the survivors of the company submitted their plays to print they had three parts which are distinguished as *1, 2,* and *3 Henry VI.* Strange's company is in no way connected directly with these other titles, nor are the other titles themselves wholly consistent with each other.

First was printed *The First part of the Contention betwixt the two famous Houses of Yorke and Lancaster, with the death of the good Duke Humphrey,* etc., 1594, which had been entered S.R. under the same long-tailed title March 12, 1594. Then followed in 1595, without entry S.R., *The true Tragedie of Richard Duke of Yorke, and the death of good King Henrie the Sixt, with the whole contention betweene the two Houses Lancaster and Yorke, as it was sundrie times acted by the Right Honourable the Earle of Pembrooke his seruants.* It is obvious that these long-tailed titles are descriptive of the contents by way of advertisement. These are for print; certainly for acting, some very much briefer title served, but we do not have indication in these title pages of what that abbreviation was. *Contention* is common to the two title pages, the one having *The First part of the Contention,* the other *the whole contention,* which are squinting distinctions, not likely representing the stage titles. Here it is pertinent to note that the word in the *Henry VI* plays is not "contention," which occurs only once.

> No quarrel, but a slight contention[3]

Thus the word "contention" is not likely to have come from the author. Instead, Halle's word "dissension" occurs half a dozen times in *1 Henry VI,* being there concentrated three in III, 1, two in IV, 1, one in V, 5; and once in *3 Henry VI.* But the usual word is neither "contention" nor "dissension" but "quarrel," as it is throughout Shakspere, being used

---

[2] Hart, *1 Henry VI,* p. viii.

[3] *3 Henry VI,* I, 2, 6.

four times in *1 Henry VI*, three times in *2 Henry VI*, five times in *3 Henry VI*. There is thus no indication that the "contention" titles were bestowed by the author or authors, rather the contrary. Similarly, the Duke of York occurs in both printed titles, first as *the Duke of Yorkes first claime vnto the Crowne*, and then as *The true Tragedie of Richard Duke of Yorke*, but again there is nothing to hint that these are the stage titles.

As we follow the records of these two printed parts, there is gradual clarification of title up to the First Folio. In S.R. April 19, 1602, we find a transfer of both plays as "The firste and second parte of Henry the Sixt," two books, double fee. But in the collection printed in 1619 the two titles are integrated into one *Whole Contention*, of which the plays are the first and second part. They have thus been harmonized here on the "contention" theme.

The First Folio of Shakspere, 1623, had already been made up when on November 8, 1623, entry was made of the plays not already entered, since the plays are named in the order of arrangement in the First Folio, probably being checked to the table of contents. It was doubtless because of this mechanical fact that the third part of *Henry VI* is entered. For the authorities had already an entry, as we have seen, of April 19, 1602, for *1* and *2 Henry VI*. So on November 8, 1623, an entry was made for *3 Henry VI*. As a matter of fact, the entry should have been for *1 Henry VI*, and the entry in 1602 should have been for *2* and *3 Henry VI*. But there were three parts, and the authorities had finally been paid for three parts, so neither side to the bargain would trouble about our confusions.

Thus it appears that Strange's company had in 1592 a play or plays on Henry VI, which by 1623 had come to be *1, 2,* and *3 Henry VI*, while the form printed in *2* and *3 Henry VI* is connected with Strange's at this early period. When the licensing authorities sought a short form for the "contention" plays in 1602, they called them *1* and *2 Henry VI*. The long-tailed printed titles had been for advertising, and give no tangible indication of the acting titles for these plays. The First Folio is still conscious, however, of the tradition in print, attaching "with the death of the Good Duke Humfrey" to *2 Henry VI*, and the adapted "with the death of the Duke of Yorke" to *3 Henry VI*.

Further, the known custom of admission charges shows that at least two parts of *Henry VI* are involved in Henslowe's entries, and that all three may be. The first entry for *Henry VI* in Henslowe's Diary is "ne . . . R7 at harey the vj the 3 of marche 1591 . . . iij^{11} xvj^s 8^d." It will be seen that the entry does not indicate which of the three parts of the Henry VI trilogy was new March 3, 1592; but Henslowe's receipts throw some light on the probabilities. It is, of course, well known that higher prices were charged for new plays than for old. The custom at the Rose may be gathered from the accompanying tabulation of receipts from the

NEW PLAYS IN HENSLOWE'S DIARY, JUNE 26, 1594, TO JUNE 3, 1595

	First	£	s	d	Second	£	s	d	Third	£	s	d	Fourth	£	s	d
Galiaso[a]	June 26, 1594	3	4		July 12, 1594	2	6		July 23, 1594	1	11		Aug. 5, 1594	1	3	6
Philipo and Hippolito	July 9, 1594	3	2		July 13, 1594	2	0		July 18, 1594	1	10		July 24, 1594	1	10	0
Godfrey of Bulloigne	July 19, 1594	3	11		July 26, 1594	2	7		Aug. 6, 1594	1	17		Aug. 13, 1594	1	9	0
The Merchant of Emden	July 30, 1594	3	8													
Tasso's Melancholy	Aug. 11, 1594	3	4		Aug. 18, 1594	2	7		Sept. 3, 1594	2	6		Sept. 18, 1594	1	7	6
The Venetian Comedy	Aug. 25, 1594	2	10	6	Sept. 5, 1594	1	16	6	Sept. 15, 1594	1	16	6	Sept. 22, 1594	1	5	0
Palamon and Arcyte	Sept. 17, 1594	2	11		Oct. 16, 1594	1	7		Oct. 27, 1594	2	7		Nov. 9, 1594		12	0
The Love of an English Lady	Sept. 24, 1594	2	7		Oct. 24, 1594	1	3									
A Knack to Know an Honest Man	Oct. 22, 1594	2	0		Oct. 29, 1594	2	7		Nov. 1, 1594	3	3		Nov. 7, 1594	2	4	0
Caesar and Pompey	Nov. 8, 1594	3	2		Nov. 14, 1594	1	15		Nov. 25, 1594	1	12		Dec. 10, 1594		12	
Dioclesian	Nov. 16, 1594	2	14		Nov. 22, 1594	2	3									
The Wise Man of Westchester	Dec. 2, 1594	1	13		Dec. 6, 1594	1	14		Dec. 29, 1594	3	2		Jan. 16, 1595	3	0	0
The Set at Maw	Dec. 14, 1595	2	4		Jan. 2, 1595	1	4		Jan. 17, 1595	1	5		Jan. 28, 1595	1	7	0
The French Comedy	Feb. 11, 1595	2	10		Feb. 27, 1595	2	0		May 12, 1595	1	8		May 31, 1595		15	0
The Mack	Feb. 21, 1595	3	0													
Selio and Olimpo	March 5, 1595	3	0		May 2, 1595	2	10		May 9, 1595	1	6		May 19, 1595	1	3	0
Hercules, Pt. I	May 7, 1595	3	13		May 20, 1595	3	9		May 27, 1595	2	0		June 12, 1595	3	1	0
Hercules, Pt. II	May 23, 1595	3	10		May 28, 1595	3	2		June 13, 1595	3	2		Sept. 2, 1595	3	0	0
The Seven Days of the Week	June 3, 1595	3	10		June 6, 1595	2	4		June 10, 1595	3	6		June 14, 1595	3	9	0

[a] The titles are Greg's; the dates Henslowe's uncorrected.

new plays for the year June 1594–June 1595, this being the first complete year available for testing.

While there were exceptions, it will at once be noticed that normally a play returned at first performance either about £3 5s or £2 10s. Those that returned £3 5s at first performance returned about £2 10s for the second performance and £1 10s for the third. Those that returned £2 10s for the first performance returned about £1 10s for the second, and the same approximate amount thereafter, this latter being about the normal return for plays at this period. It is thus evident that there were three scales of prices that might be charged at the Rose, these running in approximately one, two, three ratio. Usually the highest price was used for a new play, the second highest for its second performance, and the regular scale for the third and succeeding performances. A play might, however, begin with the second highest rate and come to the regular scale at the second performance. Presumably there was some reason to believe that such a play would not draw a full audience at the highest price. On the other hand, a few plays were held at the highest price for many performances. Presumably, these were exceedingly popular plays. These same ratios hold good throughout Henslowe's itemized accounts, showing that this was the general custom of the theater.

HENRY VI PERFORMANCES, 1592[4]

	£	s	d
March 3	3	16	8
7	3	0	0
11	2	7	6
16	1	11	6
28	3	8	0
April 5	2	1	0
13	1	6	0
21	1	13	0
May 4	2	16	0
7	1	2	0
14	2	10	0
19	1	10	0
25	1	4	0
June 12	1	12	0
19	1	11	0

Now an examination of the Henry VI entries shows that the new play of March 3, 1592, was at the highest price, at which it was held for a second performance March 7, dropping at its next performance to the second scale, March 11, and to the regular prices March 16.[5] Then, after

---

[4] Greg, *Henslowe's Diary*, I, 13-15.

[5] Sir Walter Greg notes "The 'harey' of 16 Mar. 1591/2 is probably *Henry of Cornwall*" (Greg, *Henslowe's Diary*, II, 152), explaining "From its position one would expect the 'harey' . . . to refer to *Henry VI* . . . but the takings were too

a short interval, we find the highest price is charged March 28, directly after Easter, followed by the second scale April 5, and the third April 16. Though Henslowe does not mark it new, this is evidently another part, so not marked, running the regular gamut. After this, there are only two performances above the regular scale, both at the second highest prices. Since fairly popular plays were sometimes raised to the second highest or even the highest scale, no doubt to see if the traffic would bear it, it is likely that the performance May 4 was of the part recorded March 3 and that of May 14 of the part recorded March 28, especially since each is followed by a drop to the regular scale. It is to be noticed, too, that under this interpretation the part raised in price May 4 had not been performed since March 16 and was thus making its second bow, the same being true of the part raised May 14. We appear then to have record of at least two parts of *Henry VI* beginning at the Rose in March, 1592. There could have been three parts, of course, since there are three entries at the highest price, the first two of them consecutive. More likely, however, one part was sufficiently successful to warrant the highest price for a second day. Even so, *Henry VI* shows no extraordinary success at the box-office, nothing, for instance, like *Hercules* in 1594-95, nor several of the old stalwarts at almost any time. An extraordinary number of tears may have been shed over *Henry VI*, but not of pennies — which were the things the actors and their creditors could count.[6]

I believe we may take it as certain that in March, 1592, Strange's company was acting in two and possibly all three of the parts of *1, 2, 3 Henry VI* in approximately the forms that they bear in the First Folio. Some form of *2* and *3 Henry VI* in some way passed to Pembroke's to become eventually *Contention* and *True Tragedie* (York) — how prophetic those names! When did this occur? We would infer later than March, 1592, when at least two parts of *Henry VI* were new. The known facts concerning the origins of Pembroke's company indicate the same date. It "was at Leicester in the last three months of 1592 and made its only appearances at Court on 26 December 1592, and 6 January 1593. In the following summer it travelled, and is found at York in June, at Rye in July, and in 1592-93 at Ludlow, Shrewsbury, Coventry, Bath, and Ipswich. But it had little success. Henslowe wrote to Alleyn on 28 September 'As for my lorde a Penbrockes wch you desier to knowe wheare they be they ar all at home and hausse ben this v or sixe weackes for they cane not saue ther carges wth trauell as I heare & weare fayne to pane

---

small, 31*s* 6*d*" (Greg, *Henslowe's Diary*, II, 151). On the contrary, they are exactly right for their position. Henslowe merely condensed the 6 and the 16 of March into "at harey [the 6] the 16 of marche."

[6] Since Professor Alfred Harbage's account (*Shakespeare's Audience*) depends wholly on the assumption that only *3 Henry VI* is involved, it is completely without foundation in fact.

ther parell for ther carge.' About the same time three of their plays came to the booksellers' hands. These were Marlowe's *Edward the Second* (1594, S.R. 6 July 1593), *The Taming of A Shrew* (1594, S.R. 2 May 1594), and *The True Tragedy of Richard Duke of York* (1595). Probably the play to which this last is a sequel, *1 Contention of York and Lancaster* (1594, S.R. 12 March 1594) was also theirs, although the name of the company is not on the title-page. It is on the title-page of *Titus Andronicus* (1594),"[7] along with Derby's and Sussex's.

Thus Pembroke's makes its appearance the latter part of 1592. It should not have had its derivatives of *2* and *3 Henry VI* before that time, this fact in turn correlating with our previous fact that Strange's had the originals in the first half of 1592. Nor would the derivatives affect the rights of Strange's men to the originals. When Strange's men returned to the Rose December 29, 1592, for twenty-nine performances through February 1, 1593, they performed *Henry VI* January 16, 1593, with a receipt of £2 6s, and January 31 at £1 6s. This was evidently some part of *Henry VI* at second and then at normal rates. The *Henry VI* plays had evidently run their normal course; at least, for that audience.

Our total facts are now reasonably conclusive that Sir Edmund Chambers (*E.S.*, II, 129) has given the correct solution for Pembroke's men. "It seems to me, on the whole, likely that the origin of Pembroke's men is to be explained by the special conditions of the plague-years 1592-93, and was due to a division for travelling purposes of the large London company formed by the amalgamation of Strange's and the Admiral's. Such a division had been foreshadowed as likely to be necessary in the petition sent by Strange's men to the Privy Council during the summer of 1592 or earlier, and may actually have become necessary when, after all, the plague rendered travelling imperative." Travel or not, at least the evidence is surely now clear that Pembroke's company as such was not directly concerned with such work as Shakspere may have done on *2* and *3 Henry VI*, but in some way had connection only with the derivatives from those plays.

In view of these dates and relationships, the appearance of at least two new parts of *Henry VI* in Henslowe's Diary in March 1592 would appear to give the conclusive fact. These would be *2* and *3 Henry VI*, at least, also paired against *1 Henry VI* by the nature of their text. Some form of these two plays in some way then passed to Pembroke's company, which appears also to have had at least part, if not all, of its personnel from the Strange-Admiral combination which had acted *2* and *3 Henry VI*.

Facts in connection with the other Pembroke plays also fit these conclusions. Marlowe's *Edward II* was written about 1592 and belonged to the Admiral's. *Titus* was acted by both Derby's and Sussex's, and had

---

[7] Chambers, *E.S.*, II, 128-129.

been constructed for the Admiral's. *A Shrew* belonged probably to the Admiral's, by August, 1589. It is thus clear that however it happened, Pembroke's were in these cases merely using old plays from the Admiral's stock, in some of which both the Strange (Derby), and Sussex companies had at some time also performed. Pembroke's were traveling in June and July, 1593. Naturally, therefore, Alleyn had asked about them, and on September 28, 1593, Henslowe reported that the company had been back in London for five or six weeks and he hears they had been obliged to pawn their apparel. Had they pawned or otherwise parted with any of these plays, Henslowe would certainly have informed Alleyn. Pretty certainly, therefore, the connection of Pembroke's with the Admiral's stock was before they set out and before Alleyn's own departure about May, 1593. It would, therefore, have been before or during the season 1592-93, when the company presented two plays at court. Exactly where Pembroke's were and how Alleyn came to furnish them we do not know.

But again these facts dovetail with the known ones. For instance, Strange's men performed one or more parts of *Henry VI* before the Rose was closed in June 1592 and after they returned in December. Pembroke's evidently fit into the hiatus with their version of *2* and *3 Henry VI*. Apparently, part one had completed its run but the other parts were considered active when Pembroke's took up the succession. This would account also for the fact that while the Pembroke version is essentially a damaged abbreviation of the form retained by Strange's, yet there were minor differences. Pembroke's would presumably have been using some form of copy. Further, the quarto of 1594 gives the order of companies acting *Titus Andronicus* as "the Earl of Darbie, Earle of Pembrooke, and Earle of Sussex their Seruants." This also places the Pembroke company in succession to the Strange-Derby company, as do the *Henry VI* plays. Further, Strange's had performed a *Titus* in 1592 and Sussex just before publication. It seems clearly indicated, therefore, that when the Rose was closed and Strange's went to the country, Pembroke's had access to the stock, necessarily through Alleyn, in London. This would be between June 23 and early September, 1592, when the plague stopped all London acting till December. But wherever the company acted, it was not at the Rose, so that we have no record from Henslowe; and if Alleyn kept records of his part of these transactions, as he certainly would have done, they do not appear to have survived among his papers. The company, being apparently a new one, may well have been at Newington Butts. Exactly what its relationship was to Strange's, if any, must await further facts. But it is clear that Shakspere did not write any of these plays for Pembroke's.

It must be emphasized, however, that Pembroke's possession of any of these plays may have been, and so is to be presumed to have been, completely legitimate according to the arrangements of the time. We simply do not know the exact agreements under which these various aggregations acted in these plays. The relationship of Marlowe's *Edward II* to *2 Henry VI* shows that Marlowe found the Pembroke version underlying *Contention* quite respectable. Most likely it was a cut acting version, and may in fact have been — most likely was — essentially a copy of the acting version for Strange's, whether with or without further "improvements" we do not know. The present degradation of *Contention* is not likely to be chargeable to Pembroke's official copy, though it is clear that it happened through Pembroke's copy.

The other known facts concerning the chronology of *1, 2, 3 Henry VI* correlate exactly with our previous conclusions. For *1 Henry VI*, Nashe in *Pierce Penniless*, S.R. August 8, 1592, exclaims "How would it haue ioyed braue *Talbot* (the terror of the French) to thinke that after he had lyne two hundred yeares in his Tombe, hee should triumphe againe on the Stage, and haue his bones newe embalmed with the teares of ten thousand spectators at least (at seuerall times), who, in the Tragedian that represents his person, imagine they behold him fresh bleeding."[8] Nashe's first parenthesis uses the same phrasing as *1 Henry VI*, I, 4, 42, "Here, said they, is the terror of the French." Presumably his reference is to *1 Henry VI*, with at least this phrase already in the form found in the First Folio.

We have seen also that Marlowe used a passage from *1 Henry VI* for *Edward II*, probably not later than 1592. The echoes by Nashe and Marlowe thus indicate a date not later than August, 1592, for *1 Henry VI*.

At the opposite end, Hart[9] suggests various parallels with *Faerie Queene*, though only one of these seems strong enough to be considered.[10] Gloucester describes Henry V

> His brandish'd sword did blind men with his beams:
> His arms spread wider than a dragon's wings;
> His sparkling eyes, replete with wrathful fire,
> More dazzled and drove back his enemies
> Than mid-day sun fierce bent against their faces.[11]

In describing a dragon, Spenser wrote

> His blazing eyes, like two bright shining shieldes,
> Did burne with wrath, and sparkled liuing fyre;
> As two broad Beacons . . . . .
>
> . . . . . warning giue, that enemies conspyre,
>
> .   .   .   .

---

[8] McKerrow, *Nashe*, I, 212.

[9] *1 Henry VI*, pp. xxvi-xxviii.

[10] The parallel at I, 1, 124 is also possible.

[11] *1 Henry VI*, I, 1, 10-14.

So flam'd his eyne with rage and rancorous yre:

. . . .

Then with his wauing wings displayed wyde.[12]

The parallel is extended. The brandished sword has in some way caused the author of the passage in *1 Henry VI* to make Henry "spread-eagle" with both arms — surely such a pose would have been instantly fatal in practice! That is, the author has here presented an unvisualized figure (surely, therefore not Shakspere's), taken from dragon lore. While dragons were numerous, that of Spenser probably has enough of differentiating characteristics to justify a claim of paternity to that in *1 Henry VI*. If accepted, this borrowing probably indicates a date not earlier than 1590, when the *Faerie Queene* was published.

I believe it is also clear that at least sections of *1 Henry VI* are not earlier than the autumn of 1591. It will be remembered that in III, 2, Rouen is captured by the ruse of soldiers dressed as market men and women. Boswell-Stone says: "No date can be assigned to this scene. Chronology and facts are utterly scorned. Rouen was not surprised and recovered, but willingly received Charles VII. within its walls on October 19, 1449. . . . The fictitious capture of Rouen was, perhaps, an adaptation of a story told by Holinshed, upon Halle's (197) authority."[13] But what suggested the taking of Rouen at all, and being suggested, why did the author take it by this particular stratagem? The answer, I believe, is found in contemporary events. A picked body of English troops under Essex arrived in Normandy August 2, 1591. As the prime object of the expedition, "The queen had set her mind firmly on an immediate siege and capture of Rouen." There was an abortive attempt at surprise in October and the siege was regularly begun on the twenty-ninth of that month.[14] It seems clear that as the dramatist shaped his play for the winter 1591 the national wish became father to his thought of capturing Rouen.

But why should he capture it by this particular device? Another of England's national heroes, fighting Vere, had in May of that same year won the outlying defences of Zutphen in the Netherlands, the whole city following in a week, by precisely this stratagem of soldiers dressed as market men and women.[15] Possibly the author does get the details of his

---

[12] Spenser, *Faerie Queene,* Bk. I. C. XI. 13, 17.

[13] Boswell-Stone, *Holinshed,* 224.

[14] Cheyney, *History,* I, 259-271.

[15] Cheyney, *History,* I, 237. Vere "caused sundry of his Souldiours, secretly to be apparrelled in the habite of poore Market folks, as well of men as women, som driuing of Oxen, some of Kine, some of Sheepe, some of Hogs, and some driuing of Goates. These people thus being driuing of Cattle, were pursued & chased by some Souldiours, as though they had beene their enemies, by meanes whereof the Cattle

story from Holinshed, but he was doubtless attracted to it by Vere's famous use of the device in May, and wished and expected that Essex in the autumn might capture Rouen in the same way. But alas! and alack! Essex was not Vere. He was no more successful in capturing Rouen the autumn of 1591 than he was in bringing back Irish rebellion broached on his sword in the summer of 1599. Since we have mentioned Essex, perhaps this is as good a place as any to point out that the first appearance of Talbot's epitaph in printed form is not likely to give any evidence of the date of *1 Henry VI*, since, as Sir Edmund Chambers most dryly remarks, "travellers went to Rouen, although Essex and his soldiers failed to take it in 1591."[16]

In this connection, Mr. John Munro[17] interprets the phoenix lines in *1 Henry VI* (IV, 7, 92-93) as a reference to Essex, who landed at Dieppe August 3, 1591.[18] The same figure is used again, however, by York in *3 Henry VI*, I, 4, 35-36, where the reference appears to be to his sons. Still, it is hard to see what else the allusion in *1 Henry VI* could be to if not to the English armies in France 1589 and following. The figure was used of another army in France, and that use may have suggested those in *1* and *3 Henry VI*. A pamphlet of 1590 warns that Parma "came to plant a Colony of Spaniards in Fraunce, but he did but sowe it abroad in the fieldes, which haue lyne couered with their dead, out of whose ashes they shall not spring againe as dooth the Phenix."[19]

But if *1 Henry VI* was written in its present form in 1591-92, was it the first of the sequence to be written? After an analysis of relationships between the parts, Professor J. Dover Wilson concludes, "Apparently, therefore, Part I was from the outset intended as a preface to Part II; and most critics following Johnson have naturally, if illogically, jumped to the conclusion that it must have been written first."[20] His argument for later writing in spite of earlier planning — which to most people is likely to be the illogicality! — is that "whereas *1 Henry VI* was written by a person or persons who knew all about *2 Henry VI*, and I think

---

and poore people were receiued by the enemie, intending to succour thē, while without any suspition those poore people being couragious souldiors, hauing got the gates opened, seazed vppon the Keepers thereof" (*A Particuler, of the yeelding vppe of the Towne of Zutphen, and the beleagering of Deuenter* (1591), pp. 8-9; entered S.R. June 2, 1591).

[16] Chambers, *Shakespeare*, I, 293.

[17] *T.L.S.*, October 11, 1947, p. 528.

[18] I find an old note of mine raising the same query.

[19] *A Breefe Description of the Battailes Victories and Triumphes, atchiued by the D. of Parma, and the Spanish Armye* (tr. by E. A.). The fact that Rhodope is mentioned in *1 Henry VI*, I, 6, 22, while the company had presented her in *2 Seven Deadly Sins* about 1591 is interesting but can hardly be made to show chronological order.

[20] Wilson, *1 Henry VI*, p. xi.

3 Henry VI also, those two plays display complete ignorance of the drama which ostensibly precedes them."[21] The first part of the statement is correct and important, the second is unimportant if correct. In such work one must look forward; he need not look backward.

Professor Wilson alleges three instances in proof. First, Henry is not represented as an infant in Part I, though in both *2* and *3 Henry VI* we are three times informed that Henry was only nine months old when he became king, as we are told in *Richard III* also. As Professor Wilson himself points out, the functional stage exigencies of Part I demanded something more than a nine-months-old babe for presentation. Exactly how much more there is no indication, though Professor Wilson appears to have a definite idea. The fact is that the arguments here are in different planes. Whatever the represented age of Henry in Part I, that age was dictated by stage presentation. The references in *2* and *3 Henry VI,* and *Richard III* are to the actual historical fact, without any consideration to stage presentation. The stage presentation of Part I would have no meaning in their context.

A second point is that the author of Part I knew the character of Gloucester from Part II; specifically, "inasmuch as his single reference to Gloucester's duchess is demonstrably derived, not from the chronicles, but from what he understood about her in *2 Henry VI*."[22] But, as we have seen,[23] the reference in both instances is from the *Mirour,* and echoes the source verbally both in *1* and *2 Henry VI,* the two instances being besides in proper order. The specific point, therefore, does not hold but indicates exactly the opposite. This point is placed in a general background argument that Gloucester is two different characters in the two plays. But if so then history is to blame, since both Gloucesters are in every available historical source. The circumstances of Part I demanded that one historical phase of Gloucester be emphasized; those of Part II demanded another. Surely one does not need to emphasize the argumentations surrounding the two parts of *Henry IV,* of *Tamburlaine,* etc. A character simply cannot be the same in two parts; for one thing, the story in which he appears reflected cannot be the same. The upshot of the specific argument is that it counts definitely for Part I as written before Part II.

A third point concerns the "strange" conundrums of Part II, I, 1, 73-82. We must remember that there Gloucester is making a speech of persuasion and referring to kin and present company only. He makes no flourish of allusion to the glorious dead, where many more than Talbot would have had to be included. Also, Somerset and "brave York" were very much

[21] Wilson, *1 Henry VI,* pp. xi-xii.

[22] Wilson, *1 Henry VI,* p. xiii.

[23] See above, pp. 285 ff.

alive and present. So they needed to be persuaded, however grand rascals Gloucester may have considered them to be. Since this is another play and another day, that would also permit a different emphasis in deference to the new circumstances. If these plays happen not to be of single authorship — and Professor Wilson contends that they are not — then that fact would itself readily account for the differences, without indicating anything as to order of composition. These three points, therefore, give no indication that Part I was written after Part II. We shall see further evidence that Part I was at least planned before Part II, as Professor Wilson contends.

Professor C. A. Greer[24] has made a detailed study of these inconsistencies between *1 Henry VI* and the remaining plays of the tetralogy, concluding that the author was revising an old play and adapting it to the other plays. "It can hardly be supposed that the adapter working in *1 Henry VI* wrote an entirely new play and thus adapted it to the other plays of the tetralogy. This would mean that he sat down with a group of completed plays before him, or close at hand, and that he wrote another play, an entirely new one, and made it harmonious with the group. He should have had no great difficulty in harmonizing what he had to write with what he had before him. If he had been writing a new play from the chronicle sources and adapting it to the other plays, he would probably have made a much better adaptation. Or if he had been writing a new play from his own creative imagination and from what he had before him in the other plays, he would hardly have adapted so poorly. Certainly nothing was to be gained dramatically by the confusion of Henry the Sixth's age, Suffolk's proxy marriage, and Suffolk's demand for pay in transporting Margaret; by the failure even to refer in one play to much highly dramatic and important matter in another; and by the failure to utilize characterization in one play that would have greatly strengthened, and harmonized with, the characterization in another.

"But if the person working in *1 Henry VI* revised an old play written by some one else and adapted it to *2* and *3 Henry VI* and *Richard III,* he would have had much more justification for overlooking the discrepancies that we have noted."[25]

"As for the play of which *1 Henry VI* was a revision and adaptation, it probably was the 'Harry the Sixth' attested to by Henslowe and Nashe in 1592. It might possibly, however, have been some other Henry VI play now lost."[26] The great amount of "dissimilar or disconnecting

---

[24] C. A. Greer, "Revision and Adaptation in *1 Henry VI,*" *Studies in English* (U. of Texas Publication, No. 4226: July 8, 1942), pp. 110-120.

[25] Greer, p. 114.

[26] Greer, p. 116.

material shows the adaptation was not a perfect one but rather a very poor one, quite hasty, not extensive, and inconsistent."[27]

Professor Wilson will have *1 Henry VI* at least outlined before *2* and *3 Henry VI;* Professor Greer will have a play written and then hastily and superficially revised to conform with *2* and *3 Henry VI,* as also *Richard III.* Both agree that certain major features of structure are in conformity with the later plays, and it will appear upon analysis that these features go beyond the possibilities of insertion at a hasty and superficial revision. The fundamentals are in harmony and are from the historical sources. Either way, these major features of structure are granted. Most of Professor Greer's further arguments, especially as to when his supposed adaptation was made, are bound up with the question of authorship and cannot be considered here in detail. But it should be pointed out that once divided authorship of any kind is postulated, then almost anything can happen, especially if one also postulates the right authors. Let one examine the treatment of English history in the acknowledged plays of Greene and Peele and remember how persistently they have been suspected of having had their hands in these plays! Anyone attempting to present "real" history must have found these two trying, even beyond the patience of Job. Present evidence, therefore, indicates that Part I was written or revised in 1591-92, in its expected order, before Part II.

It will be well to examine next the evidence of date for *3 Henry VI.* A passage in this play is later than Spenser's *Faerie Queene,* S.R. December 1, 1589, printed 1590, but earlier than *Venus and Adonis,* S.R. April 18, 1593.[28] As we have seen, Marlowe's *Massacre at Paris,* new January 26, 1593, borrows from *3 Henry VI;* and *Edward II* may do so. It is only too well known that in *Groats-Worth of Wit,* S.R. September 20, 1592, Robert Greene parodied "tiger's heart wrapp'd in a woman's hide."[29] This line, therefore, in a key speech was already as it appears in the First Folio.

There has been no question, I believe, that *2 Henry VI* precedes *3 Henry VI.* In *Edward II,* Marlowe has several borrowings from *2 Henry VI* and may possibly have a few from *3 Henry VI,* while the chief borrowings from *3 Henry VI* are in *Massacre,* January 26, 1593, apparently Marlowe's last play. Incidentally, this warrants at least the suggestion that the *Henry VI* which was being put on in January, 1593, was Part III. It seems indicated, therefore, that these two plays of Marlowe's are interlocked with the second and third parts of *Henry VI.* This should

---

[27] Greer, p. 119.

[28] Baldwin, *Literary Genetics,* pp. 4-8.

[29] *3 Henry VI,* I, 4, 137.

mean that *2* and *3 Henry VI* were not merely before September, 1592, but also that they were not many months before. We need also to remember that *Edward II, True Tragedie* (from *3 Henry VI*), and probably *Contention* (from *2 Henry VI*) are all connected with Pembroke's company, *Edward II* being more closely connected with *Contention* than with the parent play as represented by *2 Henry VI*. Our facts of chronology indicate that this connection was not before the latter part of 1592.

There is one other curious connection of *2 Henry VI* with 1592. "Among those slain at St. Albans, *Stow* (661) specifies 'the olde Lord Clifforde.' ('olde' first appears in the ed. of 1592, p. 651.) Lord Clifford is not, I believe, called 'old' in any other chronicle printed before the date of this play; and he is not thus distinguished from his son in the *Contention*. In *2 Hen. VI.* we find *'old Clifford'* (Entry, IV. viii. 5), and *'Old Clif.'* is prefixed to several speeches in V. i. His son is 'young Clifford' in the *Contention* and *2 Hen. VI.* The son's name does not appear in a contemporary list (*Paston*, i. 332, 333) of the chief persons present at the battle of St. Albans, and I do not know of any book or MS. which records that he was there."[30] The distinction appears to have arisen naturally in the play from the necessity of distinguishing the Cliffords, but Stow had no such compelling necessity. Was Stow aware of the play? It does not seem likely that the play was aware of Stow.

From all this, it seems clear that Strange's company had three parts of *Henry VI* in some form in 1591-92, and that at least *2* and *3 Henry VI* as printed in the First Folio give that form approximately. So far, there is no tangible evidence that at this period *1 Henry VI* did not already precede *2* and *3 Henry VI*. When we come to examine the structure of the surviving plays, it will become even more certain that *1 Henry VI* at least approximately in the form we now have it already preceded the other parts in 1591.

When we consider the date of *Richard III*, I believe it is universally admitted that it is later than *3 Henry VI*. The relationship of the two plays would appear to make that certain.[31] Strange's company was still performing the parts of *Henry VI* till they ceased acting June 23, 1592. Strange's were still performing some part or parts of *Henry VI* when next we have record the following December 1592 and January 1593, but there was no sign of a play on *Richard III*. It seems clear, therefore, that if *Richard III* was written for the Strange-Derby-Chamberlain company, as inclusion as Shakspere's in the First Folio indicates, then it was done later than January, 1593. We have seen that it was written before *Lucrece*, S.R. May 9, 1594. Because of its relationship to the *Henry VI* plays, we

---

[30] Boswell-Stone, *Holinshed,* p. 289, n. 2.

[31] See below, pp. 382 ff.

naturally infer that it was written as soon as conditions permitted. The disturbed conditions of the latter part of 1592 evidently had not permitted, and conditions through the summer of 1593 were equally disturbed, affording Shakspere the opportunity or the necessity of writing *Venus and Adonis* before April 18, 1593, and its companion *Lucrece* before May 9, 1594. In fact, there is a passage in *Richard III* which was written between *Venus and Adonis* and *Lucrece*.[32] These various interlocking facts indicate composition between April, 1593, and May, 1594.

Here an anachronism noted by Theobald becomes significant. Stanley is at times given the title of Derby, though Thomas Lord Stanley was not created Earl of Derby till October 27, 1485, after the accession of Henry VII.[33] Wright sums up the facts, "He is called 'Derby' (the word being, of course, variously spelt) throughout the first and second Acts. He is called 'Lord Stanley' for the first time in Act III. Scene 2. In Act III. Scene 4, he is called 'Derby' in the stage directions and 'Stanley' in the text. He is 'Stanley' in Act IV. Scene 1. In Act IV. Scenes 2 and 3 [4], we find in the Folio 'Stanley' both in the stage directions and the text. In the Quarto it is 'Derby' in the stage directions, the name not occurring in the text. In Act IV. Scene 4 [5], he is called 'Derby' in the stage directions. In Act V. Scene 2, Richmond speaks of him as 'my father Stanley,' and in the next scene he is called 'Derby' in the stage directions, and 'Stanley' in the text. The error must have been due to the author, who would not have written 'my lord of Stanley,' and therefore we have retained 'Derby' wherever both Quarto and Folio agree in reading it."[34] Why this "error" on the part of the author of *Richard III*, which, incidentally, does not occur in *The True Tragedie of Richard the third*, where the father is Lord Stanley and the son is George Stanley?

The anachronism is most likely to have been caused by the patron of the company for which *Richard III* was written. This was "Ferdinando Stanley, 2nd s. of Henry, 4th Earl of Derby; *nat. c* 1559; m. Alice, d. of Sir John Spencer of Althorp, 1579; summoned to Parliament as Lord Strange, 28 Jan. 1589; succ. as 5th Earl of Derby, 25 Sept. 1593; *ob.* 16 Apr. 1594."[35] Now one should notice that throughout the play Derby has been given a prominence which he does not have in the chronicles, nor in the *True Tragedie*, where he is not brought in until the chronicle story demands him. I take it that his role has been "fattened" in honor of the patron of the company, and that the inconsistent titles are the result of the conflict between the actual title of the chronicles and the actual title of the patron of the company. If this inference is warranted, then

[32] Baldwin, *Literary Genetics,* pp. 252-253.

[33] Boswell-Stone, *Holinshed,* p. 350, n. 1.

[34] Cambridge Shakespeare (1892), V, 591.

[35] Chambers, *E.S.,* II, 118.

Richard III was written before the death of the patron April 16, 1594. Since the inconsistency is between Stanley and Derby, not between Stanley and Strange, the play was likely composed after Strange succeeded as Earl of Derby September 25, 1593. So *Richard III* was likely written between September 25, 1593, and April 16, 1594. There is evidence, not to be given here, that *Richard III* is earlier than *King John,* and that *King John* is earlier than *Richard II,* which would also place *Richard III* about this date.

If *Richard III* was written between September 25, 1593 and April 16, 1594, this would strengthen a suggestion by Sir Edmund Chambers that *Buckingham* performed by Sussex's men at the Rose between December 30, 1593 and January 27, 1594 is "a title which might fit either *Richard III* or that early version of *Henry VIII,* the existence of which, on internal grounds, I suspect."[36] Under the conditions then existing at the Rose, Sussex's company may as well have acted *Richard III,* as they are said to have acted *Titus Andronicus.* Buckingham was, however, also a character in the Queen's old *True Tragedie of Richard the third,* which could have been in this conglomerated stock at the Rose, though we have no evidence that it was. A much more serious objection is that neither Richard play gives Buckingham sufficient prominence to permit him to steal the title. One would rather expect a *Mirour* play centered upon Buckingham.

Our evidence then indicates that the present three parts of *Henry VI* were put together for Strange's in 1591-92, before the disturbed conditions broke up their acting in London, so that they did not find opportunity to complete the tetralogy with *Richard III* until the autumn of 1593.[37]

---

[36] Chambers, *E.S.,* II, 95, 130, 202, 217.

[37] Having analyzed in detail the relationship of *Richard III,* I, 4 to a passage in *King Leir* (*M.S.R.,* scene xix, lines 1431 ff.), Professor Law concludes, "first, that there is some close connection between the two scenes under discussion; second, that the probability is that Shakespeare is the borrower and not the source; third, that the *Historie of Fryer Bacon* may have served as the inspiration of the *Leir* scene, though this is not established. Whatever the conclusions, the bearing of this matter on the date and even the text of *Richard the Third* is, I think, obvious" (R. A. Law, "Richard III, Act I, scene 4," *P.M.L.A.,* XXVII (1912), p. 141). It would appear that *Leir* was not earlier than 1590. See p. 230, n. 5.

CHAPTER XVII

The Five-Act Structure of the Lancaster-York Tetralogy: The First Part of *King Henry the Sixth*

In the case of the three parts of *Henry VI,* we have frequently failed to see the forest for the trees. Usually, because of prepossessions from *Contention* and *True Tragedie* (York), we have been diverted from looking squarely at this trilogy as it stands in the First Folio. When we do look directly, we may be surprised to find that the architectonics of the plays are much better than we had supposed. They are by no means the inchoate mass, formless and void, which we may have thought them to be. Instead, they show in bulk careful planning. Nor, when once we grasp their plan, are they so focusless in detail. They are far from being mere shapeless chronicles.

In fact, it is doubtful if any of the plays in the First Folio should be called chronicles at all. There is not even much point in calling them history plays.[1] Meres in 1598 classified as tragedies those plays of Shakspere's upon English history which he included in his list. Of these, *Richard II* and *Richard III* had already been printed in 1597 as tragedies. If the first part of *Henry IV* had appeared in print before Meres made his list, it was labeled as history. But since the two parts formed a "life and death," it was also tragedy, as was *John* for the same reason. Meres was, therefore, quite within his rights in classifying all these as tragedies. But in the three parts of *Henry VI* the title role is not sufficiently strong to make the "life and death" theme at all strong, not to mention that there were three parts instead of the conventional two. Of course, if to Meres these three parts of *Henry VI* were neither comedies nor tragedies but *tertium quid,* then naturally he would not include them in his list of comedies and tragedies, and, consequently, his failure to do so could have no bearing on the question of authorship, date, etc.

Since the matter of structure is of vital importance[2] for these three

---

[1] For the background of classification into "history" as a type of play, see M. T. Herrick, *Tragicomedy,* pp. 215 ff. This squinting triple classification of F₁ occasioned the old fallacy of Shakspere's four periods by withdrawing the history plays from the tragedies. Meres in 1598 found that Shakspere had hitherto been equally tragic and comic; and so must we.

[2] My summaries are based upon the Cambridge edition of 1892, unless otherwise stated. I have tried to include every step in the action, quoting the text itself where-

plays of *Henry VI*, we may as well follow the run of them in detail. For
1 Henry VI, I, 1 *"Dead March. Enter the Funeral of* King Henry the
Fifth, *attended on by the* Duke of Bedford, *Regent of France; the* Duke
of Gloucester, *Protector; the* Duke of Exeter, *the* Earl of Warwick, *the*
Bishop of Winchester, Heralds, *&c."* Bedford imprecates the bad revolting stars that have consented unto Henry's death. This suggestion of evil
stars was, of course, a serious one, and would be taken seriously as a
possible explanation. One need only mention here the case of Romeo and
Juliet.[3] Gloucester pronounces a panegyric upon Henry as England's only
king. Exeter then asks why curse the planets of mishap instead of thinking that the subtle-witted French have been conjurers and sorcerers by
their magic verses (cf. Ovid) to contrive Henry's end. This also would
be taken seriously as a possible explanation, and is reflected throughout
the play in the witch Joan of Arc. The Bishop of Winchester says that
Henry fought the battles of the Lord of hosts and hence was more dread-
ful to the French than will be the judgment day; the church's prayers
made him so prosperous. That the Lord of hosts had been with Henry
would, of course, be accepted; but that the prayers of the Roman Catholic
church had been the efficient cause was another matter. So Gloucester
scoffs that the church (in the person of Winchester) likes none but an
effeminate prince whom like a schoolboy it may over-awe. Winchester
answers that Gloucester is protector and looks "to command the prince
and realm," but that his proud wife keeps him more in awe than God or
religious churchmen may. Gloucester replies that Winchester loves the
flesh and goes to church only to pray against his foes. Bedford calls for
peace.

> Cease, cease these jars and rest your minds in peace
>
> . . . .
>
> Henry the Fifth, thy ghost I invoke:
> Prosper this realm, keep it from civil broils,
> Combat with adverse planets in the heavens!
> A far more glorious star thy soul will make
> Than Julius Caesar or bright —

---

ever it seemed pertinent to do so. I have found this procedure necessary for myself
in order to be certain I had the evidence before me. If the reader wishes, he may
skip each time to the conclusions and check the evidence in case of disagreement. In
Appendix II, I have omitted detail from my summaries of other authors, since little
depended upon it.

[3] In the *Mirour,* Henry VI laments

> Alas what should we count the cause of Wretches cares,
> The Starres do stirre them vp, Astronomy declares:
> Our humours sayth the Leach, the double true deuines
> Toth' will of God, or ill of man, the doubtfull cause assignes.
>
> *(Mirour,* 1578, f. 90[r])

In the play, the Leach is omitted; but the stars, which can be affected by witchcraft,
and God, with the ill of man, are retained. *Mirour* and play have the same world-view.

Here Bedford refers again to the supposed power of the stars to control one's destiny, and prays that Henry's soul will, like that of Julius Caesar (cf. Ovid), become a star to combat planets adverse to England, which are stirring such civil broils as have just been sketched between the Protector Gloucester and the Bishop of Winchester, each of whom hopes to control the boy-king, Henry VI.

With the explosive and disruptive situation in England thus clearly and expeditiously sketched, we turn to news from France. A Messenger announces

> Guienne, Champagne, Rheims, Orleans,
> Paris, Guysors, Poictiers, are all quite lost.

These were lost through "No treachery; but want of men and money." So the soldiers mutter

> That here you maintain several factions
>
> . . . .
>
> Awake, awake, English nobility!
>
> . . . .
>
> Of England's coat one half is cut away.

Bedford, Regent of France, calls for his steeled coat, as a second Messenger enters to announce that

> France is revolted from the English quite,
> Except some petty towns of no import:
> The Dauphin Charles is crowned king in Rheims;
> The Bastard of Orleans with him is join'd;
> Reignier, Duke of Anjou, doth take his part,
> The Duke of Alençon flieth to his side.

Gloucester and Bedford resolve to fight. A third Messenger enters to tell how Lord Talbot with scarce six thousand troops has been overthrown by the French with twenty-three thousand. Even so, Talbot was winning when Sir John Falstaff[4] played the coward and ran away. Talbot was wounded basely in the back and taken prisoner; most of the others killed or taken prisoners. Bedford will take an army to France immediately to ransom and avenge. The Messenger says Salisbury at Orleans is also hard pressed. Exeter reminds the lords of their oaths sworn to Henry

> Either to quell the Dauphin utterly,
> Or bring him in obedience to your yoke.

Bedford goes to prepare an army; Gloucester goes to view the artillery and munitions at the tower, then to "proclaim young Henry king";

---

[4] He is always Falstaff here, as Professor J. Dover Wilson has emphasized, and as elsewhere in Shakspere, never Fastolfe, this latter being Theobald's "correction" to agree with the chronicles.

Exeter, as governor of the Prince, will devise for his safety. Winchester says

> Each hath his place and function to attend;
> I am left out; for me nothing remains.
> But long I will not be Jack out of office:
> The king from Eltham I intend to steal
> And sit at chiefest stern of public weal.

The first scene has thus shown the situation from the English view, expeditiously sketching the factions involved and predicting future objectives. The man who planned and executed this scene was at least a deft workman.

I, 2. We now go directly to France. *"Enter* Charles, Alençon, *and* Reignier," before Orleans. Charles remarks that the English formerly were victorious, now the French. Reignier says Talbot is taken and none remains but mad-brained Salisbury. In the assault upon Orleans, they are beaten back by Salisbury, and have about decided to let the famished English alone. The Bastard of Orleans enters to tell Charles of a holy maid

> Which by a vision sent to her from heaven
> Ordained is to raise this tedious siege,
> And drive the English forth the bounds of France.

Reignier and Charles exchange places to test the skill of the maid, but she rejects Regnier and detects your true Dauphin at once. She then tells Charles in private of her vision and mission to free France. Charles says that if Joan overcomes him in single combat he will receive her, which she does. Charles professes love, but Joan must first complete her mission

> I must not yield to any rites of love,
> For my profession's sacred from above:
> When I have chased all thy foes from hence,
> Then will I think upon a recompense.

To give this statement emphasis, the author put it into rhyme. He wanted the audience to be impressed with it. The bawdily jesting lords reenter, and Joan says Orleans is to be taken. She will raise the siege that night.

Having thus developed with equal expedition the situation in France, the dramatist returns us to England. I, 3. Gloucester, the Protector, appears to survey the Tower, as he said he would at the end of the first scene; but is refused admittance, since Winchester[5] has forbidden it. As Gloucester's men threaten to break in, Winchester enters with his men. Gloucester and Winchester quarrel, and Winchester's men are beaten out. The Mayor of London enters with his officers. Gloucester accuses Winchester of having "distrain'd the Tower to his use," and Winchester in turn accuses Gloucester of attempting to get armor from the Tower "To

---

[5] Winchester is "in thy broad cardinal's hat," "scarlet robes," "cardinal's hat," and is a "scarlet hypocrite."

crown himself king and suppress the prince," whereupon they fight again. The Mayor proclaims that no one may wear arms on pain of death. Gloucester will obey the law but he and Winchester "will meet." Winchester says

> Abominable Gloucester, guard thy head;
> For I intend to have it ere long.   *Exeunt.*

Having exhibited the open feud of Gloucester and Winchester in England, the dramatist returns to France. I, 4. A Master Gunner and his Boy enter on the walls of Orleans. The Chief Master Gunner has been watching three days to get a shot at the English when they use a certain tower to spy upon the town. As he goes out, leaving the Boy to watch, who steps aside, Salisbury, Talbot, Glansdale, Gargrave, and others enter on the turrets. Talbot tells Salisbury how he was exchanged, and imprecates the cowardice of Falstaff, who betrayed him. The French were ludicrously afraid of him. The Boy enters with a linstock to watch, and Salisbury steps to the grate to view the town. As the lords discuss modes of attack, the Boy shoots and Salisbury and Gargrave fall. Talbot vows to avenge them. A Messenger enters to announce that the Dauphin and Joan, "A holy prophetess new risen up," are come with a great power to raise the siege. Talbot will "try what these dastard Frenchmen dare."

I, 5. Talbot pursues the Dauphin; Joan pursues the English. Talbot enters and fights with Joan ("thou art a witch"), but she finally withdraws to enter Orleans. Talbot says

> A witch, by fear, not force, like Hannibal,
> Drives back our troops and conquers as she lists.

He cannot rally the English forces, who retire to their trenches, leaving him in shame.

I, 6. Joan has performed her promise by rescuing Orleans from the English, and all France will rejoice. Charles says

> 'Tis Joan, not we, by whom the day is won;
> For which I will divide my crown with her

and will see that various other things shall be done in her honor.

In this first act, the dramatist has consciously contrasted the English and the French. The English had been successful under Henry V, but now the faction at home between Gloucester and Winchester leaves Talbot and Salisbury (each gets the spotlight in turn) impotent in France. The French had been unsuccessful, but now are leagued together, and under the leadership of Joan have won Orleans as a first success. The structure is, consequently, balanced to bring out these contrasts, and this necessary business has been expeditiously executed. Few first acts of the date have been so clearly planned and so deftly executed.

II, 1. The French set their guard before Orleans. "*Enter* Talbot, Bedford, Burgundy, *and forces,*" prepared to scale the walls, now that the French have caroused and banqueted all day. Talbot says the French victory was "Contrived by art and baleful sorcery"; Bedford says Charles has joined "with witches and the help of hell"; but Talbot concludes

> Well, let them practice and converse with spirits:
> God is our fortress, in whose conquering name
> Let us resolve to scale their flinty bulwarks.

Bedford, Burgundy, and Talbot attack at separate spots. The alarm. The Bastard, Alençon, and Reignier enter unready and thinking "this Talbot be a fiend of hell." Charles enters, amid insinuations aside, scolding Joan and everybody else. All flee to lay other plans.

II, 2. Talbot, Bedford, and Burgundy enter within the town. Talbot has kept his vow and will bury Salisbury in the chiefest temple of the city. Burgundy says he

> scared the Dauphin and his trull,
> When arm in arm they both came swiftly running,
> Like to a pair of loving turtle-doves
> That could not live asunder day or night.

The Countess of Auvergne sends a messenger to invite Talbot to visit her. Talbot accepts but whispers directions to a captain as he goes.

II, 3. The Countess of Auvergne attempts to entrap Talbot, but his men come to the rescue.

II, 4. In London, the Temple-garden, *"Enter the* Earls of Somerset, Suffolk, *and* Warwick; Richard Plantagenet, Vernon, *and another* Lawyer." Plantagenet and Somerset seek judgment between them,[6] but Suffolk and Warwick disclaim competence in the law. Plantagenet asks that each one who thinks he has pleaded truth pluck a white rose. Somerset asks his sympathizers to pluck red roses. Warwick plucks white, Suffolk red. Vernon wishes them to agree that fewest roses means yielding the point, to which Plantagenet and Somerset agree. Vernon plucks a white rose, a Lawyer plucks another, deciding the question (whatever it was) against Somerset. The quarrel continues, in which Plantagenet is taunted as a yeoman through tainture of his father Richard Earl of Cambridge, though

---

[6] The fundamental quarrel and its consequences are emphasized in Halle and Holinshed, of course. "Although the duke of Yorke was worthie (both for birth and courage) of this honor and preferment [regent in France], yet so disdeined of Edmund duke of Summerset being cousine to the king, that by all means possible he sought his hinderance, as one glad of his losse, and sorie of his well dooing. . . . The duke of Yorke perceiuing his euill will, openlie dissembled that which he inwardlie minded, either of them working things to the others displeasure, till through malice & diuision betweene them, at length by mortall warre they were both consumed, with almost all their whole lines and ofspring" (Holinshed (1587), III, 612, 625, 630; Halle, *Vnion* (1548), Henry VI, f 129ᵛ).

His grandfather was Lionel Duke of Clarence,
Third son to the third Edward King of England.

Somerset and Suffolk leave, vowing vengeance on Plantagenet. Warwick promises in the next parliament to wipe out all blots against Plantagenet and to have him created Duke of York.

And here I prophesy: this brawl to-day,
Grown to this faction in the Temple-garden,
Shall send between the red rose and the white
A thousand souls to death and deadly night.

Says Plantagenet

I dare say
This quarrel will drink blood another day.

II, 5. Broken Edmund Mortimer in prison has sent for his nephew Richard Plantagenet, who is equally wronged with himself, he having been sequestered by Henry of Monmouth, while Plantagenet was deprived of honor and inheritance. Plantagenet enters and tells his uncle Mortimer that Somerset has just taunted him with the ignoble death of his father, Earl of Cambridge. Mortimer explains the reason

Henry the Fourth, grandfather to this king,
Deposed his nephew Richard, Edward's son,
The first-begotten and the lawful heir
Of Edward king, the third of that descent:
During whose reign the Percies of the north,
Finding his usurpation most unjust,
Endeavour'd my advancement to the throne:
The reason moved these warlike lords to this
Was, for that — young King Richard thus removed,
Leaving no heir begotten of his body —
I was the next by birth and parentage;
For by my mother I derived am
From Lionel Duke of Clarence, the third son
To King Edward the Third; whereas he
From John of Gaunt doth bring his pedigree,
Being but fourth of that heroic line.
But mark: as in this haughty great attempt
They laboured to plant the rightful heir,
I lost my liberty and they their lives.
Long after this, when Henry the Fifth,
Succeeding his father Bolingbroke, did reign,
Thy father, Earl of Cambridge, then derived
From famous Edmund Langley, Duke of York,
Marrying my sister that thy mother was,
Again in pity of my hard distress
Levied an army, weening to redeem
And have install'd me in the diadem:
But, as the rest, so fell that noble earl
And was beheaded. Thus the Mortimers,
In whom the title rested, were suppress'd.

Mortimer has no child, but Plantagenet is his heir. Mortimer dies and Plantagenet concludes

> And for those wrongs, those bitter injuries,
> Which Somerset hath offer'd to my house,
> I doubt not but with honour to redress;
> And therefore haste I to the parliament,
> Either to be restored to my blood,
> Or make my ill the advantage of my good.

In this second act, the dramatist has again balanced France and England. He continues with France from the first act, so as not to change his scene and because his crucial resolution for the end of the second act must be in England. In France, Talbot turns the tables on Joan and has an adventure for mere interest, with the Countess of Auvergne. The dramatist then turns to England to prepare for the origins of the wars of the roses, which are to form the backbone, not only of *1 Henry VI* but also of the other plays of the sequence. This origin is thus the thing toward which the protasis tends, and must come at the end of the second act. The rose quarrel in the Temple-garden finds its explanation in Mortimer's unriddling of the rival claims to the throne. Plantagenet at the end of the act becomes the rival claimant for the throne, and plans are afoot to restore him to his blood, which will be a first overt step, and so cannot occur before the third act. If one fixes his attention upon the dramatist's objective, it is hard to see how he could have reached it more expeditiously. Nor should we quarrel with him because he has not reached some objective which we would set. He has prepared the protasis, not only of *1 Henry VI,* but also of *2* and *3 Henry VI,* as well as in a way of *Richard III.* It is the protasis of one play indeed, but also of a tetralogy.

III, 1. As parliament assembles, Winchester and Gloucester continue their quarrel. Gloucester intimates treason:

> I fear me, if thy thoughts were sifted,
> The king, thy sovereign, is not quite exempt
> From envious malice of thy swelling heart.

Winchester retorts that Gloucester wishes to rule the king alone. Gloucester calls Winchester "bastard of my grandfather" and is called by him "one imperious in another's throne." When Winchester threatens "Rome shall remedy this," Warwick intervenes with "Roam thither, then," and Somerset sides with Winchester. Plantagenet, his foe, would naturally like a fling at Winchester but decides it is best to keep quiet. The two sets of factions — Gloucester-Winchester, Plantagenet-Somerset — are here aligned with each other. The King wishes to reconcile his "Uncles of Gloucester and of Winchester." There is an uproar and the Mayor enters to complain of the broils between Winchester's and Gloucester's men, which are exhibited. At the King's request, Winchester and Gloucester pretend to be reconciled, but in asides tell us that they mean it not. Warwick then presents a scroll for Richard Plantagenet, which Gloucester favors with the King, who directs that "Richard be restored to his blood." For once, Winchester concurs. The King creates Plantagenet Duke of York, as Somerset aside curses his foe. Gloucester suggests that the King should now be crowned in France. Exeter remains to sum up the true situation.

> This late dissension grown betwixt the peers
> Burns under feigned ashes of forged love,
> And will at last break out into a flame:
>
> . . . .
>
> And now I fear that fatal prophecy
> Which in the time of Henry named the fifth
> Was in the mouth of every sucking babe;
> That Henry born at Monmouth should win all
> And Henry born at Windsor lose all:
> Which is so plain, that Exeter doth wish
> His days may finish ere that hapless time.

The factions are lining up, and Plantagenet has taken his first step toward the throne.

III, 2. Joan gets her soldiers into Rouen as market men, who open the way for the French forces. Talbot says

> Pucelle, that witch, that damned sorceress,
> Hath wrought this hellish mischief unawares,
> That hardly we escaped the pride of France.

The two sides taunt each other. Talbot says to Joan, who has taunted Bedford

> Foul fiend of France, and hag of all despite,
> Encompass'd with thy lustful paramours!
> Becomes it thee to taunt his valiant age,
> And twit with cowardice a man half dead?
> Damsel, I'll have a bout with you again,
> Or else let Talbot perish with this shame.

Talbot challenges the French to the field, and when they refuse, vows with Burgundy to take the town or die, with the dying Bedford looking on. Falstaff is exhibited flying again. As the French flee, Bedford dies in peace. Talbot rejoices that the town is taken and will to Paris to the King, as soon as he has given burial to Bedford.

III, 3. *"Enter* Charles, *the* Bastard *of Orleans,* Alencon, La Pucelle." Joan says

> Let frantic Talbot triumph for a while
> And like a peacock sweep along his tail;
> We'll pull his plumes and take away his train,
> If Dauphin and the rest will be but ruled.

All agree. Joan says

> By fair persuasions mix'd with sugar'd words
> We will entice the Duke of Burgundy
> To leave the Talbot and to follow us.

Charles thinks

> if we could do that,
> France were no place for Henry's warriors;
> Nor should that nation boast it so with us,
> But be extirped from our provinces.

Talbot passes by on his way to Paris, but Burgundy lags behind and is summoned to a parley. Joan exhorts him to look with pity on his native France, especially since the English are only using him as a tool and will thrust him out like a fugitive as soon as Henry is established. They have already slighted him by freeing his enemy the Duke of Orleans even without ransom. Burgundy decides to forsake Talbot and join the French. Says Joan aside, completely out of character one would think, "Done like a Frenchman: turn, and turn again!"

III, 4. Talbot at Paris pays homage to the King, who creates him Earl of Shrewsbury. After the others exeunt, Vernon and Basset continue the quarrel of the white rose and the red. The audience is not to be permitted to forget it.

In the third act, the dramatist has again balanced England against France. He continues in England from the end of the second act, but also to bring the beginning of the epitasis properly at the first of the third act, as Plantagenet takes his first step toward the throne by being created Duke of York, and as the factions align with and against him. In France, Joan wins Rouen, though Talbot immediately regains it. But Joan wins Burgundy from Talbot to her side, and it is prophesied that this will force the English from France. This shift is thus the beginning of the end so far as France is concerned, and consequently comes as the chief point of the third act. The King, who has come to Paris, creates Talbot Earl of Shrewsbury, as the English factions continue for and against York. So Joan and Talbot each takes a balanced step at the end of the third act, though that of Talbot is purely personal. Thus the third act begins a double epitasis, for Plantagenet in the tetralogy; for Joan and Talbot, that is, for France and England, in the struggle for France of Part I.

IV, 1. King Henry the Sixth is crowned at Paris, and the Governor of Paris is sworn to obey him alone. Sir John Falstaff enters with a letter from the Duke of Burgundy — a fit messenger! Talbot tears the garter from Falstaff's craven leg because at the battle of Patay he ran away. In fact, he had run away twice, once by report, at Patay, and once by presentation, in a fictitious engagement. The King banishes Falstaff on pain of death. Burgundy's letter proclaims his change of side. The King says Talbot shall give Burgundy chastisement for this abuse, a task which Talbot accepts gladly and exits to perform. Vernon and Basset bring their quarrel of the end of the preceding act to the King, demanding combat, as York and Somerset each acknowledges and supports his servant. Vernon had said that Basset's red rose represented the blushing cheeks of Somerset about the argument in law with the Duke of York. Vernon claims that Basset had first said that his pale rose bewrayed the faintness of York's heart. York and Somerset show their antipathy to each other. The King begs

> Good cousins both, of York and Somerset,
> Quiet yourselves, I pray, and be at peace.

They ask the combat, but their servants wish the quarrel to remain with them, where it began. Gloucester rebukes them all for disturbing the King and kingdom with their factions. The King commands them to forget their quarrel and to remember that any show in France of dissension encourages rebellion

> let us not forgo
> That for a trifle that was bought with blood.

He himself puts on a red rose but not to show favor to Somerset. He institutes York to be regent in these parts of France, and commands Somerset to aid him. One should know what to expect of this wise coupling of fighting cats. Henry himself will return to Calais and England. As the others exeunt, Warwick things the King did well, but York does not like the fact that Henry wore Somerset's red rose. Exeter remains as a kind of chorus again to voice his fears for England. Of York he says

> had the passions of thy heart burst out,
> I fear we should have seen decipher'd there
> More rancorous spite, more furious raging broils,
> Than yet can be imagined or supposed.

Every simple man knows that this jarring discord of nobility doth presage some ill event.

> 'Tis much when sceptres are in children's hands:
> But more when envy breeds unkind division;
> There comes the ruin, there begins confusion.

The Biblical[7] authority, of course, gives certainty to his warning.

IV, 2. Talbot commands the General of Bordeaux to yield the town. The General says Talbot is surrounded and has not an hour to live. Says Talbot

> Sell every man his life as dear as mine,
> And they shall find dear deer of us, my friends.

---

[7] Ecclesiastes, 10, 16.

IV, 3. York hears that three French armies are closing in on Talbot at Bordeaux and says

> A plague upon that villain Somerset,
> That thus delays my promised supply
> Of horsemen, that were levied for this siege!

Sir William Lucy calls for aid to Talbot and his son, but York cannot aid because of the failure of Somerset. Says Lucy

> Thus, while the vulture of sedition
> Feeds in the bosom of such great commanders,
> Sleeping neglection doth betray to loss
> The conquest of our scarce cold conqueror,
> That ever living man of memory,
> Henry the Fifth: whiles they each other cross,
> Lives, honours, lands and all hurry to loss.

The seditious division between Somerset and York, the representatives of the roses, must cause the loss of France, which Henry V had won.

IV, 4. Somerset tells a captain of Talbot's that he cannot aid.

> the over-daring Talbot
> Hath sullied all his gloss of former honour
> By this unheedful, desperate, wild adventure:
> York set him on to fight and die in shame,
> That, Talbot dead, great York might bear the name.

Sir William Lucy enters to lament that Somerset and York are betraying Talbot to death. Somerset says

> York set him on; York should have sent him aid.

Lucy pronounces

> The fraud of England, not the force of France
> Hath now entrapp'd the noble-minded Talbot:
> Never to England shall he bear his life;
> But dies, betray'd to fortune by your strife.

Somerset will have horsemen to Talbot's aid in six hours, but Lucy says it is now too late, "His fame lives in the world, his shame in you."

IV, 5. Talbot urges his son John to escape by flight, who in turn entreats his father, but they bid each other farewell as they exeunt together to battle.

IV, 6. Talbot rescues John, relates their great deeds, and again asks him to fly, but he refuses and again they exeunt to battle.

IV, 7. Talbot relates the death of his son. He clasps the body of his son in his arms and dies.

The fourth act has now worked up to the brink of the catastrophe. Charles is to point out at the beginning of the fifth act that "All will be ours, now bloody Talbot's slain." And Talbot had been slain, as Lucy[8] is caused to emphasize, because of the quarrel of York and Somerset, the representatives of the roses, which in the first part of the act Henry VI had tried to heal. The defection of Burgundy in the third act and the dissensions of York and Somerset in the fourth have necessitated the coming catastrophe of the fifth, which is assured by the death of Talbot, which is thus the end of the fourth.

We must now pause to notice, however, that the First Folio does not place the act-division here, though it has marked all acts of *1 Henry VI* except this, and even attempts to mark that. Here the final scene of the play is headed simply "Actus Quintus," without the addition of "Scena Prima" as in the preceding acts, this latter being a normal form of statement in the First Folio. It does not seem probable that any of the scenes of Acts IV and V can have been transposed from their present position. If there has been no omission, then the situation would appear to be clear. The fourth act would end properly with the death of Talbot. There would next have been a new scene V, 1, with the entry of the French to discover the bodies, since the victory of France is the catastrophe, and the death of Talbot the occasion of it. Therefore, the death of Talbot, according to the formula belongs to the end of the fourth act, the victory of France to the beginning of the fifth. So the Second Folio is unquestionably correct in placing "Actus Quintus. Scaena Prima" after the death of Talbot and in omitting the "Actus Quintus" of the First Folio at V, 5, of modern editions. It will be seen that the error was a purely mechanical one. Since according to the First Folio, there is only one scene in what modern editions consider to be the fourth act, omission of the heading for V, 1, caused scenes two and three of the fifth act to come in proper sequence with the one scene of the fourth act, thus concealing any sign of displacement.

---

[8] Notice the "structural" prominence given to Sir William Lucy, who is in fact an interloper. In the thirty-eighth year of Henry VI, various men "departed from London, toward the kyng, lyeng at Couentre." In a battle near Northampton July 9, 1460, "were slayn, Humfrey duke of Buckyngham, Jhon Talbot erle of Shrewsbury, a valeant person, and not degenerating frō his noble parent: Thomas lord Egremond, Jhon viscont Beaumond, and syr William Lucy, which made great hast to come to parte of the fight, and at his first approche was strikē in the hed w^t an axe" (Halle, *Vnion* (1548), Henry VI, f clxxvi^v; Holinshed (1587), p. 654). So through this son John Talbot, second son by the first marriage, not the son John by the second marriage, who gets killed with his father in 1453, this ardent Sir William gets attached to the major Talbot incident. He is not Sir William of Charlecote indeed, and actually he is not killed with the right John, nor apparently killed at all; but the mention of Coventry and Sir William Lucy in connection with the death of John Talbot, worthy son of the great Talbot, would suggest a bit of local patriotism. At any rate, the dramatist certainly was not prejudiced against the name of Lucy. It would seem clear that Shakspere, even if he were only toucher-up of the play, had not yet heard that the Lucy family had chased him out of Stratford for stealing the deer which it did not have.

After the Second Folio made the proper correction, all was well enough till Capell considered that the stage was not clear at this point and so removed the heading of V, 1, to its present position, thus attaching the scene with the French to the Talbot scene as in modern editions. But one should remember here the now famous case in *Midsummer-Night's Dream,* where "They sleepe all the Act."[9] Dead bodies would also stay put till called for. It is thus clear that according to the conventions of Shakspere's day the Second Folio made the proper correction and that Capell's further adjustment is without authority.

The fact, however, that in the First Folio only the final scene is set off as "Actus Quintus," without scene, and not as the fourth scene, as one would have expected, might be due to another entirely mechanical accident. This scene of 108 lines is almost certain to have been a single leaf. If it was marked for attachment to the fifth act, it may by consequent accident have become the fifth act. This final scene might thus be suspected of being a revised ending to the play. But however this division between the fourth and fifth acts came to exist in the First Folio, yet modern editors from the Second Folio have been agreed that it is wrong. I believe it is clear that the modern editors since Capell are wrong only to the extent of failing to mark the latter part of their IV, 7, as V, 1, and the remaining scenes in sequence. I continue my summary in accordance with this conclusion.

[V, 1] The French enter saying

> Had York and Somerset brought rescue in,
> We should have found a bloody day of this.

They discover the dead Talbots. Lucy enters to learn from the French what persons have been taken prisoners and what persons killed. He demands the bodies of the Talbots for burial, which are insultingly granted.

> I'll bear them hence; but from their ashes shall be rear'd
> A phoenix that shall make all France afeard.

Says Charles

> And now to Paris, in this conquering vein;
> All will be ours, now bloody Talbot's slain.

It is thus made clear in balanced form and prophecy that the French are to have the present victory, but that the English are some day to "make all France afeard" — probably a reference to the English army in France in the early 'nineties. Here we have the proper topic-sentence beginning of the catastrophe which is to be developed in the fifth act.

---

[9] Compare *King John* also, where modern editors have wrongly revised the division between the second and third acts as given in the First Folio, exactly as here.

[V, 2] V, 1. Henry VI is told that the pope, emperor, and Earl of Armagnac have sent letters in which

> They humbly sue unto your excellence
> To have a godly peace concluded of
> Between the realms of England and of France.

Gloucester favors peace and says the Earl of Armagnac has offered his daughter in marriage to Henry, who will abide Gloucester's decision. Gloucester will accept the offer but Winchester says aside

> I'll either make thee stoop and bend thy knee,
> Or sack this country with a mutiny.

[V, 3] V, 2. The French hear that the Parisians are turning from the English, but that the English army is now one.

[V, 4] V, 3. Before Angiers, Joan says the regent conquers, and calls up her fiends for aid; but she can no longer bribe them with blood, body, or soul and all.

> My ancient incantations are too weak,
> And hell too strong for me to buckle with;
> Now, France, thy glory droopeth to the dust.

York captures Joan.

> Curse, miscreant, when thou comest to the stake.

Suffolk enters with Margaret, daughter of the King of Naples, as prisoner. He is smitten with her beauty and decides to win her for his king, though the English nobles are certain to object to the poverty of the match. Margaret is willing if her father be. Her father, Reignier, consents if he may quietly enjoy his own, Maine and Anjou. Suffolk will take the bargain to Henry. Suffolk is thus to offer his bargain of beauty to Henry as a substitute for Gloucester's; the daughter of Reignier instead of the daughter of the Earl of Armagnac.

[V, 5] V, 4. Joan, condemned to burn as a sorceress, scorns her father as "no father nor no friend of mine," claiming noble birth. Her father disowns her. York orders her burned but she claims inspiration of divine grace. She next claims to be with child by various French nobles. She is led out cursing. Cardinal Beaufort, Bishop of Winchester, enters to announce a parley for peace. York says to Warwick

> I foresee with grief
> The utter loss of all the realm of France

The Cardinal tells Charles that Henry says

> upon condition thou wilt swear
> To pay him tribute, and submit thyself,
> Thou shalt be placed as viceroy under him,
> And still enjoy thy regal dignity.

Charles at first objects to the terms, but Reignier and Alençon advise him
to accept, the latter saying

> And therefore take this compact of a truce,
> Although you break it when your pleasure serves.

Someone by or before 1623 accepted this as the end of the fourth act.
Part of his reason, if he had any, may have been that we now have a Joan
for a Talbot. But while the two are in fact balanced, yet they are only
pawns in the main structure of the play. Neither death is presented as
having effect actually on the end of the play. The catastrophe has been
arranged fully before the death of Joan, and her fate has no bearing
upon it one way or another.

[V, 6] V, 5. Suffolk has fired King Henry with desire of Margaret.
Gloucester says it is a sin for him to consent, since Henry is already
betrothed to another; but Suffolk overpersuades. Suffolk says

> Margaret shall now be queen, and rule the king;
> But I will rule both her, the king and realm.

Suffolk has won from Gloucester and continued contentions are thereby
assured.

The dramatist has thus developed his theme that through faction the
English lost France. As Boswell-Stone points out,[10] this suggestion of
factionalism is in Halle and Holinshed, but it is the author of *1 Henry VI*
who has developed the suggestion into the whole cause and motive force
for his play. The first act presents the developing cooperation of the
French under Joan of Arc, with the result that the French win their first
success. Here material from the chronicles has been freely rearranged,
supplemented, and oriented to bring out the main theme.

In the second act, after Talbot has given Joan a Roland for her Oliver,
the quarrel of Plantagenet and Somerset is developed, forecasting the
wars of the roses. Most of the material is fictional, especially that which
surrounds the quarrel of the roses. Here the formula of construction
called upon the author to make clear the objectives of the protasis to this
play, and in this case to his tetralogy also. Consequently, he was obliged
to invent most of his material in order to point properly his story. He
docs so, however, in accord with the spirit of the chronicles.

In the third act, Plantagenet becomes Duke of York and the earlier
factions are merged into the quarrel of York and Somerset, which is to

---

[10] Boswell-Stone, *Holinshed,* p. 206. The reader will find in this, the standard
work, detailed presentation of the historical facts. It has been argued, however, that
Boswell-Stone does not give sufficient weight to Halle (Edleen Begg, "Shakespeare's
Debt to Hall and to Holinshed in *Richard III,*" *S.P.* (1935), XXXII, 189 ff.;
W. Gordon Zeeveld, "The Influence of Hall on Shakespeare's English Historical
Plays," *E.L.H.* (1936), III, 317 ff.). In his edition, Professor J. Dover Wilson gives
a convenient summary of the "Material" for each scene.

be the final and overt cause of the losses in France. In France, Talbot and Joan give tit for tat, but Joan wins Burgundy over to the French side, which is the first of the crucial losses, while Talbot merely gets an earldom. Again the chronicle situations have been very freely interpreted.

In the fourth act, the losses in France are continued and made conclusive by the death of Talbot for lack of support from York and Somerset. The author has freely rearranged main events, and has invented details to point his story.

The fifth act patches up a peace which is in fact a victory for the French, and incidentally disposes of Joan also. Basic materials are to be found in the chronicles, but they have been very freely adapted to the purposes of the play.

It will now be seen that the fundamental structure of *1 Henry VI,* into which the facts are fitted, is derived directly from the historical sources. Halle and Holinshed had placarded Henry's decision to restore Plantagenet in blood as cardinal, he "not foreseeing that this preferment should be his destruction, nor that his seed should of his generation be the extreame end and finall conclusion."[11] This is the epitatical action which leads on not only through *1 Henry VI* but also to and through the remaining three plays of the tetralogy. Consequently, the author places it at its proper place, in the beginning of the third act. The decision which necessitates it must be made in the second act, hence the latter part of that act is spent in explicating the background to the origins of the wars of the roses, which occasion the crucial action in the third act. This beginning of the wars of the roses is the thing toward which the protasis tends in the first two acts, and we have seen how carefully the author works out the various factional steps leading up to it. In the third act, the faction of Gloucester and Winchester is aligned with what is to become the chief factional focus, the wars of the roses. That there may be no mistaking the significance of what has happened, Exeter is caused to point out the true situation and to warn of the prophecy that Henry VI is to lose all. The objective of the third act then becomes Burgundy's defection, which is labeled as the move which will drive the English out of France. The fourth act has as its objective the death of Talbot, which occasions the catastrophe of a real victory for the French in the fifth act, as is specifically pointed out.

Thus the author has plotted *1 Henry VI* carefully and consistently upon the idea or ideas which he has taken from the sources, and he has freely rearranged and supplemented historical facts from these sources to serve these ideas. This fundamental plan, therefore, evidently belongs to the original play. And *1 Henry VI* was certainly planned as a unit on

---

[11] Boswell-Stone, *Holinshed,* p. 223.

its own; it is not merely a haphazardly agglomerated "lean to" or portico. If there are inconsistencies, they are of detail, not of fundamental plan.

For what it is, a political moral, the plot is well constructed, even though we probably do not wish what it is. Talbot and Joan are forced to fit into the framework of this political moral, instead of being permitted to occupy the center of the story, as we probably wish; and even the dash of would-be romance at the end merely illustrates factionalism. Not even the champion of the Lord of hosts, Talbot, can withstand factionalism — though, of course, that emissary of the devil, "that witch, that damned sorceress" Joan, must get her just deserts!

For our present purposes, it is beside the point to ask whether the result is a good or a bad play. "There is nothing either good or bad, but thinking makes it so." "If she be not so to me, / What care I how fair she be?" Objective means are dependent on subjective effect. Here one objective means, structure, has been carefully attended to. Such a means is supposed to be an important part of procuring an effect. That *1 Henry VI* did procure an effect we have the word of Nashe. But it would appear that it was Talbot who "made" the play for the contemporary audience. It was, however, a Talbot who was losing his life and France because of the factionalism the play was constructed to warn against. Doubtless this careful construction did play its part in procuring this effect, whether it has the same effect on us or not. At any rate, the careful construction is there and should never again be overlooked in evaluating the play.

CHAPTER XVIII

The Second Part of *King Henry the Sixth*

The act divisions[1] have not been marked for *2* and *3 Henry VI* in the First Folio, but the only place where doubt has been recorded, according to the Cambridge Shakespeare (Wright), among modern editors has been concerning one scene as between the fourth or the fifth act in *2 Henry VI,* the same kind of problem we have found in *1 Henry VI.* Analysis in the light of the five-act formula confirms these divisions and seems conclusive in the one case of doubt. I shall, therefore, proceed on the basis of the accepted divisions.

I, 1. Suffolk reports to Henry VI and his assembled court that he has married Princess Margaret by proxy and now presents her to the King. Henry salutes her as queen and the lords acknowledge her. Suffolk then

---

[1] The sixteen plays printed in more or less "good" quartos before the First Folio are not in the quartos divided into acts. But all these except *Romeo and Juliet, Hamlet,* and *Troilus and Cressida* — if these be "good" quartos — are divided into acts in the First Folio. Of the thirty-six plays in the First Folio, twenty-nine are divided into acts, though with occasional errors, six are marked as to act one only, one as to acts one and two. All comedies are in acts, and all histories except *2* and *3 Henry VI* (preceded by "bad" quartos). But of the tragedies *Troilus and Cressida, Romeo and Juliet, Timon of Athens,* and *Antony and Cleopatra* mark only the first act, *Hamlet* marks acts one and two. Similarly, when Sir Walter Greg sums up the characteristics of fifteen manuscripts which he considers to be "prompt books," he finds twelve divided into acts, and but three wholly undivided (Greg, *Dramatic Documents,* p. 210). Thus this type of stage manuscript almost universally preserves the acts. Necessarily, however, it was the author who wrote the plays in these units which are labeled acts — and as he composed was regularly paid in instalments proportionate to the acts he handed in. There can be no question that Shakspere wrote his plays in units, which the First Folio has attempted to label as acts. These units are discriminated in accordance with the five-act formula, and except for a few evident errors, are labeled accordingly.

These act-divisions, therefore, were made in manuscript, at whatever time and by whomever they were made. If they are free editorial insertions for the First Folio, the editor did not work consistently, and found most difficulty with the irregular plays. This situation is more likely to mean that in these cases he had no manuscript with authentic divisions to guide him, and that he did not on his own insert divisions — later editors have not been so deterred. Life-long actors in these plays, as were Heminges and Cundall, could readily have pointed out the proper divisions, if they had been editing or had been asked by an editor. If the author's manuscript survived for any play, it should have had the act-divisions in some way indicated. These act-divisions are likely to mean, therefore, that for the plays which include them the author's own manuscript, or a fairly close copy thereof was available, at least for consultation.

presents the articles of peace to Gloucester, the Protector. The articles of peace for eighteen months provide that Henry marry Margaret, release Anjou and Maine, pay Margaret's expenses, and receive no dowry. Gloucester cannot read the articles through, but his old foe, Cardinal Beaufort, Bishop of Winchester, can. Henry creates Suffolk a Duke, discharges York from being regent in France for eighteen months, thanks the others for entertaining the Queen, and goes in with the Queen and Suffolk to provide for her coronation. Gloucester laments that his brother Henry V conquered France, his true inheritance, that his brother Bedford toiled his wits to keep what Henry got, that Somerset, Buckingham, York, Salisbury, and Warwick received deep scars there, that his uncle Beaufort and himself with all the learned counsel of the realm had debated long

> How France and Frenchmen might be kept in awe,
> And had his highness in his infancy
> Crowned in Paris in despite of foes.
> And shall these labours and these honours die?

He concludes

> O peers of England, shameful is this league!
> Fatal this marriage, cancelling your fame,
>
> .   .   .   .
>
> Undoing all, as all had never been!

The Cardinal, of course, takes the opposite view

> Nephew, what means this passionate discourse,
> This peroration with such circumstance?
> For France, 'tis ours; and we will keep it still.

Gloucester replies

> Ay, uncle, we will keep it, if we can;
> But now it is impossible we should;

for "Suffolk, the new-made duke that rules the roast" has given away Anjou and Maine. Salisbury, Warwick, and York also lament. The Cardinal objects and Gloucester departs saying

>   if I longer stay,
> We shall begin our ancient bickerings.
> Lordings, farewell; and say, when I am gone,
> I prophesied France will be lost ere long.

The Cardinal says that Gloucester is his enemy, an enemy of all, and no great friend to the king,

> Consider, lords, he is the next of blood,
> And heir apparent to the English crown.

Hence he is displeased. Though the people call him the good Duke of Gloucester,

> I fear me, lords, for all his flattering gloss,
> He will be found a dangerous protector.

So Buckingham says

> Why should he, then, protect our sovereign,
> He being of age to govern of himself?
> Cousin of Somerset, join you with me,
> And all together, with the Duke of Suffolk,
> We'll quickly hoise Duke Humphrey from his seat.

The Cardinal goes to Suffolk at once to put the plan into operation. Somerset and Buckingham like the Cardinal no better than they do Gloucester, and exeunt saying one or the other of themselves shall be protector. Salisbury says

> While these do labour for their own preferment,
> Behoves it us to labour for the realm.

Gloucester has always borne himself like a gentleman, but the haughty Cardinal demeans himself unlike the ruler of a commonwealth. So Salisbury invites his son Warwick and "brother" York

> Join we together, for the public good,
> In what we can, to bridle and suppress
> The pride of Suffolk and the cardinal,
> With Somerset's and Buckingham's ambition;
> And, as we may, cherish Duke Humphrey's deeds,
> While they do tend the profit of the land.

Warwick agrees and York says aside "And so says York, for he hath greatest cause," alluding to his own designs upon the crown.[2] Warwick says that once again he will win Maine from France or else be slain. York remains to say to himself; that is, to the audience

> 'Tis thine they give away, and not their own.
> . . . .
>
>   for I had hope of France,
> Even as I have of fertile England's soil.
> A day will come when York shall claim his own;
> And therefore I will take the Nevils' parts
> And make a show of love to proud Duke Humphrey,
> And, when I spy advantage, claim the crown,
> For that's the golden mark I seek to hit:
> Nor shall proud Lancaster usurp my right,
> Nor hold the sceptre in his childish fist,
> Nor wear the diadem upon his head,
> Whose church-like humours fits not for a crown.

Henry is surfeiting in love, and when Gloucester is fallen at jars with the peers, then he himself will raise the milk-white rose of York and force

---

[2] See *1 Henry VI*, II, 5, etc.

the crown from Lancaster (who had assumed Somerset's red rose). So all factions are now declaring their attitudes toward the crown.

I, 2. Gloucester's wife Eleanor advises him

> Put forth thy hand, reach at the glorious gold.

Gloucester will harbor no ambitious thoughts but is troubled by his dream that his staff of office had been broken, as he thinks by the Cardinal, and that the heads of Somerset and Suffolk were placed on the broken pieces. Incidentally, there is no "tie-back" to this dream, when Suffolk and Somerset fulfill it. Eleanor scoffs and says she dreamed that she had been crowned queen. Gloucester chides Eleanor for such thoughts, which will

> tumble down thy husband and thyself
> From top of honour to disgrace's feet

and forbids her to mention the subject again. A messenger summons Gloucester to the King and Queen. The Duchess says she will play her part in Fortune's pageant (Gloucester had just warned her of Fortune's wheel). Hume enters, salutes her as majesty, and says Margery Jourdain, the witch, and Roger Bolingbroke, the conjurer, have promised to raise a spirit to answer her questions. As she exits, Hume says Eleanor gives him gold, but intimates that he is really in the pay of the Cardinal and Suffolk to betray the Duchess (the Cardinal had gone to Suffolk to lay a plan against Gloucester).

> Hume's knavery will be the duchess' wreck,
> And her attainture will be Humphrey's fall;
> Sort how it will, I shall have gold for all.

I, 3. Peter, the armourer's man, and other petitioners wait for the Lord Protector but mistake Suffolk and the Queen.[3] One petition is against the Cardinal's man for having taken house, lands, and wife, and all. Another is against Suffolk himself for enclosing the commons of Melford. Peter petitions against his master Thomas Horner "for saying that the Duke of York was rightful heir to the crown," "and that the king was an usurper." Peter is sent with a pursuivant for his master; the Queen tears up the other supplications. The Queen thinks Henry would get rid of Gloucester as protector if he were not so bent to holiness; he ought to be made pope.

> Beside the haughty protector, have we Beaufort
> The imperious churchman, Somerset, Buckingham,
> And grumbling York; and not the least of these
> But can do more in England than the king.

Suffolk adds,

> And he of these that can do most of all
> Cannot do more in England than the Nevils:
> Salisbury and Warwick are no simple peers.

---

[3] It may be well to note that in I, 3, 3, "quill" is only "coil" or "quoil," though editors have kept quite a "quill" about it.

But the Queen likes least the presumptions of Gloucester's wife, and wishes to be revenged upon her. Suffolk says he has "limed a bush for her," and they must stay on good terms with the other lords until they have brought Gloucester into disgrace.

> As for the Duke of York, this late complaint
> Will make but little for his benefit.
> So, one by one, we'll weed them all at last,
> And you yourself shall steer the happy helm.

The King and his party enter discussing whether the regent in France shall be York or Somerset. Warwick is for York, the Cardinal and Buckingham reprove him. Salisbury asks Buckingham to show cause why Somerset should be chosen and the Queen interposes, "Because the king, forsooth, will have it so." Gloucester retorts

> Madam, the king is old enough himself
> To give his censure: these are no women's matters,

only to get the equally tart query,

> If he be old enough, what needs your grace
> To be protector of his excellence?

Suffolk demands that Gloucester resign as protector, since under him as king

> The commonwealth hath daily run to wreck;
> .   .   .   .
> And all the peers and nobles of the realm
> Have been as bondmen to thy sovereignty.

The Cardinal, Somerset, Buckingham, and the Queen each chimes in with charges against Gloucester, who exits. The Queen drops her fan, orders the Duchess to pick it up, and boxes her ear for not stooping quickly enough. The Duchess warns the King

> look to't in time;
> She'll hamper thee, and dandle thee like a baby:
> Though in this place most master wear no breeches,
> She shall not strike Dame Eleanor unrevenged.

The Duchess exits and Buckingham tells the Cardinal he is following to see what she and Gloucester are about. Gloucester returns after he has cooled down to discuss whether York or Somerset shall be regent of France. Suffolk objects that York is most unfit of any man, and York retorts that he would be so because Somerset would not send him supplies, as was true last time, when Paris was lost. This Warwick also affirms. Horner and Peter now enter to enable Suffolk to make his charge against York. Horner denies having said

> that Richard Duke of York
> Was rightful heir unto the English crown,
> And that your majesty was an usurper.

Horner denies the charge, Peter affirms, and York is indignant. Gloucester says let Somerset be regent in France, since this breeds suspicion of York, and let Horner and his man have a day appointed for single combat. Peter is afraid to fight, but must or be hanged.

I, 4. The Duchess consults the wizards. The first question is, "First of the king: what shall of him become?" The answer is

> The duke yet lives that Henry shall depose;
> But him outlive, and die a violent death.

The second

> What fates await the Duke of Suffolk?

The answer

> By water shall he die, and take his end.

The third

> What shall befall the Duke of Somerset?

The answer

> Let him shun castles;
> Safer shall he be upon the sandy plains
> Than where castles mounted stand.

The prophecies for Suffolk and Somerset are tied in at fulfillment, but not that concerning Henry and York. York and Buckingham break in with the guard to arrest all the crew. York reads the predictions and says

> These oracles are hardly attain'd,
> And hardly understood.

He will take the news to the King, which Gloucester will not like. Buckingham will be the messenger. York orders that Salisbury and Warwick be invited to sup with him tomorrow night.

In this first act, the dramatist has outlined the various objectives of the different factions, most of which demand that Gloucester be deposed as protector. Cardinal Beaufort, Bishop of Winchester, is still antagonistic to Gloucester, of course. The Queen and Suffolk also wish to pull him down that they may rule. And York wants Gloucester removed from his path to the crown. The demand that Gloucester be removed has been voiced, and at the end of the first act comes the incident which will occasion Gloucester's downfall.

II, 1. As the King's party go hawking, the sport is moralized against Gloucester, whom the Cardinal accuses of designs upon the crown. They challenge each other in asides as the King suspects dissension and tries to compound their strife. A townsman of St. Alban's enters proclaiming a miracle; a blind man at St. Alban's shrine has received sight. The man Simpcox is brought in by the Mayor and his brethren. Gloucester proves him to be a fraud both as a blind man and as a cripple. Buckingham enters with news of the Duchess' practice. The Cardinal taunts Gloucester in an aside, and Gloucester replies aside that he is now vanquished. Gloucester answers the Queen that if his wife be guilty she shall be punished. The King will return to London on the morrow to see justice done in this matter.

II, 2. York, Salisbury, and Warwick have met at supper as planned at the end of the first act. York recites to them his pedigree to substantiate his claim to the crown as issue to an elder son than the ancestor of Henry VI.

> Henry doth claim the crown from John of Gaunt,
> The fourth son; York claims it from the third.

Salisbury and Warwick in consequence salute York as rightful king. York must wait, and directs

> Do you as I do in these dangerous days:
> Wink at the Duke of Suffolk's insolence,
> At Beaufort's pride, at Somerset's ambition,
> At Buckingham and all the crew of them,
> Till they have snared the shepherd of the flock,
> That virtuous prince, the good Duke Humphrey:
> 'Tis that they seek, and they in seeking that
> Shall find their deaths, if York can prophesy.

Warwick will one day make the Duke of York king, and that king will place Warwick next himself. Thus the downfall of Gloucester will bring an epitasis to the play.

II, 3. Henry VI condemns the witch to be burned in Smithfield, the three assistants to be strangled on the gallows, the Duchess after three days of open penance to live in banishment with Sir John Stanley in the Isle of Man. Gloucester cannot justify Eleanor, asks leave to go, and is by Henry commanded first to give up his staff, with the Queen chiming in. Gloucester gladly lays his staff at Henry's feet. The Queen rejoices that Henry is now king, herself queen, and Gloucester twice maimed. Suffolk also rejoices at the fall of Gloucester and Eleanor. York reminds them that it is now time for the combat between Horner and his man. Horner, well drunk, declares his innocence, but when his dead-frightened man Peter Thump strikes him down he confesses treason. York tells Peter to thank God and the good wine his master had drunk, but the King considers that God has shown Peter to be innocent.

II, 4. Gloucester philosophically but sympathetically waits to see his wife as she passes in penance. His servants would take her away from the officers but he forbids. Eleanor reproaches Gloucester for having permitted his wife to be punished thus

> But be thou mild and blush not at my shame,
> Nor stir at nothing till the axe of death
> Hang over thee, as, sure, it shortly will:

> For Suffolk — he that can do all in all
> With her that hateth thee and hates us all —
> And York and impious Beaufort, that false priest,
> Have all limed bushes to betray thy wings.

But Gloucester relies upon his innocence and will not break the law, exhorting his wife to patience. A Herald summons Gloucester to a parliament about which he has not been consulted. Gloucester asks Sir John Stanley to be kind to his wife and promises to do him kindness if the world laughs again. The Duchess wishes for death as she departs for the Isle of Man.

The second act has prepared for the final downfall of Gloucester. The conspirators have forced him out of office and have brought his wife to shame. He also receives the summons to parliament, which will prove his final undoing. That parliament, therefore, must wait for the third act,[4] since Gloucester's downfall marks the epitasis in the plans of the various factions, especially in those of York, who is to win in this first contention, and has specifically laid his plan of action in the second act, which will lead to final success in the fifth.

One matter of technique is particularly significant. Structurally, the claim by pedigree must be made in the second act, for the sake of the plays which are to follow. But in the second act it must give pride of place to preparation for the specific epitatical business of this particular play, the pulling down of Gloucester, and its consequences, which is also, therefore, an epitasis in the trilogy (tetralogy). Throughout, the dramatist must provide for a double structure, that of the trilogy (tetralogy), and that of each play. And since each play is a unit as well as a member of a trilogy (tetralogy), the crucial points of structure for the trilogy (tetralogy) must at crucial places be repeated. The amount and emphasis required in the repetitions would be a matter of judgment, and presumably the presentation would be varied and not verbatim.

III, 1. King Henry wonders that Gloucester has not yet arrived at the parliament, since he is usually first. The Queen advises that Gloucester is rancorous, and next in succession to Henry. He ought, therefore, to be kept away from the King. Also, the commons love him. Suffolk says the Duchess began her practice, no doubt, by his subornation, and Gloucester is full of deep deceit. The Cardinal, York, and Buckingham add other allegations of similar tenor. The King replies that Gloucester is innocent of treason to his person. The Queen warns

> Take heed, my lord; the welfare of us all
> Hangs on the cutting short that fraudful man.

---

[4] Notice the corresponding position and function of the parliament scene in *1 Henry VI*, which guarantees the correctness of the act-division here.

Somerset enters to say that in France, "all is lost." King Henry says, "God's will be done!" York says aside

> But I will remedy this gear ere long,
> Or sell my title for a glorious grave.

Gloucester enters and is arrested by Suffolk for high treason. York accuses him of having stayed the soldiers' pay, causing the loss of France. Gloucester replies that on the contrary he spent much of his own. York accuses Gloucester of having devised strange tortures for offenders; Gloucester replies that only the murderer was tortured. Suffolk arrests Gloucester nevertheless and assigns him to the Cardinal to be kept for trial. The King hopes Gloucester will clear himself. Gloucester replies

> I know their complot is to have my life;
> And if my death might make this island happy,
> And prove the period of their tyranny,
> I would expend it with all willingness:
> But mine is made the prologue to their play;
> For thousands more, that yet suspect no peril,
> Will not conclude their plotted tragedy.

He accuses the Cardinal, Suffolk, Buckingham, York, and the Queen of plotting against him. They object but Gloucester says

> Ah! thus King Henry throws away his crutch,
> Before his legs be firm to bear his body.
> Thus is the shepherd beaten from thy side,
> And wolves are gnarling who shall gnaw thee first.
> Ah, that my fear were false! ah, that it were!
> For, good King Henry, thy decay I fear.

As Gloucester exits, Henry laments that these lords and Margaret seek Gloucester's life, but he cannot prevent. As he exits with his train, the Queen advises

> This Gloucester should be quickly rid the world,
> To rid us from the fear we have of him.

The Cardinal says they must have some color for his death. Suffolk says Henry would strive to save Gloucester if they proceeded openly, and the commons might rise to save his life. York whets the conspirators on, and Suffolk advises that they slay Gloucester as they would a fox, by any means possible — what a sentiment for an English "gentleman"! Suffolk says if they agree he will be Gloucester's priest. The Cardinal will not wait for a priest (he is already one) but will provide an executioner, to which the other three agree. A Post enters to announce a rebellion in Ireland. York advises ironically that Somerset be sent, seeing the luck he has had in France. Somerset now enters the conversation to say that York could not have done as well. York retorts he would have died, but

Somerset has not even a scar. The Queen tries to stop the quarrel. The Cardinal asks if York will try the Irish, and it is so decided. York remains alone to say

> Now, York, or never, steel thy fearful thoughts,
> And change misdoubt to resolution
>
> . . . .
>
> Well, nobles, well, 'tis politicly done,
> To send me packing with an host of men
>
> . . . .
>
> 'Twas men I lack'd, and you will give them me
>
> . . . .
>
> Whiles I in Ireland nourish a mighty band,
> I will stir up in England some black storm
> Shall blow ten thousand souls to heaven or hell;
> And this fell tempest shall not cease to rage
> Until the golden circuit on my head,
> Like to the glorious sun's transparent beams,
> Do calm the fury of the mad-bred flaw.

He has set on John Cade to claim the crown as John Mortimer. York will then come from Ireland and reap the harvest Cade has sown

> For Humphrey being dead, as he shall be,
> And Henry put apart, the next for me.

III, 2. Two murderers are on the way to report to Suffolk that they have killed Gloucester. Suffolk will reward them well. The King enters and commands that Gloucester be brought before him for a fair trial. Suffolk reports that Gloucester is dead in his bed. The Cardinal says it is God's secret judgment; the King swoons; all the conspirators act the hypocrites; and the King loathes Suffolk, causing the Queen to put on an exhibition of the forlorn wife. Warwick and Salisbury report the commons are angry because they have heard that Gloucester was murdered by means of Suffolk and the Cardinal. Warwick is sent in to investigate, while the King forebodes. Warwick brings in the body and announces that he believes that Gloucester died a violent death. Suffolk resents the implied accusation, and the two leave to do battle to the death. They return, swords drawn, Suffolk complaining that the commons have set upon him. Salisbury enters with the demand of the commons that Suffolk be put to death or banished because he killed Gloucester and will kill the King. The King banishes Suffolk within three days on pain of death, and refuses to be moved by the Queen's plea. As he leaves, she pronounces a curse upon the group and Suffolk joins in. The Queen says

> I will repeal thee, or, be well assured,
> Adventure to be banished myself:
> And banished I am, if but from thee.

Suffolk answers in kind. Vaux passes on his way to ask the King to visit the dying Cardinal, who is

> Blaspheming God and cursing men on earth.
> Sometime he talks as if Duke Humphrey's ghost
> Were by his side.

Suffolk and the Queen part, with interchanged hearts.

III, 3. The Cardinal raves in presence of Henry and his party of the death of Gloucester. The King tries to remind the Cardinal of God, but "He dies, and makes no sign."

The third act begins to fulfill Gloucester's dream. His staff has been broken, and his life taken by the Cardinal. Suffolk is also in fact already on one end of Gloucester's staff. If Somerset can be made to grace the other end, this will leave the world for York, as York himself points out that it will — if he can manage Margaret. The remainder of the play must show what use York makes of his offered opportunities.

IV, I. A Captain who has captured Suffolk and his party is distributing the prisoners. Suffolk falls to the lot of Walter Whitmore. Others put their prisoners to ransom, but Whitmore has lost an eye and in revenge will put Suffolk to death, fulfilling the prophecy that Suffolk should die by water (Water, Walter, Gualtier). The Captain reads the bede roll of Suffolk's offenses to him before he is beheaded, blaming him for most of England's ills. So Suffolk's head is now officially to grace one end of Gloucester's broken staff, as in the dream, and Somerset will in no long time balance the other end, though no reference is made to the dream here or at the death of Somerset. The Gentleman who is to go for the ransom money says

> His body will I bear unto the king:
> If he revenge it not, yet will his friends;
> So will the queen, that living held him dear.

IV, 2. Jack Cade is gathering a clownish army to support his claim to be a Mortimer and rightful heir to the crown. England is to be reformed. The Clerk of Chatham is condemned to death because he can write, read, and cast account (petty school curriculum). Sir Humphrey Stafford and his brother command Cade's followers to depart to their homes. Cade claims the throne, and is told "the Duke of York hath taught you this." Stafford and his party depart to gather an army.

IV, 3. Cade has overcome and slain the Staffords, and is now to go to London.

IV, 4. The Queen has received Suffolk's head, and wishes she might embrace the body. The King will send a holy bishop to entreat Cade's followers, or he himself will parley with Cade that so many simple souls may not perish by the sword. Cade has arrived in Southwark, vowing that he will be crowned in Westminster.

> All scholars, lawyers, courtiers, gentlemen,
> They call false caterpillars and intend their death.

The King and his party, except Lord Say, flee to Killingworth as they hear that Cade has captured London bridge.

IV, 5. Lord Scales at the Tower will send Matthew Goffe to Smithfield to help the Lord Mayor cope with Cade.

IV, 6. At London stone Cade hears that an army is gathering in Smithfield. He orders London bridge to be burned and the Tower too, if possible.

IV, 7. Cade has slain Goffe and his army, and is deciding to be the sole law of England. Lord Say "which sold the towns in France" is brought in prisoner. Cade orders him put to death, as also Sir James Cromer his son-in-law, and their heads to be brought to him on poles. These heads are to be borne before Cade through London instead of maces, and at every corner they are to be made to kiss.

IV, 8. Buckingham and Clifford proclaim free pardon to Cade's followers, if they will return to their homes. They decide to follow Clifford against the French. Cade flies and Buckingham offers a reward of a thousand crowns for his head.

IV, 9. King Henry resents the fact that he was born a king. He pardons the followers of Cade. A Messenger announces

> The Duke of York is newly come from Ireland,
> And with a puissant and mighty power
> . Of gallowglasses and stout kernes
> Is marching hitherward in proud array,
> And still proclaimeth, as he comes along,
> His arms are only to remove from thee
> The Duke of Somerset, whom he terms a traitor.

Henry laments that he has no sooner been rid of Cade than York appears. He will commit Duke Edmund and Somerset to the Tower, and sends Buckingham to parley with York.

The fourth act ends Suffolk; York brings on the rebellion of Cade and as it ends, York himself returns from Ireland, demanding the imprisonment of Somerset his foe. York is appearing at the end of the fourth act to bring on the catastrophe in the fifth. This is, of course, according to the *Andria* formula.

[V, 1] IV, 10. Iden kills Cade, will dishonor the body and take the head to the King. I think Capell was unquestionably correct in beginning the fifth act with this scene instead of with the next as does Pope. In fact, I was forced by the formula to place the division here and then found that Capell had been before me.

[V, 2] V, 1. York enters with his army

> From Ireland thus comes York to claim his right,
> And pluck the crown from feeble Henry's head:
> Ring, bells, aloud; burn, bonfires, clear and bright,
> To entertain great England's lawful king.

He will also "toss the flower-de-luce of France." Buckingham enters from Henry to know why York should come with so great an armed force. York replies

> The cause why I have brought this army hither
> Is to remove proud Somerset from the king,
> Seditious to his grace and to the state.

Buckingham answers that Somerset is in the Tower. York will dismiss his army and will send his sons or anything else as pledge of his fealty, if only Somerset may die. King Henry enters and receives York's submission. York has brought an army

> To heave the traitor Somerset from hence,
> And fight against the monstrous rebel Cade.

Iden presents the head of Cade and, at Buckingham's suggestion, is created knight for his service. The Queen brings in Somerset, saying

> For thousand Yorks he shall not hide his head,
> But boldly stand and front him to his face.

York upbraids Henry for weakness and concludes

> Give place: by heaven, thou shalt rule no more
> O'er him whom heaven created for thy ruler.

Somerset would arrest York, who sends for his sons, and the Queen sends for Clifford. Edward and Richard enter, followed by Old Clifford and his son. Clifford will not recognize York as king but would have him put to death as a traitor, York calls for his "two brave bears," the earls of Salisbury and Warwick (cognizance, a bear and ragged staff, hence the "bear" allusion). Clifford threatens, and York's party taunt him. King Henry reproaches Warwick for failing in his duty and leading his son astray. Salisbury replies for both that York is rightful king and their oath to Henry must be broken as the lesser sin.[5] The King calls for Buckingham to put down York, who says "I am resolved for death or dignity." Warwick and Clifford, Young Clifford and Richard bid each other defiance.

[V, 3] V, 2. Warwick seeks Clifford, who has slain York's horse, as York slew his. They engage again and York slays Clifford. Young Clifford mourns his father and bears his body out. Richard kills Somerset.

---

[5] Compare the dilemma of the King of France in *King John*.

Margaret urges Henry to fly to London to raise another army. Young Clifford enters to urge the same course; exeunt.

[V, 1] V, 3. York inquires after Salisbury, and Richard reports his valiant deeds. Salisbury enters saying

> Well, lords, we have not got that which we have:
> 'Tis not enough our foes are this time fled,
> Being opposites of such repairing nature.

York advises to pursue the King to London before he can call a parliament. Warwick agrees.

> Saint Alban's battle won by famous York
> Shall be eternized in all age to come.

The fifth act thus brings the catastrophe of York's victory and Henry's defeat, though York is not yet king.

The objective of this play is the success of York. As the various factions band together to pull Gloucester down, York consents and aids because it suits his purpose, and at the end of the first act plans to confer with Salisbury and Warwick. In the second act, York presents to Salisbury and Warwick his claim to the crown, and they agree one day to make him king. To further York's plans, Gloucester is forced out of office and has intimation of worse to come. The pulling down of Gloucester is the objective, not only of *2 Henry VI*, but has been the objective from the beginning of *1 Henry VI*. Just as the end of the protasis, and the epitasis of Part I served those functions for the whole tetralogy, so the end of the protasis, and the beginning of the epitasis of Part II form a continuation of Part I, and look forward to the remainder of the tetralogy.

The significance of Gloucester's downfall for succeeding events had, of course, been properly moralized by Halle and Holinshed. "Oft times it hapneth that a man, in quenching of smoke, burneth his fingers in the fire: so the queene, in casting how to keepe hir husband in honor, and hir selfe in authoritie, in making awaie of this noble man, brought that to passe, which she had most cause to haue feared; which was the deposing of hir husband, & the decaie of the house of Lancaster, which of likelihood had not chanced if this duke had liued: for then durst not the duke of Yorke haue attempted to set foorth his title to the crowne, as he afterwards did, to the great trouble of the realme, and destruction of king Henrie, and of many other noble men beside."[6] The person who constructed the framework for *2 Henry VI* simply took over this epitatical action for its proper place in his five-act formula, for this part and for his tetralogy. Again, therefore, the fundamental structure is directly from the sources.

---

[6] Boswell-Stone, *Holinshed,* pp. 264-265.

Naturally, the *Mirour* had also seen the significance of this act of the Queen, giving it full moralization, set in its total background. Gloucester's "case was the more lamentable, in that hee suffered without cause. And surely thoughe the Cardinal against nature was the Dukes mortall Foe, yet the chiefe causers of his confusyon, was yᵉ Quene, and William Dela-poole Erle of Suffolke and afterwards Duke, whose counsel was chefely followed in the contryuing of this noble mans destruction, She through ambicion to haue soueraynty and rule and he through, flattery to purchace honour and promotion, which as he in shorte time obtayned: so in as short tyme he lost agayne, & his life withal by the iust iudgement of God, receiuing such measure as he before mette to this good Prince. This drift of his turned to the vtter ouerthrow of the king himselfe, the Quene his wife, & Edward their son a most goodly prince. & to the subuersion of the hole house of Lancaster, as you may see at large in the Chronicles."[7]

The Roman Catholics could use the argument. "*Quene Margarets* to much fauour and credit (by him not controled) towards the *Marques of Suffolke,* that after was made *Duke,* by whos instinct and wicked Counsail, she made away first the noble *Duke of Glocester,* and afterward com-mitted other thinges in great preiudice of the Realm, and suffred the said moste impious & sinful *Duke,* to range & make hauock of al sorte of subiectes, at his pleasure, (much after the fashion of the *Earle of Ley-cester* now, though yet not in so high and extreme a degre:) this I say was the principal and original cause, both before God and man, (as *Polidore* wel noteth [Pol. lib. 23 hist. Angl.]) of al the calamitie and ex-treme desolation, which after ensued both to the kinge, Queene, and theyr onelie child, with the vtter extirpation of theyr familie."[8] This was the official view, promulgated by Henry VII through his mouthpiece Polydore Vergil; so known and necessarily accepted by all. This goodly moral was not likely to be lost on any sixteenth-century person.

And the *Mirour* further enforces the tragedy of Gloucester "for vertu cald (the good)"[9] as occasioned by his wife. "I haue here ready penned ii. notable tragedies, the one of Humfrey Duke of Glocestre, the other of the Duches Elienor his wife which as (me semeth) be two of yᵉ most memorable matters fortuning in yᵗ time But whether of thē is fyrst to be placed in the order of our boke, I somewhat stande in doute. For albeit the sayde Dukes death happened before the deceasse of the Duches, yet was her fall first, which fynally was cause of ouerthrow to both. why shoulde you doubte then (quod the rest of yᵉ company) for seyng yᵉ cause doth alwaies go before theffect and sequel of any thing: it is good reason

[7] *Mirour* (1578), FC4ᵛ.
[8] *The Copie of a Leter* (1584), p. 188.
[9] *Mirour* (1578), FC2ʳ.

you should begin w[t] her first."[10] The Duchess was cause of the overthrow of Gloucester, and Gloucester's overthrow caused that of the house of Lancaster. The *Mirour* brings these events specifically into mesh, as do the plays.[11] Halle furnishes the fundamental materials, and Holinshed borrows them; but *Mirour* had further shaped them by moralization to its tragic view, and the tetralogy follows suit. We cannot arrive at the relative importance of Halle, Holinshed, and the *Mirour* for the tetralogy by a merely statistical method, however important statistics may be. And we must remember that all these works grew out of and in turn shaped a common point of view, even for the majority of people who had never heard of these works.

But to return, in the third act, York gets sent to Ireland with an army, which, he says, will give him the crown. Gloucester is removed from his path by murder, procured by the Cardinal, who also dies, thus removing another obstacle from York's path. In the fourth act, Suffolk, too, is put to death and Cade raises a rebellion, which is finally put down. The time is now ripe for York's return from Ireland, as he claims to force Somerset, his enemy, from the King. In the fifth act, Somerset is killed, and York has put the King and his party to rout. York's plans have succeeded to the stage where all his opponents have been vanquished. This play sets forth the victory of York, and does it in the regular five stages in accord with the five-act formula. In its fundamentals, this part is also based squarely upon the historical sources, though it deals very freely with details of fact, as had Part I, and as will Part III.

---

[10] *Mirour* (1578), f 39[v].

[11] See also the source of the rivalry of Margaret and the Duchess, above, pp. 285-286.

CHAPTER XIX

The Third Part of *King Henry the Sixth*

I, 1. We begin with a résumé of the battle of Saint Alban's, which occurred at the close of the second part. Henry escaped; Northumberland, old Clifford, Stafford, Buckingham, Wiltshire, and Somerset (York's long-time special foe) were killed. Since they are now at London before the parliament house, Warwick advises York to possess the throne. The Queen has called a parliament to meet this day, where York and his faction will win his right by words or blows.

> The bloody parliament shall this be call'd,
> Unless Plantagenet, Duke of York, be king,
> And bashful Henry deposed, whose cowardice
> Hath made us by-words to our enemies.

Henry's followers wish to eject York from the throne by force, but Henry tries talk. Henry claims through his grandfather Henry IV, is reminded that Henry won the crown by rebellion, says aside, "I know not what to say; my title's weak," but claims that Richard II made Henry IV his heir, which Exeter claims can not be done.[1] Fearful of defection, Henry suggests a compromise, whereby he shall reign during life, but York and his heirs shall then succeed. Henry's followers pronounce a curse upon him and depart in search of the Queen. "Now York and Lancaster are reconciled." As all exeunt except Henry and Exeter, who attempts to steal away, Margaret enters with the Prince of Wales. Margaret will divorce herself from Henry's board and bed till the act of disinheritance has been repealed, and she will take the field against York's faction. Henry will send Exeter to attempt to win back Northumberland, Clifford, and Westmoreland.

I, 2. Two of York's sons and his brother are disputing who shall "play the orator" to York as he enters. His sons, Edward and Richard, advise York to seize the crown now. York demurs at his oath, but is over-persuaded. He is about to send Montague to Warwick, Richard to Norfolk, Edward to Cobham and his Kentishmen, when a messenger brings news that the Queen is leading an army to besiege York. So Montague is to go alone to summon aid while York and his sons defend themselves.

---

[1] See Swinburne on wills, below, pp. 400-401.

The Mortimers arrive and York decides with his five thousand men to meet the Queen's twenty thousand in the field.

I, 3. To avenge the death of his father, Clifford kills the boy Rutland, son of York.

I, 4. York says the battle has gone against him. Margaret and her party demand his surrender. Margaret taunts him with the death of Rutland and the defeat of his other sons, and mocks him with a paper crown. York delivers a tirade and curses Margaret. Clifford and Margaret stab York to death, and Margaret orders his head to be set on York gates.

The first act presents the compromise of Henry and York, which Margaret rejects, killing York. The death of York fulfills one of the prophecies of the first act of *2 Henry VI*, so that these sections were probably planned together, though the fact is from the source.

II, 1. As Edward and Richard are wondering what has happened to their father, they see three suns. Edward thinks this signifies that the three sons of York shall take the field. A messenger announces York's death. Warwick and Montague enter and hear the news. Warwick has fought with the Queen at St. Alban's and has been beaten. Norfolk is a short distance away, and George, Duke of Clarence to be, is bringing soldiers also. They will to London to fight the Queen, proclaiming Edward king on the way. A messenger announces that the Queen is seeking them, and they prepare to meet her.

II, 2. Henry prays that God will not punish him for having broken his oath unwillingly. Margaret and Clifford try to persuade him that he should never have taken an oath to disinherit his son. Henry knights his son Edward, who will fight for the crown. A messenger warns that Warwick and York are at hand. The two parties do a deal of wrangling. Margaret will not permit Henry to speak. The sides part for battle.

II, 3. Warwick, Edward, George, and Richard tell how the battle has been going against them, but vow to win or die.

II, 4. As Richard fights with Clifford, Warwick enters and Clifford flies.

II, 5. As King Henry laments his situation, a son enters who has killed his father, then a father who has killed his son. King Henry wishes his death would end these fearful deeds. Margaret, the Prince, and Exeter enter to warn Henry that Edward and Richard are in pursuit to kill them all.

II, 6. Clifford enters wounded, lamenting that Henry had not swayed as his ancestors but had given ground to the house of York. As he faints, Edward, George, Richard, Montague, and Warwick enter victorious. Clifford dies. Warwick advises the putting of Clifford's head upon the gates of York in the place of that of the Duke of York, whom Clifford

had slain. Edward is to go to London to be crowned; Warwick will go
to France to ask the Lady Bona to be Edward's queen.

> So shalt thou sinew both these lands together;
> And, having France thy friend, thou shalt not dread
> The scatter'd foe that hopes to rise again.

Richard is created Duke of Gloucester; George of Clarence. Richard
says

> Let me be Duke of Clarence, George of Gloucester;
> For Gloucester's dukedom is too ominous.

Warwick thinks this "a foolish observation."

The second act has given York's party control, and Edward is to be
crowned king.

III, 1. Two keepers capture King Henry as he returns from Scotland

> even of pure love,
> To greet mine own land with my wishful sight.

King Henry says

> My queen and son are gone to France for aid;
> And, as I hear, the great commanding Warwick
> Is thither gone, to crave the French king's sister
> To wife for Edward: if this news be true,
> Poor queen and son, your labour is but lost.

III, 2. King Edward solicits the Lady Grey, but she will consent only
in marriage.

> I know I am too mean to be your queen,
> And yet too good to be your concubine.

Edward tells his brothers he will marry her. News is brought to Edward
that Henry is taken prisoner. Richard of Gloucester remains to sum up
the situation. He would himself be king

> And yet, between my soul's desire and me —
> The lustful Edward's title buried —
> Is Clarence, Henry, and his son young Edward,
> And all the unlook'd for issue of their bodies,
> To take their rooms, ere I can place myself.

He cannot be a lover; he must dream of the crown. He will set all his
villainous abilities awork to get the crown. *Richard III* begins with a
rephrasing of this speech.

III, 3. Margaret presents her case to Lewis of France. Warwick
enters to propose a league of amity and Lady Bona, Lewis's sister, as
Edward's queen. Margaret protests, but is asked to stand aside. Lewis
decides to accept Warwick's proposal and calls Margaret to be a witness.
As Warwick and Margaret berate each other, a post enters with letters for
Warwick, Lewis, and Margaret. The news is that Edward has married

Lady Grey. Warwick renounces Edward and returns to Henry. Lewis will aid in restoring Henry. Warwick will marry his daughter to Henry's son, Prince Edward. Warwick will avenge himself on King Edward.

The third act has prepared serious opposition for Edward, even though Henry VI is in his power. Richard plans to get the crown; the French King and Warwick will aid Henry VI.

IV, 1. Gloucester, Clarence, Somerset, and Montague are disgusted with "this new marriage with the Lady Grey." Edward enters with the Queen and attendants, asks Clarence "how like you our choice?" who answers "As well as Lewis of France, or the Earl of Warwick." Gloucester will not openly admit that he is "offended too." Hastings scorns French alliance, since Edward has rewarded him with "the heir of the Lord Hungerford." Gloucester and Clarence say he has provided for his wife's kindred but has not considered his brothers in a rich match, and Clarence is going to arrange for himself. The Queen is sorry because of their displeasure, and Edward bids her "forbear to fawn upon their frowns"; he will force his brothers to "obey, and love thee too." Gloucester will stay mum. A Post enters with defiance from King Lewis, Lady Bona, Queen Margaret, and Warwick. Warwick and Margaret have decided "That young Prince Edward marries Warwick's daughter," and Clarence says, "Belike the elder; Clarence will have the younger" as he bids King Edward farewell with Somerset in tow; but Gloucester remains, "not for the love of Edward, but the crown." Edward will levy men, and Hastings, Montague, and Gloucester will side with him against "Warwick with his foreign power."

IV, 2. Warwick says all goes well. Clarence and Somerset enter. Warwick plans to surprise Edward.

IV, 3. Warwick captures Edward, though Hastings and Richard escape. Edward shall be but Duke of York and Henry shall be King. So to London to free King Henry.

IV, 4. Queen Elizabeth has heard the news and that Warwick comes to London, so she is taking sanctuary.

IV, 5. Gloucester, Hastings, and Stanley rescue Edward, and set out for Flanders.

IV, 6. Henry, though he retains the crown, will, to conquer fortune's spite and avoid thwarting stars, resign his government to Warwick, who chooses Clarence as protector, the two to yoke together. Margaret and Prince Edward are to be brought back from France. Henry prophesies of young Henry, Earl of Richmond, "This pretty lad will prove our country's bliss."[2] News comes of Edward's escape. Somerset and Oxford will send Richmond to Brittany for his safety.

IV, 7. King Edward is returning with aid from Burgundy, and gains

---

[2] See *Richard III,* IV, 2, 99-101.

admission to York as Duke of York only. Montgomery enters with an army to put Edward back upon the throne, not to claim a dukedom for him. All agree and proclaim Edward king, who will go forth on the morrow to meet Clarence and Warwick.

IV, 8. Henry's adherents will leave him in London while they raise troops to meet at Coventry. Henry thinks the people should love and support him for his justice and mercy. Edward's party capture Henry and will go to Coventry to overwhelm Warwick before he gathers his power.

So in the fourth act Edward has been overthrown, but at the end has captured Henry and is on his way to force a catastrophe with Warwick.

V, 1. As Warwick's reinforcements are expected from all parts, Edward's troops arrive. Recriminations are in order. Oxford brings his forces into the city to Warwick, then Montague arrives, and next Somerset. But Clarence defies Warwick and turns to Edward. The opposing forces will fight at Barnet.

V, 2. Edward brings in Warwick wounded and exits in search of Montague. As Warwick laments, Oxford and Somerset enter to tell him that Queen Margaret has brought a power from France. Montague is dead; Warwick dies; and Oxford and Somerset go to meet Margaret.

V, 3. Edward is victorious, but Margaret is bringing an army of thirty thousand, and has been joined by Oxford and Somerset. Edward has conquered at Barnet and will now to Tewksbury.

V, 4. Queen Margaret, with Prince Edward, cheers her forces for loss of Warwick and Montague. Edward's party enters.

V, 5. Edward has conquered, orders Oxford to be kept a prisoner, Somerset executed. Prince Edward enters prisoner for a railing match, and is stabbed by King Edward, Gloucester, and Clarence. Gloucester would also kill Margaret, who swoons. Gloucester slips away to London to the Tower. Margaret prays that if Edward and Clarence have children they may meet the same fate as Prince Edward.[3] Margaret begs death but

---

[3] This prayer, but not all its details, is suggested by the source, and in *Richard III* becomes Margaret's famous curse. Halle says that "George duke of Clarence Rychard duke of Gloucester, Thomas Marques Dorset, and Williā lord Hastynges, sodaynly murthered, & pitiously manquelled [Prince Edward]. The bitternesse of which murder, some of the actors, after in their latter dayes tasted and assayed by the very rod of Justice and punishment of God. . . . [Margaret] in her very extreme age . . . passed her dayes in Fraunce, more lyke a death than a lyfe, languishyng and mornyng in continuall sorowe, not so much for her selfe and her husbande, whose ages were almost consumed and worne, but for the losse of prince Edward her sonne (whome she and her husband thought to leue, both ouerlyuer of their progenye, and also of their kyngdome) to whome in this lyfe nothyng coulde be either more displeasant or greuous" (Halle, *Vnion* (1548), King Edward IV, f CCXXI[v]). So when Prince Edward is here murdered in *3 Henry VI*, V, 5, Margaret prays a similar fate upon the children of King Edward and Clarence, and in *Richard III* the device is expanded to and beyond the full list in Halle.

is taken out forcibly. Clarence tells Edward that Gloucester has gone to make a bloody supper in the Tower. Edward hopes his queen has a son for him.

V, 6. As Henry rails at Gloucester, the latter stabs him. Now that Henry and his heirs are out of the way, Gloucester will be rid of Clarence, Edward, and their heirs, "Counting myself but bad till I be best."

V, 7. King Edward sums up the enemies he and his brothers have conquered that his son "Young Ned" may possess the crown in peace, while Gloucester mutters of his intentions. King Edward says

> Now am I seated as my soul delights,
> Having my country's peace and brothers' loves.

Margaret is being ransomed by her father, so to France. Edward welcomes peace, "For here, I hope, begins our lasting joy."

In the first act, York is killed in battle. His personal success in *2 Henry VI* is thus cancelled, and some other member or members of his house must carry on the opposition to Lancaster, which is now uppermost. In the second act, the Yorkists reverse the situation upon the Lancastrians. The Yorkists plan to crown Edward as oldest son, who has now become titular leader, but with Richard as the real military force. This is the thing toward which the protasis of the play has tended, and consequently the remainder of the play will be concerned with establishing Edward as king. In the third act, Edward brings on an epitasis for himself by jilting Bona of France and marrying Lady Grey. This puts the King of France and Warwick on the side of Margaret, and even Clarence eventually on the side of Warwick; but Richard remains firm for Edward, since he himself plans finally to get the crown. The fourth act presents the give and take of this new struggle, with Edward first losing completely but at the end of the act gathering power and on the brink of forcing a catastrophe in the fifth. The fifth ends the Lancastrians and puts Edward, as he thinks, securely on the throne; but Richard is muttering aside that we had better wait and see him get the crown.

It will be seen that the three parts of *Henry VI* are clearly demarcated from each other and that Henry VI is himself a mere figure head. The fundamental interest is in a political moral; how factionalism had once ruined England, and will again do so unless suppressed. This factionalism centered in the contentions of the houses of York and Lancaster but was not confined to them. There is thus *1 Henry VI* as prologue, setting the stage of these interlocking factionalisms and showing how their beginnings in effect lost France. Then *2 Henry VI* presents the personal success of York and his house against Henry VI and Margaret with the house of Lancaster. Finally, *3 Henry VI* presents the ultimate triumph of Edward and the house of York over Henry VI, Margaret, and the house of Lancaster. But the political moral is not yet done. So *3 Henry VI* introduces and keeps before us the faction within the house of York itself, namely Richard's designs upon the crown, and also has Henry VI bless officially the role which Richmond is to play in finally ending all these factions. That is, *3 Henry VI* has clearly and carefully planned for the main features of *Richard III* as we have them now. And this planning is in the fundamental plot of *3 Henry VI,* not merely thrust in. The essential plot of *Richard III* as we have it was determined along with the plots of *1, 2, 3 Henry VI.* These four plays were plotted as a sequence, whoever did it and when, and whoever executed the plans and when. Also, the real pairing is between *1* and *2 Henry VI,* on the one hand, and *3 Henry VI* and *Richard III* on the other, with one Duke of Gloucester (Humphrey) tugging at one end and another (Richard III) at the other, and with contentions loosely holding together the middle.

These are not merely chronological chronicle plays. Each has its definite subject, and the three are clearly delimited as a trilogy covering the reign of Henry VI. The first contains the loss of France through faction, principally that of the roses, and this same faction has yet two further stages of progress in the reign of Henry VI, which are delimited as the first and second contentions between the houses of York and Lancaster. Now so far as the most general features of delimitation are concerned, it would have been possible to begin by writing a first and second contention between the houses of York and Lancaster, since these two phases are fundamental to the original facts. It would then be possible later to write an introductory play leading up to those facts, just as *Richard III* was written as a summary. But such a hypothesis will not satisfy the detailed plotting of these three parts in the complete harmony which we have observed. For the five acts of each unit have been pointed with relationship to the sequence of the other units. Such detailed and correlated delimitation can only mean that this trilogy was basically so planned or plotted at original construction, though some changes of fact and emphasis are possible within the plotted framework.

Whether there were earlier forms of the *Henry VI* plays, especially of Parts II and III, as has so long been assumed, is quite decidedly a question, now that *Contention* and *True Tragedie* cannot be alleged in evidence. The casting pattern of the plays does not bear witness to earlier forms. They show no kinship in structure to the history plays constructed for the Queen's before 1590, nor do they remind one of the Admiral's pattern, particularly as represented by Marlowe. They are "too large" for the earlier Strange's. And in fact their total point of view as well as structure points to construction in the 'nineties.

CHAPTER XX

The Tragedy of *King Richard the Third*

I, 1. Richard soliloquizes that now all is peace in which he is unfitted to shine

> And therefore, since I cannot prove a lover,
> To entertain these fair well-spoken days,
> I am determined to prove a villain
> And hate the idle pleasures of these days.[1]

He has already laid a plot which should soon get his brother Clarence out of the way. This speech repeats and condenses a position at which he had arrived in *3 Henry VI,* III, 2, 124 ff., where he had decided to attain the crown in spite of the apparently insuperable difficulty of several older brothers and their children. Thus *Richard III* begins with the epitasis of *3 Henry VI.* Richard had also reminded the audience of this purpose at the end of *3 Henry VI,* V, 6, 84 ff., in the catastrophe of that play. Now he begins the protasis of his own play with that position. The reader will remember the exactly similar case of York in *1* and *2 Henry VI,* though it is not so heavily pointed. Richard is now ready to begin removing these difficulties from his path, and Clarence is to be first.

> This day should Clarence closely be mew'd up,
> About a prophecy, which says that G
> Of Edward's heirs the murderer shall be.

It turns out that Gloucester himself is the G who murders Edward's heirs; but he has managed to get the prophecy applied as George, Duke of Clarence. Clarence enters on his way to the Tower. Richard says it is "My Lady Grey," King Edward's wife, who is causing Clarence's trouble. Only the Queen's kindred and night-walking heralds to Mrs. Shore are safe. These two control everything. Richard promises Clarence that his imprisonment will not be long, and as Clarence passes on, tells the audience that he hopes shortly to send Clarence's soul to heaven. Hastings, who has just been delivered from prison through Mrs. Shore's intercession, brings news that King Edward is seriously ill. Richard remains to say

> Clarence hath not another day to live:
> Which done, God take King Edward to his mercy,

---

[1] I have used the Cambridge Shakespeare (W. A. Wright, 1892) here as usual, since the differences between quarto and folio do not affect the fundamental structure.

> And leave the world for me to bustle in!
> For then I'll marry Warwick's youngest daughter.
> What though I kill'd her husband and her father?

I, 2. Anne, "Warwick's youngest daughter," is following as mourner the corpse of Henry VI, father of her murdered husband Edward. Gloucester stops the procession and in a long and highly rhetorical debate woos and wins her.

> Was ever woman in this humour woo'd?
> Was ever woman in this humour won?
> I'll have her; but I will not keep her long.

I, 3. Queen Elizabeth laments the illness of her husband, for her son

> Is put unto the trust of Richard Gloucester,
> A man that loves not me, nor none of you.

King Edward plans to reconcile Gloucester and Hastings with the Queen's brothers. Gloucester enters with Hastings and Dorset, complaining of the false accusations against him to the King. He accuses the Queen of causing Clarence and Hastings to be imprisoned, which she denies and says she will complain to the King. Queen Margaret enters, in asides to point out what each has done against her faction of Lancaster, and eventually to put her curse upon these her enemies for their deeds. In the recriminations, most of the violent deeds of the past contention between Lancaster and York are alluded to. Richard claims that his father's curse has fallen on Margaret, which suggests to her that she try a bit of cursing herself by way of tit for tat. The tie-in is with York's speech in which the phoenix feather was "O tiger's heart wrapp'd in a woman's hide!"[2] The dramatist evidently still preened his feathers over this key speech in spite of the fact that Greene had ruffled them some months before. This shaft did not kill cock robin. After all, there is nothing to show that Greene disapproved the line; he thought it admirable for his purpose, and we have agreed only too well. Shakspere himself evidently still thought it was a good curse — else he would have changed it. Margaret invokes specific punishment on each — including Richard but not Buckingham, who is merely warned — for some deed against her party, and as each later in the play meets his doom he remembers and reminds the audience of Margaret's curse. These curses serve to tie the threads of the play together, presenting the eye for an eye and tooth for a tooth between Lancaster and York. This device is the more significant in that it is fictitious; indeed Margaret was already dead before the historical date of this scene. The whole device of Margaret and her curses in Shakspere's "invention," though the device as such had already been used and had its

---

[2] *3 Henry VI*, I, 4, 137.

inception in Halle.[3] After Margaret leaves, the others are summoned to King Edward. Gloucester remains long enough to turn over to the murderers a warrant for the death of Clarence.

I, 4. Clarence has presentiments of retaliation in the hereafter and is murdered.

The stage is now set to present the nemesis of the house of York for its sins against the house of Lancaster, which had not itself been less guilty. The agent of this nemesis is Richard, himself a member of the house of York. He has now determined to remove all those of his own house who stand in his way to become king. He has announced his purpose at once, and in the first act removes Clarence from his path. He has hastened to get this done before Edward dies, and on Edward's authority, not his own. Also, Clarence, like Buckingham, is outside the scheme of Margaret's curses. Richard plans to marry Anne as soon as Edward is dead, and has wooed her successfully in the first act. Richard has begun to act, but nemesis has not yet set in. It will begin when Edward dies to balance Henry VI, as Margaret had prophesied. But it is necessary to have Clarence out of the way first, as in fact he was. Consequently, he is sacrificed at the end of the first act, and this serves to precipitate the chief problem or action of the play.

II, 1. King Edward thinks he has set his friends at peace on earth, and is ready for heaven. Richard alone is needed

> To make the perfect period of this peace.

Richard enters and begs pardon of all. The Queen asks pardon for Clarence to crown this reconciliation, and Richard pretends that she is insulting the dead. Edward says the order was reversed; Richard says it came too late. Edward laments that no one sued for Clarence. Richard remains to insinuate to Buckingham and others that the Queen's party did this, but "God will revenge it."

II, 2. The Duchess of York is talking with the children of Clarence, who think that the King has done this, and "God will revenge it"; but the Duchess admonishes that it was not the King and intimates that it was Richard. Queen Elizabeth enters lamenting Edward's death, and the Duchess and the children of Clarence join in the round of grief. Rivers advises that Prince Edward be crowned at once. Richard enters with others, and Buckingham also proposes that Edward be crowned. Buckingham advises Richard privately to separate the Queen's kindred from Edward.

II, 3. The citizens lament the death of King Edward and, remembering the Bible and Henry VI, fear the worst from the factions.

II, 4. News is brought to the Queen, the Duchess, and the Archbishop

---

[3] See above, p. 379, n. 3.

of York, with little York, that the Queen's kindred have been separated from Prince Edward and sent to prison. The Duchess laments the civil war of her descendants. Queen Elizabeth will take sanctuary with York.

Richard now has Prince Edward in control, but Queen Elizabeth is taking the second son to sanctuary. Here are the opposing plans in their proper place at the end of the second act. They will clash in the third.

III, 1. Buckingham and Richard welcome Prince Edward to London, though he laments his uncles. Hastings brings Edward news that his mother and brother have taken refuge. Cardinal Bourchier is to persuade or to force her to send York out. York is brought in and the two princes are to be lodged in the Tower till the coronation. Buckingham is sounding out the lords for crowning Richard instead of the prince. Richard promises him the earldom of Hereford, as well as King Edward's moveables, when he becomes king.

III, 2. Stanley sends news of an ominous dream to Hastings, who scoffs at his fears. Catesby suggests that Richard must wear the garland of the realm; but Hastings will not consent to Richard's having it against the "true descent" of Edward's children, though he rejoices at the news that the Queen's kindred die today. Stanley invites Hastings to the Council, and he goes rejoicing at the misfortunes of his enemies. Buckingham meets him and intimates to the audience that Hastings will not return from the Tower.

III, 3. Rivers, Grey, and Vaughan pass by to their death.

> *Grey.* Now Margaret's curse is fall'n upon our heads,
>   For standing by when Richard stabb'd her son.
> *Riv.* Then cursed she Hastings, then cursed she Buckingham,
>   Then cursed she Richard. O, remember, God,
>   To hear her prayers for them, as now for us!
>   And for my sister and her princely sons,
>   Be satisfied, dear God, with our true blood,
>   Which, as thou know'st, unjustly must be spilt.

III, 4. Hastings thinks himself close enough to Richard to speak for him at the council upon the time of the coronation. After Richard has heard of Hastings' stand against making Richard king, he accuses him of protecting witchcraft, and orders his immediate death. Hastings remembers his joy at the death of the Queen's kindred

> O Margaret, Margaret, now thy heavy curse
> Is lighted on poor Hastings' wretched head!

III, 5. As Richard and Buckingham pretend great fear of imminent danger, the Mayor and Catesby enter, to whom Lovel and Ratcliff enter with Hastings' head. Hastings had planned, they say, to murder Richard and Buckingham in the council house. The Mayor will explain to the citizens. Buckingham is to follow and infer the bastardy of Edward's children, Edward himself, etc. He is to bring the Mayor and citizens to Baynard's Castle. Richard will "draw the brats of Clarence out of sight."

III, 6. A Scrivener enters with the indictment of Hastings, ruminating upon the fact that it is a "palpable device."

III, 7. Buckingham reports to Richard that the citizens are mum, but the Mayor is coming. Richard, accompanied by two bishops, is finally persuaded to receive the Mayor. Buckingham says the citizens blame Richard for not accepting the crown as his by right. Richard demurs but finally is overpersuaded. He is to be crowned tomorrow.

Richard has the crown about to be placed upon his head; but Margaret's curse has begun to work, and that through Richard himself. The tragedy of the house of York has now arrived at its epitasis.

IV, 1. Queen Elizabeth, the Duchess of York, and Dorset meet Anne and Clarence's daughter, all on the way to the Tower to see the princes, but Brakenbury refuses them entrance on orders from Richard. Stanley summons Anne to be crowned at Westminster. Queen Elizabeth sends her son Dorset to join Richmond

> Lest thou increase the number of the dead;
> And make me die the thrall of Margaret's curse,
> Nor mother, wife, nor England's counted queen.

Anne remembers the curse she had pronounced on Richard's wife, as it now begins to come true on herself. Anne goes to Richard, Elizabeth to sanctuary, the Duchess to her grave. Elizabeth bids the rough cradle of her sons farewell.

IV, 2. Richard enters crowned by Buckingham's efforts, and hints that "Edward lives"; but "High-reaching Buckingham grows circumspect." Richard sends for Tyrrell to do the deed. Stanley reports the flight of Dorset. Richard tells Catesby it is rumored that Anne is "sick and like to die"; he intends to marry Clarence's daughter to some mean-born gentleman, the boy is foolish

> for it stands me much upon,
> To stop all hopes whose growth may damage me.
> I must be married to my brother's daughter,
> Or else my kingdom stands on brittle glass.
> Murder her brothers, and then marry her!
> Uncertain way of gain! But I am in
> So far in blood that sin will pluck on sin.

Tyrrell enters and undertakes to kill the princes. Buckingham returns to put Richard in mind of the promised earldom of Hereford but Richard is so wrapt up in Richmond, now the rival claimant to the throne, that Buckingham gets no attention. Richard remembers that Henry VI prophesied Richmond would be king;[4] and that a bard in Ireland told him once

---

[4] *3 Henry VI,* IV, 6, 68 ff.

"I should not live long after I saw Richmond." Buckingham says,

> O, let me think on Hastings, and be gone
> To Brecknock, while my fearful head is on!

IV, 3. Tyrrell reports to Richard that the princes are dead and buried. Richard says he has attended to the children of Clarence, "Anne my wife hath bid the world good night," and now he will marry young Elizabeth, his brother's daughter, whom Richmond wants. Catesby announces that Ely is with Richmond, and Buckingham is in the field.

IV, 4. Margaret says

> So, now prosperity begins to mellow
> And drop into the rotten mouth of death.

Queen Elizabeth and the Duchess of York enter lamenting, and the three play the game of swap out. Margaret sums up the score

> Thy Edward he is dead, that stabb'd my Edward;
> Thy other Edward dead, to quit my Edward;
> Young York he is but boot, because both they
> Match not the high perfection of my loss:
> Thy Clarence he is dead that kill'd my Edward;
> And the beholders of this tragic play,
> The adulterate Hastings, Rivers, Vaughan, Grey,
> Untimely smother'd in their dusky graves.
> Richard yet lives, hell's black intelligencer,
> Only reserved their factor, to buy souls
> And send them thither: but at hand, at hand,
> Ensues his piteous and unpitied end:
> Earth gapes, hell burns, fiends roar, saints pray,
> To have him suddenly convey'd away.
> Cancel his bond of life, dear God, I pray,
> That I may live to say, The dog is dead!

After Margaret has finally wrung the subject dry, Richard enters for pages of recriminations with the ladies. His mother finally curses him and leaves. Richard thinks he has persuaded Elizabeth to give him her daughter in marriage.

> Relenting fool, and shallow, changing woman!

(Richard forgets that he is in exactly the wrong place in the fourth act!) Ratcliff and Catesby report that Richmond only waits for Buckingham to welcome him aland. Richard orders that troops be raised at once. Stanley's son George is kept as hostage of his faith. Messenger after messenger announces the rising of important forces against Richard, but Buckingham's army has been destroyed and other catastrophes have happened to Richmond's side. Buckingham is captured, but Richmond lands at Milford.

IV, 5. Derby tells Urswick that his son George is hostage but the Queen has consented heartily to Richmond's marriage with her daughter. So ends the fourth act.

All have now fallen, as Margaret had prayed and prophesied in her curses, except Richard; and she leaves the stage confidently renewing her curse upon him. At the end of the act, Richmond stands ready to precipitate the catastrophe, strictly according to the Terentian formula. Margaret declares officially that the epitasis is complete, and awaits the catastrophe.

V, 1. Buckingham passes to execution, with a recognition of divine retribution and a remembrance of Margaret's curse and prophesy. Since Buckingham's error is wholly within the house of York and not against Lancaster, Margaret's curse was rather a prophecy in his case, and consequently his catastrophe is incidental to the catastrophe of York; hence is saved for the fifth act.

V, 2. In God's name, Richmond seeks Richard, who has no friends but friends for fear.

V, 3. Richard, with three times the men that Richmond has, gloomily pitches his tent on one side of Bosworth field; Richmond hopefully pitches his on the other and sends a message to Stanley. Richard in melancholy sends a threat to Stanley and prepares to sleep; Richmond is encouraged by Derby (Stanley) and, as God's champion, in confidence also sleeps. Then we hold the masque review of the ghosts; Prince Edward first, son of Henry VI, who comes second, next Clarence, then Rivers, Grey, and Vaughan together, next Hastings, followed by the two young princes, with Anne in sequence, and Buckingham as rear guard. Each curses Richard and blesses Richmond. Both Lancaster and York thus invoke catastrophe upon Richard through Richmond Tudor. Says Clarence as first of the Yorkists in line.

> Thou offspring of the house of Lancaster,
> The wronged heirs of York do pray for thee.

Richard's conscience is shaken with his fearful dream, and he goes to play the eavesdropper on those who might plan to desert. Richmond has had sweet sleep and reminds his soldiers.

> God and our good cause fight upon our side

while Richard is

> One that hath ever been God's enemy.

Richard himself forebodes

> A black day will it be to somebody

and gives directions for the imminent battle. His motto is

> Conscience is but a word that cowards use,
> Devised at first to keep the strong in awe:
> Our strong arms be our conscience, swords our law.

Richard orders the death of George Stanley when the elder Stanley (ancestors of the patron of Shakspere's company) refuses to aid Richard, but the execution must be deferred till after the battle.

V, 4. Richard seeks a horse; he has already slain five Richmonds, but never the right one.

V, 5. Richmond is victorious and Derby (that ancestor again) crowns him. George Stanley lives. Richmond gives healing orders.

> We will unite the white rose and the red.
>
> . . . .
>
> O, now let Richmond and Elizabeth,
> The true succeeders of each royal house,
> By God's fair ordinance conjoin together!
> And let their heirs, God, if thy will be so,
> Enrich the time to come with smooth-faced peace,
> With smiling plenty and fair prosperous days!

And a curse is invoked upon those traitors who would "reduce these bloody days again."

CHAPTER XXI

The Moral of the Lancaster-York Tetralogy

Richard III is not only a play at the conclusion of a tetralogy; it is also the conclusion of the tetralogy on the wars of the roses, with the moral of the whole series brought to a final focus. It brings together the highlights of the preceding events, in such a way as to picture the way of God to England.

It will be noticed that the structural idea of the play is expressed through the device of Margaret's curses upon the house of York for that of Lancaster, supplemented in the catastrophe by way of summary with the review of the ghosts from both houses, all damning Richard and approving Richmond. Now Margaret was dead before the historical time of this play. But like a Senecan ghost she calls for revenge. The revenge, however, is not for a single deed or for a single person, but for the accumulated sins of the house of York against the house of Lancaster. Margaret or Henry VI would be the natural mouthpiece for Lancaster, and Henry, since he had been a king, could have appeared at this period only as a ghost, but Margaret can have her life lengthened and appear in the flesh. As the actual former leader of the house of Lancaster, she is also the natural choice. She has, therefore, been projected into these later events by way of connecting these effects with their causes. Margaret and Margaret's role are, therefore, wholly unhistorical. She is the champion of Lancaster against York.

But this idea of Margaret's curses had grown up in *3 Henry VI*. York had cursed Margaret in a speech made memorable for us by Robert Greene's citation of a line from it,[1] and Richard has set Margaret cursing by reminding her of that speech.[2] Since Richard claims that "God, not we, hath plagued thy bloody deed," Margaret decides to try her luck at the same game. She had already made a trial run in *3 Henry VI*, V, 5, 63-67, where, following a suggestion to be found in Halle, she prays that if Edward and Clarence have children they may meet the same fate as has her Prince Edward. That idea is merely expanded in *Richard III*. Margaret's curses for topic-sentence, with constant reference by way of tie-in,

---

[1] *3 Henry VI*, I, 4, 111-149.
[2] *Richard III*, I, 3, 174-181.

then suggested the parade of the cursing ghosts for a summing-up sentence. Here then is the genesis and maturation of this structural idea.

Lancaster has had its tragedy completed in *3 Henry VI*. God is now in *Richard III* to exact from York an eye for an eye and a tooth for a tooth in punishment for its sins; but He is also to reward England with peace through joining the guiltless survivors of the two factions. The agent of this divine vengeance upon York is Richard, himself a Yorkist. He first destroys all others and then himself is last destroyed. Richard had been in fact prominent in this destruction of the other members of his house and had in fact benefitted by their destruction whether or not he himself had been directly concerned in their taking off. Consequently, he becomes the representative of the house of York. Then Richmond is left guiltless of the crimes of both houses, inheriting only their virtues.

Not only is the device of Margaret unhistorical, but also the idea of opposing in this way sin against sin of the two houses. This idea, to express which Margaret was continued in life and Richard was caused to be the sole scapegoat of his house — this balance of sins between the houses is also new to this tradition. There had been a "contention," and both Margaret and Richard had played important parts therein. But no one had thus represented them as moralized representatives of their houses. Such a representation, however, was not new to Shakspere. Romeo and Juliet find that the stars use their houses to confound them, innocent though they be. Instead of the stars with their chance, in *Richard III* we have God unerringly avenging murders committed, and restoring the right. In *Romeo and Juliet* the stars work through the warring houses by a succession of accidents to cause the tragedy of the lovers. In *Richard III*, God works unswervingly through the warring houses to punish crime and to reward virtue. Clearly, the motive force of the stars acting upon the houses in *Romeo and Juliet*, the germ of which is from the source, Brooke, has suggested to Shakspere the device in *Richard III* of having God exact punishment upon and through the contending houses of Lancaster and York. That is, Shakspere constructed *Richard III* after he had constructed *Romeo and Juliet*.

On the background of *Romeo and Juliet* and the three parts of *Henry VI* the genesis and development of this framework idea is quite clear. Shakspere himself did not use it again. He was beginning to attempt to put the motive force into the individuals, not in some external agency as the stars or God working through some instrument upon the individual. Nor do I recall anyone else before him in English drama who has used opposing families quite or at all in this way. Since the families had the power of arranging marriage, they regularly enter as a determining factor into the background of the lovers' fortunes in Latin drama. This social fact continued to reflect itself in Romantic drama and story in Shakspere's time. Hence its assumption in the background of the story of Romeo and Juliet, where Shakspere in his search for machinery through which a motive-force could work brought it into the foreground and made it crucial. I do not think of any other Englishman who has thus consciously and pointedly used the houses in the technical structure of a tragedy before Shakspere did so. The idea of moralizing historical events is, of course, a traditional one in England and elsewhere, in drama and other forms of literature. In fact, the Old Testament naturally encouraged this attitude toward history, and fundamentally that attitude still prevails with the majority, whether or not they interpret specifically in terms of divine guidance.

In *Romeo and Juliet* the stars had used chance or accident against the lovers at the crucial points. Their tragedy is not shown to have had any necessary connections with what they are. In *Richard III*, responsibility for the tragedy is indeed fixed upon individuals. But the handling is external. They have sinned and the wages of sin is death. Thus saith the Lord. Blessed be the name of the Lord. Richard announces that he is a villain, then consistently and with impishly conscious pride acts the part. There can be no question of what ought to happen to him, and his enemies threaten him with God. At the appointed time God delivers him to Richmond. So with the other characters; each is caused to recognize God's punishment for sin. Here is a sermon on political hell-fire and damnation, with a pearly gate at the end wherethrough to glimpse the coming glories of the Tudor heaven, from which even in Shakspere's day a few Lucifers yet needed to be thrown.

It may not be amiss to point out that some have been unduly impressed with the pearly gate of *Vnion* and forget the hell-fire of *Continual Discension* through which that heaven had finally been attained. In the tetralogy, no one sees the pearly gate save by prophecy till Richard III has been removed from before it. The promised reward of union comes only in the final speech, as in a good morality play, and even in that, the final place is given to the curse upon traitors who would "reduce these bloody days again." The sequence is not continued (as Halle does) to show the blessings of the union in the reigns of Henry VII, Henry VIII, Edward VI, and then Elizabeth. No one had a vision of an eight-play epic celebrating the union of the houses of Lancaster and York. Instead, someone who believed in the real and present glories of that union under Elizabeth planned to warn against falling again into the "discension" of those old days of the wars of the roses, and to do so began logically where the historians placed the origins of that particular trouble, with the struggle of Somerset and York, the result being the present tetralogy. At the conclusion of this tetralogy was Richard III, so supreme a political exemplum in his own right that Harington in 1591 uses him in defense and praise of all tragedy. "For Tragedies, to omit other famous Tragedies; That, that was playd at S. *Iohns* in Cambridge, of *Richard* the 3. would moue (I thinke) *Phalaris* the tyraunt, and terrifie all tyrānous minded men, frō following their foolish ambitious humors, seeing how his ambition made him kill his brother, his nephews, his wife, beside infinit others; and last of all after a short and troublesome raigne, to end his miserable life, and to haue his bodie harried after his death."[3] In the Shaksperean tetralogy, Richard is all this as well as the scapegoat for the accumulated sins of his house. Richmond and union are merely a touch of "moonlight and roses" after Shylock has stumbled off the stage.

It may now be well to notice the suggestion that the construction of *Richard III* has been affected by that of *The True Tragedie of Richard the third*. If there is connection — and there well may be — it does not go very deep. Basing upon the excellent structural analysis of *Richard III* by Professor Law,[4] Professor Wilson[5] points out "When we consider . . . the construction of . . . *Richard III* . . . the play can, I think, be shown to owe more to its predecessor than would appear on the surface. Noting that the initial dramatic problem of *Richard III* was to impose at least the form of unity upon the miscellaneous jumble of events in the chronicles between the death of Henry VI and the accession of Henry VII, Law points out that one method pursued by the dramatist was, after a first act, which is mainly invented, to confine the action as far as possible to the happenings of a single year in the chronicles. Thus in Acts 2, 3, 4, and the first scene of Act 5 our attention is wholly directed to 1483, after which it is immediately switched to the Battle of Bosworth (22 August 1485), with which the play concludes. Now this is precisely the structure of *The True Tragedy*, which begins, after an Induction, with a scene at Edward's death-bed; and though dramatizing some episodes in 1483 from the chronicles which Shakespeare either passes over or merely alludes to, those which it omits he omits also, notably the coronation of Richard III. It would seem, therefore, as if the framework of *Richard III,* at any rate in its main outline, may have been constructed by the dramatist responsible for the old play." This coincidence may in fact be due partly to direct influence, but it is probably sufficiently accounted for by the shaping ideas behind the two plays.

For we must remember that, whatever his subject, the dramatist under the rules of that day always had an "old play" upon which to base, consisting of the traditional type, the five-act formula, the casting pattern of his company, etc. Any two dramatists, therefore, in treating the same

---

[3] Harington, *Orlando Furioso* (1591), ¶6ʳ.

[4] R. A. Law, *"Richard III:* A Study in Shakespeare's Composition," *P.M.L.A.* (1945), LX, 689-696.

[5] J. D. Wilson, *Richard III,* p. xxxi.

body of events would inevitably have a considerable degree of coincidence. Consequently, coincidence must be specific and extended if it is to prove direct connection.

So with the wars of the roses as an exemplum of primogeniture. If an Englishman chose to use this idea at all, its main outlines were already shaped. It was an epic already sketched. If, therefore, any Englishman wrote any one of these histories on this background, he would consciously or unconsciously be writing an epic or part thereof. Since the Henry VI plays came first among these history plays, and since the original author or authors did shape them in conformity with this idea, they did write this tetralogy in accordance with this epic idea, which later they filled in with four more plays. This fact does not mean, however, that all eight plays were planned to form an epic.[6] Such as it is, the epic was already there, and for whatever reason, the beginning was made *in medias res* with Henry VI, instead of with the actual beginning in *Richard II*. As we have seen, sufficient reason for beginning here would be the political situation at the time, with the English again fighting in France.

After this first tetralogy, a second was planned and executed to deal with the origins and development of the whole dissension which lay behind the struggle of York and Lancaster, but that tetralogy is beyond the scope of our present work.

In all this, these history plays merely follow their chief sources. These were Halle, Holinshed, and the *Mirour*. Holinshed embodies most of Halle, and the *Mirour* presents the moralized tragedies of various people, taking its facts for the most part avowedly from Halle, with some reference to Fabian, the interpretation of the *Mirour* being also usually at least implicit in Halle. So Halle's view is fundamental here. And Halle was at considerable pains to state what that view was. His title in 1548 runs: *The Vnion of the two noble and illustre famelies of Lancastre & Yorke beeyng long in continual discension for the croune of this noble realme, with all the actes done in bothe the tymes of the Princes, bothe of the one linage and of the other, beginnyng at the tyme of kyng Henry the fowerth, the first aucthor of this deuision, and so successiuely proceadyng to the reigne of the high and prudent prince kyng Henry the eight, the vndubitate flower and very heire of both the sayd linages.*

Halle's over-all view is this, "For as kyng henry the fourthe was the beginnyng and rote of the great discord and deuision: so was the godly matrimony [of Henry VII and Elizabeth], the final ende of all discensions, titles and debates" (Preface). This is the official and conventional view which had been promoted and promulgated by Henry VII himself

---

[6] See Law's objections to Tillyard.

and enforced by all succeeding Tudors.[7] Since Henry IV displaced Richard II, the latter sovereign becomes a possible starting point, as in Halle himself, and the success of Henry VII forms the real conclusion of this process, though one could then bring the history triumphantly to date as did Halle.

Halle's headings for the various reigns are themselves significant. There is "An introduccion into the history of Kyng Henry the fourthe," "The victorious actes of Kyng Henry the fifth," "The trobleous season of Kyng Henry the sixt," "The prosperous reigne of Kyng Edward the fourthe," "The pitifull life of Kyng Edward the. v.," "The tragical doynges of Kyng Richard the thirde," "The politique gouernaunce of Kyng Henry the. vii.," "The triumphusant reigne of Kyng Henry the. VIII." Anyone looking for tragic material would naturally turn to Henry VI and Richard III. Significantly, even the prosperous reign of Edward IV has been overwhelmed in our tetralogy.

Halle begins his work with a proper statement of view, in his "introduccion into the deuision of the two houses of Lancastre and Yorke." "What mischiefe hath insurged in realmes by intestine deuision, what depopulacion hath ensued in countries by ciuill discensiō, what detestable murder hath been cōmitted in citees by seperate faccions, and what calamitee hath ensued in famous regiōs by domestical discord & vnnaturall controuersy: Rome hath felt, Italy can testifie, Fraunce can bere witnes, Beame can tell, Scotlande maie write, Denmarke can shewe, and especially this noble realme of Englande can apparantly declare and make demonstracion. For who abhorreth not to expresse the heynous factes comitted in Rome, by the ciuill war betwene Julius Cesar and hardy Pōpey by whose discorde the bright glory of the triūphant Rome was eclipsed & shadowed? Who can reherce what mischefes and what plages the pleasant countree of Italy hath tasted and suffered by the sedicious faccions of the Guelphes and Gebelynes? Who can reporte the misery that daiely hath ensued in Fraunce, by the discorde of the houses of Burgoyne and Orliens: Or in Scotland betwene the brother and brother, the vncle and the nephew? Who can curiously endite the manifolde battailles that were fought in the realme of Beame, betwene the catholikes and the pestiferus

---

[7] For instance, on November 8, 1529, King Henry VIII said, "But when we remember our mortalitie and that we must dye, then we thinke that all our doinges in our life tyme, are clearely defaced, and worthy of no memorye, if we leaue you in trouble at the tyme of our death. For if our true heyre be not knowen at the time of our death, see what mischiefe and trouble shall succeede to you and to your children. The experience therof some of you haue seene after the death of our noble grādfather, K. Edward .4. & some haue heard what mischiefe & manslaughter cōtinued in this realme betwene the houses of Yorke & Lancaster: by the which dissension, thys realme was lyke to haue bene clearely destroyed" (Foxe, Actes (1570), p. 1193, col 1 — one book supposed to be available to every Englishman).

sectes of the Adamites and others? What damage discension hath dooen in Germany and Denmarke, all christians at this daie can well declare. And the Turke can here good testimony, whiche by the discord of christen princes hath amplified greatly his seigniory and dominion. But what miserie, what murder, and what execrable plagues this famous region hath suffered by the deuision and discencion of the renoumed houses of Lancastre and Yorke, my witte cannot comprehende nor my toung declare nether yet my penne fully set furthe." (How inevitably are we reminded of Bottom).

The reader should notice that *Julius Caesar* belongs to this sequence, and is treated by Shakspere from this view; refusal to see and admit the fact is at the bottom of most of the major disputes as to interpretation of the play. *Romeo and Juliet* too might have been forced to conform had Shakspere not already written it before he came into contact with this sequence. As it was, *Romeo and Juliet* served instead to point the way for balancing the houses in *Richard III*. Shakspere's *King John* also belongs to this sequence, being the earliest instance of a broken succession in modern English history. And the *Mirour* recognizes the fact.

> Was not Richard, of whom I spake before,
> A rebel playne vntil his father dyed,
> And John likewise an Enmie euermore
> To Richard againe, and for a rebel tryed?
> After whose death, it cannot be denyed,
> Against all right this John most cruellye
> His brothers children caused for to dye.

> Arthur and Isabell (I meane) that were
> Geffreyes children, then Duke of Britaine
> Henries third sonne, by one degree more neere;
> Then was this John, as stories shew most playne,
> Which two children were famisht or els slayne,
> By John their Eame cald *Saunzterre* by name,
> Of whose fowle act, al countries speake great shame.[8]

So John is also fitted into this theme of dissension.

First, then, we have the three parts of *Henry VI* and *Richard III* treating of the York-Lancaster dissension, the wars of the roses. Next, *King John* was reworked as the earliest instance of the theme in English history. Then came the Lancaster division, including *Richard II, 1, 2, Henry IV,* and *Henry V,* which was the occasion of the Lancaster-York dissension. Finally came *Julius Caesar* as the illustration from Roman history, quite pertinent for the descendants of Brute.[9] Shakspere has taken his theme

---

[8] *Mirour* (1578), f 42[r].

[9] Halle causes York to say, "But as Preachers say: euill gotten gooddes, do not long continue, nor vsurped power, hath no prosperous successe. I will not molest you, with the rehersyng of the calamitie, whiche fell emõgest the Israelites, when Athalia

through English and Roman history. It is to be found also, with a difference, in the lack of degree in *Troilus and Cressida,* eventually from Homer, the Greek, though the theme in *Troilus* is only explanatory and incidental.[10] Here, then, is the principal theme upon which Shakspere exercised himself to maturity. It deserves more consideration as such than it has ordinarily received. But that consideration should be historical not hysterical.

Halle might plan to give the complete cycle from the deposition of Richard II through the settlement with Henry VII, and Baldwin and his cohorts might also decide to begin with the reign of Richard II, when they examined Halle for moralizable downfalls, yet they quickly found themselves concerned with the reign of Henry VI, and used about five-sixths of their space upon it and its consequences. By folio 29, they request, "Let vs . . . come to . . . Henry the syxte: whose Nonage broughte Fraunce and Normandye oute of Bondage, and was the cause that so few of our noble men dyed aged."[11] Here is where the tragic conflict between Lancaster and York really began. Till then Lancaster's crime had paid quite well. Loss of France was the first major catastrophe

---

slew all the bloud Royal, except litle Joas, and tyrānously vsurped the croune: nor troble you with the cōtinual warre, which happened emōge the Romaines, when Julius Cesar toke vpon hym, without lawe or aucthoritie, the name and stile of Emperor," but instances instead some early English history (Halle, *Vnion* (1548), Henry VI, f CLXXVIII^v and f CLXXIX^r). We may add another instance, "and this indignation of due honour not giuen to them which had fought valiantly, induced many agaynst their countrey, to subuert the libertie thereof. *Coriolane,* the *Gracchi, Scylla, Marius, Sertorius, Catiline,* and *Caesar* be an example hereof" (Cornelius Agrippa, *Vanitie* (1575), f 127^v). In Lydgate's *The Serpent of Deuision* . . . *Romes ouerthrowe,* 1590, Lucan is alleged as the authority for the statement that "the denying of *Iulius* his purchast honor . . . was the cheefe ground and occasion of all the war that after began in *Rome*" (B2^r; cf. B4^r, bottom). Caesar was everywhere a stock exemplum of "ambition" resulting in upset order.

[10] Halle, of course, takes the conventional point of view of moralizing-historians generally. "I would desire of God, that all men would in egall balance, ponder & indifferently consider the causes, of these misfortunes and euill chaunces, the whiche beyng eleuate in aucthoritie, dooe mete and measure, Justice and iniury, right and wrong, by high power, blynd aucthoritie, and vnbridled will" (Halle, *Vnion* (1548), Edward IV, f CCXIX^r). Edward IV is caused to say, "Suche a serpente is ambicion and desire of vainglory and souereingtie, which emongest estates when he is once entred he crepith furth so far, till with deuision and variaūce he turneth all to mischiefe. Firste longynge to be next to the beste, afterwarde egall with the beste, and at the laste chief and aboue the beste. Of which immoderate appetite of worship and the debate and discension that grewe there by, what losse, what sorowe, what trouble hath within these fewe yeres growen within this realme, I pray God as well to forget as we well remembre" (Halle, *Vnion* (1548), Edward V, f III^r). Edward; that is Halle, is as well aware of the serpent ambition as is Ulysses and of its effect upon estates, with the "Firste longynge to be next to the best," etc., in a well-worn progression. In fact, Edward says in brief, as had many another, what Ulysses dilates at large; it was merely the commonplace view of the political moralists of the time.

[11] *Mirour* (1578), f 29^v.

(rather amusing this — since Lancaster won France under Henry V, had it not a right to lose it under Henry VI!) to overtake England for the sin of the Lancastrians in breaking the succession in primogeniture. The interest in French affairs in the early 'nineties made this a natural subject for discussion, and the *Mirour* a natural guide for interpretation. So it happens that the first tetralogy begins naturally with the loss of France as its first unit. Contemporary interests being what they were, it was the inevitable place to begin.

The *Mirour* leaves no more doubt as to its attitude toward primogeniture than does the tetralogy. Writing in the reign of Mary, Baldwin had said toward the end of the *Mirour:* "The matter is notable to teache al people aswel officers as subiects to cōsyder their estates, and to lyue in loue & obedience to the highest powers, what so euer they bee, whom God eyther by byrth, law, succession or vniuersal election, doth or shall auchthorise in his owne rowme to execute his lawes and iustice, among any people or nation: for by all these meanes God placeth his deputies, and in my iudgemēt there is no meane so good either for the cōmon quiet of the people, or for gods free choise, as the natural order of enheritaunce by lyneal discent: for so it is left in Gods hands, to create in the wombe what prince hee thinketh meetest for his purposes: the people also know their princes and therfore the more gladly and willinglie receiue and obay them."[12] "For what soeuer man, woman, or childe, is by the consent, of the whole realme established in the royal seate, so it haue not bene iniuriouslye procured by rigour of sword and open force, but quietly, by title, eyther of enheritaunce, succession, lawful bequeste, common consent, or election, is vndoubtedlye chosē by God to be his deputie: and whosoeuer resistethe any such, resisteth against God himselfe, and is a ranke traytour and rebel."[13] For the English, primogeniture alone was God's way, and God had always stood ready to punish dissenters.

It should not need to be pointed out that this theme of warning against dissension was very much to the fore in the 'eighties and the 'nineties, so that these plays are very directly aimed at the interests of the time, hence also the clear indications of their success. According to the author or authors of the tetralogy and to the historians of that day, the cause of the dissension was the broken succession in primogeniture, where the oldest should have succeeded the oldest. Thus we have the elaborate genealogical presentations to prove the claim of York against Lancaster. Even Henry VI is caused to admit that his claim is weak. If Henry VII and Elizabeth were the rightful successors by primogeniture, then by this rule Mary Queen of Scots, a Roman Catholic, would be the rightful claimant until

---

[12] *Mirour* (1578), f 174ᵛ.

[13] *Mirour* (1578), f 175ᵛ.

she was removed,[14] when her son James, who had been separated early from his mother and carefully reared as a protestant, became "apparent."[15] After the beheading of Mary, the Roman Catholics tried by this same rule of primogeniture to find some other candidates either more suitable to them, or who would at least start another contention which would enable the Roman Catholics to gain control. This is no place for a volume on that background. But one can turn to Robert Parsons, *A Conference about the next Succession to the Crowne of Ingland*, 1594, for one of the clearest available expositions of the family backgrounds for these claims. If one examines Parsons' "Perfect and exact Arbor and genealogie of al the kynges Queenes and Princes of the blood royal of Englād," he will see that after the descendants of Henry VIII, then James VI of Scotland was the claimant through Margaret, eldest daughter of Henry VII, with Lady Arabella next in line (which was the cause of all her woe). Next, through Mary, second daughter of Henry VII, were Edward and Henry Seymour (house of Hertford), and Ferdinando Lord Strange and his brother (house of Derby). So one comes very close to Strange's company when he reads the report on September 14, 1592, of the priest George Dingley on what he has heard in Spain. "Has heard the Earls of Oxford and Cumberland, and Lords Strange and Percy talked of as much alienated by discontent. Their chief hope is the death of Her Majesty. The Spaniard gives that as a reason of his lingering in re-attempting a new assault, because time may call her away whose life makes the attempt three times more perilous, and they confirm their opinion with the certain hope of a debate between the two houses of Hereford and Derby, who, they think, will seek the Crown, each one for himself, during which contention the Spaniard thinks the entry into England would be without danger.

"They greatly rejoiced in the muttering of the Martinists translating the book into Spanish, and presenting it to the King, judging by the hot words of 100,000 fists about their ears, and such like in the book, that some uproar would shortly be moved by the faction, which would find favour amongst the noblemen, in hopes of enjoying the bishops' and other spiritual revenues. They also hope to have Scotland as their back friend."[16] Our tetralogy is pointed exactly against such disunion, and extra-special care has been taken in *Richard III* to play up the loyalty of Derby, the patron of the company.

---

[14] As Antony Colynet in his *True History of the Ciuill Warres of France* (1591) puts it, "the hope which the Leaguers had of *England* was dead with the Queene of *Scottes*" (p. 142).

[15] As Robert Bruce reminded him in an *Epistle Dedicatorie*, dated December 9, 1590, "And suppose zee be ane King, Sir, of this kingdoome presentlie, and Apparent of ane vther" (*Sermons vpon the Sacrament*, A3ᵛ). This was one excellent reason to "go to Scotland" at this period.

[16] *C. S. P. Domestic, 1591-94*, p. 270 (Vol. CCXLIII. 11).

For there was not merely the Roman Catholic question, with the Pope through Spain attempting to bring England back into the fold, and through the Guise, etc. to suppress the Huguenots in France. The English had met their direct threat in '88, and in '89 and the early 'nineties were helping to meet that in France. Of this concern most of us are at least vaguely aware, though in these days of atomic brotherhood[17] it is not quite polite to take those old differences too seriously. Few of us, however, are aware of the concern the various "puritan" elements were causing — Marprelate and the rest. The fundamental accusation against them was that they were in fact traitors and would pull down all government.[18] Whether the accusation was true is beside the question. It happens that W. Burton states the case accurately for his time in a reference to Lyly's *Pappe with an Hatchet,* "we shal geue no occasion iustly to feare the sheading of bloud, except by some butcherly Machiuel, who belike hauing lost his penknife, knew not how to make his pen but with a hatchet. You knowe my meaning . . . come Spaniards, and we hold together: goe Spaniards, we fall asunder."[19] But one must also remember what did happen a half-century later. The fears were real and in not too long a time they were justified. The established order must be maintained at all costs, and that could be done only by continuing the fundamental principles of primogeniture and lawful succession, as God had determined. For disobedience one could expect the same dire punishments as in the past.

So in the early 'nineties there was a great deal of whistling in the dark to keep courage up. Swinburne puts the case all too pragmatically. He refers to the rulings that "aswell by the ciuill law as by the cannon lawe, (with the which lawes the lawes of this our realme of England, doe in this point seeme to ioyne hands:) It is vnlawfull for a king to giue awaie his kingdome from his lawfull heires, for the confirmation whereof diuers writers vse diuers reasons." Nevertheless, "this princelie controuersie, as it hath seldome receiued ordinarie triall heretofore; so hereafter if the case were to be argued in verie deede, verie likelie it is to bee vrged with more violent arguments and sharpe syllogismes, then by the vnbloodie blowes of bare words, or the weake weapons of instrumentes made of paper and parchment: And on the other side to bee answered with flatte denials of greater force, and distinctions of greater efficacie, then can proceede from anie legall or logicall engine; and in the end to be decided and ruled by the dead stroke of vnciuill and martial cannons, rather then by anie rule of the ciuill or cannon lawe."[20] In the blank space below, he

---

[17] Modern version of a "shot-gun marriage" between the nations.

[18] See above, pp. 147 ff.

[19] Burton, *A Sermon . . . 1589,* H4[r].

[20] Henry Swinburne, *A Briefe treatise of Testaments and Last Willes* (1590), f 68[r&v].

adds ominously, *Videant quorum interest*. That is only too exactly what Englishmen feared in 1590, and so in that dark to keep their courage up they whistled for all they were worth the tune of due succession in primogeniture. As their own recent history had taught them, they were dealing with no academic question.

It was evidently the interest in French affairs which occasioned the Henry VI plays, specifically, therefore, *1 Henry VI,* which could thus hardly have been planned as we have it before say 1590. England had once claimed and controlled France, and now English armies were in France to help subdue the country for the protestant Navarre. The analogy of Talbot was exact. At least Navarre would hardly have been so enthusiastic about Henry V, and himself took proper precautions to see that the English armies did not again play such a part in France. But in the early 'nineties the English were particularly interested in the subject of wars in France. The first part of *Henry the Sixth* was necessarily the point of departure at this time, but as necessarily it demanded the scope of the first tetralogy to give it the proper horrific background. The theme, therefore, was not the loveliness of union, but the horrors of dissension.

CHAPTER XXII

The Work of Peele and Shakspere
on *Titus Andronicus*

Another play in which Shakspere's company is supposed to have acted in 1592 is *Titus Andronicus,* which was entered S.R. February 6, 1594, and printed that year. It has been suggested indeed that the entry could have been for the prose *History of Titus Andronicus.*[1] But the evolution of rhetorical pattern in the titles to the various items involved will clear the direction of change and indicate that the entry was for the play.

Chapbook	The			History of Titus Andronicus, The Renowned Roman Gener
S.R.	a	Noble	Roman	Historye of Tytus Andronicus
1594	The Most Lamentable Romaine			Tragedie of Titus Andronicus
	head-title: the same			
	running-title: omits "Romaine"			
1600	As 1594			
1611	The Most Lamentable			Tragedie of Titus Andronicus
	head- and running-title as 1594			
1620	Eine sehr klägliche			*Tragœdia von Tito Andronico* und der hoffertigen Kayserin
1623, head	The	Lamentable		Tragedy of Titus Andronicus
running	The			Tragedie of Titus Andronicus

It will be seen that the S.R. entry changed the subtitle of the chapbook, "The Renowned Roman General" into "Noble Roman" and inserted it into the main title, also substituting "a" for "The." Then the quarto of 1594 substituted "Most Lamentable" for "Noble," and "Tragedie" for "Historye," also reversing "a" back to "The." It shortened its running-title by omitting "Romaine." The quarto of 1600 duplicated. Next, the quarto of 1611 took for its title the running-title of 1594, continued in 1600. This is the form which was translated into the German title of 1620. Since the agreement is caused, however, by the omission of the one word "Romaine," which is non-essential and did not maintain itself, it may very well be merely coincidental. Finally, the head-title of the First Folio omitted "Most" from the title of 1611, and the running-title further omitted "Lamentable."

Probably the most important fact demonstrated by this rhetorical evolution is that before the records in 1594 the chapbook title was exactly as it

---

[1] J. Q. Adams, *Shakespeare's Titus Andronicus, the First Quarto 1594.*

is now; and that it was almost certainly the title in English — not the title of its alleged original in Italian — which was used to evolve the phraseology of the S.R. entry. Even if the S.R. entry should have been based on the Italian title, it still follows that the material of the chapbook was available by 1594. Further, the adaptation of the title in S.R. was made toward the play title, not for the chapbook, which even in the eighteenth-century edition still retained its pre-1594 title exactly. The fact that the title of the play as entered S.R. was further adapted in the edition of 1594 raises the suspicion, nothing more, that the S.R. title is for the play at some stage before the revision of late 1593 or early 1594. If so, it would be the first title for the play, as shown by its close connection with the chapbook title.[2] It would not follow, however, that the play was ever acted under that title.

Along with the entry of the play Feb. 6, 1594, was "the ballad thereof." The ballad title as attached to the eighteenth-century chapbook shows awareness of both the chapbook title and the play title of 1594, *The Lamentable and Tragical History of Titus Andronicus.* The ballad is a "History of Titus Andronicus" as is the chapbook, necessarily; but it is also "Lamentable and Tragical" as is the play. The connections with the play title are with the printed version, not that in S.R. As for the ballad as attached to the eighteenth-century chapbook, it was in print by 1620 in Richard Johnson's "The golden garland of princely pleasures, the third time printed," and so was presumably in the earlier prints of this collection. Of the ballad Sir Edmund Chambers says, "it rested on the play as we have it."[3] If the entry in 1594 was for the play, then the entry for the ballad says it rests on that item. The evolution and concatenations make it reasonably clear that the chapbook and the ballad at least approximately as we have them in the eighteenth century are as they were in 1594, when a ballad was entered.

After entry, the play was printed this same year of 1594 as having been acted among others by Sussex's men, and since Henslowe's Diary shows that company performing it in January and February, 1594, we apparently have one fact that we can reasonably trust; the form printed in 1594 should be the form used by Sussex's men. Henslowe distinguishes this play acted by Sussex's men as new, and other facts show that there was at least some revision at that time.

---

[2] The S.R. scribe found some difficulty in transcribing this title, "a[n . . . Rom *deleted*] Noble Roman Historye of Tytus [& *deleted*] Andronicus." Sir Walter Greg, whose transcription I have quoted, observes, "The deletions were made at the time of writing" (Greg, *Bibliography,* I, 10). It could be argued that the scribe was shortening, *currente calamo,* the title of the prose history. But in that case, how could the author of the printed title to *Titus Andronicus* have had access to this form, upon which he has modeled?

[3] Chambers, *Shakespeare,* I, 321.

These other facts concern principally the work of George Peele, where it appears that the history of the "invention" of the word *palliament* may establish an important point. Peele in his *Honour of the Garter* writes

Anon I saw

.   .   .   .

A goodly king in robes most richly dight.
The upper, like a Romaine Palliament,
In deede a Chapperon, for such it was.[4]

Professor Price has suggested that "The context makes it quite certain that Peele is referring to the robes of the Knights of the Garter, which in those days were purple. Peele says in effect that Edward III in his purple robes of the Garter was like a Roman Emperor wearing the purple."[5]

But Cooper, by 1590 "Doctor *Cooper* Bishop of *Winchester,* Prelate" of the order (1584-94)[6] and the standard authority on such words in Peele's day, does not fully agree with Professor Price's interpretation of *pallium.* In his *Thesaurus* of 1565, Cooper defines *"Pallium . . .* A mantell such as knightes of the garter do weare: a longe robe: a garment that philosophers vsed: a coape: a cloke." Cooper had inherited the first part of this definition from Elyot, who in 1538 had written, *"Pallium,* a mantelle, suche as knyghtes of the garter do weare." Then Cooper in his first revision of Elyot in 1548 expanded the definition to practically its final form. Thomas Thomas continues Cooper's definition; but Rider omitted the reference to the Knights of the Garter. Thus from 1538 Elyot and his successors[7] informed Englishmen that the proper word in Latin for the "Romaine Palliament" which the Knights of the Garter wore was the Greek *pallium,* and that the word had reference to the form of the garment only, not to its color at all. Bishop Cooper would certainly not have permitted the members of the order to be ignorant of the proper word, and its implications, for their mantle.

In their ruling that *pallium* was the proper word in Latin and *mantle* in English, the Renaissance dictionary makers were no doubt quite correct that *pallium* was one proper word in Latin, only they came too late to advise the Founder. Ashmole says of this garment, "In the Founder's Statutes it is called *Mantellum,* and in *Hen. V. Manteau,* both which we render *Mantle.* But the Exemplar of the Founder's Statutes entred in the black Book, and the Statutes of King *Henry* VIII. call it *Trabea,* which *Rosinus* reckons among the different Kinds of *Mantles* or *Gowns.* And in

---

[4] Horne, *Peele,* p. 249; Bullen, II, 324-325; *Honour* [1593], B2ᵛ.

[5] H. T. Price, "The Language of *Titus Andronicus," Papers of the Michigan Academy of Science Arts and Letters,* XXI, 506.

[6] Segar, William, *The Booke of Honor and Armes* (1590), Bk. V, p. 16.

[7] Even resolute John Florio chimes in, as frequently, "Pallio, *a mantle, cloke, robe, or other long garment as the knights of the garter weare. Also a cope or a surplis.*

20 *Art.* of King *Hen.* VIIIth's Statutes it is applied both to the *Mantle* and *Surcoat;* sometime it is stiled *Chlamyda* [pl.]; sometime *Stola;* but in other Places more pertinently, *Pallium* and *Toga.*"[8] King Henry VIII's English term had been regularly *mantle.*[9] It would appear, therefore, that while the dictionary makers preferred the Greek *pallium,* yet that those who made the statutes of the order had not been so meticulous, and along with the more "pertinent" *pallium* and *toga,* used also *chlamyda* and *stola.* Not only so, but they could use the one term *trabea* for both mantle and surcoat.

It is evident that Ashmole thinks the terms *pallium* and *toga* more "pertinent" because he had been properly taught by the teachers from the dictionaries and text books, which were constructed later than the statutes. For Thomas Godwyn would have told Ashmole that "The *Grecians* had their *Mantile* called *Pallium;* the *Romanes* their gowne called *Toga,* and by this different kinde of garment the one was so certainly distinguished from the other, that this word *Togatus* was often vsed to signifie a *Romane,* and *Palliatus* a *Grecian.*"[10] From similar sources, Peele would have acquired this very elementary information in grammar school. He would have known that *pallium* was Greek, not Roman.

But Peele was not thinking in terms of either *pallium* or *toga.* Instead, he was adapting another closely connected official term. On occasions of state, officials of the Heralds' College appeared *suis Paludamentis.*[11] Again, Godwyn will inform us that, "The fifth sort of gowne was called *Paludamentum;* It was a military garment, which none but the L. Generall or the chiefe captaines did vse to weare. *Isidorus* saith it was not only garded with purple, but with skarlet, and gold lace, whence it was sometimes called *toga purpurea,* somtimes *coccinea.* It was much like the habit which the *Grecian* Emperour was wont to weare called *Chlamis;* yea now it is called *Chlamis;* wee may english it an *Heralds* coate of Armes."[12] So Peele bestows the purple *paludamentum* of Roman chief captains, which might also be equated with the chlamys of Grecian Emperors, upon the King, and equates with it the purple *pallium* — or whatever else one chooses to call it — of the Knights as chief captains. As Singer pointed out, "The writer [in *Titus Andronicus*] was evidently thinking of the *plaudamentum,* which Valerius Maximus says was *white or purple,* but has confounded it with the white costume from which *candidate* is de-

---

[8] E. Ashmole, *The History of the most Noble Order of the Garter* (1715), p. 159 (second).

[9] *Ibid.,* pp. 548, 552, 554, 556, 559.

[10] T. Godwyn, *Romanae Historiae Anthologia* (1614), p. 78.

[11] Smith, *Camdeni . . . Epistolae* (London, 1691), p. lxvii.

[12] Godwyn, *Anthologia* (1614), p. 82. Notice the *chlamyda* of the statutes. Godwyn is merely summarizing some such author as Rosinus, admittedly.

rived."[13] But, as we shall see, the author has not "confounded" anything in error. Clearly, *palliament* has been coined from *paludament*[*um*], presumably under the influence of *pallium*.

Immediately, however, Peele in error equates this garment with another.

> The upper, like a Romaine Palliament,
> In deede a Chapperon, for such it was.

Now the *chaperon* was another part of the habit. "The Hood and Cap comes in the next Place to be spoken of, which Hood in King, *Henry* VIII's Statutes, and the Black Book of the Order is called *Humerale;* but in the Rolls of the Great Wardrobe, *Capucium.* In the *French* it is *Chaperon,* a Word used in the Statute, *Anno I. Richard* II. *C. 7.* and also retained in the Old *English* Copy of *Henry* VIII's Statutes made of his Reign, and annexed to this Treatise."[14] Thus *pallium* and *chaperon* would appear to have been merely words to Peele, and from some written or printed account he confused the two.

There is an illustration at p. 63 of Segar's *Honor Military, and Ciuill* (1602) of Lord Admiral Charles Howard, Earl of Nottingham, in full regalia, and an accompanying detailed description of the habit.[15] "The habit of these Knights is an vnder garment, or gowne of Crimsin veluet, of some called a kirtle, ouer which he weareth a mantle of Purple veluet lined with white sarsnet, on the left shoulder thereof is embroidred in a Garter an Eschuchion of *S. George,* and ouer his right shoulder hangeth his hood of Crimson veluet lined with white, the *Cordons* to the mantle are purple silke and gold" (p. 65). Peele has confused the mantle or *pallium* with the hood or *chaperon.* In the illustration, the hood itself, since it hangs "ouer his right shoulder," does not show.

How came Peele to commit this error? We look naturally to his sources. The fundamental version of the story which Peele retells goes back to Polydore Vergil. This Holinshed adapts. Then in 1590 Segar adapts Holinshed. But Peele is closest to Holinshed, and it seems clear that here Holinshed is in fact his basic, if not his only literary source. For instance, Peele's list of the first Knights of the Garter is very close to that of Holinshed. Peele gives Nicholas as the name of the Earl of Warwick, which is corrected in the Ashmole copy of Peele's poem to Thomas. Holinshed had given the name as "N. earle of Warw.,"[16] and Peele, not recognizing the symbol for *nomen,* or name to be inserted, which he should have remembered even from his catechism, expands into Nicholas.

---

[13] Singer, *Shakespeare* (1856), VIII, 12.

[14] Ashmole, *Garter* (1715), p. 168.

[15] See also the description in Victor Von Klarwill, *Queen Elizabeth and Some Foreigners,* p. 377. Ashmole, *Garter* (1672), between pp. 202 and 203 illustrates the various items.

[16] Holinshed, *Chronicles* (1587), I, *Description,* 160.

Other printed lists of the time known to me make no statement of the given name. Again, Peele inserts Southampton for Salisbury, but that was willful in order to enable him to insert a bit of flattery for the young Earl, whom Shakspere, as well as others, was courting at the time.[17] In fact, Southampton himself had been "proposed" at this time, but did not make it.[18] Peele has Walter Pagannell where Segar has Sir Walter Pauelly, to which the Ashmole copy corrects Peele. Here Peele is using the Latin form, as in Camden's *Britannia,* "Guilielmus Paganellus."[19] Peele's source is again Holinshed, who gives "Sir Walter Pannell *alias* Paganell." Peele has also Sir Haunchet Dambricourte, which is an evident misprint for Holinshed's "Sir Sanchet Dambricourt." Others regularly give the name as Sir Sanchet Dabridgecourt. Peele is clearly nearest to the list in Holinshed,[20] but since the author claims here to be printing a treatise upon the subject, we must face the possibility that Peele had also seen that treatise, though no such printed treatise is known.

Peele's use of sections of Holinshed which are not alleged to be from the treatise would appear to settle the matter in favor of Holinshed. That author had sketched the founding of this order under Edward III, and had there given reference to the *Description of Britain* for a fuller treatment, where we read,

The other order of knighthood in England, and the most honorable is that of the garter, instituted by king Edward the third, who after he had gained manie notable victories, taken king Iohn of France, and king Iames of Scotland (and kept them both prisoners in the Tower of London at one time) expelled king Henrie of Castile the bastard out of his realme, and restored *Don Petro* vnto it (by the helpe of the prince of Wales and duke of Aquitaine his eldest sonne called the Blacke prince) he then inuented this societie of honour, and made a choise out of his owne realme and dominions, and throughout all christendome of the best, most excellent and renowned persons in all vertues and honour, and adorned them with that title to be knights of his order, giuing them a garter garnished with gold and pretious stones, to weare dailie on the left leg onlie: also a kirtle, gowne, cloke, chaperon, collar, and other solemne and magnificent apparell, both of stuffe and fashion exquisite & heroicall to weare at high feasts, & as to so high and princelie an order apperteineth. Of this companie also he and his successors kings and queenes of England, be the souereignes, and the rest by certeine statutes and lawes amongst themselues be taken as brethren and fellowes in that order, to the number of six and twentie, as I find in a certeine treatise written of the same, an example whereof I haue here inserted word for word, as it was deliuered vnto me, beginning after this maner . . .
The order of the garter therefore was deuised in the time of king Edward

---

[17] Exactly what were they all aiming at, and who got the prize?

[18] C. C. Stopes, *Southampton,* p. 55.

[19] W. Camden, *Britannia* (Frankfort, 1590), p. 213.

[20] Stow's list is also close to that of Holinshed, being probably from it (Stow, *Annales* (1592), pp. 384-385).

the third, and (as some write) vpon this occasion. The queenes maiestie
then liuing, being departed from his presence the next waie toward hir lodg-
ing, he following soone after happened to find hir garter, which slacked by
chance and so fell from hir leg, vncespied in the throng by such as attended
vpon hir. His groomes & gentlemen also passed by it, disdaining to stoope
and take vp such a trifle: but he knowing the owner, commanded one of them
to staie and reach it vp to him. Why and like your grace (saieth a gentleman) it is but some womans garter that hath fallen from hir as she followed
the queenes maiestie. What soeuer it be (quoth the king) take it vp and giue
it me. So when he had receiued the garter, he said to such as stood about
him: You my maisters doo make small account of this blue garter here (and
therewith held it out) but if God lend me life for a few moneths, I will make
the proudest of you all to reuerence the like. And euen vpon this slender
occasion he gaue himselfe to the deuising of this order. Certes I haue not read
of anie thing, that hauing had so simple a begining hath growne in the end
to so great honour and estimation.[21]

The author continues to quote his treatise as to the original membership (which we have examined above), election, admission (which includes a description of the different articles of apparel, installation), etc.;
but we need not for our present purpose quote it further. Under the
reign of Edward III Holinshed had given a much briefer statement and
had given a cross-reference to this fuller account; both accounts are also
easily accessible through the indexes. I quote only such items as seem
pertinent. "The K. of England is euer cheefe of this order. They weare
a blew robe or mantell, & a garter about their left leg, richlie wrought
with gold and pretious stones, hauing this inscription in French vpon it,
Honi soit qui mal y pense, Shame come to him that euill thinketh. This
order is dedicated to S. George, as cheefe patrone of men of warre . . .

"The cause and first originall of instituting this order is vncerteine.
But there goeth a tale amongst the people, that it rose by this means. It
chanced that K. Edward finding either the garter of the queene, or of
some ladie[22] with whom he was in loue, being fallen from hir leg, stooped
downe and tooke it vp, whereat diuerse of his nobles found matter to iest,
and to talke their fansies merilie, touching the kings affection towards the
woman, vnto whome he said, that if he liued, it should come [t]o passe,
that most high honor should be giuen vnto them for the garters sake: and
there vpon shortlie after, he deuised and ordeined this order of the garter,
with such a posie, wherby he signified, that his nobles iudged otherwise
of him than the truth was. Though some may thinke, that so noble an
order had but a meane beginning, if this tale be true, yet manie honorable
degrees of estates haue had their beginnings of more base and meane

---

[21] Holinshed (1587), Vol. I, *Description,* p. 159. Segar, *Honor and Armes* (1590),
Bk. V, pp. 14 ff. simply extracts Holinshed for much of his materials.

[22] The countes of Salisburie.

things, than of loue, which being orderlie vsed, is most noble and commendable, sith nobilitie it selfe is couered vnder loue, as the poet *Ouid* aptlie saith,

Nobilitas sub amore iacet."[23]

This version of the story is merely a translation from Polydore Vergil.[24]

It may now be noticed that Peele used both of Holinshed's accounts. Peele enverses them thus:

> Anon I saw
> Under a Canapie of Crymsin bysse,
> Spangled with gold and set with silver bels,
> That sweetlie chimed, and luld me halfe a sleepe,
> A goodly king in robes most richly dight.
> The upper, like a Romaine Palliament,
> In deede a Chapperon, for such it was;
> And looking neerer, loe upon his legge,
> An[25] auncient badge of honour I espyed,
> A Garter brightly glistring in mine eye,
> A worthy ornament. Then I cald to minde,
> What Princely Edward, of that name the third,
> King Edward for his great atchivements famed,
> What he began; The Order of S. George,
> That at this day is honoured through the world.
> The order of the Garter so ycleepd.
> A great effect, grown of a slender cause,
> Graced by a King, and favoured of his feeres,
> Famed by his followers, worthy Kings and Queenes,
> That to this day are Soveraignes of the same.
> The manner how this matter grew at first.
> Was thus. The King disposed on a time
> To revell, after he had shaken Fraunce,
> (O had he bravely helde it to the last)
> And deckt his Lyons with their flowre de Lyce,
> Disposed to revell: Some say otherwise,
> Found on the ground by Fortune as he went
> A Ladies Garter: And the Queenes I troe
> Lost in a daunce, and tooke it up himselfe.
> It was a silken Ribban weaved of blewe.
> His Lords and standers by, seeing the King
> Stoope for this Garter, smiled: as who would say,
> Our office that had beene, or somwhat els.
> King Edward wistlie looking on them all,
> With Princely hands having that Garter ceazd,
> From harmelesse hart where honour was engraved,
> Bespake in French (a could the language well)
> And rife was French those dayes with Englishmen;

---

[23] Holinshed (1587), III, 366.

[24] The quoted sections of these accounts stood in the edition of 1577 of Holinshed practically as in that of 1587, which I have used.

[25] Horne reads "And," but notes no variant.

> They went to schoole to put together Townes,
> And spell in Fraunce with Feskues made of Pikes.
> Honi Soit Qui mal y pense, quoth he,
> Wherewith upon advizement, though the cause
> Were small, his pleasure and his purpose was
> T'advance that Garter, and to institute
> A noble order sacred to S. George:
> And Knights to make, whom he would have be tearmed
> Knights of the Garter. This beginning had
> This honourable order of our time.[26]

The reader will notice how Peele versifies Holinshed. For instance, "And euen vpon this *slender* occasion he gaue himselfe to the deuising of this order. Certes I haue not read of anie thing, that hauing had so simple a begining hath *growne* in the end to so great honour and estimation" (italics mine) becomes

> The Order of the Garter so ycleepd.
> A great effect, *grown* of a *slender* cause.

Peele accepts the version in Holinshed's treatise that Edward found the queen's garter "as he went." But as in the translation from Vergil, where an *amica* is insinuated, the lords jest "merrily," causing Edward to speak his motto in French and to decide to use that garter as a badge of honor. The touch that the garter was blue is from the treatise, etc. But I take it that sufficient has been pointed out to establish Holinshed as Peele's source.

It will now be seen how Peele has procured his Roman palliament for King Edward. Holinshed says, "The K. of England is euer cheefe of this order. They weare a blew robe or mantell & a garter about their left leg, richlie wrought with gold and pretious stones." This mantle and garter are also the only items in Peele's description; but he has equated the mantle, which he calls a Roman palliament, with the *chaperon* of Holinshed's other itemized list. For such an error there seems to be no accounting save by his sheer ignorance and inattention. The process by which the blue mantle (not purple here, though at this period it seems actually to have been purple) became a Roman *palliament* appears to be quite clear. Peele has Holinshed's statement before him that "They weare a blew robe or mantell" and remembers the term *chaperon* from Holinshed's previous complete description of the costume. So Peele erroneously equates the two. He wants besides a fine sounding variant for that blue (purple) mantle. He should have known from his dictionary that the official Latin for that mantle is *pallium,* and he should also have known that the *pallium* was Greek apparel. From some source, he knew of the similarly ceremonial Roman *paludamentum.* So Holinshed's blue mantle becomes neither a Greek *pallium* nor a Roman *paludament,* but a "Roman

---

[26] Horne, *Peele,* pp. 249-251; Bullen, II, 324-326; *Honour* [1593], B2ᵛ-B3ᵛ.

palliament." Such is one result of the ingrained habit, fixed by the schools, of striving for high-sounding variation.

In view of the actual origin of Peele's word *palliament*, it is rather instructive to behold the dictionaries. According to the *N.E.D.*, this word *palliament* is "ad. med. L. *palliāmentum*, f. *palliāre* to cloak." The *Century Dictionary* had earlier given the same derivation, though I have not thought it necessary to trace it to its source. Now I have found no instance in the Latin writers on the Order of the Garter of any such term as *palliāmentum*, and, as we have seen, Ashmole assures us from his examinations that the word in Latin was *pallium*. In Du Cange and the word lists which I have examined I have found no instance of such a form as *palliāmentum*. At least, it is not likely to have been a common word. It may have existed, and Peele may in some way have known it; but most likely he himself coined his word directly from *pallium* and *paludamentum*. On this background it appears reasonably certain that Peele is the inventor of *palliament*. If so, then anyone else using the word is certainly a borrower from him.

Thus we inevitably turn a suspicious eye with Mr. Robertson[27] upon the only other known use of the word *palliament*, which is in *Titus Andronicus*.

> *Titus Andronicus,* the people of Rome,
> Whose friend in iustice thou hast euer beene,
> Send thee by mee their Tribune and their trust,
> This Palliament of white and spotles hue,
> And name thee in election for the Empire,
> With these our late deceased Emperours sonnes:
> Be *Candidatus* then and put it on.[28]

Here is another Roman *palliament*, and since this is the robe of a *candidatus*, the *toga candidata*, the color is now quite correctly specified as white. Peele also had referred to loyalty's

> weedes of spotlesse white:
> Like those that stoode for Romes great offices.[29]

In both Peele and *Titus* we have a *palliament*, and in both a reference to the white robe of a *candidatus*. But the etymology of *candidatus* was known to everyone with any tincture of learning in that day, and the author of the passage in *Titus* makes it clear that he knew it. So there is

---

[27] J. M. Robertson, *An Introduction to the Study of the Shakespeare Canon*, pp. 176 ff.

[28] *Titus Andronicus*, I, 1, 179-180; Adams' facsimile of 1594 quarto, B2ʳ.

[29] Horne, *Peele*, p. 256. These "weedes," however, are not connected with the Roman palliament. *N.E.D.* is thus in error when it groups the use of *palliament* in *Honour* with that in *Titus* as referring to "the white gown of a candidate for the Roman consulship."

no significant coincidence on this point, except possibly for the already well-worn phrase "spotless white."

There is no evidence, then, that the author of this passage in *Titus* mistook the color of a *palliament* as Professor Price thought, or that he drew his alleged mistake from Peele, and hence could not have been Peele himself. On the contrary, Peele himself appears to have invented the word *palliament,* and if so, we also know quite exactly when he did it. For he refers to Marlowe's death on May 30, 1593, and received £3 for his poem on June 23, 1593, three days before June 26, 1593, when Northumberland was stalled.[30] The poem was composed, therefore, in June, 1593. Further, Peele's use of the word *palliament* is a direct one, growing out of Peele's source, while that in *Titus Andronicus* is a derived one. Thus *palliament* went into *Titus* most likely between the invention of the word by Peele in June, 1593, and the probable entry of the play February 6, 1594; presumably, therefore, just before Henslowe listed the play as "ne" for Sussex's men January 24, 1594. The person who inserted it was the last reviser, or a last reviser, of the form of the play printed in 1594, which is essentially the form printed in 1623 as Shakspere's. Under these circumstances, Peele as the inventor and only known purveyor of the word must remain grievously suspect in connection with this word *palliament* in *Titus Andronicus.*

A second set of parallels, also pointed out by Robertson, can now be put sufficiently into their complete relationships to become significant.[31] These have as their base a passage in Spenser's *Faerie Queene* and involve a passage in *3 Henry VI* and one in *Titus Andronicus* in such a way as to show that this is the order of composition. But one line of the passage in *Titus* also fits into an evolving set of figures by Peele in such a way as to make it highly improbable that anyone else would have written it so.

It should now be noticed that neither in the case of *palliament* nor the line from *Titus* are we dealing with parallels as such. In both cases we have tried rather to reconstruct the complete pertinent background for our facts. It is not a matter of merely two coinciding points each time; but a whole mesh of interrelated circumstances, in which our fact can apparently fit at only one place. It is a theorem of imposition in geometry, where the key points are shown to coincide, thus proving identity. Our interpretation may still be wrong through inadequate, inaccurate, or misinterpreted facts. But when we get a sufficient body of pertinent and accurate facts, the method itself is of necessity sound.

A parallel case to the last has some degree of probability, but of itself not so high a degree as the two preceding. The case may be stated in Robertson's own words. "In *Titus* we have the lines:

---

[30] Horne, *Peele,* p. 173; Bullen, II, 316.
[31] Baldwin, *Literary Genetics,* pp. 5-8.

> And *faster* bound to Aaron's charming *eyes*
> Than is *Prometheus tied to Caucasus,*

which point to two separate lines in Peele's *Edward I* (sc. iv, 21; x, 201):

> To *tie Prometheus' limbs to Caucasus* . . .
> *Fast* by those *looks* are all my fancies *tied.*

In *Titus* the two figures are combined in one eminently grotesque trope. Are we then to suppose either (1) that Shakespeare made this absurd combination immediately after reading *Edward I* (published in 1593), or that Peele got his ideas yet again from hearing *Titus* played in the theatre, and frugally turned one stolen trope to account by making two uses of it? Are not both inferences alike fantastic? Is not the natural explanation this, that Peele, writing the two plays about the same time, used up his own rhetoric twice over, one of his lines with 'tie' in it recalling to him the other?"[32]

The difficulty here is that, for our purposes, Robertson has stated the case much too narrowly; we are not shut up to Shakspere or Peele. The world used these figures separately, as Mr. Robertson himself indicates in a footnote. "Echoes of Lilly: — 'My thoughts are stitched to the stars' (*Endymion,* I, 1) and of Greene: —

> Fast-fancied to the keeper's bonny lass . . .
> And lock'd him in the brightness of her looks.
> (*Friar Bacon and Friar Bungay,* Dyce, pp. 150-1)

— and various other passages. In *Locrine* (V, iv) we have: —

> As Tityus *bound* to houseless *Caucasus.*"[33]

The fundamental figure from which the first figure evolved is probably that of the ears of an audience tied to an orator's tongue, so frequently used in the school discussions of oratory; and Caucasus also belonged to the conventional figures.

The significant parallel between *Edward I* and *Titus* is in the echoing phraseology and in the known contiguity in time. What we know is that Peele had used these figures separately by 1593, and that if he had then combined them he would have got very much the result in phraseology which we find in *Titus.* Since someone did revise *Titus* about the end of 1593, since no other person is known to have combined the figures, and since no one else is known to have phrased either figure as did Peele, it is highly probable that the reviser of *Titus* did combine these figures used by Peele. It then in turn becomes more probable that Peele himself combined the two than that anyone else did. But we are not certain that we have a sufficient number of surviving instances to determine the tradition

---

[32] Robertson, *Introduction,* p. 178.
[33] Robertson, *Introduction,* p. 178, n. 2.

in these figures, and we have had to combine a sequence of uncontrollable probabilities. So far the evidence indicates a higher probability for Peele as the author of these combined figures in *Titus* than for any other known person. Peele's known habits in such matters as demonstrated in the preceding instances raise the probability somewhat. But this instance of itself does not attain anything like so high a degree of probability as the preceding.

Yet something else must now be considered. This and the preceding instance are the first seventeen lines of the same speech; they do not stand alone.

> *Aron.* Now climeth *Tamora* Olympus toppe,
> Safe out of fortunes shot, and sits aloft,
> Secure of thunders cracke or lightning flash,
> Aduaunc'd aboue pale enuies threatening reach,
> As when the golden sunne salutes the morne,
> And hauing gilt the Ocean with his beames,
> Gallops the Zodiacke in his glistering Coach,
> And ouer-looks the highest piering hills.
>   So *Tamora.*
> Vpon her wit doth earthly honour wait,
> And vertue stoops and trembles at her frowne.
> Then *Aron* arme thy hart, and fit thy thoughts,
> To mount aloft with thy Emperiall Mistris,
> And mount her pitch, whom thou in triumph long
> Hast prisoner held, fettred in amourous chaines,
> And faster bound to *Arons* charming eies,
> Than is *Prometheus* tide to *Caucasus,* etc.[34]

It will be noticed that the Caucasus figure is a part of the fundamental theme of the speech. Now that Tamora is mounting the top of Olympus with Jupiter-Saturninus, then Aaron must also mount since he holds her faster prisoner than ever Jupiter did Prometheus on the top of Caucasus. This figure belongs to the fundamental thesis of the whole speech and is not an insert. The zodiac figure is detachable, but is now attached by way of further elaboration of the first fundamental figure. It thus belongs to the final form of the speech.

Our pattern of known coincidence with Peele is now enormously more complicated by the structural conjunction into one theme of these two in themselves complicated instances. The coinciding patterns are now complicated beyond the bounds of chance. Either Peele wrote the speech, or someone else has expended an unusual degree of effort in order to write it in Peele's style. He must have combined a passage from *Descensus Astraeae* (1591), and two from the at-the-time-unprinted *David and Bethsabe,* as probably an unprinted revision to *A Tale of Troy* for his zodiac figure; and have combined two figures from *Edward I* for his

---

[34] *Titus Andronicus,* II, 1, 1-17; Adams' facsimile of 1594 quarto, C2ᵛ-C3ʳ.

Caucasus figure. Incidentally, the combination of the two figures from *Edward I* into "one eminently grotesque trope" is not so surprising as Mr. Robertson thinks. For the fundamental figure is of the ears of an audience tied to an orator's tongue, and it was Prometheus who procured *Rhetorica,* or this oratorical ability, for men.[35] This is no doubt the associational background which brought the separate figures into juxtaposition. It is more likely to have operated in Peele's mind, which is known to have had the two figures in solution, than in that of any other known individual of the time. When the total of this exceedingly complicated pattern of inter-relations is considered, I do not see that any conclusion is possible other than that Peele wrote this speech. Therefore, I do here and now accuse George Peele of having revised *Titus Andronicus* about the end of 1593.

There are other tantalizing parallels with Peele, but none that I can tie down as definitely as the preceding. It may be of some significance, however, that when Mr. Robertson lists, not altogether accurately, the words and accentuations special to *Titus* in the Shakespeare Concordance and then lists the ones found in Peele,[36] there are as many parallels with the first act of *Titus* as with the whole of the last three. The same concentration is evident for the first three scenes of the second act. If these parallels indicate anything, they indicate that the bulk of Peele's work is concentrated before the fourth scene of the second act. This is the section where our extended parallels have been located, and also where most of the other noticeable parallels with Peele are to be found. Further, the vocabulary parallels are about equally from *Edward I, David and Bethsabe, Arraignment of Paris,* and *Battle of Alcazar* — but not so from *Locrine,* if it should be Peele's. Of the poems, the *Honour of the Garter* ranks with the plays, and most of the others would do so if they were of comparable length. The comparison is with Peele's fundamental vocabulary, not with a chance period of it.

There are a few further probabilities to be deduced from the known body of facts. For if the present form of *Titus Andronicus* represents a revision at the end of 1593, and if the author of at least part of the revision, whether Peele, Shakspere, or Tertium Quid, borrowed the word *palliament* from Peele's *Honour of the Garter,* then we have some further significant facts. In that case, the other significant parallels with the *Garter* as well as those with Peele's *Edward I,* S.R. October 8, 1593, and printed the same year, can only have been borrowed for *Titus* at the revision about the end of 1593, if there has been any borrowing at all. Further, the known concatenation of dates would make it highly probable

[35] Erasmus, *Adagia* (Basle, 1574), p. 304. See note in Hillebrand, *Troilus,* I, 3, 73-74.

[36] Robertson, *Introduction,* p. 193.

that the parallels are due to influence upon *Titus* from *Garter* and *Edward I*. There would then be the added question of why the reviser of *Titus* was so noticeably influenced by these two works of one author from the many works published in 1593. If the reviser was Peele, the answer is easy. If it was Shakspere, the answer is anything but easy, and consequently is the more significant; Shakspere must in that case have taken such a fancy to Peele that these two works would influence still others of his plays shortly after 1593. I believe no such claim has yet been made and demonstrated. Until this has been done, if it can be done, the weight of argument is very heavily for Peele. "Why should Shakespeare so determinedly echo in one play, and in that only, one third-rate contemporary, who echoed him in return?"[37] To that very pertinent question I should be able to furnish no answer.

Thus mere weight of genuine parallels would have its significance here, whether we could show direction of borrowing, or even borrowing at all. Sir Edmund Chambers has a sound statement from that point of view. Speaking particularly of Robertson, he says, "The methods employed inspire me . . . with very little confidence, in view of the amount of 'common form' in plays of the period and the number of little-known writers who may have been at work. In particular 'parallels,' whether 'echoes' or not, are insecure evidence. There are many in *Titus Andronicus* to both plays and poems of Shakespeare. Those to Marlowe, Kyd, Greene, and others seem to me slight. But there are many also to Peele, and some, chiefly to his *Edward I* and his poem *The Honour of the Garter,* both printed in 1593, go rather beyond a repeated use of out-of-the-way words or of short collocations of words. As a whole the play does not very strongly remind me of any of Peele's known plays, although I think that he wrote with different degrees of care at different times."[38]

We have tried to take three nuclei out of that "common form" about which Sir Edmund is quite correct. My impression as to the further parallels of *Edward I* and *The Honour of the Garter*[39] with *Titus Andronicus* also agrees with Sir Edmund's. If we can put a few more of these parallels into their complete pertinent background, we shall be able to get something more definite than impressions.

We must now notice that there is also an important parallel to *Titus Andronicus* in Nashe's *Unfortunate Traveller.*[40] As the climax of a horrific story, Nashe writes, "Her Husbands dead bodie he made a pillow

---

[37] Robertson, *Introduction,* p. 183.

[38] Chambers, *Shakespeare,* I, 317.

[39] I do not know, however, why Sir Edmund confines his parallels to these two works of Peele.

[40] John Dale Ebbs, "A Note on Nashe and Shakespeare," *M.L.N.* (1951), LXVI, 480-481; rediscovered by Ernest C. York, "Shakespeare and Nashe," *N.Q.,* Sept., 1953, 198, 370-371.

to his abhomination," and the forced widow laments, "Haue I liud to make my husbands bodie the beere to carrie mee to hell? had filthy pleas- ure no other pillow to leane vpon but his spredded lims?"[41] The first sentence has a close verbal parallel in *Titus Andronicus,*

> Drag hence her husband to some secret hole,
> And make his dead trunke pillow to our lust.[42]

The concidence in phraseology, as well as situation, between the first sentence quoted from Nashe and the second line from *Titus Andronicus* cannot be due to chance; there is certainly close connection of some sort between the passages.

Both passages are set in a similar context. In Nashe the sentences describe the climax of a lurid story, which is certain to be a retelling, though apparently no one has located the source story. Because of the nature of the story, this detail is also certain to have been in it, for it describes the climactic action of the story and Nashe gives it a double billing, as it were. In *Titus Andronicus,* on the other hand, the detail is merely a threat, and there is no intention of acting it out; the brothers are under orders from Aaron as to how to dispose of the husband's body more advantageously to the plot. In *Titus Andronicus,* the threat is purely fictional, while it is the actual story of Nashe.

The same is true of the background setting of the detail. In Nashe the full story is given; in *Titus Andronicus* it is again merely allusively fictionalized.

Demetrius   .   .   .   .

> This minion stood vpon her chastitie,
> Vpon her Nuptiall vow, her loyaltie,
> And with that painted hope, braues your mightenes,
> And shall she carrie this vnto her graue.

Chiron.   And if she doe, I would I were an Euenuke,
> Drag hence her husband to some secret hole,
> And make his dead trunke pillow to our lust.[43]

No doubt Lavinia would have argued thus had she been given the oppor- tunity. The wife in Nashe's story was given the opportunity and did argue at length from the topic sentence that "it is the spoil of my honor thou seekest in my soules troubled departure." She wished to carry that to her grave but was not permitted.[44] In Nashe, the wife goes through this horror; Lavinia is only threatened with it. The presumption of originality

---

[41] McKerrow, *Nashe,* II, 292-293.

[42] *Titus Andronicus,* II, 3, 129-130; Adams' facsimile of 1594 quarto, D3^r.

[43] *Titus Andronicus,* II, 3, 124-130; Adams' facsimile of 1594 quarto, D3^r.

[44] If we mentally substitute "honor" for "her chastitie . . . her Nuptiall vow, her loyaltie" in *Titus,* we shall find no reason to put an obelus before the line following, as do the Cambridge editors. In the second speech below, all this is summed up for Lavinia as "That nice preserued honestie of yours."

is wholly with Nashe's story. If the dead body as "pillow" proves to be in the source of Nashe's story, then we shall be certain it was the original of the two.

It is significant that the publication of the two versions was at the same period. *The Unfortunate Traveller* is dated at the end June 27, 1593, was entered S.R. September 17, 1593, but both surviving editions are dated 1594. *Titus* was acted as "ne" January 23 (24), 1594, and printed that year. Thus priority in print cannot be determined, and since Nashe was a dramatist and had been connected with the dramatists of this aggregation, priority in print would not necessarily be significant. The threat does not now appear in precedent versions of the Andronicus story, but they have been too wretchedly preserved to warrant any confidence that it had not been in any of them. The most that can be claimed on present evidence is the probability that *Titus Andronicus* is the borrower, and that the borrowing was for the present version, which was "ne" January 23 (24), 1594. Nor does the evidence indicate who did the borrowing.

But if Peele was a reviser of *Titus* about the end of 1593 for the version which was printed in 1594, then for that particular final revision Shakspere could at most have been only a co-reviser of the play. It would seem certain that several passages by Shakspere do belong to this version. *Titus* appears to have a passage later than one in *Venus and Adonis,* S.R. April 18, 1593.[45] Another elaborate figure, that of the double-hunt is also later than *Venus and Adonis.* This figure clearly begins life for Shakspere in the chase of "poor Wat" in *Venus and Adonis* (695-696) as a simple chase, with Echo personified and reflecting the earthly chase into the skies.

> Then do they [the hounds] spend their mouths: Echo replies,
> As if another chase were in the skies.

This becomes specifically an assumed, but not developed, "double hunt" in *Titus Andronicus.*

> whilst the babling eccho mocks the hounds,
> Replying shrillie to the well tun'd hornes,
> As if a double hunt were heard at once,
> Let vs sit downe and marke their yellowing noyse.[46]

The basic figure is developed in *Venus and Adonis.* In *Titus* it is then assumed and described as a "double hunt." But personified Echo, who had doubled the hunt into the skies, is now only "the babbling echo," mocking the hounds and replying to the horns. The skies are not even mentioned as a reflector, though they are implied in the "double hunt." It is thus clear that the passage in *Venus and Adonis* is the earlier. In *Titus,* music of the hounds is also given an attentive and appreciative

---

[45] Baldwin, *Small Latine,* II, 435.
[46] *Titus Andronicus,* II, 3, 17-20; Adams' facsimile of 1594, quarto, D1ᵛ.

audience. Venus had been attentive to catch the sound of the fatal hunt of the boar instead of "poor Wat" as she had recommended.

> She harkens for his hounds and for his horn;
> Anon she hears them chant it lustily (868-869).

But in neither the chase of the hare nor that of the boar was Venus appreciative of the music.

Now that we know the relationship between these passages, we should add the ending of the speech in *Titus*, as does Professor Parrott.[47]

> Whiles hounds and horns and sweet melodious birds
> Be unto us as is a nurse's song
> Of lullaby to bring her babe asleep.[48]

We may now be certain that this echoes

> By this, far off she hears some huntsman hollo;
> A nurse's song ne'er pleased her babe so well.
> (*Venus and Adonis*, 973-974)

In *Midsummer Night's Dream*, as in *Titus*, there is also to be an attentive and very appreciative audience for the hunt.

> We will, fair queen, up to the mountain's top,
> And mark the musical confusion
> Of hounds and echo in conjunction.
>
> . . . .
>
>   besides the groves,
> The skies, the fountains, every region near
> Seem'd all one mutual cry.[49]

The figure has now bifurcated. In its first statement the hounds and echo produce "the musical confusion" which is to be enjoyed. As reflectors, in the second statement, we now have groves, skies, fountains, every region near. It is no longer a single hunt redoubled in the skies as in *Venus and Adonis,* or a double-hunt in earth and sky as in *Titus Andronicus,* but a myriad hunt echoed from innumerable reflectors. So far, the authorship and evolution of the figure are clear.

Then comes in *The Shrew* (Ind. ii, 43-44), a false-ringing and washed out version of the original figure

> Thy hounds shall make the welkin answer them
> And fetch shrill echoes from the hollow earth.

---

[47] T. M. Parrott, "Shakespeare's Revision of 'Titus Andronicus,'" *M.L.R.*, XIV, 28. See also the parallels between *Titus*, II, 3, 199-201, and *Venus and Adonis*, 665-666, 1055-56.

[48] *Titus*, II, 3, 27-29.

[49] *Midsummer-Night's Dream*, IV, 1, 106-108; 112-114. The occasion of this hunt was the statement in Chaucer's *Knight's Tale* that Theseus delighted to hunt the great hart in May, "With hunte and horn and houndes hym bisyde."

Now the hounds make "the welkin" answer them and get echoes from "the hollow earth"; that is, the hounds are echoed by sky and earth. There is no longer even a hunt actually; merely someone's attempt to be ornamentally "classical."

The fundamental passage in *Venus and Adonis* was ready for print in April, 1593. Thus the passage in *Titus* must have belonged to the version which was "new" in January, 1594, and that in *Midsummer-Night's Dream* can hardly be earlier than 1594.[50]

Titus also connects closely in certain other passages with *Lucrece,* S.R. May 9, 1594, apparently being there the later.[51] Some of these relationships hold irrespective of authorship. But if Shakspere had a hand in *Titus,* these relationships would imply that he was working upon both productions at the same time in 1593-94. Further, as my revered master, Professor T. M. Parrott, has shown[52] (accepted and "improved upon" by Professor Wilson), the parallels of *Titus* with Shakspere's other work concentrate upon *Lucrece.*[53] Whatever these parallels may indicate about authorship, yet it is certain that *if* Shakspere had anything to do with writing *Titus,* then he worked upon the play about the time he was writing *Lucrece.* I believe the evidence indicates conclusively that Shakspere did some work upon *Titus* in 1593-94. This should mean that Shakspere and Peele were co-writers or co-revisers for the version which appeared in Henslowe's Diary as "new" January 24, 1594, and was entered S.R. February 6, 1594, and printed the same year. Evidence we shall examine later will indicate that they were only revisers at this time. It looks, therefore, as if we begin to have one solid "place to stand" in dealing with the question of the date and authorship of *Titus.*

---

[50] I must leave it to Professor Wilson to defend his statement that "All these [passages] are themselves echoes of *Arcadia* (1590), Bk i, ch. 10" (Wilson, *Titus Andronicus,* p. 117).

[51] Baldwin, *Literary Genetics,* pp. 131, 234.

[52] Parrott, *M.L.R.,* XIV, 16 ff.

[53] See also pp. 301-302, 316 ff.

CHAPTER XXIII

The Five-Act Structure of *Titus Andronicus*

Since there are several versions of the Andronicus story, it will be well to get before us immediately, as a basis of comparison, a detailed analysis of *Titus Andronicus* as it was printed in 1594 and 1623. As only the First Folio gives the act divisions, I have based upon it, since there are no important differences of structure between it and the first quarto as published in 1594.

I, 1. The Tribunes and Senators enter "aloft." Below, Saturninus enters with his followers at one stage door, Bassianus and his at the other, both in warlike mood. They are sons of the former emperor, and Saturninus claims the crown as "the first borne Sonne"; that is, by primogeniture, while Bassianus claims by "Desert in pure Election." Marcus Andronicus, brother of Titus, enters aloft as Tribune with the crown to tell Saturninus and Bassianus that the people of Rome have chosen Titus Andronicus for his deserts, who by the Senate is accited home. Marcus Andronicus proposes that all claims be left to the Senate. Bassianus agrees because he loves Lavinia, the daughter of Titus, while Saturninus trusts his right. So Saturninus and Bassianus dismiss their followers and "go vp into the Senat house" to join the Tribunes, Senators, and Marcus Andronicus, thus clearing the lower stage for the grand entry of Titus, with various sons, coffin, prisoners, etc., "as many as can bee." The coffin is committed to the tomb. Lucius, son of Titus, demands "the proudest prisoner of the Gothes" to sacrifice *Ad manus fratrum* and Titus assigns Alarbus, eldest son of Tamora, Queen of the Goths, who is taken out by Titus' sons to be sacrificed. The sons promptly return and Titus concludes the burial ceremonies. Lavinia enters to greet her father Titus and to pay her tributary tears. Marcus Andronicus welcomes the family and announces to Titus that the people of Rome have sent by him, their Tribune, a candidate's robe of white that he may stand in candidacy along with Saturninus and Bassianus for the crown. Titus wants a staff, not a crown, Saturninus will use force, Bassianus wishes to ally himself with Titus for Lavinia's sake. The Tribunes agree to accept the decision of Titus, who nominates Saturninus. Saturninus is acclaimed with a long flourish to enable everybody left above to "come downe." Saturninus will marry Lavinia in gratitude to Titus, who presents his trophies to Saturninus, including Tamora, by whom Saturninus is immediately impressed, though Lavinia is not jealous. Bassianus snatches Lavinia as his "lawfull promist Loue," and Titus kills his son Mutius for aiding. Saturninus, Tamora, her two sons, and Aaron the Moor have gone out and now "Enter aloft." Saturninus renounces Lavinia and denounces Titus and his sons. Instead, he chooses Tamora as his bride. Exeunt to be married, leaving Titus alone, to whom Marcus and Titus' sons return and finally persuade Titus to permit Mutius to be buried. Titus thinks Tamora should be thankful to him for her advancement. Saturninus with Tamora and followers enter at one door, while Bassianus, Lavinia, and followers enter at the other for mutual recriminations. Tamora advises Saturninus to dissemble and take Titus to favor lest the people revolt to him.

> Ile finde a day to massacre them all,
> And race their faction, and their familie,
> The cruell Father, and his trayt'rous sonnes,
> To whom I sued for my deare sonnes life.[1]

So Saturninus pardons all faults, and all are friends. There is to be a panther hunt on the morrow.

The first act, therefore, is built on the rivalry of Saturninus and Bassianus for the crown, into which Titus refuses to enter, and also their rivalry for Lavinia, where again Titus had not wished to interfere. These rivalries end with Saturninus, the rightful claimant by primogeniture, as Emperor, thanks to Titus, and Tamora as Empress, again thanks to Titus, as he thinks. But in fact Tamora informs us that she intends to destroy Titus and all his house. Here is the crowded presentation, and here at the end of the first act is Tamora's decision to massacre all the opponents of herself and Saturninus. The first act has been made regular at the expense of very great pains.

II, 1. Aaron the Moor gloats over the fact that his mistress Tamora has mounted so high.

> Away with slauish weedes,[2] and idle thoughts,
> I will be bright and shine in Pearle and Gold,
> To waite vpon this new made Empresse.
> To waite said I? To wanton with this Queene,
> This Goddesse, this *Semerimis,* this Queene,
> This Syren, that will charme Romes *Saturnine,*
> And see his shipwracke, and his Common weales.

Tamora's sons Demetrius and Chiron enter quarreling over who shall have Lavinia. Aaron warns them of Bassianus, but when he finds "some

---

[1] Antony Colynet would have said this was a Machiavellian policy worthy of "old Cathy" herself.

[2] In the German play Morian says "Let me now put off these old rags, as I see that my secret mistress has the good favour of the Emperor," and ["Takes off the old mantle"].

certaine snatch or so" would serve their turns, he suggests rape during the coming hunt.

> Come, come, our Empresse with her sacred wit
> To villainie and vengance consecrate,
> Will we acquaint with all that we intend,
> And she shall file our engines with aduise.

II, 2. The party spreads to the hunt, with Demetrius and Chiron watching their chance to get at Lavinia.

II, 3. Aaron buries some gold; Tamora wishes to play Dido to his Aeneas, but Aaron says

> Vengeance is in my heart, death in my hand,
> Blood, and reuenge, are Hammering in my head.
>
> . . . .
>
> This is the day of Doome for *Bassianus;*
> His *Philomel* must loose her tongue today,
> Thy Sonnes make Pillage of her Chastity,
> And wash their hands in *Bassianus* blood.

Tamora is to deliver a scroll to Saturninus and to be cross with Bassianus, who enters with Lavinia as Aaron leaves to fetch Tamora's sons. After much recrimination as to horns, Tamora's sons enter, Tamora accuses Bassianus and Lavinia of threatening to bind her there to die, etc., the sons stab Bassianus, Tamora would stab Lavinia also, but her sons have other uses for her. Lavinia thinks Tamora should be grateful to Titus, but Tamora plans revenge on all the house for Alarbus. The sons throw the body of Bassianus into the pit as directed by Aaron and take Lavinia, with Tamora's blessing, to satisfy their lust. Aaron then lures Quintus and Martius, two sons of Titus, into the pit, and brings Saturninus to discover them there. Tamora enters, with Titus and his son Lucius. Tamora presents the incriminating letter, which Titus had found, Aaron finds the gold, and Saturninus orders the two sons of Titus to prison, though Tamora promises Titus to intercede.

II, 4. Demetrius and Chiron mockingly advise Lavinia to tell or write what they have done, since they have ravished her, cut off her hands, and cut out her tongue. As they exeunt, her Uncle Marcus finds her bleeding at mouth and arms, and will take her to Titus.

Tamora has begun her revenge upon Titus, though the actual plan of villainy is Aaron's. By the end of the act, two sons of Titus are under accusation of murder, as he knows, and his daughter has been raped and maimed as he does not yet know. Titus is about to acquire something to revenge in a big way. That something is prepared for in two installments pat at the end of the second act as in the *Andria* formula, being the thing toward which the protasis tends. Titus must become aware of his task, and set about the accomplishment of it in the third act. The protasis is complete, the epitasis of preparation for revenge must occupy the third and have reached the occasion for the catastrophe by the end of the fourth.

III, 1. As the Judges and Senators pass over the stage with the two sons of Titus to the place of execution, Titus goes before, pleading in the name of his age and service done. He lies down, but the Judges pass by him, and the Tribunes exeunt. Lucius enters to say that he had attempted to rescue his brothers and has been banished by the Judges. Marcus presents Lavinia as consuming sorrow for Titus' age. Titus does rhetorical justice to the mounting sea of his ills. Aaron enters with an alleged promise from the Emperor that if Titus or Lucius or Marcus or any one of you will send him a hand chopped off, the sons of Titus will be returned to him alive. Lucius and Marcus wish to supply the hand but as they go to get an axe Titus persuades Aaron to operate on him. Aaron tells the audience aside that this is a villainy and that Titus will receive the heads of the boys. As Titus "passions," a messenger enters with the two heads and the hand sent as a mockery. Titus vows vengeance; Lucius will to the Goths to raise an army.

III, 2. Titus suggests that Lavinia take a knife between her teeth and commit suicide with it; a pretty "passion" of a fly. Grandson is to read sad stories to Lavinia and Titus. (This scene forecasts the means of discovery in the fourth act.)

Titus is now crazed with grief and bent upon revenge, though he does not yet know exactly from whom to seek it. But at the end of the third act he and his family are on the way to read sad stories, which will enable Lavinia to reveal the culprits. We can then have a plan of revenge at the end for a perfect fourth act.

IV, 1. Lavinia is pursuing grandson Lucius with his books. By signs she directs Titus and Marcus to Ovid's story of Philomela. Then using staff in mouth and stumps to guide it, as Marcus taught her, she writes in the sand *"Stuprum, Chiron, Demetrius."* Marcus calls on all to kneel and vow "Mortall reuenge vpon these traytorous Gothes," though Tamora will be hard to match. Titus will send grandson Lucius with a message to Tamora's sons. Marcus laments that Titus is

> so iust, that he will not reuenge,
> Reuenge the heauens, for old *Andronicus.*

IV, 2. Grandson Lucius presents from Titus to Tamora's sons weapons with a verse from Horace. They do not catch the point, but Aaron does, and wishes Tamora were afoot. As all gloat over their revenges upon Titus, the trumpets announce that the emperor has a son. The nurse enters with a blackamoor child, which is clearly Aaron's, with the request from the Empress that Aaron christen it with his dagger's point. Aaron takes the child, kills the nurse so that she will not talk, and will do as much for the midwife. A white child will be substituted and all will be well. Aaron will take his child to the Goths.

IV, 3. Titus looks "for iustice, and for aide," as his kindred watch lamenting over him, and talk of joining the Goths. They shoot into the court arrows with messages soliciting each of the gods for justice. A clown is commissioned to deliver an oration to Saturninus with a knife wrapped in it.

IV, 4. Saturninus has collected the arrows with their messages, and resents the insinuation that the sons of Titus did not receive justice. Tamora pretends to calm his anger against Titus, but intimates aside that she has plans to get rid of Titus, if only Aaron has managed to carry out his share of covering up. The clown delivers the letter from Titus and is ordered hanged. Saturninus orders that Titus be dragged in by the hair, but Aemilius arrives with the news that Lucius is bringing an army of Goths. Saturninus fears the common people will make Lucius emperor. Tamora promises to manage Titus and bids Aemilius to have Lucius meet Saturninus, so as "To plucke proud *Lucius* from the warlike Gothes." Tamora goes to try out her plan.

Titus is crazily appealing for justice, while his son Lucius is at the end of the act bringing an army of Goths to force justice. Tamora has her counterplan at the end of the act to outwit Titus and Lucius. Here is the occasion of the catastrophe exactly in place, and according to the *Andria* formula.

V, 1. The Goths will follow Lucius to right their wrongs from Rome. Aaron and the child are brought in and ordered hanged, but Aaron promises valuable information if the child be spared. Aaron says Tamora is mother of the child, that he engineered the rape of Lavinia and the death of her two brothers by Tamora's sons, etc.; and that he is sorry only that he has not committed worse crimes. Hanging is too good for him. Aemilius gets the consent of Lucius to meet the emperor at the house of Titus.

V, 2. Tamora visits Titus dressed as Revenge, but Titus recognizes her. He asks her to destroy Rape and Murder (her sons). Tamora plans to get Titus to send for Lucius, so that she can persuade the Goths to scatter while Lucius is away. Consequently, she promises Titus, if he will send for Lucius, to get all his opponents into his power. Titus sends Marcus. Tamora leaves her sons with Titus while she goes to get the emperor. Says Titus

> I know them all, though they suppose me mad,
> And will ore-reach them in their owne deuises.

Titus causes the sons of Tamora to be bound, and with his one hand cuts their throats while Lavinia with her stumps holds a basin to catch the blood, after he has told them that their mother shall eat of them at the feast.

V, 3. Lucius has come, but gives orders that Aaron be kept safe and that the ambush of their friends be strong. Enter Saturninus, Tamora and court to debate the quarrel with Lucius at the feast. Titus serves in the food as cook. He kills Lavinia, discovers that Tamora has fed on her own sons before he kills her. Saturninus kills Titus and is killed by Lucius. Marcus and Lucius explain to the Romans, who make Lucius emperor. Lucius laments Titus and sentences the unrepentant Aaron. Funeral orders for the dead. And here is a proper catastrophe!

The whole play is motivated by revenge and counterrevenge. Theoretically, Tamora plans a Machiavellian revenge upon Titus and all his house for the sacrifice of her son Alarbus. Actually, Aaron formulates and executes the dirty work until he gets captured, just as in the chapbook the Moor was "the main Engine to bring about her Devilish Designs." Opposed is the nobly patient Titus, who will believe no evil till it is piled high upon him at its proper place in the third act. The whole plot is marshalled with meticulous accuracy in the *Andria* formula, as our analysis has shown. For that reason, it would have been a more straightforward play for its contemporaries than it is to us, with our different reaction complexes.

CHAPTER XXIV

The *Old Titus Andronicus*

We have seen earlier that the casting-pattern of *Titus Andronicus* as printed in 1594 is that of the Admiral's men before 1590. The various other surviving forms of the Titus story throw further light on the form and content of the original play. Quite important here is the eighteenth-century chapbook on Titus in the Folger Shakespeare library, which the late Professor J. Q. Adams has described, concluding that if the original chapbook was not the source of *Titus,* yet it represents "an early English rendering of that source."[1] The title of the chapbook runs, *The History of Titus Andronicus, The Renowned Roman General, Who, after he had saved* Rome *by his Valour from being destroyed by the barbarous* Goths, *and lost two-and-twenty of his valiant Sons in ten Years War, was, upon the Emperor's marrying the Queen of the* Goths, *put to Disgrace, and banish'd; but being recall'd, the Emperor's Son by a first Wife was murder'd by the Empress's Sons and a bloody Moor, and how charging it upon* Andronicus's *Sons, tho' he cut off his Hand to redeem their Lives, they were murder'd in Prison. How his fair Daughter* Lavinia *being ravish'd by the Empress's Sons, they cut out her Tongue, and Hands off, &c. How* Andronicus *slew them, made Pyes of their Flesh, and presented them to the Emperor and Empress; and then slew them also. With the miserable Death he put the wicked* Moor *to: then at her Request slew his Daughter and himself to avoid Torments.* It is said to be "Newly Translated from the *Italian* Copy printed at *Rome,*" and was printed and sold by C. Dicey of London and Northampton. Chapter I presents the saving of Rome, II the ten years war, with the loss of the twenty-two sons of Titus, and death of the King of the Goths, III the peace concluded by marriage of the Emperor to the Queen of the Goths, who with her sons slew the Emperor's son. In IV, the wicked Moor betrays the three sons of Andronicus, gets them killed and the hand of Titus cut off, V the Queen's sons ravish and mutilate Lavinia, but she informs on them nevertheless, VI Titus feigns madness, entraps the culprits, makes pies of

---

[1] J. Q. Adams, *Shakespeare's Titus Andronicus* (1936), pp. 7-9; Ralph M. Sargent, "The Source of *Titus Andronicus,*" *S.P.,* XLVI, 167-183, summarizes the known facts concerning the previous history of the chapbook, accepts the conclusions of Adams, and adds to the arguments.

them, serves them to the Emperor and Empress, slays the two, punishes the Moor, and kills his daughter and himself.

According to the story, Theodosius, Emperor of Rome, is oppressed by "a barbarous Northern People out of Swedeland, Denmark, and Gothland," who were led by their king Tottilius. Theodosius was besieged in Rome, with famine, etc. Titus Andronicus, who was a Roman Senator, and Governor of the province of Achaia in Greece, came to the rescue and put Tottilius to rout. Titus was given a triumph. He was then made general and finally slew Tottilius, and captured his queen, for which he had a second triumph, marred somewhat by the loss of five sons in battle. But the two sons of Tottilius, by name Alaricus and Abonius, carried on the war, so that the Emperor finally agreed, against the wishes of Titus, to marry Attava, Queen of the Goths. If Theodosius had no issue by her, then Attava's two sons were to succeed to the Empire. Attava vowed revenge on Titus, and had procured a decree of banishment against him but the people forced revocation. A Moor begot a "Blackmoor Child" upon Attava, and was banished but recalled. Lavinia, daughter of Titus, was wooed and won by the Emperor's son by a former marriage. To cut off rivalry with her sons from this direction, Attava, the Moor, and Attava's sons invited the prince to a hunt "in the great Forest, on the Banks of the River Tyber, and there murder him." They shot him with a poisoned arrow, threw him in a deep pit, covered lightly with boughs and earth, and reported they had lost him. Lavinia sent her brothers (two, later three) to look for the prince, but they fell into the deep pit and could not get out. So Attava, the Moor, and her two sons, who had been watching, hastened to the court and sent the guards searching, who found the sons of Andronicus in the pit with the murdered prince. The sons were cast into a noisome dungeon, and Attava sent the Moor to say that the sons would be spared if Titus would cut off and send his right hand to court. The Moor cut off the hand, which was later returned with the bodies of his three sons. Lavinia went moaning into the woods and groves and was there betrayed to the queen's sons by the Moor. They ravished her, and by the advice of the Moor, cut out her tongue and cut off her hands. She would have died if her Uncle Marcus had not soon after come in search of her. Lavinia, without prompting, took a wand between her stumps and wrote

> The Lustful Sons of the proud Emperess
> Are doers of this hateful Wickedness.

Titus vowed revenge. Titus "feigned himself distracted, and went raving about the City, shooting his Arrows toward Heaven, as in Defiance, calling to Hell for Vengeance," but could get no justice. So he and his friends ambushed the two sons of Attava in the forest a hunting, bound them to a tree, and Andronicus cut their throats while Lavinia held a bowl between her stumps to catch the blood. Conveying the bodies home, Titus made two mighty pasties of them and invited the Emperor and Empress to dinner. They ate and were then killed. The Moor told how he had killed the Prince, betrayed the three sons of Titus, and advised the abuse of Lavinia. He was buried alive to the middle, smeared with honey, and the bees and wasps stung him as he starved to death. Titus killed Lavinia at her request, and then himself.

Since I believe there can be no question that the chapbook represents the source, I shall refer briefly to one confirmatory point, and then let the further presentation demonstrate the relationship. That the original of the chapbook precedes the plays, as Adams concluded, is indicated also by the pseudo-historical setting of the chapbook.[2] In the chapbook, Theodosius, Emperor of Rome, is grievously besieged by "a barbarous Northern People of Swedeland, Denmark, and Gothland," under Tottilius their king. There was, of course, a Gothic king Totilas or Totila — impressive enough for me to remember him from the history which was early thrust upon me! "An East-Gothic king in Italy. He overran the peninsula; opposed Belisarius and Narses; took Rome 546 and 549; and was defeated and mortally wounded at the battle of Taginae in July, 552."[3] His first siege of Rome involved the inhabitants in such desperate straits as are described in the chapbook. Theodosius I was a famous opponent of the Goths. "Roman Emperor . . . was made joint emperor by Gratian and ruler over the East in 379; defeated the Goths and other invaders; and after 382 enrolled the Goths in the empire."[4] So the actual Theodosius brought the Goths into the empire, as does the fictitious one. Other details of the prose pamphlet could be matched from the history of the Romans and the Goths, but these show sufficiently that the chapbook has a pseudo-historical setting. I believe it does not need to be argued that this fact places it earlier than the plays upon Titus Andronicus. This fact makes it probable also that the title page of the chapbook is correct in stating that it was originally translated from the Italian. If one could find out at what time, that would help to date the Titus plays.

We have seen that the rivalry for the crown by Saturninus, Bassianus, and Titus forms the framework of the first act of Titus as printed in 1594. This framework was evolved from the situation in the chapbook. There the unnamed son of the Emperor is to marry Lavinia, daughter of Titus, and is killed by the Gothic Queen and cohorts to prevent succession to the crown. So the projected Bassianus succession is in the source.

---

[2] Sargent refers to Totila as possibly the suggestion for Tottilius, as I now notice. Dr. J. G. McManaway tells me he had noticed this setting years ago. I owe my direct acquaintance with and information from the chapbook to his courtesy in making his photostat of it available to me.

[3] *Century Dictionary of Names.*

[4] *Ibid.*

The author of the *Old Titus* retains the son, "renews" his father, like old Aeson, into an older brother and rival for the crown, and brings also his father-in-law Titus involuntarily into the rivalry. The first act, therefore, of the *Old Titus* was at least in general content and consequent organization much as it is in the *Titus* of 1594. We shall see that the German version of 1620 (G) retains part of this rivalry, but the Dutch play of 1641 (D) completely recasts the first act because of Senecan necessities.

There is an important corollary to our information that the rivalry was developed from the source, and that concerns the names of the characters in the *Old Titus*. The only names which survive in S (Titus, as given in the First Folio) from the chapbook are Titus, Marcus, and Lavinia. Clearly, therefore, it is D which has changed from Lavinia to Rozelyna, but retaining Titus and Marcus. Since D and S agree quite fully in the names of their *dramatis personae,* it is thus indicated that the few variants in names of minor characters between D and S are also probably due to change on the part of D. But G agrees with these three (chapbook, D, and S) only in the name of Titus, the title character; all others are different. It is clear, therefore, that G has purposely varied some of its names from those in the common source — certainly so in Victoriades for Marcus, and Andronica for Lavinia, also certainly in Aetiopissa for the Gothic Queen. This fact of conscious change casts doubt on the supposition that any play in the direct line from chapbook to S contained a son of Titus named Vespasian instead of Lucius, as does G.

But since this son of Titus is a complete invention without even existence in the source, this objection is not as strong as it might at first appear. We must remember also that in the source Titus was never a rival for the crown in any way. But when in the original invention for the *Old Titus* Titus became an emperor *in posse,* with a son to succeed as actual emperor in his right, it was almost inevitable that the son thus created should be Vespasian in honor of that very prominent father and son, the emperors Titus and Vespasian. I believe this is clearly the origin of the name Vespasian, whether it was in the original play, or whether it was only a variant on the part of G. If this had been the idea of the person who hashed *Titus* into G, we would expect him to have altered the title also in honor of his invention; but he merely adorns the common title into "A Most Lamentable Tragedy of Titus Andronicus and the Haughty Empress, Wherein are found Memorable Events." It is not likely, therefore, that the name Vespasian is the invention of the person guilty of G. It likely goes back to the original invention of the play, along with the invention of Titus as potential emperor. Obviously the actual Titus and Vespasian combination of emperors impelled everyone to feel the necessity of coupling Titus by and with someone, whether "the Haughty Empress," "Aran," or merely "Andronicus," as frequently. Titus needed companionship; his natural companion was Vespasian, and that is the combination we have certainly in G, probably deriving from the original play. This fact, however, argues caution in assuming that because Henslowe had "vespacia" in his title there was still a character called Vespasian in the play. That I, at least, do not assume.

Incidentally, the creation of Vespasian (Lucius) threw the mathematics of the sons out of plumb. In the chapbook, Titus "lost two-and-twenty of his valiant Sons in ten Years War," as we are told on title page and in chapter heading II. In the text, we learn that the second triumph of Titus, for killing the Gothic King, was somewhat marred by the loss of five sons. All this appears in the *Titus* of 1594. As Titus is about to enter, we are told

> Ten yeares are spent, since first he vndertooke
> This Cause of Rome, and chasticed with Armes
> Our Enemies pride. Fiue times he hath return'd
> Bleeding to Rome, bearing his Valiant Sonnes
> In Coffins from the Field, and a[s] this day
> To the Monument of [the] *Andronici*
> Done sacrifice of expiation,
> And slaine the Noblest prisoner of the *Gothes*.[5]

Here are the ten years and the five sons. Then as Titus later pleads for the lives of his two condemned sons he says

> For two and twenty sonnes I neuer wept (III, 1, 10).

Here are the two and twenty sons in proper phraseology. It will be seen that these passages belong to the *Old Titus*,[6] also that the author of them has not harmonized his data. But besides the two and twenty in battle, in the chapbook Titus lost his last three to the Gothic Queen. So in *Titus* we are told of

> fiue and twenty Valiant Sonnes,
> Halfe of the number that King *Priam* had (I, 1, 79-80).

In the play, the last three sons have been subdivided. Titus himself kills one for disobedience and loses two to the Gothic Queen. This exhausts his generous allowance of twenty-five. So Vespasian (Lucius) is extracalary. It will be seen also that the author of the *Old Titus* did not get his statistics as to numbers, alive or dead, completely harmonized, but simply took over separate statements of the chapbook.

For the second act, we have seen that in the *Titus* of 1594 this act is built upon the hunt, with the murder of Bassianus, the incrimination of

---

[5] I, 1, 31-38. The emendation of "at" to "as" clears the succeeding lines, which were omitted from Q₂ and by consequence from the First Folio. This sixth occasion will follow the ritual, "Our Romaine rightes," used in the preceding five. Critics appear not to have grasped this fact fully.

[6] Harold De W. Fuller's parallels (*P.M.L.A.*, XVI, 48 ff.) could also be made to yield considerable information as to the probable details of the *Old Titus*.

certain sons of Titus, and the rape of Lavinia. All these are in the chapbook, so were in the *Old Titus*. These are all in D also, and were in the ancestor of G, though the latter omits the incrimination of the sons.

The third act of the *Titus* of 1594 exhibits the mounting seas of Titus' woes; the condemned sons, the mutilated Lavinia, the chopped hand. All these are from the chapbook and hence were in the *Old Titus*. They are also in both G and D. The banishment of Lucius is added in D and S.

The fourth act of the *Titus* of 1594 is built upon the discovery of the culprits in the rape of Lavinia, the black babe, and the plan and counterplan of Titus and Tamora for a catastrophe. The discovery by the stump-driven cane is in the chapbook, as is the black babe. The specific plans, however, are not there. The discovery and the black babe must thus have been in the *Old Titus*. Incidentally, by its device of an amputated tongue and stump-driven cane for communication the chapbook has suggested to some author in *Titus* the story of Tereus, which "is constantly in Shakespeare's mind in *Titus*,"[7] if Shakspere was the author. But though the chapbook device suggested the story, it does not follow that the author of the *Old Titus* was the one who caught the suggestion. The discovery is in both G and D, the black babe is in G but has been omitted from D because of Senecan necessities. The plans and counterplans are in G and D basically as in *Titus* of 1594. They must, therefore, in some form have been in the *Old Titus*.

The fifth act of *Titus* of 1594 involves the butchery of Tamora's sons, the Thyestean banquet, and the meting out of punishment. The butchery, the banquet, and the meting out of punishment are in the chapbook, with slightly different details, as they are also in G and D. They were, therefore, in the *Old Titus*.

It becomes apparent that the *Old Titus* ran in much the same fashion as the *Titus* of 1594. An examination of the German and Dutch versions will enable us to fill in more details and to arrive at conclusions as to its original act structure.

---

[7] J. C. Maxwell, *Titus* (Arden), p. 55.

CHAPTER XXV

The Dutch *Aran en Titus* of Jan Vos

Of the other surviving versions of the Titus story the Dutch play of Jan Vos[1] is nearest *Titus Andronicus* as it was printed in 1594. It is clear that D (the Dutch version of Vos, as printed 1641) rests upon a play with the same act-divisions as those of S (*Titus Andronicus*) as given in the First Folio, 1623. D was to conform to the Senecan unity of time, as is specifically pointed out in the printed play; "het Treurspel begint, met den dagh, en eyndight, inde andere nacht." There were thus some things in the original story that a time-starved Senecan would be obliged to forego. One remembers immediately English Sidney's objection more than half a century earlier to the begetting of children in a play; the natural and irreducible process requires too much time. So the black babe business, which was in the chapbook of Titus also, had to go. This left a gaping hole in the fourth act. To fill it, D readjusts the catastrophe, putting only the actual Thyestean banquet and the burning of Aran into the fifth act. The fourth act now becomes the discovery and punishment of the perpetrators of the crime against Rozelyna, in preparation for the grand catastrophe. This leaves the capture of Aran isolated, and since it is no longer dependent upon the black babe, it is thrown back to the end of the third act, to be out of the way.

Here S quite clearly represents the original organization, inasmuch as it has all the catastrophe in the fifth act; Aaron, the sons, etc. It is D which has been forced to redistribute because of the omission of the black babe business. Getting set to stage the grand burning of Aran may also have had something to do with the new division. So the divisions between the third and fourth and fourth and fifth acts in the play underlying D were the same as those in S. That still remains true of the division between the first and second acts. For the division between the second and

---

[1] Whether the play underlying the Linz program was a German translation of the play of Vos or of an earlier Dutch version used by Vos (Fuller, *P.M.L.A.* (1901), XVI, 17-18) has little bearing here. Such a change as from Rozelyna to Lavinia is hardly significant so late as 1699, or even 1650 in a German sufficiently literate to translate from the Dutch. More weighty perhaps is the motive given in the Linz program and the early German version for cutting off the hand of Titus. But surely a German sufficiently interested to translate a Titus play would know of the *Titus Andronicus* printed as early as 1620, even if he did prefer Lavinia to Andronica — or Rozelyna.

third, the discovery of Rozelyna by Marcus gets four lines at the beginning of the third act in D instead of being the occasion of the epitasis at the end of the second act as in S. Physically, the incident belongs immediately after the mutilation of Lavinia as in S, since, as the chapbook specifically points out, she would have bled to death if Uncle Marcus had not happened along immediately. She could not wait for first-aid till the third act. Though this reason is not specifically stated in S, yet it is implied by the fact that Marcus happens upon Lavinia as the villains exeunt, and points out to the audience that a

> Crimson riuer of warme blood,
> Like to a bubling fountaine stir'd with winde,
> Doth rise and fall betweene thy Rosed lips,
> Comming and going with thy hony breath.

> notwithstanding all this losse of blood,
> As from a Conduit with their issuing Spouts," etc.

But D permits Rozelyna to go the greater part of an act without attention while other grisly subjects for rhetoric are long drawn out. The reason is readily apparent. D has chosen to end the second act with a very long antiphony of woe between Saturninus and Titus, the one "rhetoricizing" upon the loss of a brother, the other of his sons. There was no room in that balance of bale for Rozelyna-Lavinia. So she was thrown into the beginning of the catchall third act, as the capture of Aran was thrown back to the end of it. It thus appears that the ancestor of D had exactly the same act-divisions as S.

The material in the first act was also the same. We have seen that the disputed succession, with the three rivals, which involves the Bassianus-Lavinia match, was developed from the chapbook. But there was no sacrifice there, either threatened or actual, as in D and S. The sacrifice was, however, in some form clearly in the common ancestor of D and S. If so, the question is which is the substitute; the actual sacrifice of the son, as in S, or the threatened sacrifice of Aran as in D. In the chapbook and specifically in S, it is the Gothic Queen who vows to extirpate the house of Titus, with the Moor assisting, though in fact even in S Aaron steals the show as devil incarnate; in D it is specifically the Moor Aran who vows, with Thamera assisting. In order to get his proper Senecan balance, the author responsible for the situation in D has substituted the threatened sacrifice of Aran for the actual sacrifice of Alarbus in order to have a balanced act of rhetorical pleading. Now Saturninus pleads for the love of Thamera, as Thamera pleads for the life of her lover Aran.

If D has substituted the proposed sacrifice of Aran, that was also the occasion for the changed motivation. In the chapbook and S, Attava-Tamora vows vengeance against Titus and his family for full value received; in D Aran takes the lead in this because Titus had ordered him to be sacrificed. The Dutch play is even by title that of *Aran en Titus,* not *Titus and Vespasian,* or *Titus Andronicus.* This changed motivation, with Aran as driving force, has superseded all others. The rivalry for the crown in the parent play of D was necessarily cut. But it is still implied in the unexplained succession of Lucius at the end of D. In S, all three claimants to the crown are dead, and Lucius is the only "apparent." Naturally, therefore, he succeeds, as in the German play also. In D, however, Titus has no claim on the crown; but Marcus hands it over as a matter of course, as in S.

Marcus.

> Uw' Keyzerlijke banden
> Zijn nu voor Lucius, en wat aan't rijk behoort:
> Nu zal het noodig zijn, dat gy des Tibers oord,
> En't ruyme marrektveld, omheyningt met uw' troepen,
> Dan zalmen's Vorsten dood, en u voor Vorst, uytroepen;
> En wie 'er tegens streeft, alwaart de Ridderschap,
> Die zal naa Pontus Meyr, in eeuw'ge ballingschap.

It is thus clear from these various pieces of evidence that the rivalry for the crown was in the parent play of D, but has been cut because of Senecan necessities.

It is now apparent that in D, as the chorus tells us, the first act has been contrived to exhibit the power of Love. Saturninus falls in love at first sight with Thamera, and the decree of Titus against Aran precipitates a long drawn out argumentative "passioning," with Thamera and her sons pleading for Aran, while Saturninus, now aided by Bassianus, pleads for the love of Thamera in return for the life of Aran. This first act has been cast into the form of a beloved Senecan argumentation.

The second act in D has been similarly manipulated. Its grand objective is to be the antiphony of grief by Saturninus and Titus, so that, as we have seen, Rozelyna-Lavinia had to be deferred to the third act. Other manipulations will appear as we examine the details on the background of the chapbook and S. In the chapbook, Attava, the Moor, and her sons use the hunt to murder the son of Theodosius and conceal the body in a pit, into which two (or three) of the sons of Titus fall and are accused. Attava sends the Moor to demand the hand of Titus in return for the lives of his sons. The Moor cuts off the hand for Titus, which is later returned with the corpses of the sons. These misfortunes send Lavinia mourning into the woods and groves, where the Queen's sons ravish her, and by the advice of the Moor mutilate her hands and tongue. She would have died had not Uncle Marcus happened along at the right time.

Here the parent play condensed and rearranged. It wove the two wood scenes together, deferring the interposed hand-chopping of the chapbook in order to get both the sons and the daughter into position to precipitate all the epitatical woe properly in the third act. It is also clear that D has made some changes in the interests of its Senecan form. As we have seen, one of these was to defer Rozelyna-Lavinia in order to preserve the balance between Saturninus and Titus. That balance evidently occasioned the addition of two more sons of Titus — he had plenty already — to get murdered in the pit, so that Titus could mourn two dead sons while Saturninus mourns one dead brother. Incidentally, the addition also occasioned the renaming of these sons in D. Similarly, Bassianus and Rozelyna-Lavinia are given a chance to fall in love in this second act, since the Senecan necessities of the first act had not given time.

So in D the Queen's sons quarrel over Lavinia-Rozelyna, overhear Bassianus, the King's brother, courting Rozelyna; and Aran, who intends to destroy the whole house of Titus, suggests that both satisfy their lust upon her and mutilate her so that she cannot tell. After a jealous fit, Aran tells Thamera his plan to finish off Rozelyna, get Bassianus and two sons of Titus, Klaudillus and Gradamard, into this pit, and implicate in fratricide the two youngest sons, Pollander and Melanus, by means of a helmet of gold. Bassianus and Rozelyna come upon the couple as they kiss and part. After a scene, Thamera calls her son Quiro, Bassianus is killed and hung on a bush, and Rozelyna is to have her rose plucked. As Klaudillus and Gradamard enter, Thamera calls to Aran it is time, who gets them into his pit, as Marcus, Saturninus, Lucius, and Titus enter, find them dead, and discover the incriminating evidence. Thamera and Aran enter to accuse Pollander and Melanus. Titus rises to the heights.

In S, the sons of Tamora also quarrel, and Aaron tells them he will lay a plan by which they may have Lavinia in the hunt. The love scene in D between Bassianus and Lavinia does not occur in S, since that had been attended to in the first act. In S they had already been married, and in the chapbook were at least about to be, but D could not take time to get them properly attached. Nor is any quarrel necessary between Aaron and Tamora in S and the chapbook, as in D. But in S as in D Aaron takes the lead in plotting against the sons of Titus, with gold and a letter playing their parts as in D. In S, Tamora is to be cross with Bassianus, while Aaron slips away to call her sons, who enter to stab Bassianus and with Tamora's blessing take Lavinia off to be raped. Aaron then lures the two sons of Titus into the pit, where the body of Bassianus had been thrown, and brings Saturninus to discover the horror. Tamora brings in the incriminating letter, etc., and the sons of Titus are sent to prison. This is essentially as D except that D kills one brace of sons along with Bassianus, and accuses another brace of having killed all three. As we have seen, this was no doubt in order to give Saturninus and Titus a balanced duet of high rant to end the act, and I suppose this was the reason Rozelyna-Lavinia had to bleed till she could be spared four lines for her misfortune at the beginning of the third act. S had no such necessity, and gave her full presentation at the end of the second act, as the five-act formula demanded. It is thus clear that most of D's variants from S in the second act are caused by its attempt to keep the unity of time, and by its climactic purpose to balance Titus and Saturninus in pages of grief. That is, S represents the run of the second act in the parent play of D.

The hand-chopping of the chapbook becomes the highlight of the third act. Preliminary to it in both D and S Titus pleads unsuccessfully in closely similar stage business for the lives of his sons before the Judges and Tribunes. In both, Lucius, another son, gets banished. In both, Rozelyna-Lavinia is next added to the mounting woes of Titus. Then we have the hand-chopping in both. D gives an alleged reason for reversing the sentence on the sons and exacting this ransom instead; the chapbook and S do not; it is evidently extra ornamentation. In D, Lucius and Marcus wish to substitute for Titus in sparing a hand, though only the hand of Titus is demanded, as in the chapbook. But in S the hand may be of Titus, Marcus, Lucius, or any of you. In both D and S, Titus fills the interval with raving till the hand and heads are brought back — more manageable than the hand and bodies in the chapbook. Titus rises to the occasion in both D and S, but more fantastically in D, where the heads speak, instead of merely being invoked to do so as in S, ghosts swear, etc., this being evidently extra-ornamentation. In both D and S, Lucius departs to gather troops, as there was no need to do in the chapbook. This is evidently the run of the parent play of D, and here S ends its third act, but D, as we have seen, throws the capture of Aran by Lucius back to this position, and Aran makes a clean breast of anything but clean material.

As we have seen earlier, D was obliged to advance its division between the fourth and fifth acts because it omitted the incident of the black babe. In the chapbook, the Empress explains the black babe after the fashion of Laban's sheep and Jacob's rods — she looked too hard at Aran — but Aran is banished, then recalled on condition that it should not happen again. S presents the story in the fourth act — it happened in the chapbook immediately after the Emperor's marriage, before the betrothal of Lavinia, the hunt, etc. In S, the discovery of Aaron as the father of a child by Tamora is coupled with the discovery of Tamora's sons, instigated by Aaron, as the offenders against Lavinia. In the chapbook, Lavinia took a wand between her stumps and wrote

> The Lustful Sons of the proud Emperess
> Are doers of this hateful Wickedness.

Titus vowed revenge and, like Hamlet, "feigned himself distracted, and went raving about the City, shooting his Arrows toward Heaven, as in Defiance, calling to Hell for Vengeance." S or an ancestor has combined

this and the black babe to make up the fourth act. D has omitted the
madness along with the black babe, retaining only the discovery of the
culprits. In chapbook, D, and S the discovery is made by Rozelyna-
Lavinia's handicapped writing. In D and S, Ovid's story of Philomela
precipitates the discovery. The parent play thus had approximately the
same materials as S. It is D which has made the changes.

D next pulls some of the material from the fifth act to make up its
fourth. In the chapbook, Titus and his friends ambushed Attava's sons
and bound them. Titus butchered them while Lavinia caught the blood in
a bowl with her stumps. Then came the pies and the party, with death for
everybody. In S all this is presented in the catastrophe of the fifth act,
along with the capture as well as the disposal of Aaron. But there the
sons are not ambushed. Instead, they and their mother are hoisted with
their own petard as they think they are deceiving crazy Titus. Also,
Lucius, not in the chapbook, takes over the kingdom, for which purpose
he was invented for the *Old Titus*.

D readjusts its material to center the fourth act upon Rozelyna-Lavinia.
With Ovid to give the suggestion, she uses her cane to disclose the culprits.
Thamera and her sons then play into the hands of Titus by appearing as
Revenge and attendants to persuade Titus that his son Lucius is at the
bottom of the trouble. Titus persuades Revenge-Thamera to invite the
Emperor and Empress to his house on business, leaving her attendant-sons
with him to spur on his revenge. The sons are slaughtered, with Rozelyna-
Lavinia biting out their hearts and spitting them in their faces. The
chorus then laments Rozelyna's plight and indicates that worse is to come.
So the chorus shows exactly how and why the redistribution has been
made.

With the preliminary butchery thrown to the fourth act, D now has the
Thyestean banquet left for the fifth act, which is strengthened by a more
"fitting" punishment of Aran. In the chapbook, the Moor was buried alive
to the middle, smeared with honey, and left to the bees and wasps till he
starved to death. S spares him the smearing with honey and the consequent stinging. D burns Aran on the stage — see the pictures in the first
edition!

It is thus clear that S tends to reproduce the structure of the common
ancestral form underlying D and S, while D adapts it to a different set of
literary ideas. Indeed, I find nothing in structure to indicate that D was
not dependent upon S itself. Since S was in print as early as 1594, there
is nothing improbable about that solution. The fact that D rests on a form
with the act-divisions of S might even be held to point to the First Folio
in 1623, where these were first made available in print. As a matter of
fact, the author of D would not need to have the actual act-divisions

marked, since the material itself shows the five units which D manipulates. But while structure is not conclusive, yet such a detail as that in the chapbook and D the hunting was to be on Tiber, but was not so localized in S points strongly to an earlier version than S as the parent play, though D was otherwise also aware of the localization on Tiber. I think an earlier version than S is also certainly indicated by the positive relationships of D with the German version, to which we now turn.

CHAPTER XXVI

Titus and Vespacia

Another piece of evidence can now be supplemented to show that some form of *Titus* was being performed in London either in or shortly before 1592. In *A Knacke to knowe a Knaue,* performed by Strange's company as a new play June 10, 1592, and thence till January 24, 1593, seven performances, printed in 1594, a character Osrick says

> My gratious Lord, as welcome shall you be,
> To me, my Daughter, and my sonne in Law,
> As *Titus* was vnto the Roman Senators,
> When he had made a conquest on the Goths:
> That in requitall of his seruice done,
> Did offer him the imperiall Diademe:
> As they in *Titus,* we in your Grace still fynd,
> The perfect figure of a Princelie mind.[1]

In no surviving version do the senators actually offer Titus the imperial diadem. They come nearest to doing so in the present *Titus Andronicus.* The allusion makes it clear, therefore, that some form of *Titus* was on the stage in London by June, 1592.[2]

The surviving German play of *Titus,* printed in 1620 (G), also helps to make it clear that there was a precedent play. As we shall see, G preserves only the pieces and patches of its parent play. We cannot reason, therefore, from its omissions, but only from its inclusions, remembering, however, that even they are probably in very mangled form. As we have seen, the Dutch play (D) has completely reworked the material of its parent play to a different set of standards. We can, therefore, use only its inclusions. After such known drastic alterations, coincidence between G and D in omission is not significant, nor is variation in omission. This omitted evidence is simply non-existent. But coincidence in inclusion by G and D is significant, especially if S agrees. Coincidence by G and D against S will mean that the two have a common ancestor either preceding or suc-

---

[1] *Knacke* (1594), F2ᵛ.

[2] Paul E. Bennett, "An Apparent Allusion to 'Titus Andronicus,'" *N.&Q.,* 200, 422-424, believes that *A Knack* "is a bad quarto, memorially reconstructed by some of the Earl of Derby's men early in January 1594 or late in December 1593," and that the Titus allusion came in at that time; but to turn his own phrase, this date for the allusion is "desperately conjectural."

ceeding S. When we consider Fuller's "Points common to G and D, but not found in S," the first two are coincidence in omission and so invalid. But we have positive agreement in

3. The information that the Empress's first husband has been killed to quiet his suspicions.

4. The Moor in effect boasts himself the "Lightning and Thunder" of his people.

5. The Moor is angry at the Empress when he meets her alone in the forest.

6. The charge of insulting the Empress upon which the sons of Titus are arrested.

7. The hand of Titus only is demanded in return for the lives of his sons, instead of (as in S) the hand of Titus, Marcus, Lucius.

8. Extreme obscenity in the Moor's confession of his past life.[3]

Some of these six points are rather tenuous and might well be coincidence, but such items as six and seven are not likely to be so. That is, G and D share a common ancestor against S. Since the hand business of seven belongs to the chapbook, it is S which has varied. That is, a common ancestor of G and D precedes S. It is thus clear that there was an earlier form than the present *Titus*. G and D may, however, have branched from that preceding form or forms at different stages. But it is at least clear that there was an earlier form of *Titus* than that printed in 1594, and that some form of *Titus* was being performed in London by June 1592. The surviving German play of 1620 is some kind of offshoot of that precedent form.

We may now return to the Roman senators and Titus of our allusion in *Knacke*. As we have seen, *Titus* of 1594 comes nearest to presenting the complete conditions of the allusion. It is clear that G presents a simplified version of the first act as it appears in the English *Titus*. In G, Vespasian (not Marcus) enters with the Roman crown in his hand, Titus Andronicus with a laurel crown on his head, and the Emperor of Rome that is to be. Also the captives of Titus, consisting of the Queen of Ethiopia (Aetiopissa), her two sons, and Morian, with Andronica, daughter of Titus, tagged on. Vespasian offers the crown to Titus, "as every body loudly says that the Roman crown is due to him by right." The Emperor objects, "I am the next heir and it belongs to me by right." Titus renounces the crown in the interest of "concord and unison between the Emperor, the Senate, and the commonalty." So he places the crown on the Emperor's head. In turn, the Emperor solicits the fair Andronica to be his bride, to which Titus assents, with his blessing. Titus then presents the Queen of Ethiopia and the other prisoners as a present to the Emperor, who tells

---

[3] Fuller, *P.M.L.A.*, XVI, 40.

Aetiopissa to cheer up. All exeunt except Morian, who remains to tell of his hopes for Aetiopissa, who had poisoned her former husband, the King of Ethiopia, for his sake. Morian had been "The Lightning and Thunder of Ethiopia" till Titus overcame him. The Emperor, Queen (Aetiopissa), her two sons, and Morian enter. The Emperor has sent Andronica back to Titus "with the message that I liked her not." Instead, he crowns Aetiopissa and hastens to "enjoy your stately person." All exeunt except the two sons, who remain to brew more mischief.

Thus the rivalry of Titus and Saturninus for the crown appears here in the simplest possible terms. Bassianus does not even appear in the first act, much less rival Saturninus for the crown and Lavinia. But here the nature of the German play must be taken into consideration, and that is now quite clear. It is a version cut to the minimum for a company which had neither the numbers nor the theater to put on the elaborate "upstairs-downstairs" action of *Titus,* with "Scene individable." Bare floor space and simple declamation had to serve their turn. We have exactly the "peeces and patches" of a play, such as Fynes Moryson and his English companions could not bear in the English comedians in Germany of the early 'nineties. From these tattered rags of structure, therefore, we cannot tell, at least in this act, whether the German version preceded or succeded *Titus* of 1594, though it was based upon a form of the story which was more nearly that of *Titus* than of any other version.

We must now notice that G (the German version) has certainly omitted a great deal of its parent play, in fact presenting only scenes from it arranged in print as eight acts. So in the Bassianus (Andronicae Gemahl) — Lavinia (Andronica) business, this couple appears first in the second act as married, without any explanation of how they got that way. Similarly, the whole business of incriminating the sons of Titus is omitted. Since the pit business is in the chapbook, it was in the ancestor of G in some form, whether it involved the details of a bribe of gold and a letter as in D and S or not. Instead of the pit incrimination, at the necessary moment we are told that the sons had been imprisoned because they had insulted the Empress, which is also a supplementary accusation in D, though not in S. For the material corresponding to the first two acts of S, the action and motivation of S are regularly implied, even when they are not presented. So in the third act, there is no pleading by Andronicus before the Tribunes, since only the Empress is to blame.[4] Instead, the hand-cutting follows immediately. Then in the interval between the sending of the hand and the return of it and the heads, the sons turn Lavinia-Andronica adrift, and Marcus-Victoriades discovers her and sets out in

---

[4] Incidentally, the cutting of the pit incrimination has cut two actors from the play. It will have been cut to a minimum cast, as all such plays had to be.

chase. After the fragments of the sons, etc. have been presented, Marcus (Victoriades) adds Lavinia (Andronica) to increase the woe. These differences are clearly due to simplification and rearrangement on the part of G. Then, without any necessity, G defers the discovery of the villains to the next scene, which is called an act. But G uses only the simple discovery by stump-directed writing as in the chapbook, without the aid of Ovid as in D and S. This is presumably another simplification by G. Lucius has been held over for this business, and only now is sent to raise an army. G has not the business of the message to Tamora's sons, nor has D, nor the chapbook. It may be an addition of S; it may be an omission of both G and D. But G preserves the black babe along with the chapbook and S, which D omits. G does not present the arrow shooting, though it later alludes to it, showing that it has been cut, as was the case in D. The Messenger of defiance is presented by G, as in S, but not in the chapbook, nor by D, which has cut all the crazy antics of Titus, along with the black babe. The remainder of the action in G is essentially as in S.

It will be seen that G gives us only the "peeces and patches" of the Titus play. Most of its differences in material from S are clearly due primarily to cutting for simplification. The original act-structure, as indicated by S and D, has been completely lost, being replaced in print, at least, by eight divisions called acts, which are more nearly scenes. The material and organization, however, of the ancestor of G is so nearly that of S as to make it certain that the ancestor of G had the same five-act division as in S. Even if they were not marked as acts, the five units were there. It is thus also clear that this division belonged to the *Old Titus*, as did the casting pattern for the Admiral's men before 1590. That is, the plot and structure of the *Old Titus* before 1590 were essentially the same as those of the *Titus* of 1594. If there was difference, it was in details and phraseology.

Here a very brief postmortem on Fuller's work[5] should be instructive. Its chief disease was the fallacy of negative, omitted, and so non-existent, evidence. It was and is known that G was cut heavily, and that D had also made drastic changes. Their common omissions, therefore, cannot be put in evidence. Similarly, their disagreements may as readily be the result of the same cause of omission, etc. on the one side or the other, and so must be laid aside. Their negative relationships with S are equally invalid. When reduced to the positive, but little is left of Fuller's elaborate tabulations of agreements in disagreement. This same fallacy of negative or non-existent evidence has vitiated and still vitiates much of the evidence adduced on the *Old Hamlet*, not to mention various "bad" quartos.

Now returning once more to Titus and the Senators, in the chapbook

---

[5] Fuller, *P.M.L.A.*, XVI, 1-65.

and in the Dutch play of Vos, there is no rivalry for the crown on the part of Titus or anyone. In the German play, Vespasianus (Lucius) offers the crown to Titus in the name of everybody. There is no mention of the senators specifically in the offer itself and they play no part. But Titus claims all voices, and states that both the senators and the commonalty must be in harmony with the emperor. Thus the senators *may* have been involved more directly in the parent version, though that is not likely. At any rate, there was a Titus play preceding the *Titus* of 1594, and this *Titus* of 1594 comes nearest to satisfying the allusion in *Knacke*.

This German version also contributes one other important fact. In it, the first person to speak is Vespasianus, and he is offering the crown to Titus. It later appears that Vespasianus is that son of Titus who is called Lucius in *Titus,* to whom the crown eventually devolves. It is thus a fact that, though its title is *Titus Andronicus and the Haughty Empress,* yet the German play is one of Titus and Vespasian, however the fact be explained. This grouping of Titus and Vespasian has been repeatedly equated with one of Henslowe's titles. " 'tit(t)us & vespacia' 'tit(t)us.' Performed by Strange's men, as a new play, 11 Apr. 159[1/]2, and thence till 25 Jan. 1593, 10 performances."[6] As a matter of fact, "vespacia" is included consistently in the seven performances before June 22, 1592, but not in the three the following January. If both titles refer to the same play, its range is thus that of the *Henry VI* plays. If it was some form of the Titus story, it paralleled those plays also in the range of companies performing it. For the title page of *Titus* in 1594 (S.R. February 6, 1594) informs us that "it was Plaide by the Right Honourable the Earle of *Darbie,* Earle of *Pembrooke,* and Earle of *Sussex* their Seruants." That Sussex's company was the final one we have Henslowe's Diary to show. " 'tit(t)us & ondronic(o)us' 'andronicous.' Performed by Sussex' men, as a new play, 23 (24) Jan. 1593/4 and again 28 (29) Jan. and 6 Feb."[7] Later it was "Performed by the Admiral's and Chamberlain's men, 5 (7) and 12 (14) June 1594."[8] Final possession was by the Shaksperean company, this being the reason that "the Lorde Chamberlaine theyr Seruants" was added to the other three titles on the title page of the quarto of 1600, though not within the quarto.

If Sussex's men had the play just before publication in 1594, then Strange's and Pembroke's must have preceded in performance, in whatever order they did it. The succession of these plays was from Strange's to Pembroke's about the autumn of 1592, as shown specifically by the case of *3 Henry VI.* This means that Strange's had some form of this play of

---

[6] Greg, *Henslowe's Diary,* II, 155.

[7] Greg, *Henslowe's Diary,* II, 159.

[8] *Ibid.,* II, 159.

Titus before the autumn of 1592, confirmed by the allusion in *Knacke,* a Strange play, new June 10, 1592. Since such an allusion to a story not otherwise well known must be to a current production, and since the German play is a Titus and Vespasian play, though its title is *Titus Andronicus,* we are probably safe enough in accepting Henslowe's entries of April 11 and following as being to *Titus* in a form very badly represented by the German version. If not, we must throw Strange's first connection still further back than the beginning of Henslowe's Diary February 19, 1592.

If the reference to *Titus and Vespasian* is to *Titus,* then the form presented on April 11, 1592 was "new," and the "new" form of January 24, 1594, was a new revision. It is also clear that there was a still earlier form than any "new" form of 1592. As we have seen, the casting pattern of the surviving *Titus* is that of the Admiral's men before 1590. We have seen also that the *Old Titus* had the same materials, organization, and consequent five-act structure as the *Titus* of 1594. Since the Admiral's split about 1590, one half going to Germany to act their plays in "peeces and patches," that fact also gives some indication for an *Old Titus* before 1590. And these various indications fit in with Ben Jonson's statement in the Induction to *Bartholomew Fair;* "Hee that will sweare, *Ieronimo,* or *Andronicus* are the best playes, yet, shall passe vnexcepted at, heere, as a man whose Iudgement shewes it is constant, and hath stood still, these fiue and twentie, or thirtie yeeres." This statement would date *Titus* and *Spanish Tragedy* between 1584 and 1589. We have seen that the *Spanish Tragedy* belongs near the former date. The indications are that the *Old Titus* belongs about or before the latter date.

It seems clear, therefore, that the general form of the present play was given it for the Admiral's men before 1590. At some time thereafter the "peeces and patches" of the English play were taken to Germany, and the resultant tatters appear in print in 1620. The Admiral's play probably appears as a "new" play *Titus and Vespasian* in Henslowe's Diary for Strange's company while it was cooperating with the Admiral's, April 11, 1592. The "new" should mean at least a revised form. The play was acted in succession by Strange's, Pembroke's, and Sussex's, the last of the three putting it on under the title of *Titus Andronicus* January 24, 1594. Later, the cooperating Chamberlain-Admiral's group performed it in June, 1594, and the Chamberlain's men retained it. When it was printed in 1594, the title page began with Strange's, who had it in or shortly before 1592.

Now what of Shakspere's hand in the play? I believe it is clear that he would not have written the original play for the Admiral's before 1590. If this be granted, then Shakspere did not write the *Old Titus,* as he did not write the *Old Hamlet.* Since the "new" *Titus and Vespasian* of 1592 was for Strange's, cooperating at the time with the Admiral's, Shakspere may well have had something to do with that revision, if indeed this is a revision of the *Old Titus*. But the chief demonstrable connections of Shakspere's plays and poems are with the *Titus Andronicus* which was "new" in 1594 and printed that year. At least, we know enough now about the history of the play's evolution to understand why there has been such dire disagreement about Shakspere's authorship. But on the details of Shakspere's actual lines in the play this history throws little light — "By God's sonties, 'twill be a hard way to hit!" — and I have resolutely expressed no opinion — not that I do not have at least one!

CHAPTER XXVII

The Merry Wives of Windsor

When Strange's returned to the Rose December 29, 1592, they acted twenty-six week-days till January 31, 1593. *"Muly Mollocco, The Spanish Tragedy, A Knack to Know a Knave, The Jew of Malta, Sir John Mandeville, Titus and Vespasian, Friar Bacon and Friar Bungay, 1 Henry VI, and 2 Tamar Cam* all made their appearance again. In addition, there were a comedy called *Cosmo,* and two news plays, *The Jealous Comedy,* which may, I think, be *The Comedy of Errors,* and *The Tragedy of the Guise,* which is usually accepted as Marlowe's *Massacre of Paris."*[1] It may be pointed out that we do not know which *Henry VI* was involved; from the history of the plays, I would rather suspect *3 Henry VI.*[2] Nor does the identification of *The Comedy of Errors* as *The Jealous Comedy* appeal to me, since it certainly was not a new play on January 5, 1593, and I have found no valid evidence of a revision at this time.[3]

We must, however, examine "the notion of Fleay that the *Jealous Comedy* produced by the Alleyn company for Henslowe on 5 January 1593 . . . may have been an early form of *Merry Wives.* It may, of course, have been any play with jealousy as a prominent motive in it, *Comedy of Errors* . . . or another."[4] There is nothing, of course, to suggest that *The Jealous Comedy* was Shakspere's, and certainly the title is general. But if Shakspere did have a "new" play put on by this company at this period, then *The Jealous Comedy* is it.

It will be well, therefore, to examine the structure of *Merry Wives* to see if it throws any light on origins.

I, 1. Shallow, Slender, Evans enter before Page's house. Shallow will procure revenge on that Falstaff. Evans thinks all would be better employed in securing the pretty heiress Anne Page for Slender. Page thanks Shallow for some venison, which Shallow says was ill-killed; and Page would do a good office between Shallow and Falstaff, who enters with Bardolph, Nym, and Pistol. Shallow proffers his complaint against Falstaff; "you have beaten my men, killed my deer, and broke open my

---

[1] Chambers, *E.S.,* II, 123.
[2] See above, pp. 326 ff.
[3] Baldwin, *Five-Act,* pp. 665 ff.
[4] Chambers, *Shakespeare,* I, 435.

lodge" (100-101), which Falstaff does not deny. Evans thinks Page, himself, and mine Host of the Garter should be umpires. Slender also has a complaint, which proves to be that Pistol picked his purse, or maybe it was Nym, or Bardolph. Falstaff concludes, "You hear all these matters denied, gentlemen" (168). Enter Anne Page, Mistress Ford and Mistress Page. Page invites all to a hot venison pasty for dinner and hopes "we shall drink down all unkindness" (178). All exeunt except Shallow, Slender, and Evans. As Slender wishes for his *Book of Songs and Sonnets,* his servant Simple enters but is unable to help Slender locate the *Book of Riddles,* while Evans with the help of Shallow tries to get him interested in a marriage with Anne Page. Slender will do a greater thing at the request of his cousin Shallow. Anne Page invites them to dinner, to which Shallow and Evans hasten, and Slender sends his servant Simple to wait on Shallow, but is himself unpersuaded by Anne Page. Slender prefers to boast of fencing, of his exploits with Sackerson the bear at bearbaiting, etc., but Page returns and manages to get him in to dinner.

I, 2. Evans is directing Simple to the house of Dr. Caius to give Mrs. Quickly a letter "to desire and require her to solicit your master's desires to Mistress Anne Page" (8-9).

I, 3. Falstaff parts with Bardolph to mine Host of the Garter to be a tapster, since Bardolph was too careless in his stealing. Falstaff plans to make love to Ford's wife, because "she has all the rule of her husband's purse" and "he hath a legion of angels" (49-50). Falstaff has written letters to both Mistress Ford and Mistress Page, who are to be his East and West Indies of wealth. Pistol and Nym will not be panders, so Falstaff turns them off also, and will keep only his "skirted page" (Robin) to carry on his intrigue. Nym and Pistol will get revenge by telling Ford and Page.

I, 4. Mistress Quickly sets the prayerful John Rugby as a guard to watch for Dr. Caius, while she talks with Simple. As she is agreeing to help Slender with Anne Page, Rugby warns of the approach of Dr. Caius, and Simple gets concealed in the closet, where Caius finds him. Simple blurts out his mission, and Caius challenges Evans, since Caius also wants Anne Page. Mine Host of the Garter will measure the weapons. As Caius exits with Rugby, he threatens that if Mistress Quickly does not aid him with Anne, she will lose her place. Fenton enters, also to hire Mistress Quickly's good graces with Anne Page.

The first act presents the proposed intrigue of Falstaff with Mistress Ford and Mistress Page, and the plans of the three rival suitors for Anne Page, with Mistress Quickly as intermediary for all three. Accordingly, Falstaff's followers have been dispersed into strategic positions to play their parts.

II, 1. As Mistress Page resents her letter from Falstaff and plans revenge, Mistress Ford enters with her duplicate missive, also seeking revenge. "Let's appoint him a meeting; give him a show of comfort in his suit, and lead him on with a fine-baited delay, till he hath pawned his horses to mine host of the Garter" (82-85). They retire as the jealous Ford enters with Pistol, and the trusting Page with Nym, who are imparting Falstaff's designs. Mistress Ford and Mistress Page come forward as Mistress Quickly enters, whom, as they go out, they plan to use as messenger to Falstaff. Ford is suspicious of his wife, Page is not suspicious of his. Enter "my ranting host of the Garter" (170), followed by Shallow, who have a jest to be played upon Caius and Evans, beginning with sending them to different places for the duel. The Host is to give Ford, as Brooke (F Broome), access to Falstaff. As the others exit, the jealous Ford remains to tell the audience he plans to test his wife and Falstaff.

II, 2. Falstaff will not lend Pistol a penny, since Pistol would not bear his letter. Robin announces Mistress Quickly, who makes an appointment with Falstaff for Mistress Ford, and conveys the intentions of Mistress Page, to whom Falstaff must send his page. Pistol follows Mistress Quickly and Robin out, and Bardolph, as drawer, enters to exulting Falstaff, announcing Brooke (Ford in disguise), who fees Falstaff to lay siege to Mistress Ford, and is promised that he shall enjoy Ford's wife, is told of the appointment and is to return at night to hear of progress. Falstaff exits, and Ford exhibits his jealousy.

II, 3. As Caius waits impatiently for Evans, who has not come, the Host, Shallow, Slender, and Page enter and let Caius exhibit. They will get him around to Evans under the pretence of seeing Anne Page.

Falstaff's wooing is planned as the proper end of the protasis in that thread of the story, but there is no corresponding step in the Anne Page rivalry, though it is represented in the final scene of the act. The story of Falstaff and the merry wives is to furnish the fundamental structure of the play.

III, 1. Evans, with Simple, awaits impatiently for Dr. Caius. Simple reports that Page, Shallow, and Slender are approaching without arms. The Host, Caius, and Rugby enter. Evans sees that he and Caius are to be made laughing-stocks and in asides "cues" Dr. Caius. The Host confesses his trick and reconciles the two. As Slender (now sighing like furnace for sweet Anne Page), Shallow, Page, and Host exit, Caius and Evans agree to be revenged on the Host.

III, 2. Mistress Page, preceded by Robin the page, meets Ford as she is on her way to visit Mistress Ford. Ford cannot understand how Page can be so obtuse, and will expose everybody. As Page, Shallow, Slender, Host, Evans, Caius, and Rugby enter, Ford invites them all to go with him, but Shallow and Slender have an appointment to dine with Anne Page. Slender has Page's good will, but Page's wife is for Caius; the Host is for Fenton, who "kept company with the wild prince and Poines" (62-63), but Page will not consent to him.

III, 3. Mistress Page and Mistress Ford instruct their servants in the art of bearing a heavily loaded buck-basket without staggering when they carry it out to dump its contents "in the muddy ditch close by the Thames side" (12-13). Robin the page reports Sir John is in at the back door and requests Mistress Ford's company. As Falstaff bepraises Mistress Ford and befouls Mistress Page, who hears all, Robin announces the hurried arrival of Mistress Page, who says Ford is coming with all the officers in Windsor to search for a man, and Falstaff gets packed among foul clothes in a basket to be sent to Datchet Mead. Ford, Page, Caius, and Evans enter to search. Ford permits the "buck" washing to pass before he locks the door and institutes his search, while Mrs. Ford does not know whether to be more pleased at outwitting her husband or Falstaff, and she suspects some leak in communications to her husband, so Mistress Ford and Mistress Page plan to send Mistress Quickly to Falstaff for a second duping. As Ford returns saying "may be the knave bragged of that he could not compass" (176-177), the merry wives understand how Ford found out, and Mistress Ford acts properly the injured wife. Page invites the group for breakfast in the morning and then to go a-birding. Evans and Caius have some private scheme for getting even with mine Host.

III, 4. Anne Page coaches Fenton in his suit, and communicates secretly a plan if her father will not consent. Shallow, Slender, and Mistress Quickly "Break their talk" (22) to give Slender his chance at courtship, with Shallow prompting him. Page and Mistress Page enter. Page favors son Slender, while Fenton gets a rebuff from Page and an ambiguous promise from Mistress Page, who really favors Caius; but Anne will have neither the fool nor the physician. Mistress Quickly is neutral and will do what she can for all three suitors, especially Fenton; but now she must do the errand of Mistress Ford and Mistress Page to Falstaff.

III, 5. Falstaff orders Bardolph to bring him sack as he informs the audience of how he was thrown in Thames. Mistress Quickly enters to explain the "mistake" and invites Falstaff again to Mistress Ford, when the husbands go a-birding in the morning. Brooke (Ford) enters to learn from Falstaff how the latter escaped as foul clothes but has another assignment with Mistress Ford. Ford informs the audience that this time he will surely catch Falstaff.

In the third act, Falstaff has made his first attempt upon the merry wives and is duped, but falls into the trap of an invitation to a second attempt. For the Anne Page plot, each rival has hopes, but Anne favors Fenton, who is forbidden by her father.

IV, 1. Mistress Quickly reports on Falstaff's anger and bears Mistress Ford's invitation to Mistress Page to come suddenly, which Mistress Page will do as soon as she gets her son William to school. This introduces a wholly extraneous comic interlude, with Evans posing Master William Page upon his Accidence, while Mistress Quickly aids in misunderstanding, and Mistress Page enjoys the fun.

IV, 2. As Mistress Ford has Falstaff in fool's heaven, with her husband supposedly out of the way a-birding, Mistress Page rushes in with the news that Ford is coming in a rage to search for the fat knight. After a discussion of ways and means, it is decided that Falstaff shall escape in the clothes of "the fat woman of Brentford" (identified in the quarto of 1602 as Gillian of Brainford, a name of notorious fame), whom Ford detests; but the merry wives will also send the buck-basket before.

> We'll leave a proof, by that which we will do,
> Wives may be merry, and yet honest too:
> We do not act that often jest and laugh;
> 'Tis old, but true, — Still swine eats all the draff (90-93).

Ford and his crew meet the basket bearers, and he calls for his wife in order to make the grand exposé, but finds only dirty clothes. Ford is now in good fettle to give Mother Prat of Brentford; that is, Falstaff, a thorough cudgelling, while Evans likes not his beard, which he has espied under the muffler. As Ford pursues his search, the merry wives decide to tell their husbands what they have done and to invite their aid in further punishing Falstaff by publicly shaming him.

IV, 3. Bardolph tells the Host that the Germans desire three of his horses to meet the duke himself at court tomorrow. The Host has heard of no duke at court and will charge the Germans a-plenty for the horses and for their use of his house the past week.

IV, 4. The merry wives plan with their husbands and Sir Hugh to punish Falstaff by making an assignation with him in the park at midnight, where he is to come as the ghost of Herne (quarto of 1602, Horne) the hunter, with horns on head, to Herne's oak. Nan Page, William, and others dressed as urchins, ouphs, and fairies will pinch Falstaff soundly and burn him with tapers till he tells the truth. Evans will train the children and be a jack-an-apes also in the show (this is how his function of schoolmaster came to be emphasized). Page plans aside to have Slender steal Nan away and marry her at Eton, while Mistress Page makes similar plans for Dr. Caius. Ford will visit Falstaff again as Brooke.

IV, 5. The Host shows Simple the chamber of Falstaff, who will wait till the fat woman comes down, but Falstaff says she has already gone.

Simple wants to find out from her for Slender whether Nym stole his chain, and Falstaff answers for her ambiguously as to the chain, and as to Slender's chances with Nan Page. As Simple departs, happy with supposedly favorable answers, Bardolph enters to tell the Host how the three Germans had "ditched" him and stolen the horses. Evans happens in to improve the occasion by telling the Host how three cozen-Germans had fleeced various inn-keepers of horses and money, followed by Dr. Caius, who happens by also to improve the fears of the Host, who rushes out with Bardolph to see what can be done. As Falstaff ruminates on his washing and cudgelling, Mistress Quickly enters from the merry wives to explain again and give him another invitation.

IV, 6. Fenton fees the melancholy Host to assist him in abducting Anne Page, whom Slender intends to steal with the blessing of her father, and Dr. Caius with the connivance of her mother, but Anne intends to run away with Fenton.

The fourth act has brought us to the brink of catastrophe in both plots. Falstaff has been duped a second time and a plan has been laid to beguile him even a third time to his final public exposure and punishment, while Anne Page is to be abducted from among the actors in that punishment. In a minor thread, Evans and Caius have had revenge upon the Host, just as earlier Nym and Pistol had their revenge upon Falstaff and were dropped without being given a chance to gloat over it.

V, 1. Falstaff hopes for good luck the third time as Mistress Quickly leaves to provide horns and a chain for him as Herne's ghost. Brooke learns from Falstaff of the plan for the night and is to get an account of Falstaff's misadventure as the old woman, but Falstaff will be revenged.

V, 2. Page is coaching Shallow and Slender on the plan to steal his daughter Anne.

V, 3. Mistress Page, Mistress Ford, and Doctor Caius rehearse the plan to steal her daughter Anne, as the ladies approach Herne's oak.

V, 4. Evans "tribs" in to the pit of concealment with his fairies.

V, 5. Falstaff enters at midnight as Herne, invoking Jove to favor his expectations (after the model of Chaerea in Terence). As he promises the entering wives that he will divide his favors between them, there is a noise and Falstaff is left to the mercy of Sir Hugh, Pistol, Mistress Quickly, Anne Page, and their retinue of fairies with tapers, who pronounce a blessing upon Windsor, and the order of the Garter particularly, and then discover Falstaff and punish him. While this performance is going on, each of the three suitors steals one of the fairies away. The Pages and Fords shame Falstaff, who perceives he is made an ass. Falstaff must also repay Brooke (Ford), but Page promises Falstaff a posset tonight to laugh at his wife because Slender has stolen Anne, while Mistress Page says aside that Anne has married Caius. Slender returns blurting out that his Anne was a great lubberly boy. Mistress Page is about to crow over her husband when Caius enters to report like luck with a boy and not Anne. Fenton enters with Anne and all is forgiven. Even Sir John is to be admitted to the sport by a country fire (after the fashion of Terence's braggart soldier).

The principal structure of the play is in the duping of Falstaff, with the courting of Anne Page as a dependent and totally unnecessary part. The first act introduces the characters and their plans, both in the intrigue of Falstaff and in the courtship of Anne Page. The second act presents the end of the protasis in Falstaff's intrigue, with the usual plans; that of Falstaff against Mistress Ford and that of Mistress Ford to see the biter bit. In the third act, Caius and Evans are tricked and vow revenge upon mine Host, who has tricked them. This does not forward the Anne Page rivalry, to which Caius and Evans belong, and is merely a comic by-thread to exhibit these two fritter-makers of the Queen's English, one of whom happens to be a suitor, the other the chief champion of Slender in the rivalry for Anne Page. As its proper business, the third act presents the first duping of Falstaff. In the rivalry for Anne, she favors Fenton and indicates that if her father does not consent she has a plan, while father indicates his wishes for Slender, and mother hers for Caius. Thus all issues are joined in this epitasis. The fourth act presents the second duping of Falstaff and the plan for the third and final one. The three rivals for Anne also lay their plans to steal her during this final duping and punishment of Falstaff. The Host is duped in the fourth act to get the revenge of Caius and Evans out of the way. Then the fifth act exposes Falstaff and gives Anne to Fenton as a proper catastrophe.

It will be seen that the structure lies in the duping of Falstaff, and that for the final three acts it follows a conventional one, two, three pattern, as in *The Comedy of Errors,* for instance. The rivalry for Anne Page is made to intermesh with this main structure, while the Caius-Evans by-plot in turn intermeshes with that rivalry. The various intrigues are kept moving, without the machinery making itself mechanically conspicuous. The deceptively easy flow of events is really controlled tightly, but with enough of the extraneous to camouflage the tightness with which the plot controls the story.

It is also quite enlightening to see how Falstaff and his motley crew of attendant comedians have been "laid into" this plot, where by right no one of them belongs, least of all the Falstaff of the *Henry IV* plays. Evidently these "humours" were in demand and had to be fitted into parts, willy-nilly. For this is a Windsor merry wives story of courtier intrigue, and not a Falstaff story at all. To introduce the play, Justice Shallow is duped again by Falstaff and his men, as a device to get Falstaff connected with the Ford and Page households. Shallow, "in the county of Gloucester, justice of peace" (I, 1, 4), has beeen transplanted near enough to Windsor upon the pretext that "The council shall hear it" (I, 1, 31, 106), to bestow the ill-killed venison upon Page, and is given a cousin Slender, whom he wishes to marry Anne Page. He is thus merely attached to the play. The name of Falstaff is attached to the duper-duped of the merry wives story. In order to distribute Falstaff's comrades, he is caused to part with his three "men." Because of his careless stealing, Bardolph is placed with mine Host of the Garter. Because they will not be panders for Falstaff to Mistress Ford and Mistress Page, Falstaff cashiers Pistol and Nym, who, for revenge, tell the husbands of Falstaff's plans, thus arousing Ford's jealous suspicions. They have now served their purpose, as any one servant of any would-be duper could have done; but Pistol is brought back once more to "fall for" Mistress Quickly, whose husband he had become by *Henry V*. He had, of course, known her in *1* and *2 Henry IV*, but Shakspere had not there decided to pair them. Falstaff is now left with his "skirted page" Robin, with whom he also parts to Mistress Page. This retinue is that of *Henry V* as a projection of that in *2 Henry IV*, where Nym does not appear. Mistress Quickly, regularly hostess of a tavern in Eastcheap, now becomes the servant of Dr. Caius and is the go-between in both stories.

It will be seen that Falstaff and his fellows have been merely attached to the play. The duper-duped has been labeled with the name of Falstaff, and Falstaff's crew have been used in various positions, most of them completely non-essential, at least for them. Falstaff and his crew do not belong to either thread of the story; they have merely been "let into" this conventional intrigue plot. These characters were simply "turned" for *Merry Wives* after they had won popularity in some or all of the Henry plays. I suppose this "turning" could have happened when the play was originally constructed, but in that case I cannot conceive how Shakspere could have made their connections so superficial, and could so have warped their fundamental humors. It is far more likely that Shakspere let them into an old play, his or another's, which he was revising.

Notwithstanding these superficial inlays, the structure of the play has in general been surprisingly well done, whether we do or do not think that such a job should have been done at all. The eighteenth century accounted for the play as hasty work at the Queen's command. Even if we could be certain that this play was in fact done in haste, it is not in its structure nor in the execution of that structure hasty work, but a well-planned whole, though it has suffered minor damages in transmission, as is usual for plays of the time. We may prefer a tightly knit Italianate intrigue, as we may prefer the Italianate sonnet; but Shakspere, as evidently did his audience, preferred a less mechanically obvious form.

As we have seen, the duper duped by the merry wives is the fundamental plot, to which the triple-wooing of Anne Page has been added. It is easy enough to recover the minimum outlines of the fundamental plot at first construction. In the first place, as I have pointed out elsewhere,[5] some author was conscious that Falstaff was a Thraso, and so he consciously echoed and in some respects modelled upon *Eunuchus*. Malone pointed out but did not connect two specific echoes of that play in speeches of Falstaff, one at III, 3, 36-38, the other at V, 5, 10-11. Besides, at the end Falstaff, after ignominy, is forgiven and gets his invitation to take part in the festivities, as does Thraso in *Eunuchus*. The author has thus indicated the type of play he is consciously writing.

Knowing the type, we can recover the outlines of the original play. Whatever the names attached, and wherever they were localized, the primary nucleus consisted of Falstaff, the merry wives, and their husbands. For the men actors in the company this supplied the high comedian, and the two contrasted "young" men, the one jealous, the other placid. Falstaff is the high comedian, and as braggart soldier shows many characteristics in common with Armado and Parolles. Like them, Falstaff is "war-like, court-like, and learned." Armado, like Falstaff, is certainly a "high-falutin Euphuistic lover," as Sir Arthur Quiller-Couch labels Falstaff, though not having been born an Englishman and reared in the right circles, I am naturally not qualified to say whether either is an "attenuated prig of a character."[6] Jealous Ford pairs with Antipholus of Ephesus and Proteus. His foil is equable Page to match Antipholus of Syracuse and Valentine. Since, as we shall see, the wives planned originally to make Falstaff pawn his horses to mine Host, evidently the Host was a principal aider and abetter in their devices. He has the humorous turn of ladies' manager Boyet, of Lafeu, or Capulet, though that turn is now much exaggerated. The Host would need a man, now Bardolph, to assist him in various ways, and such an assistant would regularly be a clown. The Falstaff duping was, and still shows that it was, constructed to the five-man pattern for the Shaksperean company in its first period, not later than 1594. It has then been enlarged by adding the triple rivalry for Anne Page as a minor thread in order to provide for three more male roles. It is thus exactly parallel in method of structure with *Fair Em* about the end of 1590, the difference being that the subplot of *Fair Em* was apparently added at construction to meet the particular conditions, while the subplot was added in *Merry Wives* probably later, as we shall see, doubtless also to meet changed conditions.

It is readily apparent, also, how the five-act structure was built up.

---

[5] Baldwin, *Five-Act Structure,* pp. 554-559.

[6] See O. J. Campbell, "The Italianate Background of *The Merry Wives of Windsor*" (U. of Michigan Publications, Language and Literature, Vol. VIII), pp. 86 ff., for detailed discussion of these characteristics.

Since it was to be a Thraso play, the duper-duped had to go through the conventional one, two, three stages from epitasis to catastrophe of the five-act formula. The game of hide the lover, real or supposed, was a favorite international sport in the literature of the time. From this background, the original author selected certain stock devices to go with his stock characters. The principal device is of the lover, would-be or actual, who confides in the husband. He must confide twice and then be exposed in order to get the one, two, three demanded by the formula as adapted to Thraso or the duper duped. The would-be lover must thus be provided with two gruelling escapes and then be exposed for the catastrophe. For the first escape, the author here adapts the device of a movable receptacle, with the would-be lover as uncomfortably hidden as is possible under old documents, clothes, etc., the device taking the purely English and localised form of a buck-basket full of clothes on its way to Datchet Mead. For the second escape, the author uses another purely localised device, the disguise as a suspected and disliked witch, which would procure a sound beating. The third device was even more local, disguise as Herne or Horne of Windsor Forest, to be properly punished by fairies.

It appears not to have been noticed that in the first of these three, when Falstaff is carried out as dirty clothes, *Merry Wives* combines two previous devices. So far as I know, these two devices occur together only in Straparola's story *Le Tredeci Piacevoli Notti* (1550-53), iv. 4 and its derivatives. There at the first alarm the wife bade the lover "lie down upon the bed, and remain there with the curtains drawn, till her husband was gone . . . she hid me in the bed, and drew the curtains that he might not see me."[7] At the second, the wife "hid her lover in a chest, before which she placed a quantity of clothes, in such a manner that they should not see him . . . took a chest and placed me therein, and put a number of clothes before it, which she so disposed that they should not see me; and he, turning the bed over and over, and finding nothing, went away."[8] The third time, the wife "opened a large desk which was in her chamber, and hid him in it." The husband searched the bed and the chests in vain, and then set the room on fire; but the wife said "you shall not burn this desk, where are the writings belonging to my fortune. And calling four able porters, she made them take the desk from her house and put it in that of the old woman her neighbour."[9] Having been three times foiled, the husband planned to expose the wife and lover; but they yet again turned the jest upon him. Thus the lover confesses to the husband and escapes three times.

Straparola had expanded his story from an analogous one in "Il Peco-

---

[7] Hazlitt, *Shakespeare's Library* (1875), I, iii, 57.

[8] Hazlitt, p. 57.

[9] Hazlitt, p. 58.

rone di Ser Giovanni Fiorentino," where the wife at the first alarm "hid her lover under a heap of clothes from the washing, which were not yet fully dry, and had been thrown for a time on a table under a window . . . she had hidden me under a heap of wet clothes from the wash."[10] At the second and only other attempt, "the lady putting out the light, and, putting Bucciuolo behind her, opened the door, and put her arm round her husband, and with the other hand pushed her lover out of the door, without her husband's perceiving it."[11] The wife then pretends her husband is mad, and Bucciuolo leaves town.

These two stories are combined in a play by Duke Henry Julius of Brunswick, printed in 1594, which is described as *Tragedia Hibeldeha von einer Ehebrecherin, wie die jren Man drey Mal betreucht, aber zu letzt ein schrecklich Ende genommen habe. Mit acht Personen.* 8 vo. Wolfenbüttel 1594.[12] In *Hibeldeha,* the Duke has a combination of *Il Pecorone* and Straparola's tale. The husband incites a student to attempt his wife, though the student does not know this relationship. In the first attempt, "The wife had shewn him a hiding-place under the window, and after her husband had searched the house for some time, she had led him up stairs, and then called out to him in a loud voice, 'Now, sweetheart, go, it is time,' " whereupon he "jumps out of the window." This is the hiding place under the window of *Il Pecorone* adapted. At the second attempt, the wife demonstrates to her husband how, if she did have a lover in the house, she would blind the husband's eyes by covering them with his cloak, whereupon the lover escapes again. This is the second and final attempt of *Il Pecorone* adapted. In the third attempt, the husband threatens to burn the place down. "When the wife heard this she hid me in a tub, and threw some old linen over me. Then she ran out to her husband, and begged, that if he was determined to set the house on fire, he would at least spare her linen, and help her carry it out. He did so, and so he carried me out of the house too. But as soon as he had gone in again, I ran away." Here the second and third devices of Straparola's story have been combined. At the threat of fire, the goodwife, much more in character, bethinks her of her linen instead of legal documents, and the linen is transferred to a tub as a proper container, so that she and her husband can lug out tub, lover, and linen. So far as I know, this is the only other place besides *Merry Wives* where the two devices have been fused; and in both plays the end result is the same; a lover, real or supposed, is hidden in a tub or buck-basket, under linen or dirty clothes, and is taken out by the husband and wife, or the wife's servants. In this

[10] Hazlitt, pp. 29-30.

[11] Hazlitt, p. 31.

[12] W. L. Holland, pp. 401-444; summarized and abstracted in English by Cohn, *Shakespeare in Germany* (1865), pp. XLIII ff.

intricate fusion the two plays cannot possibly be independent of each other. But the Duke's play takes all three of its devices from the two Italian stories, while *Merry Wives* has only the fused device ultimately from Straparola. *Merry Wives* is thus further away from the common ancestor of this device than is *Hibeldeha*.

Now the Duke of Brunswick, author of *Hibeldeha*, is known to have had connections with English plays and players. "Unfortunately the exchequer-accounts of the years 1590-1601 are missing from the Brunswick Court Archives," and our first surviving record there of Thomas Sackville (formerly of the Admiral's men) is 1597, but Cohn presents sufficient evidence for his statement that "In all probability the whole company . . . appeared on the stage of this Prince in Wolfenbüttel immediately after its arrival in Germany."[13] In this particular play, the clown apologizes for not understanding German very well because he is English. The situation more than suggests that *Hibeldeha* was based upon such "peeces and patches" of an English play as the German branch of the Admiral's men provided. If so, Strange's company would have had access to the original Admiral's play during their cooperation with Alleyn. But *Merry Wives* is not a version of this hypothetical Admiral's play. From it or from some other source it has borrowed the single fused device of the lover transported in some receptacle as clothes or linen.[14]

It will be seen that Duke Julius has in some respects himself varied the device. In Straparola's story and in *Merry Wives*, the wife has her men carry the receptacle out. With only eight "persons," Duke Julius has economised on his man-power by having the wife and husband do the job themselves. Thus the hypothetical Admiral's play doubtless had the receptacle carried out as in Straparola and *Merry Wives*.

It is also apparent that *Tarltons Newes out of Purgatorie*, about 1590, is not the source of either our hypothetical Admiral's play or *Merry Wives*. The author of the *Newes* discards Straparola's bed — the most obvious place to look! — but saves the feathers and puts them into "a great driefatte" (66) as a suitable receptacle. The lover is now hidden in the vat under the feathers instead of in a chest hidden by clothes, thus combining Straparola's first two devices. Having combined the first two devices, the author introduces a new one of hiding the lover in "a priuie place between two seelings of a plauncher . . . betweene two seelings of a chamber in a fit place for yᵉ purpose."[15] The third device is adapted from Straparola. Now at a grange the wife has hidden the lover in a chest full of her husband's legal papers. When the husband threatens fire, she

---

[13] Cohn, XXXIII-XXXIV.

[14] In connection with Falstaff's characteristics in *Merry Wives*, it will be well to remember that the lover in these stories is a student.

[15] Hazlitt, pp. 67-68. Sounds like hiding a priest!

threatens to throw the chest into it, and so the husband causes two of his men to take the chest out and cart it back home, where the lover could be released at leisure. Here the clothes device has been metamorphosed into a feather device.

Merry Wives has its over-all multiple-confessional device and the fused device of the buck-basket ultimately from Straparola's tale; but certainly, I think, through an Admiral's play on the subject, which is represented by the *Hibeldeha* of Duke Julius. The author of *Merry Wives* has adapted the clothes device to the circumstances of a merry wife of Windsor. The clothes are now foul, in a buck-basket, with the lover rammed down under them on the way to washing at Datchet Mead. The other two devices are independent of those in the source analogues, and also are given a local Windsor setting, the final one being probably an adaptation of a Windsor legend. Incidentally, both of these are disguises and are in the tradition of Chaerea's ludicrously inappropriate disguise as a eunuch. It will be remembered that Falstaff fancied himself as Chaerea in his first and third adventures but proved to be only a Thraso in all.

The origin and nature of these three devices furnish a corollary of fundamental importance. Regardless of source, these three devices are a unified set, beginning, ending, centered upon Windsor. The original play was not merely a duper-duped; the duping was set at Windsor. Even if there should be a few "pure London" touches in the play, these are incidental, and are the kind of thing we know to expect of a play written for the London stage. And the play was so written, to be put on by the London company with no possible hypothetical aid there from Windsor. Since the company was obliged to put the play on with its own resources in London, there is nothing to imply that the company had any assistance at Windsor[16] — if it ever performed the play there, as it well may have done. But Herne's oak was represented on the London stage, and we may take it as certain that the play was never performed by these actors at the actual Herne's oak in Windsor Forest, if such an oak existed. Shakspere's fairies seem always to lead our wits a wool-gathering!

---

[16] We must remember the practicalities of the situation. Quite clearly the company had at the period continuous use of several well trained boys. *Richard III,* for instance, has four women with major parts, surpassing *Merry Wives* and about equalling *Midsummer-Night's Dream* in its demands upon the boys. Other plays and facts also indicate that an unusually able group of boy actors was coming to maturity in the company at this time (See Baldwin, *Organization and Personnel*). There is, therefore, conclusive evidence that the company had as a regular part of its personnel at the time an unusually able group of boys, and there is no evidence whatever that the company ever at any time "borrowed" boy actors for special occasions. Conceivably, some such "cooperation" for boys could have happened quite occasionally, but I know of no evidence that it ever did. Certainly it was not a normal routine. Cooperation with a company of professional tumbling boys, as with that of Simonds, was, of course, quite another thing.

Incidentally, if there was a Herne's oak in Windsor Forest, then also it is even more clear that this framework belongs to the original construction. It is at least the fundamental occasion of the deer-stealing story in the play, causing Robert Shallow to be moved all the way to Windsor to serve again as Falstaff's dupe. For the deer-stealing belongs evidently to Herne, the hunter of Windsor Forest, in whose likeness Falstaff is to be punished. This impersonation made a deer-stealer of Falstaff. Since Falstaff was to wear the horns, he might as well kill his own deer. So Shallow and his entourage are moved to Windsor, etc. Thus, so far as this evidence goes, the deer-stealing may have belonged to the original plot, but also it may have been added later.

It will be seen that the author has simply adapted stock devices and characters to his local conditions and needs. Any dramatist of the time (or his company of actors) must have known many such, and the author of *Merry Wives* shows knowledge of some he does not use, such as the lover up a chimney. Falstaff says, "I'll creep up into the chimney" (IV, 2, 46), but Mrs. Ford objects, "There they always use to discharge their birding-pieces." Anyone who has suffered through Fenton's *Certaine Tragicall Discourses* is likely to remember Cornelio's anxious vigil so ensconced, "beynge in continuall expectacion that some roostye halbarde shoulde bee throste vpp into the chymney where he stood."[17] It is not at all likely, of course, that our dramatist was thinking of this particular instance. But to suggest such an author's literary sources for such a play we can only continue to accumulate and catalogue these parallel devices and characters. For this is not primarily a "story" comedy, but one of situations.

The original play underlying *Merry Wives* in its five-man character pattern pairs most nearly with *Comedy of Errors, Two Gentlemen,* and the first form of *Love's Labor's Lost,* which belong before the middle of 1590.[18] With the triple rivalry for Anne Page added, the parallel is with *Fair Em,* probably the end of 1590. The addition of this rivalry could, therefore, have been made at any time after 1590. Incidentally, the Anne Page rivalry also consists of Anglicized stock characters from the same general conventional sources as the main plot.

Certain dislocations, shared by folio and quarto, show that this addition of the Anne Page rivalry was not at first construction. In the final version of *Merry Wives* as we now have it there are two plots concerning horses, each of which was evidently essentially the same in the folio and in the parent of the quarto. The first of these plots concerns Falstaff's

---

[17] Fenton, *Discourses* (1567), f 117[r].

[18] Furnivall was scandalized to find that his interpretation of Fleay's rhyme test in terms of proportion of rhyme to blank verse placed *Merry Wives* next to *The Comedy of Errors* (*New Shak. Soc. Transactions* (1874), pp. 32-33).

horses. In II, 1, of the First Folio, the merry wives decided to lead Falstaff on "till he hath pawned his horses to mine host of the Garter" (84-85). In the grand exposé, Ford, who had passed himself off on Falstaff as Brooke (quite fitting for a Ford!), says to Falstaff, "And, Master Brook, he hath enjoyed nothing of Ford's but his buck-basket, his cudgel, and twenty pounds of money, which must be paid to Master Brook; his horses are arrested for it, Master Brook" (V, 5, 109-112). Ford is parodying in style Falstaff's last speech to Master Brooke, and does not yet give away the fact that he himself was Brooke, though he thus indicates that he has close connection with him. Later, Ford reminds Falstaff, "Marry, sir, we'll bring you to Windsor, to one Master Brook, that you have cozened of money, to whom you should have been a pandar: over and above that you have suffered, I think to repay that money will be a biting affliction" (V, 5, 158-162). The reference is to the money Brooke had thrust upon Falstaff at the first interview toward the end of the second act. Ford does not give the identity of Brooke to Falstaff till the final couplet

> To Master Brook you yet shall hold your word;
> For he to-night shall lie with Mistress Ford.

The same approximate action is indicated in the quarto of 1602. The wives decide at the corresponding place to be revenged upon Falstaff but do not specify how. Falstaff receives money from Brooke; and is told at the exposé that he must repay twenty pounds he borrowed from Brooke; but no mention is made of his horses being arrested. Mrs. Ford then assumes that Ford has now been identified as Brooke and says

> Nay husband let that go to make amēds,
> Forgiue that sum, and so weele all be friends (1561-62)

But Ford still has his jesting couplet, slightly modified, at the end.

It will be seen that the folio version makes a false start of Falstaff's horses, since the merry wives do not lead Falstaff on to pawn his horses to the Host. Instead, Ford says that Falstaff's horses have been arrested for the twenty pounds owed to Brooke. But these details indicate an intention for this version, since it has its proper beginning, though it proves to be a false one, in the second act, and has a consequent end in the fifth, even though this end has forgotten the original beginning. What has happened is that a different beginning has been substituted in the second act in the form of borrowed money, and the original beginning has not been canceled. It is not really obtrusive, of course, since it can be taken as a first reaction by the merry wives which was not followed up. One would have expected here that Bardolph would be the agent of the merry wives with the Host, and would attach himself to the Host to procure revenge upon Falstaff, just as Nym and Pistol informed the husbands in order to procure revenge. But we have no direct indication of how the merry wives originally planned to make Falstaff pawn his horses to the Host. Instead, Falstaff's horses are now alleged to be arrested for debt. Falstaff's horses belonged to the main plot and must once have been more prominent there.

A second piece of horse business now also concerns the Host, as was originally intended, but not Falstaff. It is an entirely different scheme from both the projected and the resultant one in the preceding. In this second business, Caius and Evans agree in III, 1, to be revenged on mine Host, because as Evans puts it, "he has made us his vlouting-stog." So as Bardolph reports how the post horses were stolen, Evans comes hot on his heels to report other cozenings, and to remind mine Host, "you are wise, and full of gibes and vlouting-stocks, and 'tis not convenient you should be cozened" (IV, 5, 73-75), while Caius follows immediately with more coals for Newcastle. Evans and Caius have hastened in behind Bardolph to remind the Host that he has received tit for tat — "vlouting stog" against "vlouting-stocks." Evans and Caius could come so pat because they had engineered the hoax. As Page is issuing his invitation for the morrow of the fourth act when in his second attempt he expects to expose Falstaff and his wife, Evans says to Caius, "I pray you now, remembrance to-morrow on the lousy knave, mine host. . . . A lousy knave, to have his gibes and his mockeries!" (III, 3, 213-217). The echoing words in the various passages make it clear that this is the planned revenge of Caius and Evans. The second scene before the denouement, in fourteen lines, Bardolph had told mine Host that the Germans wanted three horses to meet the duke who was to be at court tomorrow, and the Host says he is going to make them pay a plenty for the horses, since for a week he had turned away all other guests because of the Germans. These Germans never appear on the stage, and the Host asks if they speak English, thus indicating that he is not supposed to have associated with them. Since they did not appear on the stage, it is idle to guess who would have acted the parts if they had done so. The fact is that the dramatist makes no statement even as to who are supposed to have been the Germans. But it is clear that Evans and Caius engineered the hoax upon mine Host. This hoax is clearly an insert upon the original plot, to show off Caius and Evans. Since Caius is one of the suitors for Anne Page, and Evans is "business manager" for another, the horse-stealing plot came in with the triple rivalry for Anne Page. As it stands now, it is really incomplete, since mine Host should have had his horses restored. Instead, Fenton promises to reimburse him for further aid to himself. But money is not a horse! It is likely, therefore, that there has been further adjustment after the insertion of the horse-stealing. Was the horse-stealing also intended in the surviving version to be cut?

The source and inspiration for the hoax is indicated in the account of its execution. For Bardolph reports, "they threw me off, from behind one of them, in a slough of mire; and set spurs and away, like three German devils, three Doctor Faustuses" (IV, 5, 62-64). Bardolph is thinking of the "dunking" of the horse courser in Marlowe's *Doctor Faustus*. This is a sufficient and known source for the invention. There may, in fact, have been other sources in life or in literature, but they are not necessary, since the dramatist has himself indicated a sufficient source. I suppose this relationship could be considered as giving some very slight preference for the period when Shakspere's company was acting *Faustus,* but the preference could be but very slight.[19]

If we do seek a source in real life, we should remember what the conditions are. Three Germans who are said to be followers of a duke who is said to be coming to court steal three horses from mine Host. Evans reports also "three cozen-germans that has cozened all the hosts of Readins, of Maidenhead, of Colebrook, of horses and money" (IV, 5, 70-72), and Caius follows to say that the court knows of no duke who is to come from Germany. In the Folio, the duke has nothing to do with the transaction, and it is denied by the perpetrators of the hoax that there is a duke. In the Quarto, this has been evidently jumbled. Even a German duke may have been suggested by *Faustus,* though the author of *Merry Wives* might well have had his suggestion from some other source, including actuality.

An actual German duke was long since nominated for the honor, and here we may call on Sir Walter Greg for some carefully considered opinions. When he examines in the quarto of 1602 "the second and main fragment of the horse-stealing plot" he concludes, quite correctly I think, "A careful comparison of the texts makes it clear that the original passage was substantially as in the folio, the discrepancies being due to corruption in the quarto text."[20] Whatever has happened to the horse business, it was essentially the same in the folio and in the parent of the quarto. Sir Walter is thus further justified in noting upon *cosen garmombles* of the quarto, "The folio reads: 'Cozen-Iermans.'" The question whether 'cosen garmombles' is or is not an inversion of 'our cousin Mumpellgart,' as Elizabeth called her persistent suitor for the honour of the Garter, has been debated by editors at a length and with an erudition which make emulation vain. I would only call attention to one point. I have been forced above to the conclusion (line 1344) that the whole of this passage is unoriginal, being a substitution for a more elaborate scene which had for some reason to be cut out. Moreover, of this substituted passage the authoritative text is preserved in the folio. It is therefore

---

[19] The reference to Mephostophilis has been noted, and Falstaff's magnificent horns are likely to be the very ones which were clapped on the disrespectful knight.

[20] W. W. Greg, *Merry Wives,* p. 85.

unreasonable to suppose that the quarto, which is particularly corrupt at this point, can retain original readings which have been revised in the folio. If 'garmombles' is anything but a wild blunder of the compositor, it must be, not a fragment of the original text, but a sly allusion to the censored episode introduced by the actor . . . for the benefit of an audience familiar with current dramatic scandal."[21] Granting all this, there might still be "Germans in both"; "Cosen-Iermans," which is a clear enough pun upon cozening Germans, as they are otherwise said to be, and "cosen garmombles," supposed by some to be an allusion to "our cousin Mömpelgard," who was a German. It should not be forgotten in this connection that the quarto makes the Duke of Germany directly responsible, so that "cosen garmombles" is an even more appropriate reference. This relationship, therefore, between folio and quarto text does not in itself preclude the possibility that the reference is to Mömpelgard, nor does Sir Walter infer that it does.

It should probably be added that shortly after Mömpelgard's visit, and just about the time *The Jealous Comedy* was about to appear as "new," Thomas Nashe was certainly giving prominence to the word "geremumble." In *Strange Newes,* Nashe says of Harvey, "A litle before this, the foresaid fanaticall *Phobetor, geremumble, tirleriwhisco,* or what you will, cald forth the biggest gunshot of my thundring tearmes, steept in *Aqua fortis* and gunpowder, to come and trie them selues on his paper Target."[22] Nashe composed this pamphlet not earlier than December, 1592, and a considerable period before March 25, 1593.[23] In this notorious bout, Nashe labels Harvey a "geremumble" — whatever that was! Anyone who had "geremumble" prominently in mind, before or after Nashe, was heavily predisposed to such a metamorphosis as that of "cousin Mömpelgard" into "cosen garmombles."

And while we have Nashe on the witness stand we would also like him to explain about "the horses lately sworne to be stolne"[24] in *Summer's Last Will and Testament,* about 1592. Here is an alleged horse-stealing of the period, notorious enough to be referred to in a play, whether or not it was connected with Mömpelgard.[25] And in the same play Nashe refers to the legacies in Gillian of Brainford's will, an instrument to which he makes reference elsewhere — as do numerous others. One feels that Nashe could tell us a great deal. But so far Thomas Nashe stands mute.

It may be, therefore, that "garmombles" is a kind of anagram for Mömpelgard. It is true that there is not much parallel in the play with the

[21] Greg, *Merry Wives,* pp. 85-86.

[22] McKerrow, *Nashe,* I, 321.

[23] McKerrow, *Nashe,* IV, 152-153.

[24] McKerrow, *Nashe,* III, 241.

[25] Chambers, *E. S.,* III, 452; *Shakespeare,* I, 435.

known acts of Mömpelgard. But we must not forget that it was the duty of Edmund Tilney[26] to see that there was none, or at least not enough to be provable. The suggestion would necessarily be by not too obvious innuendo. At the time of the visit, Frederick was Count of Mömpelgard, "cosen garmombles." Technically, he was not a German Duke till August 8, 1593, when he succeeded his cousin as Duke of Württemberg, still remaining, of course, Count of Mömpelgard.[27] Technically, therefore, no German Duke was expected at court when Count Mömpelgard came. No pretended followers of his are known to have caused trouble by stealing horses — not specifically post horses in the play, but only by long-range inference. All that we have, in fact, is the possibility that "cosen garmombles" may have been intended to suggest "cousin Mömpelgard," who was a German, did visit Windsor in 1592, and became a Duke in 1593. Perhaps the garter echoes might as another feather be thrown into the balance. And it must be repeated that if the censor did his duty this is all we are entitled to expect — even for a court performance, with Queen Elizabeth all but writing the play! At least, no other German is known in the possible period who attracted such public attention. The audience is to think of a German Duke, and if it does think of one, it has no other of whom to think. I may add that other suggested parallels known to me do not have even a "cosen garmombles" to recommend them, and so shall be unnoticed here.

Since the horse-stealing third plot is the revenge of Caius (one of the three rivals in the Anne Page plot) and of Evans (manager of Slender as another rival in the Anne Page plot) it came in with or after the addition of the triple rivalry for Anne Page. Since the horse-stealing is a substitute for the horse-pawning of the main plot, it evidently came in with the Anne Page business, as an addition to the main plot.

Merry Wives shows one further connection with an early play of Shakspere's, the *Midsummer-Night's Dream,* which is usually dated not later than 1595 at furthest. This connection we shall examine later.

As we look back at our conclusions so far, it is clear, I believe, that the fundamental plot of *Merry Wives* was shaped for the Shaksperean

[26] In our favorite diversion of interpreting various plays as allegories of current events at home and abroad we have almost consistently ignored the existence of Edmund Tilney, whose duty it was to regulate such matters and whose reaction in such a case as the old play of *Sir Thomas More* is well known. If his life collections on the historical backgrounds of his time (in a folio volume belonging to the Ernest Ingold collection in the University of Illinois Library) ever become generally available, they ought to demonstrate to the most obtuse that if such possible interpretations were unsuspected by Tilney, they would certainly be unsuspected by his contemporaries. And if they had been suspected by Tilney, his contemporaries would never have had a chance to suspect them.

[27] W. B. Rye, *England as seen by Foreigners,* pp. lv ff; Victor von Klarwill, *Queen Elizabeth and Some Foreigners,* pp. 345 ff; J. Crofts, *Shakespeare and the Post Horses.*

company before 1594. If the horse-stealing addition in any way reflects Mömpelgard, the triple rivalry for Anne Page would likely have been added about 1592-93. This form of the play might well be *The Jealous Comedy,* which was "new" on January 5, 1593; and "cosen garmombles" would at that time be a sure-fire joke.

But if *The Jealous Comedy* was an earlier form, then the Falstaff crew as such had not yet been let into it. The time at which the Falstaff crew did enter the play can be determined approximately, and has important bearing on fundamental questions. The characters represent the situation between *2 Henry IV* and *Henry V.* It is objected, however, that Nym does not appear in the *Henry IV* plays. The problem resolves itself, therefore, to the question of whether Nym was invented along with Slender for *Merry Wives,* or for *Henry V.* According to Slender, Nym acts as fully in character in *Merry Wives* as he does in *Henry V.* Besides, Shakspere has killed off the principals of this set of characters in *Henry V,* probably including Nym himself. Further, under the conditions of the plot in *Merry Wives,* Falstaff needed three cashiered men, one for the Host (Bardolph), and a pair for the husbands (Pistol and Nym). A third follower of the braggart-duper (Falstaff) had to be invented, and he had to receive a fitting embodiment and significant name. It would seem reasonably clear, therefore, that this Corporal, "your coach-fellow Nym" (II, 2, 6-7), was invented as a "side-kick" for Ancient Pistol in *Merry Wives.*

Other evidence is conclusive, I believe, as to this relative position of the play. This is concerned with the Oldcastle imbroglio. Greg[28] suggested that "his Castle" is an allusion to Oldcastle. Robertson then pointed out that the metrics called for such a word as Oldcastle where Falstaff now is made to answer.[29] Apparently, the conclusion that Falstaff was Oldcastle is now generally accepted.[30] It is also generally accepted that Falstaff elsewhere, except in *1 Henry VI,* was originally Oldcastle before family objections were raised, supposedly by the Cobhams. The objections had arisen before *1 Henry IV* was printed (entered S.R. February 25, 1598), but not till after *2 Henry IV* and *Merry Wives* had been written, since traces of Oldcastle survive in both. Now William Brooke, seventh Lord Cobham succeeded Henry Carey, first Lord Hunsdon, who died July 22, 1596, as Lord Chamberlain. Cobham himself died March 5, 1597. If any one of the Oldcastle plays was performed at court the season of 1596-97, then unavoidably the Lord Chamberlain would see his ancestor exhibited, and could hardly be expected to find

---

[28] Greg, *Merry Wives,* p. 84, Scene xvi, line 1305.

[29] J. M. Robertson, *The Problem of The Merry Wives of Windsor,* p. 29.

[30] Chambers, *Shakespeare,* I, 434 hesitates on Oldcastle, but accepts Brooke, apparently without seeing any discrepancy.

the jolly reprobate as amusing as did his contemporaries. *Merry Wives* would also add Brooke to Oldcastle, as he still is in the cut acting version of 1602, but changed to Broom for the folio version, though Brooke still shows through. Other evidence could be added in connection with the *Henry IV* plays, but I believe it is already clear that it was William Brooke who objected to Oldcastle, and hence that the objection, which he could enforce, was made certainly before March 5, 1597.[31] The apology is attached to *2 Henry IV*, and the company had proceeded to *Merry Wives* before the objection was made known. It must, therefore, have arisen when one of the plays was presented at court. Since Cobham was not favorable to players anyway, this must have been serious for Shakspere's company, and they probably regarded his taking off as providential. The upshot is that the Oldcastle crew were let into the old play shortly before March 5, 1597 in consequence of their popularity in the two parts of *Henry IV*.

In fact, it is alleged that it was Queen Elizabeth herself who ordered Shakspere to exhibit Falstaff in love within ten days or two weeks. Mr. P. A. Daniel in his introduction to the facsimile of the quarto of 1602 gave the basic facts of this legend of the Queen's command, to which a few additions have since been made. In an essay attached to his *Comical Gallant*, which was an "improved version" of *Merry Wives*, John Dennis in 1702 wrote of Shakspere's play "I knew very well, that it had pleas'd one of the greatest Queens that ever was in the World. . . . This Comedy was written at her Command, and by her direction, and she was so eager to see it Acted, that she commanded it to be finished in fourteen days; and was afterwards, as Tradition tells us, very well pleas'd at the Representation. . . . I had observed what success the Character of *Falstaffe* had had, in the first part of *Harry* the Fourth. And as the *Falstaffe* in the Merry Wives is certainly superiour to that of the second part of *Harry* the Fourth, so it can hardly be said to be inferior to that of the first."[32] Dennis could make such astounding statements because Falstaff's "real" character had not yet been suspected, and he was still taken to be the fat, jolly rogue of the seventeenth-century, as anyone may see by tracing him through the *Shakspere Allusion Book!*

In a prologue to his play, which thus was presumably earlier than the defense, Dennis wrote

> But *Shakespear's* Play in fourteen days was writ,
> And in that space to make all just and fit,
> Was an attempt surpassing human Wit.
> Yet our great *Shakespear's* matchless Muse was such,
> None e'er in so small time perform'd so much.

[31] For the bearing of this fact on certain theories concerning *Merry Wives*, see *T.L.S.*, October 8, 1931, p. 778.

[32] E. N. Hooker, *Critical Works of John Dennis*, I, 279; II, 391.

With more time at its command, the musing wit of John Dennis was to improve that of Shakspere.

In a reply to Jeremy Collier in 1704, Dennis further "improves" his story. "Nay, the poor mistaken Queen her self encouraged Play-Houses to that degree, that she not only commanded *Shakespear* to write the Comedy of the *Merry Wives,* and to write it in Ten Days time; so eager was she for the wicked Diversion; but ev'n with that Hand that wielded the Scepter descended poorly to translate a Play that was writ by a *Grecian* Poet."[33] In the two years, the round fortnight has shrunk to the still round sum of ten days — influence of Falstaff's arithmetic, no doubt! If "tradition" specified the exact time, why couldn't John Dennis keep it straight?

The story is not known again till in 1709 Rowe in his *Life of Shakespear* took up the theme. "She was so well pleas'd with that admirable Character of *Falstaff,* in the two Parts of *Henry* the Fourth, that she commanded him to continue it for one Play more, and to show him in Love. This is said to be the Occasion of his Writing *The Merry Wives of* Windsor. How well she was obey'd, the Play it self is an admirable Proof."[34]

Then Gildon in the supplementary volume of poems in 1710 writes of *Merry Wives* in his *Remarks on the Plays of Shakespear,* "The *Fairys* in the fifth Act makes a Handsome Complement to the Queen, in her Palace of *Windsor,* who had oblig'd him to write a Play of Sir *John Falstaff* in Love, and which I am very well assured he perform'd in a Fortnight; a prodigious Thing, when all is so well contriv'd, and carry'd on without the least Confusion."[35] The story is now lodged in 1709-10 in the fundamental reference books and thus assured of eternity.

Gildon combines "Falstaff in Love" from Rowe with the fortnight of composition from Dennis, so he makes no contribution. As usual with Rowe, a little is made by deduction to go a long way. How had the Queen become interested in Falstaff? Obviously by seeing the two parts of *Henry IV,* which Dennis had also mentioned, and obviously also the characters in *Merry Wives* show that this play was later. Why had the Queen wanted to have Falstaff in a third play? Since the precedent two plays present Falstaff in war, the third must present him in love. It does, doesn't it? Of course, Rowe forgets that, with Doll Tearsheet, the Queen had seen Falstaff in all the love of which he was capable. As usual with him, Rowe is simply putting his source story into the facts which the plays themselves furnish. From the great deep to the great deep — Rowe's bootstraps were well worn with lifting! His addition of

---

[33] Hooker, *Dennis,* I, 300.

[34] N. Rowe, *Shakespear,* I, VIII-IX.

[35] C. Gildon, [*Poems*] (1710), p. 291.

Falstaff "in love" is his own deduction from the three plays themselves. We are thus thrown back on John Dennis, who was engaged in a defense of plays, and did not keep his story straight. The play simply could not have been "written at her Command, and by her direction . . . in fourteen days," much less in ten as Dennis says elsewhere, and no one in recent years has been able to swallow that story anything like whole.

Sir Arthur Quiller-Couch sums the facts inimitably. "These are all the 'authorities' for the legend, which (as Malone conjectured) may have come down to Dennis through Dryden, who had it from D'Avenant [neither of whom, being notoriously close-mouthed characters and not given to writing, gave the slightest hint of such knowledge!] We must observe (1) that it crops up precisely a hundred years after our play first saw print, in a Quarto of 1602; (2) that Dennis was born in 1657, Gildon in 1665, Rowe in 1674; and (3) that the first-named allows Queen Elizabeth's delight in the play to be a 'tradition.' Indeed the whole story is that and no more."[36] It should be added that this "tradition" belongs to a network of such "traditions," which were taking their characteristic forms at this time; deer-stealing,[37] native ignoramus,[38] and the rest. I cannot, therefore, concur in Sir Arthur's conclusion: "Nevertheless we accept it." In fact, he and his colleague accept only the "tradition" that Queen Elizabeth showed some kind of interest in Falstaff. Perhaps. But if so, we have no convincing evidence of it. "Nevertheless I wish we had!" It would explain why the Falstaff crew was thus so superficially let into an old play, be its name *The Jealous Comedy,* or already *Merry Wives,* or what not.[39]

Most of the required tinkering involved the first act, upon which incidentally we center most of our praise. That the first act was tinkered about the time of the Falstaff craze is indicated also by at least two of its allusions. Our first dated allusion to Sackerson the bear (I, 1, 269), who scared all the women but not Slender, is in the *Epigrams* of Sir John Davies, probably c. 1598. Also, Falstaff says of Page's wife, "she is a region in Guiana, all gold and bounty" (I, 3, 65-66). Sir Walter Raleigh's expedition of 1595 to capture Eldorado at least captured the attention of the public. Lawrence Keymis published his *Relation* in 1596, and numer-

---

[36] A. Quiller-Couch and J. D. Wilson, *Merry Wives,* p. ix.

[37] Baldwin, *Small Latine,* II, 681 ff.

[38] Baldwin, *Small Latine,* I, 53 ff.

[39] I think of two other analogous "tall stories." In 1613, Walter Burre stated that *The Knight of the Burning Pestle* "in eight daies (as lately I haue learned) was begot and borne" (Greg, *Bibliography,* III, 1214). William Alabaster says in 1632 that *Roxana* as a "morticinum . . . duarum hebdomadarum abortum . . . non aevi integri" (Greg, *Bibliography,* III, 1232). Were there enough of such stories to form a "tradition" for Dennis?

ous references to the riches of Guiana follow thereupon.[40] These references thus most likely belong to 1596-98, and so probably were inserted along with the Falstaff crew.

It may be added that there were no further surviving main alterations, since the version of 1602, with Brooke still in it and Oldcastle submerged, is cut down from the same plot as that which appears in 1623. Daniel and Greg long since established in other ways that fundamental relationship between the versions. There are only a few rearrangements in the quarto of 1602 and a few omissions which might be held to affect the plot. These are all connected with the wooing and wedding of Anne Page. In the technically crucial third act, the end is given by the First Folio quite properly to the Falstaff plot, whereas the quarto of 1602 quite improperly places the Anne Page plot, itself rearranged, in this position, after the Falstaff plot. Since the Falstaff plot is the one on which the play is constructed, it is quite certain that the quarto has here for some reason been rearranged. Sir Walter Greg is also certainly quite correct in his conclusion that, except for a fragment of the first scene, the first four scenes of the fifth act in the folio version have been omitted from the quarto.[41] They are preparatory to the triple-stealing of Anne Page, and are really superfluous, since the denouement itself of the stealing was intended to explain all that needs to be known as to how it happened. This thread of the story has, therefore, been severely cut,[42] and the remainder partially rearranged. The effect is to reduce the wooing and wedding of Anne Page to a vestigial minimum. The cutting in the quarto of 1602 brings the play back to and toward the old five-man pattern,[43] and doubtless was intended to meet certain acting conditions. The cutting was done, however, upon the play approximately as it is found in the folio version.[44] So, if there was an old play, as we have seen there was, it is

---

[40] See Hart's edition for these various parallels.

[41] Greg, *Merry Wives* (1910), p. xxxi.

[42] For tabulations of abridgement, see William Bracy, *The Merry Wives of Windsor* (University of Missouri Studies, XXV, No. 1), pp. 79 ff.

[43] See under *Jealous Comedy* in the tabulation opposite p. 229 in Baldwin, *Organization and Personnel*.

[44] Certain statistical facts form a supporting corollary to this relationship. If we assume for convenience in statement that Q_1 is a cut version of that in F_1, then considering the five male characters by quantity, the Host has been least cut (75 per cent of F_1), Falstaff but little less (65 per cent), and Page not much less (60 per cent). In any case, the effect has been to give the comedians more prominence. So, if mine Host reported the text, why should Falstaff, a major part with nearly four times as many lines as the Host in F_1, fare almost as well as the Host himself, in spite of the great number of his lines? Perhaps mine Host was Falstaff's "understudy"! Then why should mine Host do so well by the serious Page, while he fails so miserably on Evans (37 per cent), and Ford (47 per cent)? Looked at in another way, the major parts for men retain their relative position in Q_1, except that Evans has been dropped from third man to an equality with the Host, who is sixth, while

not represented by the quarto of 1602. It follows also, that since the quarto of 1602 has the full Falstaff-Oldcastle crew, it is not earlier than the *Henry IV* plays, nor later than March 5, 1597. It does not, therefore, belong to the bad quartos emanating from 1593-94 — as I would have liked it to do! This cutting and consequent or subsequent mangling was of a later date, showing that similar forces were still operative.

As to authorship, the final version of *Merry Wives* is attributed to Shakspere, and I suppose no competent person will doubt that the Falstaff crew is his. Whether Shakspere constructed the original duper-duped plot and whether he added the Anne Page rivalry does not appear from direct evidence. The fact that Shakspere was so fully aware in *Midsummer-Night's Dream* of the fairy scene in *Merry Wives* would argue that he had already had some close connection with the latter. At any rate, the play is in the First Folio as his, and it is said that possession is nine points in the law.

Slender has been cut to a minor part. So have Caius, Fenton, and Shallow been severely cut. Mine Host, a comedian, has singularly bad luck with most of his fellow comedians. Such relationships as we have here noted would indicate purposeful changes, whether for cutting or for "fattening," not any form of mere chance alone, whether an actor's memory of other parts, or what not. And, of course, we must remember that *theoretically* Q_1 could represent a cut form of a fuller version, and this cut form might itself have later been expanded into the version in F_1 — most emphatically, I make no suggestion that it was. Nor do I even suggest other possible permutations and combinations.

CHAPTER XXVIII

A Midsummer-Night's Dream

Shakspere's company appears only once more in Henslowe's Diary, this time again with the Admiral's men, but at Newington Butts, in June, 1594. "Four plays . . . (*Hester, Titus, Hamlet,* and the *Taming of a Shrew*) do not occur in the later Admiral's lists and may therefore be assigned to the Chamberlain's men. They are not, however, new, and they do not appear in the earlier Strange's lists."[1] *Titus,* however, may have appeared as *Titus and Vespasian.* Three of these, *Titus, Hamlet,* and probably *A Shrew,* had belonged to the Admiral's before the split of 1590, and there is evidence that *Hester* probably also did. We have considered Shakspere's connection with *Titus.* His connections with *Hamlet* can best be treated in the light of the full evolution of the play, which cannot be undertaken here. The title *A Shrew* indicates the old play and not Shakspere's revision. That is also indicated by the fact that Shakspere's *The Shrew* shows the casting pattern of plays after the reorganization in 1594. We shall not, therefore, consider it here. Nor shall we consider how these four plays came to be grouped, and how at least three of them continued with Shakspere's company.

One other play of Shakspere's, *A Midsummer-Night's Dream,* has its affinities with the early plays, though it does not appear under that title in Henslowe's Diary. But neither does any other of Shakspere's early comedies appear there under its surviving title. Nor does *Romeo and Juliet.* That is, Shakspere had not yet produced any play which was kept continuously in stock at this period, nor that had been revived, so far as we have record, before this summer of 1594. His name in connection with his plays has not yet been directly mentioned. It is certainly not yet headline material.

We turn, then, to *A Midsummer-Night's Dream,* as the last probable representative of early work, and begin with an examination of its structure.[2]

I, 1. Theseus and Hippolyta are to be married at the new moon, four

---

[1] Greg, *Henslowe's Diary,* II, 163.

[2] For an analysis of E. A. J. Honigmann's thesis that *King John* precedes *Troublesome Raigne* and hence is early, see the review by Professor T. M. Parrott, *J.E.G.P.* (1956), LV, 297 ff., and the article by Professor R. A. Law, "On the Date of *King John,*" *S.P.,* LIV, pp. 119-127.

days hence, "With pomp, with triumph and with revelling" (19). Egeus enters to complain that his daughter Hermia wishes to marry Lysander, whereas Egeus has chosen Demetrius for her. Egeus demands that Hermia shall obey or die, as Athenian law provides. Egeus tells Hermia that if she does not obey, she must die or become a nun. She must decide "by the next new moon" (83). Lysander pleads that he may have Hermia, pointing out that Demetrius has made love to Helena, who dotes in turn on him. Theseus will look into that, and takes Egeus and Demetrius off the stage, very stupidly leaving Hermia and Lysander alone, who plan to elope to Lysander's Aunt, seven leagues from Athens, and there be married. They are to meet tomorrow night "in the wood, a league without the town" (165), where Lysander had met Hermia and Helena once, "To do observance to a morn of May" (167). Helena enters wishing to be translated to Hermia so that she might make Demetrius love her. Hermia tells Helena that she and Lysander plan to elope tomorrow night. Left alone, Helena decides to tell Demetrius, just in order to get to go to the forest and back with him.

I, 2. The mechanicals are getting cast for their "most lamentable comedy, and most cruel death of Pyramus and Thisby" (10-11), to be performed before the Duke and Duchess on their wedding night. The actors are to con their parts by tomorrow night, when they meet "in the palace wood, a mile without the town, by moonlight" (90), to rehearse "At the duke's oak" (97).

The first act has introduced Theseus and Hippolyta as background machinery, has exhibited the crossed loves of the two pairs of lovers, the plan of one pair to elope tomorrow night, and the plan of one of the other pair to prevent it. The antecedent square of two pairs of lovers has by parental interference been reduced to a triangle of two men and a woman, with one woman left over. The mechanicals form plans for their play which will bring them also to the appointed scene of action. The human action is ready to begin.

II, 1. Puck and a fairy say that Oberon, king of fairies, is vexed with Titania, queen of fairies, because she will not give him a changeling boy. Both are to keep their revels in the wood tonight and there will be trouble. Oberon and his train enter at one door, Titania and hers at the other and begin to quarrel. Titania is jealous because Oberon has come with his love the Amazonian Queen to bless her marriage to Theseus. Oberon in turn accuses Titania of having aided Theseus in four former affairs (partial list only!). Titania says Oberon has disturbed her revels with brawls ever "since the middle summer's spring" (82), so that the winds in revenge for the fairies not dancing have caused floods, upsetting the seasons. After Titania still will not give him the changeling boy and exits, Oberon decides to be revenged. He sends Puck for the flower love-in-idleness, whose juice laid on sleeping eyelids causes the person to love whatever next appears in sight. This he will use on Titania and will not undo the charm till she gives him the changeling.

Demetrius wishes to find Lysander and Hermia, and to be rid of Helena, who still pursues him off stage. Oberon says

> Fare thee well, nymph: ere he do leave this grove,
> Thou shalt fly him, and he shall seek thy love (245-246).

Oberon will use the magic juice on Titania, and Puck is instructed to use some on the youth who disdains the Athenian lady, so that he will see her first upon waking and be "More fond on her than she upon her love" (266). Titania comes into position and gets her juice from Oberon. Lysander and Hermia come into position, and Puck gives him a dose. Demetrius gives Helena the slip. She finds and wakes Lysander, who, of course, now loves and pursues her, leaving Helena to wake from a prophetic dream, when she exits, leaving Titania asleep on her flowery bank (cf. Lyly's lunary bank) all the act.

In the second act, the magic juice has found the wrong eyes, and now we have no couple left from our square, but instead a circle. Hermia still loves Lysander, who now loves Helena, who still loves Demetrius, who has been directed to love Hermia. Both men have shifted, but the women both remain true. For the clown plot, a similar ludicrous situation is prepared, with Titania loving Bottom.

III, 1. The mechanicals find a green plot for their stage, a hawthorne-brake for a tiring house, and proceed to rehearse their play, till Bottom gets translated by means of an ass-head, donated at unawares by Puck. Titania awakes, sees the ass-headed Bottom, and falls in love with him.

III, 2. Oberon hears from Puck that Titania has fallen in love with a monster. Puck thinks he has attended to the young Athenian also as directed until Demetrius enters pursuing Hermia, and Oberon tells Puck he has put the juice in the wrong eyes. Hermia thinks Demetrius has killed Lysander. Demetrius finally lies down to sleep. Puck is to bring Helena, and Oberon will charm Demetrius' eyes to love her when he awakes. Lysander is to come with Helena.

> Then will two at once woo one (118)

Lysander and Helena enter, Demetrius wakes, and begins courting Helena, who thinks both Demetrius and Lysander are mocking her, since she knows they both love Hermia. Hermia enters seeking Lysander, who tells her he loves Helena and hates Hermia. Helena thinks all three have plotted against her. After much recrimination at cross purposes by all four, Demetrius and Lysander exeunt to fight, and the girls go separately. Puck is to lead the men astray so that they cannot fight but will go to sleep, and then he is to crush the herb in Lysander's eyes to make him love Hermia. This will clear the Athenian couples. Oberon will beg Titania's Indian boy and uncharm her. Lysander and Demetrius wander in and out seeking each other till they lie down to sleep. Helena and Hermia also come in and lie down to sleep, so that now "Two of both kinds make up four" (438). Puck applies the juice to Lysander's eyes and all is to be well.

The circle is now by shifting the first man to his first allegiance resolved back into a triangle of two men and a woman, with one woman left over, only this time the women have swapped places at the tip of the triangle. The resultant complications are, of course, only too fully exploited. But the four are put to sleep and after they have slept all the act[3] are to wake as the original square of two couples. Titania is also to be uncharmed.

IV, 1. Titania helps Bottom admire himself till he goes to sleep, when she also sleeps, enabling Oberon to undo his charms, since Titania has sent him the changeling boy. Puck removes the "transformed scalp" of Bottom (undisturbed, of course), and Oberon restores Titania. Oberon promises that he and Titania

> will to-morrow midnight solemnly
> Dance in Duke Theseus' house triumphantly,
> And bless it to all fair prosperity:
> There shall the pairs of faithful lovers be
> Wedded, with Theseus, all in jollity (85-89).

Oberon and Titania exeunt, leaving Bottom and the couples sleeping. Theseus, Hippolyta, Egeus, and others enter on May day morning a hunting, discover the sleeping couples, and wake them with their horns. Lysander admits that he was stealing away from Athens with Hermia, and Egeus invokes the law. Demetrius says he pursued the couple, and Helena pursued him. Now he wants only Helena, to whom he was betrothed before he saw Hermia. To Helena he will forever be true. Theseus will overbear Egeus, give up the hunt, and three couples shall be married at once. The couples exeunt, and Bottom wakes (the horns didn't disturb him; neither blast was his cue!) from Bottom's dream.

IV, 2. The mechanicals cannot proceed with their play without Bottom. The duke and others are married, and Bottom has lost a pension of sixpence a day (half-pay) for life. Bottom turns up "large as life and twice as ugly," and the play is to go forward without onions or garlic.

---

[3] One is reminded of an analogous device. In *James IV*, the "chorus" is asleep without comment at the end of the third act, since no further comment is needed here to point out these two acts of the epitasis. Similarly, in *The Spanish Tragedy*, Revenge as chorus sleeps symbolically for the third and fourth acts, causing someone to miss his cue and label both of them the fourth act. In *A Shrew*, Sly as chorus also goes to sleep. So Shakespere's device of sleeping through the act was not a startling deviation.

The actual play is now over, even including the marriages; but we are to have still the ensuing celebration and the fairy blessings.

V, 1. Theseus thinks these reported wonders are mere imagination, but Hippolyta thinks there is something to the stories. As the four lovers enter, Theseus asks about the masques and the dances

> To wear away this long age of three hours
> Between our after-supper and bed-time (33-35).

Philostrate presents the list of offerings, and Theseus selects

> A tedious brief scene of young Pyramus
> And his love Thisbe; very tragical mirth (56-57)

to be played by the mechanicals.

> For never any thing can be amiss,
> When simpleness and duty tender it (82-83).

The play follows till midnight. Then Puck with his broom cleans house, and Oberon and Titania at "fairy time" after midnight give their blessing, and the fairies are to bless "each several chamber" with consecrated field-dew. Puck as epilogue begs the plaudits of the Gentles.

The fifth act does not belong to the play proper at all, which ended with the fourth act. The fifth act belongs, not by virtue of Aristotle or the five-act formula, but in the right of the wedding customs of the time. Within this framework, we in fact get two plays, that of the Athenian lovers, and that of the mechanicals of Athens.

As I have pointed out elsewhere,[4] this is a variant on an Italianate type of plot. The first act breaks by parental interference an antecedent square of two couples into a triangle of two men and a woman, with one woman left over. In the second act, the triangle is by Oberon's interference also broken, so that we have a complete circle of four. Here is the involution from square to circle. Then we reverse to evolve from circle back to square. In the third act, the circle is resolved back into a triangle of two men and a woman, with one woman left over; but, of course, the women have now reversed positions. In the fourth act, the triangle is so broken that we have again the same square of two couples with which the play began. The obligatory fifth act is then provided by the framework to the story of the two couples.

This framework has been handled exactly as in *The Comedy of Errors* — for here is another set of errors. Theseus and Hippolyta have been introduced in the first scene as are the Duke and Aegeon in *The Comedy*. They are then left unused till they are needed at the end of the play. They do not even "sit and see" as in an earlier type of framework play. The Duke and Aegeon in *The Comedy* are left to the last lines of the

---

[4] Baldwin, *Five-Act Structure*, p. 479.

play. Theseus and Hippolyta also are brought back only to end the play of the Athenian lovers at the end of the fourth act. They then continue to preside over the fifth. In the meantime, within this framework the story of the Athenian lovers goes through its purely mechanical permutations and combinations exactly as was the case in *The Comedy,* only on a different system. In *The Comedy,* however, the five-act formula is exactly preserved; in *Midsummer-Night's Dream,* the purely mechanical permutations and combinations determine the first four acts, when an external fifth act is added.

This external fifth act is in consequence in parallel with *Love's Labor's Lost,* where since love's labor is lost if it were a comedy there can be no proper catastrophe of marriages, so that the fifth act must necessarily be faked. In *Midsummer-Night's Dream* the mathematical permutations have forced this external ending. So the ending was made for the play, not the play for the ending. That is, it is not at all likely that the play was constructed for such an occasion as is represented in the fifth act, but rather that such an occasion was invented to round out the play.

Here the parallel in handling with the ending of *Love's Labor's Lost* is significant. As Alden notes "esthetically," "We . . . have the wedding pageant as produced by the clown-workmen, — a reworking, it will be noticed, of Armado's pageant of the Worthies in *Love's Labor's Lost;* Shakespere even repeats the detail of representing the chief persons as giving gracious welcome to the crude efforts of 'tongue-tied simplicity,' thus gently linking the farce-scene with the dignity of its setting."[5] One will remember the words of the Princess as she overrules the King.

> Nay, my good lord, let me o'errule you now:
> That sport best pleases that doth least know how:
> Where zeal strives to content, and the contents
> Dies in the zeal of that which it presents:
> Their form confounded makes most form in mirth,
> When great things labouring perish in their birth.[6]

In *Midsummer-Night's Dream* the roles are reversed. Besides the speech to which Alden refers, we have

> *The.* The best in this kind are but shadows; and the worst are no worse, if imagination amend them.
> *Hip.* It must be your imagination then, and not theirs.
> *The.* If we imagine no worse of them than they of themselves, they may pass for excellent men.[7]

I take it that there will be no question as to which of these speeches has the priority in time. In both plays, the shows proceed with comment by

---

[5] Raymond Alden, *Shakespeare,* p. 205.

[6] *Love's Labor's Lost,* V, 2, 513-518.

[7] *Midsummer-Night's Dream,* V, 1, 210-214.

the court, but there is no direct baiting of the actors in *Midsummer-Night's Dream* as there is in *Love's Labor's Lost*. So in *Midsummer-Night's Dream* Shakspere has decided to stuff his fifth act with a play at court as he had done in *Love's Labor's Lost,* and the execution is consciously in parallel.

As to the system of permutation and combination employed in *Midsummer-Night's Dream,* it is closest kin to that used in *Two Gentlemen of Verona.* In the latter, we begin with a couple and an unattached man. Then we get two couples by attaching the second man. Then the first man breaks his coupling and forms a triangle against the second man. Finally the first man is "reduced" to his original allegiance, and we have the desired two couples. In *Two Gentlemen of Verona* we evolve our square, break it into a triangle plus one, then reverse to the square, without complicating into the circle. In *Midsummer-Night's Dream* we begin with a square, complicate through triangle, and shifted triangle, to circle, and then reverse. In both plays the women remain constant. In *Two Gentlemen of Verona* one man remains faithful, and one shifts and returns. In *Midsummer-Night's Dream,* both men shift, the one by nature, the other by art (magical compulsion), and both are returned by magical compulsion. That is, Shakspere has merely doubled the complication of *Two Gentlemen of Verona* to form the plot of *Midsummer-Night's Dream.* He did the same thing to the plot of *Menaechmi* at the suggestion of *Amphitruo*[8] to get the plot of *The Comedy of Errors.* Fortunately, he did not twin the sisters in *The Comedy of Errors,* nor shift the women in *Midsummer-Night's Dream.* That would have been complication with a vengeance! It will be seen that the more complicated permutation and combination of *Midsummer-Night's Dream* is simply a development of the less complicated in *Two Gentlemen of Verona.* All such mechanically manipulated plots — *Love's Labor's Lost, Comedy of Errors, Two Gentlemen of Verona, Midsummer-Night's Dream,* etc. — belong to Shakspere's early work before he had learned how to make the characters furnish their own motive force to run the necessary machinery.

As we look at the machinery of *Midsummer-Night's Dream,* it becomes immediately apparent that Oberon and Titania manipulate our permutations and combinations through the fourth act, and provide the blessing to round off the fifth. It is important to notice that "both ends" of their function are derived from *Merry Wives.* It has not escaped the acute observation of Professor J. Dover Wilson that the "rounds of waxen tapers on their heads" for the fairies of *Merry Wives* (IV, 4, 50) are also used in *Midsummer-Night's Dream* (p. 151). Incidentally, the fact that these are described in *Merry Wives* probably indicates that they were a

---

[8] Baldwin, *Five-Act Structure,* 700 ff.

novelty to the author if not to the audience. The fact that they are only implied in *Midsummer-Night's Dream* probably indicates that they were then "old stuff." But even more important is the fact that for the fairy revels the two plays use the same set. One will remember that the punishment of Falstaff was at Herne's oak in Windsor Forest. In *Midsummer-Night's Dream,* the mechanicals are to meet "At the duke's oak" (I, 2, 97). Also Lysander and Hermia were to meet "in the wood, a league without the town" (I, 1, 165), where they had met before. The spot proves to be the same as for the mechanicals. This is not actual Athens. Patently it is one of the English palaces, with palace woods a mile without the town. If this is not Windsor Forest, then what is it? At any rate, Herne's oak within the forest is now the duke's oak. The same forest set evidently served for both plays. If this is the explanation — and what else can it be? — then the *Merry Wives* forest came first from reality and later served for the escapades of the fairies in *Midsummer-Night's Dream.*

The company still had this set, as well as the rounds (compliments of Professor Wilson!) and the one and only ass-head (compliments of Professor Gaw!) in stock, so that Herne's oak becomes the duke's oak. Also, in *Merry Wives* the fairies not merely detect and punish the lust of Falstaff, but they also purify and bless every room of Windsor Palace, especially the chairs of the Order of the Garter. In *Midsummer-Night's Dream* they purify and bless "each several chamber" in the palace of Theseus, especially those of the newly wedded. The same palace set, no doubt, the same idea.

Of course, the company would have been obliged to provide and keep in stock the proper fairy regalia.

> For they must all be mask'd and vizarded.[9]

When Master Page hastened out to buy the equipment of the fairies, he and the actors would go ordinarily no further than to their stock. With a bit of refurbishing and adaptation the same equipment would serve for *Merry Wives* and *A Midsummer-Night's Dream,* or any other fairy group they might present. These properties would also tend to "type" their presentations, not merely in outer symbols, but also in such things as certain persons acting certain parts in certain ways, be it the fairy queen or what not. It was inevitable, therefore, that there should be some fundamental likeness between the fairies of *Merry Wives* and those of *Midsummer-Night's Dream.* The two presentations have the same setting, the one of Herne's oak in Windsor Forest, the other at the duke's oak in the palace woods a mile out of Athens, which is the same stage oak and

---

[9] *Merry Wives of Windsor,* IV, 6, 40.

forest,[10] but that in *Midsummer-Night's Dream* later. Windsor Palace would also serve for the palace of Duke Theseus.

The reader should not overlook one important implication of this particular relationship between *Merry Wives* and *Midsummer-Night's Dream*. Whichever came first, both were written to use the same properties and stage sets, those belonging to the company. Neither play was written initially for an occasion. Both were written for the public stage, though both show signs of performance at court, as was normal. *Midsummer-Night's Dream* was certainly not constructed for a wedding any more than *Merry Wives* was written to expose some would-be cuckold-maker at Windsor. Indeed, there is no indication that any play at this period was written for a wedding; a masque would have been the proper form there. Of course, if anyone were willing to pay sufficiently for a performance upon any occasion at off hours, I have no doubt that he would have been accommodated.[11]

We have, then, another important point in our genetics. The fairies were used as an incident in one scene of *Merry Wives* to help provide the denouement. That has suggested using them as the machinery for a complete play, under the appropriate description of *A Midsummer-Night's Dream*. So now we have both the King and Queen of fairies to produce the desired effects. Here then is the very heart of our play structure. They must be provided with mortals to be mixed up in the oak setting, and with a palace to bless at the end as in *Merry Wives;* that is, they are to follow the same tradition.

The mortals to be mixed up and then unscrambled with a blessing come fundamentally from two literary sources; the one the story of Theseus, the other Ovid's story of Pyramus and Thisbe. The story of Theseus is itself ultimately from two sources, Chaucer's *Knight's Tale* and Plutarch's Theseus in North's translation. Since any competent edition of *Midsummer-Night's Dream* will cite conclusive details from Plutarch, we need trouble no further about it, inasmuch as it was details that it furnished. But fixing their eyes upon details, many critics have failed to see the significance of Chaucer's story for the structure of the play.

Fleay[12] pointed out one solid and inescapable fact. The name Philostrate is in Chaucer's *Knight's Tale* of Theseus; it is not in Plutarch's story.

---

[10] For Lyly's "treelogy," see Baldwin, *Five-Act Structure*, 525.

[11] G. L. Kittredge, *Midsummer-Night's Dream* (1939), p. viii, n. 1, lists the suggestions of "ingenious scholars" for weddings. "(1) Robert Earl of Essex and Frances, the widow of Sir Philip Sidney, in April or May, 1590; (2) Sir Thomas Heneage and Mary Countess of Southampton on May 2, 1594; (3) William Stanley, Earl of Derby, and Elizabeth Vere, daughter of the Earl of Oxford, on January 26, 1595; (4) Thomas Berkeley and Elizabeth Carey on February 19, 1596; (5) Henry Earl of Southampton and Elizabeth Vernon in 1598; (6) Henry Lord Herbert and Anne Russell on June 16, 1600."

[12] F. G. Fleay, *Life and Work of William Shakespeare*, p. 185.

From the point of view of plot, there are other important coincidences with Chaucer. Knight[13] pointed out that, "The very expression 'to do observance' in connexion with the rites of May, occurs twice" in Chaucer's story. Once it is Emelye, young sister of Hippolyta, to whom May said "Arys, and do thyn observaunce (1045)." Again it is Arcite, principal squire of Theseus, who rose "to doon his observaunce to May (1500)." The important fact is not the coincidence in phraseology, but that May day is likely to be impressed upon any one sensitive to it who reads *The Knight's Tale*. There should be no difficulty in accounting for May day. Nor do we need to seek further for the suggestion of the hunt, for, as Knight also pointed out,[14] "The Theseus of Chaucer was a mighty hunter":

> This mene I now by myghty Theseus,
> That for to hunten is so desirus,
> And namely at the grete hert in May,
> That in his bed ther daweth hym no day
> That he nys clad, and redy for to ryde
> With hunte and horn and houndes hym bisyde.
> For in his huntyng hath he swich delit,
> That it is al his joye and appetit
> To been hymself the grete hertes bane,
> For after Mars he serveth now Dyane.[15]

Here is a hunt in May, with horn, dogs and all. In May, "he serveth now Dyane"; that is, Titania. This could underlie Oberon's twitting of Titania with Theseus, though the scandals he twitters are from Plutarch.

Staunton is thus as completely wrong as he is completely right in his summary of the case. "The persistence [of the commentators] in assigning the groundwork of the fable to Chaucer's *Knight's Tale* is a remarkable instance of the docility with which succeeding writers will adopt, one after the other, an assertion that has really little or no foundation in fact. There is scarcely any resemblance whatever between Chaucer's tale and Shakespeare's play, beyond that of the scene in both being laid at the Court of Theseus. The Palamon, Arcite, and Emilie of the former are very different persons indeed from the Demetrius, Lysander, Helena, and Hermia of the latter. Chaucer has made Duke Theseus a leading character in his story, and has ascribed the unearthly incidents to mythological personages, conformable to a legend which professes to narrate events that actually happened in Greece. Shakespeare, on the other hand, has merely adopted Theseus, whose exploits he was acquainted with through the pages of North's *Plutarch,* as a well-known character of romance, in subordination to whom the rest of the *dramatis personae* might fret their

---

[13] C. Knight, *Shakspere,* note to I, i, 177.

[14] Note IV, i, 117.

[15] F. N. Robinson, *Chaucer* (1933), pp. 38-39 (1673-1682).

hour; and has employed for supernatural machinery those 'airy nothings' familiar to the literature and traditions of various people and nearly all ages. There is little at all in common between the two stories except the name of Theseus, the representative of which appears in Shakespeare simply as a prince who lived in times when the introduction of ethereal beings, such as Oberon, Titania, and Puck, was in accordance with tradition and romance."[16]

All this is essentially true. And yet the very parallels which Staunton admits are the ones we need to complete our genetic pattern. We do have fairies, but they serve the same function of furnishing "unearthly incidents" as do the mythological personages. The fairies are merely the modern equivalent of the ancient mythological machinery. The fairies also fit with the observance of May day in the tale and with the vigorous hunting of Theseus in May. It is quite true that "Palamon, Arcite, and Emilie . . . are very different persons indeed from . . . Demetrius, Lysander, Helena, and Hermia." But they are at least lovers in a triangle. Here we will permit Sir Edmund Chambers from his green and salad days to put the case, as usual correctly. "Clearly the framework of the story, so far as it centres in Theseus, is adapted from the *Knightës Tale* of Chaucer. In the tale, as in the play, the action has its rise in the celebration of Theseus' wedding; there, too, the characters go forth to 'doon their observance to May,' and there the theme of friendship broken across by love is illustrated in Palamon and Arcite, as here, though differently, in Hermia and Helena. Several slighter parallels of incident and phrase are recorded in the notes,"[17] which those whom it may concern will fail to consult at their peril. Further, "As Ten Brink has pointed out in his excellent study of the play, the motive of this story [of the Athenian lovers] is varied from that of Chaucer's *Knightës Tale*. In the *Knightës Tale* the friendship of Palamon and Arcite is broken by their common love for Emilia. This corresponds very closely to the relation of Proteus and Valentine in *The Two Gentlemen of Verona*. But both in *The Two Gentlemen of Verona* and in *A Midsummer-Night's Dream* Shakespeare has complicated the situation by introducing a second woman, and in *A Midsummer-Night's Dream* he has still further modified it by making the broken friendship that of the women, not that of the men."[18] This evolution of the plot is itself fundamentally important, as we have already seen above. Given the *Knight's Tale* and *Two Gentlemen*, the result is a complication into the plot of the Athenian lovers in *Midsummer-Night's Dream*. These various pieces of machinery are adapted, therefore, from

---

[16] H. H. Furness, *Midsummer-Night's Dream,* pp. 271-272.

[17] E. K. Chambers, *Midsummer-Night's Dream* (1897, Warwick ed.), p. 17.

[18] Chambers, *Midsummer-Night's Dream* (1897), p. 22.

Chaucer's *Knight's Tale,* and in fact give us the over-all framework of the play.

The play is to be a fairy story after the fashion of the fairy thread in *Merry Wives.* So Oberon is provided, by his magic juice to manipulate by mathematical permutation the four Athenian lovers through a triangle into a circle and then reverse through another triangle, and that triangle adapted, to square the circle into two couples. Oberon is a substitution, as we have seen, of a modern equivalent for the original mythological machinery. These efforts, however, are incidental to his own endeavors to force Titania to give him a changeling boy, in which Bottom of the mechanicals becomes entangled, involuntarily but with perfect aplomb. But Oberon and Titania have as their main purpose to watch over and bless Theseus and Hippolyta, as Oberon watched over and brought good fortune to Huon of Bordeaux. When, therefore, Oberon has driven his geese to Camelot, Theseus impounds them by giving the orders he could just as well have given in the first few lines, except that there would have been no play. Theseus now presides over the wedding festivities of the final act, mostly the mechanicals' play from Ovid, and the fairies bestow the blessing they had come all the way from India to give.

While Oberon is the motive force, his interference in the love affairs of the Athenian couples which form the play proper was purely accidental. Equally accidental was his interference in the play of the mechanicals by translating their principal actor into the semblance of the perfect ass he so eminently was. Only in the fifth act does Oberon, with his fairy queen, perform his proper function to tie the whole together. After pranks performed, the blessing is bestowed; so must all good faires do.

It may come as a surprise to find that Oberon is the motive force, since we are much more conscious of Titania, who is the occasion of Oberon's interferences. A very brief look at her origins may help us to a better understanding of her role. The worst of her reputation may be given at once. Reginald Scot in 1584[19] quotes in translation the decree of a general council. "It may not be omitted, that certeine wicked women following sathans prouocations, being seduced by the illusion of diuels, beleeue and professe, that in the night times they ride abroad with *Diana,* the goddesse of the *Pagans,* or else with *Herodias,* with an innumerable multitude, upon certeine beasts, and passe ouer manie countries and nations, in the silence of the night, and doo whatsoeuer those fairies or ladies command, &c." On the same page, Scot also equates "fairies or witches."[20]

---

[19] Reginald Scot, *Discouerie* (1584), p. 66.

[20] The other supposed instances of Diana as queen of fairies cited by Miss M. W. Latham (*The Elizabethan Fairies,* p. 181) do not in fact apply. In Golding's translation of Ovid's *Metamorphoses,* some nymphs who serve Diana are made out to be water fairies (Rouse's ed., IV, 370), but Diana is not Queen of Fairies. By

It is upon this idea that King James in 1597 enlarges, when he writes of "That fourth kinde of spirites, which by the Gentiles was called *Diana,* and her wandring court, and amongst vs was called the *Phairie* (as I tould you) or our good neighboures, was one of the sortes of illusiones that was rifest in the time of *Papistrie:* for although it was holden odious to Prophesie by the deuill, yet whome these kinde of Spirites carryed awaie, and informed, they were thought to be sonsiest and of best life. To speake of the many vaine trattles founded vpon that illusion: How there was a King and Queene of *Phairie,* of such a iolly court & train as they had, how that they had a teynd, & dutie, as it were, of all goods: how they naturallie rode and went, eate and drank, and did all other actiones like naturall men and women: I thinke it liker VIRGILS *Campi Elysij,* nor anie thing that ought to be beleeued by Christians, except in generall, that as I spake sundrie times before, the deuil illuded the senses of sundry simple creatures, in making them beleeue that they saw and harde such thinges as were nothing so indeed . . . For may not the deuil object to their fantasie, their senses being dulled, and as it were a sleepe, such hilles & houses within them, such glistering courts and traines, and whatsoeuer such like wherewith he pleaseth to delude them."[21]

To King James, these fairies were only a midsummer-night's dream, and to Theseus, as to James, they were merely the products of shaping fantasy such as are to be found in "Antique fables" and "fairy toys," to which lovers and madmen are subject, for

> The lunatic, the lover and the poet
> Are of imagination all compact.[22]

But old-wife Hippolyta demurs. It seems clear that Theseus had been reading up on his life in Plutarch. "What hath bin written before, is but of strange faynings, and full of monstrous fables, imagined and deuised by Poets, which are altogether vncertaine, and most vntrue."[23] Quite clearly, Professor Wilson is in error in saying that the poet "was an afterthought";[24] he is the author of the antique fables. He appears, however, to be probably correct in saying that the lines we have quoted belong to an insert, and it seems also clear that the lines were inserted at original

---

implication Spenser connects Diana with the Fairy Queen in the person of Queen Elizabeth. For Elizabeth is not merely the Faerie Queene, she is also Belphoebe, compounded of "Phoebe and Cynthia being both names of Diana" (Spenser, *A Letter of the Authors*). But there is no direct statement that Diana is the Queen of Fairies. In Lyly's *Endimion,* IV, 3, there is a reference to Actaeon's ill-luck with Diana's bathing, but it is merely another warning coupled with "Nor pry into our Fairy wooing," which was directed by Tellus, not Diana.

[21] James I, *Daemonologie* (1597), pp. 73-74.

[22] *Midsummer-Night's Dream,* V, 1, 7-8.

[23] Thomas North, *Plutarch* (1595), p. 1.

[24] Wilson, *Midsummer-Night's Dream,* p. 85.

composition,[25] at the suggestion of Plutarch. Titania and her court are "*Diana,* and her wandring court." We have it on the highest possible authority. This synonym of Titania for Diana would certainly be known to Shakspere from Ovid and from Virgil. One such passage from Virgil occupied the bad eminence of a "flower" in the *Flores* of Mirandula, which was an anthology of excerpts upon which the grammar school boys learned to model their verses.[26] But in *Midsummer-Night's Dream* Titania is as lovely in name and act as the moonlight itself; Oberon must bear all the blame!

The genetics of the structure of the play now aids us in clearing some difficulties. I suppose we may as well begin with the moon. Fairies demand midnight and moonlight for their most successful operation, though Oberon insists here as pointedly as in *Huon of Bordeaux* that he is not evil and so can abide even the morning light, and Ovid demanded an effective moon for Pyramus and Thisbe as the mechanicals knew. So on both counts the outdoor night of the play must be moonlit. Indeed, it is customary to say that the play is "bathed in moonlight." In consequence, a favorite method of attempting to date the play has been by the moon. Here we had best begin with known fact so as to see what is left to conjecture. For the mechanicals, we know that the moon came in with the story of Pyramus and Thisbe from Ovid. In the original story, Thisbe saw the lioness, not lion as in Shakspere, *ad radios lunae.* Hence the mechanicals must have their innings with the moon. In I, 2, Quince directs his fellow mechanicals to con their parts "by to-morrow night; and meet me in the palace wood, a mile without the town, by moonlight" (89-90), so that, as Bottom puts it, they "may rehearse most obscenely and courageously," without being spied upon. They expect a good moon by which to see in the evening. As they proceed in their rehearsal (III, 1), they find it necessary to provide a method of supplying the moonlight for the meeting of Pyramus and Thisbe on the night of the show. Bottom calls for a calendar to see whether the moon is to shine the night of their play, and the provident Quince, though in the woods, has an almanac to show that it will. They are, in fact, represented as rehearsing under a full moon and should need no calendar to tell them that the moon is to shine the night of their play; that is, unless we are to have double-moon time and permit them one moon the same time and place that the lovers have another — and mayhap Theseus and Hippolyta still another! It must be evident that here Shakspere has consulted neither calendar nor common sense. For such a mad mistaking crew why should he, especially when all is midsummer madness? We cannot, therefore, derive any aid from the

---

[25] One should remember that for ordinary human beings composition consists mostly of inserts — and, alas, some of them are certain to show in the finished form.

[26] Baldwin, *Small Latine,* II, 411.

almanac of the mechanicals. They have one moon for themselves and another for Ovid's lovers. And they do not use Ovid's moon after all but the man in the moon to symbolize it!

We do not fare much better with the lovers. They are in the same wood with the mechanicals, who have met by moonlight. Just before they arrive Oberon and Titania are "Ill met by moonlight" (II, 1, 60). Later Titania invites Oberon to stay "And see our moonlight revels" (141). As they clear the stage, Demetrius and Hermia arrive. Then come the mechanicals to rehearse by moonlight. After Bottom gets translated, Titania orders her fairies "To fan the moonbeams from his sleeping eyes" (III, 1, 159). Later Titania says

> The moon methinks looks with a watery eye (III, 1, 183).

Certainly the lovers could not have avoided all this moonshine. But they have no moon of their own, only Venus. Demetrius says that Hermia looks

> as bright, as clear,
> As yonder Venus in her glimmering sphere (III, 2, 60-61).

A few lines later Oberon echoes this when he puts the juice into the eyes of Demetrius, so that Helena may

> shine as gloriously
> As the Venus of the sky (III, 2, 106-107).

One Venus is to replace another, and no actual Venus star is needed in either case, bright or dim, morning, noon, or night. It is clear, therefore, that there was plenty of moonlight in the palace wood the night before the wedding day, which was May day.

But the palace itself was ill-provided.

> Four happy days bring in
> Another moon: but, O, methinks, how slow
> This old moon wanes! (I, 1, 2-4).

This hoped for new moon of crescent promise is all that the palace can command; and in spite of all the moonlight in the palace wood on the night before May day, Theseus and Hippolyta must wait till May day for their sliver of deliverance. This inconsistency is in keeping with the whole time scheme of the play, as indicated in the same speech. Perhaps Professor Kittredge makes the very best possible of this bad matter. "The time-scheme of the drama has worried the critics a good deal and has helped them in spinning tenuous theories of revision. We need only observe that the four days and four nights contemplated by Hippolyta in i, 1, 7-11, are not fully spanned. The action begins on the first day of the four, accounts for the second and the third, and ends shortly after midnight on the third day or, in other words, very early on the fourth. No audience would note the discrepancy, for the night in the enchanted forest is long enough to bewilder the imagination."[27] But surely it is now evident that the new moon and the four days at the beginning are only a false start, on a discarded plan. No dramatist who had worked through the mechanics of this plot and had exuded all this moonlight could have written those lines — not even one full of North Carolina moonshine!

Why then did the Theseus-Hippolyta framework ever have a new moon of promise on May day? The favorite answer has been that of actuality; there was to be such a new moon when the dramatist wrote his lines. At least, we know nothing to indicate that the traditional story of Theseus and Hippolyta demanded such a setting. After summing up the time scheme and losing two days, W. A. Wright very cautiously suggests, "It is a curious fact, on which, however I would not lay too much stress, that in 1592 there was a new moon on the 1st of May; so that if A Midsummer Night's Dream was written so as to be acted on a May day when the actual age of the moon corresponded with its age in the play, it must have been written for May day 1592."[28] Others, however, have laid great stress and have even improved.

Draper[29] points out first that there is a reference to Venus as a bright and clear morning star (III, 2, 60, cf. 380). Venus is bright, but it is only a plausible inference that she is a morning star. In 1595, Venus "was a bright and very obvious morning star from the latter part of April into June; and further computation shows that this is the only year between 1592 and 1598 in which Venus was clearly visible at this season as a morning star."[30] "The last two nights of Shakespeare's comedy are supposed to be graced by a new moon . . . Dates agree in showing an astronomical new moon on April 29, 1595 O.S.; and the thin crescent might be dimly visible on the following evening and more clearly on May first. On the years immediately preceding and following, moreover, no new moon fell near to May Day. This date, furthermore, would show Venus as a morning star at its greatest brilliance."[31] This argument assumes exactly the one thing which we know is not the fact, that Shakspere has harmonized his astronomical references by the almanac, whereas we know that he did nothing of the kind. We are not told directly that Venus was shining as a morning star. And this directly mentioned Venus is not used as a time-indicator at all. And since under the assumed conditions Shakspere is writing before the fact, not after it, he must use a calendar, not observation. Wright cites the calendar for a new moon on

---

[27] Kittredge, *Midsummer-Night's Dream* (1939), p. ix.

[28] W. A. Wright, *Midsummer Night's Dream* (1877), p. xxiii.

[29] J. W. Draper, "The Date of *A Midsomer Nights Dreame*," *M.L.N.*, LIII, 266-268.

[30] Draper, 267.

[31] Draper, 268.

May 1, 1592. As I understand Draper, his calendar for 1595 would place
the new moon on April 29, though I have not looked up an actual calendar
— if one exists — to see. If, therefore, this new moon represents actuality, then the time would be May 1, 1592. Everything is against the
assumption that Shakspere actually checked upon his astronomical facts,
but anyone of that time might readily have known whether the first of
May was to have a new moon. There is no known reason, however, why
this wedding in Athens long ago should be celebrated on a May day with
a new moon. I am afraid that with present information most of this is
"just so much moonshine." At any rate, the crescent moon of May day
four days hence seems certainly to be vestigial and to belong to a discarded time-scheme. In the play proper, the moon is evidently full and
functional; nor does anyone have any thoughts of its being otherwise in
the single outdoor night of the second, third, and fourth acts. The man
in the moon must serve indoors the next night for the fifth act.

Here are the ultimates; but they may not all be proximates. The false
start of four days till the new moon suggests that there may have been
a precedent Theseus play, and if so along the line of Chaucer's story, and
embodying the elements which have come over into *Midsummer-Night's
Dream*. There was interest in the story of *Palamon and Arcyte* easily
accessible to Shakspere at this time, since the Admiral's, with whom
Shakspere's company had been cooperating as late as the preceding June,
put on a play as new under this title in September, 1594.[32] We do not
have the play, and there is no suggestion that Shakspere used it; simply
the theme was of interest at the time and easily available to Shakspere.
Also, there was certainly a current old play of *Huon of Bordeaux* at the
Rose in December and January 1593-94,[33] played by Sussex's men, who
followed Strange's men in various plays. It does not survive, and we do
not know directly that Oberon was in it; but because of his relationship
to Huon how could he have been kept out? He must have had some part
in directing events, exactly as he does in *Midsummer-Night's Dream*. But
details do not come from *Huon of Bordeaux*, nor likely from a play. Still,
that bit of machinery was evidently ready at hand.

This interest in these subjects would reflect upon and through Shakspere and his audiences. There is nothing, however, to indicate that
Shakspere used either *The Knight's Tale* or *Huon of Bordeaux* directly.
But Plutarch and Ovid are different. The *Metamorphoses* of Ovid he
had known, of course, from grammar school days. But his first at all
considerable use of Plutarch is in *Midsummer-Night's Dream*. Of this
ponderous tome Shakspere's fellow townsman and schoolmate, Richard
Field, was to publish a second edition in 1595, after having printed for

---

[32] Greg, *Henslowe's Diary*, II, 168.

[33] Greg, *Henslowe's Diary*, II, 158.

Shakspere the flimsy pamphlets of *Venus and Adonis* in April, 1593, and *Lucrece* in May, 1594. It would be worth our while to find out exactly at what time Field began upon this second edition of Plutarch, since Shakspere under the conditions could not have avoided some contact with it, and the life of Theseus, significantly enough, was the first in the volume. At that time, Shakspere's effective acquaintance with Plutarch's lives evidently began — at the beginning casually by hap! Plutarch had not yet — if ever — become Shakspere's pillow, to percolate by osmosis as it were! Later Plutarch was to teach Shakspere some of his most fundamental lessons in tragedy, as well as to furnish him stories for plays.

As we now look back, the genesis of the plot shows that both its analysis and its synthesis represent a single "thinking" on the part of Shakspere. If there was a play to supply the Chaucer material, it supplied only material, not the present plot. The new moon and proposed four-day time scheme may have come from such a play. It is more likely an original plan which the mechanics of the Athenian lovers forced Shakspere to abandon — or permit the lovers to sleep all day, unmissed in Athens, as one remarkably fertile commentator has suggested! Shakspere settled for letting them sleep all of an act, almost. He may not then have troubled to harmonize his original statement of time scheme. What difference did it make anyway? Especially on his stage, not ours?

When, then, did this fundamental construction of the plot occur? *Midsummer-Night's Dream* shows the five-man pattern before the company was reorganized about June, 1594.[34] It is exactly the five man pattern of *Two Gentlemen*. It has the two young men, would-be faithful Lysander — Valentine, and fickle Demetrius — Proteus; the two comedians, the clown Bottom — Launce, the higher comedian Quince — Speed; and the old man father Egeus — Duke. Only this time the plot demanded that Duke Theseus have a prominent part instead of father Egeus. There are other adjustments also in relative importance, arising, no doubt, from a different set of circumstances. It is clear, therefore, in character pattern as well as in the structural relations we have just examined that *Midsummer-Night's Dream* belongs to the first period.

There is one insert which is clearly of 1594. While the events are such as befit the madness of a midsummer-night's dream, the setting throughout is insistently around the first of May. An ornamental plum from Ovid, however, is presented from the point of view of still another season. Ovid's pattern involves all four seasons, as here.[35] This ornamental passage now is adapted as a specific reference to disturbed seasons. Since these have their origin at "middle summer's spring" (II, 1, 82), we

---

[34] Baldwin, *Organization and Personnel,* pp. 82, 236 ff.

[35] Baldwin, *Literary Genetics,* pp. 298-300.

will require the end of the year to know that summer and winter have exchanged places. So we are told

> The human mortals want their winter here;
> No night is now with hymn or carol blest (101-102).

This is "now" *A Midsummer-Night's Dream* at Christmas,[36] not the May day of the setting. Throughout the May-day setting of the play itself the weather is evidently ideal. The actual bad weather has evidently caused an insert.

Latham noticed the power of Oberon in *Huon of Bordeaux* to raise storms,[37] and Munro[38] has suggested that this power occasioned Shakspere's explanation of the bad weather. But Oberon is not represented as having caused the bad weather, though Titania alleges that he was the occasion of it. Since fairies were mixed up with the weather anyway, doubtless no special suggestion was needed. At any rate, the actual bad weather to disturb Ovid's seasons is sufficient to account for the result. Since basically the speech itself is a literary plum from Ovid's tree, the details which come from Ovid, some of which are themselves confused, need not come from actual English weather. It is, however, clear that this bad weather is an insert from the point of view of Christmas.

The reason for the Christmas view is immediately apparent. For we proceed within a few lines to the courtly compliment for the "fair vestal throned by the west."[39] The weather and the courtly compliment are thus inserts for a Christmas performance at court. The Christmas is also said to be the first after the disturbed weather began at "middle summer's spring" (II, 1, 82).

We can now quote "the history book" on the weather. As Cheyney points out, the year 1596, "was the third and hardest of a series of five continuous years of dearth. The main cause is abundantly indicated in the literature of the time. It was the rain. In 1594, the first of these five years, it was declared, on contemporary authority,

> 'The ox hath therefore stretched his yoke in vain,
> The ploughman lost his sweat, and the green corn
> Hath rotted ere his youth attained a beard.'

---

[36] Professor Wilson gives no sufficient authority for his contention that line 102 "refers, not to Christmas carols as many commentators seem to have imagined, but to the songs and dances of May-time or the summer 'wakes,' semi-religious merry-makings that lasted all night" (*Midsummer-Night's Dream*, pp. 114-115). Where were these ever referred to in such terms? All the seasons are alleged to have been involved, and Professor Wilson himself thinks "the whole passage was written late in 1594 when the wet summer had been followed by a mild winter" (p. 115).

[37] Latham, *Fairies*, p. 187.

[38] John Munro, *T.L.S.*, September 27, 1947, p. 500.

[39] II, 1, 155 ff. Why must the little flower be anything but a flower? And certainly Elizabeth was always complimented as the virgin Queen.

In 1595 the pious Churchyard testifies that

> 'A colder time in world was never seene;
> The skies do loure, the sun and moon wax dim,
> Summer scarce known, but that the leaves are greene,
> The winter's vaste drives water o'er the brim . . .
> Nature thinks scorn to do his dutie right
> Because we have displeasde the Lord of Light.'

A preacher at York [in 1594] reminds his hearers that 'Our July hath been like to a February, our June even as an April, . . . our years are turned upside down, . . . our summers are no summers, our harvests are no harvests. . . . For a great space of time scant any day hath been seen that it hath not rained upon us.' The chroniclers tell the same story Camden speaks of continual rains in summer, and Stow reports that 'this summer, by reason of much raine and great floods, corne waxed scant.' "[40] Since in *Midsummer-Night's Dream* the Christmas is the first after the difficulties began at "middle summer's spring" (II, 1, 82), it is that of 1594. Also, while the weather continued unfavorable, it was that of 1594 which impressed contemporaries, especially that in June and July at "middle summer's spring."

Once it be granted that there was a Christmas performance at court in 1594, then, as Sir Edmund Chambers says, another "allusion also tells in favour of 1594, and, moreover, points distinctly to the latter part of that year. In act i. sc. 2 and in act iii. sc. 1, there is some alarm amongst the clowns lest that 'fearful wild fowl,' the lion, should frighten the ladies. It can hardly be doubted that this is a reminiscence of what actually happened in the Scottish court at the baptism of Prince Henry on August 30th, 1594, when a triumphal car 'should have been drawn in by a lion, but because his presence might have brought some fear to the nearest, or that the sight of the lights and torches might have commoved his tameness, it was thought meet that the Moor should supply that room.' "[41] This parody would have been particularly effective at court the Christmas of 1594, and still stands on its own today.

Our indications so far then are that *Midsummer-Night's Dream* was constructed in its present form by the summer of 1594, and contains matter inserted for a Christmas performance at court the Christmas of 1594. The court performance would indicate that the play was current in 1594. At least a few lines of the play date themselves as belonging to this current version. Lines I, 1, 17-78, are not earlier than 1594.[42] These

---

[40] Cheyney, *A History of England* (1926), II, 4-5; most of these instances, plus Forman, are given in full in Chambers' ed. of *Midsummer-Night's Dream* (1897), Appendix C; the reader should not overlook Sir Edmund's concluding sentence, which contains one of his best sly "digs."

[41] Chambers, *Midsummer-Night's Dream* (1897), pp. 10-11.

[42] Baldwin, *Literary Genetics,* p. 221.

immediately precede a reference to that new moon which some would
have to be that of 1592. If so, this speech would indicate that the reference
was made not earlier than 1594.

Another passage is of similar date. In *Richard III*

> The tiger now hath seized the gentle hind (II, 4, 50).

A. H. Thomson[43] notes that the figure is also used in *Lucrece, 543,*

> Like a white hind under the gripe's sharp claws

and reversed in *Midsummer-Night's Dream,* II, 1, 232-233,

> The mild hind
> Makes speed to catch the tiger.

The passage in *Midsummer-Night's Dream* exactly reverses the line in
Richard III, even preserving the adjective by variation, *gentle, mild.*
Clearly, the passage in *Midsummer-Night's Dream* is later than that in
Richard III. The relationship of the passage in Lucrece, where the
figure concerns the hind and the gripe, not the hind and the tiger, is not
clear. We have seen cause to date *Richard III* the winter of 1593-94; and
Lucrece was printed in May, 1594.

Another elaborate figure, that of the double-hunt, also belongs not
earlier than 1594.[44] All our indications, therefore, are that *A Midsummer-
Night's Dream* was constructed about the first half of 1594 and received
some addition or change for court performance the Christmas of 1594.
There are minor touches of staging, etc. which apparently came in later;
but there was clearly no fundamental revision. We have the original
structure of 1594.

---

[43] Arden ed., p. 84.

[44] See above, p. 419; *Midsummer-Night's Dream,* IV, 1, 113-115; 119-121.

CHAPTER XXIX

Iohannes Factotum

There is a tide in the affairs of men
Which taken at the flood leads on to fortune;
Omitted, all the voyage of their life
Is bound in shallows and in miseries.
On such a full sea are we now afloat,
And we must take the current when it serves,
Or lose our ventures.[1]

William Shakspere came in on the tide of *The Expansion of Elizabethan England,* which occurred within the expansion of Europe, occasioned in part by a new world into which to expand. Not that anyone wanted a new world; it was an unwelcome block to access to the old world, and efforts were for long directed to getting through or around it. No new world was sought; all that was wanted was fuller and freer access to the old. The analogy holds for all the intellectual endeavors of the time, including the literary, for they emanated from the same minds. Some minds were more sensitive to some stimuli than to others, and their conditioning circumstances varied. Shakspere's mind was literarily one of the most sensitive which has ever worked itself out on earth, and its conditioning circumstances were at times such as to elicit and permit what we generally consider to be very great works of art.

Shakspere arrived in London just as the current of drama was eddying into the full sea upon which he was to float till he was "bound in shallows and in miseries" of eventual tragicomedy. But drama was only one form of literary expression, and literary expression was only one emanation of life. William Shakspere was continuously in London from the autumn and winter season of 1587-88, when he saw two plays of John Lyly's from which he procured the framework for one play by himself. Politically, the Armada was about to strike — and give the name Armado to the braggart Spaniard of that play; literarily, Robert Greene was currently championing "university" ideals of literature against certain popular innovations in drama, but was himself about to succumb to the popular stage. Behind all this lay the whole history of the human race. Here we can notice only a few of the more obvious proximate facts.

Shakspere begins under the spell of John Lyly, and Lyly was, and was

---

[1] *Julius Caesar,* IV, 3, 216-222.

493

at the time recognized as, the acme in literary drama of a long evolution. But Lyly was only one dramatist, and Shakspere was to try his hand in succession upon most of the types of current popular drama and from them eventually to develop — and then tear down — something of his own. This seeking must have been a conscious, though not necessarily a systematic, process. So had his age sought consciously and more or less systematically literary excellence in various forms.

Thomas Cooper, at the time only a bookseller's hack, tinkering up other men's works, but by 1587-88 a leading bishop and being taunted by Martin Marprelate with his humble days — Thomas Cooper was conscious shortly before 1549 of what was happening, as he busied himself in helping to make it happen. He is summing up briefly the achievements of the reign of Henry VIII. "In knowlage of good letters he farre passed all kynges of Englande before his tyme. . . . He . . . greatly aduanced and set foorth the true knowlage of goddes woorde and all other honest learnynges and sciences. He founded .ii. colleges, one at Oxenforde, an other at Cambridge: and set vp dyuers free scholes in other partes of the realme.

"The knowlage of good letters by continuall warres beyng neglected and driuen out of Italie, encreased greatly in Germanie, France, Englande and Scotlande. For augmentyng and furtheryng wherof, Margaret the kynges grandmother builded .ii. colleges in Cambridge. In like maner Wylliam bishop of Lincolne, and Rycharde of Winchester builded .ii. other in the vniuersitee of Oxenforde: of the whiche one is called Brasennose, the other Corps Christie College."[2] A little later Cooper pays his respects also to Erasmus and to Colet.[3]

Because of the wars in Italy, these other countries, Germany, France, England, and Scotland, had been forced to strengthen their own provisions for "good learning." Cooper might have added that these countries had themselves also been retarded culturally by intestinal wars; in England, the wars of the roses. But through it all was aspiration and the beginning provision for better things, when times should be more conducive. And Cooper could point with pride to what had been done, and could confidently make his contributions to the cause.

In the next decade, Jasper Heywood can sum up with a pride akin to elation what was already being accomplished in literature. He had himself begun to turn Seneca into English verse of sorts, and in his preface to *Thyestes,* printed 1560, he exhorts his translation to

> goe where Mineruaes men,
> And finest witts doe swarme: whome she
> hath taught to passe with pen.

---

[2] Thomas Cooper, *An Epitome of Cronicles* (Lanquet, [1549]), p. 27[2]ʳ.
[3] Cooper, p. 27[2]ᵛ.

In Lyncolnes Inne and Temples twayne,
    Grayes Inne and other mo,
Thou shalt them fynde whose paynfull pen
    thy verse shall florishe so,
That Melpomen thou wouldst well weene
    had taught them for to wright,
And all their woorks with stately style,
    and goodly grace t'endight.
There shalt thou se the selfe same Northe,
    whose woorke his witte displayes,
And Dyall dothe of Princes paynte,
    and preache abroade his prayse.
The Sackuyldes Sonetts sweetely sauste,
    and featly fyned bee,
There Nortons ditties do delight,
    there Yeluertons doo flee
Well pewrde with pen: suche yong men three,
    as weene thou mighst agayne,
To be begotte as Pallas was,
    of myghtie Ioue his brayne.
There heare thou shalt a great reporte,
    of Baldwyns worthie name,
Whose Myrrour dothe of Magistrates,
    proclayme eternall fame.
And there the gentle Blunduille is
    by name and eke by kynde,
Of whome we learne by Plutarches lore,
    what frute by Foes to fynde.
There Bauande bydes, that turnde his toyle
    a Common welthe to frame,
And greater grace in Englyshe geues,
    to woorthy authors name.
There Gouge a gratefull gaynes hath gotte,
    reporte that runneth ryfe,
Who crooked Compasse dothe describe,
    and Zodiake of lyfe.
And yet great nombre more, whose names
    yf I shoulde now resight,
A ten tymes greater woorke then thine,
    I should be forste to wright.[4]

Like Mark Antony, Heywood could say,

Now let it work. Mischief, thou art afoot,
Take thou what course thou wilt.[5]

But before the end of the next decade Roger Ascham was much less than pleased with the course literary mischief was taking. Writing about 1567, he fulminates against the "English man Italianated" by actual resi-

---

[4] Jasper Heywood, *The Seconde Tragedie of Seneca entituled Thyestes* (1560), *7ᵛ-*8ʳ. See also "T. B. To. the Reader" in *The Eyght Tragedie of Seneca* (1566).

[5] *Julius Caesar*, III, 2, 261-262.

dence in Italy, who then brings his infection back to England. "These be the inchantementes of *Circes,* brought out of *Italie,* to marre mens maners in England: much, by example of ill life, but more by preceptes of fonde bookes, of late translated out of *Italian* into English, sold in euery shop in London, commended by honest titles the soner to corrupt honest maners: dedicated ouer boldlie to vertuous and honorable personages, the easielier to begile simple and innocēt wittes. It is pitie, that those, which haue authoritie and charge, to allow and dissalow bookes to be printed, be no more circumspect herein, than they are."[6] "There be moe of these vngratious bookes set out in Printe within these fewe monethes, than haue bene sene in England many score yeare before."[7]

Ascham's objection, of course, is not to translations as such. Translations had long formed a very solid part of English literary fare,[8] and Ascham was as admiring of the content of most of these as was Heywood, though he would have preferred people to become acquainted with the content in Greek or at worst in Latin. It was "these vngratious bookes" — these "baggage books" — to which Ascham objected. And one has only to check any bibliography of prose fiction to see that Ascham was correct about the flood of such translation that had actually set in within a few months of the time he was writing. Ascham pretty clearly is thinking of Painter's *Palace of Pleasure,* which appeared in 1566, and Fenton's *Tragicall Discourses,* which followed in 1567, both of which were to be thoroughly pillaged by the dramatists. Boccaccio's *Philocopo,* published probably in 1566, was doubtless also disturbing to Ascham, and *Chariclea and Theagines* of 1567, Greek in provenance though it was, was likely no more reassuring. There were several other pieces in the lighter vein in these years, and they were but the first of a large supply to rush through the flood-gates of translation. From Italy, France, and Spain, the translators imported a bountiful supply of these "Amorous and Tragicall Tales." Along with these came translations of the Greek romances also — one form of Greek that Ascham could doubtless have spared. And the translators belonged to the same group of university men, mostly at the inns of court, whom Heywood had hailed. They had now about completed the translation of Seneca into English and were ransacking world sources for bloody enough narratives to be treated on the stage in the Senecan manner. And in their ransacking they had come also upon a wealth of amorous as well as tragical tales. All began now to pour into print.

And we must never forget that the literature of the time was based upon

---

[6] R. Ascham, *Scholemaster* (1570), 26ᵛ.

[7] Ascham, 27ᵛ.

[8] See, for instance, the tabulation in Professor H. S. Bennett's *English Books & Readers 1475 to 1557,* pp. 277 ff.

the tale, even if it was ornamented into *rigor mortis* by Lyly or allegorized into desiccation by Spenser. The drama immediately used this source of supply. Fortunately, we have the titles of plays at court for most of the years in the 'sixties and the 'seventies — though probably even more fortunately, the plays themselves have not survived. The plays for the season 1568-69 through that of 1570-71 are missing. Before this break in the late 'sixties, the titles indicate plays of heavily moral import and form, with only an occasional hint at a moralized story. But with the season of 1571-72, the scales are reversed. Now story plays predominate, whether classical or romantic. Brawner sums up acceptably. "According to my classification of the sixty-five plays whose titles we have, they fall into the following groups: Classical Narratives, 21; Romantic Narratives, 31; Moralities, 4; Comedies, 4; Native Realistic Plays, 2; Episode Plays, 2; "Antick" Play, 1. Of the twenty-one classical narrative plays, eighteen were performed by child actors and only three by adult companies; and of the thirty-one romantic narrative plays, twenty-eight were acted by adult companies, three by children's. The two plays of native realism were acted by men, the four moralities by children."[9]

So, in this period 1570-85, the boys continued slightly the old peda-gogical morality plays, but turned mostly to classical narrative for their sources, these stories, however ornamented, being also used fundamentally as moral exempla. That is, these were schoolboys, and were simply con-tinuing the school tradition. Along with the traditional morality plays of grammar school, they were now emphasizing the moral ideas which had been devised for the various classical stories as exempla. We must not forget that these classical narratives and the plays built on them were a part of the grammar school educational process. When eventually these boys were coming to be used as professionals, their public activities were suppressed, and they reverted to mere schoolboys again — witness the proud tradition of Westminster and others at the present day.

The men, in contrast, dealt principally in love and adventure. There are numerous pairings of male and female names in the titles, as well as various knights and adventurous figures, all from the tales that were flooding in. There are four comedies of sorts, two so labeled; and two murder plays. There was evidently very little interest at the "profes-sional" and court level in comedy or tragedy as such. The interest was in story, classical or romantic, just as the statistics of publication show that was the predominant literary interest of the period. Incidentally, this

---

[9] J. P. Brawner, *The Wars of Cyrus* (1942), p. 64. See also the introduction to the companion doctoral dissertation (unpublished) by Robert L. Blair on the *Old Wives Tale,* Urbana, 1936; Brawner classical, Blair romantic. Charles W. Roberts, *An edi-tion of John Phillip's Commodye of pacient and meeke Grissill,* Urbana, 1938, unpub-lished, treats of an earlier stage of the romantic.

posed a problem for the dramatists. Classical comedy and tragedy were expository in structure; even more so were the morality plays. The miracle plays were on too large a scale in their narrative scope, and their smaller units were tied together with expository doctrine. So since the clientele demanded narrative, the dramatists had to learn how to expose a narrative in the two-hours traffic of the stage. In the 'seventies, there is little indication that anyone was trying very hard to solve the problem, and we get such a play as *Common Conditions,* printed 1576, where the author calls time in the middle — or maybe not so far — of his story, and promises more of it on some other occasion, if the audience desires. From titles and survivals it is evident that these plays were but very loosely driven by some moral; hence the scandalized remarks of a Sidney. Under the goadings of the classicists, most dramatists were later to do somewhat better at exposing a narrative, notably Shakspere; but many were still quite lax with their machinery.

Fortunately, we have only enough surviving plays for this period 1570-82 to serve as sufficient samples. For the classical narrative of the boys, there is the *Warres of Cyrus* for the Chapel at Farrant's Blackfriars in 1576-77 to indicate the kind of drama Lyly was to inherit and continue.[10] There is also the morality *Misogonus* (1577), probably for performance at Kettering grammar school, and *The Marriage between Wit and Wisdom,* 1572-79, evidently for boys. For the romantic narrative of the men, we have *Common Conditions* (printed c. 1576), *Clyomon and Clamydes* (c. 1570), *The Rare Triumphs of Love and Fortune* (probably performed by Derby's Men at court December 30, 1582).[11]

It might be well also to glance briefly at the inns of court for the 'sixties and 'seventies, since tragedy, of an Italianate tincture, was there a-brewing, diluted with some Italianate comedy. As we have seen, Jasper Heywood commended his Senecan effort (1560) to the literary coterie at the inns of court in London, where the inevitable *Gorboduc* was about to be produced by Sackville and Norton, to whom he pays his respects in other capacities. We need not catalogue here the *disjecta membra,*[12] but the first fine fury of the Senecan form appears to have passed from the lawyers with the 'sixties, though there are occasional indications as late as the 'eighties that the form was still relished at the inns of court. It had not, however, been so sedulously cultivated in the 'seventies as in

---

[10] Brawner, *The Wars of Cyrus* (1942).

[11] This has been placed in its relevant background by John I. Owen, *An edition of the Rare triumphs of love and fortune,* Urbana, 1952 (available on microfilm).

[12] The fullest and clearest analysis available of how a literary dramatist put together a play of the general type and time is to be found in the work of James L. Jackson, *An edition of Richard Edwardes' Damon and Pithias,* Urbana, 1949 (available on microfilm).

the 'sixties, and in the 'eighties it passed to the public stage, there to be staled and clapperclawed by the vulgar. Needless to say, the elite of the law circles then abandoned it. For comedy, Gascoigne at Gray's Inn in 1566 had translated Ariosto's *Suppositi*. These inns of court men, then, during the 'sixties fostered Italianate Seneca, Italianate comedy, as well as translations of tales and romances from the "romance" languages. But the lists of plays at court show that up to 1582, their interest in tragedy and comedy as types had not spread to the companies of boys or to the professional companies of men, though the dramatists of the men's companies gladly availed themselves of the translated tales.

Thus the popular stage of the 'eighties still needed to be introduced to comedy and tragedy of the classical variety. As Nashe points out in his preface to *Menaphon,* mere learned grammarians, not university men, were by 1589 taking over the business of translating, and were presuming to raise their hands to the classical ark in various other capacities. Christopher Marlowe was also leading a rebellion against "university" ideals in the drumming decasyllables of his blank verse for the popular stage. This had begun to happen in the business of making plays when grammarian Thomas Kyd about 1583 had brought down tragedy to the popular stage with *The Spanish Tragedy*. Anthony Mundy, another grammarian, had helped in the movement by adapting Pasqualigo's *Il Fedele,* which received performance at court before publication in 1585, probably about the time of *The Spanish Tragedy*. Italianate tragedy and comedy had now both been brought down to the popular stage, to accompany Lyly's semi-professional grammar school plays. Much more was happening in popular drama around 1583 than we have usually been aware of, and the process had gone much further by 1587-88, when Shake-scene arrived and was by 1592 to concede that he was better at this business of making plays than even the doubly artful university men, even though he had only the "small Latine and Lesse Greeke" of a learned grammarian. Should we add to our list that very learned grammarian Ben Jonson of a few years later?

In the 'eighties, the "expansion" of drama in the Elizabethan period began to take conscious shape, as did the other activities of life. When Shakspere made his entrance in 1587-88, the show was just ready to begin; the tide in the affairs of drama was just ready to flow. In what direction did William Shakspere choose to go? He did not — he could not — choose any of the goals we now "hindsee." Instead, he was *Iohannes Factotum* — "I thank thee, Jew, for teaching me that word"; never said Robert Greene a truer thing — bobbing around everywhere. He began to swim where he fell in, from the grammar school wharf. Nothing more natural. As a more or less learned grammarian, he began with what he knew best.[13] Besides, the admittedly greatest literary figure in semi-popular narrative and drama in 1587-88 was John Lyly, with George Peele reflecting a somewhat more erudite reputation from the *Arraignment of Paris*. If Shakspere was already attached to acting, as tradition says, a purely mechanical fact may have had its bearing on Shakspere's direction of interest. Shakspere's two hours traffic on the popular stage was from two to four; Lyly's plays at Paul's had to be acted between four and six. If Shakspere could raise the price, he could find the time to see the plays at Paul's, but not easily those performed by the other companies of men. It is a significant fact that with the exception of Lyly, the contemporary dramatists made use of by Shakspere as models wrote or had written for his company. Their plays were compulsorily available to him as actor.

So grammarian — and country schoolmaster? — William Shakspere began naturally with John Lyly's type of play for schoolboys. Taking the typical school idea of love versus learning for *Love's Labor's Lost,* he adapted machinery for it from two of Lyly's plays to produce a school morality for men, not boys. He flourishes his well-beaten rhetorical tricks in very competent fashion. No learned grammarian — nor his master — need be ashamed of this display.

The Comedy of Errors is even more a school piece. Taking the complications of two of the plays of Plautus ordinarily read in grammar school, Shakspere complicates the complications to out-Plautus Plautus.[14] This is the unornamented type of grammar school play. The form of the name Dromio is Lyly's invention, and the play upon complications was evidently suggested by the highly complicated and Italianate *Mother Bombie.* The witchcraft theme which points the acts and in a way is supposed to motivate the unfolding complications was also doubtless in part suggested by *Mother Bombie* and localized to the Biblical Ephesus. This witchcraft theme was beginning a run; *Mother Bombie,* 1588-89, *Orlando Furioso,* 1588-89, *Faustus,* 1588-89, *Bacon,* 1589, *John a Kent and John a Cumber,* 1589-90 etc. Shakspere is in 1589 using a current theme, but not borrowing specifically from any known contemporary dramatist, though other relationships indicate that Lyly's *Mother Bombie* was probably the inciting force here. It was doubtless the sensational Faust story from Germany which incited this run of witchcraft at this time, though Lyly is for the most part independent of this run and had regularly used the classical magic of metamorphoses throughout his plays. Perhaps *Mother Bombie* becomes an actual, not a classical, "witch" in

---

[13] The size of Shakspere's Latin and Greek has no bearing on the question. Here is what has been done, whoever did it and whatever languages were involved, Greek, Latin, English, what not, or just the air.

[14] For a detailed analysis, See Baldwin, *Five-Act Structure,* pp. 665 ff.

deference to this actuality. But only Marlowe in *Faustus* uses the theme seriously for the very heart of his play. Lyly, Greene, Mundy, Shakspere, etc. use it as Hallowe'en machinery. To Marlowe it was thinkable and deadly earnest; it *did* happen, and he makes it rehappen for us.

Outside the drama, Shakspere borrows Menaphon from Greene, who had borrowed the name from Marlowe's *Tamburlaine.* Along with him from *Menaphon* came certain ancient plot devices for separation and reunion, which in turn brought in the Apollonius device. A current execution outside his theater door also made its contribution. And if we only knew, many another current idea or event doubtless enters into the composition of the play. But the essential process is fully clear. Shakspere does not slavishly imitate. From myriad current sources in literature and in life he gathers and recombines world-old materials to make something new and in many respects different. This is the fundamental process of creation in so far as it is yet possible for human beings. It was a most "artful" process; it was at the same time the most natural of processes, but done with outstanding intellectual skill.

The *Two Gentlemen of Verona* brings the romantic interest more to the fore than it had been in *Love's Labor's Lost* and *Comedy of Errors,* but the same kind of machinery and materials are being used.[15] It also is idea driven, grammar school-Lyly style, love versus friendship. This was the motive idea of *Endimion,* a play upon which Shakspere had modeled fundamentally in *Love's Labor's Lost.* There is nothing to show certainly that *Two Gentlemen* borrows this aged idea from *Endimion* (1587-88). We simply happen to know that this is one place where Shakspere had come in contact with it. This idea too was starting a dramatic run under the incitement of *Bacon,* 1589.[16] Greene had managed in *Bacon* to make a love story transcend his feeble machinery, and it was this achievement which was generally imitated. Shakspere in *Two Gentlemen* also brings the love story to the fore, but in the end his well-polished machinery proves too much for it, though the story almost succeeds. There is nothing to show specific influence from Greene, but Greene proved to be the sensation here, and Shakspere is fitting into the movement. Of course, Shakspere himself, along with his fellow dramatists and literary writers generally, had been feeling his way in this direction, very slightly in *Love's Labor's Lost,* much more fully in the added material to *The Comedy of Errors,* and now almost principally in *Two Gentlemen.* For his love theme, Shakspere uses a simple triangle story which is ultimately connected with a Spanish romance, the *Diana* of Montemayor. No details certainly come over, and there is nothing to show that the triangle is taken directly from the romance. In the 'seventies, there were numerous knights,

---

[15] For a detailed analysis, see Baldwin, *Five-Act Structure,* pp. 719 ff.

[16] See above, pp. 236 ff.

etc. from similar sources, and in 1585 the Queen's men gave a *Felix and Philiomena* at Court.[17] Many people would know this story, though there is nothing to indicate that Shakspere knew the play himself.[18] In the 'eighties and 'nineties, Anthony Mundy was translating volumes of such materials, but the English *Diana* did not become available till 1598. Mundy himself was probably readily available to Shakspere at the time he was writing *Two Gentlemen*. Greene accuses Mundy of writing *Fair Em*, 1590, and according to the title page *Fair Em* was acted by Strange's company. If Mundy's brains — "our best plotter" — were available to Shakspere or to his employers, there is no mystery as to how Shakspere *could* have become possessed of this wraith of a plot ultimately from a voluminous Spanish romance. In any case, Shakspere is drawing from materials which were variously current and were of outstanding current interest.[19]

A much more important event for Shakspere's love story was his discovery of Brooke's *Romeus and Juliet,* which occasioned a shift in the very heart of his play.[20] Now Valentine gets banished in the shoes of Romeus, which in their wanderings upset the original geographical scheme of the play. But along with this bit of machinery from *Romeus and Juliet* had evidently come something else, which is indefinable and intangible, a strengthened concept of romantic love — almost strong enough to escape from the shining machinery with which it is to be encumbered. The banishment evidently occasioned other bits of borrowing, such as the Robin Hood forest, instead of the Arcadian forest of Montemayor. This again was current material. Mundy used it in *Fair Em,* 1590, Peele used it in *Edward I*, etc. There is nothing to show that Shakspere is borrowing specifically from any of these. Simply, this was currently attractive material, and Shakspere added it to his frippery. The same process is at work throughout, as in preceding plays.

The newly discovered *Romeus and Juliet* of Brooke now demanded its own play. Here there is no previous love tragedy of the kind surviving. No previous known dramatist, Lyly, Peele, Mundy, Marlowe, Greene, was capable of writing such a play — and few, if any, after. To them, even to

---

[17] Chambers, *E.S.,* IV, 160.

[18] Baldwin, *Five-Act Structure,* p. 720.

[19] We have not done justice to the corporate knowledge of Shakspere's organization and its clientele. There must have been dozens of people who knew stories that the actors simply must get made into plays. Any story so known might become compulsorily available to any hireling dramatist — as all dramatists for the popular stage were. Shakspere certainly had an uncanny ability in picking the brains of both the past and his present; so great that some have wanted to bestow on him the ability also to pick the brains of the future. We would like to know more about Shakspere's living syndicate of brains, not merely his business associates, but particularly about the "diuers of worship" who approved — and no doubt did their best to improve — his art.

[20] See Baldwin, *Five-Act Structure,* pp. 759 ff.

Greene, love was only a game, and to Marlowe it was not even a game. But Brooke spoke to Shakspere, and he awoke to a realization, of which he had always been dreaming. Love is a basic human need and is stronger even than death. So he sets himself to let Romeo and Juliet make us feel their side of the story, as they do in spite of enswaddling machinery.

Of course, the ornamental machinery is still there; but it usually serves, or we can make it serve, Romeo and Juliet, instead of dominating them. True, the stars, as in Brooke, are supposed to cause all their woe; but that was a valid cause to contemporaries, and is ignored by us. The story itself and the characters in it are sufficient to carry us along without any aid from the stars, and that must also have been true for even those who took the stars seriously. There is still machinery for driving the characters and their story, but they are not driven, though at crucial times the machinery of the stars does interfere with and determine their earthly course. They and their love are above the stars and every other earthly thing. The story has now transcended the machinery. Significantly, the story suffices; it is not complicated or padded from other sources. It is merely embodied in the current machinery of the stage as a vehicle.

One other important fact here dawns upon Shakspere. The love of Romeo and Juliet is a lyric love, not a rhetorical game of wits, as with Biron and Rosaline. There had been some touches in *The Comedy of Errors* and in *Two Gentlemen,* but now the lyric takes complete precedence of the merely rhetorical. Perhaps it would be better to say that rhetoric subserves lyric, for lyric had its own ornamentation of rhetoric, and of this ornamentation the lyric of *Romeo and Juliet* certainly has enough, even though lyric is predominant and rhetoric subservient. One need only to call to mind the lines he remembers from the play and notice their nature. Verse, poetry as such, highly and "artificially" ornamental though it be, was getting a grip on Shakspere, and was eventually to get from him relatively simple and sincere expression, dominating all the artificialities. The earlier plays give no indication that Shakspere thought of himself as a poet rather than as an artfully rhetorical playwright, hardly even a dramatist. These early plays show skilful maneuvering of words, whether in or out of some formal metrical pattern, always smoothly running, never or very seldom harsh. But in *Romeo and Juliet* Shakspere obviously sings with all the power of which he was capable at the time. He was here consciously trying to be a lyric poet. But no predecessor of his is known to have made such an attempt, and he himself had not occasion for attempted repetition. This story and this alone had called for exactly this treatment. Still, it showed the way to later adaptations and approximations.

Shakspere had now attained a stage in his thinking and practice which enabled him to grasp and to execute an idea which many of the best minds of his age, on the background of many ages, had been developing. *1 Henry VI* begins with the question of how this universe is governed — God's way to man. Specifically, why had these evils happened to England? Was it because of the "bad revolting stars," as Bedford advocated, and as Shakspere had accepted for motive force to his machinery in *Romeo and Juliet?* Was it witchcraft, as Exeter contended, and as Shakspere had accepted for motive force in *Comedy of Errors,* there fitting into a run of witchcraft plays? Was it the will of the Lord of hosts, as argued by Winchester, a suspect source for such a doctrine? The answer which the historians had given was God's will, directing man in the way he should go. And this is the answer which is developed in the three parts of *Henry VI,* and so elaborately applied in *Richard III.* As to the Hebrew prophets, so to those of English history, God was working through history to chasten and purify man, and this doctrine these four plays fully grasp and to the best of their skill apply.

And for Shakspere it makes ultimately little difference whether he found the idea in the historical sources and executed it in these four plays completely unaided, or whether he found it already more or less fully executed in old plays. The significant thing is that Shakspere did from some source come to grips with the long developed idea and had the necessity of trying to embody it concretely in his work. Doubtless he had given the idea lip service from earliest glimmerings of intelligence. But now he must enter into the idea and the idea must enter into him. He has been feeling for a motive force for each of his plays, and has each time used directly or indirectly some small facet of this world view; sin against the holy ghost of love in *Love's Labor's Lost,* apparent witchcraft in *Comedy of Errors,* and on full scale the stars in *Romeo and Juliet.* Only *Two Gentlemen* is moralized without direct religious connection. Shakspere from the beginning at least felt dimly the need of a motive force which was acceptably religious as well as literary. His universe was at the beginning and remained throughout conventionally religious. The development lay in his grasp of and ability to apply the principles which he had been taught. There is no rebellion here, only acceptance; if his religious villains are literally "heroes," they are none the less consciously villains. They do not forget it; nor do they permit us to forget it.

In his application of ideas of motive force, Shakspere had now gone far enough in his thinking to appreciate the grandeur and the magnitude of this one already made to his purpose. And, characteristically, it must have been Shakspere who improved the idea by moralizing the two houses, as he had learned to do in *Romeo and Juliet.* But what of the other dramatists who have been suspected of having had a hand in these plays? In these history plays characterization is still fundamentally moralization, as it was in their sources in Halle, Baldwin, Holinshed, etc., and as it was in the Terentian criticism of the time; and that moralization was theological, rather than ethical.[21] To state the case crudely, Marlowe of his age most nearly escaped this moralization because he had no morals, and so Greene accuses Tamburlaine of "daring God out of heauen." The difference is particularly noticeable in such a character as Richard. In these plays as in history Richard III is a thoroughly Christian son of the devil, so stigmatized from birth; Marlowe's Tamburlaine with the giants rebels against all the gods in heaven. All Marlowe's characters are "godless"; that is one reason why they have such strong appeal to us; they are so human, we say! Certainly we cannot suspect Marlowe with his rebel giants. I believe there is no necessity to labor the point that this is neither Marlowe's world view nor his construction. That must be self-evident to anyone who has any competent grasp on Marlowe. It must be equally evident that Greene had not the intellectual strength to grasp, nor the architectonics to execute such an idea. If anyone thinks otherwise, let him read through carefully the whole of Greene's writings — just once. Peele's relics in history and elsewhere certainly carry no suggestions in their view nor in their construction by pageant scenes of either the quality or the quantity of thinking found in the tetralogy. For other suspects, we may not have a sufficient body of work to give certainty, but surviving work does not cast suspicion on any of them.[22] For known dramatists, present evidence indicates *aut* Shakspere *aut diabolus.* And yet the second tetralogy gives us pause. *Richard II* is constructed as a proper prologue to the total eight, but the theme of factionalism as such is then no more emphasized structurally for the following three plays. Perhaps we had better keep *diabolus* prominently in mind.

But even if Shakspere should be responsible for the structure of the plays, this would not mean that he wrote every word of these plays *de novo* from the sources. Others may have written plays on Henry VI and Richard III, even embodying to some degree this fundamental idea, which Shakspere later welded together into a consistent whole. But no such play on English history or any other subject survives. Sententious Senecan Roman and English history we do have, and miracle play English patches from the chronicles, but nothing to compare with or to suggest the quality and scale of execution in the three parts of *Henry VI* and *Richard III.* The scale upon which the idea is grasped and executed is one which Shakspere had progressively attained, and no one else is known to have been working in similar directions. But the significant fact is that he has attained it, whether under the primary guidance of the sources, whether

---

[21] See E. W. Robbins, *Dramatic Characterization in Printed Commentaries on Terence 1473-1600,* and the various works of Professor Marvin T. Herrick on the international critical background.

[22] See Appendix II.

already rough hewn in some old play, or for that matter whether already fully shaped in three or four plays. It is in any case a landmark in the development of his thinking. It was by following up this fundamental attainment through English and Roman history that Shakspere eventually arrived at the view of his great tragedies. But that does not belong to our present undertaking.

After these five plays, *Romeo and Juliet, 1, 2, 3 Henry VI*, and *Richard III*, our remaining plays, *Titus, Merry Wives*, and *Midsummer-Night's Dream* may at first appear to be anticlimax. I believe the evidence, external as well as internal, is now clear that Shakspere did not construct *Titus*. It is a Senecan tragedy of the popular slaughter-house type, where the objective is to spatter as much blood as ingeniously as possible. But the play did bring Shakspere to close quarters with Senecan tragedy, which was at the time considered to be the only tragedy worthy of the name — *Romeo and Juliet* had been without the pale, fortunately. The universities had admired, performed — and paid for — Seneca as part of the educational process; and had encouraged — and paid for — frigid imitations in Latin. University men at the inns of court had adapted Seneca in English on Italian models into a more direct and gory form. Thomas Kyd, son of a scrivener, thus connected with the humbler branches of the law, is the first, so far as we know, to bring this Senecan type to the popular stage, by transmuting as completely as he was able the gory rhetoric of Seneca into the actual vinegar and paint of stage blood. In this slaughter-house type, surely *Titus* is the grandest of the lot. But it did not grip Shakspere, nor did its kind. He might revamp progressively a *Hamlet* into a play with quite a different emphasis from that of the first *Hamlet,* of this type; but he wrote originally no play of this type, and he pursued *Titus* itself no further. Before 1594 he had done with it. Quite evidently it was thrust upon him.

But Shakspere had grasped some things from this Senecan background, as we see in *Richard III*, where Sir Thomas More had early directed Richard in the Senecan way he should go. This Senecan shaping in the source accounts for much in the concept of Richard. The dominant concept in his presentation, however, comes from Marlowe's variant rebels. In Tamburlaine, Marlowe had taken a figure from the romances of history, bent on world conquest and striving to perform superhuman feats. He is not a pagan character of Senecan type; neither conventional saint nor sinner of the Christian concept. He is neither moral nor immoral in accordance with any accepted standard, but an a-moral rebel with his own standards. Faustus, the Jew of Malta, etc., reflect this same fundamental attitude. Richard belongs here in general scope of concept, though like those other devils he believes and finally trembles, as Marlowe's characters do not. There is no direct imitation of Marlowe, and Richard is consciously a jauntily impudent sinner against God's law. But without the Marlovian magnitude and drive in the background, Richard would have lacked a great deal of his heroic proportions in sin. Marlowe had prepared the way that Richard might be a magnificent sinner. Shakspere now has a character of sufficient size, even if he is but a single characteristic; but he is conceived in sin, and born and devoted to iniquity. The problem henceforth is sufficiently to humanize the concept into neither saint nor sinner, but into a human being understandably suffering on his way to purification, as in the great tragedies. Shakspere's contacts with old line tragedy here at this stage of his development through Kyd and Marlowe show him able to grasp a fundamental concept which was to be important in his later thinking.

The attempt at conventional tragedy in *Richard III* had, of course, involved also conventional trappings. The "height of Seneca his style" was conventional, and in *Richard III* Shakspere "rolls in rhetoric as an ape in his tail." As *Love's Labor's Lost* is his supreme rhetorical exhibition in morality-comedy, so is *Richard III* in tragedy. Between these the *Comedy of Errors* forms a kind of bridge. For it tries out a highly complicated plot. So *Love's Labor's Lost* magnifies the complicated rhetorical verbiage, *Comedy of Errors* the complicated plot (also a rhetorical device), *Richard III* both the complicated rhetorical verbiage and the complicated plot. *Richard III* is thus Shakspere's most "artificial" play. In each case, the type called for the treatment, and each time Shakspere rose to the occasion. But the extreme graces of rhetoric satisfied him no more in tragedy than they had in morality comedy. Rhetoric could not be a fundamental end but only a subservient means. Once each he tried *in extremis,* and not again. But, characteristically, he tried to the limit. In this first period, he tried each thing in extreme; nothing could be too much of the particular subject of experiment, as by trial and error he gradually evolved his own nothing too much — though he is still blamed more for too much than for too little. Each time he grasped the fundamental of some type and then developed it as fully as he could at the time. And each time he turned to something else. But each time something that he had learned from the preceding experiment passed with him to the next. And so it remained to his very last play. This was his strength; it was also his weakness. He never had, he never arrived at, an ideal for a perfect play, though he worked within the accepted ideals of his day. He never had, he never arrived at, an ideal formula which could automatically ensure the perfect life, though he was taught, accepted, and worked within the conventional concepts of his day.

In tragedy, then, Shakspere has fortunately written the lyrically romantic *Romeo and Juliet,* principally as a projection of his own attainments in romantic comedy.[23] Then in the history plays, he faced a type which had not fully been domesticated into either comedy or tragedy, but which was by him to be constructed always as tragedy, never as comedy, even in the most comic of them, never as "chronicle," if one can differentiate structurally such a type at all. In *Richard III* particularly, he shaped within the evolved Senecan tradition. In *Titus,* he accepted what had been shaped in a more direct Senecan vein. But he did not attempt to repeat any of these. In *Romeo and Juliet,* he has attained a poetic picture of persons whom we can love and regret. In *Richard III,* he has produced a character of tragic size but a villain, not a hero, except in technical literary paradox. The knowledge acquired here will be used later, but he does not know it; he does not know what he is to attain any more than does anyone else, then or now. There was no far-off divine event; simply a human being was groping his way into himself, and that final self we approve highly, whether Shakspere himself considered it a success or a failure. We can now trace in some detail the process and see how, here a bit and there another, Shakspere eventually found and built up the human being he was to be. But how he knew himself in these bits and not in their surrounding materials we do not know any more than did he or does anyone else. There is the mystery of human existence, whose heart we would all gladly pluck out.

As to the remaining comedies of this early period, we do not know enough about the early *Merry Wives* to judge in detail. But here was an Italianate intrigue domesticated into English conditions. The intrigue was evidently conducted smoothly, as one would expect of the author of *The Comedy of Errors.* In fact, the early play was probably a much more neatly finished play structurally than is the present form. Falstaff and his crew make the play for us, but they overlayed and distorted its structural form. The domestication to plausible citizens of Windsor represents a continuation of what was done germinally in *The Comedy of Errors.* The merry wives, at least, are much more plausible as human beings — not as ideals — than are Adriana and Luciana. This difference is characteristic of Shakspere's growing grasp upon living human beings in an accountable universe. But I believe there are few or none who would champion the early *Merry Wives* as one of Shakspere's really great comedies.

As for *Midsummer-Night's Dream,* "Lord, what fools these mortals be!" Whatever Puck's intonation, that of Shakspere is of amused toleration, delighted with all their foibles. And so these poor mortal lovers are put through a charade of mishaps, with Bottom-Dogberry and his crew playing their stolid-stupid parts. Stolid Bottom serves the same plot function as does stupid Dogberry later. Here by common consent is

---

[23] See Baldwin, *Five-Act Structure,* pp. 810-811.

Shakspere's first great clown. But he is not created for himself; he and none but he can serve this story. As for the actual machinery of the play, it is for four acts a smoothly working mathematical involution and evolution, though a small Gordian knot had to be cut by having the characters sleep through an act division. The fifth act is then an appended conclusion. As machinery, it is as external and mechanical as that in *The Comedy of Errors*, though it is less complicated. It neither drives the story, nor does the story drive it. The two just amble along amicably together. Nor do the characters as such drive the story, although when we stop to analyze we become aware that Puck with characteristic puckishness pulls the determining strings, even though the puckish results were set in motion by accident, not by his plan. Puck is not Prospero.

Here we may notice the interesting and significant fact that so many of these early plays have a framework structure. In the *Comedy*, the story from Plautus was put into the setting of a family to be reunited, partially suggested by the source, and this problem is given a Duke to act as umpire. In *Romeo and Juliet*, the source contributed the background framework of the houses and the malignant stars to work evil through them. In *Richard III*, the houses, eventually from history and proximately as developed in the *Henry VI* plays, have been moralized into the framework, with God punishing political sin in and through them. In *Midsummer-Night's Dream*, one house objects (not two as in the tragic *Romeo and Juliet*), and a partial Duke (being himself *particeps criminis*) serves as umpire to end all well, while puckish love is permitted by the errors of magic and accident (not mistaken identity as in *Comedy of Errors*, but changed identity)[24] to run the show. While the framework structure is a fundamental device in these early plays, it is turned and varied in numerous ways, in combination with still other devices which have also their interconnections. A framework setting was something to and through which to apply the motive force. The use of an idea for framework, as in *Love's Labor's Lost* and *Two Gentlemen of Verona* is a cognate device. In all these plays, Shakspere is consciously trying to apply an adequate motive force, and gradually but not systematically he is trying to make it an actual and driving internality, not an abstract externality.

As background to all this analysis, we must remember that we are dealing with an age which founded its compositional theory upon imitation by analysis and synthesis, and drilled upon the *Copia Rerum et Verborum* of Erasmus as a basic text book. If ye know not me, ye know nobody. If Shakspere had directly or indirectly any knowledge of compositional theory and practice, this is the only knowledge he could have. Otherwise,

---

[24] *Midsummer-Night's Dream* shares with *Two Gentlemen* this device of changed identity, or shifting affections in an ordered sequence.

he must have been impossibly ignorant, or transcendently learned. Older critics may have excuse for not being sufficiently aware of that fact and its bearings; we have none. But the fundamental fact has been common knowledge with the best of our older critics. We will still do well to remember a title from Coleridge: *Shakspeare's Judgment Equal to His Genius.* Shakspere shows not merely a high degree of deftness in the purely intellectual side of the process of analysis and synthesis as practiced in his age, but especially an uncanny feeling for what the ages have come to consider as the right things, upon which to use his intellect. There was method in his madness, even though it is his madness which has counted.

By common consent *Midsummer-Night's Dream* is one of Shakspere's better plays, and by common consent we praise it most for what we call its poetic qualities. These transcend all the techniques of versification, plot, characterization, etc., to give us a favorite play, though it is hardly outstanding in any mechanical technique. This poetic quality we can recognize, we can attempt to describe; we cannot explain. We can see that Shakspere is growing, but like the dial's shade, his growth is not seen.

And this is the really significant attainment. In the romantic tragedy of *Romeo and Juliet,* in the romantic comedy of *Midsummer-Night's Dream,* this poetic quality transcends the subserving mechanics to give us a satisfying experience, not as plays technically, not as verse technically, but as themselves, without consciousness of the techniques of attainment. One is likely to forget completely the technical point he is pursuing, just to read and enjoy. The poetry of these plays does not reside in the technique of verse, no more does Shakspere's verse generally. In this first period particularly, Shakspere experiments with numerous verse techniques, as he does with prose techniques. He has explored fully the technicalities of formal rhetoric as applied to either verse or prose. For verse, one can turn to the laborious statistics of the metrical tables to find Shakspere trying a little bit of almost anything available in his day, complicated sonnet, various other lyric forms, etc., as well as blank verse. But there is no systematic experimentation to give a neat chronological succession of statistics. Rather, there is the trial upon various emergent occasions of various conventional modes of attaining desired effects. We simply feel that gradually Shakspere is learning to use his technical devices to attain his aesthetic ends as had no one before, nor has any one since. This transcendent adaptation is the thing.

As we look at this first period then, Shakspere has produced an outstanding romantic tragedy *Romeo and Juliet,* and an almost equally outstanding romantic comedy *Midsummer-Night's Dream,* both marked by their poetic qualities. He also produced a *Richard III,* which has maintained itself, usually in a seriously mangled form, and hardly for what Shakspere himself intended it to be. But in it Shakspere had attained a figure of sufficient size for tragedy. As we look back from the vantage of later accomplishments, we can see the promise of greatness to come.

But what of Shakspere himself; what of his contemporaries? Had Shakspere received a dagger in his eye along with his coetanean Marlowe, we should now have no suspicion that the world's greatest dramatist had failed of fruition. It is distressing to think what we should now be saying of him. No play had reached print under his name; no play was to be so graced for several years to come. A parody of his name would survive in Greene as that of some obscure upstart, and that would be all for drama, except Chettle's apology, which few under the circumstances would trouble to take seriously. His poetic fame would rest on *Venus and Adonis,* just coming off the press of a pious fellow townsman; so, no doubt, we would say.

We ought, therefore, to acknowledge the exceeding great debt we owe to Shakspere's masters, who believed in him and gave him a chance to develop his potentialities. And what did the master-actors see in this hireling Shakescene? He was a man with and through whom they could work. Not merely could he write plays acceptable to their clientele. He could also shake a scene well enough to demand admission to their controlling group as an actor. Not only was he admitted as a master-actor, but he was put into a key practical position in their business, where he must sue and be sued. Their financial lives they placed in his hands; they could hardly have given a greater token of confidence in their ability to work with and through him in the practical affairs of life. Greene indicates that Shakspere as well as his masters had also by August, 1592, the highest opinion of his abilities as a dramatist, and Chettle can a few weeks later add a favorable opinion from "divers of worship," which Shakspere soon had occasion to follow up. For while Greene thought in August, 1592, that Shakescene stood at the height of Fortune's wheel, still that wheel was already revolving into a period of intermittent plague which brought ruinous financial difficulties. Shakspere himself found it advisable to make a bid for the patronage of one so high-placed as the Earl of Southampton. In April, 1593, came the hesitant *Venus and Adonis,* as the first fruits of his purely poetic invention, and in May, 1594, the more assured *Lucrece.* He had notions of being a poet. But when later in 1594 his company itself broke connections with the Admiral's men and reformed, Shakspere was taken into the membership and so made no further known overt moves toward Southampton, though he doubtless kept the connection — as in the sonnets, for instance — just in case! And the poetic efforts were themselves not wasted; their plums found themselves warmed over in many a later theatrical pie!

By August, 1592, Shake-scene thought himself able to bombast out a blank verse with the best of the dramatists, and his masters would not accept as substitute even Robert Greene. "Divers of worship" also approved his facetious grace in writing, and under the emergent circumstances of the plague in 1593-94, he was to capitalize upon that ability in *Venus* and *Lucrece*. But with better days Shakspere's masters tied him into the golden heart of their future, and fortunately for us as for them, he sought no more to be a poet. To this loyal, though self-interested belief and devotion of his masters become fellows we owe much in the opportunity and incitement it gave Shakspere to grow and develop. To them he was a man of potential promise as well as of present performance. It is to be hoped that we all know the confidence and sense of dedication which such trust brings.

We now know, therefore, a great deal of the essential how and what of Shakspere's literary beginnings and of how they fitted into the known background of his life. But why? The one thing which is apparent from all our knowledge is Shakspere's "power of growth" — that assumption by which Aristotle begs the universe and we can do no better. This power shows itself in this first period seeking in myriad directions, and beginning to attain a few settled bases, upon which, as we can now see after the fact, he was later to build.

But granting the power of growth, how did that power know in what directions to grow in order to become the supreme unity we call Shakspere? We need as well the shaping form of Plato's heavenly ideas or ideals for this power to grow into. Simply, we ought to recognize that in accounting for Shakspere's ontology we usually beg the whole question. Until we know more of such matters, it will probably be best to be content with establishing the process and progress of growth, without invoking any postulate of any faith, literary or religious, to explain it.

It is not that Shakspere was not developing in this period; it is that along many lines he was developing into a final whole. But that final whole would have been visible to a contemporary only by faith, and could not be known in its eventual actuality. In myriads of ways Shakspere was a promising young man; in none of them as yet, if ever, supreme. To Robert Greene merely *Iohannes Factotum;* to his masters and fellows the actors, the most promising of dramatists. Besides the animus, Greene was judging by his interpretation of the culturally accepted dogma of his day of what was literarily right; the actors were judging primarily by pragmatic results. They agreed with divers of worship that his facetious grace in writing approved his art. Shakspere's plays approved themselves to a gainful audience; they were, therefore, good. Neither the box office nor theory has ever proved itself by past experience to be infallibly "right." In the case of Shakspere we now vote with those who were obliged to judge primarily by the box office, but we do not vote with them because they so judged. Nor do we know that some future time will not agree with Greene. *De gustibus non disputandum est.*

We are still left with the heart of our mystery unplucked. How did Shakspere — how does anyone — know to attain himself?

Robert Greene and *Fair Em*

In addressing *Greenes farewell to Folly* "To The Gentlemen Students of both Vniuersities" Greene is certain that

Others will flout and ouer read euerie line with a frumpe and say tis scuruie, when they them selues are such scabd Iades that they are like to dye of the fazion, but if they come to write or publish anie thing in print, it is either distild out of ballets or borrowed of Theologicall poets, which for their calling and grauitie, being loth to haue anie prophane phāphlets passe vnder their hand, get some other Batillus to set his name to their verses: Thus is the asse made proud by this vnder hande brokerie. And he that can not write true Englishe without the helpe of Clearkes of parish Churches, will needes make him selfe the father of interludes. O tis a iollie matter when a man hath a familiar stile and can endite a whole yeare and neuer be beholding to art? but to bring Scripture to proue any thing he sayes, and kill it dead with the text in a trifling subiect of loue, I tell you is no small peece of cunning. As for example two louers on the stage arguing one an other of vnkindnesse, his Mistris runnes ouer him with this canonicall sentence, A mans conscience is a thousand witnesses, and hir knight againe excuseth him selfe with that saying of the Apostle, Loue couereth the multitude of sinnes. I thinke this was but simple abusing of the Scripture. In charitie be it spoken I am perswaded the sexten of Saint Giles without Creeple gate, would haue beene ashamed of such blasphemous Rhetoricke.[1]

As Bernhardi noted,[2] Greene's illustrative quotations are from *Fair Em*. Em had said to the unfaithful Manville, "Thy conscience, Manuile, is a hundred witnesses" (V, 1, 157), which in the form Greene quotes is not scriptural but classical. And it was not her knight, as Greene says, who excused himself with the words of the apostle. Neither was the false lover merely a knight. It was King Zweno who forgave his daughter saying

> Yet loue, that couers multitude of sinns,
> Makes loue in parents winke at childrens faults (V, 1, 121-22).

Greene's malice sought something to laugh at as absurd, and so he wrested these passages of "blasphemous Rhetoricke" to his own purpose. As a matter of fact, he would only have heard the play on the stage anyway and so could not have been completely accurate had he wished. This uneducated man, whose matter is either "distild out of ballets," or is the work of theological poets who give it to him because they are ashamed to sign their own names, whose ignorance is so great that he cannot write true English without the help of a parish Clerk, yct "will needes make him selfe the father of interludes" — this ignoramus must be laughed out of business lest true art suffer. *Fair Em* was indeed "distild out of ballets," as Greene intimates. The story of William the Conqueror was taken from Henry Wotton's *Courtlie controuersie of Cupids Cautels* (1578). The story of the Miller's daughter of

---

[1] *Greenes farewell to Folly* (1591), A4ᵛ; Grosart, *Greene*, IX, 232-233.

[2] Bernhardi, *Greene's Leben*, pp. 40 ff., with a reference to "Collier hist. of dram. Part II, 441."

Manchester was also pretty certainly ballad material, though the exact source is not known.[3] With the help of ballets, and with Greene's *Friar Bacon* as a model, this degreeless person had managed to produce a play which doubtless was being compared favorably with the work of Robert Greene, Master in Arts of either university. Such a situation was intolerable.

Who was the author of *Fair Em?* Greene expected his contemporaries easily to recognize him from his description. We ought, therefore, to be able eventually to do so. This author has not only written, but he has also published, prophane pamphlets. These pamphlets are "either distild out of ballets or borrowed of Theologicall poets, which for their calling and grauitie, being loth to haue anie prophane phāphlets passe vnder their hand, get some other Batillus to set his name to their verses." So the author's pamphlets are in verse, either of ballad quality, or of theological cast. But the author himself "can not write true Englishe without the helpe of Clearkes of parish Churches," this again pointing to the source of the author's inspiration. Still, "In charitie be it spoken I am perswaded the sexten of Saint Giles without Creeple gate, would haue beene ashamed of such blasphemous Rhetoricke," as this author has been guilty of. Greene is saying that, after all, the work must be the author's own, since not even the Sexton, let alone the Clerk, would be guilty of such blasphemy. But why has Greene now localized the parish by referring to the Sexton of St. Giles without Cripplegate? Evidently because that was the author's parish, and these the church officials to whom he would turn. For Greene has in mind one unofficial social function of the parish clerk, that of general scribe for his illiterate parishioners. This man, who is so illiterate as to need the aid of the parish clerk in his writing, is the author who besides his pamphleteering activities "will needes make him selfe the father of interludes," and write such a play as *Fair Em.*

What writer of plays had also published pamphlets of ballad and moralizing characteristics, and lived in St. Giles Cripplegate in 1591? The only possible answer is Anthony Mundy. The records of St. Giles contain various entries of the christenings and burials of his children from June 28, 1584, through September 5, 1589.[4] The records of this parish have been thoroughly searched for players and poets. Long since, Collier, who would not easily have overlooked a writer, made the search, and more recently the records have been checked by Bentley.[5]

The only other possible candidate is the Robert Wilson, who was buried as an actor at St. Giles on November 20, 1600. Storojenko[6] arrived at Robert Wilson by the following set of circumstances. One R. W. evidently alludes to Greene among others in his *Epistle Dedicatorie* before *Martine Mar-Sixtus* (S.R. November 8, 1591, printed 1591). Storojenko assumes that R. W. is the outraged author of *Fair Em,* and from the initials identifies him as Robert Wilson, Sr.

In this dedication to Master Edmund Bowyar, Esq., this R. W. speaks of "this short treatise, the fruites of a schollers study," and says,
Loath I was to display my selfe to the world, but for that I hope to daunce vnder a maske, and bluster out like the winde, which though euery man heareth, yet none can

---

[3] Brooke, *Apochrypha*, p. xl; Chambers, *E.S.*, IV, 11-12. Rollins, *Index*, No. 1765 and references would identify this ballad with one which survives, but could not have been the source of *Fair Em*.

[4] These may be found conveniently summed up from Collier in Turner, *Mundy*, p. 77, n. 14.

[5] G. E. Bentley, "Records of Players in the Parish of St. Giles, Cripplegate," *P.M.L.A.*, XLIV, 789-826.

[6] Grosart, *Greene*, I, 235 ff.

in sight descrie, I was content for once to become odious, that is, to speake in print, that such as vse to carpe at they know not what, may for once likewise condemne they know not whome, and yet I doo not so accuse the readers, as if all writers were faultles, for why? We liue in a printing age, wherein there is no man either so vainely, or factiously, or filthily disposed, but there are crept out of all sorts vnauthorized authors, to fill and fit his humor, and if a mans deuotion serue him not to goe to the Church of God, he neede but repayre to a Stationers shop and reade a sermon of the diuels: I loath to speake it, euery rednosed rimester is an author, euery drunken mans dreame is a booke, and he whose talent of little wit is hardly worth a farthing, yet layeth about him so outragiously, as if all *Helicon* had run through his pen, in a word, scarce a cat can looke out of a gutter, but out starts a halfpeny Chronicler, and presently *A propper new ballet of a strange sight* is endited: What publishing of friuolous and scurrilous Prognostications? as if *Will Sommers* were againe reuiued: what counterfeiting and cogging of prodigious and fabulous monsters? as if they labored to exceede the Poet in his *Metamorphosis;* what lasciuious, vnhonest, and amorous discourses, such as *Augustus* in a heathen common wealth could neuer tolerate? & yet they shame not to subscribe, *By a graduate in Cambridge; In Artibus Magister;* as if men should iudge of the fruites of Art by the ragges and parings of wit, and endite the *Vniuersities,* as not onely accessary to their vanitie, but nurses of bawdry; we would the world should know, that howsoeuer those places haue power to create a Master of Artes, yet the art of loue is none of the seauen; and be it true that *Honos alit artes,* yet small honor is it to be honored for such artes, nor shal he carry the price that seasoneth his profit with such a sweete; It is the complaint of our age, that men are wanton and sick of wit, with which (as with a loathsome potion in the stomack) they are neuer well till all be out. They are the Pharisees of our time, they write al, & speak al, and do al, *vt audiantur ab hominibus;* or to tel a plaine truth plainely, it is with our hackney authors, as with Oysterwiues, they care not how sweetely, but how loudely they cry, and cōming abroad, they are receaued as vnsauory wares, men are faine to stop their noses, and crie; Fie vpon this wit; thus affecting to bee famous, they become notorious, that it may be saide of them as of the *Sophisters* at *Athens: dum volunt haberi celebriter docti innotescunt insigniter asinini,* & when with shame they see their folly, they are faine to put on a mourning garment, and crie Far well. If any man bee of a dainty and curious eare, I shall desire him to repayre to those authors; euery man hath not a Perle-mint, a Fish-mint, nor a Bird-mint in his braine, all are not licensed to create new stones, new Fowles, new Serpents, to coyne new creatures; for my selfe, I knowe I shall be eloquent enough, I shal be an Orator good enough if I can perswade, which to be the end and purpose of my heart, he knoweth who knoweth my heart.

Thus R. W. is venturing into print for the first time, and that anonymously. His sole ambition is to be a good enough orator to "perswade," the fundamental business of an orator. He does not aim to profit and delight [*Aut prodesse . . . aut delectare,* "seasoneth his profit with such a sweete," *miscuit utile dulci*], the poet's aim, as do the various classes of more or less belles lettres he has enumerated. Even his worst fears could not have guessed that Zoilus would slander him with such an identification as Robert Wilson and with the authorship of *Fair Em.* What R. W. does actually is first to translate the oration of Sixtus the fifth, September 11, 1589, in which that pope defended the assassination of Henry III of France, and then to mar Sixtus for his position. One gets the impression of a very serious young man. As Grosart and Nicholson also conclude,[7] R. W. cannot possibly be Robert Wilson.

R. W. begins with ballad materials, and so the red-nosed rimester — not rednosed minister! — is clearly Elderton. Finally, R. W. turns to the Ovidians, where Greene is as clearly the chief offender, though Mundy's

[7] Grosart, *Greene,* I, lxv-lxvi. One A. S. corrects the red-nosed minister and suggests Richard Willes as the author of *Martine Mar-Sixtus* (*N. & Q.,* 10th S., II, 483-484).

Honos alit artes is coupled with Greene's *In Artibus Magister*. Thus R. W. is taking the line which Gabriel Harvey was to follow the next year in his *Foure Letters,* where Elderton and Greene are "two notorious mates and the very ringleaders of the riming and scribbling crew,"[8] and where "Eldertons ale-crammed nose" plays its accustomed part. Had Grosart troubled to read the copy of *Martine Mar-Sixtus* in the British Museum, he would have found a red-nosed rhymester instead of a red-nosed minister, so painful to him, a minister. There is nothing in this passage about a minister, let alone a red-nosed one. And there is nothing new on Greene, except that R. W., whoever he was, did not approve of him, among very numerous others.

It has also become customary to point out that Robert Wilson has in a very general form the sentiments which Greene pillories in *Fair Em*. But so has many another. There is, therefore, really no tangible evidence for Robert Wilson as the author of *Fair Em*.

In this connection, it is pertinent to notice that Wilson has also been identified by some as the manager caricatured by Roberto in *Groats-Worth of Wit,* 1592. We have seen that this caricature is a reworking of a gibe by Nashe in 1589, and is certainly for the most part fictional. But if one assumes that Greene's caricature in 1592 is autobiographical (one need not and I myself do not), then Greene was hired by a manager, apparently of the Queen's and presumably in 1589, as the ownership and beginning dates of Greene's plays would indicate, to write for the company. This season John Dutton and John Laneham received the pay for the court performances; but in 1590-91 John Dutton and his brother Laurence received pay for four plays, while Laneham received pay for only one, showing that Laneham at that time controlled only some minor branch, while Greene apparently had been with the main body. Thus John Dutton would be the most likely man to suspect as Greene's managing player of 1589-92, though something could be said for Laurence. Unfortunately, there appears to be no indication as to the types of characters they acted or as to whether either made any pretence to authorship.

It has been suspected, indeed, that Robert Wilson is the object of Greene's attack. But he does not at all fit Greene's conditions. It is either significant or suspicious that both of our principal references to Robert Wilson couple him with Tarleton. Meres wrote in 1598, "As *Antipater Sidonius* was famous for extemporall verse in Greeke, and *Ouid* for his *Quicquid conabar dicere versus erat;* so was our Tarleton" of whom Doctor Case said, *"Cicero suum Roscium: nos Angli Tarletonum, in cuius voce & vultu omnes iocosi affectus, in cuius cerebroso capite lepidae facetiae habitant.* And so is now our wittie *Wilson,* who, for learning and extemporall witte in this facultie, is without compare or compeere, as to his great and eternall commendations he manifested in his chalenge at the Swanne on the Banke side."[9] Since the Swan theater was established only a few years before Meres wrote, this reference must be to the Robert Wilson who wrote for the Admiral's men, and this Wilson is likened in extemporal ability to Roscius, the great Roman comedian, and Tarleton, the greatest English clown.

Wilson and Tarleton are coupled together in the same general way, but with some difference, in Howes' continuation of Stow's *Annales* in 1615.

---

[8] Grosart, *Harvey,* I, 164.

[9] Meres, *Palladis Tamia* (1598), pp. 285^v-286^r. See D. C. Allen's edition of this section, index, under Wilson.

Howes notes under 1583 the formation of a company of twelve to be Queen's men; "amongst these xii players, were two rare men, viz. *Thomas* (*sic*) *Wilson* for a quicke delicate refined extemporall witte, hee was the wonder of his time."[10] The notice by Howes is suspiciously like that of Meres. Howes evidently had seen the patent, which names the twelve men. Here he would learn the fact that Tarleton and a Robert Wilson were members of the group in 1583. If he knew the passage in Meres also, his total information on Wilson would be accounted for. But there is nothing to show certainly that Howes did know the passage in Meres. If the two are independent, then as Sir Edmund Chambers says, "The common use by Meres and Howes of the phrase 'extemporall witte' renders it almost impossible to suppose that they are not speaking of the same man."[11] But since this is only a cant phrase of the day, the evidence is not quite so convincing as at first sight it might appear. The fact that Meres characterizes Wilson's extemporal wit as marked by "learning" and Howes speaks of it as "quicke delicate refined" is much more significant, especially since it is brought first and then Tarleton's extemporal wit is varied from it. If the reader will examine the specimens of this extemporal wit attributed to Tarleton, and also Armin's *Quips Upon Questions* he will get some idea of what the usual clown did, and will notice that something a bit higher is attributed to Wilson then this ordinary clowning. The evidence is thus in favor of identifying the Robert Wilson mentioned by Meres with the one mentioned by Howes.

This identification, however, appears to raise difficulties. Heywood in a publication of 1612 includes Wilson in a list of early "English actors . . . these, since I never saw them, as being before my time, I cannot (as an eye-witnesse of their desert) give them that applause, which no doubt they worthily merit."[12] Since Heywood's time must go back to the middle nineties, this actor Wilson would be earlier, and since all others in this list except one belonged to the Queen's in 1583, it is clear that Heywood is referring to Robert Wilson as an actor. Further, there is no certain record of any Wilson as an actor after the beginning of the nineties. It is true that " 'Robert Wilson, yoman (a player)' . . . was buried at St. Giles's, Cripplegate, on 20 November 1600. . . . A Wilson is in the suspected Admiral's cast of *c.* January 1600."[13] The second of these cannot be accepted as evidence, and the first means only that Robert Wilson was at some time an actor. The proper explanation appears to be that of Sir Edmund Chambers. "I take it the explanation is that, at or before the virtual break-up of the Queen's men in the plague of 1592-3, Wilson gave up acting, and devoted himself to writing, and occasional extemporizing on themes."[14] Wilson's withdrawal, however, as an actor from the Queen's men appears to have been earlier than June 30, 1588. "Of the twelve members belonging to the original Queen's company in 1583 [Wallace, *First London Theatre*, p. 11], only three — Robert Wilson, John Bentley, and Tobias Mills — do not appear in a certificate of Lay Subsidies, June 30, 1588 [Malone Soc. *Coll.*, I, 354-5]. Now Tobias Mills was buried July 11, 1585" [Chambers, *E.S.*, II, 330], and John Bentley August 19, 1585.[15] This evidence might indicate that Robert Wilson, the early actor-

[10] Stow, *Annales* (1615), p. 697.
[11] Chambers, *E.S.*, II, 349.
[12] Chambers, *E.S.*, IV, 252.
[13] Chambers, *E.S.*, II, 350.
[14] Chambers, *E.S.*, II, 349.
[15] T. W. Baldwin, "Nathaniel Field and Robert Wilson," *M.L.N.*, XLI, 33-34.

dramatist, was also dead by June 30, 1588. Wilson might, however, already have withdrawn from the Queen's. In view of all the evidence, it seems best to agree with Sir Edmund Chambers and Sir Walter Greg that there was probably but one Robert Wilson, actor-dramatist. It would seem certain that the Queen's man had withdrawn from that organization or died before June 30, 1588.

But Greene's picture does not coincide with the known facts concerning Wilson. Greene's player controlled a company and hired Greene to write a play for it. There is no record to indicate that Wilson was ever in such position, and it seems certain that he was not in such a position with the Queen's men at the proper period. Greene's actor had been "a countrey author, passing at a Morrall . . . teaching education," though "now my Almanacke is out of date." While Robert Wilson wrote morality plays, he was certainly no country author of the antiquated type Greene is satirizing. Greene can hardly have been satirizing Robert Wilson. For ought I can see, we shall need to await further information before we can identify certainly the object of this attack in *Groats-Worth,* if in fact Greene is attacking any particular individual.

Thus Robert Wilson does not fit as the object of Greene's satire in *Groats-Worth,* or in *Farewell to Folly* as the author of *Fair Em.* Besides, even if all the work attributed to Robert Wilson belonged to one man and not to two or three, still it does not include the classes of literature alluded to by Greene. Wilson had not printed under his name pamphlets of ballad and moralizing characteristics. In fact, there is no indication that by 1591 any Wilson had been a pamphleteer at all. Certainly, Wilson's pamphleteering activities could not have been either of the quantity or of the quality implied in Greene's attack.

Just as clearly Mundy's pamphlets had been both of the quantity and of the quality implied. For the quantity, one may turn to any bibliography of Mundy's work. Nor will the ballad quality need demonstration for one who is usually identified as "Antonio Balladino." Similarly, the moralizing vein runs heavily through his work. He had published numerous anti-Catholic pamphlets, growing out of his visit to Rome, as also other "godly" works.[16] Mundy had referred to Master Robert Crowley, the vicar of St. Giles,[17] as authority, though not I believe to the clerk or to the sexton. But the chief point to Greene's gibe lay in the fact that Mundy himself was a Messenger of the Chamber, and, among other things, "was employed as a pursuivant to execute the Archbishop of Canterbury's warrants against Martin Marprelate in 1588."[18] Indeed, Greene may be charging Mundy specifically with having written for the Archbishop in the controversy, as seems implied also by another allusion.[19] Whether so or not, Mundy's connection with the Archbishop made him a fair mark for Greene's insinuation that he really only published under his own name work which theological poets would not publish under theirs, and that even in the writing of his own work he sought the help of parish clerks and sextons. This moralizing tendency runs very heavily through Mundy's work. And Mundy lived in St. Giles, and had the "theo-

---

[16] The fullest account of Mundy's work will be found in Celeste Turner, *Anthony Mundy An Elizabethan Man of Letters.* Besides the text, which brings out these characteristics of Mundy's work, see the bibliography, pp. 201 ff.

[17] Turner, *Mundy,* pp. 75-76.

[18] Chambers, *E.S.,* III, 444.

[19] J. D. Wilson, *M.L.R.,* IV, 489.

logical" connections which gave point to Greene's satiric jesting. Greene could not possibly be referring to anyone else than Mundy.

Greene in 1591 charges the author of *Fair Em* with blasphemy. We are reminded, as others have been, that he brought the same charge against Marlowe's companion gentleman poet early in 1588. Now in the years preceding, Anthony Mundy had been taking extra special care to get himself labeled as a poet and by implication a gentleman.[20] One remembers that Mundy had been a government agent, as had Marlowe, and was a pamphleteer, as was Greene. It would, therefore, be quite the expected thing for Mundy and Marlowe to be associated, and for them to be antagonistic to Greene. As to the play which contained the mad priest of the sun, apparently by Marlowe's companion poet, the best guess, as we have seen, is that it was *Heliogabalus,* which was entered S.R. June 19, 1594, but of which no copy is known.[21]

---

[20] Turner, *Mundy,* pp. 75 ff.
[21] Chambers, *E.S.,* IV, 401.

Five-Act Structure in Peele, Marlowe, and Greene

The principal suspects in the *Henry VI* plays show, in their known works, characteristic habits of structure, and these are not those of the *Henry VI* plays. We shall consider briefly Peele, Marlowe, and Greene, since they have left enough known work to be significant.

Peele constructs always by pageants, with minimum regard to five-act structure. For *The Arraignment of Paris,*[1] the framework is furnished by the conventional five-act formula. The first act properly introduces the principal characters; gods and goddesses in scene one, human beings in scene two. The second act presents the fateful decision by Paris, as a second act should do. The third act summons Paris to his arraignment because of that decision, which is regular. The fourth act presents the consequent arraignment of Paris, with its suspended catastrophe for Paris, which ought to occur in the fifth act if this were the tragedy of Paris. Instead, the goddesses appeal the case at the end of the fourth act from the decision which Paris made in the second, and which is consequently the occasion of the decision on that appeal in the fifth act. Paris has been excluded from the fifth act of his play.

Peele has used the five-act formula merely as a framework on which to hang as many pageants as possible. He shifts his whole structure at the end of his fourth act in order to get a pageant-ending of courtly compliment for Queen Elizabeth. Incidentally, the play must have been so constructed originally; else its ending was completely rewritten, and in that case what its original ending was I cannot guess.

Not only does Peele warp the formula for his pageant purposes, but he also pads very heavily throughout. This is particularly true of the third act, where the story of Colin the faithful is developed anachronistically in contrast to the story of Paris the unfaithful, who in fact has not actually been unfaithful yet, though Oenone puts on her sad pastoral plaints as if he had. Throughout, Peele is intent on his pastoral pageantry, with its singing, etc. The story is only a slight structural thread, which everybody knew anyway. Incidentally, here is Peele's idea of a "contention" play, a very far cry from the *Henry VI* plays. For Peele, the presentation, ornamentation, was the thing, and for it contemporaries praised the play in highest terms.

Alcazar is constructed as the tragedy of Sebastian, occasioned by the Moor. The first act presents the political background in Barbary, which results in the flight of the Moor before his uncle Abdelmelec. In the second act, Sebastian decides to enter the war on the side of the Moor, and the presenter warns that this is the beginning of Sebastian's tragedy. This is the crucial decision, properly in place. In the third act, Sebastian prepares for the war in Barbary, though he is being deceived by Spain, while the Moor actually hopes to use him and ruin him. The fourth act gets the forces into the field and to the

---

[1] I use Bullen's edition for Peele.

brink of Alcazar, with the Moor looking forward to a Christian tragedy for his ally Sebastian. In the fifth act, Sebastian does meet his Christian tragedy, but the Moor is also killed, and Abdelmelec establishes the rightful succession. The units are further demarcated by a Presenter to summarize the significance of the coming act, and for the first two acts the Presenter has the aid — or hindrance — of dumb shows.

As usual, Peele works in and by spectacle as much as possible. But he does not now have a singing organization, as in the *Arraignment* and *Edward I*. He must rely, therefore, more on spectacle groupings, speeches, sensational effects.

The title of *Edward I* indicates the main ingredients of this "Famous Chronicle." It is Edward's "returne from the holy land. Also the life of Llevellen rebell in Wales. Lastly, the sinking of Queene Elinor, who sunck at Charingcrosse, and rose againe at Potters-hith." This reminds one of the formula for *David and Bethsabe,* where the three parts are demarcated by choruses; and Peele may have intended no further divisions than these three in *Edward I*. But it is possible to divide the play into five acts.

The chief "contention" of the play is for Wales. The first scene shows Edward's return from the holy land, the second introduces Lluellen, Prince of Wales, who plans to fight Edward in order to get Lady Elinor. Here then could be the first act, presenting the inciting incident at the end.

In the third scene, Edward will meet Lluellen, Prince of Wales, who plans in the fourth to trick him, and does in the fifth, so that Lluellen gets Lady Elinor, which displeases Mortimer. Edward supposes he has won Wales from Lluellen and in scene 6 Queen Elinor arrives to bear a son, who shall be Prince of Wales. This could be the second stage or act, in which Edward thinks he has won Wales.

In the seventh scene, Mortimer turns over Lady Elinor to Lluellen, who is going to play Robin Hood against Edward, but Mortimer is going to play the Potter for Lady Elinor. Scene 8 is a Robin Hood play. Scene 9 presents Baliol sending defiance to Edward. In scene 10, Edward prepares to christen the Prince of Wales, to whom the powerful barons are bringing gifts. Scene 11 is music for the Queen. So both Wales and Scotland are creating an epitasis, but Edward has his remedy for Wales. This should be the third act.

In scene 12, Longshanks and Lluellen have a personal encounter. In scene 13, the Prince of Wales is christened, Baliol's challenge is presented, Edward is to conquer Baliol, while Mortimer is to conquer Lluellen, and Queen Elinor is to go to London. Scene 14 presents Baliol's reaction to Edward's answer. In scene 15, Mortimer pursues the Welsh rebels. In scene 16, Queen Elinor puts the Mayoress to death with a serpent. In scene 17, Lluellen is killed. In scene 18, the Friar sings farewell to his old service, and in scene 19, attaches himself to Mortimer, who now has Lady Elinor. In scene 20, Queen Elinor sinks at Charing Green. Everything is now ready for settlement, though some settlement begins with scene 16. But it is Queen Elinor's sinking which will occasion the real catastrophe for Edward, and so should signalize the end of the fourth act.

In scene 21, Edward brings in Baliol prisoner, whose life he spares, thus putting a catastrophe to that thread of the story. In scene 22, Queen Elinor rises at Potter's Hive, stricken in body and conscience. In scene 23, Edward hears that Lluellen is dead, and Elinor risen. Edward will go and confess Elinor, though Lancaster advises against it. In scene 24, David and his fellows go to execution, fulfilling Harper's prophecy, and so we have the

final catastrophe of this thread of the story. In scene 25, Queen Elinor
laments her sins; Edward and Lancaster enter as friars; Elinor confesses
sin with Edmund Lancaster. Joan is a Friar's daughter, but young Edward
is true begotten. Elinor dies, Lancaster denies sin, but is sent out and Joan
called in to hear the news and die, after which her husband Gloucester is
informed. Orders for a magnificent funeral. Mortimer is to present signs
of victory; Baliol threatens Northumberland; Edmund laments, Gloucester
laments, and the play stops.

But while the play could have been divided into five acts, yet these units
are neither emphasized nor even clearly demarcated. We have simply a
succession of pageants, presenting the chief spectacles which could be attached to Edward's reign, strung loosely together upon certain threads of
story. There is no beginning, no middle, no end; simply a start, a continuation,
a stop; that is, a "chronicle," as it is labeled.

The Old Wiues Tale is constructed as a continuous pageant, before its own
"sit and see" audience, and so needs no further discussion.[2]

In *David and Bethsabe,* Peele has divided David's life into three "discourses," officially marked by choruses. The first "discourse" consists of
three scenes and covers the period through David's decision to procure the
death of Urias, with attendant circumstances. Chorus then laments and tells
us to pass on to the death of Bethsabe's child. The second "discourse" presents David's sorrow over the child, followed by the story of Absalom's
revolt and death. Chorus again improves the occasion, and promises "a third
discourse of David's life, / Adding thereto his most renowmèd death." The
third part contains scenes 14 and 15, in which David mourns for Absalom but
is reconciled to Joab's solution. Thus Peele has written a life and death of
David, in three parts. There is nothing to indicate that he thought of the
story as divided into five acts. There is only a modicum of singing.

It appears then from this analysis of his plays that Peele was on speaking
terms with the five-act formula, and used and abused it perfunctorily upon
occasion, as in *The Arraignment of Paris* and *The Battle of Alcazar.* But
Peele was more interested in pageant or chronicle presentation as in *Edward
I* and *David and Bethsabe.* In *The Old Wive's Tale,* Peele presents within a
story a story acted out in pageant sequence. In fact, Peele is not interested
in drama as drama at all, but in story presented in pageant form. This is as
true in the two plays where Peele uses the five-act formula overtly as it is
in the others. In none of them does the five-act formula have any shaping
effect. In both the plays where it is marked it is only a piece of machinery
perfunctorily and not very intelligently used. Certainly, Peele did not construct the well-knit three parts of *Henry VI,* or any one of them.

MARLOWE

Marlowe used the five-act formula in a general way, on which to hang
episode in a "life," as Peele used it occasionally on which to hang pageant.
In *1 Tamburlaine,* the structure has been largely determined by the episodes,
especially for the first three acts, with the final episode divided into two for
the fourth and fifth acts. The first act prepares for the first episode, the
taking of Persia, in the second act. Normally, the crucial resolve does not
come till the end of the second act. But Zenocrate is only a symbol of attain-

---

[2] On a possible five-part structure within the pageantry, see Robert L. Blair, *An Edition of
George Peele's* Old Wives' Tale (Abstract of a Thesis, Urbana, Illinois, 1936), pp. 10-14.

ment. So she is placed at the end of the first act as the inciting force. The real objective is Tamburlaine's capture of Egypt (ruled by Zenocrate's father), toward which the taking of Persia is a first step, and of Africa a second. So this first step is assigned to the second act, and the second step to the third act. The third and final step is then divided for the fourth and fifth acts. Thus the first act prologues the first episode in Tamburlaine's rise, and the fifth act concludes the third episode. Zenocrate becomes the symbol of purpose at the end of the first act, becomes willing as epitatic symbol in the third, and is claimed in the fifth. The five-act formula has been quite thoroughly dominated by the episodes. And Tamburlaine personally, not the structure, makes the whole a unity. Tamburlaine is a man of action, to be exhibited episodically, not a man of thought to be manipulated into the logical stages of the five-act formula, which is quite roughly handled.

Tamburlaine is the wandering knight of romance, performing high deeds of adventure for his lady fair. The whole five-act structure of the play lies in that convention. In the first act, the Scythian shepherd Tamburlaine dons his armor to conquer the world and become worthy of the fair Zenocrate, who is already betrothed to Arabia. In the second act, Tamburlaine wins Persia. In the third, Zenocrate makes the epitatical disclosure that she loves Tamburlaine and not the Arabian Prince, to whom she had been betrothed. Tamburlaine has reached the epitasis of having won Zenocrate's love, and his eventual objective must thus be to overcome the Arabian Prince and Zenocrate's father, the Souldan of Egypt, who favors him. Tamburlaine conquers Bajazeth, king of the Turks, to be crowned by Zenocrate as "Emperor of Africa." Tamburlaine has now won Zenocrate and another kingdom, if only he can hold both. But there is still the Souldan and the rival Arabia for him to oppose in the fourth act and overcome in the fifth. They and their city Damascus oppose in the fourth act, with Bajazeth cursing for them; but all are overcome in the fifth, and Tamburlaine kills his rival, gets the consent of Zenocrate's father, whom he gives further power, and takes truce with the world to marry Zenocrate. So should a hero of romance act.

In *2 Tamburlaine,* there is but one country to take, and Tamburlaine, the man of action, has little opportunity to force episode and five-act formula into unity. Instead of three episodes to be dominated by Tamburlaine, as in the first part, there is but one for him; and he can not get to it till the fourth act. To occupy the time for three acts, there is the episode of Sigismund to fill the second act, in order to free Callapine's forces against Tamburlaine in the third. But the best Tamburlaine can do in the third act is to burn a town in honor of dead Zenocrate. Only in the fourth act does the man of action really begin to act. He then finishes the episode, and is himself finished in the fifth act. The man of action gets little chance to dominate the episodes into unity, as he had done in *1 Tamburlaine.*

The five-act formula fares no better, though it is given more opportunity than in *1 Tamburlaine.* There is the over-all theme of the son seeking revenge for his father, and this runs completely through the play. But the son appears mostly by proxy, as it were, and is no worthy opponent of Tamburlaine. His supporters eventually get themselves into position to be conquered by Tamburlaine, and the son himself manages to be in at the death — his own. But the son is merely supposed to be a dummy for Tamburlaine to exhibit upon, and he proves to be a very poor one. Marlowe has consequently resorted to balanced structure in the first three acts, driving two teams, as it were. The five-act formula has to content itself with the Tamburlaine side of the balance. It is the death of Zenocrate which sends Tamburlaine berserk, to become Tamburlaine Furioso, after the fashion of the romances, not the opposition of son Callapine for father Bajazeth. And the results are mostly mad rant, daring God out of heaven, not an ordered sequence leading to a catastrophe. At this stage, Marlowe knew only how to make conquering action dominate for a kind of unity. In losing action, he had insufficient thought unity to dominate the action. In all his plays, Marlowe will keep his episodes, and he will never learn to harmonize with any considerable success the action episodes with the thought units of his plays.

In the first act of *Faustus*, Faustus decides to investigate necromancy. In the second, after investigation, Faustus signs away his soul. This is the crucial decision. In the third, Faustus is perturbed with ideas of repentance, but is diverted with pastimes, such as the pageant of the seven deadly sins, seeing hell (not exhibited), and traveling to Rome. In the fourth, after his "journey through the world and air," Faustus exhibits his acquired knowledge before the Emperor, and will return to Wirtenberg, for "Thy fatal time draws to a final end." In the fifth, Faustus pays up.

Faustus is not a man of action but a man of thought. Consequently, the five-act formula fares somewhat better than usual. Faustus needs to decide to investigate necromancy as the first step or first act. He needs next to decide for it as the second step or second act. All this fits nicely with the formula. Faustus has doubts as he actually embarks, which is a good start for an epitasis in the third act, calling for a double dose of good and evil angels to mark the struggle. Then there is no more struggle, merely an allusion or two, until the Old Man of the fifth act. The latter part of the third and most of the fourth are filled with the rewards of the bargain Faustus has made. In the third, Faustus acquires further art by travel. In the fourth, he exhibits his acquirements at home till time is up, with only a passing reference to his coming end, and an attempt to sleep off remembrance, which is used only for horse play. There is no development of epitasis after the initial struggle. Faustus spends his time in diversion until the end of the twenty-four years demands the highest epitasis of catastrophe in a fifth act. The third and fourth acts are distinguished principally as episodes with minor episodes in the twenty-four years. Thus the whole play is episodic; but the episodes, as such, simply fill the necessary time. They have no increasing order in themselves, and in their sequence they have no consequential bearing on the outcome. It is Faustus himself who holds the play together, even though for a considerable space we are permitted to forget that he is a doomed Faustus. But the initial struggles and the final consummation grip us to unify the whole in the thoughts of Faustus, just as *1 Tamburlaine* succeeds by the acts of Tamburlaine, which *2 Tamburlaine* attempts to repeat but fails.

Marlowe has constructed the *Jew of Malta* by episodes, in general conforming to the principles of five-act structure. In the first act, all the possessions of Barabas are confiscated by Malta to pay tribute to the Turk; but he plans to get a store of hidden wealth from his house by having his daughter Abigail become a nun in the nunnery which his house has become. In the second act, with the treasure procured by Abigail Barabas sets up in business again under the protection of the Governor of Malta, whom naturally he hates. He foments rivalry between the Governor's son Lodowick and Mathias for Abigail, with the aid of Ithimore, whom he has purchased as a worthy tool. He sends a feigned challenge from each to the other. Thus the first act has given the occasion and the second a plan for revenge. In the third act, this plan is executed. Lodowick and Mathias kill each other; but Abigail finds out why and returns to the nunnery, whereupon Barabas poisons the nuns, in order to kill Abigail, who confesses the secret, however, to two friars before she dies. Thus in the third act the first plan of vengeance has been executed but has occasioned an attempt to cover up. In the fourth act, the friars attempt to blackmail Barabas, who strangles one and gets the other executed for the murder, thus ending this source of danger. But a Curtezan and her man worm the secrets of Barabas out of his servant Ithimore and begin to blackmail him. Barabas poisons the lot. Thus Barabas has cut off one peril of exposure, but is now exposed to a new one, which he attempts to meet. The third and fourth acts have each an episodic move and a countermove which proves ineffective, thus necessitating the business of the next act. In the fifth act, the poison has not worked quickly enough to prevent accusations before the Governor of Malta. The accusers die and Barabas is thrown over the walls as dead, but has only taken a sleeping potion. Barabas shows the besieging Turks how to enter Malta, and is himself made Governor. He plots with the former Governor to destroy the Turk, but gets caught in his own trap.

Marlowe has an occasion in the first act, an epitatical plan in the second, followed by the one, two, three of execution in the third, fourth, and fifth acts. He gets this one, two, three, by two recoiling episodes, leading to a conclusion. In fact, the total structure is really episodic, presenting the life and death of Barabas in five units, tied together by the moves for revenge for his confiscated wealth.

The *Massacre at Paris* is in fact "the tragedey of the gvyes" as Henslowe labels it when new on January 30, 1593, though actually it is also "the comedy" of Navarre's attaining the crown as Protestant champion. In the first act, Navarre, the Protestant, marries into the royal house in spite of the fact that Guise, with the Cardinal, and Dumaine, his brothers, stormed thereat. Guise now plans to kill the Queen of Navarre (Navarre's mother) and the Lord High Admiral, who are the champions of the Protestants. Says Guise, the King

> barely bears the name;
> I execute, and he sustains the blame.
> The Mother Queen works wonders for my sake (Sc. II, 74-76).

More than 30,000 Catholics in Paris will aid him. He will be king, though Navarre is also in his way; but France itself is first to be won. So the plot is laid. In the second act, the Queen of Navarre and the Admiral are killed, and the Protestants of Paris massacred. The Queen Mother does away with her son Charles because he and Navarre vow vengeance for the massacres. She will replace Charles with Henry. Navarre will now claim his own kingdom. Thus the Protestant champion has made the crucial resolve, which will bring on the Protestant epitasis. Navarre is to become the Protestant champion to oppose Guise as Catholic, and this leads to the downfall of Guise and the succession of Navarre. In the third act, the Queen Mother intends with the Cardinal and Guise to run the kingdom, while Henry amuses himself. If Henry is not compliant, he shall follow Charles, and Katherine will be Queen. An army is being sent against Navarre, who says he will fight

> Against the proud disturbers of the faith,
> (I mean the Guise, the Pope, and king of Spain,
> Who set themselves to tread us under foot,
> And rent our true religion from this land (Sc. XIII, 3-6).

Open conflict is prepared against the Protestant champion by the Catholic, and the Protestant prepares to meet it. In the fourth act, Navarre overcomes. The King orders Guise to put down arms. Navarre will aid the King against Guise and revolted Paris.

> For his aspiring thoughts aim at the crown:
> And takes his vantage on religion,
> To plant the Pope and Popelings in the realm,
> And bind it wholly to the see of Rome (Sc. XVII, 24-27).

In the fifth act, all remaining principals get killed except Navarre, who is to succeed as Protestant King and champion against the Catholics.

The play is thus constructed on the opposition between Guise as Catholic champion and Navarre as Protestant. But Navarre is only an incident in the over-all plans of Guise, and is to be last attended to. Most of the play is devoted to this dog Guise eating the other dogs, with Navarre mostly taking an occasional occasion when it arises, and surviving finally all the other contenders for the crown. It is the tragedy of the Guise, Navarre being the shining knight with little to do, exactly as Richard III is the villain and Richmond the residual hero. Only, Richard far out-Guises Guise. Marlowe could have profited by *Richard III,* had it been written, as much as *Richard III* profited by Marlowe. That is, Guise needed more of the drive of Tamburlaine and Richard III. Apparently, he did not have the right kind of deeds to give this drive, and much of his big talk has certainly been excised from this mere torso of a play. The result is that the play has two ends but little middle. The one, two, three of the final acts is mostly three. In the third act (one), Navarre has a minor victory against the King's army; in the fourth (two), he prepares to aid the King against Guise, his ultimate opponent; in the fifth (three), all opponents are eliminated, but Navarre does not eliminate them. For the most part, Navarre is a donothing hero. The different stages are not sufficiently centered on either Guise or Navarre.

In *Edward II,* Marlowe presents the wars of the Barons, led by Mortimer, Jr., with Edward. In the first act, the Barons cause Gaveston to be banished by parliament, but at the Queen's entreaty recall him. At recall, in the second act, Gaveston is worse than ever and Edward dotes worse than ever, raising Gaveston to the heights. The Barons tell Edward, "Look next to see us with our ensigns spread," and Edward resolves, "Have at the rebels, and their complices." Here are the crucial resolves to point properly a second act. In the consequent fighting of the third act, after the Barons have executed Gaveston they are broken by Edward and the Spencers. In the fourth act, counterplots from France overthrow Edward, who is captured and forced to give up his crown to the Prince, who is to be under the tutelage of the Queen and Mortimer, Jr., who has led the Barons. In the fifth act, Edward is murdered; but his son takes over and orders the Queen, his mother, to the Tower, Mortimer to execution.

It will be seen that the five episodes of the struggle between Edward and the Barons, specifically Mortimer, Jr., have been determined broadly by the five-act formula, with each episode leading to the next. (I) Gaveston is banished but repealed. (II) Gaveston is repealed but aggravates matters to war. (III) The war brings death to Gaveston and defeats the Barons, but they flee to the brewing trouble in France. (IV) The trouble brewed in France overthrows Edward but Edmund and the Prince sympathize with Edward. (V) Edward is murdered but the Prince avenges. Marlowe gets the one, two, three of the final acts by permitting Edward to win in the third, then the Barons in the fourth, and finally both to lose in the fifth.

We may glance briefly at the *Dido and Aeneas.* In the first act, Aeneas and his men are herded toward Dido's court, where the action is to begin. In the second, they are welcomed and Cupid is to make Dido love Aeneas, and consequently to furnish him again for his voyage to Italy. This is the crucial plan. In the third act, Dido and Aeneas consummate love, and Aeneas is to remain in Carthage, which is a greater epitasis than was planned. In the fourth act, Aeneas tries to obey orders to leave for Italy, but is caught. In the fifth act, Aeneas leaves and everybody commits suicide. There are thus five story episodes. There is also a two, three of first failure and then success for the fourth and fifth acts, but not a one, two, three of two attempts and success. The one, two, three has been attained by a plan in act three (one), and a counterplan in four (two), followed by success in five (three).

Thus in a general way Marlowe uses the five-act formula. The first act always presents the inciting problem. Except in *1 Tamburlaine,* the second act then presents the crucial resolves or plans, occasioning an epitasis in the third act. Marlowe's first two acts are usually praised for their construction, and this is the fundamental reason. But for the heart of his play in the third and fourth acts, Marlowe relies upon sensational episode, with little or no necessary progression in thought or in emotion between the acts or necessarily leading through these acts to an inevitable catastrophe. When time is up, he aims at a sensational catastrophe, which is always plausible, but hardly inevitable, except that the source story ended that way. Fundamentally, Marlowe constructs by episodes in a "life," loosely made to conform to the five-act formula. Nor is there much sign of progress from play to play. Very broadly speaking, one can say that in construction Marlowe does not learn; he merely becomes more experienced. Marlowe is as over-loose as youthful Shakspere is over-tight in his construction. It is amusing to find the learned grammarian as the stickler for the rules, while the Masters of Arts are all but contemptuous.

Without exception, Marlowe constructs by episodes in a life: Tamburlaine, Faustus, Barabas, Guise, Edward II, even Aeneas. These episodes are made to conform roughly to the five-act formula, but are not dominated nor even controlled by it. Since Marlowe depends fundamentally on episode, he succeeds best where some character dominates the episode, as Tamburlaine (first part), and Faustus. Barabas would be as successful if we could sympathize sufficiently with Marlowe's view, as Marlowe's age did. In *Massacre,* Marlowe is actively sympathetic with the person who does not dominate the episode but merely benefits by it. In *Edward II,* historical fact and current interpretation interfered. Edward was too weak to be a hero or a heroic villain, but he was a king. Gaveston and Mortimer had to be villains, but not sympathetic ones. Marlowe, therefore, cannot present a dominating personality if he would. The result is a broader and to us more interesting interaction of characters, but a less unified play. The same forces were at work in *Massacre*. In a way, therefore, this "progress," which we praise in *Edward II* was thrust upon Marlowe by inescapable circumstances, and is not the result of improvement in construction. The construction in *Massacre* and *Edward II* is particularly significant in that both deal with the evils of civil war, as do the *Henry VI* plays. Evidently, the handling is quite different. Marlowe's strength was not in construction but in a character dominating episode. When the character does not dominate, the structure as such does not bind the episodes together.

Robert Greene

Since Robert Greene was as progressively repetitive in his fundamental plotting as he was in details, it will be well to examine here his five-act structure in further confirmation of the canon and chronology of his plays. This procedure is particularly desirable because of Greene's suspected connections with the *Henry VI* plays. We shall examine the four plays which Greene certainly wrote completely or partially, in the order which we have already established. For some purposes, structure of the late romances would have a bearing here, but for our present purpose, it may be omitted.

The act-divisions for *Orlando Furioso* have not been preserved and are quite shadowy. The first act should end with the first scene in Collins' edition, since the characters are introduced and the problem stated. The suitors have presented their cases and Angelica chooses Orlando, whereupon the majority of the suitors will make war upon Orlando and his faction, with Sacripant against all. With the second scene the action begins, since Orlando is attacking two of the rival suitors, and drives them out in the third. Then in II, 1 of Collins' edition Sacripant puts his plan into execution against Orlando and drives him mad. Tacked on is the information that one of the rivals has been overcome with generosity and will not fight against Orlando's side. So Orlando has been victorious against all rivals except Sacripant, who has driven him crazy to provide an epitasis. The end of the second act is thus properly discriminated in Collins' edition. The third act exhibits the epitasis of mad Orlando, who manages incidentally to kill Brandimart in defence of Angelica, whom he does not recognize. We learn later that Rodamant has also been killed and that Mandricard is on the side of Marsilius and Orlando, so that Sacripant is left as the chief opponent. In the fourth act, the twelve peers enter to hunt down and punish Angelica, whom Marsilius will not defend, and at the end Orlando is restored to sanity and goes out to kill Sacripant. This restoration is thus the occasion of the catastrophe and marks correctly the end of the fourth act. The fifth, of course, ends Sacripant and reunites Orlando and Angelica.

It will be seen that Greene thinks he has observed the five-act formula. He evidently considered Orlando's madness as both the thing toward which the protasis tends and as the occasion of the epitasis. So the first act sets the problem, and the second presents the action to the occasion of the epitasis. But the occasion of the epitasis *is* the epitasis and leaves the third act with little to do and the fourth with not much more. Evidently, however, the restoration of Orlando to sanity is both the thing toward which the epitasis tends and the occasion of the catastrophe, so marking properly the end of the fourth act. But this occasion is as external as it is in a play of Terence. As a result, the third and fourth acts "tend" mostly by presenting Orlando's madness till the external machinery of the twelve peers and Melissa can get into position to restore Orlando and help him right his wrongs. If one is interested in Orlando furious, as he evidently is supposed to be, then the epitasis is strong. If not, it is a weak waste of clownish buffoonery. The surviving evidence makes it clear that the play was successful, though much of the clownery was excised.[3] Thus Greene divides his narrative into five episodes loosely conforming to the theory of the five-act formula.

I have made a rather detailed analysis of *Bacon* elsewhere,[4] to which I refer the reader.

The quartos do not mark the acts and scenes of *Looking Glasse,* and the acts are only mechanically demarcated. There are three threads of story set in the "sit and see" commentary of Oseas, who is eventually relieved by the somewhat recalcitrant Jonas for the catastrophe. The main thread of story is of Rasni, paralleled by the story of the Usurer's victims, and by that of the Clown. Each of the two minor threads has four appearances before the catastrophe, evidently therefore intended to be in four acts. For the most part these two minor threads pursue their own way with no connection with each other and hardly any really organic connection with the main thread. This main thread of Rasni does not go through any clearly functional stages rising to a catastrophe. In his first appearance, Rasni boasts and announces his intention of taking his sister Remilia to wife. In his second, he is about to marry Remilia, who is blasted by lightning, whereupon Rasni decides to console himself with Alvida, who is willing. Rasni's third appearance is tacked on to the Clown business and leads to Alvida's poisoning of her husband. Rasni's fourth appearance connects with the Usurer story and ends in his loss of his favorite, but again he will console himself with Alvida. In his fifth appearance, Rasni is warned of ominous happenings but refuses to heed. His further appearances are in what is obviously the catastrophe. The story of Rasni is hardly even episodic and has no climactic progression. As divided, the only question would be whether the second appearance of the Rasni thread belongs to the first "act" of the play or to the second. The fact that it does not belong to the introduction but begins the action indicates that it belongs to the second "act," as does also the purely mechanical division into fifths. With this exception, the Rasni thread gets its fair rotation with the other two threads. All are exhibited for a moral purpose, which is heavily emphasized at every stage. The handling, therefore, is wholly mechanical and external, not anywhere functional. I see no indication that the five-act formula has had any further effect than to occasion five mechanical divisions.

James IV is a "guided" narrative in a "sit and see" framework. But, as a matter of fact, the framework serves principally as an excuse for the extra-ornamentation of dancing and pageantry. It guarantees, however, that the present major divisions belonged to the original structure. In a general way, the five narrative episodes do conform to the formulae for five-act structure. The first act introduces the characters, and sketches their attitudes toward what is to be the problem of the play. The King of Scots has married the daughter of the King of England, but has fallen in love with another and lays plans to procure her. An interested possible suitor for the second lady is introduced, though to the King of Scots he is never anything except at the end the man who had now married the second lady. In this case, the King loses to a subject as the Prince does in *Bacon.* But the subject is not

[3] See Greg, *Abridgements,* pp. 306 ff.

[4] Baldwin, *Five-Act Structure,* pp. 737-740.

his, and there is no overt rivalry. The clowns are attached to the upper groupings. In the second act, the prospecting suitor is smitten with the second lady. But without overt knowledge of this the second lady because of her modesty has refused the advances of the King's agent, so that the King realizes that he can have her only in marriage and consequently plans the death of his wife. The King also loses all his virtuous supporters in favor of the wasters. Here are properly the crucial decisions of a second act. As Greene causes Bohan as chorus to say

> now it beginnes to worke in kinde.
> The auncient Lords by leauing him alone,
> Disliking of his humors and despight,
> Lets him run headlong, till his flatterers,
> Soliciting his thoughts of lucklesse lust
> With vile perswations and alluring words,
> Makes him make way by murther to his will.
> Iudge, fairie King, hast heard a greater ill?[5]

Oberon caps the speech with

> Nor seen more vertue in a countrie mayd.
> I tell the⟨e⟩, *Bohan,* it doth make me sorry,
> To thinke the deeds the King meanes to performe.[6]

In the third act, the King's intention is discovered to his wife, who flees in disguise. Thus an epitasis has been produced for the King and his wife. The rival lady and her suitor are not represented, since their story hinges upon that of the King and his wife. But in this crucial spot Bohan-Greene must poke his head out of the tragicomic lion's skin to reassure the audience.

> since shee scapes by flight to saue her life,
> The King may chance repent she was his wife.
> The rest is ruthfull; yet, to beguile the time,
> Tis interlast with merriment and rime.[7]

In the fourth act, the rival lady gives her honorable suitor some encouragement — after his financial rating is found to be satisfactory. The Queen is hunted down, and is reported as dead to the King of Scots, who immediately sends a proposal to the rival lady. At the exact end of the act, one of the characters is about to report events to the King of England, which will be the external occasion of the catastrophe. In the fifth act, the King of Scots learns that the rival lady has married an honorable suitor, and the English King comes to avenge his daughter. But the Queen was not killed and reconciles all.

The episodes (pageants) of the narrative do follow in general the five-act formula. But the play is consciously constructed as a "moral," with Bohan as chorus to point it. And as consciously the episodes of the King's wrongdoing and repentance go through the proper "moral" stages. The story is a highly ornamented exemplum, much of the ornamentation being extraneous or unessential both for the moral and for the story. The love story is not permitted to stand on its own structurally or actually. But it comes near enough to doing so to make us think that it does. The structure is much tighter than in *Bacon,* to which *James IV* is very closely akin.

---

[5] Collins, *James IV*, 1100-1107.

[6] Collins, *James IV*, 1108-10.

[7] Collins, *James IV*, 1459-62.

As a matter of fact, *Bacon, Looking Glasse,* and *James IV* share the same plot. A wild to wicked young prince (Edward) or king (Rasni, James IV) hesitates between wife, already (Dorothea) or to be (Elinor, Remilia), and a rival attraction (Ida, Margaret, Alvida). The women in the case are equally good (Dorothea-Ida, Elinor-Margaret), or comparably wicked (Remilia-Alvida), the very wicked Rasni requiring darkly shaded ladies, though one of them is caused to repent and is permitted to go scot free.

In all four of the plays, the love story is put through the five-act division in closely similar ways. In *Orlando Furioso,* Melissa's magic is called in at the end of the fourth act to "untie the knot" of Orlando's furiosity. In *Bacon,* the magician loosely guides the whole narrative. He is called in at once and interferes with the love story at various points. In consequence, the love story has a more evident and coherent evolution than in *Orlando.* There is some logical sequence and consequence in its development, not merely a chronological order. But again the epitasis of the third and fourth acts consists of separate perturbations rather than a developing sequence. We settle the Edward-Lacy-Margaret triangle at the beginning of the third act, and then leave it till we are ready to unsettle it again at the end of the fourth act. The interval is filled with various other more or less epitatical and perturbed incidents. But on the whole the narrative has much more expository guidance than in *Orlando.*

The framework of magical guidance is more overt but less functional to the story itself in *James IV.* It is now a "sit and see" framework, with the story as an alleged moral exemplum. But while the framework comments and forecasts, it does not direct, and Oberon merely helps furnish the enveloping spectacle. He takes no part in the story except to save one of the roguish comedians from a deserved hanging. In *James IV,* the moral is now supposed to be dominant, as befitted Greene's period of repentance. The narrative is told as a moral lesson, with a commentator. Like Prince Edward, King James loves another woman than his destined queen, and like Edward he loses that woman to a subject, though that subject is neither his, nor a trusted noble, nor even an acquaintance. Both finally settle upon the destined queen. But in the framework King James is moralized as an exemplum and in the play repents, Prince Edward is not moralized and he merely does the fitting thing. The repentance theme and its exemplification in *Looking Glasse* have done their work. Rasni also is attracted to Alvida, already a subject's wife, even while he is infatuated to marriage with his sister. Rasni's story is dragged at the chariot wheels of the theme of repentance. Having (with Lodge's aid) triumphed over Rasni as a moral exemplum, Greene was prepared to force the Edward theme into submission for *James IV.* But fortunately, he did not now have the moral fervor of Lodge breathing down his neck, so that James IV is only moderately exemplified, mostly in the framework, and his story itself is permitted to take its immoral course, with the bystanders in the play shaking their heads, and the chorus observers condemning but doing nothing. For James IV himself now recognizes from the beginning that he shouldn't, that he is transgressing the moral law; Edward is never troubled by such scruples, and Rasni is forced to become conscious and repent only at the end. And this theme now guides the story into its epitasis. Recognizing the wrong, but as infatuated as Rasni, James IV produces an epitasis by ordering the death of his wife. And that epitasis does not flounder quite so badly as previously through the third and fourth acts, till the fifth act can mete out justice. For now we have at least the Queen's discovery of the King's order and her consequent flight in the third act, and the pursuit and supposed murder of the Queen in the fourth to give sequent and consequent stages to the epitasis. Greene now finally has a fairly firm exposition within his narrative. But it does not center upon the King. Though he has set the sequence off, he does not control it. Greene, however, is interested fundamentally throughout his plays in the actual narrative of his story, as are neither Peele at all, nor Marlowe very much.

Greene's authenticated plays, including even the one of partial authorship, are quite distinctive in their structural characteristics. With them *Alphonsus King of Aragon* does not harmonize. *Alphonsus* is a simple conqueror play. In Act I, Alphonsus lays his plans to get back Aragon. In Act II, Alphonsus wins not only Aragon, but other crowns as well. In Act III, Alphonsus rewards his supporters, even giving away the crown of Aragon, since he is going to take the far greater one of Turkey. Amurack of Turkey is warned by prophecy to submit to Alphonsus, and give him his daughter Iphigina in marriage besides, but Amurack will resist. The wife and daughter are also warned of impending fate. It will be noticed that here in the third act we meet the major objective as in *1 Tamburlaine,* to which objective the battles of the second act have been a stepping stone. And since Alphonsus himself has found no Zenocrate to play to his Tamburlaine, the author gives him one by prophecy — "unbeknownst" to him, as it were. In Act IV, Alphonsus conquers Amurack. In Act V, Amurack, Fausta, and Iphigina are brought to accept their fated roles, and so Alphonsus has conquered Turkey as he set out to do, and gets Iphigina to boot. The author has thus modeled this play on *1 Tamburlaine,* and evidently planned to write also a second part.

In its masque machinery, the play is closely allied to *James IV.* These two plays are very much more carefully planned and executed than *Bacon* and *Orlando,* even though they are still loosely constructed, romance style. Somewhat more of a middle is thrust upon them, though they never go of their own momentum.

If the inscriptions on a copy of the quarto of *George a Greene,* printed 1599, were made by Sir George Buc, as competent authority now believes,[8] then Buc had heard two stories as to its authorship. The one runs, "Written by .... a minister, who act⟨ed⟩ the piñers pt in it himself. Teste W Shakespea⟨re⟩." The other, "Ed. Juby saith that the play was made by Ro. Gree⟨ne⟩."[9] The structure of the play gives no support to Ed. Juby.

The play consists of successive incidents loosely connected with George a Greene. In the first act, as divided by Collins, Kendall intends to fight James of Scotland for himself, not for Edward of England, but George a Greene opposes him. Bettris loves George a Greene, but her father is opposed. In the second act, Musgrove takes James of Scotland prisoner. George a Greene is ambushed by Kendall and his men, and prepares a ruse. In act three, Bettris escapes from her father, George outwits Kendall and takes him prisoner, and Bettris joins him. In act four, Edward decides to go with James in disguise to see George a Greene. Robin Hood also decides to have a bout with him. Robin's men are beaten and Robin himself driven to a stay. In the fifth act, Edward arrives and eventually sets all right.

The play has neither a protasis nor an epitasis. It has an "incidental"

---

[8] See above, p. 218.

[9] Greg, Three Manuscript Notes, *The Library,* 4th ser., XII (1932), p. 308.

beginning, a string of incidents for a middle, and an "incidental" ending. It is merely a string of incidents revolving around George a Greene. The author may have divided it into five sections and have called them acts, but no such original divisions survive, and I see no certain indication that they were ever made. Neither in plot nor in structure does it show any kinship with Greene's four authenticated plays.

Since Lodge and Greene are accused of some variety of joint authorship in *Looking Glasse,* it will be well to look also at Lodge's single surviving play, *The Wounds of Civil War.* This is especially desirable because its theme of civil war is that of the *Henry VI* plays. Here Marius claims the place which is said "By lot and by election" (*M.S.R.,* 59) to belong to Scilla, who is accused nevertheless of being proud and factious. The play proceeds by balance in this contention. The first act presents this contention, with Marius winning the first round against Scilla, who is rallying. In the second act, Scilla has already won, and Marius flies; but young Marius is to bring old Marius back to Rome. In the third act, Scilla and Marius head for Rome and a showdown. In the fourth act, Marius wins Rome but dies, and Scilla hastens to Rome for the catastrophe. In the fifth act, Scilla triumphs in Rome and accuses the Romans of causing these civil horrors by their "seditious innouations" (*M.S.R.,* 1944). Scilla metes out punishment and retires to the country to die.

This is a straight contention play, with the crucial points at the right places; but the demarcation between Acts I and II is particularly weak, and the structure as a whole rather shambling. It is not as clear-cut, nor the theme kept so insistently before us as in *Gorboduc,* the first of them all in regular form. To me, at least, the workmanship does not suggest that in the construction of the *Henry VI* plays. Nor does the general outlook of Dr. Lodge in literature or life suggest those plays.

I do not think that Peele, Marlowe, Greene, or Lodge can be justly suspected of having constructed any or all of the *Henry VI* plays.

Indexes

The following indexes are divided into four separate categories, as follows:

    I. Index to Bibliographical References (below).
    II. Index to Citations from Shakspere's Plays (page 541).
    III. Index to Characters from Shakspere's Plays (page 543).
    IV. General Index (page 546).

For the principles on which these indexes have been constructed, see the Preface, p. vii. Since an index is no respecter of persons, I have cut titles and have otherwise abbreviated to bare identification.

I. INDEX TO BIBLIOGRAPHICAL REFERENCES

II. INDEX TO CITATIONS FROM SHAKSPERE'S PLAYS[1]

---

[1] I have used the Cambridge, 1893, edition throughout, unless otherwise specified.

III. INDEX TO CHARACTERS FROM SHAKSPERE'S PLAYS[1]

Aaron, 316, 318, 413-414, 422 ff, 433
Adriana, 508
Aegeon, 242
Aemilius, 425
Alarbus, 423, 426
Alençon, 344
Angelo, 318
Anne (Lady), 383 ff
Anne Page, 447 ff
Antipholus of Ephesus, 242, 262, 455
Antipholus of Syracuse, 242, 255
Antony, Mark, 495
Archbishop of York (Thomas
 Rotheram), 385
Armado, 455, 477, 493
Arthur, 321-322
Bardolph, 447 ff
Basset, 350 ff
Bassianus, 421 ff, 434 ff
Bedford, Duke of, 342 ff, 360 ff, 504
Biron, 110-112, 503
Bolingbroke (Henry IV), 294
Bottom, 474 ff, 483, 508
Boy (son of Master Gunner), 345
Boyet, 455
Brakenbury, Sir Robert, 386
Brooke (Ford), 449 ff, 467, 470
Broome (Ford), 449 ff, 467, 470
Buckingham, 315-316, 360 ff, 383 ff
Burgundy, 346 ff, 378
Cade, Jack, 368 ff
Caius, Doctor, 448 ff
Captain, 369
Capulet, 455
Cardinal Bourchier, 385
Catesby, 385 ff
Charles VII (of France), 344
Chiron, 417, 422 ff
Clarence (George, Duke of), 288-289,
 305, 309, 314, 376 ff, 382 ff, 390
Clarence's children, 384 ff
Clarence's daughter, 386

Claudio, 318
Clifford, Old, 338, 371 ff, 375
Clifford, Young, 287, 300, 338, 371 ff,
 375 ff
Clown (*Titus*), 425
Constance, 321-322
Coriolanus, 397
Countess of Auvergne, 346, 348
Demetrius, 417, 422 ff, 473 ff
Dogberry, 508
Dorset, 383 ff
Dromio of Ephesus, 242
Dromio of Syracuse, 242
Duchess of York, 384 ff
Edmund Mortimer, 347
Edward IV, 280, 289, 303, 314, 371 ff,
 375 ff, 382 ff, 390, 395
Edward V (Prince Ned), 304-305,
 307, 309, 385 ff, 390, 395
Edward Prince of Wales, 375 ff
Egeus, 472 ff
Eleanor (Cobham, Duchess of
 Gloucester), 279, 285-286, 290, 294,
 318, 335, 362 ff, 374
Elizabeth (Queen to Edward IV),
 309-310, 377 ff, 387 ff, 394, 398
Ely (John Morton, Bp. of), 387
Evans, 447 ff
Exeter (Thomas Beaufort, Duke of),
 342 ff, 375 ff
Falstaff, 343 ff, 447 ff, 458, 479, 508
Fenton, 448 ff
Ford. *See* Brooke, Broome
Gargrave, Sir Thomas, 345
Gaunt, John of, 294, 318, 365
General of Bordeaux, 357
Glansdale, Sir William, 345
Gloucester (Humphrey, Duke of),
 279-283, 285-286, 288, 290, 297, 326,
 332, 335-336, 342 ff, 360 ff
Grey, Lord, 385 ff
Hal, Prince, 450

---

[1] If a person appears as a character in any of Shakspere's plays, all references to
him are given here.

543